Critical Issues in Indian Politics

General Editors

FRANCINE R. FRANKEL, ZOYA HASAN, AND KANTI BAJPAI

Critical Issues in Indian Politics is a series dealing with decisive events, processes, and institutions in Indian politics. It focuses on the ideas, events, decisions, and social forces, which underlie key debates and complex changes that have transformed India in the past two decades. The volumes serve both as unique introductions and comprehensive discussions aimed at undergraduate and graduate students in India and abroad who specialize in South Asian and comparative politics. They will also interest advanced researchers and scholars in the field, policymakers, and informed general readers.

Francine R. Frankel is Professor of Political Science and South Asian Studies at the University of Pennsylvania and Founding Director of Penn's Center for the Advanced Study of India.

Zoya Hasan is Professor of Political Science at Jawaharlal Nehru University and Member of the National Commission for Minorities.

Kanti Bajpai is Professor of International Politics, School of International Studies, Jawaharlal Nehru University, New Delhi.

D1527184

Critical Issues in Indian Politics

India's Economic Transition
The Politics of Reforms

edited by

Rahul Mukherji

OXFORD
UNIVERSITY PRESS

OXFORD
UNIVERSITY PRESS

YMCA Library Building, Jai Singh Road, New Delhi 110 001

Oxford University Press is a department of the University of Oxford. It furthers the
University's objective of excellence in research, scholarship, and education
by publishing worldwide in

Oxford   New York

Auckland   Cape Town   Dar es Salaam   Hong Kong   Karachi   Kuala Lumpur
Madrid   Melbourne   Mexico City   Nairobi   New Delhi   Shanghai   Taipei   Toronto

With offices in
Argentina   Austria   Brazil   Chile   Czech Republic   France   Greece   Guatemala
Hungary   Italy   Japan   Poland   Portugal   Singapore   South Korea   Switzerland
Thailand   Turkey   Ukraine   Vietnam

Oxford is a registered trademark of Oxford University Press
in the UK and in certain other countries

Published in India
by Oxford University Press, New Delhi

ISBN-13: 978-019-806967-6
ISBN-10: 019-806967-7

Typeset in Adobe Garamond 10/12.8 by Jojy Philip
Printed in India at De-Unique, New Delhi 110 018
Published by Oxford University Press
YMCA Library Building, Jai Singh Road, New Delhi 110 001

Contents

Tables and Figures

TABLES

FIGURES

Acknowledgements

This book's journey began in 2003 with the good wishes of the series editors: Francine R. Frankel, Zoya Hasan, and Kanti Bajpai. They saw the goodness of fit between my interests and dearth of existing literature on India's economic transition from a political economy of self-sufficient, state-driven development to one that depended to a much greater extent on private initiative, competitiveness, and export promotion. India's globalization had become a fact of life by the 1990s. I am grateful to them for their suggestions and encouragement over the years. Oxford University Press ensured that this volume did not get unduly delayed.

The book was aided by a series of fortuitous circumstances. Ashutosh Varshney invited me to the Network of South Asian and Politics and Political Economy (NETSAPPE) coordinated by the Centre for South Asian Studies, University of Michigan, Ann Arbor. The yearly conferences of the NETSAPPE helped build enduring relationships with scholars who have supported this volume. They included Lloyd and Susanne Rudolph, Rob Jenkins, John Gent, Sunil Khilnani, Supriya RoyChowdhury, Atul Kohli, Pradeep Chhibber, Devesh Kapur, and Aseema Sinha. I am especially grateful to Prabhat Patnaik, C.P. Chandrasekhar, John Gent and Jason Kirk for writing excellent fresh contributions for this volume. Jagdish Bhagwati, Montek S. Ahluwalia, Ashutosh Varshney, Rob Jenkins, Lloyd and Susanne Rudolph, Baldev Raj Nayar, AnnaLee Saxenian, Supriya RoyChowdhury, and Stanley A. Kochanek secured copyright permissions for publishing their papers in this volume. The suggestions and encouragement offered by Montek S. Ahluwalia, Baldev Raj Nayar, Sumit Ganguly, Vikram Chand, E. Sridharan, Pratap Mehta, Sudha Pai, Medha and Gyanesh Kudaisya, Jack Snyder, David Baldwin, Helen Milner, Robert Jervis, Joseph Gusfield, C.P. Bhambri, and Balveer Arora are gratefully acknowledged.

My students Sitaram Kumbhar, Siddhartha Mukerji and Vasudha Dhingra cheerfully aided the completion of this project.

Colleagues at the Centre for Political Studies, Jawaharlal Nehru University, have encouraged this project by acknowledging the importance of teaching and research in political economy. I spent a delightful fourteen months at the Institute of South Asian Studies, Singapore, under the directorship of Tan Tai Yong. Tai Yong and Hernaikh Singh facilitated the completion of this project in more ways than one. Parts of this book have benefited from visits to the Saltzman Institute of War and Peace, Columbia University; the Australia South Asia Research Centre, Australian National University; the School of Advanced International Studies, Johns Hopkins University; and, the Centre for the Advanced Study of India, University of Pennsylvania.

Friends and family take the hardest toll in a project such as this. Those who worried that this book should not get delayed indefinitely due to other respon-sibilities included, Pravrajika Prabuddhaprana, Bijoya Mukherji, Indra Nath Mukherji, Subhadra Mukherji, Deepa Mukherji, Suman and Jayashree Mukherji, Dhiman and Shyamla Mukherji, Abhimanyu Mukherji, Basudeb Ghosal, and, John and Christie Vincent. Ayon cheerfully accepted my preoccupations, even though it meant less time reading and playing with dad. My father Partha Nath Mukherji taught and protected me in innumerable ways that inspired me towards the scholarly pursuit. Anjali made my projects hers as well. The book is dedicated to my mother, late Goparani Mukherji, and, the motherly and infinitely loving, Swami Tathagatananda of the Vedanta Society of New York.

Publisher's Acknowledgements

The publisher acknowledges the following for permission to include articles/ extracts in this volume.

Clarendon Press for Jagdish Bhagwati, 'What Went Wrong?', in Jagdish Bhagwati, *India in Transition: Freeing The Economy*, Oxford, 1993, pp. 39–69.

Journal of Economic Perspectives for Montek S. Ahluwalia, 'Economic Reforms in India since 1991: Has Gradualism Worked?', 16 (3), Summer 2002, pp. 67–88.

Cambridge University Press for Rob Jenkins, 'Political skills: introducing reform by stealth', in Rob Jenkins, *Democratic Politics and Economic Reform in India*, Cambridge, 1999, pp. 172–207.

Asian Survey for Baldev Raj Nayar, 'The Limits of Economic Naturalism in India: Economic Reforms under the BJP-led Government, 1998–1999', XL (5), September/October, 2000, pp. 792–815.

Economic and Political Weekly for Lloyd I. Rudolph and Susanne Hoeber Rudolph, 'Iconisation of Chandrababu: Sharing Sovereignty in India's Federal Market Economy', 5 May 2001, pp. 1541–52.

India Review for Rahul Mukherji, 'Managing Competition: Politics and the Building of Independent Regulatory Institutions', 3 (4), October 2004, pp. 278–305.

Frank Cass for Supriya RoyChowdhury, 'Public Sector Restructuring and Democracy: The State, Labour and Trade Unions in India', *The Journal of Development Studies*, 39 (3), February 2003, pp. 29–50.

Frank Cass for Stanley A. Kochanek, 'Liberalization and Business Lobbying in India', *The Journal of Commonwealth & Comparative Politics*, 34 (3), November 1996, pp. 155–73.

Introduction
The State and Private Initiative in India[1]

RAHUL MUKHERJI

This reader deals with the political and economic processes that shaped the extent of state intervention in the Indian economy. Why did the Indian economy move towards greater reliance on private initiative after 1991, with significant consequences for growth and development? What was the impact of this economic transition on the political economy of India? This introduction summarizes the context of state-market relations in India since independence, in order to throw light on significant shifts in economic policies and institutions in India's plural setting.

India's tryst with economic reforms began immediately after independence in 1947. Political disputes about the role of the state in the development of Indian industry and agriculture began with the debates about the nature of Indian socialism and its economic planning. On one side were the landlords and Indian industrialists who emphasized productivity and growth, and on the other were those who wished greater redistribution through the direct intervention of the state. The extent of political power wielded by these groups had a substantial impact on policy. Technical assessments about the results of the planning experience—along with exogenous shocks such as wars and balance of payments crises—also influenced policy outcomes.

In this story of the relative importance of the state and the market, one could divide the Indian experience into three broad phases. The first period from independence till 1968 witnessed political battles which produced a compromise that gave birth to a large public sector, trade protection, and incentives for Indian industry to operate within a protected Indian market. Capital had some room for manoeuvre even though it substantially depended on the state. Indian agriculture suffered during this period. The second phase between 1969 and 1974 witnessed an intensification of state intervention in economic activity coupled with agricultural reforms. The third phase, which began around 1975, saw the evolution of a model that increasingly began to rely on price incentives and efficiency. The third phase was a slow and evolutionary process. The shift away from import substitution towards trade promotion and efficiency occurred slowly, and, unlike in the case of China, it was Indian industry and its interests that drove the reforms process rather than the interests of foreign capital. In the post-1975 period, the phase of economic reforms beyond 1991 marked the most radical departure from the past.

This reader has contributions to the development debate, the content of reforms, the politics that produced the reforms, and the impact of reforms on the political economy of India. The post-1991 period has witnessed institutional or structural changes favouring competition and private investment in areas such as telecommunications and capital markets. Economic policies have shifted from emphasizing import substitution to vigorously promoting exports, driven by shifts in industrial and trade policy. Reforms have given a distinct meaning to Indian federalism. Regional inequalities, slow rates of growth in the agrarian sector, and challenges to redistribution and the provision of physical and human infrastructure pose challenges for the story of India's development.

THE STATE-PRIVATE ENTERPRISE COMPROMISE, 1947-68

During this period, the politics of economic policy occurred largely within the Congress Party. Right-wing parties like the Swatantra Party and the Jan Sangh could pose the threat of weaning people away from the Congress Party if a radical version of social and economic transformation were imposed on those who had favoured private property and price incentives. The socialists within the Congress, who favoured radical redistribution and abolition of private property, had the sympathy of Prime Minister Nehru.[2] On the other hand, Sardar Patel and many state-level party leaders, who were a powerful political force to reckon with, were uneasy with the idea of radical redistribution.[3] The compromise that emerged between the radical version and the status quo lasted till about 1968.[4] Prime Minister Shastri tried to introduce reforms, but his tenure was short-lived. Prime Minister Indira Gandhi pursued economic reforms for a brief period at the time of a balance of payments crisis in 1966. This section will briefly describe the politics of the 'state–private property compromise' from examples drawn from industrial and agricultural policies in India.

Sardar Patel's influence between 1947 and 1950 set the stage for a compromise that would give private industry some room for manoeuvre in India. He enjoyed enormous powers, which were deployed for deciding the composition of the Congress Working Committee. Patel facilitated the formation of a Socialist Party outside the Congress Party, which was a major loss for Nehru and the Congress socialists.[5] Patel and the doyen of Indian nationalist business G.D. Birla had shared a common vision. Birla played an important role in working out a mechanism that would determine the transfer of assets between India and Pakistan in the aftermath of partition. He had helped Patel's candidate Purshottamdas Tandon get elected as the Congress President in 1950, against the wishes of Nehru.[6] He was relied upon to brief Patel about the state of industrial sectors like jute and cotton, and, as Patel's emissary in the late 1940s, made high-profile visits to the US and the UK.[7]

The compromise was most clearly evident in industrial policy. The report of the Economic Programme Committee of the Congress Party in January 1948 was very different from the Industrial Policy Resolution (IPR) of April 1948. The report had suggested nationalization of public utilities and key industries, public ownership of monopolies, and the abolition of the managing agency system.[8] Homi Modi and Birla had criticized the report on behalf of the Federation of Indian Chambers of Commerce and Industry (FICCI). They were satisfied that the watered-down IPR of April 1948 had allowed public ownership of assets in only three sectors of the economy. In the six other sectors, the government had the right to begin new enterprises while the old privately owned enterprises could continue. The rest of the sectors were open for private investment.[9] The late 1940s had witnessed the removal of price controls on sugar, cotton, and foodgrains. The Company Law enacted in 1956 gave a new lease to the managing agency system, which had been criticized in the Report of the Economic Programme Committee in 1948. Withdrawal of this provision would have created a disruption in the managerial environment of private companies.[10]

Indian industry had opposed the Industrial Development and Control Bill introduced in parliament in 1949.[11] The final compromise was the Industrial Development and Regulation Act of 1951. Arguments against production controls and investment pessimism were made on behalf of Indian industry by the FICCI. Patel had even urged Birla to mobilize opposition to the bill. The proponents of government regulation were empowered by the rising inflation in the aftermath of the de-regulation of prices in 1948.[12] The Industrial Development and Regulation Act of 1951 was a compromise between those who wanted extensive controls and those who wished the self-regulation of industry. A number of sectors were brought under licensing but development councils were also established to give industry a voice in sectoral policies. These development councils and the Central Advisory Council on Industry with representatives from Indian industry would work closely with the government on licensing issues. While Indian industry wished greater room for manoeuvre within India, it sought help from the state to protect it from foreign competition.[13]

The Planning Commission came into existence in March 1950, as a compromise between those who wanted the commission to enjoy powers of policy implementation, and those who wished that it remain just an advisory body. Strong proponents of planning like Nehru and Gulzarilal Nanda desired a powerful Planning Commission. Industry needed the state for finance but was opposed to directions from the state with respect to the modalities of doing business. Patel was opposed to a powerful Planning Commission. Several ministers were also opposed to a Planning Commission with powers of implementation, as this would rob them of their executive power. Matters came to a head when Finance Minister John Mathai tendered his letter of resignation, owing largely to the proposal of setting up the Planning Commission as a super-cabinet.[14]

The Planning Commission was to be an arm of the government with powers to decide the size and allocation of resources but devoid of substantial powers to interfere with the work of other ministries. Indian industry had worried about direction from the Planning Commission.[15] G.D. Birla lost no time in organizing FICCI into a cohesive organization. FICCI conducted an extensive orientation programme for Members of Parliament (MPs). The *Hindustan Times* and the *Eastern Economist*, both of which were owned by Birla, argued the perspective of Indian industry.[16]

The First Five-Year Plan was sympathetic to the concerns of Indian industrialists in the private sector. The final draft of the Plan, which was approved in December 1952, allocated Rs 15 billion out of a total of Rs 35 billion for the private sector.[17] Financial organizations such as the Industrial Finance Corporation of India (IFCI), the National Industrial Development Corporation (NIDC), and the Industrial Credit and Investment Corporation of India (ICICI) were born between 1950 and 1955.[18] The First Five-Year Plan allocations emphasized a more prominent role for Indian private industry and agriculture than would be the case with the Second Plan, which began in 1956.[19]

The politics of the Second Five-Year Plan was quite different from that of the First Five-Year Plan. This period witnessed the ascendance of heavy capital intensive industrialization, largely within the public sector. The death of Patel enabled Nehru to garner greater authority within the Congress Party after assuming the Presidency of the Congress Party. By the mid-1950s, at the height of Nehru's power, the Planning Commission had assumed overarching importance. Nehru could now obtain approvals from the Cabinet, the All-India Congress Committee and the National Development Council.[20] The Planning Commission was manned typically by about five respected technocrats as full members; the prime minister was chairman and the deputy chairman enjoyed the rank of a cabinet minister. The Cabinet Secretary—the first among the secretaries in the Indian administrative service—was a secretary of the Planning Commission; and the Finance Ministry's Chief Economic Advisor was an advisor to the Planning Commission. I.G. Patel, the Deputy Economic Advisor of the Ministry of Finance (1954–8), had played an important role in coordinating the work between the Planning Commission and the Ministry of Finance on the eve of the Second Plan.[21]

The rise of Nehru and the Planning Commission gave birth to a certain kind of technocratic thinking. Voices favouring the importance of consumer goods and light industrial projects did not gain much ground in the policy debates.[22] Foreign advisors from the US, USSR, and China were consulted.[23] Finally, it was the Nehru–Mahalanobis model of heavy industrialization that won the day. Capital-intensive industrialization was considered a necessary investment for the long-term development of the country. This was supposed to promote the goal of economic self-sufficiency. To a great extent, this strategy of modernization drew inspiration from the Soviet success with centralized planning.[24] The allocations for organized industry and minerals grew from 7 per cent in the First Plan to about 20 per cent in the Second Plan.[25]

The emphasis on heavy industry in the public sector was a distinct characteristic of the Second Plan. Lobbying by Indian industry was less effective in the mid-1950s.[26] The Industrial Policy Resolution of 1956 brought more areas of industrial activity under regulation. Private investment in organized industry in the First Plan was about twice the level of public investment. This sequence stood reversed, and there was much greater investment in large-scale public sector industries than in industries in the private sector in the Second Plan. Even though private capital had some room for manoeuvre, the state's powers over private capital through licensing and financial controls, rendered the private sector in a position of dependence with respect to the state.[27]

The emphasis shifted to heavy industrialization, with reduced resources for the development of Indian agriculture. The reduction in the outlay on agriculture and irrigation was to the tune of 20 per cent of the Plan expenditure from the earlier 33 per cent. Despite reduced outlays in agriculture, India faced its first balance of payments crisis in 1956–7.[28] Shorn of resources to fund both industry and agriculture, India's agricultural strategy during the Second Plan emphasized institutional changes such as land reforms, cooperatives, and economies of scale using abundant manpower to boost productivity without having to make substantial investment. State trading was pursued with the aim of containing the price level. It was believed that the availability of abundant manpower, coupled with redistribution via land reforms and economies of scale to be realized through the cooperative farming effort, would enhance agricultural productivity without having to invest much in agriculture.

The Congress Party at the local level could neither sustain the radical redistribution programme, nor could it enthuse a substantial number of unemployed people towards the cooperative movement. Agriculture ministers at the Centre like A.P. Jain and S.K. Patil were critical of the approach of the Planning Commission towards Indian agriculture. They argued for price incentives and subsidies rather than price controls through state trading. The surplus labour failed to respond to the call of the cooperative movement, while the landed elite suspected cooperatives in agriculture as an attempt to introduce communist-style collectivization. The cooperative effort did not take into account the crop specificity of regions. It lumped all regions as equally suited for all kinds of agricultural activities, creating a paucity of resources for all the districts.[29]

Political opposition against the Congress Party was brewing. By the late 1950s, the Swatantra Party posed a threat to the Congress Party's claim to represent the landed and the propertied classes. The Chinese invasion of Tibet in 1959 and the war in 1962 were dampeners for the lessons in collectivization that India had wished to learn from China. In the parliamentary bye-elections of 1963, Rammanohar Lohia (Socialist Party), J.B. Kripalani (independent)[30] and Minoo Masani (Swatantra Party) won seats against the Congress Party candidates. This called for self-reflection within the Congress Party. Nehru felt the challenge and requested Kamraj and a few others to step down from political positions, urging them to devote themselves to the cause of the Congress Party. The Kamraj Plan especially picked right-wing Congress Party functionaries in high political positions and entrusted them the task of party-reorganization.[31] Nehru's attempt to put some weight behind the redistributive ideal failed to take shape after the war with China in 1962. The war had taken a serious toll on his health.

The economic scenario was gloomy towards the end of Nehru's tenure. The agriculture sector, which is the base for industrial expansion, was in shambles by the late 1950s and the early 1960s. Land reforms had failed miserably. Whereas in 1953–4 three-fourths of the agricultural households owned 16 per cent of the land, in 1961–2 the same proportion of households owned 20 per cent of the land. In June 1966, 60 per cent of all agricultural families remained outside the cooperative movement. The rural elite was averse to redistribution of resources.[32] Foodgrain production in 1962–3 declined below the levels of 1961–2. While industry was growing, even if at a lower than targeted rate of growth of 8 per cent, the economy was in dire need of agricultural growth.[33]

The period between 1964 and 1968, beginning with the prime ministership of Lal Bahadur Shastri and lasting till the early years of Mrs Gandhi's tenure, witnessed greater attention to India's agriculture. The power of the Planning Commission, which was a firm supporter of capital-intensive industrialization, was reduced. Members of the Planning Commission now had fixed tenures, and the Cabinet Secretary would no longer be the secretary of the Planning Commission. Finance Minister T.T. Krishnamachari, who felt the need for heavy industrialization rather than price and technological incentives, had to resign. Sachin Choudhury and Morarji Desai, the two finance ministers who succeeded Krishnamachari, were not in favour of sacrificing agriculture for industry. Shastri's secretariat had more cordial relations with the Federation of Indian Chambers of Commerce and Industry than was the case during the Nehru period.[34]

Shastri increased the powers of the Prime Minister's Office (PMO). His secretary L.K. Jha, who was more inclined towards viewing government as regulator rather than as an entrepreneur, became influential. Shastri's office systematically engineered a reduction in the importance of the Planning Commission and tried to change the mindset of the Ministry of Finance. He brought in the technocratic minister of Steel and Heavy Industries, C. Subramaniam, as minister of Food and Agriculture. Subramaniam advanced arguments to justify the need for better seeds, pesticides, irrigation, and price incentives for ensuring agrarian development and food self-sufficiency that were reminiscent of the reasons advanced for increasing self-sufficiency in iron and steel as the engine of India's industrial growth during the Second Five-Year Plan. The reduced power of the Planning Commission and the increased role of the National Development Council, composed of state chief ministers who favoured a pro-agriculture policy, aided Subramaniam's designs of boosting Indian agriculture.

The Planning Commission became more of an advisory body composed of technocrats. It was to give technical guidelines in consultation with the NDC after taking into account political considerations.[35] The famous Gadgil formula was worked out as a means of distributing resources to the states.[36] The paucity of resources ensured that there could only be annual plans for the years 1966–7, 1967–8 and 1968–9. The Fourth Five-Year Plan had to wait till 1969. Mrs Gandhi reinforced efforts to reduce the Planning Commission's opposition to the new agricultural strategy by making the Minister of Food and Agriculture, C. Subramaniam, a member of the Commission. In 1966, the differences between the Ministry of Food and Agriculture and the Planning Commission had been removed.[37]

Last but not least, the donors became less tolerant of India's anti-agriculture position after 1963.[38] India's dependence on the Western Aid India Consortium and the World Bank was very substantial at this time. Moreover, in 1966, President Johnson refused to renew shipments of foodgrains to India under Public Law 480 at the time of a drought, which left India's strategy of independent economic development vulnerable to Western designs. While the US government's policy of carrot and stick, working in conjunction with the initiatives of the Rockefeller Foundation, drove India to self-sufficiency in foodgrains, the consensus about laying greater emphasis on agriculture was an internal decision, which was taken during the time of Prime Minister Shastri and was supported by Mrs Indira Gandhi.[39]

The results of this strategy of agrarian self-sufficiency were quite spectacular, even though its gains remained restricted to the wheat-growing areas of Punjab, Haryana, and western Uttar Pradesh. India's food output increased from 72 million tons to 108 million tons between 1967–8 and 1970–1. India had imported 10 million tons of wheat from the US in 1965. By 1971, its food reserves were about 8 million tons.[40]

Trade liberalization was short-lived in the aftermath of a balance of payments crisis in 1966. Unlike in the area of agriculture, where an internal consensus on reforms had emerged, the technocratic and political elite was not convinced that increasing India's export orientation would be good for reducing India's dependence on foreign aid. A variety of powerful arguments made in favour of export pessimism overshadowed the ones that favoured exports. First, the political class was largely opposed to the devaluation of the rupee, which was a condition for securing finances for the Fourth Five-Year Plan. Second, Indian industry, which was well adjusted to a protected home market, did not favour trade reforms. Third, the devaluation and liberalization policies pursued by the government did not engender levels of aid and export growth that would have made these policies more durable. The policies favouring trade reforms were reversed by 1969. India lost an opportunity to benefit from globalization at a time when East and Southeast Asia engaged global capital and markets for pursuing their strategy of economic development.[41]

THE RISE OF STATE CAPITAL, 1969–73

The period between 1969 and 1973 saw conflicts emerge between the old guard of the Congress Party called the 'Syndicate', and Prime Minister Mrs Indira Gandhi, whose support base was the Left-oriented members of the Congress Party in the Congress Forum for Socialist Action, and the Communist Party of India. The conflict became full-blown in the Faridabad session of the Congress Party in April 1969, when Mrs Gandhi directly attacked Congress president Nijalingappa. When the Congress president proposed the name of Neelam Sanjeeva Reddy for presidency of the country, Mrs Gandhi opposed this move by proposing the name of the trade union leader V.V. Giri. Mrs Gandhi was worried that a president elected by the Syndicate would try to dislodge her from power. V.V. Giri won the election to presidency only by a narrow margin. A majority of the Congress members of parliament and the state-level members of legislative assemblies had voted for Neelam Sanjeeva Reddy. Giri could not have won the election without support from the left within the Congress and from the Communist Party of India.[42]

Mrs Gandhi's policies subsequently needed to follow the course of satisfying the Left. The traditional Congress support base was not likely to be of much help under these circumstances. The state very quickly came to acquire the commanding heights of the economy in a manner that surpassed Nehru's record of encouraging public ownership of assets. All the major banks were nationalized, covering over 85 per cent of the bank deposits in 1969. In the same year, the Monopolies and Restrictive Trade Practices Act barred all commercial enterprises valued at greater than Rs 200 million from expansion or diversification. The industrial licensing policy was made more stringent in 1970. Between 1969 and 1971 the government nationalized the coal, copper, general insurance and significant parts of the steel industry. The wheat trade was nationalized in 1973.[43] The Foreign Exchange Regulation Act (1974) brought down the permissible level of foreign equity in Indian firms from 51 per cent to 40 per cent. Indian company law requires 51 per cent of the votes for the passage of ordinary resolutions dealing with the closure of business and the appointment and removal of directors.

EXPERIMENTS WITH LIBERALIZATION

The radical economic stance favouring state control and inward oriented industrialization began to change slowly but perceptibly after 1974. This was a response to the continuing crisis of public policy in dealing with social mobilizations. It is plausible to argue that the politics of command directed from the state now turned into a politics of aggressive demands made on the state by social actors seeking a better quality of life.[44]

The deprivations that the people were willing to bear when the prices of essential commodities rose in the mid-1960s now produced violent unrest, which could not be brought under control by the regular coercive machinery of the state. Jayaprakash Narayan was the charismatic leader who brought the social forces together in the mid-1970s.[45] Mrs Gandhi failed to contain student unrest in Gujarat and Bihar, which was fuelled by inflation. She gave up the idea of nationalizing the foodgrain trade in 1974. The deflationary macroeconomic policy introduced to curb inflation resulted in worker unrest. In May 1974, 1.7 million railway workers went on strike. Mrs Gandhi's position became politically weak after the Allahabad High Court found in June 1975 that she had committed corrupt practices under the Representation of People's Act. Her inability to deal with the protest led to the proclamation of Emergency in June 1975. The period between June 1975 and the elections in March 1977 produced the only period of authoritarian rule in India's post-colonial political history.[46]

Mrs. Gandhi initiated a policy change that would seek to promote exports and interfere less with the activities of private capital. The pro-business tilt in India's economic policy began in 1975. These policies began having a cumulative effect on growth rates after 1980, which was a major break from growth rates of the past. The growth in India's per capita income, which was 1.4 per cent per annum between 1950 and 1980, accelerated to 3.6 per cent per annum between 1980 and 2004.[47]

This policy shift, even though it was not very significant compared to developments in other parts of East and Southeast Asia, was significant in relation to policies pursued in India between 1969 and 1974. Moreover, these shifts reflected India's own learning with previous experiences in policy-making. The steady devaluation of the rupee, deflationary economic policy, and the decision not to take over wheat trade in 1974 signalled a quiet departure from previous practices. The New Economic Programme of 1975–6 gradually liberalized the procedure for increasing production capacity beyond what was stipulated in the license. It made it easier for private industry to conduct research and development; procure licenses for production, imports and exports; and encouraged foreign collaborations.[48]

The Janata Party government that came to power in 1977 pursued private sector-enabling politics. Its electoral victory had resulted from the movement spearheaded by Jayaprakash Narayan. The new dispensation emphasized agriculture over industry. It tried to promote small-scale industries. The government was averse to public sector undertakings and removed the 10 per cent price preference for these enterprises. It abolished price controls on sugar and the food zoning system. The government eased procedures for private sector credit and imports.[49] These measures may have aided the realization of 8 per cent growth in Indian industry in 1980.[50]

Several reports and policy documents critical of government policy came to characterize the Janata government (1977–9) and the Congress governments of Indira Gandhi (1980–3) and Rajiv Gandhi (1984–9). Various reports of the Government of India beginning from the late 1970s began arguing the case for increasing export orientation for financing India's development.[51] The influential report of Vadilal Dagli[52] demonstrated the adverse consequences of the system of controls, which resulted in delays and corruption. Narasimham (1985) argued against controls and in favour of exposing the Indian economy to the winds of competition. Abid Hussain[53] argued for making trade an integral part of India's development strategy.[54] Mrs Gandhi was surrounded by liberal-minded technocrats like P.C. Alexander, L.K. Jha and Manmohan Singh in the early 1980s, who thought differently from earlier economic policy influentials like D.P. Dhar and P.N. Haksar. It is not a coincidence that L.K. Jha, who was influential during the mid-1960s when liberalization had been attempted, was to become an important player again in the early 1980s.

The idea of homegrown conditionality was emphasized when India successfully sought a large IMF drawing of SDR 5 billion in the aftermath of the second oil shock in 1979. India pre-empted IMF conditionalities by embedding reforms relating to macroeconomic adjustment within the Sixth Five-Year Plan (1980–5). 53 per cent of the loan was for public sector investments. Export promotion and import liberalization were emphasized, along with import substitution in power, fertilizer. and insecticides. While the Indian state did not work out a pro-market compromise with the IMF, it moved towards pro-business deregulation against opposition from the Left in India. The US, UK, and Australia had opposed this loan within the IMF but did not use the veto.[55]

Rajiv Gandhi's tenure was unabashedly more tilted towards promoting Indian business for engendering efficiency and growth than any regime in the past. Big business was redefined: the Monopoly and Restrictive Trade Practices (MRTP) Act would now regulate businesses worth more than Rs 1 billion as compared with the earlier size limit of Rs 200 million. Fewer firms would now come under the MRTP's regulatory sway. Eighty-two intermediate industries, such as electronic machinery and machine and drug-related industries were delicensed, and it became easier to obtain a license in others. Broadbanding permitted entrepreneurs greater freedom to choose between product types without seeking permissions for production. Capacity expansion became much easier.[56]

Physical infrastructure was viewed as a critical component of private sector-oriented growth. The National Thermal Power Corporation funded by the World Bank became one of largest power producers in the world using coal. The Mahanagar Telephone Nigam Limited (MTNL) providing telecom services in the metropolitan areas of Delhi and Mumbai, was made autonomous of the Department of Telecommunications and corporatized against the wishes of the majority of the telecom unions. Corporatization or creating government-owned entities autonomous from their respective ministries was designed to make the government-owned telecom service provider more efficient. Private production of telecommunications equipment was also allowed in the mid to late 1980s.[57]

Rajiv Gandhi's pro-business budget of 1985 was criticized at the Congress Party's session in 1985 for not having invoked socialism as an explicit goal.[58] Organized labour opposed the corporatization or privatization of public assets wherever it was attempted. The opposition to economic liberalization was further complicated by the allegation that Rajiv Gandhi was involved with the Bofors scandal concerning financial kickbacks due to the acquisition of a Swedish gun for the Indian Army.[59]

The state began to retreat from the liberal agenda from 1986 onwards. In 1986 the customs duty on some capital goods and machine tools was raised. In 1987 customs duty on imports of all machinery, except those for power and fertilizers, was raised to 85 per cent. Direct taxes were not raised but indirect taxes were raised to shore up revenue. Anti-poverty programmes were initiated in 1987 to garner a pro-poor image. The 1988 budget aided the large farmers by increasing outlays in agriculture, irrigation, fertilizer, and pesticides. Protection for capital goods industries was increased. In the face of impending elections, the 1989 budget was designed as a pro-poor budget. The Jawahar Rojgar Yojana was to uplift 44 million rural people out of poverty.[60]

The retreat of the state from the agenda of promoting India's competitiveness could be viewed as reflecting the increasing power of both the rich agrarian and indigenous business communities in economic policy. The rich- and middle-farmer agrarian community got mobilized in the 1980s and demanded investments and subsidies. It would not tolerate the discrimination against rural India by urban India, which became famously dubbed as 'Bharat versus India'. A state inclined towards protecting indigenous business could not discipline capital by accepting external competition. The traditional industrial houses maintained their clout in the context of a protected economy. Reliance was perhaps the only major new corporate player to emerge during this regime. Its growth was premised on excellent relations with the state, which enabled the company to obtain the permissions it needed. Economic liberalization promoting competition would therefore not be easy, even though there was a considerable consensus within the government to pursue it.[61]

THIS BOOK

This reader carries a mix of published essays—suitably updated—written over the last ten years, and fresh contributions to the field. Divided into three sections, the first engages with development thinking on the causes and consequences of the far-reaching reforms introduced in 1991. The analysis in the preceding sections has demonstrated how import substitution was locked in a political economy that could not easily be disciplined towards accepting the greater competition associated with promoting exports. 1991 was a major break in the pace of freeing the state from direct intervention in the economy and promoting competition. How was this political economy overturned and with what consequences? After 1991, the state sought to focus more attention on government failure and took upon itself the role of creating and regulating markets in sectors such as power, telecommunications, stock exchanges, and the like.

The reader begins with two diametrically opposite views on the economic conditions that produced the reforms beyond 1991. In Chapter 1, Jagdish Bhagwati points towards the low levels of productivity due to the nature of India's import-substituting industrialization and the vested interests that it spawned within the business community, the bureaucracy, and the political class. These policy failures, which were well understood by the technocracy, could be addressed at the time of the balance of payments crisis in 1991, despite opposition from the vested interests who had resisted it during the 1980s. In Chapter 2, Prabhat Patnaik and C.P. Chandrasekhar suggest that there was no imminent need to undertake the kind of policy reforms that were dictated by the Fund–Bank lobby in 1991. There was no crisis in the real economy. The crisis was caused largely by finance capital, which decided to withdraw from India at the time of an exogenous shock. The chapter points to contradictions within India's model of import substitution and highlights the problems facing structural adjustment in India. It argues the case for an alternative development paradigm. In Chapter 3, Montek Ahluwalia describes the achievements and challenges facing India's gradual reforms. This macro picture of India's economic liberalization describes the evolving relationship between the state and the market in areas such as industry, trade, agriculture, infrastructure, the financial sector, and the social sector.

Chapters 4–7 in Section II explain the political economy of reforms beyond 1991. In Chapter 4, Rahul Mukherji traces the roots of ideational changes within the Indian political and technocratic elite. The chapter presents a mechanism for comprehending conditions under which the crisis of 1991 produced a bargaining situation in a two-level game between multilateral agencies like the International Monetary Fund and the World Bank; the executive; and capital and labour. This enabled the Indian executive to pursue a policy line which was impossible in the absence of a crisis. Ashutosh Varshney argues in Chapter 5 that economic reforms in India could occur due to the distraction of identity politics, which became so vivid in public memory after the demolition of the Babri mosque in Ayodhya. Also, reforms occurred in areas that concerned 'elite politics', such as trade, investment and finance, and not in areas dominated by 'mass politics' like fiscal deficit and labour laws. In Chapter 6, Rob Jenkins argues that economic reforms in India occurred by stealth, which emphasizes change in the garb of continuity. In Chapter 7, Baldev Raj Nayar describes how bi-partisan support for economic reforms was born after the advent of the Bharatiya Janata Party government. The political economy of reforms had now become so entrenched that a liberal policy line had come to stay, irrespective of the party in power.

Section III covering chapters 8–14 deals with the impact of economic reforms on the political economy of India. The nature of the sub-national state in India had been an important source of variation for determining the investment climate in India before 1991. This variation has been explained in terms of the nature of the developmental bureaucracy, the political roots of developmentalism located within a social structure, and the nature of the relationship between the central and the state government.[62] Lloyd and Susanne Rudolph in Chapter 8 enlighten us about the reasons why state-level strategies at the sub-national level have become more important for growth after 1991, when the Centre's contribution to providing finances to the states became much less. This dynamic has led to growing regional inequality between the better-governed investment-attracting states and those where investors do not find a safe refuge. The bad news is that poor states like Bihar, Orissa, and Uttar Pradesh, which are not governed effectively, also account for that vast majority of India's population.[63]

Jason Kirk in Chapter 9 explains the political economy of how the World Bank went sub-national in India. The Bank began to focus on certain states and would provide conditional funds to that state in return for pursuing the good-governance agenda. Both the Central government in India (especially the Ministry of Finance) and the World Bank understood that they needed to be able to deal with states if they were to seriously pursue their development agenda. The Bank approached the Ministry of Finance for permission to initiate sub-national funding, and the Ministry agreed because it was hopeful that the World Bank leverage through its ability to fund development might engender good governance in the states. The relationship between Bank involvement and good governance in Indian states is a promising area for further research.

Economic reforms have entailed the creation and regulation of markets that would work efficiently towards creating infrastructure. India is embarking on regulation in areas such as airports, roads, ports, and a variety of sectors where competition needed to be promoted against the monopolistic propensities of state and private capital. Chapter 10 by Rahul Mukherji tries to discern why India's telecommunications reforms succeeded but power sector reforms were impeded by political bottlenecks.[64] Chapter 11 by John Echeverri-Gent explains the success of India's stock market reforms.

India's success in reforming the stock market and the telecommunications sector was aided by technological developments, which facilitated institutional change, promoting efficiency by enhancing competition. Second, both these sectors were regulated at the level of the central government, and the necessity of efficient stock exchanges and telecommunications for engendering development was clearly understood by the technocratic elite. Third, the fiscal crisis of the Indian state made stock-market reforms and private investment in telecommunications critical. In both cases, reforming existing institutions and engendering greater efficiency was not politically feasible, and competition had to be promoted from outside. In the case of stock-market reform, a government-controlled National Stock Exchange was made to compete with the broker-driven Bombay Stock Exchange. In the case of telecommunications reform, competition from the private sector nudged the government-owned companies to become more efficient. Promoting competition rather than privatization may hold the key to enhancing productivity and growth in India.

The power sector was less amenable to competition because power tariffs could not easily be realized in rural areas. The sector was affected by what Ashutosh Varshney called the logic of 'mass politics' in Chapter 5. Competition could only work in the context of a market when consumers were willing to pay. It was necessary to evolve political support for the rationalization of power subsidies, which would benefit the needy from the revenues derived from those who could afford to pay. Rationalizing power sector tariffs was as much a political as an economic issue, which the World Bank and the Government of India had failed to take note of in their experiments with privatizing the sector. Since power is a state subject, there needed to be a better understanding of what produces good regulatory governance at the state level, and of the impact of the Electricity Act 2003 in promoting or debilitating such governance. Taken together, Chapters 9–11 provide insights for scholars and policy-makers who are trying to understand how efficient markets are created, and the ways to deal with market failure.

Chapter 12 by AnnaLee Saxenian, dealing with the the growth of India's information technology sector, shows how the state aided the IT sector to realize its potential in world markets via export-oriented trade policy and the creation of infrastructure. However, there is a fundamental difference between Bangalore and the Silicon Valley. While Silicon Valley plays a vital role in enhancing US productivity, India's export-oriented IT sector does not. India's software sector needed to play a more central role in promoting India's development by making IT applications for domestic use that could bring advantages to the common citizen.

In Chapter 13, Supriya RoyChowdhury discusses the trends in trade union politics in India. Roychoudhury argues that trade union power has declined in an era of sub-contracting, voluntary retirement schemes, and improved worker-management relations. This analysis begs the question of how India's trade unions can succeed in checking the exploitative informalization of labour by becoming more inclusive. While India's trade unions typically carry less than 10 per cent of the work force with them, the same figure for Scandinavian countries is 90 per cent. Higher membership is likely to reduce privileges for some but increase them for the vast majority of the workforce. This is an important issue because India's growth has been criticized for not being an employment-engendering process.[65]

Stanley Kochanek's chapter on the organization of Indian industry divides the story into three phases (Chapter 14). The first phase between 1951 and 1969 was the golden age for private capital protected from competition and aided by the state. The second phase between 1969 and 1979 was a period of 'briefcase politics', which was based to a great extent on the ability of firms to establish a working relationship with the state. From the 1980s, there have been greater demands for transparency and good corporate governance. This is also the period that witnessed the rise of the Confederation of Indian Industry (CII). A vigorous constituency for reform of trade and foreign investment policies is yet to take shape.

THE CHALLENGES AHEAD

Human development has not been one of India's successes, even though growth rates picked up after 1980, and may have accelerated further in the last few years. Economic growth during an era of reforms needed to be converted into human development. Nutrition, health, education, and sanitation for the vast majority of Indians would require efficient public service delivery for the poor who are not within the purview of the market.[66] Since the logic of competition has limitations in this area, scholars and policy-makers need to comprehend the sources of social power that impede the maturing of the welfare state in India. To give one example, Myron Weiner found an explanation embedded in India's social structure that throws light on the lack of universal elementary education in India.[67] Poverty reduction was found to be seriously affected by the social bases of the power of the ruling party in an Indian state.[68] The poorest districts in India like Kalahandi, Koraput and Bolangir suffered neither from lack of agricultural productivity nor central-level funds. Yet, these districts, with a high concentration of tribal population, were among the most malnourished in India.[69] A major telecommunications initiative for improving rural connectivity was used by big corporations to increase their profits in urban areas.[70]

Another pressing challenge for India's political economy is the decline of Indian agriculture and rural employment.[71] The political economy of agrarian distress might well turn out to be a political economy of subsidies to rich farmers at the expense of the poor. Why will the rich farmer forego free power, water, and subsidized fertilizers, in order to enable the state to focus on amenities to improve the lot of the poorer farmers? If such redistribution is not possible, additional investments would be required to take care of poverty in rural areas. This question of agrarian redistribution has vexed policy makers since the time of Jawaharlal Nehru.

A globalizing state needed welfare to a greater extent than a closed economy, because globalization and specialization can produce growth and social disruption. The states of Scandinavia, which were more dependent on the world economy than the United States, also played a more central role in securing their citizens lives. All developed countries which view trade as an important factor in development policy have a reasonable provision for social security. As India's promising economic growth becomes more dependent on the global economy, the state will need to produce not only competitive firms but will also need to secure its citizens from the ravages of uncertainty.[72] Ensuring growth with redistribution in India would require the transformation of state-society relations towards a more inclusive growth paradigm. India's democracy should facilitate an inclusive political economy of development in an era of globalization. Students of politics and sociology would need to contribute as much as economists for comprehending the social bottlenecks obstructing the politics of growth and redistribution in India.

NOTES AND REFERENCES

1. The author would like to thank Francine R. Frankel, Baldev Raj Nayar, Susanne Rudolph, Lloyd Rudolph, Montek S. Ahluwalia, Sumit Ganguly, C.P. Bhambri, Medha Malik Kudiasya, Gyanesh Kudaisya, Partha Nath Mukherji, Siddhartha Mukerji, Sitaram Kumbhar, and Anjali Mukherji for suggestions. The Institute of South Asian Studies, National University of Singapore, and the Centre for Political Studies, Jawaharlal Nehru University's project on political institutions supported this research. The shortcomings, as usual, rest with the author.

2. Nehru's views about the role of the state were quite sophisticated. Even though Nehru was in favour of redistribution and the role of state in development, he understood the need for growth and efficiency. Consequently, he did see an important role for the private sector as well. P.N. Dhar, *The Evolution of Economic Policy in India* (New Delhi, Oxford University Press, 2003: 230–3).

3. Sardar Patel was not only India's first Home Minister and Deputy Prime Minister; he wielded enormous power within the Congress Party and the government.

4. This broad characterization holds true when compared with the period

1969–74. The period between 1954–64, which saw the rise of Nehru and the Second Five-Year Plan, saw a greater role of the state in the economy compared with the sub-periods 1947–54 and 1964–8. This section will explain why this was the case.

5. Francine R. Frankel, *India's Political Economy 1947–2004* (New Delhi, Oxford University Press, 2005).

6. Nehru's candidate was J.B. Kripalani. See also Frankel, *India's Political Economy*, pp. 88–90.

7. Medha M. Kudaisya, *The Life and Times of G.D. Birla* (New Delhi, Oxford University Press, 2003), chap. 11.

8. The managing agency system was considered to be a colonial device by which managers could control a large number of commercial and financial enterprises.

9. The three sectors reserved for government were arms and ammunitions, atomic energy, and railways. The government would not abolish existing enterprises but reserved the right to introduce new commercial activity in areas such as coal, iron and steel, minerals, shipbuilding, aircraft manufacturing, and telephone and telegraph equipment.

10. Frankel, *India's Political Economy*, pp. 84–6, 94–6; Dwijendra Tripathy, *The Oxford History of Indian Business* (New Delhi: Oxford University Press, 2004), p. 85. There is evidence to suggest that I.G. Patel, who chaired a committee on the managing agency system in the 1960s, was sympathetic to its contribution the management of private enterprises in India in an era of scarce managerial talent. I.G. Patel, *Glimpses of Indian Economic Policy* (New Delhi, Oxford University Press, 2003), pp. 99–100.

11. The bill heralded the beginning of industrial licensing alongside a comprehensive system of controls that could interfere with management practices in private enterprises.

12. Michael Brecher, *Nehru: A Political Biography* (London, Oxford University Press, 1961), p. 197; Kudaisya, *The Life and Times of G.D. Birla*, pp. 305–11.

13. Vivek Chibber, *Locked in Place* (Princeton and Oxford, Princeton University Press, 2003), chap. 6

14. Ibid., pp. 146–52.

15. Jagdish N. Bhagwati and Padma Desai, *India: Planning for Industrialization* (London and New York, Oxford University Press, 1970), pp. 114–20.

16. Kudaisya, *The Life and Times of G.D. Birla*, pp. 309–11.

17. India's First Five-Year Plan began in 1951, even though the final plan document was ready only in 1952.

18. Kudaisya, *The Life and Times of G.D. Birla*, pp. 311–2.

19. A.H. Hanson, *The Process of Planning* (London, Oxford University Press, 1966), chap. III.

20. The National Development Council had been formed in order to give the states the opportunity to review the plans and recommend social and economic policies.

21. Hanson, *The Process of Planning*, chapter V; Frankel, *India's Political Economy*, chap. 4; Patel, *Glimpses of Indian Economic Policy*, chap. 2.

22. B.R. Shenoy favoured the consumer goods sector and greater emphasis on the market mechanism. Even though a compromise was reached between the 'big planners' and the 'small planners', the big planners won the day. *India: Planning for Industrialization*, pp. 114–20. C.N. Vakil and P.R. Brahmananda were also critical of the Second Five-Year Plan. Terence J. Byres (a), 'The Creation of "The Tribe of Pundits Called Economists": Institutions, Institution Builders and Economic Debate', in Terence J. Byres (ed.), *The Indian Economy* (New Delhi, Oxford University Press, 1998), pp. 20–73. Terence J. Byres (b), 'From Ivory Tower to the Belly of the Beast: The Academy, the State, and Economic Debate in Post-Independence India', in Terence J. Byres (ed.), *The Indian Economy* (New Delhi: Oxford University Press, 1998), pp. 74–158.

23. Patel, *Glimpses of Indian Economic Policy*, pp. 38–46.

24. Mahalanobis was a gifted statistician who got interested in planning. His intellectual prowess as a scholar had won worldwide acclaim. He was a close associate of Nehru. Apart from his contribution to planning, Mahalanobis was the founder of the Indian Statistical Institute and the National Sample Survey. Byres, 'The Creation', pp. 41–50. On India's strategy of heavy industrialization typified in the Second Five-Year Plan, see Sukhamoy Chakravarty, *Development Planning* (Oxford, Clarendon Press, 1987), chap. 2; Baldev Raj Nayar, 'Political Mainsprings of Economic Planning in the New Nations,' *Comparative Politics*, 6, 3, April (1974), pp. 361–3; Hanson, *The Process of Planning*, chap. V.

25. Bhagwati and Desai, *India: Planning for Industrialization*, pp. 115–16, chap. 9; Patel, *Glimpses of Indian Economic Policy*, pp. 46–9; Frankel, *India's Political Economy*, p. 131.

26. Kudaisya, *The Life and Times of G.D. Birla*, pp. 313–16.

27. Frankel, *India's Political Economy*, pp. 129–31; Rudolph and Rudolph, *In Pursuit of Lakshmi*, pp. 23–6.

28. Bhagwati and Desai, *India: Planning for* Industrialization, pp. 115–16.

29. Frankel, *India's Political Economy*, chaps. 4–5, Ashutosh Varshney, *Democracy, Development, and the Countryside: Urban-Rural Struggles in India* (Cambridge and New York, Cambridge University Press, 1998), chap. 2.

30. Kripalani was earlier Nehru's candidate for the Congress President in 1950, when he had lost the election to Tandon.

31. Frankel, *India's Political Economy*, chap. 6. The six right-wing cabinet ministers who resigned in 1963 included S.K. Patil (Agriculture) and Morarji Desai (Finance).

32. Francine R. Frankel, 'Ideology and Politics in Economic Planning: The Problem of Indian Agricultural Development Strategy', *World Politics,* 19, 4, July (1967), pp. 621–45; Francine R. Frankel, 'Compulsion and Social Change: Is Authoritarianism the Solution to India's Economic Development Problem?' *World Politics* 30, 2, January (1978), pp. 215–40.

33. Even though land reform failed, about twenty million tenants came to acquire a substantial proportion of the fourteen million hectares of land that was redistributed. These tenant bullock capitalists subsequently became a force in Indian politics from the 1970s (Rudolph and Rudolph, 1987, chapters 12–13); Frankel, *India's Political Economy,* p. 216.

34. Ibid., chap. 7; Varshney, *Democracy, Development, and the Countryside,* chap. 3; Kudaisya, *The Life and Times of G.D. Birla,* pp. 205–29.

35. D.R. Gadgil, the new deputy chairman of the Planning Commission, was a well-known critic of the Commission since the First Plan. He believed that role of the Commission ought to be technical and advisory rather than political. Hanson, *The Process of Planning,* pp. 71–2, 97–8; Frankel, *India's Political Economy,* p. 309.

36. Of the total central assistance to be given to the states, 60 per cent would be distributed on the basis of population, 10 per cent on the basis of the tax effort in relation to per capita income, and 10 per cent would depend on commitments to major projects in areas such as irrigation and power. The Centre's grants would be equal to about 20 per cent of the state's revenue mobilization effort. There would also be grants to states like Jammu and Kashmir or states in Northeast India, which would not follow this logic. Frankel, *India's Political Economy,* p. 312.

37. Frankel, *India's Political Economy,* chaps. 7–8; Varshney, *Democracy, Development, and the Countryside,* chap. 3; Gurcharan Das, *India Unbound* (New Delhi, Penguin Books, 2002), chap. 9.

38. Patel, *Glimpses of Indian Economic Policy,* chap. 4; Bruce Muirhead, 'Differing Perspectives: India, the World Bank and the 1963 Aid-India Negotiations', *India Review,* 4, 1, January (2005), pp. 1–22. For a sympathetic account of the Indian planning and development experience, which reflected the donor position in the early 1960s, see John Lewis, *Quiet Crisis in India* (New York, Anchor Books, 1964).

39. Varshney, *Democracy, Development, and the Countryside,* chap. 3.

40. Ibid., pp. 48–9.

41. Rahul Mukherji, 'India's Aborted Liberalization – 1966', *Pacific Affairs,* 73, 3, Fall (2000), pp. 375–92; P.N. Dhar, *The Evolution of Economic Policy in India* (New Delhi, Oxford University Press, 2003), pp. 20–1. On the growth strategies deploying trade as a route to development in East Asia, see Stephan Haggard, *Pathways from the Periphery,* Ithaca, Cornell University Press, 1990);

Robert Wade, *Governing The Market* (New Jersey, Princeton University Press, 1990); and Alice Amsden, *Asia's Next Giant* (New York, Oxford University Press, 1990).

42. Frankel, India's Political Economy, chap. 10; Dhar, *The Evolution of Economic Policy*, chap. 1.

43. Baldev Raj Nayar, 'When Did the 'Hindu Rate of Growth End?' *Economic and Political Weekly,* May 13 (2006), p. 1886; Baldev Raj Nayar, *India's Mixed Economy* (Bombay: Popular Prakashan, 1989), chap. 7.

44. Lloyd I. Rudolph and Susanne H. Rudolph, *In Pursuit of Lakshmi* (Chicago, The University of Chicago Press, 1987), chaps. 9–13.

45. Jayaprakash Narayan, a radical socialist and close associate of Mohandas Gandhi and Nehru, was one of the leaders who had spearheaded the formation of the socialist group within the Congress Party in 1933. He was actively involved with the Bhoodan and Gramdan movements for redistributing land in post-colonial India.

46. Frankel, *India's Political Economy*, pp. 515–47. For an argument regarding how Mrs Gandhi's inability to garner votes from the reliable Congress support base led to the politics of patronage between 1969–74, see Charles Hankla, 'Party Linkages and Economic Policy: An Examination of Indira   Gandhi's India', *Business and Politics,* 8, 3 (2006). For a description of how Mrs Gandhi could not use emergency powers to nudge India in a developmental direction, see Jyotirindra Dasgupta, 'A Season of Ceasars: Emergency Regimes and Development in Asia', *Asian Survey* 18, 4, April (1978), pp. 332–7.

47. Deepak Nayyar, 'India's Unfinished Journey: Transforming Growth into Development', *Modern Asian Studies,* 40, 3 (2006), pp. 800–10.

48. Nayar, 'When Did the 'Hindu Rate of Growth End?', pp. 1885–90; Baldev Raj Nayar, *India's Globalization* (Washington, East-West Centre, Policy Studies No. 22), pp. 10–13; Siddhartha Mukerji, 'State and Industrial Transformation in India: 1966–1987', unpublished M.Phil. dissertation, Jawaharlal Nehru University (2007), pp. 49–53.

49. Baldev Raj Nayar, *The Political Economy of India's Public Sector* (Bombay, Popular Prakashan, 1990), p. 34.

50. Atul Kohli, *Democracy and Discontent* (New York, Cambridge University Press, 1990), pp. 311–2.

51. P.N. Dhar, 'The Indian Economy', in Robert E.B. Lucas and Gustave F. Papanek (eds), *The Indian Economy* (New Delhi, Oxford University Press, 1988), pp. 13–14.

52. Dagli, Vadilal (chair), *Report of the Committee on Control and Subsidies* (New Delhi: Government of India, 1979).

53. Hussain, Abid (chair), *Report of the Committee on Trade Policies* (New Delhi: Government of India, Ministry of Commerce, 1984).

54. Nayar, *The Political Economy of India's Public Sector*, pp. 56–8.

55. Praveen K. Chaudhry, Vijay L. Kelkar and Vikash Yadav, 'The Evolution of "Homegrown Conditionality" in India-IMF Relations', *Journal of Development Studies*, 40, 6, August (2004), pp. 64–81; John G. Ruggie, 'Political Structure and Change in the International Economic Order: The North-South Dimension', in John G. Ruggie (ed.), *Antinomies of Interdependence* (New York, Columbia University Press, 1983), pp. 453–89.

56. Nayar, *The Political Economy of India's Public Sector*, pp. 58–63.

57. Rahul Mukherji, 'Managing Competition', *India Review* 3, 4, October (2004), pp. 278–305; Biswatosh Saha, 'State Support or R&D in Developing Countries: Telecom Equipment Industry in India and China', *Economic and Political Weekly*, August 28 (2004), pp. 3917–21.

58. Rajiv Gandhi, *Selected Speeches and Writings – 1986* (New Delhi, Publications Division of the Ministry of Information and Broadcasting, 1989), pp. 66–72.

59. Atul Kohli, *Democracy and Discontent* (New York, Cambridge University Press, 1990), chap. 11; Nayar, *The Political Economy of India's Public Sector*, pp. 83–7; Rahul Mukherji, 'Promoting Competition in India's Telecom Sector', in Vikram Chand (ed.), *Reinventing Public Service Delivery in India* (Washington and New Delhi: World Bank and Sage, 2006), pp. 65–6.

60. Nayar, *The Political Economy of India's Public* Sector, pp. 98–104. The Jawahar Rojgar Yojana initiated in 1989 led to the creation of about 697 billion persondays by 1997 and contributed to the creation of physical assets in forestry, mining, agriculture, and rural development.

61. One influential view about this class conflict is to be found in Pranab Bardhan, *The Political Economy of Development in India* (Oxford, Basil Blackwell, 1984). On the rise of the farmers, see Varshney *Democracy, Development, and the Countryside,* chap. 5; Akhil Gupta, *Postcolonial Developments: Agriculture in the Making of Modern India* (Durham, Duke University Press, 1998), chap. 1. On the relationship between mobilization, party competition and expenditures, see Pradeep Chhibber, 'Political Parties, Electoral Expenditures and Economic Reform in India', *The Journal of Development Studies* 32, 1, October (1995).

62. Aseema Sinha, *The Regional Roots of Developmental Politics in India* (Bloomington, Indiana University Press, 2005).

63. See also Montek S. Ahluwalia, 'State-level Performance under Economic Reforms in India,' in Anne Krueger (ed.), *Economic Policy Reforms and the Indian Economy* (New Delhi, Oxford University Press, 2002).

64. I have argued elsewhere that the telecommunications success is still largely an urban phenomenon and the regulator still has a long way to go in bringing rural connectivity at par with urban connectivity. Mukherji, 'Promoting Competition, pp. 82–6. This is a case of market failure that regulators must

address in telecommunications and other sectors. In that sense, the success in telecommunications is a limited success that has produced the lowest tariffs in the world and brought greater numbers of people within the purview of the market.

65. Nayyar, 'India's Unfinished Journey', pp. 820–3.

66. Ibid.; Vikram Chand, 'Institutional Innovations in Public Service Delivery in India', in Vikram Chand (ed.), *Reinventing Public Service Delivery in India* (Washington DC and New Delhi, World Bank and Sage Publications, 2006).

67. Myron Weiner, *The Child and the State in India* (New Jersey: Princeton University Press, 1991); Ashutosh Varshney, 'Why Haven't Poor Democracies Eliminated Poverty', in Ashutosh Varshney (ed.), *India and the Politics of Developing Countries* (New Delhi: Sage Publications, 2004).

68. Atul Kohli, *The State and Poverty in India* (New York: Cambridge University Press, 1987).

69. Sitaram Kumbhar, 'The Politics of Poverty in Orissa', unpublished M.Phil. dissertation, Jawaharlal Nehru University (2005), chap. 2.

70. Mukherji, Promoting Competition, pp. 80–6. For further elaboration of the political economy of elite capture of economic policy, see Atul Kohli, 'Politics of Economic Growth in India: 1980–2005, Part II', *Economic and Political Weekly,* April 8 (2006); Frankel, '*India's Political Economy*', pp. 771–88. On the problem of election funding, see E. Sridharan, 'Electoral Finance Reforms', in Vikram Chand (ed.), *Reinventing Public Service Delivery in India.*

71. G.K. Chadha and P.P. Sahu, 'Post-Reform Setbacks in Rural Employment', *Economic and Political Weekly,* May 25 (2002), pp. 1998–2026.

72. For an account of the challenges facing the Indian state in an era of globalization, see Rahul Mukherji, 'The Indian State under Globalization', Paper for the Ford Foundation's Project on Globalization and the Indian State, Working Paper Number 1 (New Delhi: Ford Foundation and National Foundation for India, 2005). This paper will be published in Subrata Banerjee (ed.), *Haksar Memorial Volume IV* (Chandigarh, India, CRRID, forthcoming). For a comprehensive account of why globalization could not substantially reduce the welfare states in the West, see Paul Pierson (ed.), *The New Politics of the Welfare State* (Oxford, Oxford University Press, 2001). Data shows that the while the welfare state may not have declined substantially in the developed world, just the opposite is true for the developing world. Nita Rudra, 'Globalization and the Decline of the Welfare State in Less Developed Countries', *International Organization,* 56 (2) (2002).

DEVELOPMENT STRATEGY

1

What Went Wrong?[*]

JAGDISH BHAGWATI

India's disappointing growth rate, over more than a quarter century, of an annual average of 3.59 per cent in the 1950s, 3.13 per cent in the 1960s, and 3.62 per cent in the 1970s,[1] must be explained. The Harrod–Domar model provides the stylized analytical categories within which this explanation is best provided.

Figure 1.1: Growth rates in real GNP in the Indian economy, 1952–86

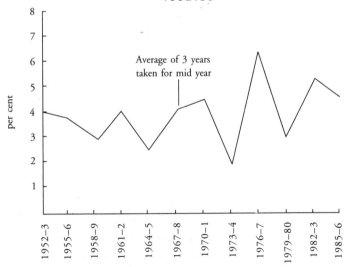

Source: Government of India.

* Originally published as 'What Went Wrong?', in Jagdish Bhagwati, *India in Transition: Freeing The Economy*, Oxford, Clarendon Press, 1993, pp. 39–69.

LOW PRODUCTIVITY, NOT INADEQUATE SAVING

In essence, the weak growth performance reflects not a disappointing savings performance, but rather a disappointing productivity performance. The Indian savings rate more than doubled during this period, from roughly 10 per cent to approximately 22 per cent between 1950 and 1984, supporting a somewhat higher domestic investment rate owing to the (relatively modest) influx of foreign savings, chiefly in the form of assistance rather than foreign investments (see Figure 1.2). But the growth rates did not step up correspondingly.

Figure 1.2: The financing of gross domestic capital formation by gross domestic saving and foreign saving (as per cent of GDP at market prices)

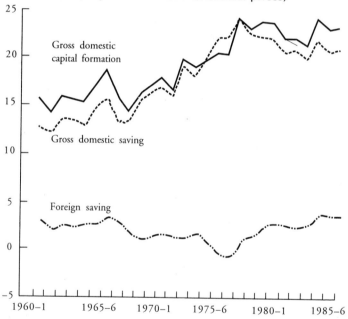

Note: Negative foreign savings are indicated by a bolder line.
Source: National Accounts Statistics: new series. From V. Joshi and I.M.D. Little, *India: Crisis, Adjustment and Growth,* World Bank mimeo, 1992 (Oxford: Oxford University Press, 1994), ch. 13.

There is an interesting parallel with the Soviet Union. The Soviet Union had falling growth rates during the period 1951–80 in the face of high and mildly rising saving rates. The productivity of investments had been abysmal there too, with the effect showing up in falling, not just stagnant, growth rates (see Figure 1.3). On the other hand, in India, with rising saving (and investment) rates, the effects of inadequacies in the policy design and framework showed up in stagnant growth rates.

Figure 1.3: Growth rates in real GNP in the Soviet economy, 1951–80

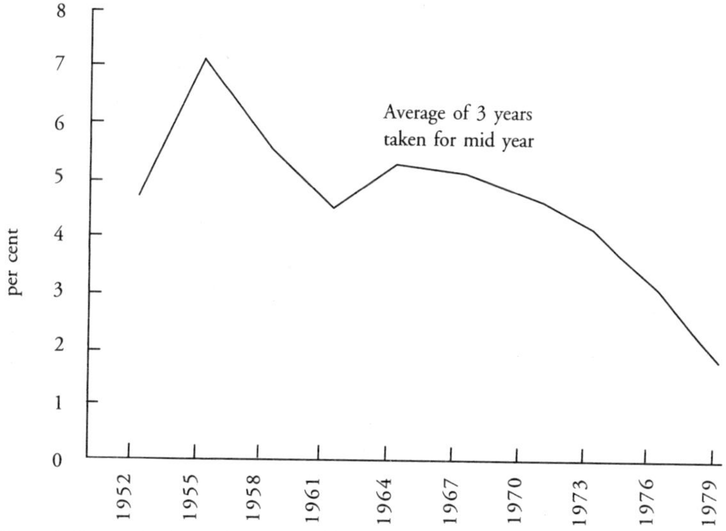

Source: P. Desai, *The Soviet Economy: Problems and Prospects* (Oxford: Basil Blackwell, 1987).

DISMISSING ALTERNATIVE EXPLANATIONS

But before I consider where exactly the Indian policy framework went wrong, it is necessary to examine more carefully the lack of correspondence between savings and growth rates in India. In particular, there are three possible alternative explanations that must be assessed and dismissed before the inference that I am drawing about the abysmally low productivity of increased savings can be firmly drawn:

1. Savings may have been overestimated.
2. Income may have been underestimated.
3. The composition of investment may have shifted efficiently towards sectors with greater capital intensity.[2]

There is something to be said for each of these possible explanations, but not much—certainly not enough to make a serious dent in the thesis that low productivity, not a failure to raise savings, lies at the core of India's failure. Thus, let me consider each of these three qualifications, in turn.

Overestimated Savings

We know, for instance, that because of shifts in relative prices of capital goods, the real savings and hence investment rates are not as high as a proportion of GNP as the estimated 22–23 per cent estimates at current prices.[3] If this correction is made, as by a Working Group under the chairmanship of Professor K.N. Raj, the real gross fixed capital formation as a proportion of GDP nonetheless increased by more than 70 per cent during the period 1950–80, on a very conservative basis (this does not even adjust for quality changes in capital goods over this period, as noted by Mahfooz Ahmed and S.P. Gupta in their dissenting note to the Raj Committee's estimates).[4]

Underestimated Growth

The underestimation of growth is presumably from the growth of the unrecorded, parallel economy. But to turn to this explanation,[5] we would have to assume either that the parallel economy's income is more unrecorded relative to its investment, or that, if both are symmetrically unrecorded, the productivity of investment in the parallel economy exceeds that in the recorded, legal economy.

The latter may well be true in so far as the parallel economy escapes the inefficient policy framework. But if this is true, it is an indictment of the policy framework itself and offers no escape from the low- productivity thesis. As for the former argument—that unrecorded investment may be exceeded by unrecorded income, each relative to its corresponding estimate in the legal economy—there is no empirical evidence that I know of. However, recently T.N. Srinivasan and I have considered formally how much such differential undeclared income and investment would have to be to make a significant contribution to explaining the lack of a satisfactory growth rate.[6] Our judgement was that it would have to be a great deal, therefore offering an unlikely escape from the low-productivity thesis.

Compositional Shift

Finally, the compositional shift escape route also promises little. There are two ways in which this argument has been made:

1. Agriculture became more capital-intensive with the Green Revolution.
2. There were shifts within the industrial sector towards capital-using industries.

Sukhamoy Chakravarty has argued that the Green Revolution created demand for capital-intensive production and the use of fertilizers, whereas the earlier expansion of agricultural production was based on extensive cultivation of land.[7] However, bringing in more land does not rule out an increase in the capital–output ratio from diminishing returns to investment as less fertile land is brought into cultivation. At the same time, the Green Revolution carried with it a significant increase in overall productivity that could outweigh the simultaneous increase in capital-intensity and reduce the capital–output ratio.[8] Moreover, within industry generally, my former student Isher Ahluwalia has already shown that a disaggregated industry analysis confirms that a falling output-to-capital ratio has afflicted nearly all industry groups, taken individually.[9]

Further examining technical change, with conventional econometric estimates of overall factor productivity change, T.N. Srinivasan and I had marshalled much evidence that showed abysmally low technical change through a two-decade period ending in the early 1970s.[10] A thorough analysis by Isher Ahluwalia in 1985 confirmed these findings for the 1970s as well, with some estimates running negative.[11] Her more recent analysis of productivity growth at a detailed level of disaggregation (for 63 industries) of the Indian manufacturing sector unambiguously establishes that there was a prolonged and broad-based phase of stagnation in total factor productivity in the manufacturing sector in the 1960s and the 1970s.[12] Industries accounting for almost 60 per cent of the total value added in manufacturing experienced negative 'total factor productivity' growth during this period.

Yet, we still have one last hurdle to cross, at least for the 1970s. Professor K.N. Raj, one of India's most distinguished economists, has argued that the rise in India's capital–output ratio during this period was matched by its rise elsewhere, the common cause being the oil shock of 1973, so that the inference of inefficient resource use resulting from an inappropriate policy framework is not warranted.[13] But I find this argument unconvincing. The macroeconomic consequences of the oil shock led to a serious rise in unemployment and reduced growth in countries so afflicted. But there is little evidence that this happened in Indian industry. Then again, we also know from Bela Balassa's work[14] at the World Bank that economies with a superior policy framework (especially in regard to outward-orientation in trade), such as South Korea, managed to surmount the adverse effects of the oil shock substantially better than other developing countries, thus showing lower worsening of the capital–output ratio, and therefore returning us after all to the question of the policy framework to explain India's low productivity performance.

WHY LOW PRODUCTIVITY?

Economists typically look for stylized explanations of economic phenomena. Economic theory, which abstracts from detail to concentrate on the essentials, trains us to do so, enabling us to focus on the forest rather than the trees. The philosopher Henri Bergson once remarked that the great advantage of time is that it prevents everything from happening at once. To us economists, the chief virtue of theory, and of associated stylized explanations, is that it enables us to avoid having to consider all explanations, minor and major, at the same time.

The main elements of India's policy framework that stifled efficiency and growth until the 1970s, and somewhat less so during the 1980s as limited reforms began to be attempted—and whose surgical removal is, for the most part, the objective of the substantial reforms begun in mid-1991—are easily defined. I would divide them into three major groups:

1. Extensive bureaucratic controls over production, investment, and trade;
2. Inward-looking trade and foreign investment policies;
3. A substantial public sector, going well beyond the conventional confines of public utilities and infrastructure.

The former two elements adversely affected the private sector's efficiency. The last, along with the inefficient functioning of public-sector enterprises, additionally impaired the public-sector enterprises' contribution to the economy. Together, the three sets of policy decisions broadly set strict limits to what India could get out of its investment.

While these policies define the major solution to the puzzle of India's disappointing growth, I would also like to draw attention to a phenomenon that has recently been noted and analysed with insight by the political scientist Myron Weiner: namely, India's failure to spread primary education and to raise literacy to anywhere near the levels that many other countries have managed (see Figure 1.4).[15]

The proximate reason, analysed by Myron Weiner, is that primary education is not compulsory in India, despite widespread belief in India and outside to the contrary. India only has 'enabling' legislation which permits local governments to enforce compulsory primary education; and the legislation has often not been used. Weiner shows persuasively that in other countries that have successfully increased literacy through primary education, the natural desire of parents to use children for work to augment family income has been countervailed in

Figure 1.4: Rates of literacy of people aged 15 in selected countries in c. 1990 (per cent)

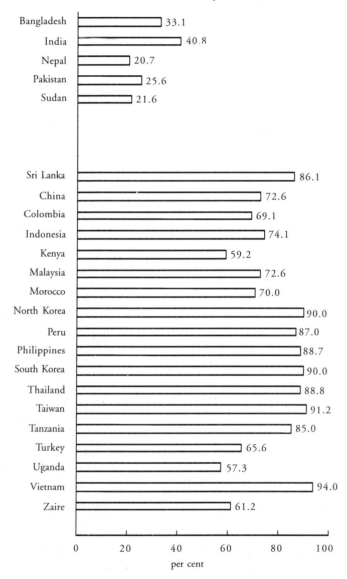

various ways. One, characterizing much of the West, was the shifting attitude to children, a process stretched out over centuries:

As Philippe Aries has documented, childhood was discovered ('invented?') in Europe in the thirteenth century, but it became more significant by the end of the sixteenth and early seventeenth centuries. In the eighteenth century, the concept of adolescence, as distinct from that of childhood, emerged. In time, the central concern of the family became its own children. Children became, as Viviana Zelizer has written, 'priceless'. Children were transformed from valuable wage earners to economically useless but emotionally priceless objects. The transformation did not occur without considerable public debate, and while the upper middle classes held this view of their own children, they did not readily apply it to the children of the poor.

It was not until the nineteenth century that governments began to regulate the conditions of employment for children and to restrict the ages at which children could work. However, much of the early legislation proved to be ineffective, although the passage of the legislation itself was indicative of changing attitudes toward children and work, and toward the responsibility of the state as protector of children against employers and parents.[16]

Another factor emphasizing the value of basic education, and obtaining in Prussia and Scotland, was the Protestant Reformation. By undercutting the intermediary role of the priesthood between Man and God, it led to the view that everyone should be able to read the Bible, and hence provided the necessary support for primary education by the Church itself.

In India, however, there has been an absence of such countervailing force in favour of primary education. Weiner persuasively documents, from extensive interviews with officials at local levels and in other ways, the pervasiveness of views that reinforce, instead of offsetting, the parental wish to use child labour. These come principally from a caste-defined view of life that undervalues economic and social mobility, and the sense of the futility of educating the children of the poor in an ethos defined additionally by the prevalence of underemployment.

With what we now know about the close relationship between literacy and growth, especially in the context of the Far Eastern economies, though else-where too, there seems to me to be little doubt that India's productivity suffered seriously from both the oppressive framework above and the illiteracy below: the pincer movement killing the prospects for efficiency and for growth. I shall concentrate, however, on the framework above, for that defines the agenda for reform.

The Control of Industry and Trade

Few outside India can appreciate in full measure the extent and nature of India's controls till recently. The Indian planners and bureaucrats sought to regulate both domestic entry and import competition, to eliminate product diversification beyond what was licensed, to penalize unauthorized expansion of capacity, to allocate and prevent the reallocation of imported inputs, and indeed to define and delineate virtually all aspects of investment and production through a maze of Kafkaesque controls. This all-encompassing bureaucratic intrusiveness and omnipotence has no rationale in economic or social logic; it is therefore hard for anyone who is not a victim of it even to begin to understand what it means.

I can illustrate this no better than by recalling the time when I wrote an op-ed piece in the *New York Times,* on the occasion of Prime Minister Rajiv Gandhi's first visit to the United States.[17] I was explaining and endorsing the moves towards liberalization of controls, and citing in that context the 'broad-banding' decisions that introduced a limited degree of product diversification. But I had great difficulty getting past an astonished editor, since he simply could not understand what broad-banding meant. When he had finally understood, he asked me whether I could explain why on earth anyone should want to rule out product diversification in the first place.

In essence, the industrial-cum-trade licensing system, whose origin and misguided rationale I shall presently discuss, had degenerated into a series of arbitrary, indeed inherently arbitrary decisions, where, for instance, one activity would be chosen over another simply because the administering bureaucrats were so empowered, and indeed obligated, to choose. It is tempting to assume 'treason of the clerks', but surely the system was conceived and its rationale initially provided by economists, not by the bureaucrats, who were by and large the functionaries entrusted with implementing the system. True, some of the bureaucrats deluded themselves into believing in the social virtues of a system that gave them these powers and the responsibility to make these arbitrary decisions. Female readers especially will appreciate my recalling a seminar on industrial policy in the Planning Commission in 1967, when I sat next to the economist-bureaucrat in charge of the industrial licensing system. With passion and puritanical zeal, he confronted my criticisms and argued that, without the industrial licensing regime, we would fritter away resources on producing lipstick. As I heard this, I could not help smelling the Brylcream in his hair.

The origins of this bureaucratic nightmare lay, for sure, in the combination of two major factors: first, the inability to trust the market when scarcities are acute and the tasks set are challenging; and, second, the failure to understand that markets will generally work better than central planning as a resource-allocational device. The former is a widespread phenomenon, not unique to India. The latter was manifest in the early assertions, from the writings of Barone, Lange, and Lerner, that centralized planning would work better than a decentralized market system because it would calculate prices better. It was left to Hayek to expose the illogicality of this position by arguing that central planners would not be able to secure the information and knowledge that micro-level decision-makers alone would have.[18] Only by ignoring this critical fact were Lange and Lerner able to prove the proposition that socialism would work better than capitalism, that centralized planning would dominate decentralized markets.

The pernicious role of economic theorizing in other ways, based on what turned out to be wrong premises, must also be reckoned with if the ideas that led to the comprehensive controls over investment and production are to be accurately assessed. Thus, recall that the Harrod-Domar model was essentially a 'flow' model, ideally assuming a single commodity, and led in practice to policy choices involving both neglect of productivity and attention to savings and hence to fiscal policy and aid policy. The 'structural' models that inherently involved multiple commodities also opened up the question of the ideal allocation of investible resources among alternative uses. There were at least three strands of influential economic argumentation at the time that complemented one another in providing intellectual support for the idea that governmental design and control of investment-allocation decisions was necessary.

Two of them, by Hirschman and by Rosenstein-Rodan, proceeded by formulating the developmental problem as one of creating the inducement to invest, but paradoxically wound up by arguing for attending to the composition of investment instead.[19] Hirschman proposed that unbalanced growth characterized the investment process and therefore argued for both the disastrous slash-imports-and-invest policy and the strategy of choosing investments that maximized the inducement to invest by focusing on industries and sectors with maximum forward and backward linkages. By contrast, Rosenstein-Rodan focused on balanced growth in an ingenious argument for co-ordination of decentralized investment decisions, each held up in a Nash equilibrium but made feasible through governmentally-contrived co-operative equilibrium: an idea that has now been elegantly formalized in a multiple-equilibrium framework by the economists Kevin Murphy, Andre Schleifer, and Robert Vishny.[20] In turn, this implied, in effect, an effort at identifying and guiding the investments to be coordinated.

The investment-allocation focus, however, grew more directly out of the subsequent theoretical literature addressed to that problem itself. The combination of the twin assumptions of export pessimism and putty-clay technology implied, in Indian thinking, a shift from the Harrod–Domar to the Feldman–Mahalanobis model where, to match the anticipated shift in future investment, there was a need to appropriately shift the investment pattern now. Additional input into this ethos came from the theoretical developments that focused on the heterogeneity of capital goods and the formulation of the optimal trajectory of investments and outputs as in the turnpike theorem. If I may paraphrase Sukhamoy Chakravarty, the logic of investment planning was the order of the day in the high theory of developmental planning.

These ideas thus predisposed the planned effort at development in India— where economists were at the frontier of developmental thought—towards guidance and control of investments. It was these ideas, bastardized to some extent but not altogether, which led to the institutions (such as the licensing system) that then grew like Frankenstein into the system that I have just described. In turn, these institutions created the interests—the politicians who profit from the corruption, the bureaucrats who enjoy the power, the businesses and the workers who like sheltered markets and squatters' rights—that now pose the threats to change as our ideas themselves have changed and reform is contemplated in light of the new ideas.

The central role of the economists, and their responsibility for India's failings, cannot therefore be lightly dismissed. It is not entirely wrong to agree with the cynical view that India's misfortune was to have brilliant economists: an affliction that the Far Eastern super-performers were spared. There is a related but distinct proposition that India has suffered because her splendid economists were both able and willing to rationalize every one of the outrageous policies that the government was adopting, by ingeniously constructing models designed to yield the desired answers.

The Indian embrace of bureaucratic controls was also encouraged by additional objectives, none of them served well by the control system in practice. One was the prevention of the concentration of economic power, by licensing the creation and expansion of capacity. But, if monopoly power was to be reduced, the virtual elimination of domestic and foreign competition (that is, the elimination of the 'contestability' of the market) was hardly the way to do it.

If the growth of large business houses was to be moderated below what it would otherwise be, that too was not to be: the control system gives better access to the haves than to the have-nots, in practice. But the myth of the efficacy of controls as an anti-monopoly instrument in both these senses remained hard to kill.

Then again, the control system was considered to be necessary to protect the small-scale sector. The large-scale or 'organized' sector, in this view, had to be controlled, its growth restrained by licensing, in order to create space for the small-scale sector. This policy, in fact, made little sense and led to big losses. In an excellent recent analysis, Dipak Mazumdar has shown how this policy handicapped India's successful textile industry.[21] The goal of protecting the hand-looms (household) sector created severe problems of competitiveness in international markets for the large-scale sector. The latter was prevented from diversifying into synthetic fibres adequately, for the sake of protecting the small frames producing cotton and the small producers of cotton textiles. Again, expansion into the domestic market was impeded. Mazumdar has correctly observed:

India has probably been unique in the way it has pursued an import substitution policy of industrialization and also placed severe restrictions on the large-scale industrial sector from expanding in the domestic market for consumer goods. This policy covered a whole range of industries, and the problems discussed in the case of the textile industry have similarly afflicted a number of the others....the failure of the large scale industry to exploit the potentially large domestic market—even while its competitiveness in exports was reduced—had a severe dampening effect on economic growth.[22]

But a larger point needs to be made. The attitude that, to protect the small-scale sector, one had to restrain the large-scale sector was symptomatic of a planning approach that presumed that the growth of the large-scale sector would necessarily reduce the growth of the small-scale sector. This was too mechanistic an approach: quite possibly, the two sectors could have grown together. After all, the soap produced by Lever Brothers is not exactly a substitute for what passes as soap in the small-scale sector. A smarter approach would have been to put in place the machinery to provide assistance to the small-scale sector if its fortunes were indeed affected in reality. In other words, rather than act restrictively on presumed outcomes that no planners could adequately forecast, it would have been sensible to think of an institutional design to cope with adverse consequences were they to materialize.

Finally, the licensing system was reinforced equally by the fact that regional balance in development was necessary for political, pluralistic, and equity reasons in a multi-state system. But here too the regulatory system of licensed capacity creation, allocating the 'going' capacities 'fairly' among different states at each point of time for each industry, was neither necessary nor desirable. Regional policy can take the form of subsidies, infrastructure, investments, etc., and does not require licensing to redirect investments on a regulated basis. Besides, it was inevitable that the licensing method of allocating investments would degenerate rapidly into politicking by the states to get a share of every bit of licensed capacity. Thus, the small capacities often licensed were split further into yet smaller plants to distribute the largesse over different claimants, accentuating the losses from lack of economic scale. I recall the witty Indian cartoonist R.K. Laxman drawing an irate politician who was complaining that his state had not been allocated a gold mine whereas another had.

If then the comprehensive set of controls over production and investment had many complementary and reinforcing rationales, none of them compelling in their logic and all of them misguided, its costs were certainly considerable. These costs have now been extensively analysed. The stifling of private initiative, the diversion of resources into unproductive rent-seeking activities stimulated by the controls, and costly bottlenecks reflecting artificial rigidities are only illustrative of the unnecessary economic costs imposed by this control-infested system. But the mounting evidence of the system's corrosive influence on the moral ethos and the integrity of political and public life—as corruption was inevitably spawned by politicians and (largely lower-level) bureaucrats tempted to exploit the control system to their advantage—cannot be dismissed from the final accounting of what this regime cost India.

Foreign Trade and Investment

Let me now turn directly to the question of foreign trade and make four observations.

1. Allied to the extensive control framework was India's persistent failure to seize the gains from trade. Indian foreign trade and domestic developmental policies were based on the now outmoded belief in 'export pessimism'. Many countries shared this belief in the 1950s. The great development economists of the time, among them Ragnar Nurkse and Raul Prebisch, accepted this pessimism as well. However, the post-war period showed this pessimism to have been ill-founded.

   But while the most successful developing countries adapted their policies in light of the emerging reality of rapidly expanding trade prospects, Indian policies continued to be based on the unrealistic and false premise of export pessimism. The failure to use the exchange rate actively to encourage exports, the inflexibilities introduced by the pervasive controls which must handicap the ability to penetrate competitive foreign markets, the protection and hence attraction of the home market: these policies produced a dismal export performance, while other successful countries expanded their exports rapidly and benefited from greater economic growth. I should perhaps remind you that the architect of India's recent reforms, Dr Manmohan Singh, wrote his D. Phil. thesis at Oxford under Ian Little in 1961, arguing precisely that India's export pessimism was unjustified: but this lesson would be ignored for a long time.[23]

You can gauge the extent to which India failed on the export front by noting that her share in world exports was only 0.41 per cent by 1981, having fallen almost continually since 1948, when it was 2.4 per cent. Figure 1.5 shows the dramatic decline that occurred in India's exports relative to both world exports and total developing-country exports.

Figure 1.5: India's export ratios relative to world exports and developing country exports, 1950–90

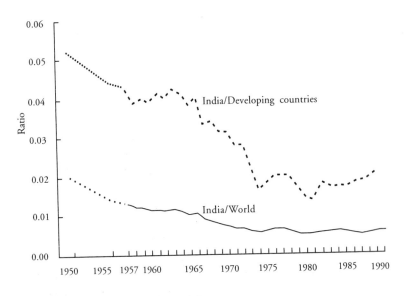

Note: Data for 1951–4 and 1956 are missing.
Source: International Financial Statistics, published by IMF.

Figure 1.6: India's exports/GNP ratio, 1950–87

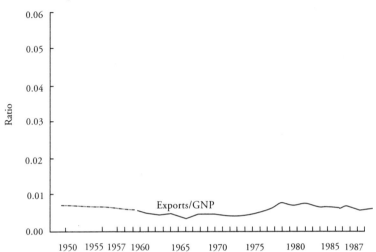

Note: Data for 1951–4, 1956, and 1958 are missing.
Source: Government of India, New Delhi.

Figure 1.6 complements this illustration and underlines further India's dismal export performance by showing an equally dramatic stagnation in her exports-GNP ratio.

2.   In turn, this surely also reduced India's success with industrialization, not merely with growth. Thus, other countries which began with a much smaller industrial base were not only exporting more manufactures than India but were also catching up with India in the absolute size of their manufacturing sector. The size of Korea's manufacturing sector, for example, was less than 25 per cent of India's in 1970 (measured at value added). By 1981, it was already up to 60 per cent. Korea's manufactured exports, negligible in 1962, amounted by 1980 to nearly four times those of India. Then again, in 1990 OECD countries imported only $9 billion worth of manufactures from India but $41 billion from South Korea.[24] Simply put, during its quarter-century of weak economic performance, India missed the bus on industrialization (even though the share of industry in national income increased through the four decades since 1950).

In this context, I should perhaps emphasize that rapid industrialization (based on foreign trade) would also have facilitated rapid growth by breaking the constraint that Professors Raj, Chakravarty,[25] and others have continually emphasized as being imposed on the Indian growth rate by the 'natural' limits on agricultural growth. These economists have typically argued that agricultural-growth-based demand constraints operate on industrial expansion; they also emphasize supply links. But this argument is only as good as its premise that foreign trade is not available to the economy at the margin. This premise, however, is unrealistic and must be rejected as one which has done no good to the design of Indian policy.[26]

3. I should also add that the deadly combination of industrial licensing and controls at home with import and exchange controls externally effectively cut off the rigours of competition from all sources and made the creation of a *rentier*, as against an entrepreneurial, economy more likely. X-inefficiency was certain to follow, with only the exceptional escaping from the consequences of the wrong set of incentives. As Herbert Spencer said eloquently a century ago, 'The ultimate result of shielding men from the effects of folly is to fill the world with fools.'[27]

4. Finally, India's trade and industrial policies handicapped the attack on poverty, not merely by reducing efficiency and growth, but also by distorting its quality. For instance, the capital-intensity of techniques of production in manufacturing was, despite the existence of excess capacity, inefficiently increased by the creation of incentives to add to capacity, simply because scarce and profitable imports were allocated to producers pro rata to capacity installed. The exchange control regime also served to eliminate any flexibility in imports of intermediates, parts, etc.: the inability to import these freely increased the incentive to hold inventories, raising both the capital-intensity and lowering the overall efficiency of production.[28] Furthermore, the reliance on capital accumulation as the engine of growth combined with a closed foreign-trade regime implied that India had to have a relatively larger machinery sector. This added to the capital intensity of her production structure and detracted from the development of labour-intensive manufactures and, ultimately, from a more equitable distribution of income.[29] Most of all, the inward orientation of the trade-and-payments regime, in drastically impairing India's export performance, simultaneously prevented the build-up of labour-intensive exports and hence a favourable impact on wages and employment and therefore *ceteris paribus* on poverty as well.[30]

TECHNOLOGY AND DIRECT FOREIGN INVESTMENT

India cannot be faulted much on her technological and scientific achievements. She has to her credit remarkable triumphs shared only with a few, often only with advanced nations. She has picked up nodules from the depths of the oceans, put men in Antarctica, fired intermediate missile rockets, won Nobel Prizes in the sciences, and has perhaps the highest number of scientific and skilled people in the developing world.

Yet, as in the Soviet Union, the state of her average technology in the communications and industrial sectors has fallen seriously behind that of the superior performers. While this remains a grey area within economics, it would be astonishing if, again as in the Soviet Union, excessive controls hindering the freedom to produce or invest, and hence to profit from innovation, have not impeded technological innovation.[31] At the same time, the controls on trade have evidently reduced the ability to invest in newer-vintage capital goods embodying technical change.

The restrictions on incoming direct foreign investment have also reduced the absorption of new technology from this source. While the Korean and the Japanese growth of domestic technological capabilities was not based on direct foreign investment, these nations did not have the baggage of India's regime of 'don'ts' that also reduced other forms of technical absorption and innovation. India therefore lost on all counts when it should have, with better policies, gained on them all.

The Public Sector

What I have said so far pertains mostly to the productivity of the private sector. The framework I described, and the consequences I have detailed, were applicable mainly to the private sector, though not entirely, since the public sector could not be shielded from most of their problems despite efforts in that direction. But the story in India would not be complete if the public sector, with its special (though perhaps universal) problems, were excluded from scrutiny.

In India, the public sector is truly substantial. From the beginning, no doubt as a consequence of the influence of socialist doctrines on Prime Minister Jawaharlal Nehru and indeed on many of us who studied economics at Cambridge and politics at the London School of Economics, the public sector was considered to be an important sector to cultivate and enlarge. Fabianism, with its anti-revolutionary thrust, probably helped define a policy of gradualism: nationalizations were not contemplated but it was expected instead that increasing shares of investment in the public sector over successive five-year plans would steadily increase the average size of the public sector to a decisive share in the nation's capital stock. A measured and slow-paced ascent up the Marxist mountain was therefore part of the ideological agenda.

In turn, the two Industrial Policy Resolutions of 1948 and 1956 shifted a number of industries to the exclusive domain of the public sector. Thus the 1956 Resolution stated:

In the first category there will be industries the future development of which will be the exclusive responsibility of the state. The second category will consist of industries, which will be progressively state-owned and in which the state will therefore generally take the initiative in establishing new undertakings, but in which private enterprise will also be expected to supplement the effort of the state. The third category will include all the remaining industries, and their future development will, in general, be left to the initiative and enterprise of the private sector.[32]

The first category turned out to be an enormous one, embracing not merely defence-related industries but also atomic energy, iron and steel, heavy machinery, coal, railways and airlines, telecommunications, and the generation and distribution of electricity. These industries provide the bulk of the infrastructure of the country; their inefficiency could thus, in turn, create inefficiencies in the user industries in the private sector. It did do so, as I argue presently.

In fact, the overwhelming presence of the public sector in India must be spelt out to see why the matter of its functioning is of great importance to Indian productivity and economic performance. Thus, the 244 economic enterprises of the central government alone, excluding the railways and the utilities, employed as many as 2.3 million workers in 1990. In manufacturing, if the small 'unorganized' sector is excluded, their employment was over 40 per cent of that provided by the private-sector firms. In fact, when state-level enterprises are counted in, the public-sector enterprises in manufacturing, mining, construction, transport and communications, banking and insurance (both now nationalized, partly and wholly respectively) provided nearly 70 per cent of the 26 million jobs in the large-scale 'organized' sector in 1989.[33]

Not merely because of its size, but also, as I have just noted, because of its composition, which is such that it can affect the supply of important productive inputs such as electricity, transportation, finance, insurance, and steel, and hence influence the efficiency of the private sector, the public sector must be efficient. But, as virtually everywhere to some degree or the other, this has not been the case in India.[34]

Overstaffing due to politics,[35] the 'goofing-off' effect of soft budget constraints, etc. have been amply documented by a series of investigations. I must confess that I was among the many who thought in the 1950s and 1960s that the public-sector enterprises could be operated better. Recall that this was also the assumption underlying the Lange-Lerner argument, now seen to be a consequence of unrealistic premises, that centralized planning would function better than the decentralized market system as an allocative device. In reality, the conditions that would make the public sector productive and efficient seem beyond reach, at least in India.

This inefficiency, directly observed and documented, is not the only cause of public-sector losses, and some of the losses are attributable also to a governmental policy of taking over so-called 'sick units' (that is, private firms making losses) to respond to political demands for the avoidance of bankruptcy. It is noteworthy, however, that the public-sector enterprises have as a rule produced abysmally low returns on the enormous amounts of employed capital. Thus, even during the decade of the 1980s when the awareness of the issue was keen, the (simple) average rate of financial return on employed capital was 2.5 per cent! And that too was heavily weighted by the profits of 14 petroleum enterprises which produced as much as 77 per cent of the 1989–90 profits. Besides, even this meagre profitability was ephemeral, based on historical-cost depreciation: corrected for replacement cost, the profits in public-sector enterprises in coal, steel, fertilizer, power, and transport were even estimated to be negative.[36]

But the public sector's economic inefficiency represents only the microeconomic aspect of its failure. The low profitability also amounted to a macroeconomic failure. And this would contribute to the fiscal and foreign exchange crisis that developed in the 1980s, gathering force at the end of the decade, forcing India into near-bankruptcy and therewith into IMF loan support and the drastic macroeconomic and microeconomic reforms that the present government has firmly embarked upon.

The failure of the public-sector enterprises to generate profits and hence contribute to governmental saving coincided with an unprecedented increase in the 1980s of budgetary expenditure on defence, governmental wages and salaries, and subsidies. As a result, the government's contribution to total savings fell dramatically through the 1980s (see Figure 1.7). The government had to resort to a mix of increased domestic and foreign borrowing and to reduce simultaneously the growth of capital expenditure, which, in fact, declined a little during the 1980s as a proportion of GDP.

Figure 1.7: The components of gross domestic savings in India: period averages (per cent of GDP at market prices)

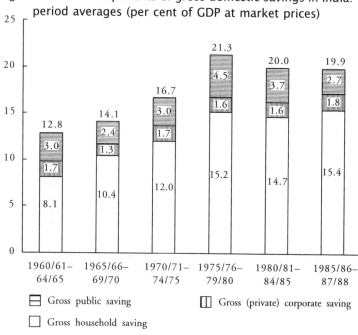

Source: Same as for Figure 1.2.

The relative decline in capital expenditure meant of course that there was a slowdown in the investment in infrastructure. Coming on top of the inefficient use of this investment, this slowdown contributed to the infrastructural bottle-necks that in turn contributed to the low productivity of investment in many user industries that I noted earlier.

The Crisis

The state of Indian public finances reached crisis proportions by the end of the 1980s. The public debt-to-GNP ratio increased through the 1980s, jumping drastically towards the end of the decade to nearly 60 per cent, a near doubling of the ratio in 1980 (see Figure 1.8). As I argued above, this had to do with the failure of the public sector to generate investible resources and the explosive growth of governmental current spending that saw the budget deficit as a proportion of GDP rise from 6.4 to 9 per cent during the 1980s.

The two OPEC shocks of 1973 and 1979 had little role to play in this drama. The external shock administered by the loss of remittances and the

Figure 1.8: India's net public debt to GNP ratios, 1970–87

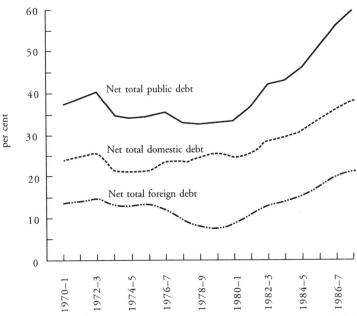

Source: W. Buiter and U. Patel, 'Debt, Deficits, and Inflation: An Application to the Public Finances of India', *Journal of Public Economics,* 47 (1992), pp. 171–205.

expenditures incurred to rescue workers in the aftermath of the invasion of Kuwait in August 1990 certainly accentuated the fiscal crisis at the end. But the crisis was almost entirely 'home-made'.[37]

The rise in foreign borrowing was a major component of the fiscal crisis. The external public-sector debt as a proportion of GNP doubled during the 1980s to 21 per cent by 1987–8. In consequence, debt service as a proportion of exports increased more than threefold to 32 per cent in 1986–7 in only seven years. The foreign exchange reserves fell through the last three years of the decade. The result was an unprecedented downgrading of India's credit rating in the international capital market.

By 1990 there was palpable fear of default. In January 1991 the government was forced to take IMF loans worth $1.8 billion by drawing from the Compensatory and Contingency Financing Facility and the first tranche of the standby facility. By October 1991 the borrowing was increased under instruments that entailed commitments and firm action both to control and reduce the budget deficit and to undertake structural reforms.

The content of the structural-reform conditionality was no more than what many in India had long seen to be necessary. The reaction of some that these were alien ideas being imposed by the World Bank and the IMF on India was ludicrous. These ideas had been evolved by some of us (and by some foreign economists as well) in the 1960s[38] and had in fact made their way into these institutions which are distinguished for the absorption and diffusion of new and important ideas rather than for their creation.[39] Those denouncing alien intrusions were in fact denying the credit to their own nationals who had contributed to the evolution of the ideas whose serious implementation was now to be India's principal challenge. Also, the structural reform agenda endorsed by the IMF and the World Bank was little different from what the new government of Prime Minister Narasimha Rao had already announced by way of reforms in July 1991, albeit with the foreknowledge and complicity of these multilateral institutions, whose lending was imminent.

India was finally at a critical turning-point. The question was no longer one of whether to undertake reforms? Rather the questions now were: in what sequence, with what speed, with what chance of success? These are issues that lend themselves more to speculation than to serious scholarship.

NOTES AND REFERENCES

1. The moving average of three-year annual growth rates is plotted in Figure 1.1, showing also the fluctuations that reflect, among other things, the agricultural harvest and its effect on the rest of the economy.

2. I deliberately add the proviso 'efficiently' to rule out the possibility that the shift in investment towards more capital-intensive sectors may itself be an inefficiency resulting from faulty policy design. Only those composition shifts which are exogenous to the policy framework must be isolated if they are to be treated as a factor detracting from the thesis of low returns from the increased savings and investment.

3. The work of M.K. Rakshit, 'Income, Saving and Capital Formation in India: A Step towards a Solution of the Savings-Investment Puzzle', *Economic and Political Weekly* 17 (14, 15, 16) (April 1982), pp. 561–72, suggests that even the nominal savings may have been overestimated.

4. Cf. Report of the Working Group on Savings, Reserve Bank of India, Bombay, February.

5. S. Chakravarty, 'Aspects of India's Development Strategy for the 1980s', *Economic and Political Weekly,* 19 (26) (1984), pp. 845–52.

6. Cf. J. Bhagwati and T. N. Srinivasan, 'Indian Development Strategy: Some Comments', *Economic and Polilcal Weekly* 19 (47) (24 November 1984),

2006–7. This article comments more broadly on Chakravarty, 'Aspects of India's Development Strategy for the 1980s'.

7. Cf. S. Chakravarty, *Development Planning: The Indian Experience,* 1985 Radhakrishnan Lectures (Oxford: Oxford University Press, 1987), p. 56.

8. Moreover, the import-substitution policy with respect to fertilizers, and their production in the public sector, avoidably increased the cost of the fertilizers.

9. Cf. I.J. Ahluwalia, *Industrial Growth in India: Stagnation Since the Mid-Sixties* (New Delhi: Oxford University Press, 1985).

10. Cf. J. Bhagwati and T.N. Srinivasan, *India* (New York: Columbia University Press, 1975).

11. Ahluwalia, *Industrial Growth in India.*

12. Cf. I.J. Ahluwalia, *Productivity and Growth in Indian Manufacturing* (New Delhi: Oxford University Press, 1991). Significantly, the study establishes a turnaround in this respect in the 1980s. Total factor productivity in the manufacturing sector grew at a rate of 3.4 per cent p.a. in the first half of the 1980s compared with no growth in the preceding decade-and-a-half (indeed, a slight decline at the rate of 0.3 per cent p.a.).

13. Cf. K.N. Raj, 'Some Observations on Economic Growth in India Over the Period 1952/53 to 1982/83', *Economic and Political Weekly,* 19 (13 October 1984).

14. Cf. Bela Balassa, 'Adjustment to External Shocks in Developing Economies', World Bank Staff Working Paper 472 (Washington, DC: World Bank, 1984).

15. Cf. M. Weiner, *The Child and the State in India* (Princeton, NJ: Princeton University Press, 1991).

16. Weiner, *The Child and the State in India,* p. 110.

17. Cf. J. Bhagwati, 'Is India's Economic Miracle at Hand?', *New York Times,* 9 June 1985.

18. Cf. F. von Hayek, *Knowledge, Education, and Society* (London: Butler and Tanner, 1983); and his earlier, seminal piece, 'Economics and Knowledge', in his essays, *Individualism and Economic Order* (London: Routledge & Kegan Paul, 1949).

19. Cf. A. Hirschman, *The Strategy of Economic Development* (New Haven, Conn.: Yale University Press. 1958); P.H. Rosenstein-Rodan, 'Problems of the Industrialisation of Eastern and South-Eastern Europe', *Economic Journal.* 1943, vol. 53 and 'Notes on the Theory of the "Big push"' (Center for International Studies, Cambridge, Mass.: MIT, 1957), later version in the International Economic Association Conference volume, *Economic Development in Latin America* (London: Macmillan, 1963).

20. Cf. K.M. Murphy, A. Schleifer, and R. Vishny, 'Industrialization and the Big Push', *Journal of Political Economy,* 97 (1989), pp. 1003–26.

21. Cf. D. Mazumdar, 'Import-Substituting Industrialization and Protection of the Small-Scale: The Indian Experience in the Textile Industry', *World Development,* 19(9) (1991), pp. 1197–213. In addition, the official import-licensing policy handicapped industry by restricting the importation of superior and more efficient machinery in favour of the domestic equipment manufacturers.

22. Mazumdar, 'Import-Substituting Industrialization', p. 1211.

23. Cf. M. Singh, *India's Export Trends* (London: Oxford University Press, 1964). This work is the first, systematic analysis of India's export performance (up to 1960, since the thesis was written during 1961) and potential. Since then, there have been other important analyses in the same vein, reinforcing the view that Indian exports could be significantly increased. In particular, see M. Wolf, *India's Exports* (London: Oxford University Press, 1982).

24. Cf. *World Development Report,* 1992 (World Bank, Washington, DC, 1992), p. 250.

25. Cf. Chakravarty, *Development Planning,* pp. 60–4.

26. A thorough evaluation of the 'demand deficiency' thesis is to be found in T.N. Srinivasan, 'Demand Deficiency and Indian Industrial Development', Yale University (Economics Department), mimeo, forthcoming in a festschrift for K.N. Raj.

27. H. Spencer, 'State Tamperings with Money and Banks', in *Essays: Scientific, Political, and Speculative,* iii (London: Williams and Norgate, 1891), p. 354.

28. These and other inefficiencies were identified and discussed in J. Bhagwati and P. Desai, *India: Planning for Industrialization* (Oxford: Oxford University Press, 1970).

29. Cf. A. Panagariya, 'Indicative Planning in India: Discussion', *Journal of Comparative Economics,* 14 (1990), pp. 736–42.

30. It is ironic that experience has not been kind to the branch of developmental thinking, fashionable in Indian academic circles in the 1950s and 1960s, which favoured the choice of capital-intensive processes and industries on the ground that they would lead to more savings, greater growth, and higher employment later despite lower employment now. For important cross-country evidence on the role of trade and industrial policies on employment and income distribution, see the synthesis volume by A. Krueger, *Trade and Employment in Developing Countries: Synthesis and Conclusions,* NBER (National Bureau of Economic Research) (Chicago: Chicago University Press, 1982), based on several in-depth country studies.

31. Cf. J. Berliner, *The Innovation Decision in Soviet Industry* (Cambridge, Mass.: MIT Press, 1976).

32. Quoted in T. N. Srinivasan, 'Reform of Industrial and Trade Policies', *Economic and Political Weekly* (14 September 1991), pp. 2143–5. For greater detail, see Bhagwati and Desai, *India: Planning for Industrialization*.

33. Cf. the excellent account in B.R. Nayyar, 'The Public Sector in India: The Dialectics of Legitimation and Rent Seeking', in L. Gordon and P. Oldenberg (eds), *India Briefing 1992*, The Asia Society (Boulder, Colo.: Westview Press, 1992). Also note that the share of public-sector to private-sector employment in the 'organized' sector has increased steadily since 1960–1 and sharply in the 1980s.

34. Below, I detail some of the reasons for public-sector inefficiency. This is, of course, compatible with the existence of some remarkably successful public-sector enterprises.

35. There was not merely overstaffing; workers earned wages for overtime too. Indeed, many workers came to believe that their salaries were rewards simply for being employed, while, for the work they did, they had to be paid an overtime. This idea was pushed to its limits when even workers of a 'sick unit', no longer in operation, began to ask for a 'notional' overtime. If the unit had been functioning, they reasoned, they would have been receiving overtime. The same should be paid in addition to the salaries because it was not their fault that the unit had been closed.

36. Cited in Nayyar, 'The Public Sector in India'; see esp. Table 4.

37. This is the adjective used by W. Buiter and U. Patel, 'Debt, Deficits and Inflation: An Application to the Public Finances of India', *Journal of Public Economics,* 47 (1992), pp. 171–205. 1 draw here on their excellent analysis of what went wrong with India's public finances. There is also a splendid treatment of the subject in V. Joshi and I.M.D. Little, *India: Crisis, Adjustment and Growth,* World Bank mimeo, 1992 (Oxford: Oxford University Press, 1994).

38. The earliest Indian economists include T.N. Srinivasan, V.K. Ramaswami, and Padma Desai. The foreign economists include, among others, Bela Balassa, Arnold Harberger, Anne Krueger, and Ian Little.

39. This is, of course, as it should be. The universities are naturally the major source of innovation in economics. The evolution of the monetarist approach to the balance of payments by Jacques Polak, and the influential theoretical work of Marcus Fleming and Robert Mundell, at the IMF nearly a quarter-century ago, are among the exceptions that underline this rule.

2

The Indian Economy under 'Structural Adjustment'*

Prabhat Patnaik and C.P. Chandrasekhar

Post-independence India was one of the classic cases of dirigiste economic development. Not only was the state highly interventionist, but the economy came to acquire a sizeable public sector, especially in areas of infrastructure and basic industries. The 'mixed' economy which thus came into being, together with the fact that the polity was characterized by multi-party parliamentary democracy with a largely free press and significant freedom of expression, invested the Indian experiment with a novelty and uniqueness that attracted worldwide attention and gave rise to a vast theoretical literature. Not only did a rich literature on development planning take shape within India, starting with the celebrated plan models of Professor P.C. Mahalanobis, who was a pioneer theoretician of Indian planning, but issues like the class nature of the Indian state, the class character of Indian planning, etc. became matters of intense debate, especially in Marxist and radical circles, both within the country as well as internationally.[1]

India's transition in 1991 to a regime of 'structural adjustment' is therefore an event of great historical significance, which merits serious study but is shrouded in a great deal of misconception, some of it nurtured for ideological reasons precisely because of the significance of the event itself. The first such misconception is that 'structural adjustment' became inevitable because the earlier regime had brought the economy to a point of 'collapse'. Let us examine this proposition at some length.

* This paper was commissioned for this volume.

THE IMMEDIATE BACKGROUND TO
STRUCTURAL ADJUSTMENT

The fact that the economy, prior to approaching the IMF for credit under a range of facilities,[2] faced an acute crisis in terms of very high rates of inflation and sharply declining foreign exchange reserves is not in question. But, first, this crisis was almost entirely speculative in origin, having little to do with the developments in the real sectors of the economy; second, it cannot even be contended that the genesis of speculation, even if unrelated to the immediate performance of the real economy, could be located in some long-term tendency towards stagnation or collapse of the economy—on the contrary, the second quinquennium of the 1980s saw the most pronounced industrial boom ever witnessed in the history of the Indian economy; and, third, the vulnerability of the economy to speculative forces was itself in part a result of its gradual 'liberalization' and the confusion about the future of dirigisme which came to prevail during this quinquennium.

To say all this is not to whitewash the fundamental flaws of the dirigiste regime, or to gloss over its basic contradictions, but merely to avoid making facile judgements about it. The nature of these basic contradictions, we argue below, was altogether different from what the ideologues of structural adjustment would have us believe. In the current section, however, we confine ourselves to showing the essentially speculative nature of the crisis immediately preceding structural adjustment; the longer-term issues are dealt with in subsequent sections.

Table 2.1 provides a summary picture of economic performance in 1990–1 and 1989–90. In terms of the performance of the material production sectors, at any rate, one can scarcely look upon 1990–1 as being in any sense a disappointing year. What did happen, however, is a sharp acceleration in the inflation rate, especially that affecting agricultural labourers, who are among the poorest in the society, notwithstanding substantial increases in agricultural output in general and in foodgrains output in particular. What also happened was a worsening of the trade balance, largely because of a higher oil import bill and reduced exports to West Asia, consequent to the Gulf War. The increase in the current account deficit was even larger than the increase in the trade deficit. Not only had remittances by Indian emigré workers from the Gulf countries, which had been an important source of foreign exchange, reached a plateau for a couple of years, but in 1990–1 there was an absolute drop in their size because of reverse migration. Whatever possible economic benefits the country could have derived from this reverse migration were not exploited: when owing to the uncertainty over the fate of the Kuwaiti currency many Indians wished to shift their accumulated savings into Indian banks, the latter refused to accept them because they themselves were uncertain about the fate of the Kuwaiti currency. As a result anywhere between $5–7 billion were lost to the Western banks, which had no such hesitations about accepting the Kuwaiti currency; if this money had come into India, then the foreign exchange crunch would have been easily averted.

Table 2.1: Annual percentage change in selected indicators: 1990-1

(Figures in brackets refer to change in 1989–90 over 1988–9)

1	GDP at factor cost (1980–1 prices)	4.9 (6.9)
2	Index of Agricultural Production	3.2 (0.6)
3	Foodgrain Production (m.tonnes)	3.0 (1.6)
4	Index of Industrial Production	8.3 (8.6)
5	Index of Wholesale Prices (1980–1= 100)	12.1 (9.1)
6	Consumer Price Index for Industrial Workers (Base 1982= 100)	13.6 (8.6)
7	Consumer Price Index for Agricultural Labourers (1960-61=100)	16.6 (1.0)
8	Exports (US$)	9.2 (18.9)
9	Imports (US$)	13.5 (8.8)

Notes: Figures relate to financial years, that is, April–March. The increase in the wholesale price index is calculated by comparing the last week of the April–March year with the last week of the previous corresponding year; the increases in the other price indices are obtained by comparing the last months.
Source: Government of India, Ministry of Finance, *Economic Survey* (Annual), various issues.

But the increase in the current account deficit, significant though it was, was not in itself primarily responsible for the foreign exchange crunch. The current account deficit stood at $4,853 million in 1987–8, $7,996 million in 1988–9, $6,837 million in 1989–90, and $9,438 million in 1990–1, which gives some idea of the order of increase involved. But this increase by $2.6 billion in 1990–1 over the previous year was more than offset by loans *without condition-ality* from the IMF totalling $2.5 billion and an *additional* running down of reserves, over and above the decline recorded in the previous year, of about $250 million. And yet, the magnitude of reserves at the end of March 1991 was still large enough to cover almost three months' imports. Since three months' import cover is generally considered to be 'safe' enough in the Indian context, the shortfall in reserves in March 1991, when severe import compression measures through quantitative restrictions were imposed on the economy, was by no means excessive. It was definitely less than a billion dollars, which is the estimated magnitude of illegally non-repatriated exchange earnings during the last two quarters of 1990–1—a figure that more than doubled by the time structural adjustment came into force.

In other words, by March 1991, when import restrictions were imposed (which soon converted the trade deficit into a surplus), it was not the trade or current account deficit as such which was responsible for the foreign exchange crunch but the speculative outflow of funds, partly in the form of non-repatriation of exchange earnings in violation of the country's laws, and partly in the form of non-resident Indians taking money out of the country, which was not illegal but constituted speculation nevertheless.[3] After March 1991, as import compression began to reduce the trade deficit, affecting the performance of the real sectors of the economy, the balance of payments continued to be under severe pressure because the speculative outflows persisted and even got enlarged.

One can argue quite persuasively that, *even so*, India could have managed her payments and restored confidence in her currency with a relatively *low-conditionality* IMF loan, without going in for the whole gamut of structural adjustment measures. The reason that she did go in for structural adjustment was not because of any objective necessity being faced by the economy but because the 'liberalization' lobby, consisting of both the Fund and the Bank as well as elements within the Indian government and business class (more on these groups later), considered this a heaven-sent opportunity to tie the country down to structural adjustment, to jettison altogether, and not just rectify, the dirigiste regime which had prevailed since Independence. In other words, the event of historical significance that we referred to at the beginning of this chapter was achieved as a silent coup, behind everybody's back as it were, by trapping the country into structural adjustment. (It is interesting that the government never brought out a white paper on the balance of payments crisis as demanded by several opposition parties at the time). We shall however be content in this chapter to develop not this strong proposition, but a much weaker one, namely, that the balance of payments crisis, such as it was, was a contribution of speculative forces and did not represent a 'collapse of the economy under the earlier regime'. We have seen that there was no collapse in any *immediate sense*. Later on we shall discuss the more long-term performance of the earlier regime.

The other aspect of the 1990–1 crisis relates to inflation, and this again represented not a failure on the production side but a combination of speculation and of administered price increases in preparation for 'liberalizing' the economy. The most significant feature of the inflationary process, we have seen, was the rapid increase in the prices of the absolutely essential commodities consumed by the poorest in the society. Three commodities in particular led the inflationary process: rice, wheat, and edible oils, with price increases over 1990–1 (last week-to-last week) of 14 per cent, 49 per cent and 33 per cent respectively. Per capita availability (without taking account of private stock movements) of edible oils in 1990–1 was 5.5 kg, which was higher than in the two preceding years: the cause of the price increase was therefore private hoarding. On such occasions the usual practice of the government had been to use imports (and release them if necessary through the public distribution system) for breaking the 'bullish' sentiment of the market; but the foreign exchange crunch, itself a fallout of speculative forces, prevented it from using this, its standard weapon of supply management.

As for rice and wheat, again it was not any output or availability failure which underlay the price increase; nor was there any spontaneous speculative upsurge (since the 1990–1 output was remarkably good). The cause of the inflation lay in the government's decision to raise the issue prices of these grains through the public distribution system. In May 1990 the issue price of wheat was raised by 15 per cent while that of the common variety of rice was raised by 18 per cent. The reason for doing so was supposedly to control inflation by reducing the fiscal deficit through cuts in food subsidy: this idea, which is an important component of structural adjustment, had already crept into the thinking of the Indian government for quite some time under the influence of the World Bank. As a matter of fact it ended up sharply accentuating the inflationary pressures upon the poor.

A point needs to be clarified here: first, the agricultural labourers, apart from those in a few states like Kerala, West Bengal, and more recently a couple of other southern states, do not generally have access to the public distribution system, a fact which has been used by the 'liberalization' lobby to demand a whittling down of food subsidies on the grounds that it would not affect the really poor anyway. What this argument misses however is the fact that the open market price *invariably* moves up with the issue price of the public distribution system. A rise in the issue price creates self-fulfilling 'bullish' expectations among the sellers in the open market; and, given the inelastic demand for foodgrains, this brings in a large bonanza even with small accretions to private stocks (which

again can be unloaded in the next period at the government's fixed procurement price). This is exactly what happened in 1990–1 and would happen, as
we shall see, with a vengeance the next year when structural adjustment was
officially enthroned as the basis of government policy. To be sure, the exact
magnitude of an open market price increase for a particular crop for a particular
period may not match the magnitude of issue price increase owing to the
existence of lags and of other specific considerations, but that does not negate
the basic relationship.

If we have discussed developments in 1990–1 at some length, this is only to
dispel the facile notion that the Indian economy was collapsing under the
weight of dirigisme.

CONTRADICTIONS OF THE DIRIGISTE REGIME

This phenomenon of financial globalization was bound to affect the domestic
economy, sucking domestic wealth holders into its vortex and in the process
undermining the viability of the dirigiste alternative. For any state intervention
to be even remotely effective, it is essential that there be some 'control area'
within the domain of the state over which it can ensure a degree of correspondence between the intentions behind its policy–actions and their outcome. If
finance can flow in or flow out in response to pressures emanating from
abroad—in other words, if the domestic wealth holders' behaviour defies the
very concept of a 'control area' under the domain of the nation-state over which
it can ensure some semblance of correspondence between the intentions behind
its actions and their outcome—then the possibility of state intervention gets
eroded. It is not surprising that virtually all forms of interventionism, not only
traditional socialism but even Keynesianism, welfarism, conventional social
democracy, third world nationalism, and its necessary accompaniment, the
dirigiste developmental model, have all run into rough weather in recent years.
The reason for this is not some sudden realization on the part of 'everybody' of
the alleged superiority of the market, but the profound change in the context
which has taken place in recent years through the phenomenon of financial
globalization. To say this however is not to suggest that all prospects of progressive economic policies being pursued in particular countries (it will have to be
necessarily in particular countries to start with) have disappeared; the point is
merely to underscore the changed context.

It would be a gross mistake, however, to hold this changed context alone as
the reason for the eventual transcendence of the dirigiste regime. The regime

had serious internal contradictions, which contributed to an erosion of its social stability as well as of its economic viability, and propelled it towards a situation where it had no alternative viable responses left to the changed context that we have underscored. In other words it is the interplay between the changed international context and the accentuating domestic contradictions within the earlier regime which gave rise to the 'totality' of circumstances that permitted the enactment of the event of historical significance referred to at the beginning of this chapter. In the present section, we shall discuss these internal contradictions.

A brief clarification is however in order here. The economic policy regime erected in the 1950s was not just a brainchild of the then prime minister Nehru and the group around him, as is often made out by its admirers as well as its critics. Its roots lay in the freedom struggle itself. The economy had been dominated by metropolitan capital and metropolitan commodities in the pre-Independence period. Freedom meant freedom from this domination; and this could not be ensured without giving the state in independent India a major role in building up infrastructure, expanding and strengthening the productive base of the economy, setting up new financial institutions, and regulating and coordinating economic activity. This was necessary for building capitalism itself, though some no doubt entertained the fond hope that all this would add up to a transition to socialism. State capitalism and state intervention in other words were essential instruments for the development of a relatively autonomous Indian capitalism, displacing metropolitan capital from the pre-eminent position it had occupied in the colonial economy. It is this displacement which drew the ire of international agencies like the Fund and the Bank (more explicitly, as we have seen, of the latter). The manner of their intervention has been alluded to earlier; let us move on now to the internal contradictions.

Three mutually reinforcing and interrelated contradictions need to be noted.[4] First, the state within the old economic policy regime had to simultaneously fulfil two different roles which were incompatible in the long run. On the one hand it had to maintain growing expenditures, in particular investment expenditure, in order to keep the domestic market expanding. The absence of any radical land redistribution had meant that the domestic market, especially for industrial goods, had remained socially narrowly based; it had also meant that the growth of agricultural output, though far greater than in the colonial period, remained well below potential, and even such growth as occurred was largely confined, taking the country as a whole, to a narrow stratum of landlords turned capitalists and sections of rich peasants who had improved their economic status. Under these circumstances, a continuous growth in state spending was essential for the growth of the market; it was the key element in whatever overall dynamics the system displayed. At the same time however the state exchequer was the medium through which large-scale transfers were made to the capitalist and proto-capitalist groups; the state in other words was an instrument for the 'primary accumulation of capital'.

It was not of course the only instrument; direct means such as the eviction of tenants, private encroachment on common resources and private encroachment on State-owned resources such as forests from whose use the poor were simultaneously excluded, all played their role. But the state exchequer remained the pre-eminent mechanism for 'primary accumulation'; through the non-payment of taxes (to which the state generally turned a blind eye), through a variety of subsidies and transfers, and through lucrative state contracts, private fortunes got built up at the expense of the state exchequer.

The contradiction between these two different roles of the state manifested itself, despite increasing resort to indirect taxation and administered price hikes, through a growth in the government's revenue deficit. A result of this of course was that the fiscal deficit also went up; this however reflected not a step-up in public investment but a decline in public savings. In the 1950s and the 1960s the revenue account of the central government at least was in surplus, but in the 1970s even this went into a deficit, which climbed steadily from Rs 17,150 million in 1980–1 to Rs 105,140 million in 1988–9, Rs 119,140 million in 1989–90 and Rs 185,610 million in 1990–1. The implications of this growing fiscal crisis were obvious: the government had either to cut back the tempo of its investment or to maintain this tempo through increased recourse to borrowing. If the borrowing is from abroad, then the building up of pressure for a change in the policy regime is obvious. If the borrowing is domestic, then private wealth holders may be willing to hold claims upon the state only after they have increased their holdings of other assets, such as urban property or consumer durables or commodity stocks, in which case, *ceteris paribus*, the inflationary impact of a given tempo of public investment keeps increasing. And, since rampant inflation cannot be allowed in a system of parliamentary democracy with virtually non-existent indexation for the vast bulk of the workers, the state would sooner or later have to cut back its expenditure, especially investment expenditure, which would slow down the economy and eventually arouse capitalists' demands for an alternative policy regime. Even if private wealth holders are willing temporarily to hold government debt without there being any inflationary pressures immediately, this only accentuates the inflation-proneness of the economy in the long run, with identical results.

In short, the regime gets progressively engulfed in a crisis. In its efforts to combine political legitimacy with economic dynamism, it increasingly comes a cropper.

The second contradiction lay in the inability of the state to impose a minimum measure of 'discipline' and 'respect for law' among the capitalists, without which no capitalist system anywhere can be tenable. Disregard for the laws of the land, especially tax laws, was an important component of the primary accumulation of capital. The same disregard—the same absence of a collective discipline which a capitalist class imposes upon itself in any established capitalist country—also meant that a successful transition could not be made from a Nehruvian interventionist regime to an alternative viable capitalist regime with state intervention, but of a different kind. After all, the state is strongly interventionist even in a country like Japan, but it is interventionism based on close collaboration between the state and capital, which simultaneously promotes rigorous discipline among the capitalists. To be sure the extent and nature of state intervention in Japan is itself a result of specific features of Japanese civil society as it has developed historically, which cannot simply be emulated elsewhere. Indeed the point being made here—namely, the inability of the Indian state to promote a measure of discipline among the Indian capitalists—is obviously merely a descriptive one, the analysis of which has to be located in the specific nature of the Indian society and polity—a task outside the scope of this chapter. But the description is important; it provides a proximate explanation of why the retreat from Nehruvian dirigisme, instead of leading to an alternative viable capitalist regime carving out a space for itself in the international economy, through an alternative mode of state intervention, has resulted in a situation where the economy is left to the caprices of international capital. Indeed many advocates of a retreat from Nehruvian dirigisme had turned explicitly to the Japanese 'model' and had hoped for a new consolidation of Indian capitalism, much in the way that Japanese capitalism had consolidated itself. They were of course being unhistorical; an important aspect of their unhistoricity was their refusal to recognize the inability of the Indian state to impose a measure of 'discipline' on Indian capital.

The third contradiction had its roots in the cultural ambience of an ex-colonial society like India. The market for industrial goods was from its very inception, as we have seen, a socially narrowly based one. Capitalism in its metropolitan centres is however characterized by continuous product innovation, the phenomenon of newer and ever newer goods being thrown on to the market, resulting in alterations of lifestyles. In an ex-colonial economy like India, the comparatively narrow social segment to whose hands additional purchasing power accrues in a large measure, and whose growing consumption therefore provides the main source of the growth in demand for industrial consumer goods, is also anxious to emulate the lifestyles prevailing in the metropolitan centre. It is not satisfied with having more and more of the same goods which are domestically produced, nor is it content merely with expending its additional purchasing power upon such new goods as the domestic economy, on its own, is capable of innovating. Its demand is for the new goods which are being produced and consumed in the metropolitan centres, and which, given the constraints upon the innovative capacity of the domestic economy, are incapable of being locally produced purely on the basis of indigenous resources and indigenous technology. An imbalance therefore inevitably arises in such economies between what the economy is capable of locally producing purely on its own steam and what the relatively affluent sections of society who account for much of the growth of potential demand for consumer goods would like to consume. This imbalance may be kept in check by import controls, though such controls inevitably give rise to clandestine imports, through smuggling, which are sold in local 'black markets'. But even leaving aside such clandestine imports, the more the imbalance between what is produced and what is sought to be consumed is kept in check through controls, the more it grows because of further innovations in the metropolitan economies.

The result is a powerful build-up of pressure among the more affluent groups in society for a dismantling of controls. The fact that this would result in substantial sections of domestic producers going under—that is, in a de-industrialization in the domestic economy, together with an accentuation of the already precarious balance of payments situation—does not come in the way of such pressures being built up. The inculcation of a desire to emulate the fashionable lifestyles prevailing in the metropolitan countries among segments of the underdeveloped economy acts as a powerful instrument in the hands of metropolitan capital in its efforts to prise open the market of such an economy and to wrest back the space which it had yielded as a result of granting political independence. The contradiction between the extant production pattern and the desired consumption pattern of the affluent sections of the population contributes to a dismantling of the dirigiste economic regime. And this contradiction too has been manifest in India.

The net result of the working out of all these contradictions has been evident in the Indian economy for quite some time. The growth in the index of manufacturing industrial production, which is a barometer of the expansion in the possibilities of productive accumulation, is quite revealing. The growth rate figures for different periods are summarized in Table 2.2.

Table 2.2: Growth rates of the index of industrial production, manufacturing

(Annual Average Compound Rates)

1951–2 to 1964–5	7.8%
1965–6 to 1969–70	3.3%
1970–1 to 1980–1	4.1%
1980–1 to 1984–5	5.7%
1984–5 to 1989–90	8.8%
1990–1 to 1994–5	3.9%
1994–5 to 2002–3	5.8%

Notes and Sources: The figures up to 1970 have 1960 as base; the figures for the 70s have 1970 as base; the figures for the 80s and early 1990s have 1980–1 as base; and figures for the latter half of the 1990s have 1993–4 as base. These rates are based on figures from various issues of the annual *Economic Survey* issued by the Ministry of Finance and the *Report on Currency and Finance* of the Reserve Bank of India.

After 15 years of rapid industrial expansion in the 1950s and the early 1960s, there was a dramatic decline in the rate of manufacturing growth during the next 15 years. Even though the growth rate picked up somewhat in the early 1980s, it was still nowhere near the rates witnessed in the first 15 years of planning. It is only after the mid-1980s that a pronounced boom occurred once again in the manufacturing sector of Indian industry, to be followed by the adjustment-induced recession of the 1990s. The fact that the 15 years after the mid-1960s, which were characterized by a relative stagnation in manufacturing output, also witnessed a decline in the rate of growth of public investment compared to the earlier period is well-known. The increasing fiscal difficulties faced by the state—which were manifested *inter alia* in the revenue account of the central government itself running into a deficit during the course of this period—and which were a result, as we have argued, of its role in promoting 'primary accumulation of capital'—entailed that the state could not adequately fulfil its other role, namely, as an expander of the market. A number of industries which catered to mass consumption or to the investment requirements of the state vanished. And the slower expansion of public investment also meant a slower growth in the productive potential of the industrial sector on account of the infrastructural constraints that resulted from such slower expansion.[5]

Given the sluggish growth of the home market, breaking into export markets could have provided a new stimulus to industrial expansion and a new basis for capital accumulation in productive channels. But export markets were dominated by metropolitan capital. To permit Indian capital a share of this export market as a junior partner, metropolitan capital demanded a price, namely, that it too should have a share of the Indian market. Any attempt by Indian capital to break into export markets, not as a junior partner of metropolitan capital but independently (through making use of imported technology where necessary), required a massive effort of its own backed by the Indian state. This, however, never became a serious possibility owing, among other things, to the reason mentioned earlier, namely, the unwillingness of Indian capital to accept a certain minimum 'discipline' imposed by its own state upon itself, which was necessary for the purpose and which underlay the international successes, for example, of Japanese capitalism. The export prospects of Indian capital consequently remained bleak.

In this context, a schism developed within the ranks of the Indian capitalists. A section was willing to make compromises with metropolitan capital on the terms that the latter demanded: it was all for allowing metropolitan capital to capture a share of the Indian market even at the expense of the entrenched capitalists, not to mention the public sector, in the hope of being able to better its own prospects as a junior partner, both in the domestic as well as in the international market. It was thus in favour of import liberalization, a full retreat from Nehruvian dirigisme, and accepting the kind of regime that metropolitan capital generally, and the Bank and the Fund as its chief spokesmen, had been demanding. The more powerful and the more entrenched monopoly houses were however more circumspect. They would not mind import liberalization in areas other than their own, including in areas dominated by the public sector; they would not mind collaborating with foreign capital to add to their empires and hence a degree of relaxation of controls to further facilitate such collaboration; but they would not like encroachments by metropolitan capital upon their own empires. Their attitude towards Fund–Bank style liberalization was therefore more ambiguous.

Support for Fund–Bank-style liberalization was growing not just among a section of capital. A whole new category of an altogether different kind of businessmen was coming up, who were more in the nature of upstarts, international racketeers, fixers, and middlemen, often of 'non-resident Indian' origin or having NRI links, often linked to smuggling and the arms trade; these in any case did not have much of a production base, and their parasitic intermediary status as well as the international value of their operations naturally inclined them towards an 'open economy'. On the other side, among the affluent groups of consumers, the desire for an 'open economy', where they could have access to a variety of goods available abroad but not at home, had also grown strong. And finally, as we have already mentioned earlier, one should not exclude a section of the top bureaucracy itself, which had close links with the Fund and the Bank, either as ex-employees who might return any time to Washington D.C., or through being engaged in dollar projects of various kinds, or as hopeful aspirants for a lucrative berth in Washington D.C.; the weight of this section in the top bureaucracy had been growing at an amazingly rapid rate, and its influence naturally was in the direction of adopting the Fund-Bank policy regime.[6] In short, quite apart from the growing leverage exercised by the international agencies in their capacity as 'donors', the internal contradictions of the Nehruvian dirigiste policy regime generated increasing support within the powerful and affluent sections of society for changing India's economic policy regime in the manner desired by these agencies.

It is against this background of a two-decade-long sluggish industrial growth on the one hand, and growing pressures for a retreat from interventionism and the adoption of a Fund-Bank style 'liberalization' package on the other that the economic policies of the latter half of the 80s, which in several ways marked a new departure, have to be located. Briefly, three new features characterized these policies. First, there was a significant increase in the magnitude of the government's deficit as a proportion of the GDP at current market prices. The gross fiscal deficit of the central and state governments averaged 9.5 per cent of GDP during 1985–6 to 1989–90 and touched 10.1 per cent in 1990–1. However, this was not due to any increase in the share of public investment, but largely to a decline in the share of public savings, reflected in the burgeoning revenue deficit (which rose from an average of 2.8 per cent of GDP during 1985–6 to 1989–90 to 4.5 per cent in 1990–1), with the current expenditure of the state growing at a rate far outstripping the growth in tax as well as non-tax revenues, despite hikes in indirect taxation and in administered prices. Partly this was because of the government's refusal to garner larger direct tax revenues;[7] partly because of the growing expenditure on interest payments (the sins of past deficits catching up with the government) and on subsidies, especially on fertilizers (caused primarily by wrong technological choices involving the setting-up of plants with extraordinarily high capital costs); and partly because of the general profligacy which characterized the then government to an unprecedented extent.

The second feature was the liberalization of imports of capital goods and components required for a number of commodities catering to luxury consumption, especially of electronics and automobiles. This was justified in the name of 'marching to the 21st century'. And important government officials unashamedly put forward the argument that since even the small segment of the population that demanded such goods amounted in absolute terms to a fairly large number, the country could go forward on the basis of such an industrialization strategy, whose benefits would 'eventually trickle down' to the poorer sections of the population as well.

The remarkable aspect of the policy of import liberalization of the late 1980s was that it was not necessarily tied in to a larger export effort; its main immediate thrust was towards producing more goods—luxury goods—for the domestic market. In 1985–86, the very first year that the policy was introduced, there was a dramatic increase in the trade and current account deficits, the latter from 1.24 per cent of GDP to 2.26 per cent. True it reached a plateau thereafter (1.99, 1.89 and 2.66 per cent in the three subsequent years), because of which many have argued that it would be unfair to blame the Rajiv Gandhi government for import profligacy. But this argument misses two important points: first, the high absolute level of the trade and current deficits were sustained despite the fact that owing to the development of the Bombay High oilfields, India's oil import bill came down in absolute terms between 1984–5 and 1988–9. In other words, but for the import profligacy the trade deficit should have declined significantly in absolute terms since mineral oil and related products accounted for nearly a third of India's import bill on the former date. Second, the remittance inflows during this period had flattened out and 'soft loans' were becoming more and more difficult to come by. The need was to conserve foreign exchange and the maintenance of a high, even though steady, absolute level of the trade deficit was a mark of profligacy. And over two-fifths of the increase in import value between 1984–85 and 1988–89 (barring items virtually re-exported) was on account of machinery and transport equipment, which went to a significant extent into the production of a variety of goods for the 'elite' market.

The third new feature was a systematic resort to commercial borrowing abroad, including from the NRIs. As the trade and current account deficits went up in the latter half of the 1980s, commercial borrowings were increasingly resorted to which in turn contributed with a lag to keeping up the current account deficit itself (owing to interest payments) and necessitated further borrowing, both for this reason as well as for amortising past loans. Debt has a habit of escalating rapidly, feeding upon itself; and as fresh debt is contracted to pay off old debt, the terms at the margin become stiffer, the maturity period shorter, and hence the rate of escalation of debt even steeper. And this is precisely what happened. The debt in dollar terms nearly quadrupled during the 1980s, from $20,582 million in 1980 to $81,994 million in 1990; debt to banks and private individuals increased more than 10 times from $1,997 million to $22,387 million. India's debt-service payments absorbed 31.2 per cent of her exports in 1990.[8]

If the large fiscal deficits of the late 1980s had not been accompanied by large current account deficits on the balance of payments, the inflationary overhang would have grown faster and there would have been much higher inflation in the 1980s than actually occurred. On the other hand, if the current account deficit had been as large as it was owing to import liberalization but the fiscal deficits had actually been smaller, then imported goods would have out-competed domestic goods to a greater extent (since the home market would have been narrower with a smaller fiscal deficit), and there would have been greater 'de-industrialization', and hence a smaller rate of industrial growth.

The odd thing about industrial growth, however, was that notwithstanding its impressive rate, it had limited impact upon industrial employment. Between end-March 1985 and end-March 1990, employment in the (organized) private sector went up by a mere 273,000 (or 3.7 per cent) in five years, while in the private manufacturing sub-sector it actually declined by 16,000. Even in the public manufacturing sector it went up between these two dates by a mere 109,000 (5.8 per cent). Thus the acceleration of industrial growth appears to have had no significant impact on industrial employment.

The industrial boom of this period, however, even as it tried to paper over the basic contradictions of the regime, and that too apparently successfully, left the economy on a powder-keg. The enormous external debt, a growing portion of it being in the form of short-term borrowing, made the economy acutely vulnerable to currency speculations and 'confidence crises' of international investors, a vulnerability that was an entirely new phenomenon for the Indian economy. The liquidity build-up in the domestic economy which inevitably followed made it acutely vulnerable to sudden inflationary upsurges. The consequences of both these phenomena in precipitating the crisis of 1991 have been explored earlier. What we turn to now is the fall-out of the adjustment process adopted in response to that crisis.

THE PROGRESS OF STRUCTURAL ADJUSTMENT

The most palpable impact of structural adjustment has been a deceleration in the reduction of poverty. Table 2.3, taken from Sen and Himanshu (2004)[9]

Table 2.3: Headcount poverty ratios and comparable change

(based on official poverty lines)

Year (NSS Round)	Headcount ratios (% HCR)				Comparable annual change in HCR from			
	Rural		Urban		About 5 years ago		About a decade ago	
	Uniform 30 day	Mixed 30–365 days	Uniform 30 day	Mixed 30–365 days	Rural	Urban	Rural	Urban
1983 (38)	45.6		40.8		–1.4	–0.8	–1.1	–0.6
1986–7 (42)	40.2		36.7					
1987–8 (44)	39.0	(35.2)	38.7	(34.9)	–1.5	–0.5	–1.4	–0.7
1989–90 (45)	38.1		37.5					
1990–1 (46)	33.5		36.0					
1992 (48)	41.7		37.8					
1993–4 (50)	37.2	31.6 (31.9)	32.4	27.9 (28.0)	–0.3 (–0.6)	–1.1 (–1.2)	–0.8	–0.8
1994–5 (51)	41.3	36.6	35.7	30.7	1.6 (1.4*)	–0.1 (0.3*)		
1995–6 (52)	37.1	31.5	30.2	25.5			–0.3 (–0.6*)	–0.7 (–0.8*)
1997 (53)	35.3	31.1	32.7	28.7	0.1 (–0.3*)	–0.4 (–0.4*)		
1999–2000 (55)		28.8		25.1	–0.5* (–0.5*)	–0.5* (–0.5*)	–0.5* (–0.5*)	–0.8* (–0.8)
2000–1 (56)		25.0		24.9	–1.9* (–1.9)	–1.0* (1.0)	–0.3* (–0.4*)	–0.6* (–0.7*)
2001–2 (57)		29.1		26.6				

Note: All estimates use the All-India distribution and All-India poverty lines. The MRP in the 43rd round had 365-day questions only for clothing; footwear and durable goods and the corresponding estimates for round 50 are in brackets. All other MRP estimates used 365-day questions for clothing, footwear, durable goods, education and institutional medical care. MRP estimates for rounds 51 to 53 are hybrid, replacing deciles-wise the 30-day estimates for low-frequency items in Schedule 1 with corresponding 365-day estimates from Schedule 2, and 55th round estimates are food-adjusted. All other estimates use unadjusted original distributions. Comparable annualized change is either from one thick round to another, including from rounds 27 and 32, or over the following comparable thin rounds: 42 & 52; 45, 51 & 56; and 46 & 53. Each of these sets had the same principal purpose of enquiry and the same sampling frame. The change figures are on both URP basis (unbracketed) and MRP (bracketed). The change estimates with asterisks are those for which the same reference period was not available from the two rounds compared. These cases involve rounds 42, 45, and 46 for which MRP is not available, and it was assumed that the MRP–URP difference was the same as in round 43; and rounds 55 and 56 for which URP is not available and it was assumed that the MRP–URP difference was the same as the average for rounds 51 to 53. Change figures without asterisks are direct, from comparable rounds using comparable reference periods.

Source: Abhijit Sen and Himanshu, *Poverty and Inequality in India: Getting Closer to the Truth,* available at http://www.macroscan.org/fet/may04/pdf/Poverty_WC.pdf, accessed 1 June 2004.

presents the most thorough analysis of annualized changes in headcount ratios from all comparable rounds of the National Sample Survey. These figures point to an acceleration of urban poverty reduction in the late 1980s, followed by slowdown after the mid-1990s. On the other hand, for rural areas, quinquennial comparisons show a sharp slowdown in poverty reduction during the early 1990s, followed by revival in the late 1990s. However, unlike in urban areas, the decadal pace of rural poverty reduction is found to reduce very significantly, from 1–1.5 percentage points per annum during the 1970s and 1980s to at most 0.5 percentage points per annum in the 1990s. All of these, argue Sen and Himanshu, *imply that the number of poor increased during the 1990s, by between 3 and 35 million.*

The supporters of structural adjustment attribute this fact to causes other than the process of adjustment: for instance, it is argued that the main cause of the increase in rural poverty in a year like 1991–2 was the increase in the consumer price index for agricultural labourers, which went up by 19.3 per cent in that year on an average of months basis and 21.9 per cent on the last-month-of-the-year basis; and that this increase was largely a result of a crop shortfall together with private hoarding.[10]

That this explanation would not do is obvious from the following: the output fall in 1991–2 affected only the *kharif* crop, when food grains production fell from 99.44 million tonnes to 91.59 million tonnes, and not the *rabi* harvest (comprising largely wheat), which was more or less stable at its 1990–1 record level of 76.95 million tonnes, with the 1991–2 figure being 76.79

million tonnes. Further, within the kharif crop, the principal cereal, rice, also recorded a marginal increase from 66.32 million tonnes to 66.37 million tonnes. The decline in kharif foodgrain production was due to a decline in the production of coarse cereals from 32.7 million tonnes to 26 million tonnes and of pulses from 5.4 million tonnes to 4.1 million tonnes. Further, throughout 1992 wheat stocks with the government were higher than the minimum norm for public stocks, though this was not true of a kharif cereal like rice. In short, in terms of availability (ignoring private hoarding), or in terms of the ability of the government to counter reduced supplies on account of private hoarding, there is absolutely no reason why wheat prices and perhaps even rice prices should have gone up at all, even if it is conceded for argument's sake that other kharif cereal prices could have. And yet we find that the average-of-months index of wholesale price for wheat went up by as much as 18.6 per cent in 1991–2 and by 21.9 per cent for rice. The reason for this dissociation between the pattern of price movements and the pattern of apparent demand-supply imbalances, and hence for the irrelevance of these apparent imbalances as the explanatory variable for price movements, lies in the fact, mentioned earlier, of the increase in the issue prices of the public distribution system. In December 1991, the issue price of the common variety of rice was hiked by 30.4 per cent and of wheat by 19.7 per cent, which was in addition to the increases in June 1990 mentioned at the beginning of this chapter.

Structural adjustment has in other words necessarily entailed costly food for the working people. And there is nothing in this to be surprised about, because it is part of the logic of structural adjustment: by insisting on a reduction in the magnitude of food subsidy and by insisting on an elimination of all input subsidies into agriculture (of which the fertilizer subsidy was the most important element in India), it necessarily ensures that the price of food in terms of the wage unit, especially in the unorganized sector, goes up. A rise in rural poverty is an inevitable consequence of this phenomenon.

The second notable consequence of structural adjustment was an immediate deceleration in the rate of growth of per capita income. During the period 1987–8 to 1990–1, per capita national product at 1980–1 prices went up by 17 per cent; during the subsequent three years the order of increase was 2.6 per cent. If the agricultural sector is kept out of the picture as being in some ways a *sui generis* sector, then the picture is even more dismal. The growth rate of the industrial sector (judged by the index of industrial production), which was 8.2 per cent per annum for the four years ending 1990–1, came down sharply to 4.2 per cent for the subsequent four years; the corresponding figures for the manufacturing segment of the industrial sector were 8.5 per cent and 3.9 per cent respectively.

Of course, in judging the impact of Fund–Bank-style reforms on macroeconomic performance, one has to exercise particular caution. These reforms are inevitably associated with deflation in the short run, and it is only after a while that the economy is expected to pick up *on the basis of stimuli other than those which prevailed under the dirigiste regime.* In short, a transitional period of stagnation is expected (though not strictly on the basis of the IMF's theory, which does not recognize any demand constraints), and should not cause undue worry, provided growth subsequently picks up on a new basis.

Advocates of economic reform have repeatedly argued that, after the initial adjustment, the decade of reform has witnessed India's transition to a new, higher growth trajectory. The typical claim—made by the government and neo-liberal sympathisers—has been that, as compared with the old 'Hindu rate of growth' of around 3.5 per cent per annum, the Indian economy was over the 1990s set firmly on a trajectory involving a rate of growth of well over 6 per cent. It has been argued that despite the fiscal compression resulting from the government's effort to contain the fiscal deficit in a period when the tax-to-GDP ratio was falling, liberalization provided a stimulus to private 'animal spirits', so that increasing private investment more than compensated for the sharp deceleration in public capital formation during the 1990s. Optimistic projections on the basis of this perception have even suggested that the economy could easily achieve a 9 per cent rate of growth in the near future.

But such optimism has not been borne out by the actual experience. By the end of the decade official statistics had begun to reflect the slowing of economic growth in India.[11] As the Reserve Bank of India noted in its Annual Report for 2000–1: 'Filtering the data on real GDP growth to eliminate irregular year-to-year fluctuations indicates the presence of a growth cycle in the Indian economy and a discernible downturn in the second half of the 1990s.'[12] According to the RBI, this brings the average growth rate of the 'growth cycle' over the 1990s to only 4.4 per cent, which was lower than that recorded in the 1980s. This confirms that the process of liberalizing reform has not delivered the higher rates of growth that were earlier promised and anticipated.

Table 2.4 presents the growth performance of the three principal sectors over three decades. While the primary and secondary sectors registered a rise in the rate of growth between the 1970s and 1980s, that rate of growth remained relatively constant in the 1990s when compared with the 1980s. Further, there was a deceleration in the rate of such growth during the second half of the

1990s when compared with the first half of the decade. Only the tertiary sector experienced a continuous rise in growth rates. But some services growth in the second half of the 90s was affected by the increased government expenditure on salaries that was entailed in the Pay Commission award. Thus, the 1990s liberalization was not accompanied by any new dynamism in the commodity-producing sectors of the economy; rather, it could be suggested that the transition to a higher 'trend' rate of economic growth in the 1980s lost steam over the 1990s, especially during the latter half of the decade.

Table 2.4: Sectoral GDP growth rates (base 1993-4)

		Average annual rates of growth	
	Primary	*Secondary*	*Tertiary*
1971–2 to 1979–80	2.22	4.64	4.87
1981–2 to 1989–90	3.37	6.95	7.04
1991–2 to 1999–2000	3.30	6.98	8.35
1985–6 to 1989–90	5.72	8.66	8.83
1991–2 to 1994–5	3.77	8.04	6.40
1995–6 to 1999–2000	1.95	4.99	7.20

Source: CSO, *National Accounts Statistics*, various issues

It is not just that the Indian economy too had not 'turned the corner' under structural adjustment, as many have argued. The *basis for even the improved performance was an enhanced fiscal deficit*, which the government could sustain because of the manoeuvrability that consecutive good monsoons and rising foreign exchange reserves, fed by 'volatile' capital flows, had provided it. Needless to say, this strategy had been pursued against the wishes of the Fund and the Bank, owing to the compulsions of a parliamentary democracy, forcing them to openly dissociate from this component of the government's strategy. In short, the performance of the economy during the 1990s was a result not of the success of Fund–Bank reforms, but of the government's partial, surreptitious withdrawal from them. Let us turn briefly to this important issue.

The gross fiscal deficit of the Centre and the states, which averaged 9.5 per cent during 1985–90, was 10.1 per cent in 1990–91 (just before the 'reforms' were introduced), 7.5 per cent in 1991–2, and 7.4 per cent in 1992–3; it went back to 9.0 per cent in 1993–4 (the first year of industrial 'recovery'), and 8.4 per cent according to the revised estimates of 1994–5.[13] The relationship between the expansion of the fiscal deficit and industrial performance is absolutely unmistakable. As for the Centre's own fiscal deficit, if we use the older definition, which included small savings transferred to the states, the fiscal deficit to GDP ratio. which fell from 7.9 per cent in 1990–1 to 4.9 per cent in 1996–7, rose to 7.03 per cent in 1999–2000 and was at 6.8 per cent in 2000–1.

The remarkable aspect of the increase in the fiscal deficit however is the *component* of it which increased. It is not the pace of capital formation under the aegis of the state which has increased, but the *revenue deficit*. The revenue deficit of the Centre and the states as a proportion of GDP which had averaged 2.8 per cent during the quinquennium 1985–90, went up to 4.5 per cent during 1990–91 on the eve of structural adjustment, and then, having come down to 3.6 and 3.4 during the next two years (marked by industrial stagnation), climbed up to 4.6 per cent during 1993–4; the revised estimates for 1994–5 put it once again at 4.6 per cent. One reason for this faster rise in the revenue deficit was of course burgeoning interest payments which are the price of past profligacy. The other was that while the government had accepted the 'marketist' argument which comes with structural adjustment—namely, that the state should refrain from involving itself in production as far as possible and even dispose of its profit-making assets—it was encouraged by the improved food and foreign exchange reserve position and forced by the political compulsions of democracy to ignore IMF–Bank pressures to curtail overall government spending.

Three conclusions immediately follow: first, if the objective of the reforms was to introduce 'discipline' into the government's *current* account (an objective which many Indian economists and civil servants, influenced by Buchanan and others, considered to be a sufficient *justification* for IMF tutelage), then they have been a miserable failure. Second, the increase in the government's current account deficit has been camouflaged in part by a curtailment in its investment expenditure; the overall fiscal deficit has gone up but not by as much as the revenue deficit. And, third, as mentioned earlier, this deficit expansion had stimulated a conventional industrial expansion of sorts which has nothing to do with any 'successes' of structural adjustment.

This pattern has extremely serious implications, which brings us to the *third* notable feature of structural adjustment, namely a decline in the investment ratio in the economy. Table 2.5 provides estimates of gross domestic capital formation and gross domestic savings as percentages of GDP from 1980–1 onwards. While both savings and investment rates have increased over time, this is part of a trend of much longer duration, whereby savings and investment rates have tended to increase with economic development. Thus we find that savings rates have increased from an average of 9 per cent in the early 1950s, to 12 per cent in the early 1960s, to 15 per cent in the early 1970s, to 18 per cent in the early 1980s. The increase in savings and investment rates in the 1990s can thus be seen as part of this broad tendency.

Table 2.5: Rates of gross domestic capital formation and savings

(as per cent of GDP at 1993–4 prices)

	Investment rate	*Savings rate*
1980–5	20.5	18.4
1985–90	22.8	20.4
1990–5	24.3	22.8
1995–2000	24.7	23.2

Source: CSO National Accounts Statistics, various issues

However, even this process seems to have decelerated over the years of reform. The rate of investment (or Gross Domestic Capital Formation) increased from 20.3 per cent in 1990–1 to touch a peak of 26.8 per cent in 1995–6, and then declined and stagnated at around 23 per cent. Similarly, while the rate of savings reached a peak level of 25.5 per cent in 1995–6, it subsequently fell to around 22 per cent by the end of the decade.[14]

A major reason for the relative stagnation in aggregate investment was the declining role of public investment. During the years of increasing state involvement in the industrialisation process between the mid-1950s and the mid-1970s, the public sector accounted for well over half of gross domestic capital formation. When the figure peaked in 1974–5, the public-sector share of total domestic investment was as high as 65 per cent. Over the first half of the 1980s, the share of the public sector in gross domestic capital formation was roughly stable at around half, but in the latter part of the decade it began to decline both as a share of total investment and as a share of GDP. By 1999–2000, public sector capital formation was only 28 per cent of total investment.

Marketist reformers had argued that this slack would be more than filled by private investment, which would also be more efficient. But while private investment increased until 1995–6 and then tapered off, even this was dominantly due to the increase in household investment (which is the counterpart of household physical savings). The share of investment by private households rose from 35 per cent in 1993–4 to as much as 41 per cent by 1999–2000. It is possible to speculate that much of even this increase reflected increases in what could otherwise be called luxury consumption, such as in the form of luxury housing that is classified as physical asset creation, or in the purchase of luxury vehicles that are classified as transport equipment. Meanwhile private corporate investment decelerated sharply from 1996–7. Investment in manufacturing stagnated and investment in transport actually fell in real terms.

This is not surprising: a number of researchers have drawn attention to the fact that in the Indian economy, *both in the agricultural as well as in the industrial sectors*, public investment tends to stimulate private investment, that is, has a 'crowding in' rather than a 'crowding out' effect on private investment (any possible temporary 'crowding out' owing to input-shortages amounts at most to a *postponement* of private investment without disturbing the overall relationship).[15]

The government's deficit has an extremely important role to play here. If the increased deficit is used for stepping up public capital formation, then not only does it stimulate the economy from the demand side but also keeps relaxing on the supply side—both through its direct effect on the magnitude of capital stock as well as through its indirect effect via stimulating private investment— any potential inflationary constraints upon the economy's expansion. On the other hand, if the increase in the government's deficit is confined to non-capital expenditure, then revival of the economy would necessarily be brief and evanescent, since such a revival would fairly soon run into an inflationary barrier.

This consideration is particularly important for an economy where agriculture accounts for a major part of the consumer goods sector. It may for instance be argued that *any* government expenditure (even non-capital expenditure) would, by stimulating the economy, call forth private investment via accelerator effects, so that the inflationary barrier would keep getting pushed back; this argument however would certainly not hold in the case of agriculture. Private investment in agriculture is not governed by any version of the acceleration (or capacity utilization or even profit) principle. It depends essentially upon the availability of complementary inputs like supra-individual irrigation facilities, power, extension facilities, seed–fertilizer packages, etc., whose provision is contingent upon public investment effort. In short, in an India-type economy it is not just any expansion in the government's deficit which can trigger off a sustained boom, but an expansion that takes the form of a larger investment effort. And this is precisely what the last deficit expansion during the 1990s has not been used for.

To avoid possible confusion, a word on the quirks of Indian statistics is necessary here. If one looks at the areas where the recent industrial expansion has occurred, then 'capital goods' industries are significant contributors to growth. This gives the impression that the industrial recovery is indeed investment-led. But the contradiction between the assertions that the pace of capital formation has been declining and that the 'capital goods' industries are prospering vanishes the moment we realize that in India the entire 'transport equipment' sector including passenger automobiles and the entire 'electrical machinery' sector including electronic gadgets of all descriptions are lumped together under capital goods. These sectors have been witnessing a deficit-sustained boom recently; but this fact does not help an iota in pushing outwards the inflationary barrier arising from the wage-goods sector, especially in a situation where agricultural exports are being increasingly resorted to under the impact of the 'reforms' (on this more later). Underlying the decline in the pace of capital formation is the non-fulfilment of a crucial assumption of the Fund-Bank package.

This brings us to the *fourth* notable feature of the Indian experience. The assumption usually made is that once the economy starts pursuing 'market-friendly' policies, foreign direct investment (FDI) would start coming in and raise the investment ratio in the economy even if the state withdraws from its role as an investor. This assumption, often justified with reference to the East Asian (including Chinese) and South-East Asian experience, is in fact based on a *misreading* of that experience (since foreign direct investment supplements extraordinarily high domestic savings ratios in those countries, and Fund–Bank reform packages do not in any case constitute the foundation of economic policy). In the Indian case FDI inflows have been much smaller and substantially aimed at taking over pre-existing capacities through mergers and acquisitions rather than at generating new 'greenfield' projects.

While greenfield FDI inflows into the economy have been sparse, capital has flowed in in large magnitudes into foreign currency deposits and in the form of portfolio investments, which are essentially indistinguishable from 'hot money'. This points of course to an extremely important aspect of the reality of contemporary capitalism, namely that unlike what many observers, including radical ones, assert, what has really happened in capitalism is not so much a tendency towards globalization of production as a tendency towards globalization of finance. We have suggested earlier that the Fund–Bank structural adjustment package, though advocated on the grounds that its adoption would draw FDI in large quantities, has evolved through time to cater in practice largely to the requirements of international *rentier interests*. Paradoxically, the adoption of this package, even when it succeeds in attracting large amounts of 'hot money', cannot generate growth in the economy; and of course when 'hot money' flies out, growth suffers through enforced deflation for the sake of creating creditors' confidence. In other words, this package, if conscientiously adopted, binds the economy to stagnation in years of comfortable foreign exchange and retrogression in years of foreign exchange crunch, giving rise to a combination of net retrogression and 'denationalization' of the nation's assets and natural resources.

Let us analyse this mechanism briefly before discussing the Indian case. When hot money flows occur, the recipient country has two choices: either to maintain the exchange rate by adding to reserves or to prevent a swelling of reserves by letting the exchange rate appreciate. Any government wishing to prevent a gratuitous 'deindustrialization' of the economy (and hence a gratuitous 'manufacture' of a current account deficit to accommodate hot money inflows) would of course prefer to prevent an exchange rate appreciation by adding to exchange reserves. And since these enhanced reserves represent after all an additional command over resources, even hot money flows, it may be thought, can add to the pace of capital formation if properly utilized.

The problem however is twofold: the minor problem relates to the fact that using reserves built up with hot money for undertaking investment implies in essence that the country is 'borrowing short to invest long', which exposes it to potential crises. But even if this is tackled by choosing short-gestation, foreign-exchange-earning investment projects, there remains a major problem—namely, there has to be an *agency* that must take the lead in stepping up capital formation; and an economy under Fund–Bank thraldom lacks such an agency. Since the state is increasingly forced to withdraw from its investment role, it cannot step up investment directly. Since the state cannot order private investment, it can stimulate the latter only indirectly; but the obvious indirect instrument—namely, the interest rate—can scarcely be used for fear of frightening international rentiers. And portfolio investment which typically stimulates stock-market booms makes speculation more attractive than productive investment for the domestic capitalists. Finally, since 'market-friendliness' takes the form *inter alia* of trade liberalization, which brings in MNC products to the local market, this fact tends to dampen the inducement to domestic capitalists to invest.

The upshot is that foreign exchange reserves accumulate even as productive investment languishes. The reserve accumulation, it may be thought, would give rise to a *consumption-led boom*. But, for reasons already discussed, credit to finance such a boom is expensive. And even if it does play a role, the boom would be a brief and evanescent one, until domestic supply constraints begin to appear (at which point reserves would start getting used up to augment supplies and the domestic multiplier effects of higher consumption would disappear). What is even more likely however is that such consumption growth as occurs owing to the effects of hot money inflows would, in a 'liberalized trade' regime, leak out abroad without generating any domestic growth.

On the other hand, when hot money flows out, the very fact that the reserves have shrunk in the event of higher domestic consumption (or if the outflow is larger than the extant reserves can sustain), the economy has to be deflated, and a whole lot of measures, including handing over the country's natural resources 'for a song' to international creditors, have to be adopted to cope with the foreign exchange crunch. The net result is a process of gradual economic atrophy together with 'denationalization' of assets and resources.

The relevance of the above discussion becomes obvious when we note that, even as FDI inflows remained small, India's foreign exchange reserves kept increasing through the inflow of hot money: they were $5.8 billion at end-March 1991, $25.2 billion in 1995, $42.3 billion at the end of March 2001, $54.1 billion at the end of March 2002, $75.4 billion at the end of March 2003 and $113 billion at the end of March 2004. As we have already seen, this very period of increasing reserves was marked by a decline in the pace of capital formation. True, there was a recovery of the industrial sector but that was largely government-deficit-sustained rather than monetary-policy-induced, so that the increased reserves were in themselves scarcely of much significance in causing it. There was, and still is, tremendous pressure from the Fund and the Bank for liberalizing consumption goods imports on the strength of the huge reserves, and for curtailing the fiscal deficit. Listening to this advice, the Indian government has ushered in simultaneously a combination of industrial retrogression, a decline in reserves for financing a consumption splurge by the affluent, and the creation of the very conditions for the process of atrophy-cum-denationalization outlined above. Further, having succumbed to structural adjustment, the government finds it difficult to continue resisting even demand for full capital account convertibility of the currency.

Finally, there is one other aspect of structural adjustment which deserves mention. An influential argument, which was accepted by many at the beginning of structural adjustment, was that a 'retreat of the state' and the exposure of the economy to the discipline of the market forces would cut out arbitrariness of decision-making and the corruption that is inevitably associated with it. It would streamline the functioning of the economy by making it a 'rule-governed system', though admittedly the rules were those of the market. What has happened instead in the Indian economy during this period of structural adjustment is an increase in the level of corruption, cronyism, and arbitrariness to unprecedented levels. The privatization exercise, as in other countries such as Bangladesh, has been an utter scandal. Precious natural resources, hitherto kept inside the public sector, are handed over for a pittance (and alleged 'kickbacks') to private firms with dubious objectives. The case of the Enron deal where massive contracts were signed without an open tender and at inflated capital costs, with guaranteed rates of return, has already attracted international attention. In short, the so-called 'discipline of the market' has proved to be a chimera.

But this is hardly surprising. As Lenin had pointed out long ago, finance capital is associated with swindles, bribery and corruption, or what European 'professors' of his time condescendingly called 'the American ethics'.[16]

THE ALTERNATIVE

What comes through clearly from the Indian experience with structural adjustment is the dominant role of the process of globalization of finance. We have suggested earlier that indeed the very design of the current package of structural adjustment bears the imprint of this process; and the sequel to the introduction of this package shows that the real mobility witnessed is that of finance rather than that of capital-in-production. But then if globalization of finance restricts the possibility of intervention within a 'national' (or for that matter any supranational but restricted) space by undermining the concept of a 'control area', the question naturally arises: can there be any sort of an alternative to the current set of policies? To say that an alternative presupposes *international* coordination, and can no longer be based on a national, or any kind of a spatially-restricted, response—a proposition which some radicals advance—is inadequate: it amounts de facto to conceding that a feasible alternative to the current set of policies does not exist.

It is our contention however that a feasible alternative, not just a desirable one, to the current policies exists. We should draw a distinction here: obviously the East Asian and the South-East Asian cases underscore the possibility of a successful, neo-mercantilist (and in that sense nationalist) policy response in the contemporary environment. But those cases are also marked by economies where the development of financial institutions and hence the possibility of integration with global finance are limited to start with. China's stock exchange is very recent in origin, Vietnam does not even have one to date, and even in avowedly capitalist East Asia financial interests have generally played second fiddle (except briefly in Japan). One cannot of course recreate those initial conditions (and other conditions conducive to neo-mercantilism) in India: apart from being unhistorical that is not even necessarily desirable, since neo-mercantilist strategies have been associated with politically authoritarian structures. So, in discussing an alterative we have to talk of a *sui generis* alternative. And the question is: is it feasible?

In our view the fallacy lies in believing that an undermining of the 'control area' of the nation-state is tantamount to an impossibility of intervention. What such undermining does is to impose an important additional *constraint* upon the nation-state; the nation-state cannot certainly intervene in the *old* way. It can now intervene with some degree of success *only* if it takes this constraint into account.

Specifically, for economies like India this involves keeping the volatility of financial flows under check through a combination of: (i) direct regulations; (ii) an overall sound balance of payments (in relative terms, which is not synonymous with neo-mercantilism); and, above all, (iii) a development strategy which ensures economic advance with social stability.

1. The main form of direct regulation that we have in mind is of course a mix of capital flow controls with a non-convertible currency. External pressures against such regulation would be strong; but a country the size of India can, if she so chooses, show sufficient resilience to stand up to such pressures. After all even the current government, committed as it is to structural adjustment, has not moved towards full convertibility despite external pressures.

    The real problem, it may be thought, however, would be of a different kind: globalization of finance is such a strong process that direct regulation may prove ineffective in stemming illicit flows. But to believe that the existence of regulations makes *no* difference to the behaviour of economic agents is fallacious. And the effectiveness of regulations depends upon the character, and hence the social basis, of the state (a proposition which must not be confused with the view that an authoritarian state regulates more effectively; indeed we argue the contrary). The alternative we have in mind is not confined to merely having regulations by the extant state, but encompasses, as we shall see, a change in the character of the state.

2. Regulations however have to be backed by a sound balance of payments position through a sound *trade performance*. A part of the key to such a sound trade performance lies in the imposition of intelligently devised

import controls; at the same time, however, a sound export performance is essential. While the importance of boosting exports is stressed by neo-classical economists, they never distinguish between primary commodity and manufacturing exports. In agriculture, as already mentioned, private investment is predicated upon public investment; and if the latter cannot be augmented, either because the system is already agricultural-supply-constrained *pace* Kalecki (and hence up against the inflationary barrier),[17] or because the state is being made to withdraw from its investing role, then an increase in agricultural *exports* necessarily means a lower profile of domestic availability, which has the effect of both impoverishing the domestic working masses and contracting the home market for manufac-tured goods.

Manufacturing exports, however, as Kaldor had argued long ago,[18] are in an altogether different category. To the extent that investment decisions here are induced by larger capacity utilization, larger exports provide both the inducement as well as the material wherewithal (from the supply side) for larger investment. Manufacturing exports in other words can provide the basis for a self-sustaining growth process in a way that agricultural exports (except under special circumstances) cannot. The history of colonial India provides ample evidence for this proposition: the last half-century of colonial rule saw both a stagnant per capita agricultural output and a rise in the proportion of exports out of it, resulting in a sharp decline in the per capita availability of foodgrains, from about 200 kg per year at the turn of the century to about 150 kg at independence.

An alternative development strategy therefore must specifically aim at increasing the exports of manufactured goods. And this requires not 'getting prices right' in some neo-classical sense, but above all high rates of investment, which increase the flexibility of the economy's response to the changing international environment. The correlation between high in-vestment ratios and high export growth rates in cross-country data relating to a host of underdeveloped countries is strong.[19] The direction of causa-tion is always seen to lie from exports to investment; but a mutuality of causation is much more plausible, in which case it is not exports which need be the initial intervention variable but the investment ratio itself.

3.   This brings us to the main issue, namely the alternative development trajectory. *Any* meaningful development strategy for India, it seems to us, must aim to bring about an *immediate* improvement in the living condi-tions of the working masses, especially in the rural sector—that is, the

modus operandi of the development strategy itself must be such an improvement in their living standards. This is not merely an ethical proposition, but a practical necessity, both for the preservation of meaningful democratic structures, as well as for arousing the kind of enthusiasm and participation among the masses on the basis of which alone the structures of a more accountable state, a state capable of imposing discipline upon the rich and the capitalists, can be built. Such an immediate improvement must have as its cornerstone an accelerated agricultural growth based on egalitarian land reforms. The East Asian example has shown the importance of land reforms even for a neo-mercantilist strategy of economic nationalism; indeed it is important for *any* national economic programme. The Chinese example has shown the vigour of an industrialization drive based on an expansion of mass markets deriving from an accelerated agricultural growth. In their specific context, at the present conjuncture, this growth has been achieved through a break-up of communes though on the basis of the groundwork (for example, the destruction of landlordism and the erection of water-management systems) prepared earlier. In India at the present conjuncture, accelerated and dispersed (that is, not regionally concentrated) agricultural growth requires the institution of land reforms.

Together with land reforms of course a number of complementary areas have to be dealt with such as irrigation and water management, rural infrastructure, literacy, sanitation and drinking water, etc. All these would require considerable investment, but investment that is best undertaken under the aegis of elected local-level bodies. The requirement therefore is also for a devolution of resources and decentralization of planning. But the resources themselves have got to be raised and there is no escape from heavier doses of direct taxation, of property at any rate if not of incomes (though tax evasion in the latter case has to be stopped through punitive action). It is here that the conflict between the strategy just advocated and 'marketism' becomes apparent. It is often argued by 'marketists' that they are all for rural development. But if tax concessions have to be doled out to entice capital to stay in the country; if food prices have to be raised for the surplus food producers (who happen to be the rural rich), while food subsidies are cut; if all talk of land reforms is eschewed; if financial reforms do away with any system of earmarking of credit, and if even infrastructural development like power becomes the responsibility of the private sector, especially foreign capital, with profitability being the main consideration, then there is no scope left for an improvement in the conditions of the rural poor, or for rural development generally.[20]

CONCLUDING OBSERVATIONS: THE PRIMACY OF POLITICS

It is not enough however that an alternative programme exists; it is not even enough that one can identify in the abstract the class forces that are potentially capable of providing the social support for the implementation of such an alternative programme. These forces must be concretely ready for mobilization behind such an alternative. In other words, the concrete conditions for *praxis* must exist; and in our view these conditions are rapidly ripening in the Indian context.

The early euphoria generated by talk of a 7–8 per cent growth rate after the 'marketist' economic reforms has vanished; the belief that the so-called withdrawal of the state would be followed by a less corrupt, less arbitrary, more rule-governed order has also vanished. In short the credibility of the new policy-regime in the civil society at large has suffered greatly. At the same time there are very strong and unmistakable pressures from below for a betterment in living conditions, pressures that sometimes find outlets in the refracted form of 'lower-caste' demands, and are often contained through so-called 'populist' measures. The fact however that even ruling parties which are committed to structural adjustment are forced to undertake these very 'populist' measures frowned upon by the Fund and the Bank is indicative of the pressures from below for an improvement in living conditions (which does not of course nullify the observations about increasing poverty made earlier).

The only way these pressures can be met is if the basic classes—namely, the workers, both organized and unorganized, and the bulk of the peasantry—make the alternative programme their own. If large FDI inflows are precluded, then the only means of improving the living conditions of the mass of the people is by tapping the existing reserves of the economy, that is, by taking up the slack in agriculture through egalitarian land reforms as well as by more investment in rural infrastructure, and by raising the domestic savings ratio as the East Asians and South-East Asians have done. True, this appropriation of an alternative programme would take time, but the conditions for it are ripening.[21]

We shall end with two comments. An essential component of any alternative programme, over and above the mere nitty-gritty of an economic strategy, must be a strengthening of democratic institutions and structures. Only then would its appropriation by the basic classes be a productive and more durable one. In other words what is essential is not a new bout of social engineering but a genuine process of social transformation which expands the direct political intervention capacity of the basic classes. Much has been written on the state-versus-market dichotomy, and much of it, as we have seen, is facile. If the state is not sufficiently accountable to civil society then it has to be made accountable; but this cannot be ensured merely by a *formal* change in its character. Such a formal change has to be accompanied by a substantive expansion in the capacity for direct intervention on the part of the very classes in whose favour the formal change in the character of the state is supposed to have occurred. Putting it differently, the state-versus-market debate is a red herring which sidetracks the real debate: greater or lesser democracy for the broad masses of the people.

Second, the fact that globalization of finance has made the pursuit of progressive economic policies more difficult is obviously undeniable. But, in focusing upon this phenomenon exclusively, we run the risk of missing the dialectics between the external and the internal, of completely ignoring the possibility of domestic mobilization, of ignoring the effect of this mobilization upon the ability to tackle the external constraints, in short of ignoring the 'totality' of the situation which defines the scope for *praxis*. What enters into the constitution of this 'totality' is not only the changes occurring at the level of world capitalism but also the level of political mobilization of the masses domestically.

NOTES AND REFERENCES

1. Professor Mahalanobis' writings on planning have been brought together in P.K. Bose and M. Mukherjee (eds), *Statistical Essays on Planning* (Calcutta, Publishing Society, 1985). For a general discussion of Indian planning literature, see S. Chakravarty, *Development Planning: The Indian Experience* (New Delhi, Oxford University Press, 1987), and S. Chakravarty, *Selected Economic Writings* (New Delhi, Oxford University Press, 1993), and also the Special Number of *Economie Appliquee* on Adolph Lowe and P.C. Mahalanobis (No. 2, 1994). In the Marxist tradition, apart from the very substantial literature produced by Soviet scholars, there are several essays by Oskar Lange, reprinted in *Papers on Economics and Sociology 1930–1960* (Pergamon, Oxford, 1970); Charles Bettelheim, *India Independent* (Macgibbon & Kee, London, 1968); and Michael Kalecki, 'Intermediate Regimes' in *Selected Essays on the Economic Growth of Socialist and Mixed Economies* (Cambridge University Press, Cambridge, 1972). In the literature produced from within India, reference may be made to K.M. Kurien (ed.), *Indian State and Society: A Marxian Approach* (Bombay, 1975) and Ashok Mitra, *Terms of Trade and Class Relations* (London, 1977).

2. Besides drawing $666 million from the reserve tranche, India obtained loans totalling $2672 million under the first credit tranche facility and the compensatory and contingency financing facility during 1990/91 and early 1991/92. Finally, in October 1991 it arrived at a 20-month Standby Arrangement for upper credit tranche borrowing to the tune of $2262 million.

3. The World Bank's suggestion in a report in October 1990 that the rupee should be devalued by 20 percent may have started the speculative outflow. The flight of capital from the Foreign Currency Non-Resident Accounts alone added up to $1.33 billion between October 1990 and June 1991. See C.T. Kurien, *Global Capitalism and the Indian Economy* (Delhi, 1994), p. 100.

4. A discussion along these lines is to be found in Kartik Rai, 'The Indian Economy in Adversity and Debt', *Social Scientist* (1992), Jan-Feb.

5. There are a large number of papers on the question of industrial stagnation in India after the mid-60s, some of which have been collected in Deepak Nayyar (ed.) (1994), *Industrial Growth and Stagnation: The Debate in India*, Bombay: Oxford University Press, published for Sameeksha Trust, op. cit. Special reference may be made to the papers by Shetty, Srinivasan and Narayana, and Nayyar himself.

6. See C.T. Kurien, *Global Capitalism and the Indian Economy*, Delhi, 1994, p.119.

7. Figures from Reserve Bank of India, *Annual Report 1994–95* (Bombay, RBI, 1995).

8. Figures from World Bank, *World Debt Tables: External Finance for Developing Countries, 1994/95* (Washington D.C., World Bank, 1994).

9. Abhijit Sen and Himanshu, 'Poverty and Inequality in India: Getting Closer to the Truth', available at http://www.macroscan.org/fet/may04/pdf/Poverty_WC.pdf, accessed 1 June 2004.

10. Such an argument giving primacy to supply-side factors having little to do with structural adjustment as such has been put forward by S.D. Tendulkar ad L.R. Jain in 'Economic Reforms and Poverty', *Economic and Political Weekly*, Bombay, 10 June (1995).

11. This deceleration is despite the fact that the new series of national income, with 1993–4 as base, has not only increased the GDP estimates but also points to a higher rate of growth than in the old series for both overall and agricultural incomes. Thus, the GDP estimate for 1993–4 is about 9 per cent higher according to the new series than the old, both overall and in agriculture. Also, between 1993–4 and 1997–8, agricultural GDP as per the new series rose by a total of 14.2 per cent, as compared with 8.37 per cent according to the old series. Total GDP between these years increased by 31.3 per cent as per the new series, as compared with 30.4 per cent in the old series, with GDP in the

secondary sector rising by 41.6 per cent in both series and that in the tertiary sector by 37.4 in the new series against 38.6 per cent in the old.

12. Reserve Bank of India, *Annual Report 2000–01* (Mumbai, RBI, 2001), Summary, p. 17.

13. Figures from Reserve Bank of India, *Annual Report 1994–95* (Bombay, RBI, 1995).

14. Reserve Bank of India (2001), *Handbook of Statistics on Indian Economy, 2000–01* (Bombay, RBI), Table 197.

15. For the industrial sector this was argued by Prabhat Patnaik in 'Private Corporate Industrial Investment in India 1947–1967: Factors Affecting its Size, Cyclical Fluctuations and Distribution Between Sectors', unpublished D.Phil. thesis, University of Oxford, 1973; a similar argument though within a very different overall perspective was put forward by T.N. Srinivasan and N.S.S. Narayana, 'Economic Performance Since the Third Plan', *Economic & Political Weekly*, Annual No., 1977, reprinted in Nayyar *op.cit.* For the agricultural sector the argument was put forward by S.K. Rao in 'Inter-regional Variations in the Growth of Agriculture and Population in India 1951–1968', unpublished Ph.D. thesis, University of Cambridge, 1972.

16. V.I. Lenin, *Imperialism, The Highest Stage of Capitalism* (Pluto Press, Chicago) in *Selected Works* (3 vols), (Moscow, 1977), vol. 1, p. 675.

17. M. Kalecki, 'Problems of Financing Economic Development in a Mixed Economy', reprinted in Kalecki, *Selected Essays on the Economic Growth of Socialist and Mixed Economies*.

18. N. Kaldor, 'The Case for Regional Policies', reprinted in N. Kaldor, *Further Essays on Economic Theory* (Duckworth, London, 1978).

19. Patnaik and Chandrasekhar, 'Exports, Investment and Growth: A Cross-Country Analysis', *Economic & Political Weekly*, 6 January (1996).

20. The argument that simply liberalizing the economy and thereby giving price incentives to the farmers would cause a notable increase in agricultural output together with agricultural exports is an untenable one for reasons we have already discussed, namely that growth in agriculture is not a matter of prices alone but requires substantial government investment in irrigation, extension, etc., to which private investment then responds.

Moreover, even if for argument's sake it is accepted for a moment that higher prices would stimulate higher agricultural growth, its effect on employment would be minimal since this growth under the extant agrarian structure would be under the aegis of the rich farmers: the elasticity of employment with respect to output in the new Green Revolution areas is very low and for the country as a whole has sharply declined. See Sheila Bhalla, 'Trends in Employment in Indian Agriculture, Land and Asset Distribution', *Indian Journal of Agricultural Economics*, vol. 42, no. 4, Oct–Dec. (1987), pp. 5–60.

21. A detailed picture of the emerging resistance against the new policies can be found in Utsa Patnaik, 'Food Security, Class-Structure and Export Agriculture in Underdeveloped Countries and in India', paper presented to an International Conference on Agrarian Issues, Wageningen, The Netherlands (May 1995).

3

Economic Reforms in India since 1991
Has Gradualism Worked?[*]

MONTEK S. AHLUWALIA[1]

India was a latecomer to economic reforms, embarking on the process in earnest only in 1991, in the wake of an exceptionally severe balance of payments crisis. The need for a policy shift had become evident much earlier, as many countries in East Asia achieved high growth and poverty reduction through policies that emphasized greater export orientation and encouragement of the private sector. India took some steps in this direction in the 1980s, but it was not until 1991 that the government signalled a systemic shift to a more open economy with greater reliance upon market forces, a larger role for the private sector including foreign investment, and a restructuring of the role of government.

India's economic performance in the post-reform period has many positive features. The average growth rate in the 10-year period from 1992–1993 to 2001–2002 was around 6.0 per cent, as shown in Table 3.1, which puts India among the fastest growing developing countries in the 1990s. This growth record is only slightly better than the annual average of 5.7 per cent in the 1980s, but it can be argued that the 1980s growth was unsustainable, fuelled by a build-up of external debt that culminated in the crisis of 1991. In sharp contrast, growth in the 1990s was accompanied by remarkable external stability despite the East Asian crisis. Poverty also declined significantly in the post-reform period and at a faster rate than in the 1980s, according to some studies.

[*] Originally published as 'Economic Reforms in India since 1991: Has Gradualism Worked?', in *Journal of Economic Perspectives*, 16 (3), Summer 2002, pp. 67–88.

Table 3.1: India's growth performance

(percentage per year)

	Total GDP	Sectoral Growth of GDP		
	Growth	Agriculture	Industry	Services
1970–2 to 1980–1 (average)	3.2	2.0	4.0	7.2
1981–2 to 1990–1 (average)	5.7	3.8	7.0	6.7
1991–2	1.3	–1.1	–1.0	4.8
1992–3	5.1	5.4	4.3	5.4
1993–4	5.9	3.9	5.6	7.7
1994–5	7.3	5.3	10.3	7.1
1995–6	7.3	–0.3	12.3	10.5
1996–7	7.8	8.8	7.7	7.2
1997–8	4.8	–1.5	3.8	9.8
1998–9	6.5	5.9	3.8	8.3
1999–2000	6.1	1.4	5.2	9.5
2000–1	4.0	0.1	6.6	4.8
2001–2	5.4	5.7	3.3	6.5
1992–3 to 1996–7 (average)	6.7	4.6	8.0	7.6
1997–8 to 2001–2 (average)	5.4	2.3	4.5	7.8

Note: Growth rates for 2001–2 are projections of the Ministry of Finance based on partial information.
Source: Government of India, Ministry of Finance, *Economic Survey 2001–2002*, (Ministry of Finance, Government of India, 2002).

However, the 10-year average growth performance hides the fact that while the economy grew at an impressive 6.7 per cent in the first five years after the reforms, it slowed down to 5.4 per cent in the next five years. India remained among the fastest growing developing countries in the second sub-period because other developing countries also slowed down after the East Asian crisis, but the annual growth of 5.4 per cent was much below the target of 7.5 per cent that the government had set for the period. Inevitably, this has led to some questioning about the effectiveness of the reforms.

Opinions on the causes of India's growth deceleration vary. World economic growth was slower in the second half of the 1990s, and that would have had some dampening effect, but India's dependence on the world economy is not large enough for this to account for the slowdown. Critics of liberalization have blamed the slowdown on the effect of trade policy reforms on domestic industry.² However, the opposite view is that the slowdown is due not to the effects of reforms, but rather to the failure to implement the reforms effectively. This in turn is often attributed to India's gradualist approach to reform, which has meant a frustratingly slow pace of implementation. However, even a gradualist pace should be able to achieve significant policy changes over ten years. This chapter examines India's experience with gradualist reforms from this perspective.

We review policy changes in several major areas covered by the reform programme: fiscal deficit reduction, industrial and trade policy, agricultural policy, infrastructure development, financial development, privatization, and social sector development. Based on this review, we consider the cumulative outcome of 10 years of gradualism to assess whether the reforms have created an environment that can support 8 per cent GDP growth, which is now the government target.

SAVINGS, INVESTMENT AND FISCAL DISCIPLINE

Fiscal profligacy was seen to have caused India's balance of payments crisis in 1991, and a reduction in the fiscal deficit was therefore an urgent priority at the start of the reforms. The combined fiscal deficit of the central and state governments was successfully reduced from 9.4 per cent of GDP in 1990–1 to 7 per cent in both 1991–2 and 1992–3, and the balance of payments crisis was over by 1993. However, the reforms also had a medium-term fiscal objective of improving public savings so that essential public investment could be financed with a smaller fiscal deficit to avoid 'crowding out' private investment. This part of the reform strategy was unfortunately never implemented.

As shown in Table 3.2, public savings deteriorated steadily from +1.7 per cent of GDP in 1996–7 to –1.7 per cent in 2000–1. This was reflected in a comparable deterioration in the fiscal deficit, taking it to 9.6 per cent of GDP in 2000–1. Not only is this among the highest in the developing world, it is particularly worrisome because India's public debt to GDP ratio is also very high, at around 80 per cent. Since the total financial savings of households amount to only 11 per cent of GDP, the fiscal deficit effectively pre-empts about 90 per cent of household financial savings for the government. What is worse, the rising fiscal deficit in the second half of the 1990s was not financing higher levels of public investment, which were more or less constant in this period.

These trends cast serious doubts on India's ability to achieve higher rates of growth in future. The growth rate of 6 per cent per year in the post-reform

Table 3.2: Major macroeconomic indicators

(percentage of GDP)

	Combined Fiscal Deficit of Central and State Governments	Gross Savings		Gross Capital Formation	
		Private Sector	Public Sector	Private Sector	Public Sector
1990–1	19.4	22.0	1.1	14.7	9.3
1991–2	7.0	20.1	2.0	13.1	8.8
1992–3	7.0	20.2	1.6	15.2	8.6
1993–4	8.3	21.9	0.6	13.0	8.2
1994–5	7.1	23.2	1.7	14.7	8.7
1995–6	6.5	23.1	2.0	18.9	7.7
1996–7	6.4	21.5	1.7	14.7	7.0
1997–8	7.3	21.8	1.31	6.0	6.6
1998–9	8.9	22.6	−1.01	4.8	6.6
1999–2000	9.4	24.0	−0.9	16.1	7.1
2000–1	9.6	25.1	−1.7	15.8	7.1

Notes: Public sector capital formation minus public sector savings does not equal the fiscal deficit because the definition of public sector for estimate of savings and capital formation includes non-departmental enterprises. Estimates of public sector savings and capital formation distinguishing general government from non-departmental enterprises are not readily available for recent years.

period was achieved with an average investment rate of around 23 per cent of GDP. Accelerating to 8 per cent growth will require a commensurate increase in investment. Growth rates of this magnitude in East Asia were associated with investment rates ranging from 36 to 38 per cent of GDP. While it can be argued that there was over-investment in East Asia, especially in recent years, it is unlikely that India can accelerate to 8 per cent growth unless it can raise the rate of investment to around 29–30 per cent of GDP. Part of the increase can be financed by increasing foreign direct investment, but even if foreign direct investment increases from the present level of 0.5 per cent of GDP to 2.0 per cent—an optimistic but not impossible target—domestic savings would still have to increase by at least 5 percentage points of GDP.

Can domestic savings be increased by this amount? As shown in Table 3.2, private savings have been buoyant in the post-reform period, but public savings have declined steadily. This trend needs to be reversed.[3] Both the central government and the state governments would have to take a number of hard decisions to bring about improvements in their respective spheres.

The central government's effort must be directed primarily toward improving revenues, because performance in this area has deteriorated significantly in the post-reform period. Total tax revenues of the centre were 9.7 percent of GDP in 1990–1. They declined to only 8.8 percent in 2000–1, whereas they should have increased by at least two percentage points. Tax reforms involving lowering of tax rates, broadening the base and reducing loopholes were expected to raise the tax ratio, and they did succeed in the case of personal and corporate income taxation, but indirect taxes have fallen as a percentage of GDP. This was expected in the case of customs duties, which were deliberately reduced as part of trade reforms, but this decline should have been offset by improving collections from domestic indirect taxes on goods and by extending indirect taxation to services. This part of the revenue strategy has not worked as expected. The Advisory Group on Tax Policy for the Tenth Plan recently made a number of proposals for modernizing tax administration, including especially computerization, reducing the degree of exemption for small-scale units and integration of services taxation with taxation of goods.[4] These recommendations need to be implemented urgently.

There is also room to reduce central government subsidies, which are known to be highly distortionary and poorly targeted (for example, subsidies on food and fertilizers), and to introduce rational user charges for services such as passenger traffic on the railways, the postal system and university education. Overstaffing was recently estimated at 30 per cent, and downsizing would help reduce expenditure.

State governments also need to take corrective steps. Sales tax systems need to be modernized in most states. Agricultural income tax is constitutionally assigned to the states, but no state has attempted to tax agricultural income. Land revenue is a traditional tax based on landholding, but it has been generally neglected and abolished in many states. Urban property taxation could yield much larger resources for municipal governments if suitably modernized, but this tax base has also been generally neglected. State governments suffer from very large losses in state electricity boards (about 1 per cent of GDP) and experience substantial losses in urban water supply, state road transport corporations, and in managing irrigation systems. Overstaffing is greater in the states than at the centre.

The fiscal failures of both the central and the state governments have squeezed the capacity of both the centre and the states to undertake essential public investment. High levels of government borrowing have also crowded out private investment. Unless this problem is addressed, the potential benefits from reforms in other areas will be eroded, and it may be difficult even to maintain the average growth rate of 6 per cent experienced in the first ten years after the reforms, let alone accelerate to 8 per cent.

REFORMS IN INDUSTRIAL AND TRADE POLICY

Reforms in industrial and trade policy were a central focus of much of India's reform effort in the early stages. Industrial policy prior to the reforms was characterized by multiple controls over private investment that limited the areas in which private investors were allowed to operate and often also determined the scale of operations, the location of new investment, and even the technology to be used. The industrial structure that evolved under this regime was highly inefficient and needed to be supported by a highly protective trade policy, often providing tailor-made protection to each sector of industry. The costs imposed by these policies had been extensively studied,[5] and by 1991, a broad consensus had emerged on the need for greater liberalization and openness. A great deal has been achieved in this area after ten years of gradualist reforms.

Industrial Policy

Industrial policy has seen the greatest change, with most central government industrial controls being dismantled. The list of industries reserved solely for the public sector—which used to cover 18 industries, including iron and steel, heavy plant and machinery, telecommunications and telecom equipment, minerals, oil, mining, air transport services, and electricity generation and distribution—has been drastically reduced to three industries: defence aircraft and warships, atomic energy generation, and railway transport. Industrial licensing by the central government has been almost abolished, except for a few hazardous and environmentally sensitive industries. The requirement that investments by large industrial houses needed a separate clearance under the Monopolies and Restrictive Trade Practices Act to discourage the concentration of economic power was abolished, and the act itself is to be replaced by a new competition law that will attempt to regulate anti-competitive behaviour in other ways.

The main area where action has been inadequate relates to the long-standing policy of reserving production of certain items for the small-scale sector. About 800 items were covered by this policy since the late 1970s, which meant that investment in plant and machinery in any individual unit producing these items could not exceed $250,000. Many of the reserved items, such as garments, shoes, and toys, had high export potential, and the failure to permit development of production units with more modern equipment and a larger scale of production severely restricted India's export competitiveness. The Report of the Committee on Small Scale Enterprises (1997) and the Report of the Prime Minister's Economic Advisory Council (New Delhi, 2001) had both pointed to the remarkable success of China in penetrating world markets in these areas and stimulating rapid growth of employment in manufacturing. Both reports recommended that the policy of reservation should be abolished and other measures adopted to help small-scale industry. While such a radical change in policy was unacceptable, some policy changes have been made very recently: 14 items were removed from the reserved list in 2001, and another 50 in 2002. The removed items include garments, shoes, toys, and auto components, all of which are potentially important for exports. In addition, the investment ceiling for certain items was increased to $1 million. However, these changes are very recent, and it will take some years before they are reflected in economic performance.

Industrial liberalization by the central government needs to be accompanied by supporting action by state governments. Private investors require many permissions from state governments to start operations, like connections to electricity and water supply and environmental clearances. They must also interact with the state bureaucracy in the course of day-to-day operations because of laws governing pollution, sanitation, workers' welfare and safety, and such. Complaints of delays, corruption, and harassment arising from these interactions are common. Some states have taken initiatives to ease these interactions, but much more needs to be done.

A recently completed joint study by the World Bank and the Confederation of Indian Industry found that the investment climate varies widely across states, and these differences are reflected in a disproportional share of investment, especially foreign investment, being concentrated in what are seen as the more investor-friendly states (Maharashtra, Gujarat, Karnataka, Andhra Pradesh, and Tamil Nadu) to the disadvantage of other states (like Uttar Pradesh, Bihar, and West Bengal).[6] Investors perceived a 30 per cent cost advantage in some states over others, on account of the availability of infrastructure and the quality of governance. These differences across states have led to an increase in the variation in state growth rates, with some of the less favoured states actually decelerating compared with the 1980s.[7] Because liberalization has created a more competitive environment, the payoff from pursuing good policies has increased, thereby increasing the importance of state-level action. Infrastructure deficiencies will take time and resources to remove, but deficiencies in governance could be handled more quickly with sufficient political will.

Trade Policy

Trade policy reform has also made progress, though the pace has been slower than in the case of industrial liberalization. Before the reforms, trade policy was characterized by high tariffs and pervasive import restrictions. Imports of manufactured consumer goods were completely banned. For capital goods, raw materials and intermediates, certain lists of goods were freely importable, but for most items where domestic substitutes were being produced, imports were only possible with import licenses. The criteria for issue of licenses were non-transparent, delays were endemic, and corruption unavoidable. The economic reforms sought to phase out import licensing and also to reduce import duties.

Import licensing was abolished relatively early for capital goods and intermediates, which became freely importable in 1993, simultaneously with the switch to a flexible exchange-rate regime. Import licensing had been traditionally defended on the grounds that it was necessary to manage the balance of payments, but the shift to a flexible exchange rate enabled the government to argue that any balance of payments impact would be effectively dealt with through exchange rate flexibility. Removing quantitative restrictions on imports of capital goods and intermediates was relatively easy, because the number of domestic producers was small and Indian industry welcomed the move as making it more competitive. It was much more difficult in the case of final consumer goods because the number of domestic producers affected was very large (partly because much of the consumer goods industry had been reserved for small-scale production). Quantitative restrictions on imports of manufactured consumer goods and agricultural products were finally removed on 1 April 2001, almost exactly ten years after the reforms began, and that in part because of a ruling by a World Trade Organization dispute panel on a complaint brought by the United States.

Progress in reducing tariff protection, the second element in the trade strategy, has been even slower and not always steady. As shown in Table 3.3, the weighted average import duty rate declined from the very high level of 72.5 per cent in 1991–2 to 24.6 per cent in 1996–7. However, the average tariff rate then increased by more than 10 percentage points in the next four years.[8] In February 2002, the government signalled a return to reducing tariff protection. The peak duty rate was reduced to 30 per cent, a number of duty rates at the

Table 3.3: Weighted average import duty
rates in India

	All Commodities	Peak Customs Duty[1]	No. of Basic Duty Rates[2]
1991–2	72.5	150	22
1992–3	60.6	110	20
1993–4	46.8	85	16
1994–5	38.2	65	16
1995–6	25.9	50	12
1996–7	24.6	52*	9
1997–8	25.4	45*	8
1998–9	29.2	45*	7
1999–2000	31.4	40	7
2000–1	35.7	38.5	5
2001–2	35.1	35.8	4
2002–3	29.0	30.8	4

Notes: 1. Includes the impact of surcharges in the years indicated by an asterisk. In 2000–1 duties for many agricultural products were raised above the general peak in anticipation of the removal of quantitative restrictions. This explains why the average for all commodities exceeds the peak rate in 2001–2.
2. Refers to *ad valorem* duty rates. Some items attract a specific duty, and these are not included as separate duty rates.
Source: Planning Commission, *Report of the Task Force on Employment* (New Delhi, Planning Commission, 2000). Estimates for 2002–3 have been provided by Archana Mathur of the Planning Commission.

higher end of the existing structure were lowered, while many low-end duties were raised to 5 per cent. The net result is that the weighted average duty rate is 29 per cent in 2002–3.

Although India's tariff levels are significantly lower than in 1991, they remain among the highest in the developing world, because most other developing countries have also reduced tariffs in this period. The weighted average import duty in China and South-East Asia is currently about half the Indian level. The government has announced that average tariffs will be reduced to around 15 per cent by 2004, but even if this is implemented, tariffs in India will be much higher than in China, which has, as a condition for admission to the World Trade Organization, committed to reduce weighted average duties to about 9 per cent by 2005.

Foreign Direct Investment

Liberalizing foreign direct investment was another important part of India's reforms, driven by the belief that this would increase the total volume of investment in the economy, improve production technology, and increase access to world markets. The policy now allows 100 per cent foreign ownership in a large number of industries and majority ownership in all except banks, insurance companies, telecommunications, and airlines. Procedures for obtaining permission were greatly simplified by listing industries that are eligible for automatic approval up to specified levels of foreign equity (100 per cent, 74 per cent and 51 per cent). Potential foreign investors investing within these limits only need to register with the Reserve Bank of India. For investments in other industries, or for a higher share of equity than is automatically permitted in listed industries, applications are considered by a Foreign Investment Promotion Board that has established a track record of speedy decisions. In 1993, foreign institutional investors were allowed to purchase shares of listed Indian companies in the stock market, opening a window for portfolio investment in existing companies.

These reforms have created a very different competitive environment for India's industry than existed in 1991, which has led to significant changes. Indian companies have upgraded their technology and expanded to more efficient scales of production. They have also restructured through mergers and acquisitions and refocused their activities to concentrate on areas of competence. New dynamic firms have displaced older and less dynamic ones: of the top 100 companies ranked by market capitalization in 1991, about half are no longer in this group. Foreign investment inflows increased from virtually nothing in 1991 to about 0.5 per cent of GDP. Although this figure remains much below the levels of foreign direct investment in many emerging market countries (not to mention the 4 per cent of GDP level in China), the change from the pre-reform situation is impressive. The presence of foreign-owned firms and their products in the domestic market is evident and has added greatly to the pressure to improve quality.

These policy changes were expected to generate faster industrial growth and greater penetration of world markets in industrial products, but performance in this respect has been disappointing. As shown in Table 3.1, industrial growth increased sharply in the first five years after the reforms, but then slowed to an annual rate of 4.5 per cent in the next five years. Export performance has improved, but modestly. The share of exports of goods in GDP increased from

5.7 per cent in 1990–1 to 9.7 per cent, but this reflects in part an exchange rate depreciation. India's share in world exports, which had declined steadily since 1960, increased slightly from around 0.5 per cent in 1990–1 to 0.6 per cent in 1999–2000, but much of the increase in world market share is due to agricultural exports. India's manufactured exports had a 0.5 per cent share in world markets for those items in 1990, and this rose to only 0.55 per cent by 1999. Unlike the case in China and South-East Asia, foreign direct investment in India did not play an important role in export penetration and was instead oriented mainly toward the domestic market.

One reason why export performance has been modest is the slow progress in lowering import duties that make India a high-cost producer and therefore less attractive as a base for export production. Exporters have long been able to import inputs needed for exports at zero duty, but the complex procedure for obtaining the necessary duty-free import licenses typically involves high transactions cost and delays. High levels of protection compared with other countries also explains why foreign direct investment in India has been much more oriented to the protected domestic market, rather than using India as a base for exports. However, high tariffs are only part of the explanation for poor export performance. The reservation of many potentially exportable items for production in the small-scale sector (which has only recently been relaxed) was also a relevant factor. The poor quality of India's infrastructure compared with infrastructure in East and South-East Asia, which is discussed later in this chapter, is yet another.

Inflexibility of the labour market is a major factor reducing India's competitiveness in exports and also reducing industrial productivity generally.[9] Any firm wishing to close down a plant or to retrench labour in any unit employing more than 100 workers can only do so with the permission of the state government, and this permission is rarely granted. These provisions discourage employment and are especially onerous for labour-intensive sectors. The increased competition in the goods market has made labour more willing to take reasonable positions, because lack of flexibility only leads to firms losing market share. However, the legal provisions clearly remain much more onerous than in other countries. This is an important area of reform that has yet to be addressed. The lack of any system of unemployment insurance makes it difficult to push for major changes in labour flexibility unless a suitable contributory system that is financially viable can be put in place. The government has recently announced its intention to amend the law and raise the level of employment above which firms have to seek permission for retrenchment, from 100 workers at present to 1000, while simultaneously increasing the scale of retrenchment compensation. However, the amendment has yet to be enacted.

These gaps in the reforms provide a possible explanation for the slowdown in industrial growth in the second half of the 1990s. It can be argued that the initial relaxation of controls led to an investment boom, but this could have been sustained only if industrial investment had been oriented to tapping export markets, as was the case in East Asia. As it happened, India's industrial and trade reforms were not strong enough, nor adequately supported by infrastructure and labour market reforms, to generate such a thrust. The one area that has shown robust growth through the 1990s with a strong export orientation is software development and various new types of services enabled by information technology, like medical transcription, back-up accounting, and customer-related services. Export earnings in this area have grown from $100 million in 1990–1 to over $6 billion in 2000–1 and are expected to continue to grow at 20 to 30 per cent per year. India's success in this area is one of the most visible achievements of trade policy reforms, which allow access to imports and technology at exceptionally low rates of duty, and also of the fact that exports in this area depend primarily on telecommunications infrastructure, which has improved considerably in the post-reform period.

REFORMS IN AGRICULTURE

A common criticism of India's economic reforms is that they have been excessively focused on industrial and trade policy, neglecting agriculture that provides the livelihood of 60 per cent of the population. Critics point to the deceleration in agricultural growth in the second half of the 1990s (shown in Table 3.1) as proof of this neglect.[10] However, the notion that trade policy changes have not helped agriculture is clearly a misconception. The reduction of protection to industry, and the accompanying depreciation in the exchange rate, has tilted relative prices in favour of agriculture and helped agricultural exports. The index of agricultural prices relative to manufactured products has increased by almost 30 per cent in the past ten years.[11] The share of India's agricultural exports in world exports of the same commodities increased from 1.1 per cent in 1990 to 1.9 per cent in 1999, whereas it had declined in the ten years before the reforms.

But while agriculture has benefited from trade policy changes, it has suffered in other respects, most notably from the decline in public investment in areas critical for agricultural growth, such as irrigation and drainage, soil conservation and water management systems, and rural roads. As pointed out by Gulati and Bathla (2001), this decline began much before the reforms and was actually sharper in the 1980s than in the 1990s. They also point out that while public investment declined, this was more than offset by a rise in private investment in agriculture, which accelerated after the reforms. However, there is no doubt that investment in agriculture-related infrastructure is critical for achieving higher productivity, and this investment is only likely to come from the public sector. Indeed, the rising trend in private investment in agriculture could easily be dampened if public investment in these critical areas is not increased.

The main reason why public investment in rural infrastructure has declined is the deterioration in the fiscal position of the state governments and the tendency for politically popular but inefficient and even inequitable subsidies to crowd out more productive investment. For example, the direct benefit of subsidizing fertilizer and underpricing water and power goes mainly to fertilizer producers and high-income farmers, while having negative effects on the environment and production, and even on the income of small farmers.[12] A phased increase in fertilizer prices and imposition of economically rational user charges for irrigation and electricity could raise resources to finance investment in rural infrastructure, benefiting both growth and equity. Competitive populism makes it politically difficult to restructure subsidies in this way, but there is also no alternative solution in sight.

Some of the policies that were crucial in promoting foodgrain production in earlier years, when this was the prime objective, are now hindering agricultural diversification. Government price-support levels for food grains, such as wheat, are supposed to be set on the basis of the recommendations of the Commission on Agricultural Costs and Prices, a technical body that is expected to calibrate price support to reasonable levels. In recent years, support prices have been fixed at much higher levels, encouraging over-production. Indeed, public food grain stocks reached 58 million tons on 1 January 2002, against a norm of around 17 million tons! The support price system clearly needs to be better aligned to market demand if farmers are to be encouraged to shift from foodgrain production towards other products.

Agricultural diversification also calls for radical changes in some outdated laws. The Essential Commodities Act, which empowers state governments to impose restrictions on movement of agricultural products across state and sometimes even district boundaries and to limit the maximum stocks wholesalers and retailers can carry for certain commodities, was designed to prevent exploitive traders from diverting local supplies to other areas of scarcity or from hoarding supplies to raise prices. Its consequence is that farmers and consumers are denied the benefit of an integrated national market. It also prevents the development of modern trading companies, which have a key role to play in the next stage of agricultural diversification. The government has recognized the need for change and recently removed certain products—including wheat, rice, coarse grains, edible oil, oilseeds, and sugar—from the purview of the act. However, this step may not suffice, since state governments may be able to take similar action. What is needed is a repeal of the existing act and central legislation that would make it illegal for government authorities at any level to restrict movement or stocking of agricultural products.[13]

The report of the Task Force on Employment has made comprehensive proposals for review of several other outdated agricultural laws.[14] For example, laws designed to protect land tenants, undoubtedly an important objective, end up discouraging marginal farmers from leasing out non-viable holdings to larger farmers for fear of being unable to reclaim the land from the tenant. The Agricultural Produce Marketing Acts in various states compel traders to buy agricultural produce only in regulated markets, making it difficult for commercial traders to enter into contractual relationships with farmers. Development of a modern food processing sector, which is essential to the next stage of agricultural development, is also hampered by outdated and often contradictory laws and regulations. These and other outdated laws need to be changed if the logic of liberalization is to be extended to agriculture.

INFRASTRUCTURE DEVELOPMENT

Rapid growth in a globalized environment requires a well-functioning infrastructure, including especially electric power, road and rail connectivity, telecommunications, air transport, and efficient ports. India lags behind East and South-East Asia in these areas. These services were traditionally provided by public sector monopolies, but since the investment needed to expand capacity and improve quality could not be mobilized by the public sector, these sectors were opened to private investment, including foreign investment. However, the difficulty in creating an environment that would make it possible for private investors to enter on terms that would appear reasonable to consumers, while providing an adequate risk-return profile to investors, was greatly underestimated. Many false starts and disappointments have resulted.

The greatest disappointment has been in the electric power sector, which was the first area opened for private investment. Private investors were expected to produce electricity for sale to the state electricity boards, which would control transmission and distribution. However, the state electricity boards were financially very weak, partly because electricity tariffs for many categories of consumers were too low and also because very large amounts of power were lost in transmission and distribution. This loss, which should be between 10 to 15 per cent on technical grounds (depending on the extent of the rural network), varies from 35 to 50 per cent. The difference reflects theft of electricity, usually with the connivance of the distribution staff. Private investors, fearing non-payment by the state electricity boards, insisted on arrangements that guaranteed purchase of electricity by state governments with additional guarantees from the central government. These arrangements attracted criticism because of controversies about the reasonableness of the tariffs demanded by private sector power producers. Although a large number of proposals for private sector projects amounting to about 80 per cent of existing generation capacity were initiated, very few reached financial closure, and some of those that were implemented ran into trouble subsequently.[15]

Because of these difficulties, the expansion of generation capacity by the utilities in the 1990s has been only about half of what was targeted, and the quality of power remained poor, with large voltage fluctuations and frequent interruptions. The flaws in the policy have now been recognized, and a more comprehensive reform is being attempted by several state governments. Independent statutory regulators have been established to set tariffs in a manner that would be perceived to be fair to both consumers and producers. Several states are trying to privatize distribution in the hope that this will overcome the corruption that leads to the enormous distribution losses. However, these reforms are not easy to implement. Rationalization of power tariffs is likely to be resisted by consumers long used to subsidized power, even though the quality of the power provided in the pre-reform situation was very poor. The establishment of competent and credible regulatory authorities takes time. Private investors may not be able to enforce collection of amounts due nor to disconnect supply for non-payment without adequate backing by the police. For all these reasons, private investors perceive high risks in the early stages and therefore demand terms that imply very high rates of return. Finally, labour unions are opposed to privatization of distribution.

These problems are formidable, and many state governments now realize that a great deal of preliminary work is needed before privatization can be successfully implemented.[16] Some of the initial steps, like tariff rationalization and enforcing penalties for non-payment of dues and for theft of power, are perhaps best implemented within the existing public sector framework, so that these features, which are essential for viability of the power sector, are not attributed solely to privatization. If the efforts now being made in half a dozen states succeed, it could lead to a visible improvement within a few years.

The results in telecommunications have been much better, and this is an important factor underlying India's success in information technology. There was a false start initially because private investors offered excessively high license fees in bidding for licenses that they could not sustain, which led to a protracted and controversial re-negotiation of terms. Since then, the policy appears to be working satisfactorily. Several private sector service providers of both fixed-line and cellular services, many in partnership with foreign investors, are now operating and competing with the pre-existing public sector supplier. Teledensity, which had doubled from 0.3 lines per 100 population in 1981 to 0.6 in 1991, increased sevenfold in the next ten years to reach 4.4 lines per 100 population in 2002. Waiting periods for telephone connections have shrunk dramatically. Telephone rates were heavily distorted earlier, with very high long-distance charges cross-subsidizing local calls and covering inefficiencies in operation. They have now been rebalanced by the regulatory authority, leading to a reduction of 30 per cent in long-distance charges. Interestingly, the erstwhile public sector monopoly supplier has aggressively reduced prices in a bid to retain market share.

Civil aviation and ports are two other areas where reforms appear to be succeeding, though much remains to be done. Two private sector domestic airlines, which began operations after the reforms, now have more than half the market for domestic air travel. However, proposals to attract private investment to upgrade the major airports at Mumbai and Delhi have yet to make visible progress. In the case of ports, 17 private sector projects involving port-handling capacity of 60 million tons—about 20 per cent of the total capacity at present— are being implemented. Some of the new private sector port facilities have set high standards of productivity.

India's road network is extensive, but most of it is low quality, which is a major constraint for interior locations. The major arterial routes have low capacity (commonly just two lanes in most stretches) and also suffer from poor maintenance. However, some promising initiatives have been taken recently. In 1998, a tax was imposed on gasoline (later extended to diesel), the proceeds of which are earmarked for the development of the national highways, state roads, and rural roads. This will help finance a major programme or upgrading the national highways connecting Delhi, Mumbai, Chennai, and Calcutta to four lanes or more, to be completed by the end of 2003. It is also planned to levy modest tolls on these highways to ensure a stream of revenue that could be used for maintenance. A few toll roads and bridges in areas of high traffic density have been awarded to the private sector for development.

The railways are a potentially important means of freight transportation, but this area is untouched by reforms as yet. The sector suffers from severe financial constraints, partly due to a politically determined fare structure in which freight rates have been set excessively high to subsidize passenger fares and partly because government ownership has led to wasteful operating practices. Excess staff is currently estimated at around 25 per cent. Resources are typically spread thinly to respond to political demands for new passenger trains at the cost of investments that would strengthen the capacity of the railways as a freight carrier. The Expert Group on Indian Railways (2002) recently submitted a comprehensive programme of reform, converting the railways from a departmentally run government enterprise to a corporation, with a regulatory authority fixing the fares in a rational manner. No decisions have been announced as yet on these recommendations.

FINANCIAL SECTOR REFORM

India's reform programme included wide-ranging reforms in the banking system and the capital markets relatively early in the process, with reforms in insurance introduced at a later stage.

Banking sector reforms included: (a) measures for liberalization, like dismantling the complex system of interest rate controls, eliminating prior approval of the Reserve Bank of India for large loans, and reducing the statutory requirements to invest in government securities; (b) measures designed to increase financial soundness, like introducing capital adequacy requirements and other prudential norms for banks and strengthening banking supervision; and (c) measures for increasing competition, like more liberal licensing of private banks and freer expansion by foreign banks. These steps have produced some positive outcomes. There has been a sharp reduction in the share of non-performing assets in the portfolio, and more than 90 per cent of the banks now meet the new capital adequacy standards. However, these figures may overstate the improvement because domestic standards for classifying assets as non-performing are less stringent than international standards.

India's banking reforms differ from those in other developing countries in one important respect, and that is the policy toward public sector banks that dominate the banking system. The government has announced its intention to reduce its equity share to 33.3 per cent, but this is to be done while retaining government control. Improvements in the efficiency of the banking system will therefore depend on the ability to increase the efficiency of public sector banks.

Sceptics doubt whether government control can be made consistent with efficient commercial banking because bank managers are bound to respond to political directions if their career advancement depends upon the government. Even if the government does not interfere directly in credit decisions, government ownership means that managers of public sector banks are held to standards of accountability akin to civil servants, which tend to emphasize compliance with rules and procedures and therefore discourage innovative decision-making. Regulatory control is also difficult to exercise. The unstated presumption that public sector banks cannot be shut down means that public sector banks that perform poorly are regularly re-capitalized rather than weeded out. This obviously weakens market discipline, since more efficient banks are not able to expand market share.

If privatization is not politically feasible, it is at least necessary to consider intermediate steps that could increase efficiency within a public sector framework.[17] These include shifting effective control from the government to the boards of the banks, including especially the power to appoint the chairman and executive directors, which is at present with the government; removing civil servants and representatives of the Reserve Bank of India from these boards; implementing a prompt corrective action framework that would automatically trigger regulatory action limiting a bank's expansion capability if certain trigger points of financial soundness are breached; and acceptance of closure of insolvent public sector banks (with appropriate protection for small depositors). Unless some initiatives along these lines are taken, it is highly unlikely that public sector banks can rise to the levels of efficiency needed to support rapid growth.

Another major factor limiting the efficiency of banks is the legal framework, which makes it very difficult for creditors to enforce their claims. The government has recently introduced legislation to establish a bankruptcy law, which will be much closer to accepted international standards. This would be an important improvement, but it needs to be accompanied by reforms in court procedures to cut the delays that are a major weakness of the legal system at present.

Reforms in the stock market were accelerated by a stock market scam in 1992 that revealed serious weaknesses in the regulatory mechanism. Reforms implemented include establishment of a statutory regulator; promulgation of rules and regulations governing various types of participants in the capital market and also activities like insider trading and takeover bids; introduction of electronic trading to improve transparency in establishing prices; and dematerialization of shares to eliminate the need for physical movement and storage of paper securities. Effective regulation of stock markets requires the development of institutional expertise, which necessarily requires time, but a good start has been made, and India's stock market is much better regulated today than in the past. This is to some extent reflected in the fact that foreign institutional investors have invested a cumulative $21 billion in Indian stocks since 1993, when this avenue for investment was opened.

An important recent reform is the withdrawal of the special privileges enjoyed by the Unit Trust of India, a public sector mutual fund that was the dominant mutual fund investment vehicle when the reforms began. Although the Unit Trust did not enjoy a government guarantee, it was widely perceived as having one because its top management was appointed by the government. The Trust had to be bailed out once in 1998, when its net asset value fell below the declared redemption price of the units, and again in 2001, when the problem recurred. It has now been decided that in the future, investors in the Unit Trust of India will bear the full risk of any loss in capital value. This removes a major distortion in the capital market, in which one of the investment schemes was seen as having a preferred position.

The insurance sector (including pension schemes), was a public sector monopoly at the start of the reforms. The need to open the sector to private insurance companies was recommended by an expert committee (the Malhotra Committee) in 1994, but there was strong political resistance. It was only in 2000 that the law was finally amended to allow private sector insurance companies, with foreign equity allowed up to 26 per cent, to enter the field. An independent Insurance Development and Regulatory Authority has now been established, and ten new life insurance companies and six general insurance companies, many with well-known international insurance companies as partners, have started operations. The development of an active insurance and pensions industry offering attractive products tailored to different types of requirements could stimulate long-term savings and add depth to the capital markets. However, these benefits will only become evident over time.

PRIVATIZATION

The public sector accounts for about 35 per cent of industrial value added in India, but although privatization has been a prominent component of economic reforms in many countries, India has been ambivalent on the subject until very recently. Initially, the government adopted a limited approach of selling a minority stake in public sector enterprises while retaining management control with the government, a policy described as 'disinvestment' to distinguish it from privatization. The principal motivation was to mobilize revenue for the budget, though there was some expectation that private shareholders would increase the commercial orientation of public sector enterprises. This policy had very limited success. Disinvestment receipts were consistently below budget expectations, and the average realization in the first five years was less than 0.25 per cent of GDP compared with an average of 1.7 per cent in 17 countries reported in a recent study.[18] There was clearly limited appetite for purchasing shares in public sector companies in which government remained in control of management.

In 1998, the government announced its willingness to reduce its shareholding to 26 per cent and to transfer management control to private stakeholders purchasing a substantial stake in all central public sector enterprises, except in a limited group of strategic areas.[19] The first such privatization occurred in 1999, when 74 per cent of the equity of Modern Foods India Ltd (a public sector bread-making company with 2000 employees), was sold with full management control to Hindustan Lever, an Indian subsidiary of the Anglo-Dutch multinational Unilever. This was followed by several similar sales with transfer of management: BALCO, an aluminium company; Hindustan Zinc; Computer Maintenance Corporation; Lagan Jute Machinery Manufacturing Company; several hotels; VSNL, which was until recently the monopoly service supplier for international telecommunications; IPCL, a major petrochemicals unit; and Maruti Udyog, India's largest automobile producer, which was a joint venture with Suzuki Corporation, which has now acquired full managerial control.

The privatization of Modern Foods and BALCO generated some controversy, not so much on the principle of privatization but on the transparency of the bidding process and the fairness of the price realized. Subsequent sales have been much less problematic, and although the policy continues to be criticized by the unions, it appears to have been accepted by the public, especially for public sector enterprises that are making losses or not doing well. However, there is little public support for selling public sector enterprises that are making large profits, such as those in the petroleum and domestic telecommunications sectors, although these are precisely the companies where privatization can generate large revenues. These companies are unlikely to be privatized in the near future, but even so there are several companies in the pipeline for privatization that are likely to be sold, and this will reduce resistance to privatizing profit-making companies.[20]

An important recent innovation, which may increase public acceptance of privatization, is the decision to earmark the proceeds of privatization to finance additional expenditure on social sector development and for retirement of public debt. Privatization is clearly not a permanent source of revenue, but it can help fill critical gaps in the next five to ten years while longer-term solutions to the fiscal problem are attempted. Many states have also started privatizing state-level public sector enterprises. These are mostly loss-making enterprises and are unlikely to yield significant receipts, but privatization will at least eliminate the recurring burden of financing losses.

Table 3.4: Public expenditure on social sector and rural development

		(percentage of GDP)
	Central Government	*State Government*
1990–1	1.42	5.98
1991–2	1.25	5.85
1992–3	1.29	6.72
1993–4	1.49	5.57
1994–5	1.49	6.27
1995–6	1.54	5.33
1996–7	1.56	5.13
1997–8	1.60	5.18
1998–9	1.67	5.41
1999–2000	1.59	6.06
2000–1	1.58	5.46

Source: Mahendra S. Dev and Jos Mooij, 'Social Sector Expenditures in the 1990s: Analysis of Central and State Budgets', *Economic and Political Weekly,* 2 March (2002), pp. 853–66.

SOCIAL SECTOR DEVELOPMENT IN HEALTH AND EDUCATION

India's social indicators at the start of the reforms in 1991 lagged behind the levels achieved in South-East Asia 20 years earlier, when those countries started to grow rapidly.[21] For example, India's adult literacy rate in 1991 was 52 per cent, compared with 57 per cent in Indonesia and 79 per cent in Thailand in

1971. The gap in social development needed to be closed, not only to improve the welfare of the poor and increase their income-earning capacity, but also to create the preconditions for rapid economic growth. While the logic of economic reforms required a withdrawal of the state from areas in which the private sector could do the job just as well, if not better, it also required an expansion of public sector support for social sector development.

Much of the debate in this area has focused on what has happened to expenditure on social sector development in the post-reform period. Dev and Mooij[22] find that central government expenditure towards social services and rural development increased from 7.6 per cent of total expenditure in 1990–1 to 10.2 per cent in 2000–1. As shown in Table 3.4, as a percentage of GDP, these expenditures show a dip in the first two years of the reforms, when fiscal stabilization compulsions were dominant, but there is a modest increase thereafter. However, expenditure trends in the states, which account for 80 per cent of total expenditures in this area, show a definite decline as a percentage of GDP in the post-reform period. Taking central and state expenditures together, social sector expenditure has remained more or less constant as a percentage of GDP.

Closing the social sector gaps between India and other countries in South-East Asia will require additional expenditure, which in turn depends upon improvements in the fiscal position of both the central and state governments. However, it is also important to improve the efficiency of resource use in this area. Saxena[23] has documented the many problems with the existing delivery systems of most social sector services, especially in rural areas. Some of these problems are directly caused by lack of resources, as when the bulk of the budget is absorbed in paying salaries, leaving little available for medicines in clinics or essential teaching aids in schools. There are also governance problems, such as non-attendance by teachers in rural schools and poor quality of teaching.

Part of the solution lies in greater participation by the beneficiaries in supervising education and health systems, which in turn requires decentralization to local levels and effective people's participation at these levels. Non-government organizations can play a critical role in this process. Different state governments are experimenting with alternative modalities, but a great deal more needs to be done in this area.

While the challenges in this area are enormous, it is worth noting that social sector indicators have continued to improve during the reforms. The literacy rate increased from 52 per cent in 1991 to 65 per cent in 2001, a faster increase in the 1990s than in the previous decade, and the increase has been particularly high in some of the low literacy states such as Bihar, Madhya Pradesh, Uttar Pradesh, and Rajasthan.

CONCLUSIONS

The impact of ten years of gradualist economic reforms in India on the policy environment presents a mixed picture. Industrial and trade policy reforms have gone far, though they need to be supplemented by labour market reforms, which are a critical missing link. The logic of liberalization also needs to be extended to agriculture, where numerous restrictions remain in place. Reforms aimed at encouraging private investment in infrastructure have worked in some areas but not in others. The complexity of the problems in this area was underestimated, especially in the power sector. This has now been recognized, and policies are being reshaped accordingly. Progress has been made in several areas of financial sector reforms, though some of the critical issues relating to government ownership of the banks remain to be addressed. However, the outcome in the fiscal area shows a worse situation at the end of ten years than at the start.

Critics often blame the delays in implementation and failure to act in certain areas to the choice of gradualism as a strategy. However, gradualism implies a clear definition of the goal and a deliberate choice as to extending the time taken to reach it, to ease the pain of transition. This is not what happened in all areas. The goals were often indicated only as a broad direction, with the precise end-point and the pace of transition left unstated to minimize opposition—and possibly also to allow room to retreat, if necessary. This reduced politically divisive controversy and enabled a consensus of sorts to evolve, but it also meant that the consensus at each point represented a compromise, with many interested groups joining only because they believed that reforms would not go 'too far'. The result was a process of change that was not so much gradualist as fitful and opportunistic. Progress was made as and when politically feasible, but since the end-point was not always clearly indicated, many participants were unclear about how much change would have to be accepted, and this may have led to less adjustment than was otherwise feasible.[24]

The alternative would have been to have a more thorough debate with the objective of bringing about a clearer realization on the part of all concerned of the full extent of change needed, thereby permitting more purposeful implementation. However, it is difficult to say whether this approach would indeed have yielded better results, or whether it would have created gridlock in

India's highly pluralist democracy. Instead, India witnessed a halting process of change in which political parties that opposed particular reforms when in opposition actually pushed them forward when in office. The process can be aptly described as creating a strong consensus for weak reforms.

Have the reforms laid the basis for India to grow at 8 per cent per year? The main reason for optimism is that the cumulative change brought about is substantial. The slow pace of implementation has meant that many of the reform initiatives have been put in place only recently, and their beneficial effects are yet to be felt. The policy environment today is therefore potentially much more supportive, especially if the critical missing links are put in place. However, failure on the fiscal front could undo much of what has been achieved. Both the central and state governments are under severe fiscal stress, which seriously undermines their capacity to invest in certain types of infrastructure and in social development where the public sector is the only credible source of investment. If these trends are not reversed, it may be difficult even to maintain 6 per cent annual growth in the future, let alone accelerate to 8 per cent. However, if credible corrective steps are taken on the fiscal front, then the cumulative policy changes that have already taken place in many areas combined with continued progress on the unfinished agenda should make it possible for India to accelerate to well beyond 6 per cent growth over the next few years.

POSTSCRIPT

Developments since this article was written, bear out the proposition that gradualism has indeed worked. The deceleration of the growth after the mid-1990s, which had raised doubts about the reform process, has been comprehensively reversed. India's average growth rate in the Tenth Five Year Plan period 2002–3 to 2006–7 was 7.6 per cent, marginally lower than the 8 per cent target, and the last two years saw growth exceeding 9 per cent. Gradualist reforms have continued in industry, trade, and the financial sector. The fiscal deficit has come down significantly and the gross domestic investment rate has risen to 33.8 per cent in 2005–6, holding out the prospect of high growth continuing in future. The government has defined its priorities as reviving agricultural growth, expanding access to health and education, and improving quality in both areas, and also expanding and upgrading infrastructure. The latter is sought to be achieved through a combination of public investment and public–private partnership. The Eleventh Plan aims at achieving faster and more inclusive growth with an average growth target of 9 per cent. This seems eminently achievable.

NOTES AND REFERENCES

1. The views expressed in this chapter are those of the author and do not necessarily reflect the views of either the International Monetary Fund or the Government of India. Thanks are due to Suman Bery, Ashok Gulati, Deena Khatkhate, Arvind Panagariya, Parthasarathi Shome, T.N. Srinivasan, Nicholas Stern and Timothy Taylor.

2. For example, R.G. Nambiar, B.L. Mumgekar and G.A. Tadas, 'Is Import Liberalization Hurting Domestic Industry and Employment?', *Economic and Political Weekly*, 13 February, 34 (1999), pp. 417–24; and Sudip Chaudhuri, 'Economic Reforms and Industrial Structure in India', *Economic and Political Weekly*, 12 January, 37:2 (2002), pp. 155–68. This approach reflects, to some extent, the revisionist view of the role of trade policy reforms being expressed internationally, as, for example, by Dani Rodrik, *The New Global Economy and the Developing Countries: Making Openness Work.* (Washington, D.C., Overseas Development Council, 1999). For a critique of the revisionist view, see J. Bhagwati and T.N. Srinivasan, 'Outward-Orientation and Development: Are the Revisionists Right?', in Deepak Lal and Richard Snape (eds), *Trade, Development and Political Economy: Essays in Honour of Anne O. Krueger.* (London, Palgrave, 2001), Chapter 1.

3. An increase in public savings will have some negative effect on private savings, as, for example, when higher tax revenues lead to a reduction in disposable income in the private sector, which in turn reduces private savings, but the net effect will still be positive.

4. Planning Commission, *Report of the Advisory Group on Tax Policy and Tax Administration for the Tenth Plan* (New Delhi, Planning Commission, 2001). Many countries have increased revenues substantially by switching to an integrated value added tax covering both goods and services. This is not possible in India because of the constitutional division of taxation powers between the centre (which can tax production) and the states (which can tax sales). The inability to switch to an integrated value added tax is a major hindrance to tax reform.

5. For example, Jagdish Bhagwati and Padma Desai, *India: Planning for Industrialization* (London: Oxford University Press, 1970); Bhagwati and Srinivasan, 'Outward-Orientation and Development; Ahluwalia, 1985.

6. Nicholas Stern, 'Building a Climate for Investment, Growth and Poverty Reduction in India', Speech delivered at EXIM Bank, Mumbai, India, 22 March (2001).

7. Montek Ahluwalia, 'State Level Performance Under Economic Reforms in India' (2002), in Anne Knieger (ed.), *Economic Policy Reforms and the Indian Economy*, (Chicago, Chicago University Press, forthcoming).

8. The sharp increase in average duty rates in 2000–1 reflects the imposition of tariffs on many agricultural commodities in anticipation of the removal of quantitative restrictions. Since these items were protected by quantitative restrictions in the mid-1990s, the combined protection provided by tariffs and quantitative restrictions was probably higher in the mid-1990s.

9. Planning Commission, *Report of the Task Force on Employment Opportunities* (New Delhi, Planning Commission, 2001).

10. India's reforms are often unfavourably compared with the very different sequencing adopted in China, which began with reforms in agriculture in 1978, extending them to industry only in 1984. The comparison is not entirely fair, since Chinese agriculture faced an extremely distorted incentive structure, with virtually no role for markets, that provided an obvious area for high-priority action with potentially large benefits. Since Indian agriculture operated to a much greater extent under market conditions, the situation was very different.

11. Ministry of Finance, *Economic Survey 2001–02* (New Delhi, Ministry of Finance, 2002).

12. Underpricing of water and fertilizer leads to excess usage and water-logged soil. Free electricity enables larger farmers to pump water from deep wells at relatively low cost. This encourages a much more water-using cropping pattern than would be optimal and also leads to over-exploitation of ground water and lowering the water table, which in turn hurts poorer farmers relying upon shallow wells.

13. Planning Commission, *Report of the Advisory Group on Tax Policy*.

14. Planning Commission, *Report of the Task Force on Employment Opportunities*.

15. The best known of these was the Dabhol project of the Enron Corporation, which became mired in controversy because of the high cost of power from the project, especially as a consequence of a pricing arrangement that meant that most of the tariff was US-dollar denominated and that the risk of rupee depreciation against the dollar was borne by the buyer.

16. These problems surfaced in a recent effort to privatize the distribution system in Delhi. The terms offered were publicly criticized as being too generous, because tariff setting was based on a relatively modest pace of reduction in transmission and distribution losses. Nevertheless, all bids received were below the reserve price set by the government. This was a consequence of several factors: information on the quality of assets and the financial position of the system was very poor; private investors were expected to take on the responsibility of excess staff with inadequate information on the costs of retrenchment;

enforcement of payment and disconnection for non-payment can create law and order problems in parts of the city; and there was lack of regulatory certainty about the way tariffs would be set in the future. These deficiencies inevitably led to very low bids.

17. For example, Ahluwalia, 'State Level Performance Under Economic Reforms in India'.

18. Davis, Jeffrey, Rolando Ossowski, Thomas Richardson, and Steven Barnett, 'Fiscal and Macro-economic Impact of Privatization', *IMF Occasional Paper* 194 (2000).

19. The definition of 'strategic' for this purpose covers enterprises related to defence, atomic energy and the railways. This would exclude only a handful of the 232 public sector enterprises of the central government.

20. The Ministry of Disinvestment in its website (http://www.divest.nic.in) has made a valiant effort at explaining the case for privatizing even profit-making companies on the grounds that government ownership makes it impossible to achieve commercial efficiency.

21. Jean Dreze and Amartya Sen, *Economic Development and Social Opportunities* (New Delhi, Oxford University Press, 1995).

22. Mahendra S. Dev and Jos Mooij, 'Social Sector Expenditures in the 1990s: Analysis of Central and State Budgets', *Economic and Political Weekly*, 2 March (2002), pp. 853–66.

23. N.C. Saxena, 'Improving Effectiveness of Government Programmes: An Agenda of Reform for the 10th Plan', Paper presented at a conference on 'Fiscal Policies to Accelerate Growth', organized by the World Bank, New Delhi, 8 May (2001). Available at http://www.fiscalconf.org/papers/saxena.pdf.

24. For example, an explicit statement of the reduction in import duty rates envisaged over time would have encouraged domestic producers to accelerate their efforts at adjustment. Similarly, a clear indication that reservation for small-scale producers would be phased out in a defined period would have encouraged these producers to plan for the transition more effectively. The reason these changes could not be announced in advance reflects the fact that there was not enough consensus of these initiatives at the early stages, even if they were to be implemented only gradually.

THE POLITICAL ECONOMY OF REFORMS

4

Economic Transition in
a Plural Polity
India*

RAHUL MUKHERJI[1]

This chapter traces the process that led to pro-trade economic policy change in India beyond 1991. In his inaugural address to the 84th Annual Meeting of the Indian Economic Association, C. Rangarajan described the importance of that year:

The country went through a severe economic crisis triggered by a serious balance of payments situation. *The crisis was converted into an opportunity to introduce some fundamental changes in the content and approach to economic policy.*[2]

The process that led to India's transition from import substituting industrialization (ISI) towards trade-led growth (TLG), culminating in significant policy change beyond 1991, provides valuable insights about the politics of economic transition. High tariffs, an overvalued exchange rate, import controls, and industrial licensing characterized ISI in India.[3] The trade and investment reforms of 1991 occurred in a thriving democracy at a time when the ruling Congress Party had an insecure majority. Second, India's size had made it easy for it to pursue ISI, compared with countries characterized by small internal markets.[4] India's democracy and its size make it a particularly interesting economic transition, with possible lessons for present and future democracies.[5]

Democracies, it is argued, often find it tough to make trade-friendly policy change requiring a flexible labour policy, industrial deregulation, the sale of

* This paper was written for this volume.

public sector assets, increased taxation, and a tight money policy. Such policies hurt small but powerful interests such as the political party in power, the bureaucrat, the rent-seeking ISI industrialist, and managers and workers in the public sector and ISI firms.[6]

Authoritarian regimes in Taiwan and Korea have successfully initiated economic transitions. They managed labour and business consistent with the demands of TLG. They allocated credit for export promotion, increased taxes, pursued a tight money policy, and successfully reduced the risks for the exporter by providing vital information and finance. Korea, under democratically elected Syngman Rhee, muddled up economic policy, while the autocratic hand of President Park made South Korea globally competitive. President Soeharto of Indonesia was able to redefine the state's relations with labour and business by destroying old institutions and creating new ones.[7] Allende's Chile, Rawling's Ghana, and Ozal's Turkey had military governments. In the newly democratized Bolivia, Paz Estenssoro enjoyed a great deal of autonomy.[8]

India's economic transition stands in contrast to the authoritarian transitions from ISI to TLG. Prime Minster Rajiv Gandhi's reform efforts initiated in the 1980s did not succeed despite a comfortable majority in parliament.[9] Why did India transit from ISI toward TLG in 1991? India had faced a balance of payments crisis in 1966 but had sustained ISI with renewed vigour from 1967.[10] The balance of payments crisis alone is not a sufficient cause for the policy change initiated in 1991. It is puzzling that the Congress Party coalition government of Prime Minister P.V. Narasimha Rao could initiate far-reaching reforms with an unstable majority in parliament in 1991.

Synergistic issue-linkage between the IMF, the executive, and domestic interest groups, due to the IMF agreement during the foreign exchange crisis of 1991, is critical for explaining the Indian foreign economic policy change. Synergy is a situation where the executive attempts to gain domestic approval for a policy by linking it to the perceived benefits of an international agreement.[11] Policy change in India occurred when a pro-trade executive made use of the agreement with the IMF, to gain the acquiescence of Indian industry and labour, at the time of a foreign exchange crisis.

I trace the path that ISI traversed in India.[12] I locate a mechanism that began with ISI but changed to TLG.[13] The process highlights ISI's propensity to sow the seeds of its destruction by generating unsustainable fiscal deficits. These deficits were at the root of India's balance of payments crisis. The Gulf War-driven exogenous shock (1990) was less a burden on India's balance of payments than the two oil shocks (1973 and 1980) that India had weathered with great ease. Second, ideational changes in the executive due to unresolved policy puzzles arising out of ISI convinced the executive to change course.

This chapter is divided into two parts. First, I elaborate the process that began with ISI and but changed to TLG. Second, I discuss the lessons from the Indian story. Why is the study of mechanisms or processes a fruitful way to comprehend economic policy change?

FROM IMPORT SUBSTITUTING INDUSTRIALIZATION (ISI) TO TRADE-LED GROWTH (TLG)

In this section, I outline India's path from ISI to trade-led growth (TLG). This involves the creation of a series of causal chains. A path can be traced from the initial condition of ISI to TLG.[14] This method reveals a mechanism by which economic transitions may occur in any plural polity.[15]

Two Consequences of Import-Substituting Industrialization

ISI and Social Mobilization

Industrialization can create political awareness among people and encourage them to participate in political activities. That industrialization and economic development facilitate political protest is borne out by democratization taking place from southern Europe to East Asia.[16] Even Germany up to the Second World War, which was considered the exception to this rule, seems to have witnessed considerable social and political mobilization after rapid economic development in the late 1800s and the early 1900s.[17] In this section, I argue that ISI was a strategy of economic development that generated a competitive political system in India with ever-newer demands on the executive.

Import substituting industrialization (ISI) is a modernization strategy adopted by late industrializers based on rapid heavy industrialization in the context of a closed economy. India's Second Five-Year Plan (1956–61) was an attempt in planned industrialization using internal economies of scale rather than trade. Its architect, P.C. Mahalanobis, pointed to a remarkable resemblance between the Indian plan and the Soviet experiment of the late 1920s. It emphasized rapid industrialization, economic independence and socialism, reflecting Prime Minister Nehru's vision of a modern India.[18]

Industrialization encourages people to leave the village to move to towns and cities for better employment opportunities. Second, the ISI-driven industrial strategy rests on improvements in literacy. Improved literacy rates increase access to the print media. Industrialization may also improve access to mass communications by making the television and the radio set more easily available. ISI, therefore, is the breeding ground for urbanization, literacy, and mass communications—the basic ingredients of a strategy of modernization.

Modernization can generate social mobilization. Huntington has argued, 'Social and economic change, urbanization, increases in literacy and education, industrialization, mass media expansion—extend political consciousness, multiply political demands, broaden political participation.'[19] Literacy and the growing spread of mass communications produces a heightened feeling of relative deprivation. Urbanization leads to erosion of traditional loyalty to the joint family and the feudal hierarchy of the village. Breaking of old commitments and greater respect for individualism generates new time for new purposes and produces new aspirations. Patron-client relations in the village increasingly get replaced either by class-based, sector-based, or communal group demands.[20]

The mobilized people increasingly participate in politics. New groups seize opportunities and old groups feel threatened. Autonomous political participation based on voluntary action such as casting of a vote takes over old forms of coerced participation. Interest groups such as professional organizations and cultural organizations begin to have an independent voice. Political participation of the mobilized people includes voting, lobbying, organizational activity, and various forms of political protests, including political violence.[21]

The practice of ISI-driven modernization in India resulted in the rise of education, urbanization, and mass communications. The literacy rate grew by 5.34 per cent between 1961–71, by 14.22 per cent between 1971–81, and, by 8.54 per cent between 1981–91.[22] Urban population as a proportion of total population grew steadily from 18 per cent in 1960 to 21.3 per cent in 1975 to 27 per cent in 1994.[23] In 1983, only 25 per cent of India's population was within television transmission range. With the rapid growth of electronic media, the same figure grew from 50 per cent in 1985 to 75 per cent in 1990.[24]

As access to literacy, urbanization, and mass communications improved, political participation and protest witnessed a significant rise. Cases of student indiscipline increased from 93 in 1958 to 2665 in 1968 and to 9174 in 1978. Prime Minister Indira Gandhi, faced with student mobilizations against her, declared 'national emergency' or authoritarian rule (1975–7). That the period 1975–9 recorded a decline in college enrolment could be the result of policies undertaken to curb social mobilization.[25]

Participation in riots per million people was stable up to 1963, but showed a steady increase thereafter. Riots as a proportion of total cognizable offences grew steadily between 1967 and 1971. The authoritarian regime of Prime Minister Indira Gandhi brought down the incidence of rioting in 1975. When democracy returned in 1977, it was life as usual once again.[26]

Communal riots in India appear to be a modern urban phenomenon, concentrated within cities and in industrial areas. During the period 1961–70, 32.55 per cent of communal incidents occurred in villages, where 80 per cent of India resided. According to another estimate, only 3.6 per cent of the deaths due to communal violence occurred in the villages in the last fifty years.[27]

Voter turnout increased rapidly at the end of the Second Five-Year Plan. It increased from 48 per cent in 1957 to 58 per cent in 1962, but stabilized in the range of 58 per cent and 62 per cent thereafter (in 1996 the figure jumped to 67 per cent). There has been a rise in the turnout for the elections to the state legislatures since 1989. Turnout in the local level panchayat elections has also increased, even though reliable turnout figures are not available.[28]

Politics in India became competitive as a result of social mobilization. From 1947 to 1967 the Congress party was almost congruous with the Indian political system. Major contests on Indian political issues occurred within rather than outside it. The party was accustomed to winning two-thirds of the seats in the Parliament (Lok Sabha) and a majority in all the states.[29] The election in 1967 changed this pattern. Between 1967 and 1969, the Congress lost power in eight states. What was polarity within the Congress took the shape of polarity between the Congress and a united opposition. This bipolarity began to spread to other states. A variety of contests such as Congress versus the left, Congress versus the regional party or parties, and Congress versus the right wing Jan Sangh (which later became the Bharatiya Janata Party or BJP) began to surface.[30]

The Congress party under Indira Gandhi, unable to respond to an increasingly mobilized opposition, invoked 'national emergency' between 1975 and 1977. The electorate supported the movement against authoritarian rule and dislodged the Congress party from power in 1977.[31] This was the first successful united opposition against the Congress party at the national level. The opposition coalition could not remain united, and the Congress party returned to power in 1980.

Oftentimes, increased mobilization in the absence of adequate institutional mechanisms to address the concerns of the mobilized populace induces the ruling party to use nationalism for winning elections.[32] The Congress party adopted even this strategy to win its electoral battles in the 1980s. In the early 1980s, the party adopted themes that belonged to the Hindu chauvinistic right. The opposition was often branded anti-national. The Rashtriya

Swayamsevak Sangh (RSS), which belonged to the right-wing Hindu-nationalistic BJP, helped the Congress in the elections of 1984.[33]

The Janata Dal victory in 1989 was the result of a horizontal cooperation among disadvantaged and backward castes, rather than a vertical mobilization by the higher castes. The coalition of Muslims, backward castes like Ahirs, Jats, Gujars and Yadavs (comprising the better off among the backward and middle castes), and the Rajputs put up a formidable opposition to the Congress Party. In an earlier era, such cooperation between the Rajputs (ruling caste) and backwards was unthinkable. The Bahujan Samaj Party—the first party to be lead by a member of a scheduled caste, also facilitated the Janata Dal victory in 1989.[34]

In sum, India's ISI-driven modernization promoted literacy, mass communications, and urbanization. This mobilized the people to participate in political protest and voting. The decline of the Congress Party since the mid-1980s, and the rise of regional, backward-caste and minority-group-based parties has been due largely to the Congress's institutional incapacity to deal with ever increasing social mobilization.

ISI and Low Productivity

ISI also generated the classic conditions of low productivity in India. The infant-industry-protection-inspired ISI had a deleterious impact on efficiency.[35] First, it was not easy to locate an infant industry. Second, it was not easy to determine the optimal amount of protection needed to propel an infant industry into a mature one.[36] Third, ISI depended on governmental decisions with respect to protection and subsidy. With no clear guidelines about the optimal amount of protection, ISI generated lobbying or rent-seeking behaviour that is detrimental to efficiency.[37] It became economic for an industrialist to bribe the government in order to get production and import licenses.

The ISI strategy had a negative impact on productivity in India. The public sector accounted for 27 per cent of the GDP. Its turnover investment ratio was 0.79 in 1971, went up to 2 in 1981 and then declined to 1 in 1991. Any figure below 3 is considered very low. 27 out of the 129 public sector undertakings utilized less than 50 per cent of their capacity in 1977–8.[38]

Isher Ahluwalia's study on the productivity of India's manufacturing industry noted the dismal performance in total factor productivity growth in the 1970s and a positive turnaround in the 1980s, owing largely to some deregulation in the economy. However, the capital-labour ratio in the manufacturing sector of a labour-abundant economy was increasing, leading to inappropriate factor use over time. The higher was the capital-labour ratio in an industry sector, the lower was the growth in total factor productivity in that sector. India fared much worse on this count than more trade-oriented countries such as Hong Kong, Singapore, Taiwan and Korea.[39]

Timmer and Szirmai have noted that while Taiwan and South Korea were catching up with the US's level of productivity between 1963 and 1993, India did not catch up. The South Korean gross value added per worker as a percentage of the US gross value added per worker grew from 7.5 per cent in 1963 to 48.5 per cent in 1993. The same figures for Taiwan were 11.8 per cent and 31.3 per cent respectively. For India, the figures were 7.5 per cent and 10.1 per cent respectively. India, Taiwan, and Korea were at the same level of productivity relative to the US level in 1963, but in 1993 India lagged far behind Taiwan and Korea in the race for 'catch-up'. Timmer and Szirmai also found that productivity was not so much a function of moving labour and capital towards manufacturing, which was the essence of the ISI strategy. Rather, productivity has more to do with economy-wide improvements in the technical competence of the people, financial and business services, physical infrastructure, and investment ratios.[40]

India's international competitiveness declined. India's share in the manufacturing exports of all developing countries came down from 22.1 per cent in 1962 to 3.4 per cent in 1990. Its share in the manufacturing exports of the world came down from 0.84 per cent in 1962 to 0.54 per cent in 1990.[41]

Social Mobilization, Low Productivity and the Fiscal Crisis

India's ISI contributed both to low levels of productivity and competitiveness, as well as political demands for better living and work conditions. The same people who were contented with their abject poverty became more vocal about their economic demands. The politics of 'command' characterized by state autonomy transformed itself into the politics of 'demand' led by pressure groups.[42] Two things could happen under these circumstances. First, if there were few opportunities for socio-economic mobility and political participation, the feeling of relative deprivation could lead to political violence and the declining legitimacy of the government.[43] Or the government could subsidize various sectors by providing seeds, fertilizers, irrigation, housing sites, land, and concessional finance.[44] If the government spent most of its resources in a way that did not earn adequate returns on investment, this would inevitably lead to a fiscal crisis.

Indian farmers, constituting a substantial vote bank, compelled the government to subsidize their economic activities. They could never be taxed. Fertilizer subsidy rose over the decades. The agriculture sector consumed approximately 25 per cent of the electricity but accounted for the bulk of the losses of the state electricity boards. Out of total power sector losses of Rs 43.5 billion, Rs 41 billion was estimated to be losses due to the farm sector. The story of the irrigation sector was much the same. Revenues as a proportion of recurrent expenditure fell from 22 per cent in 1980 to 7.5 per cent in 1989.[45] In 1988, the National Front government of Prime Minister V.P. Singh wrote off the debts of small farmers, at a time when it had foreign exchange reserves worth $ 3.7 billion, just enough to cover two months of imports.[46]

The political clout of the industrial sector, which included labour and capital, played an important role in explaining the degree of protection accorded to various industrial sectors. The greater the clout of organized labour and industry, the greater was the degree of protection granted to that sector.[47] The government subsidized bankrupt industrial units on uneconomic grounds. In a study of 23 such industrial units, it was found that in 17 out of 23 cases, the Board of Industrial and Financial Reconstruction (BIFR) sanctioned excessive write-offs through subsidized credit.[48]

Government expenditure of a non-economic kind rose due to the demands of the farmers, organized labour, and industrialists. Total non-developmental expenditure rose from 6.5 per cent of the GNP in 1960 to 15 per cent in 1989. The percentage of subsidies in the expenditures of the central and state governments rose from 3.2 per cent in 1960 to 12.1 per cent in 1989.[49] The increasing demands of the politically mobilized people ensured that the growth rate in government expenditure, which was 6.9 per cent between 1979 and 1983, rose to 9.5 per cent between 1983 and 1987. Rising government expenditure at the time of low productivity generated the unsustainable fiscal situation.[50]

The gross fiscal deficit is total government expenditure minus government revenue plus capital grants. It measures the overall borrowing need to finance India's government expenditure. The fiscal deficit never crossed the 6.4 per cent of GDP mark till 1983. Thereafter, between 1983 and 1990 it fluctuated between 7.5 per cent of GDP to 9 per cent of GDP.[51]

The twin ISI-driven dynamics of low productivity and social mobilization played an important role in generating the fiscal crisis of the Indian government.[52] ISI-driven modernization had generated new financial demands on the Indian government. At the same time, ISI was not a strategy that generated high levels of productivity. Financial demands on the government at the time when

Indian productivity was abysmally low created the classic condition of an unsustainable fiscal situation.

The Fiscal Crisis and Ideational Change

How did the ISI 'policy paradigm' change in India? First, dissatisfaction with a policy paradigm is necessary. A 'policy paradigm', implying a variety of policy-relevant theoretical ideas sharing certain basic assumptions about development, generates expectations about behaviour. When these expectations are not met, disenchantment with the paradigm begins to occur. 'Paradigm shifts' as described by Thomas Kuhn need not occur merely as a result of disenchantment with a policy paradigm. A policy paradigm could generate long periods of continuity despite disenchantment with anomalies.[53]

It is not easy to bring about a change in policy paradigms. Thus, building on anomalies, long periods of continuity may be punctuated by the disjunctive experience of a 'paradigm shift'. According to this view, continuity is the norm, but change is sporadic and rapid.[54] It could be accompanied by major exogenous events such as depressions, wars, or a sudden change in the terms of trade.[55] On such occasions, disenchantment with policies generated by the previous paradigm needs the support of a leadership with commitment and the power to implement new policies.[56] The pro-trade technocratic orientation in India became influential in the 1980s as a result of the failures of IS policies and the international demonstration effect of the alternative paradigm. But policy change in the direction of using trade for development had to wait till the foreign exchange crisis of 1991.

Policy puzzles persisted due to the malfunction of the ISI-driven policy paradigm in India. Infant industries did not mature into competitive ones. Income distribution remained highly skewed, leading to rising aspirations of the less privileged but newly mobilized people. Increased demand for resources and low productivity led to an unsustainable fiscal crisis. It therefore became difficult for the policy-maker to marry economics with politics. Moreover, developments in East Asia, China, and the Soviet Union validated the view that trade was essential for economic growth.[57] The Chinese shift to trade for promoting growth in the 1980s may have had a greater impact on India than the success of Korea and Taiwan. While it was easy to argue that India and the East Asian tigers were not comparable, China was both larger and a source of inspiration for many in India who believed in the merits of autarky.[58]

Prime Minister Indira Gandhi began considering TLG strategies by the end of the 1970s.[59] The government set up powerful committees to review the shortcomings of the old policies. Committees on trade (Chair: Abid Hussain, 1984), financial controls (Chair: M. Narasimhan), the public sector (Chair: Arjun Sengupta) and administrative reforms (Chair: L.K. Jha) were set up to provide a critical analysis of the past for the purposes of future policy. These reports stressed that India needed imports for growth. However, these imports required increased Indian exports, because international finance was not easily available to finance the much-needed imports.[60]

The change in Mrs Gandhi's orientation is evident from a speech she delivered to the National Development Council in February 1981:

I would like to point out that not so long ago certain countries used to be mentioned as worthy of emulation by us. Yet, at least one so-called ideal society continues to import vast quantities of grain from every available market, (e)specially capitalist markets, while our 'bourgeois' policy has made us self-sufficient. The trouble with many of our leftist friends is that they continue to think in archaic terms and in grooves of ideas which have long become outdated and which even the most orthodox socialist countries have given up.[61]

Prime Minister Rajiv Gandhi initiated pro-trade policy changes, which met with severe political obstacles.[62] Montek Ahluwalia, a technocrat with World Bank experience was brought in as Special Secretary in the Prime Minister's Office. In June 1990, Ahluwalia circulated a controversial paper arguing in favour of tariff reductions, freer entry of foreign investment, an increase in administered prices, an increase in the permissible asset limit under the Monopolies and Restrictive Trade Practices Act (MRTP), and labour laws that promote efficiency.[63] The agenda for reform was therefore clear to the executive before the foreign exchange shortfall in 1991.

The pro-trade momentum gained strength during the foreign exchange crisis of 1991. Prime Minister P.V. Narasimha Rao appointed the distinguished economist and policy-maker Manmohan Singh as India's Finance Minister. In a rare tribute, the Economics Nobel Laureate Amartya Sen has praised Manmohan Singh's doctoral dissertation of the early 1960s, where Singh had argued in favour of exports for India's development.[64] The importance of trade and global economic integration was not lost to Manmohan Singh in 1991.[65]

The Fiscal Crisis and the Balance of Payments Crisis of 1991

The fiscal crisis was the major reason why an exogenous shock, the Gulf War-driven rise in oil prices, precipitated a foreign exchange crisis in 1991. Creditor pessimism driven largely by bad fiscal management and political uncertainty had led to a disastrous depletion of foreign exchange reserves. Political mobilization for a greater share of the Government's pie had raised the fiscal deficit to 10 per cent of the GDP in 1991 (see Table 4.1).

Table 4. 1: Consolidated finances of the central and state governments[66]

(figures are expressed as a percentage of GDP at market prices)

	1960–1 to 1964–5	1970–1 to 1974–5	1975–6 to 1979–80	1985–6 to 1989–90
Revenue	12.7	14.6	17.8	20.0
a) Current Expenditure	11.8	14.2	16.3	23.0
b) Defence	2.6	3.0	2.9	3.7
c) Subsidies	0.7	1.1	1.9	3.6
d) Net interest Payments	0.4	0.5	0.7	2.5
e) Current revenue balance	0.9	0.4	1.5	–2.9
f) Capital Expenditure	6.6	5.1	6.9	7.1
Total Expenditure	18.4	19.3	23.2	30.0
Fiscal Deficit	5.7	4.7	5.4	10.0

Source: Joshi and Little (1994): 226.

Table 4.1 indicates the reasons for the rising fiscal deficit. The gap between revenue and current expenditure, which was 1.5 per cent of the GDP between 1975 and 1980, rose to 3 per cent of GDP between 1985 and 1990. Over the same period, interest payments grew by 1.8 per cent of GDP, subsidies increased by 1.7 per cent of GDP, and defence expenditure rose by 0.8 per cent of GDP. Interest payments and subsidies registered the highest rise (1.7 per cent of GDP), reflecting commercial borrowings and public demand management.

The budget deficit has a negative impact on the trade deficit. The following equation gives the relationship between the trade deficit and the budget deficit:

Trade Deficit = Savings Investment Gap + Budget Deficit $\qquad$ (1)[67]

Equation (1) identifies the two major components of the trade deficit. The trade deficit is significantly affected by the savings–investment gap and the budget deficit. In India, both the savings–investment gap and the budget deficit did not augur well for the trade deficit. First, the budget deficit or the fiscal deficit during the period 1985–6 and 1989–90 at 10 per cent of GDP was much higher than any period after 1950 (see Table 4.1).

Second, the savings–investment gap was much greater in 1991 compared with the period of the two oil shocks. In 1989–90, the gap was 2.4 per cent of GDP, compared with 0.6 per cent of GDP in 1972–3 and 0.5 per cent of GDP in 1979–80. In 1989–90, public deficit (savings minus investment) was 9 per cent of GDP, corporate deficit was 1.8 per cent of GDP, and, household savings were 8.4 per cent of GDP.[68] The household savings surplus was therefore not enough to cover corporate and public investments.

Table 4.2: Components of the balance of payments on the current account, 1982-3 to 1989-90[69]

(figures should be read as percentage of GDP)

	Average 1982–3 to 1984–5	Average 1985–6 to 1989–90	Change
Trade balance (customs)	−2.7	−2.3	0.4
Trade balance (RBI)	−3.0	−3.2	−0.2
Net non-factor services	0.5	0.3	−0.2
Resource balance	−2.4	−2.8	−0.4
Net factor income	−0.5	−1.0	−0.5
Net int. payments	−0.8	−1.2	−0.4
Net current transfers	1.3	1.0	−0.3
Current a/c balance	−0.8	−1.7	−0.9

Source: Joshi and Little (1994): 185.

Table 4.2 describes the components of India's deteriorating balance in the current account. The customs trade deficit due to import liberalization became less. The trade aspect of the balance that deteriorated involved the Reserve Bank of India's purchases of public equipment for military hardware and government purchases. Transfer receipts fell as a proportion of GDP. There was a worsening of net factor income from abroad because of increased interest payments on commercial borrowing. The deficit in the category of net factor income from abroad rose from $1.5 billion in 1984–5 to $3 billion in 1989–90. The result was that the current account deficit, which was $3 billion (1.7 per cent of GDP) in the first half of the 1980s, deteriorated to about $7 billion (3 per cent of GDP) in the latter half of the 1980s.

The budget and savings deficits were the prime motors behind the deteriorating current account imbalance. The first and second oil shocks had affected the current account adversely to the tune of about 1.1 per cent of GDP and 1.5

per cent of GDP respectively. The impact of the oil price rise in 1990 on the current account balance was not more severe (1 per cent of GDP) than the oil shocks.[70] Yet, India was less capable of dealing with the exogenous shock of 1991 on its own, largely because of a combination of a large fiscal deficit and the savings–investment gap.

The adverse credit rating of the Moody's in October 1990 pointed to a rise in the debt-service ratio, high dependence on commercial borrowings, increase in the debt-export ratio, the effect of the Gulf War, the budget deficit and the public debt, and recession in the OECD countries. This led to a shutting down of all the credit windows. Political uncertainty and mismanagement led to a further downgrading of India's credit rating in March 1991.[71]

Frantic moves to gain access to foreign exchange ensued. In April 1991, the Government sold 20 tons of gold to the Union Bank of Switzerland. In July 47 tons of gold were shipped to the Bank of England. The deposits of non-resident Indians, at $10 billion, turned into a modest net-outflow of $0.3 billion between October 1990 and March 1991. There was a net outflow of $1 billion in the period between April 1991 and June 1991. In January 1991 and in June 1991, India was on the verge of a liquidity crisis, with not enough foreign exchange to cover a fortnight of imports.[72]

THE PRO-TRADE EXECUTIVE, THE BALANCE OF PAYMENTS CRISIS AND LIBERALIZATION

I have explained how the fiscal crisis transformed Indian executive orientation. Changed executive orientation alone was inadequate for generating a distinctively pro-trade policy. Political impediments stood in the way. In this section, I explain a change dynamic through synergistic issue-linkage between the IMF, the executive, and domestic interest groups, at the time of a balance of payments crisis. Next, I describe the importance of the positive role that the pro-trade executive needs to play to exploit this synergy. Finally, I briefly describe India's trade and investment liberalization beyond 1991.

The Balance of Payments Crisis and Synergy

The simultaneous occurrence of a foreign exchange crisis and pro-trade executive orientation provides a compelling reason for trade and investment liberalization in India's plural polity. *An agreement between the executive and the IMF at the time of a foreign exchange crisis opens the possibility of synergistic issue linkage in a two-level game between the International Monetary Fund, the executive, and domestic interest groups.*[73] The interests of the domestic actors (labour and industry) do not change. But their preferences can change as a result of the IMF's lender-of-the-last-resort function.

Interests may get converted into preferences depending on how they can be pursued in the context of politics.[74] Organized labour and industry may have an interest in increasing their incomes. Based on their interests within domestic politics, they should be opposed to trade and investment liberalization. Years of ISI have accustomed these interest groups to prosper within a protected home market. Trade liberalization, on the other hand, may lead to a decline of uncompetitive sectors and job losses.[75]

An IMF agreement with a debtor country can create a temporary interest in favour of freer trade. ISI is an import dependent industrialization strategy. Though organized labour and capital have an interest in ISI, they are likely to acquiesce to a trade and investment-promoting agreement with the IMF in the short term, because no one else is willing to finance the imports of IS industrialists and workers at the time of a balance of payments crisis. Thus, the interests of labour and capital in the IS sectors may not change, but their preferences may change temporarily in favour of opening trade and investment due to an agreement with the IMF.

The foreign exchange crisis of 1991 created a short-term euphoria in favour of trade and investment liberalization in the business community. The Federation of Indian Chambers of Commerce and Industry (FICCI), representing domestic capital; the Associated Chambers of Commerce and Industry (ASSOCHAM), with historic ties to foreign capital; and the Confederation of Indian Industry (CII), representing manufacturing industry, all supported the trade and investment liberalization from 1991 to 1993.[76] The CII, which had positioned itself as the most influential industry organization, prepared a theme paper in April 1991 outlining the contours of a free economy. It held numerous meetings with trade union leaders, journalists, and politicians. One cannot underestimate the importance of industry's support for trade and investment liberalization in a democracy where elections need finance.[77]

This euphoria was short-lived. The opposition to investment liberalization within industry had gained momentum in 1993. The informal Bombay Club of prominent industrialists, which included Rahul Bajaj, H.S. Singhania, L.M. Thapar, S.K. Birla and Bharat Ram, articulated the anti-multinational corporation (MNC) viewpoint. At the Sri Ram Memorial lecture, Rahul Bajaj articulated most forcefully the need for Indian industry to have a level playing field against foreign corporations.[78]

Trade unions did not oppose reduced tariffs or foreign investment but successfully opposed the exit policy, which was designed to make a dent on job security in the organized sector. The New Industrial Policy (July 1991) established the National Renewal Fund (NRF) for restructuring industries consistent with changing technology and market conditions.[79] The 29 November nationwide strike affected financial transactions, steel plants, coal mines, fertilizer factories, and the government-owned national carrier in a big way.[80] The workers strike of 16 June 1992 affected even defence installations, the Post and Telegraph Department, Income Tax and Audit, ports and docks, and the oil sector.[81]

The IMF agreement in 1991 won the temporary acquiescence of Indian industry for trade and investment liberalization because industry needed foreign exchange for ISI-related imports. Trade unions opposed the exit policy but did not oppose tariff liberalization or foreign investment. The pro-trade Indian executive team of Prime Minister Rao and Finance Minster Singh used the period between 1991 and 1993 to usher in trade and investment liberalization that would be tough to reverse.

The Role of the Pro-Trade Executive in Exploiting Synergy

For sustained liberalization, the pro-trade executive must exploit the foreign exchange crisis to liberalize the economy to an extent from where retreat to economic nationalism is not easy. ISI-dominated industry and labour organizations are likely to oppose liberalization after the foreign exchange situation has improved. Years of ISI generate pro-ISI interests whose voice can overpower the minority pro-trade groups. And exit, as an option, does not work when dealing with institutions that have a monopoly over decision-making.[82] Second, consumers favouring liberalization are likely to face greater collective action problems than ISI-oriented producers.[83]

Such a crisis is a window of opportunity for the pro-trade executive. The prime minister and the finance minister constituted the executive team in India's Westminster-style parliamentary system. First, the crisis is likely to help unify the legislature behind the executive.[84] Second, the executive's long-term vision of trade and investment liberalization will be fulfilled only through an activist policy, because global economic integration once pursued is not easily reversed. Since a pro-trade executive is likely to have more in common with the IMF's agenda than a pro-ISI executive, this is likely to increase the positive-sum elements in the negotiations. The larger the negotiating 'win-set', the greater is the chance of an agreement with the IMF.[85]

The executive team of Prime Minister Rao and Finance Minister Singh were convinced liberalizers. Rao realized that the crisis was an opportunity to give a new definition to India's development policy.[86] The importance of trade for India's development had not been lost to Singh since the days of his D.Phil. thesis at Oxford. This ensured a large negotiating 'win-set'. In his first budget speech (24 July 1991), Singh clearly stated the Indian economic problem:

The origins of the problem are directly traceable to large and persistent macroeconomic imbalances and low productivity of investment, in particular the poor rates of return on past investments....The increasing difference between the income and expenditure of the Government has led to a widening of the gap between the income and expenditure of the economy as a whole. This is reflected in growing current account deficits in the balance of payments.[87]

The combination of Prime Minister Rao and Finance Minster Singh worked well. Rao could carry the Congress party with him on reforms and leave the economic judgement to Singh.[88] Singh's conviction helped him defend stabilization and structural adjustment. When accused of having shown the Union Budget of 1992 to the World Bank before proper parliamentary debate, Singh replied convincingly:

…As long as we get external assistance, we are obliged to discuss with our creditors because it is not a world where there is charity....I want to assert that we had not and we will not accept any conditionalities which are inconsistent with our national interest.
   …The letter of development policy which I had laid on the Table of the House was the basis for our request for assistance.... If Hon. Members examine this document carefully, they will see that it talks of policy directions which have been extensively discussed and debated in this august House.[89]

IMF's mark of approval on the Government of India's initiatives between 1991 and 1995 demonstrates the common ground between the IMF and the executive team. To quote from an IMF report:

Indian authorities have made a determined effort to correct many of the distortions…The initial impetus came from a severe balance of payments crisis in 1990–1. That crisis prompted the Indian authorities to adopt an adjustment program that contained both immediate stabilization measures and ambitious structural reforms.

The report subsequently went on to praise India's achievements in reforming trade, foreign investment, industrial controls and the financial sector.[90]

Trade and Investment Liberalization

The trade and investment oriented reforms initiated in 1991 have sustained themselves at a steady and gradual pace. India's weighted average duty rate came down from 72.5 per cent in 1990–1 to 29 per cent in 2002–3. India abolished quantitative restrictions in April 2001. Industrial decontrol and comparative advantage were emphasized. Industries reserved solely for the public sector were reduced from 18 to three (defence aircraft and warships, atomic energy generation, and railway transport). Industrial licensing was abolished, except for a few environmentally hazardous industries.[91] Foreign direct investment (FDI) responded to liberalization, albeit a little slowly. India's overall FDI rank improved from 42nd in 1990 to 33rd in 1999. India opened its equity market to foreign portfolio investment early. India ranked 6th in portfolio inflows, behind South Korea, South Africa, China, Thailand and Brazil.

Exchange rate reform was successful. An increasingly market-driven rate had a positive impact on India's exports. Based on the government's research between 1989 and 1991, the Liberalized Exchange Rate Mechanism System (LERMS) allowed 60 per cent of the foreign exchange from exports and remittances to be converted at the free market rate. 100 per cent export-oriented units and export-processing zones could sell the entire proceeds at the free market rate. The success of the LERMS encouraged the liberalizers, as there was no substantial outflow of foreign exchange reserves. Import of gold was liberalized beyond the 1992–3 budget. In August 1994, India accepted Article VIII of the IMF by allowing the rupee to become convertible on the current account.

India's dependence on trade grew, as imports and exports as a proportion of GDP rose from 15.1 per cent of GDP in the 1980s to 24.8 per cent of GDP in the nine years after the crisis (1992–2000). India's share in world exports improved from 0.42 per cent in 1980 to 0.52 per cent in 1990, and to 0.67 per cent in 2000. Yet, the 12th largest economy in the world was only the 27th largest trader.[92]

CONCLUSION: THE SIGNIFICANCE OF INDIA'S PATH

India's path to trade and investment liberalization demonstrates the importance of history and process in a political explanation.[93] To assert that the simultaneous presence of a pro-trade executive and a balance of payments crisis can lead to trade and investment liberalization begs two important questions. First, why did the Indian executive become pro-trade in 1991? Second, was the balance of payments crisis of 1991 merely the result of an exogenous shock?

India's path suggests that the birth of a pro-trade executive can be traced to the executive's inability to deal with the budget deficits generated by ISI. Second, the fiscal deficit was an important cause of the balance of payments crisis. My story avoids merely describing a conjuncture when the two policy-change variables—executive orientation and the balance of payments crisis—were present at the desired level in 1991; I am able to explain *why* the variables were present in 1991.

The literature on path dependence asserts that the logic of increasing returns can lock an inefficient trajectory because any mode of organization involves high start-up costs, learning and network externalities, and adaptive expectations.[94] ISI too involved huge doses of public and private investment for the setting up of a large government sector and for subsidizing domestic industry. Thereafter, rent-seeking opportunities for the industrialist, the politician, and the bureaucrat, and job security to the worker, created vested interests. Consistent with the conventional wisdom on path dependence, every investment in ISI made it tougher to reverse it.

This argument also poses a problem for path dependence. Path dependence suggests that it may be characterized by increasing returns and positive feedback, which may reinforce a certain direction.[95] Yet, my story highlights the problems that a path may create for its sustenance. For example, Indian ISI's problem was the sustainability of budget deficits in the context of low levels of productivity. The budget deficit in my argument, a process-driven variable, played an important role in generating my key policy-change variables: the pro-trade executive orientation and the balance of payments crisis.[96]

The argument has implications for the debate on the salience of levels of analysis for explaining trade policy change. The interests of the actor (the executive) are independent of environmental constraints. But environmental constraints play a role in translating actor's interests into policy outcomes.[97] The executive may have a pro-liberalization bent. But this may produce either protection or liberalization, depending on the severity of the foreign exchange crisis. Second, the strategic situation between the domestic actors is important. If capital and organized labour are opposed to liberalization, the pro-trade executive may achieve very little.[98] Third, the simultaneous consideration of the international and domestic levels of analysis, through synergistic issue linkage, was important for explaining trade and investment liberalization in India. Showing the dynamics at the international level and then assessing their impact on the domestic level is not a fruitful strategy.[99]

Paths can generate contingent generalizations.[100] The choices at various choice-points may have a lasting impact on the trajectory. For example, authoritarian Indonesia in 1966 had a pro-trade executive (President Soeharto) and a severe foreign exchange crisis, but synergistic issue linkages were not important for policy change.[101] Similarly, Collor's Brazil, transiting from authoritarian rule towards democracy, had no foreign exchange crisis when it liberalized its trade and investment policy.[102] These examples demonstrate that regime type may have an impact on the dynamics of policy change. If the path that democracies take differs from that of non-democracies, what explains this difference? This is a fascinating area for further research.

The Indian transition has lessons for the design of IMF conditionality. If IMF conditionalities are viewed by the debtor as being too intrusive, trade-led development requiring structural adjustment is not likely. India went for funds twice before—in 1966 and 1980—but the results of 1991 were far more impressive than the previous years.[103] What the IMF wanted India to do in 1991 was already a part of the Indian technocratic consensus by 1990. An effort on the part of the IMF to promote home-grown programmes, based on country ownership of programmes, is likely to increase the IMF's ability to get a country to move towards trade-led development.[104]

NOTES AND REFERENCES

1. The author benefited from a presenting an earlier version of this paper at a conference of the Network on South Asian Politics and Political Economy (NETSAPPE) at the University of Michigan, Ann Arbor, in 2002. He benefited from discussions with Jagdish Bhagwati, Helen Milner, Jack Snyder, David Baldwin, Sumit Ganguly, Premachandra Athukorala, Bibek Debroy, Pratap Bhanu Mehta, Ashutosh Varshney, Robert Jenkins, Atul Sarma, and Kanti Bajpai. The Australia South Asia Research Centre (Australian National University), the Rajiv Gandhi Foundation, and the Centre for Political Studies, Jawaharlal Nehru University, provided material and intellectual support. The shortcomings are all mine.

2. C. Rangarajan, 'Economic Reforms: Some Issues and Concerns', *The Indian Economic Journal,* 49, 2 (2001/02).

3. Trade-led growth (TLG) strategies, on the other hand, characterize a situation where the effective exchange rate for exports is not significantly different from the effective exchange rate for imports. See Jagdish N. Bhagwati, 'Rethinking Trade Strategy', in John P. Lewis and Velleriana Kallab (eds), *Development Strategies Reconsidered* (New Jersey, Transaction Books, 1986).

4. Stephan Haggard, *Pathways from the Periphery* (Ithaca, Cornell University Press, 1990), pp. 26–30.

5. On the definition and significance of a tough case, which is very similar to a 'crucial experiment' in the philosophy of science, see Arthur L. Stinchcombe, *Constructing Social Theories* (Chicago, University of Chicago Press, 1968), pp. 25–8; and Harry Eckstein, 'Case Study and Theory in Political Science,' in Fred I. Greenstein and Nelson Polsby (eds), *Handbook of Political Science*, vol. 7, *Strategies of Inquiry* (Reading, Mass., Addison Wesley, 1975) pp. 119–20.

6. On the problems of adjustment to TLG in a democracy, see Adam Przeworski, *Democracy and the Market* (Cambridge University Press, Cambridge and New York, 1991: chap. 4); Luiz Pereira, C.B. Jose, M. Maravall and Adam Przeworski, *Economic Reforms in New Democracies* (Cambridge, Cambridge University Press, 1993, 1–11); Haggard, *Pathways from the Periphery* (chap. 10). On the interests of rent-seeking groups in perpetuating ISI, see Anne O. Krueger, 'The Political Economy of the Rent-Seeking Society', *American Economic Review*, 64 (1974). On why small interests groups might organize effectively against large ones, see Mancur Olson, *The Logic of Collective* Action (Cambridge, Mass., Harvard University Press, 1971), chap. 1.

7. For the role of the authoritarian state in facilitating economic reforms in Taiwan, see Alice Amsden 'The State and Taiwan's Economic Development', in Peter Evans, Dietrich Reuschemeyer, and Theda Skocpol (eds), *Bringing The State Back In* (New York, Cambridge University Press, 1985); and Haggard, *Pathways from the Periphery*, chap. 4. For the relationship between authoritarianism and economic transition in Korea, see Haggard, *Pathways from the Periphery*, chap. 3; and Stephan Haggard and Chung-in Moon, 'The South Korean State in the International Economy', in John G. Ruggie (ed.), *The Antinomies of Interdependence* (New York, Columbia University Press, 1983). For Taiwan and South Korea as a whole, see Robert Wade, *Governing the Market* (Princeton, NJ, Princeton University Press, 1990).

8. Joan M. Nelson 'The Politics of Economic Transformation,' *World Politics*, 45, April (1993), pp. 433–42.

9. On Rajiv Gandhi's halting reforms, see Atul Kohli, *Democracy and Discontent* (New York, Cambridge University Press, 1990), chap. 11; Jagdish Bhagwati, *India in Transition* (Oxford, Clarendon Press, 1993), pp. 73–4; and Ashutosh Varshney, 'Mass Politics or Elite Politics', in Jeffrey D. Sachs, Ashutosh Varshney and Nirupam Bajpai (eds), *India In The Era of Economic Reforms* (New Delhi, Oxford University Press), pp. 239–44.

10. Mukherji (2000).

11. Robert D. Putnam, 'Diplomacy and Domestic Politics', *International Organization*, 42, 3, Summer (1988), pp. 446–8; and Andrew Moravcsik, 'Introduction', in Peter Evans, Harold Jacobson and Robert Putnam (eds),

Double Edged Diplomacy, (Berkeley, University of California Press, 1993), pp. 25–6.

12. Alexander L. George and Timothy J. McKeown, 'Case Studies and Theories of Organizational Decision Making', in Robert F. Coulam and Richard A. Smith (eds), *Advances in Information Processing in Organizations*, vol. 2 (Greenwich, Connecticut JAI Press, 1985), pp. 21–58.

13. For an understanding of mechanisms, see Jon Elster, *Alchemies of the Mind* (Cambridge, Cambridge University Press, 1999), chap. 1.

14. George and Mckeown, 'Case Studies and Theories of Organizational Decision Making', p. 36.

15. For a discussion on mechanisms, see Jon Elster, *Alchemies of the Mind*, chap. 1.

16. Ronald Inglehart, *Modernization and Postmodernization: Cultural, Economic and Political Change in Forty-Three Societies* (Princeton, Princeton University Press, 1997), p. 8.

17. Sheri Berman, 'Modernization in Historical Perspective', *World Politics* 53, 3, April (2001), pp. 431–62.

18. For the role of the state in late industrialization, see Alexander Gerschenkron, *Economic Backwardness in Historical Perspective* (Cambridge, Massachusetts, Harvard University Press, 1962). For India's ISI, see Sukhamoy Chakravarty, *Development Planning*, (Oxford, Clarendon Press, 1987), chap. 2. For an argument that ISI in India was a strategy of modernization see Baldev Raj Nayar, 'Political Mainsprings of Economic Planning in the New Nations', *Comparative Politics*, 6, 3, April (1974), pp. 361–3; and Baldev Raj Nayar, *The Modernization Imperative and Indian Planning* (New Delhi, Vikas, 1972). If India had gone the Gandhian way, emphasizing small and cottage industries, such a strategy may have been a departure from modernization.

19. Samuel P. Huntington, *Political Order in Changing Societies* (New Haven, Connecticut, Yale University Press, 1968), p. 5.

20. Huntington, *Political Order in Changing Societies,* pp. 39–49; Samuel P. Huntington and Joan M. Nelson, *No Easy Choice* (Cambridge, Mass., Harvard University Press, 1976), chap. 3.

21. Huntington and Nelson, *No Easy Choice,* chap. 1 and chap. 3.

22. In 1997, 62 per cent of Indians were literate. See Government of India, *Selected Educational Statistics 1997–98* (New Delhi, Ministry of Human Resource Development, 1999), p. vi.

23. United Nations Development Program, *Human Development Report 1997* (New York, Oxford University Press, 1997), p. 87.

24. Victoria L. Farmer, 'Depicting the Nation', in Francine R. Frankel, Zoya Hasan, Rajeev Bhargava and Balveer Arora (eds), *Transforming India* (New Delhi, Oxford University Press, 2000), p. 266.

25. Lloyd I. Rudolph and Susanne H. Rudolph, *In Pursuit of Lakshmi* (Chicago, University of Chicago Press, 1987), pp. 227, 295.

26. Baldev Raj Nayar, *Violence and Crime in India* (Delhi, Macmillan, 1975), pp. 22–6. Rudolph and Rudolph, *In Pursuit of Lakshmi*, p. 227.

27. On the relationship between modernization and communal violence in India, see Sudhir Kakar, *The Colours of Violence* (Delhi, Penguin Books, 1995), chap. 6. On the rural urban divide in communal riots, see Ashis Nandy, 'Coping with the Politics of Faiths and Cultures', in Joanna Pfaff-Czarnecka, Darini R. Senanayake, Ashis Nandy and Edmund T. Gomez, (eds), *Ethnic Futures*, (New Delhi, Sage Publications, 1999), pp. 136–8. On the relatively low incidence of communal violence in rural India, see Ashutosh Varshney, 'Ethnic Conflict and Civil Society', *World Politics* 53, 3 (2001), p. 371.

28. Yogendra Yadav, 'Understanding the Second Democratic Upsurge', in Frankel *et al.* (eds), *Transforming India*, pp. 122–3.

29. Rajni Kothari, 'The Congress System in India', *Asian Survey* 4, 12 (1964), pp. 1161–73; W.H. Morris-Jones, *Politics Mainly Indian* (Madras, Orient Longman1968), pp. 196–232.

30. Kothari updated his analysis for the period up to 1967 in Rajni Kothari, *Politics in India* (Boston, Little Brown, 1970), chap. 2. For a more recent analysis summarizing the trends in party competition, see E. Sridharan, 'The Fragmentation of the Indian Party System, 1952–1999: Seven Competing Explanations', in Zoya Hasan (ed.), *Parties and Politics in India* (New Delhi, Oxford University Press, 2002), pp. 481–5.

31. For a description of the mobilizations that inspired Indira Gandhi to impose a 'national emergency', see Francine Frankel, *India's Political Economy, 1947–1977* (Princeton, New Jersey, Princeton University Press, 1978), chap. 10; and Lloyd I. Rudolph and Susanne H. Rudolph, 'Regime Types and Economic Performance', in Sudipta Kaviraj (ed.), *Politics in India* (New Delhi, Oxford University Press, 1997), p. 183.

32. For an argument about the rise of the nationalist sentiment due the inability of institutions to keep pace with social mobilization, see Jack L. Snyder, *From Voting to Violence: Democratization and Nationalist Conflict* (New York, Norton, 2000), chaps. 1, 2, and 6. See also Edward D. Mansfield and Jack L. Snyder, 'Democratization and the Danger of War', *International Security* 20, 1, Summer (1995), pp. 5–38.

33. James Manor, 'Parties and the Party System', in Zoya Hasan (ed.), *Parties and Party Politics in India*, pp. 446–60.

34. Francine Frankel, 'Decline of a Social Order', in Sudipta Kaviraj (ed.), *Politics in India*, pp. 375–82. For an analysis of the entry of new groups into political competition in five districts of India, see Kohli, *Democracy and Discontent*, chaps. 3–7; and Atul Kohli, 'Centralization and Powerlessness', in Joel S.

Migdal, Atul Kohli and Vivienne Shue (eds), *State Power and Social Forces* (Cambridge, Cambridge University Press, 1994), pp. 93–4.

35. For a review of the literature supporting ISI, see Anne O. Krueger, *Political Economy of Policy Reform in Developing Countries* (Cambridge, Massachusetts, MIT Press, 1993), pp. 44–5.

36. Michael P. Todaro, *Economic Development in the Third World* (New York, Longman, 1981), pp. 453–4.

37. Anne O. Krueger, 'The Political Economy of the Rent-Seeking Society', *American Economic Review*, 64, June (1974). For a review of the literature on rent-seeking, see Anne O. Krueger, 'Trade Policy and Economic Development, NBER Working Paper 5896, Cambridge, Massachusetts (1997), p. 22.

38. Atul Sarma, 'Performance of Public Enterprises in India', in Dilip Mookherjee (ed.), *Indian Industry* (New Delhi, Oxford University Press, 1995).

39. Isher J. Ahluwalia, *Productivity and Growth in Indian Manufacturing* (New Delhi, Oxford University Press, 1991), chap. 7. Although there is some controversy about the total factor productivity growth (includes labour and capital's contribution to productivity) in the 1980s, Ahluwalia's is the majority view. I am indebted to Biswanath Goldar for his insights.

40. For the India and East Asia comparison, see Marcel P. Timmer and Adam Szirmai, 'Comparative Productivity Performance in Manufacturing in South and East Asia', *Oxford Development Studies* 27, 1 (1999), pp. 61–5. For the argument that there is no need to shift factors such as labour and capital to more productive uses for increasing the level of productivity, see Marcel P. Timmer and Adam Szirmai, 'Productivity growth in Asian manufacturing: The structural bonus hypothesis examined', *Structural Change and Economic Dynamics*, 11 (1999), pp. 371–92.

41. See Sanjay Kathuria, 'Competitiveness in Indian Industry', in Dilip Mookherjee (ed.), *Indian Industry* (New Delhi, Oxford University Press, 1995), p. 154.

42. See Rudolph and Rudolph, *In Pursuit of Lakshmi* (1987), chaps. 7–13; and Rudolph and Rudolph, 'Regime Types and Economic Performance' (1997), pp. 177–86.

43. See Ted R. Gurr, *Why Men Rebel* (Princeton, New Jersey, Princeton University Press, 1970); and James C. Davies, *When Men Revolt and Why* (New York, Free Press, 1970). On mobilization, see Huntington, *Political Order in Changing Societies*, pp. 53–5; and Huntington and Nelson, *No Easy Choice*, chap. 1 and chap. 3.

44. Subrata K. Mitra, 'Room to Maneuver in the Middle', *World Politics*, 43. On the impact of social mobilization on the Indian exchequer, see Pranab Bardhan, *The Political Economy of Development in India* (Oxford, Basil Blackwell, 1984), chap. 5.

45. Chakravarty, *Development Planning*, 126–7; Ashutosh Varshney, *Democracy, Development and the Countryside* (Cambridge, Cambridge University Press, 1995), pp. 169–72.

46. Vijay Joshi and I.M.D. Little, *India: Macroeconomics and Political Economy 1964 –1991* (New Delhi, Oxford University Press, 1994), p. 65.

47. Ira Gang and Mihir Pandey, *Trade Protection in India* (New Brunswick, New Jersey, Department of Economics – Rutgers University, 1996).

48. T.C.A. Anant and Omkar Goswamy, 'Getting Everything Wrong', in Mookherjee, (ed.), *Indian Industry*, pp. 273–4.

49. Pranab Bardhan, 'A Political Economy Perspective on Development', in Bimal Jalan (ed.), *The Indian Economy* (New Delhi, Viking Penguin, 1992), pp. 324–5.

50. Sudipto Mundle and M. Govinda Rao, 'Issues in Fiscal Policy', in Bimal Jalan (ed.), *The Indian Economy*, pp. 230–1).

51. Government of India, *Economic Survey 1994/95* (New Delhi, Ministry of Finance, 1995), p. 16.

52. I associate low productivity rather than slow economic growth with the fiscal crisis because a fiscal crisis may be associated with a high-growth but inflation-generating expansionary policy. See Krueger, 'The Political Economy of the Rent-Seeking Society' (1997), pp. 16–17.

53. Thomas Kuhn, *The Structure of Scientific Revolutions* (Chicago, University of Chicago Press, 1970), chaps 4–6. For 'policy paradigm' and economic policy change, see Peter Hall, 'Policy Paradigms, Social Learning, and the State', *Comparative Politics*, 25, 3, April (1993), pp. 277–87.

54. See Kuhn, *The Structure of Scientific Revolutions*; and Stephen D. Krasner, 'Approaches to the State,' *Comparative Politics* 16, 2 (1984), pp. 240–4.

55. See Albert O. Hirschman, 'How the Keynesian Revolution was Exported From the United States', in Peter Hall (ed.), *The Political Power of Economic Ideas* (Princeton, New Jersey, Princeton University Press, 1989); and Thomas J. Bierstaker, 'The Triumph of Neoclassical Economics in the Developing World', in James Rosenau and E.O. Czempiel (eds), *Governance Without Government* (Cambridge, Cambridge University Press, 1992).

56. Hall, 'Policy Paradigms, Social Learning, and the State', pp. 286–7.

57. For the East Asian and Chinese transitions, see Haggard, *Pathways from the Periphery*, chaps. 3–4; and N.R. Lardy, *Foreign Trade and Economic Reform in China* (Cambridge, Cambridge University Press, 1992). For the fall of the Soviet system, see Marshall I. Goldman, *What Went Wrong with Perestroika* (New York, Norton, 1991); and Paul Kennedy, *The Rise and Decline of the Great Powers* (London, Fontana Press, 1988), pp. 631–64.

58. See Anne O. Krueger, 'Contrasts to Transitions to Market-Oriented

Economies: India and Korea', in Yujiro Hayami and Masahiko Aoki (eds), *The Institutional Foundations of East Asian Economic Development* (London, Macmillan, 1998), p. 203.

59. Interview with Arjun K. Sengupta, Member: Planning Commission, New Delhi, 20 August 1997. Sengupta was an advisor to Prime Minister Indira Gandhi in the early 1980s. See also Arjun K. Sengupta, *Reforms, Equity And The IMF* (New Delhi, Har Anand, 2001), pp. 44–65.

60. See Vanita Shastri, 'The Political Economy of Policy Formation In India', Ph.D. Dissertation (Ithaca, Cornell University, 1995), pp. 165–71; and P.N. Dhar, 'The Indian Economy', in Robert E.B. Lucas and Gustave F. Papanek (eds), *The Indian Economy*, (New Delhi, Oxford University Press, 1988), pp. 13–14.

61. Indira Gandhi, *Selected Speeches and Writings – Volume 4, 1980–1981* (New Delhi, Government of India, Publications Division of the Ministry of Information and Broadcasting, 1985), p. 236.

62. On the promise of Rajiv Gandhi's reforms in 1984 and 1985, see Barnett R. Rubin, 'Economic Liberalization and the Indian State,' *Third World Quarterly* 7, 4, October (1985). On his failure to adequately deal with politics see Kohli, *Democracy and Discontent*; Bhagwati, *India in Transition*; and Varshney, 'Mass Politics or Elite Politics'.

63. Shastri, 'The Political Economy of Policy Formation In India', pp. 223–6.

64. For the published version of Singh's doctoral dissertation, see Manmohan Singh, *India's Export Trends* (London, Oxford University Press, 1964). See also Amartya Sen, 'Theory and Practice of Development', in Isher J. Ahluwalia and I.M.D. Little (eds), *India's Economic Reforms and Development* (New Delhi, Oxford University Press, 1998).

65. For concluding that Singh was pro-trade in 1991, I rely on the following sources: Personal interviews with Jagdish Bhagwati, Arthur Lehman Professor of Economics, Columbia University, New York, 14 November 1997; Manmohan Singh, Member of Parliament, Ministry of Parliamentary Affairs, New Delhi, 8 August 1997; and Montek Singh Ahluwalia, Member, Planning Commission, New Delhi, 25 April 2001. See also T.J. Byres, 'The Creation of "The Tribe of Pundits Called Economists"', in T.J. Byres (ed.), *The Indian Economy* (New Delhi, Oxford University Press, 1998: 87–8); and Amit Bhaduri and Deepak Nayyar, *The Intelligent Person's Guide to Liberalization* (New Delhi, Penguin Books, 1996), p. 50.

66. Joshi and Little, *India: Macroeconomics and Political Economy 1964–1991*, p. 226. I have relied on these figures because Joshi and Little's figures have stood the test of time as an authoritative account of the Indian crises. Their figures have not been seriously challenged, even though they tell a very important

story. See also Bimal Jalan, *India's Economic Crisis* (New Delhi, Oxford University Press, 1991), pp. 1–4, 100–17.

67. For a commentary on this equation, see Paul Krugman, *The Age of Diminished Expectations* (Cambridge, Massachusetts, MIT Press, 1994), p. 50. The equation can be derived very easily from the basic national income accounts identity:

Y (national income) = C (consumption) + I (investment) + {G (government expenditure) – T (revenue)} + {X (exports) – M (imports)}

Or, Y – C = I + (G - T) + (X - M).

But, Y – C = S (savings)

Substituting S for Y – C, S = I + G – T + X – M

Or (X – M) = (S – I) + (T – G)

68. Joshi and Little, *India: Macroeconomics and Political Economy 1964 – 1991*, chap. 12.

69. Ibid.: 185.

70. Ibid.: 114, 149, 189.

71. Sunanda Sen, 'Dimensions of India's External Crisis', *Economic and Political Weekly,* 29 (1994), p. 808;. Bhaduri and Nayyar, *The Intelligent Person's Guide to Liberalization,* p. 27; Joshi and Little, *India: Macroeconomics and Political Economy 1964–1991,* p. 67.

72. Joshi and Little, *India: Macroeconomics and Political Economy 1964 – 1991*, p. 67. Bhaduri and Nayyar, *The Intelligent Person's Guide to Liberalization,* p. 29.

73. Robert D. Putnam, 'Diplomacy and Domestic Politics', pp. 446–8; and Andrew Moravscik, 'Introduction' in Evans et al., *Double Edged Diplomacy*, pp. 25–6.

74. Helen Milner, *Interests, Institutions and Information* (Princeton, Princeton University Press, New Jersey, 1997), chap. 2, pp. 241–2.

75. I am making the assumption that while the Stopler–Samuelson theorem may be good for explaining the long-term commonality or conflict of interests between the factors of production (land, labour and capital), in the short-term sectors rather than factors of production organize themselves to express their preference for trade or protectionism. For the Stopler–Samuelson view, see Wolfgang Stopler and Paul A. Samuelson, 'Protection and Real Wages', *Review of Economic Studies*, 9 (1941); and Ronald Rogowski, *Commerce and Coalitions: How Trade Affects Domestic Political Alignments* (Princeton, Princeton University Press, New Jersey), chap. 1. For the Ricardo–Viner–Cairnes view that sectors rather than factors organize themselves more effectively, especially in the short-run, see Stephen P. Magee, William A. Brock and Leslie Young, *Black Hole*

Tariffs and Endogenous Policy Theory: Political Economy in General Equilibrium (New Cambridge University Press, 1989), chap. 7.

76. Kishore C. Dash, 'India's International Monetary Fund Loans', *Asian Survey,* 39, 6 (1999), pp. 902–3; Associated Chambers of Commerce and Industry [ASSOCHAM], *The ASSOCHAM Story* (New Delhi, ASSOCHAM, 1995), pp. 213–53. Personal interview with ex -Prime Minister Rao at his residence in New Delhi, 2 February 2001. For the influence of different industry groups in 1991, see Stanley Kochanek, 'The Transformation of Interest Politics in India', *Pacific Affairs,* 68, 4, Winter (1995–1996), pp. 534–50.

77. See Dash, 'India's International Monetary Fund Loans', p. 902; Confederation of Indian Industry [CII], 'Report on Competitive Advantage of India', (New Delhi, CII, September 1994).

78. Interview with D.H. Pai Panandiker, New Delhi, 1 September 1997. Panandiker was Secretary General of FICCI up to 1992. See also Tarun Das, 'India: A New Economic Direction', *World Affairs* 1, 2, April–June (1997), pp. 104–13. Tarun Das was the Secretary General of CII at the time of the balance of payments crisis. The Sri Ram Memorial Lecture was delivered at the PHD Chambers of Commerce in New Delhi on 21 August 1997.

79. See C.S. Venkata Ratnam, 'Exit Policy,' *Indian Journal of Industrial Relations,* 27 (1992), p. 378; and R.K.A. Subrahmanya, *Some Aspects of Structural Adjustment in India* (New Delhi, Friedrich Ebert Stiftung, 1996), pp. 59–63. On India's labour laws, see Roberto Zagha, 'Labor in India's Economic Reforms', in Jeffrey D. Sachs, Ashutosh Varshney, and Nirupam Bajpai (eds), *India in the Era of Economic Reforms* (New Delhi, Oxford University Press, 1999), pp. 161–6.

80. M.K. Pandhe, 'Magnificent Response to Nationwide Industrial Strike', *The Working Class,* New Delhi, Centre for Indian Trade Unions, December (1991), pp. 1–4.

81. M.K. Pandhe, 'Magnificent Response to General Strike', *The Working Class,* New Delhi, Centre for Indian Trade Unions, July (1992), pp. 4–8. See also Sukomal Sen, *Working Class of India,* (Calcutta, K.P. Bagchi and Co., 1997), chaps. 23–4.

82. Albert O. Hirschman, *Exit, Voice and Loyalty* (Cambridge, Massachusetts, Harvard University Press, 1970), chap. 3.

83. Olson, *The Logic of Collective* Action, chap. 1, esp. p. 48.

84. On the special advantages of the executive for crafting a unified government, see Milner, *Interests, Institutions and Information,* pp. 109–112. For divided government, see ibid., chap. 4. On how unified government was achieved in India despite much opposition in 1966, see Mukherji (2000: 382–885).

85. Moravcsik, 'Introduction', in Evans et al. (eds), *Double Edged Diplomacy;*

and Peter B. Evans, 'Building an Integrative Approach', in Evans et al., *Double-Edged Diplomacy*, pp. 402–3.

86. Interview with P.V.N. Rao at his residence in New Delhi on 2 February 2001.

87. Government of India, *Budget Speeches of Union Finance Ministers* (New Delhi, Department of Economic Affairs, 1997), p. 5.

88. *Business India,* 24 February 1997, p. 68; and *Business India,* 15 February 1998, pp. 57–8.

89. Government of India, *Lok Sabha Debates* (27 February 1992) New Delhi: Lok Sabha Secretariat, 1993, pp. 572–3.

90. See Ajay Chopra, Charles Collyns, Richard Hemming and Karen Parker, 'India: Economic Growth and Reform', *Occasional Paper 134*, IMF, Washington DC (1995), pp. 1–3.

91. See Ahluwalia (2002).

92. Arvind Virmani, 'India's External Reforms: Modest Globalization, Significant Gains', *Economic and Political Weekly* 38, 2, August 9 (2003)Virmani (2003).

93. See Paul Pierson, 'Increasing Returns, Path Dependence, and the Study of Politics', *American Political Science Review*, 94, 2, June (2000), p. 252; and Robert H. Bates, Avner Greif, Margaret Levi, Jean-Laurent Rosenthal and Barry R. Weingast, *Analytic Narratives* (Princeton, New Jersey, Princeton University Press, 1998), pp. 3–18.

94. Pierson, 'Increasing Returns, Path Dependence, and the Study of Politics', pp. 253–9.

95. Ibid., pp. 265–6.

96. Readers may think that I am contradicting myself by saying that ISI perpetuates itself and its destruction. The literature describing the complexity of causal mechanisms shows that the same cause may have two different kinds of impact on the effect. What is therefore critical is the net impact on the effect. See Elster, *Alchemies of the Mind*, chap. 1.

97. See Jeffry Frieden, 'Actors and Preferences in International Relations', in David A. Lake and Robert Powell (eds), *Strategic Choice and International Relations*, (Princeton, New Jersey, Princeton University Press, 1999).

98. Helen V. Milner, 'Rationalizing Politics,' *International Organization*, 52, 4, Fall (1998), pp. 772–86.

99. Jack L. Snyder, 'East-West Bargaining Over Germany', in Evans et al. *Double-Edged Diplomacy*, pp. 104–5.

100. Pierson, 'Increasing Returns, Path Dependence, and the Study of Politics', pp. 264–5.

101. See Hal Hill, *The Indonesian Economy Since 1966* (New York, Cambridge University Press, 1996), pp. 73–6; Andrew MacIntyre, *Business and*

Politics in Indonesia (Singapore, Allen and Unwin, 1991), pp. 11–14; John Bresnan, 'Indonesia', in Robert Chase, Emily Hill and Paul Kennedy (eds), *The Pivotal States* (New York, Norton, 1998), pp. 17–18; and Vedi R. Hediz, *Workers and The State* (London, Routledge, 1997), pp. 59–76.

102. See Ronald M. Schneider, *Brazil: Culture and Politics* (Colorado, Westview Press, 1996), pp. 114–18; Ben R. Schneider, 'Brazil under Collor', in Roderic A. Camp (ed.), *Democracy in Latin America* (Wilimington, Delaware, Jaguar Books, 1996), pp. 227–8; Lourdes Sola, 'The State, Structural Reform, and Democratization', in William C. Smith, Carlos S. Acuna, Eduardo A. Gamarra and Carol Gables (eds), *Democracy, Markets and Structural Reform in Latin America* (Miami, Florida, The University of Miami North-South Center, 1994); Leigh A. Payne, *Brazilian Industrialists and Democratic Change* (Baltimore, The Johns Hopkins University Press, 1994), chaps. 4–5; and Youssef Cohen, *The Manipulation of Consent* (Pittsburgh, University of Pittsburgh Press, 1989), chap. 7.

103. On India's response to the crisis in 1966, see Mukherji (2000); on India's response to the IMF program between 1981 and 1984, see James Boughton, *Silent Revolution: The International Monetary Fund: 1979-1989* (Washington D.C., IMF, 2001).

104. On the design of IMF programmes emphasizing country ownership of programs, see Mohsin S. Khan and Sunil Sharma, 'IMF Conditionality and Country Ownership of Programs', *IMF Working Paper* 01/142 (Washington D.C., IMF, 2001). See also Joseph Stiglitz, *Globalization and Its Discontents* (London, Allen Lane, 2002).

5

Mass Politics or Elite Politics?
Understanding the Politics of
India's Economic Reforms[*]

ASHUTOSH VARSHNEY

This chapter addresses two questions: (i) why was India's minority government in 1991 successful in introducing economic reforms, whereas a much stronger government, with a three-fourths majority in parliament, was unable to do so in 1985? and (ii) why have post-1991 reforms made substantial progress in some areas but stalled in others? In answering the two questions, my argument draws a distinction between mass politics and elite politics. It is a distinction that has not been adequately appreciated in the truly voluminous literature on the politics of economic reforms.[1] Scholars of economic reforms have generally assumed that reforms are, or tend to become, central to politics. Depending on what else is making demands on the energies of the electorate and politicians—ethnic and religious strife, political order and stability, corruption and 'crimes' of the incumbents—the assumption of reform centrality may not be right. The main battle lines in politics may be drawn on issues such as how to avoid (or promote) further escalation of ethnic conflict, whether to support (or oppose) political leaders if there has been an attempted coup, or whether to forgive (or punish) the 'crimes' of high state officials. Paradoxically, it may be easier to push through reforms in

* Originally published as 'Mass Politics or Elite Politics?: India's Economic Reforms in Comparative Perspective', in Jeffrey D. Sachs, Ashutosh Varshney, and Nirupam Bajpai (eds), *India in the Era of Economic Reforms*, New Delhi, Oxford University Press, 1999, pp. 222–60.

a context like this, for politicians and the electorate are occupied by matters they consider more critical. Economic reforms may not in such a context cause the political opposition they otherwise would.

Elite politics is typically expressed in debates and struggles within the institutionalized settings of a bureaucracy, a parliament, a cabinet. Mass politics takes place primarily on the streets. Touched off by issues that unleash citizen passions and emotions, the characteristic forms of mass politics include large-scale agitations, demonstrations, and civil disobedience: riots and assassinations are also not excluded. Whether or not we like such politics, it has profound consequences. In democracies, especially poor democracies, mass politics can redefine elite politics, for an accumulated expression of popular sentiments and opinions inevitably exercises a great deal of pressure on elected politicians. Elite concerns—investment tax breaks, stock market regulations, custom duties on imported cars—do not necessarily filter down to mass politics.

What, analytically speaking, determines whether a policy—economic, cultural, or political—would enter mass politics? Three factors are typically decisive: (a) how many people are affected by the policy, (b) how organized they are, and (c) whether the effect is direct, obvious, and short-run, or indirect, subtle and long-run. The more direct the effect of a policy, the more people are affected by it, and the more organized they are, the greater the potential for mass politics.

Ethnic disputes tend to enter mass politics quickly because they isolate a whole group, or several groups, on an ascriptive basis. They also directly concern political parties—both ethnically based parties (which may defend, or repel attacks on, their ethnic group) and multi-ethnic parties (which may fiercely fight attempts to pull some ethnic groups away from their rainbow coalitions). Because they invoke ascriptive, not voluntary, considerations, the effect of ethnic cleavages and ethnically based policies are obvious to most people and, more often than not, ethnic groups are also organized, or tend to organize quickly. Not all aspects of economic policy invoke passions and have such effects; some do, others do not. For example, by affecting more or less everybody, high inflation quickly gets inserted into mass politics.[2] Contrariwise, capital markets directly concern only the shareholders, whose numbers in most developing economies are not likely to be large and who may not be organized. As a result, stock-market disputes rarely enter mass politics in developing countries.[3] Other examples of economic policies that can enter mass politics are discussed later.

It is important to keep these considerations in mind because in large parts of the developing world, two different political processes—one provoked by ethnic conflicts and the other stemming from market-oriented economic reforms—are simultaneously under way. However, scholars of economic reform and their counterparts in the field of ethnicity and nationalism have on the whole constituted two separate groups. Such segregation has made the discussion of the politics of economic reform unduly restrictive. In multi-ethnic societies, economics may simply be one of several issues on the political agenda, and not always the most contested one. Ethnicity may be more contested, stirring mass passions and determining alignments of political parties.

Consider the evidence from India. In the largest-ever survey of mass political attitudes in India conducted between April and July 1996, only 19 per cent of the electorate reported any knowledge of economic reforms, even though reforms had been in existence since July 1991.[4] Of the rural electorate, only about 14 per cent had heard of reforms, whereas the comparable proportion in the cities was 32 per cent. Further, nearly 66 per cent of the graduates were aware of the dramatic changes in economic policy, compared to only 7 per cent of the poor, who are mostly illiterate. In contrast, close to three-fourths of the electorate—both literates and illiterates, poor and rich, urban and rural—were aware of the 1992 mosque demolition in Ayodhya; 80 per cent expressed clear opinions about whether the country should have a uniform civil code or religiously prescribed and separate laws for marriage, divorce, and property inheritance; and 87 per cent took a stand on caste-based affirmative action.

These statistics should clarify that the raging debate over economic reforms in India is, for all practical purposes, confined to the English-language newspapers, the country's graduates, the discourse on the internet, the Bombay stock market, and Delhi's India International Centre and its economic ministries. That is the circle of India's elite politics. Economic reforms were simply a non-issue in the 1996 and 1998 elections.[5] Ethnic and religious disputes, secularism, caste-based affirmative action, and social justice have been driving India's mass politics over the last 10–15 years. Expressions of India's identity politics, these issues have led mass mobilization, insurgencies, riots, assassinations, and desecrations and destructions of holy places. In mass perceptions, the significance of identities has been far greater than the implications of economic reforms.[6]

Is India peculiar in this respect? Has the predominance of identity politics hurt India's economic reforms? Are there elements in the reform package that can bring it into mass politics? My answer, and the principal argument of this chapter, is that the passions aroused by identity politics have facilitated economic reforms in India, not hurt them. How to stop Hindu nationalists from gaining politically and coming to power was the primary concern of most mainstream political parties between 1990–1 and 1997–8. New alignments of political interests thus came into being. Whether or not politicians in the past were opposed to a market-oriented liberalization, they increasingly began to support reforms once it became clear that it was more important to fight Hindu nationalists on questions of religious politics versus secularism than to oppose the government of the day on economic reforms. *The political logic induced by explosions of communal passions gave the reformers room to push reforms.*

The same logic has, however, also defined the limits of economic reforms. Afraid that the masses and their own party cadres or supporters might turn against their parties, India's reformers have failed to privatize the public sector, restructure labour laws, introduce agricultural reforms, and reduce fiscal deficits to low levels.[7] These policy areas can potentially bring reforms in mass politics, which the reformers have resisted. Instead, considerable overall progress has been made on liberalizing the investment, trade, and exchange-rate regimes and on reforming capital markets. Touching very few people *in India* directly and in the short run, these latter reforms have been an elite concern, though elsewhere in the developing world they may well be an integral part of mass politics.[8]

My argument should not be construed normatively. It is primarily empirical and explanatory. It is not a celebration of ethnic conflicts, rigid labour laws, or sick public enterprises. Rather, it is an attempt to understand, and explain, why India's politicians have behaved very differently with respect to the various aspects of reform, embracing some policies warmly but showing great caution on others. The elite–mass distinction is simply to disaggregate politics and present an explanation for these puzzling, varying rhythms. In the reform literature, both on India and elsewhere, the intra-elite distinctions—for example, conflicts between the ISI-protected versus exporting sectors—have often been noted, but elite–mass differences have not been.[9] At least in a democracy, the latter differences can be a serious issue in politics.

The first section of this chapter explains why a conjunction of ethnic conflict and economic reform helped India's reformers in 1991. The second section turns its attention on why, despite a remarkable transformation of economic policy overall, India has had inadequate or little success with fiscal balances, labour laws, agriculture, and privatization. The concluding section draws some normative conclusions.

DID ETHNIC CONFLICT HELP INDIA'S REFORMS? COMPARING REFORMS UNDER RAJIV GANDHI AND NARASIMHA RAO

By now it has become customary to say that India's reforms are irreversible. It is hard to recall how gloomy the reform prospects were in July 1991. Lacking a majority in parliament, the Rao government did not even seem stable; only six years earlier, the Rajiv Gandhi government had, despite enjoying a massive majority in parliament, found it politically hard to push market-oriented reforms. India's new finance minister in July 1991, Manmohan Singh, though a highly respected economic bureaucrat, was not a professional politician. Many members of the Congress party were resentful of his rise to power, for he had never been a party man. The country was going through massive Hindu-Muslim upheaval on the one hand and serious dispute over caste-based affirmative action on the other. To make matters worse, two insurgencies—one in Punjab, another in Kashmir—were showing no signs of abatement. The nation's head of government, Rajiv Gandhi, had been brutally assassinated in the recent past. Let alone reform optimism, many commentators were concerned whether India would even make it as a nation in the 1990s.

As it turned out, despite lacking a clear majority in parliament, the Rao government was able to push many of reforms on which Rajiv Gandhi's government, even with a three-fourths majority, had had to retrace its steps in 1986. Unless the logic of this paradoxical outcome is uncovered, it will be hard to understand the political dynamics of economic reforms in India. I will argue that the economic crisis in 1991 was a necessary, not sufficient, condition for the success of reforms. In turning crisis into success, the differences in the *political context* of the two reforms were critical.

Rajiv Gandhi's Stalled Reforms (1985–9)[10]

In December 1984, two months after the assassination of Indira Gandhi, her son Rajiv Gandhi led the Congress party (the Congress hereafter) to its biggest election victory since independence. Winning 48.1 per cent of the national vote, the Congress obtained 415 out of a total of 545 seats in the lower house of Indian parliament. No opposition party could get more than 30 seats (see Table 5.1).[11]

For the new leadership, it was a moment of unrivalled power. With a remarkable groundswell of support behind it and the opposition more or less decimated, the new government felt it had considerable autonomy to institute new, market-oriented policies and programmes. Like Rajiv Gandhi himself, some of the closest associates of the new leader came from a corporate background,[12] and many of the top positions in the economic bureaucracy also went to those inclined towards pro-market economic liberalization. It was an archetypical strong executive that the reform literature considers necessary for successful economic reform.[13]

Table 5.1: Party positions in the lower house of Parliament, 1984–9 and 1991–6

Party	Seats 1984–9	Seats 1991–2	Seats 1992–6
Congress	415	220	232
BJP	2	120	120
Janata	10	59	59
CPM	22	35	35
CPI	6	14	14
TDP	30	3	13
ADMK	12	11	11
Others	46	52	53
Total	543	524	537

Notes: (i) Elections were not held in Jammu and Kashmir at all, bringing the total seats in the Lok Sabha down to 537 in the 10th Lok Sabha (1991–6). Jammu and Kashmir has six seats in the lower house.
(ii) Elections in Punjab (13 seats) were held in February 1992, and results announced in March 1992. Column II does not, therefore, include the seats in Punjab. The figures for 1992–6 include the results of the 1991 elections and the 1992 Punjab elections.
Source: Election Commission of India, various publications.

The new leadership quickly seized the opportunity and set about restructuring the country's economic policy. The first indication of the new thrust was given by the Prime Minister himself. In January 1985, within weeks of assuming power, Rajiv Gandhi argued:

Only a few decades ago, made-in-Japan was synonymous with shoddy goods. Today, and for several years past, Japanese technology, finish and servicing have become a byword for the best that is available....I am sure we in India can do the same—and in a much shorter period. And this will, of course, involve close interaction with the outside world....We are taking a judicious combination of deregulation, import liberalization and easier access to foreign technology.[14]

Two months later, in February 1985, Finance Minister V.P. Singh presented his budgetary proposals for 1985–6. The budget delicensed several industries;[15] increased the ceiling of investment by the big business houses;[16] relaxed rules for importation of foreign technology; sought to replace quantitative trade restrictions with tariffs and lowered tariff barriers overall;[17] reduced marginal tax rates on personal and corporate income, and simplified tax rules; and, finally, announced that public sector reform was necessary. Soon after the budget, Rajiv Gandhi personally launched a critique of the import substitution strategy (ISI): 'There was no point in developing each and every component...(especially if) a component priced at a few dollars abroad was manufactured locally at an exorbitant cost.'[18]

Indian politics had not earlier seen such forthright criticisms of the ISI by the prime minister.[19] The metropolitan press was ecstatic. 'Towards a New Era', editorialized *The Times of India* on its front page on 17 March 1985. Abroad, in an editorial entitled 'Rajiv Reagan', *The Wall Street Journal* wrote:

Anyone who thinks the world never learns from experience ought to look at what's happening in India these days. Prime Minister Rajiv Gandhi's new government introduced its first budget last weekend, slashing taxes and cutting regulations in a way worthy of another famous tax cutter we know. The budget amounts to a minor revolution for a country long enamored of a socialist mirage.[20]

The opposition came, first of all, from the expected quarters: the leftist parties,[21] trade unions, and left-wing economists who had traditionally dominated India's economic thinking and bureaucracy. However, with the euphoria of new government continuing, these opponents were unable to deflect the government from its new economic path. Dissent in parliament was ineffective; the opposition parties had, after all, been virtually wiped out. Elite politics was firmly in control of Rajiv Gandhi's men.

With parliamentary arithmetic so dominated by the new regime, factions *within* the ruling Congress could have been an effective source of dissent, playing in effect the role of opposition. However, so soon after Rajiv Gandhi's massive victory, intra-party dissent was still in its formative stage.[22]

The party was, moreover, beholden to its leader for a most authoritative electoral triumph.

In January 1986, a year after the elections, an economic opening for mass politics finally emerged. Indeed, it was provided 'on a platter' by a confident economic policy team. To take reforms further and attack fiscal imbalances, the Rajiv Gandhi government announced several new measures. Subsidies on petroleum and petroleum products, food, and fertilizer were scaled down.[23] To underline the importance of cutting government expenditure, especially subsidies, a long-term fiscal policy was announced. Defending the cuts in the subsidy for foodgrain and fertilizers, the finance minister said that 'the issue was subsidy versus investment. The subsidies had gone up to astronomical levels...',[24] adding, 'the prices of kerosene and cooking gas are less than their production costs.'[25]

Even as market-oriented economists and the business press applauded the continuing thrust, a political revolt began. Since the prices of some key commodities of mass consumption—food, fertilizer, and petroleum products like kerosene—had been raised, the opposition argued that the government was insensitive to the needs of the poor. It mobilized the people for protests, and called strikes. Protests in various big cities drew large crowds.[26] It was the first nationwide protest since the new government's assumption of power 14 months earlier.[27] The success of the mobilization alarmed the rank and file of the ruling Congress party. It also finally gave state-level (as well as some national-level) leaders a chance to express dissent. Some party members threatened to speak out openly against the government in parliament.[28] Others met the prime minister in groups. And still others wrote against the new policies in the press: 'Rightly or wrongly, the impression is gaining ground that the policies of the government are leaning more toward the rich and the private corporate sector is the only major concern of the government.'[29]

Given the intensity of mass reaction and dissent of party members, the Congress government offered to lower the cuts in subsidy. The administrative prices of foodgrain, fertilizer, and petroleum and petroleum products nonetheless registered a net increase, for the cuts were lowered, not eliminated. Such reductions, which left prices higher than they were before the government changed them, were hardly enough to silence the opposition. Indeed, the price increase provided new life and new bases of support to the weak opposition parties. The argument that the new leaders were pro-rich acquired a momentum of its own in the press and, more importantly, in the political process. The new government had, after all, cut taxes on corporate and personal income in the previous year, and now it was raising prices of mass consumption goods.[30]

From this point onwards, as Kohli (1987: 316) has argued, 'the society...hit back: the state lost the temporary autonomy it had gained.' The government began to make compromises. The next budget in 1987 increased allocations for poverty alleviation programmes, restored the earlier level of fertilizer and food subsidies, disallowed across-the-board cuts in excise duties, and made tariffs on capital goods higher.[31] The last two budgets of the Rajiv Gandhi government—1988 and 1989—continued the same process.[32]

Asked in 1988 why deeper reforms were not being launched, Rajiv Gandhi's chief economic advisor argued that *there seems little room for too many more concessions.*[33] By 1988, Rajiv Gandhi himself was convinced that 'the process has to be gradual', even though the direction he had selected for the country was right.[34] Only a couple of years earlier, he had been willing to confront 'vested interests in almost every field...including our own party, including industry, in business, in administration, the whole lot, the farmers'.[35]

The Success of the Rao Government (1991–6)

The progress of reforms since 1991 is a study in contrast. Compared to Rajiv Gandhi, Prime Minister Narasimha Rao was weak in parliament. Unlike Rajiv Gandhi's three-fourths majority in parliament, the Rao government did not have majority support when it came to power in July 1991. It added some more seats to its strength in March 1992 but it was still short of a majority (see Table 5.1). Yet, whereas Rajiv Gandhi delicensed only a few industries, the Rao government delicensed all but a few. Rajiv Gandhi lowered corporate and personal income taxes: the Rao government reduced them further. Average tariff rate was 87 per cent when Rajiv lost power: it was brought down to 25 per cent in 1995 through successive reductions. Under Rajiv, capital markets had no foreign investors: under Rao, foreign portfolio institutions were allowed, rules for FDI were liberalized, and in 'key' sectors, such as power, 100 per cent foreign ownership was permitted. Finally, unlike Rajiv Gandhi, the Rao government had to sign a stabilization agreement with the IMF, which is often politically controversial in the developing world. Arguments about the Rao government mortgaging the nation's economic sovereignty could easily be made.

Why, then, was the Rao government more successful? There is no doubt that the external crisis of 1991 opened the way for reforms. In and of itself, however, the depth of the crisis cannot sustain reforms. It is necessary to know how the crisis was perceived and resolved in India's political institutions. A serious change in economic policies cannot be authorized by an executive decree if parliamentary approval is a requirement. Was the latter necessary in India's political process?

Because a restructured economic policy is reflected in national budgets, and national budgets must be approved in parliament, economic reforms must necessarily pass parliamentary scrutiny in India. Unlike a presidential system, in a parliamentary system the government will most likely fall if the national budget is not approved in the legislature. *If India's parliament had not passed the budgets, the new economic policies would have been stillborn, not because of faulty economic logic but due to the institutional constraints of a parliamentary system.* Why did India's parliament, in which the Congress government did not have majority support between 1991 and 1993, pass the budgets in September 1991, May 1992, and May 1993? These three budgets contained the bulk of India's reforms.

The debate on the first two budgets—in July-August 1991 and March-April 1992—was bitter and charged.[36] Opposition politicians made trenchant arguments in parliament about the actual or impending loss of economic sovereignty to the IMF and the World Bank. In February 1992 it was alleged that the budget proposals had been submitted to the IMF for its prior permission before being presented to India's parliament. 'None of us ever thought that India will one day come to depend on the mercy of the IMF and the World Bank,' said the parliamentary leader of the BJP.[37] 'The sovereignty of parliament has been breached and the economy of the country had been subjected at the feet of the World Bank and IMF,' said the leader of the third largest party and former prime minister.[38] 'Will all the conditionalities which are being imposed on us, be imposed on the US, if their budgetary deficit is twenty times more than that of ours?' said a third important opposition leader.[39]

A second set of political criticisms was about the pro-rich and pro-urban orientation of the new policies. 'I would call this budget anti-poor, anti-farmer, anti-development, and pro-inflation,' argued an important member.[40] 'The Government television...[is] propagating unlimited consumerism of big companies through advertisements,' argued another.[41] Finally, there was the apprehension that reform would lead to retrenchment from public sector undertakings. 'What is going to be the result of all this? 9 lakh workers belonging to public sector banks will be unemployed in the next two years....Where will they find jobs?'[42]

Yet, despite these criticisms by leaders of all major non-Congress parties, the first three budgets of the Congress government (1991, 1992, and 1993) were passed. All opposition politicians were willing to launch criticisms, but only some were willing to block the budget at the time of voting and unseat the government.

Why did opposition politicians vigorously criticize the budget but not vote against it? Let us recall the political context of 1991–2. The Rao government had initiated reforms at a time when Hindu nationalism was a rising force. In 1991, having 120 seats in parliament, the Hindu nationalist BJP was the second largest party in the country. In 1990, it had led the movement for the demolition of the Babri mosque, touching off ghastly Hindu-Muslim riots, polarizing the electorate and national politics, and causing a great deal of anxiety about law and order in the country. Out of a total of 524 elected members in the lower house in July-September 1991, the Congress party had 220 seats, as also the support of 11 members of a regional party (ADMK), bringing the aggregate of its house support to 231, whereas 263 was the halfway—and winning—mark. Similarly, at the time of vote on the next budget in May 1992, the Congress tally of seats had gone up to 232 out of a total of 537 seats. Combined with 13 seats of pro-Congress regional parties, it had 245 votes in all, 24 short of a majority (Table 5.1). The 1991, 1992, and 1993 budgets would have been blocked and reforms stalled if the remaining opposition parties had coordinated their moves and jointly voted against the government.

They did not do so because by 1990, India's politics had become *triangular*.[43] Between 1950 and 1990, the principal battle-lines of politics were *bipolar*. The Congress was the party of government, and all other parties were opposed to it. Between 1990 and 1997, a triangular contest developed between the left, the Hindu nationalists, and the Congress. Coalitions were increasingly formed against the Hindu nationalists, not against the Congress. To begin with, the left—the Communists and the lower-caste Janata Dal and its allies—disliked the reforms, but *they disliked Hindu nationalism even more*. Especially to the lower-caste Janata Dal, Hindu nationalism posed the greatest threat. The Janata Dal wanted to organize the lower Hindu castes against the upper castes, whereas Hindu nationalists were trying to build a united Hindu community against the Muslims, seeking to override and displace caste as an issue in political mobilization. The triumph of one implied the eclipse of the other. The Congress party, a foe in the past but declining ideologically, was no longer the principal enemy of the Janata Dal.

For the Janata, then, economic reforms were secondary in importance. For the Bharatiya Janata Party (BJP), too, building a temple in Ayodhya, the campaign for which had brought such remarkable electoral dividends, was much more important than the economic reforms. Both the Janata and the BJP bitterly criticized several aspects of the reforms in 1991 and 1992, but neither was prepared to issue a 'parliamentary whip' to its party members in the house to vote against the budget. (On matters of high political importance, such whips are issued to enforce party discipline in voting.) The vote on the budget being left to their conscience, some Janata members would vote against the reform, others in favour, and some would simply abstain. The same was true of the BJP in 1991 and 1992.[44] Coordinated voting between the BJP and Janata and its allies was necessary to defeat the budget, but that did not happen. The 1991 and 1992 budgets, as a result, received parliamentary approval despite the Congress lacking majority in the lower house.

Once Hindu nationalists demolished the mosque at Ayodhya in December 1992, the Janata and its allies became even more convinced that Hindu nationalists had to be contained. Most Janata members voted in favour of the 1993 budget, whereas all BJP members present in parliament opposed the budget for the first time.[45] That was not enough to defeat the budget: full floor coordination between the various opposition parties was required. Thus, three annual budgets, embodying the bulk of India's post-1991 reforms, were passed in India's parliament. *India's economic reforms kept progressing because the political context had made Hindu-Muslim relations and caste animosities the prime determinant of political coalitions.*

The political context in 1985–6 was very different. Rajiv Gandhi did face a Hindu-Sikh cleavage in the state of Punjab, but this never had the same nationwide intensity as the Hindu-Muslim divide, being confined to north India. Moreover, in 1985 Rajiv Gandhi had already concluded an agreement with Sikh politicians for peaceful resolution of Sikh demands. The agreement would unravel in 1988 and violence would touch dangerous levels. But 1985 and 1986 were years of cooled passions. The BJP had a mere two seats in parliament, the movement for the demolition of the mosque was still to take off, and the Kashmir insurgency was not on the horizon. In a political context of this kind, when economic reforms were introduced, politicians could easily use the price of food, fertilizer, and petroleum for mass mobilization.

To sum up, economic liberalization became a victim of its splendid solitude on the political agenda in 1985–6. In 1991, economic reforms were crowded out of mass politics by issues that aroused greater passion and anxiety about the nation. Because they were crowded out, reforms could go as far as they did.

WHY SOME REFORMS, NOT OTHERS?

Let me now turn to a different question. Why have some reforms been successfully executed, but others neglected or unsuccessfully pursued? Economic logic alone cannot explain the selectivity and rhythm of reforms. Reforms that touch elite politics, directly or primarily, have gone the farthest: a large devaluation of the currency, a restructuring of capital markets, a liberalization of the trade regime, and a simplification of investment rules. Reforms that are economically desirable but concern mass politics have been of two types: those that have positive political consequences in mass politics (for example, inflation control) and those that have potentially negative or highly uncertain consequences in mass politics (labour laws, privatization of the public sector, agriculture). The former have been implemented with single-minded determination; the latter have either been completely ignored or pursued with less than exemplary policy resolve (for example, fiscal balances).

What arguments can be given in support of the claims above? Why are some economic issues part of elite politics, others of mass politics? To recall an earlier argument, at least three factors determine the political placement of reforms: (a) how many people are affected, (b) how organized they are, and (c) whether the effect is direct and short-run or indirect and long-run. The more direct the effect of an economic policy, the more people are affected by it and the more organized they are, the greater the potential for mass politics. Thus inflation, by affecting everybody with the exception of those whose salaries are inflation-indexed, quickly becomes part of mass politics. Affecting fewer but still large numbers of people who are, moreover, organized, a change in labour laws and privatization of public enterprises also bring reforms into mass politics. Similarly, agriculture remains politically sensitive, partly because farm lobbies have become strong in the last twenty years;[46] and partly because few understand what the benefits of agricultural reforms are, whereas everyone knows where the cuts will be made—namely, in producer, fertilizer, irrigation, and credit subsidies. Contrariwise, given India's low external dependence and relatively closed economy till 1991, currency devaluations and trade reforms could affect very few people. Investment liberalization, similarly, could hurt the heavily protected industrialists and licence-giving bureaucrats, not the masses. And capital markets directly concern shareholders, still a small proportion of the population.

Inflation

The mid-1960s and early 1970s were about the only two times in post-1947 India when annual inflation rates reached 20 per cent, low by Latin American standards but the highest-ever in independent India. Since food prices constituted a very large share of the consumer price index and so many people were close to the poverty line, the rise in food prices led to widespread hunger, raising fears of famine and provoking food riots.

What were the political results? In the 1967 elections, the ruling Congress party was defeated in many states for the first time. And in 1973–4, despite a large Congress majority in parliament, strikes, demonstrations, and anti-government movements made it difficult for the Congress party to govern the country.[47] That is why it is often said that India has low inflation tolerance. Until incomes increase substantially, reducing markedly the share of food expenses in a typical household budget, no serious politician in India can allow the annual inflation rate to touch 20 per cent or allow it to stay in double digits for very long.

It should not be surprising that attacking inflation was a matter of macroeconomic priority for Finance Minister Singh when he took office,[48] a task at which he succeeded remarkably. Between 1991–2 and 1995–6, the annual inflation rate declined from about 13–14 per cent to 4.5 per cent.[49] The voter surveys of 1991 had shown that prices were a matter of great concern, competing with the mosque in Ayodhya and affirmative action.[50] In 1996, prices were not an issue in the elections.[51]

The inflation control policy has not been an unmitigated blessing. Its sins and blessings yet again reflect the difference between mass and elite politics. Tight money supply was the primary vehicle of inflation control,[52] which led to higher interest rates, making capital for investment expensive.[53] The government was less worried about high interest rates, which are of considerable concern to businessmen, than about bringing down the inflation rate. The former, needless to add, is of direct relevance to elite politics only; the latter is an acute concern in mass politics.

Liberalization of Capital Markets, Trade and Exchange Rate Regimes

Compared to inflation, consider now the effects of capital markets. Though the numbers of stockholders in India may have risen greatly of late, India's capital markets even today affect a very small segment of the population. Stock markets make headlines in business magazines, not vernacular dailies. The latter find stock markets newsworthy if and only if scams involving leading politicians are strongly suspected. Reforms of capital markets do not yet concern the masses. Corruption of the political elite, if demonstrable, is the link through which they read or hear about stock markets.[54]

What of trade liberalization and currency devaluation? Are they necessarily part of elite politics? In countries like Mexico, they are known to have seriously affected mass politics. In Venezuela, they were followed by a military coup, and a link between reforms and the coup was explicitly made.[55]

Were a country's economy heavily dependent on foreign trade, a lowering of tariff walls, a reduction in quantitative trade restrictions and a devaluation of the currency would be of great concern to the masses, for it would immediately affect mass welfare. In 1996, trade constituted more than 50 per cent of the GDP of Singapore, Malaysia, Thailand, the Philippines, Mexico, Hungary, South Korea, Poland, and Venezuela, and between 40 and 50 per cent of the GDP of Israel, Chile, China, and Indonesia. Changes, especially dramatic changes in the trade and exchange-rate regimes of these countries have a clear potential for mass politics. However, if trade is a small part of the economy, as has been true of India and Brazil historically, changes in trade and exchange rate regimes tend not to be direct and of short-run importance to the masses.[56]

One can argue that even if the trade dependence of an economy is small, several long-run or indirect linkages can be shown to exist between mass welfare on the one hand and overvalued exchange rates or relatively closed trade regimes on the other. Anne Krueger, for example, has argued that by making 'import competing' industrial goods dearer for the countryside and also discouraging exports, ISI-type trade and exchange rate regimes systematically discriminated against the countryside all over the developing world.[57] The implication is that a majority, or large plurality, of the developing countries' population was hurt. Thus even when trade is a small part of the economy, trade regimes can have an effect on mass welfare, not simply elite welfare.

Why, then, have agrarian politicians in most developing countries rarely, if ever, agitated for an open foreign trade regime, focusing instead on the unfavourable urban-rural trade which may, as Krueger argues, have caused less overall damage? The answer should be clear by now. If such *indirect links* were not even clear to economists, who continued until the 1970s to look at rural welfare primarily from the viewpoint of internal terms of trade, how can a politician be expected to mobilize peasants over the underlying and subtle, though hugely important, links between foreign trade and mass welfare in a poor country? *Underlying long-run and indirect links do not work well in mass politics: the effect has to be simple, intuitively graspable, clearly visible, and capable of arousing mass action.* It is easy to demonstrate the differences, or links, between urban privileges and rural misery, but rather hard to make the connections between foreign trade and rural poverty. The latter has, of course, been an article of faith in elite politics in recent years, as international financial institutions have sought to change the economic discourse of policy-makers in the developing world.

Privatization and Labour Laws

India's central government is a majority shareholder in 240 enterprises, 27 banks, and 2 large insurance companies. Only some of these enterprises generate profits. To reduce public sector expenditures, the government is pushing public sector companies to raise resources from capital markets instead of providing them with budgetary hand-outs. But very few loss-making public sector companies have yet been sold by the central government. Despite the fiscal burden, privatization so far has been basically a non-starter. In June 1998, seven years after the reforms were introduced, the government finally announced its intention to push through privatization, but it did not go very far.

It should be noted, first of all, that on economic grounds alone, privatization, while desirable, may not be as critical in India as in Eastern Europe where the private sector did not exist. Since India has a long-established private sector, it has had the option to attach greater importance (compared to privatization) to increasing deregulation of the private sector and to an end of government monopolies in banking and infrastructure. In China, too, the state first deregulated the economy, embracing privatization only later.

The hurdles for privatization are primarily political in India. Given the overstaffing of the public sector and of older private sector units, privatization will entail massive lay-offs. As a result, labour in the organized sector is opposed to privatization. Compared to the unorganized and rural sectors, which account for 90 per cent of the workforce, the labour force in organized industry and services may be small in terms of numbers. But in absolute terms, it is sufficiently large and, more critically, it is also unionized. In 1992, about 20 million people were employed in the public sector and 8 million in the organized private sector. A confrontational relationship, especially between the government and public sector unions, can bring banks, railways, telecommunications, and coal and steel production to a virtual halt, and create serious political turmoil. This is not simply a theoretical point. A large railways strike in May 1975 was the immediate occasion for the suspension of democracy and for India's only authoritarian phase, which luckily lasted only eighteen months. *Unlike Mexico where a long-standing, corporatist relationship exists between the ruling party, PRI, and labour unions, and Argentina where the Peronist government has had influence over the labour movement, no single political party in India controls the unions.* An agreement between the unions and government on the necessity of retrenchment cannot be assumed. Its possibilities have to be creatively imagined and worked upon.

Moreover, in a society where millions are unemployed, the economic idea of firing existing employees on grounds of rationality is hard to present politically. There is deep irony in this situation. It can be argued that the privileges of the organized workforce are a significant explanation for why employment in India has not grown as much as the economic and industrial growth rates since the early 1980s would seem to warrant. If labour markets had been more flexible, there would have been greater employment in the country. Turning this economic logic into political rhetoric, however, requires statesmanship, or an exceptional political period when the government's popularity or legitimacy is very high. As far as the average person is concerned, it is the government's responsibility to create jobs, not take them away. It is not easy to convince the electorate that taking away jobs today is equal to giving better jobs back tomorrow. Moreover, a large proportion of the organized working class still has rural links: organizing a large part of the electorate, let us say the peasantry, is easier if the target is the state, not if the target is the industrial working class. In other words, both for ideological reasons and for the difficulties of coalition building against organized workers, a reform in labour laws or privatization poses serious political difficulties.

Can privatization be, and be shown to be, socially sensitive? Must workers be fired in a privatization programme, or can they be kept? If privatization can somehow be decoupled from large-scale retrenchment, it will be easy to make a political case for it. If not, it is likely to be launched in sectors not critical to mass politics—for example, hotels and tourist businesses, not banks and railways. Politically it will be easier to launch a bigger privatization programme after the economy has started generating enough jobs,[58] or if a large enough structural renewal fund can be created providing social security and funds for retraining.[59]

CONCLUSION

Concentrating on India's economic reforms and drawing examples from other reforming and democratic countries, this chapter has argued that if we wish to understand why some reforms are successfully initiated and implemented while others get stalled in a democracy, it will be helpful to draw a distinction between mass politics and elite politics. Mass politics often tends to be more pressing in a democracy than elite politics, as politicians must periodically renew their popular mandates, a requirement with which authoritarian governments are not routinely burdened. While at the time of elections, popular considerations may be absolutely compelling in a democracy, even between elections a vibrant and free civil society has the capacity to mobilize and press the government against reforms that, though providing benefits to the masses in the long run, may entail short-run costs. Those reforms which do not easily enter mass politics—investment liberalization or trade and exchange-rate reform in an economy where the trade–GDP ratio is low—are easier to push through than privatization, elimination of fiscal deficits, and a reform of labour laws to make labour markets flexible. The latter set of reforms inevitably affects a large number of people directly and in the short run. Trade reforms in economies that have high trade–GDP ratios may also easily enter mass politics, but that is not so in all economies. The existing trade dependence of an economy determines whether trade reforms will trigger mass politics and large-scale political mobilization.

Popular resistance can, however, be overcome if some other policies, or political issues, that can generate support for the government are also on the agenda, and are, compared to economic reforms, able to attract greater popular attention. One can, for example, show that ethnic conflicts in many pluralistic societies are more likely to arouse mass passions than disputes over economic reforms. Paradoxically, the relegation of reforms to a secondary political status can work to the advantage of reformers, for mass preoccupation with ethnic issues provides political room to push reforms. The biggest lesson of India's economic reforms, as well as other reforms briefly surveyed in this chapter, is that given a *multiplicity* of salient political issues, even minority governments can press ahead with economic reforms. Contrariwise, strong governments, with solid majorities in the legislature, can fumble if reforms become the sole focus of political contestation in a country.

It is often argued in economic circles that if only politicians paid greater attention to economic issues, economic reforms would be so much easier or more successful. That argument may work well in authoritarian settings, but has only limited relevance in democracies. Whether or not reforms succeed in democracies depends not only on how the government leverages its popular support, a point well understood, but also on the availability of political issues not related to reforms occupying popular attention and mass energies.

NOTES AND REFERENCES

1. This is also true of the two most comprehensive and widely read political economy texts on reform: Stephan Haggard and Robert Kaufmann, *Political Economy of Democratic Transitions*, (Princeton, New Jersey, Princeton University Press, 1995); and Adam Przeworski, *Democracy and the Market*, (New York, Cambridge University Press, 1991).

2. With the exception of those whose incomes are protected by inflation indexation.

3. Again, in countries where mass privatizations have taken place and shares have been distributed to the masses, this may not be true.

4. Yogendra Yadav and V. B. Singh, 'Maturing of a Democracy', *India Today,* 15 August 1996. The survey was conducted by Yadav and Singh on behalf of the Centre for the Study of Developing Societies (CSDS), India's premier research institution for election studies. For the larger audiences, the findings were summarized in *India Today,* 31 August 1996. All figures cited below are from the CSDS survey.

5. Yogendra Yadav and Alistair McMillan, 'How India Voted', *India Today,* 16 March 1998.

6. For how this might have begun to change in recent years, see Ashutosh Varshney, 'India's Democratic Challenge', *Foreign Affairs*, vol. 86, no. 2, March/April 2007.

7. The 1998 budget, presented on 1 June to parliament, made some moves in the direction of privatization, but there is no visible progress on privatization yet.

8. This is not to say that trade policies and exchange rate, by affecting a whole range of prices, do not have a bearing on mass welfare. However, in economies where trade/GDP ratio is not substantial, these policies do not have a *short-run and direct* impact on mass welfare, which can be *easily demonstrated* in electoral politics. That is why, as argued later, the impact of trade and exchange rates on mass politics is on the whole much greater in economies where trade/GDP ratios are high. Trade can easily enter mass politics in such economies.

9. Strikes and trade union politics would qualify as mass politics, but they have not been conceptualized as such in the reform literature.

10. For detailed studies of Rajiv Gandhi's economic reforms, see John Echeverri-Gent, 'India', in John Echeverri-Gent *et al., Economic Reform in Three Giants* (New Brunswick, New Jersey, Transaction Books); Baldev Raj Nayar, *The Political Economy of India's Public Sector* (Bombay, Popular Prakashan) and Atul Kohli, 'Politics of Economic Liberalization', *World Development,* 17/3 (1987). For a succinct account of India's economic policy until then, see Jagdish Bhagwati, *India in Transition* (Oxford, Clarendon Press, 1993), chaps. 1 and 2.

11. For a summary overview of the election performances of parties, see David Butler, Ashok Lahiri and Prannoy Roy, *India Decides: Elections 1952–91* (New Delhi, Living Media India Limited, 1996), chap. 9.

12. Arun Singh and Arun Nehru, two of the most powerful ministers in the Rajiv Gandhi Cabinet, had served as business executives in the private sector before joining politics. Rajiv Gandhi was himself a pilot.

13. See Stephan Haggard and Steven Webb, 'Introduction', in Stephan Haggard and Steven Webb, *Voting for Reform* (New York, Oxford University Press for the World Bank, 1994).

14. *The Times of India,* 6 January 1985.

15. The delicensed industries included special alloys, 'steel structurals', electrical equipment, electronic components, automotive ancillaries, bicycles, industrial machinery, machine tools, and agricultural implements. 'Several Industries Delicensed', *The Times of India,* 18 March 1985.

16. To avoid the formation of monopolies, investment ceilings were imposed by the MRTP (Monopolies and Restrictive Trade Practices) Act, 1969. It had the perverse effect over time of disallowing increases in plant capacity, even if technological changes and cost reduction required it.

17. Especially in sectors such as electronics that were integral to Rajiv Gandhi's philosophy of modernization. 'Electronic Policy Relaxed', *The Times of India,* 22 March 1985.

18. Prime Minister's address to industrialists, cited in *The Times of India,* 23 March 1985. Later in December 1985, Rajiv Gandhi made the clearest

announcement of his liberalizing intentions at the centenary meet of the Congress. For a report, see 'Industries on a Shaky Base Can't Last Long', *The Times of India,* 29 December 1985.

19. Only one political party, the Swatantra, had opposed ISI in the 1950s and 1960s. Winning very few seats, it could not make a political impact. The Hindu nationalists, currently represented by the BJP, had traditionally opposed planning but not ISI. They were for internal deregulation, but not for external liberalization.

20. *The Wall Street Journal,* 21 March 1985.

21. 'Budget "Anti-poor", Says CPM Front', *The Times of India,* 18 March 1985.

22. Moreover, the new government kept the new momentum of popular goodwill going by concluding agreements on Assam and Punjab, states where insurgents had begun to dominate politics. Demonstrating a refreshing ability to come to negotiated settlements, Rajiv's 'accords' promoted moderates and undermined militants. For details, see Myron Weiner, 'Rajiv Gandhi: A Midterm Assessment', in Myron Weiner, *The Indian Paradox* (Delhi and Newbury Park, CA, Sage Publications, 1989).

23. *The Times of India,* 1 February 1986.

24. *The Times of India,* 22 February 1986.

25. 'Price Hike to Fuel Development: V.P. Singh', *The Times of India,* 13 February 1986.

26. 'Parties Threaten Stir on Price Hike', *The Times of India,* 2 February 1986; 'Bengal Bandh Plan on Prices', *The Times of India,* 4 February 1986; 'Women's Stir against Price Rise', *The Times of India,* 6 February 1986; 'Trade Unions Plan Stir', *The Times of India,* 17 February 1986.

27. *The Times of India,* 20 February 1986.

28. 'Congress MPs Sulk over Price Hike', *The Times of India,* 15 February 1986.

29. See, for example, Madhav Singh Solanki, 'Congress Decline in the Past Year', *The Times of India,* 12 March 1986.

30. Reflecting a large body of intellectual and political opinion, some of the sharpest comments were made by Rajni Kothari, the country's leading political scientist of the time and ace political commentator. See Rajni Kothari, 'Flight into the 21st Century: Millions Will be Left Behind', *The Times of India,* Sunday Review, 27 April (1986).

31. For a summary, see 'A Prime Minister's Budget', *Business India,* 9–22 March 1987.

32. For reports, see *Business India,* 7–20 March 1988 and 6–19 March 1989. Commenting on the 1989 budget, the magazine said that 'it seeks to protect the poor...and it gently squeezes the rich.'

33. Montek Singh Ahluwalia, interviewed in *Business India,* 7–20 March 1988, p. 55.

34. Interviewed in *Business India,* 30 April 1988, p. 15.

35. Interviewed in *The Telegraph,* 12 March 1986.

36. *Lok Sabha Debates,* X Series. See especially speeches in 1991 by Jaswant Singh, BJP, 29 July; Atal Bihari Vajpayee, BJP, 5 August; and Indrajit Gupta, Communist Party of India, 31 July. Also relevant were speeches cited in later notes for 1992.

37. Atal Bihari Vajpayee, BJP, *Lok Sabha Debates,* 23 March 1992, p. 1015.

38. V.P. Singh, *Lok Sabha Debates,* X Series, 29 February 1992, p. 1.

39. Chandra Sekhar, former Prime Minister, *Lok Sabha Debates,* 25 March 1992, p. 962.

40. H.D. Deve Gowda, Janata party, *Lok Sabha Debates,* 31 July 1991, p. 296.

41. Atal Bihari Vajpayee, BJP, *Lok Sabha Debates,* 23 March 1992, p. 1011.

42. George Fernandes, *Lok Sabha Debates,* 25 March 1992, p. 929.

43. This situation has some similarities with the games analysed by James Alt and Barry Eichengreen, 'Parallel and Overlapping Games', *Economics and Politics,* 1/2 July (1989).

44. In 1991, both the BJP and Janata and its allies abstained from the house at the time of vote on the budget. Cf. *Lok Sabha Debates,* 14 September 1991, and *The Hindu,* 15 September 1991. In 1992, only 56 votes were cast against and as many as 227 in favour of the budget. Virtually the entire team of Congressmen voted in favour of the budget in both years. Cf. *Lok Sabha Debates,* 6 May 1992.

45. Of the 120 BJP MPs, 99 were present at the time of budget vote. All voted against the government. Most Janata MPs abstained. Cf. *Lok Sabha Debates,* 5 May 1993, and *The Hindu,* 6 and 7 May 1993. The Communist Party of India (Marxist) (CPM), not the BJP or the Janata, was the only party which voted consistently against the budget between 1991 and 1993, showing that reforms were of greater ideological importance to the Communists than to the others. The BJP and Janata were, on the whole, strategic, not ideological, about voting on the budget. After 1993, the Congress, partly by offers of patronage, managed to get a near-majority in parliament and did not have to be concerned about a parliamentary vote.

46. See Ashutosh Varshney, *Democracy, Development and the Countryside: Urban–Rural Struggles in India* (New York, Cambridge University Press, 1995).

47. See Lloyd I. Rudolph and Susanne Hoeber Rudolph, *In Pursuit of Lakshmi* (Chicago, University of Chicago Press, 1987), chap. 8.

48. Government of India (1992), 'Memorandum to IMF on Economic Policies for 1992–3' (New Delhi, Government of India, July 1992).

49. Government of India, *Economic Survey 1995–6: An Update* (New Delhi, Government of India, 1996), p. 10. These figures are based on the wholesale price index (WPI), not consumer price index (CPI). The latter was higher than the former.

50. *India Today,* 15 July 1991.

51. That, of course, did not help the Congress party electorally, but the reasons for the Congress defeat had little to do with economics per se. All one can say is that electoral damage to the Congress could have been far worse if inflation rates had continued to be as high as they were in 1991. A reasonable hypothesis for Indian electoral politics so far, though it is still to be systematically tested, is that good economic performance on the whole does not help ruling parties electorally, but bad economic performance, especially if it leads to double-digit inflation, hurts.

52. Government of India, *Economic Survey 1995–6: An Update*, p. 10. The subsidiary factors were high levels of open market sales of foodgrain and liberal import policy with respect to essential commodities.

53. The government readily admitted that there was a link between the low liquidity situation of 1995–6 and high costs of capital borrowing. See Ministry of Industry, Government of India, 'Current Industrial Performance and Future Prospects: A Note for the Economic Editors Conference', mimeographed (New Delhi, Ministry of Industry, 5–6 November 1996).

54. Thus those reforms that are normally a concern for elite politics but have the greatest potential for corruption can enter mass politics. Otherwise, they leave mass politics unaffected.

55. Moises Naim, *Paper Tigers and Minotaurs: The Politics of Venezuela's Economic Reforms* (Washington DC, The Carnegie Endowment for International Peace, 1993), chap. 5.

56. The overall size of the economy complicates the meaning of low trade–GDP ratios. Smaller economies tend generally to have a high trade–GDP ratio, making trade very important to their political economies. With the striking exception of China, however, the largest economies of the world—the US, Japan, Germany—are less trade-dependent. (Indeed, the trade–GDP ratio for India and the US was roughly the same in 1996.) Still, trade politics, as we know, has aroused a great deal of passion in the US and Japan. The meaning of the same ratios can change if the leading sectors (autos, computers) or 'culturally significant' sectors (rice for Japan, agriculture in France) of the economy are heavily affected by trade.

57. Anne O. Krueger, *The Political Economy of Agricultural Pricing Policy,* vol. 5 (Baltimore, The Johns Hopkins University Press for the World Bank, 1993).

58. In an interview with the author (Delhi, 12 January 1992), Finance Minister Manmohan Singh unambiguously stated that given the desperation for jobs, he neither had the conscience to fire people nor was it politically feasible—until alternative opportunities could be provided.

59. India's central decision-makers have talked of a structural renewal fund, but no effective fund has yet been set up, partly because the financial requirements are quite high.

6

Political Skills
Introducing Reform by Stealth[*]

ROB JENKINS

Political skills are vital to effecting a sustainable reorientation of development policy. But like the journalistic cliché 'political will', invoking the notion of political skill comes dangerously close to constructing a residual category, a last resort when substantive variables are insufficient to explain events. To argue for political will as a contributing factor in achieving any outcome is to risk entering into the realm of circular reasoning: actions which are deemed to reveal skill on the part of their practitioners can be verified as skilful only with reference to the outcome which the skill itself was meant to explain. Thus, A occurred because B is skilful; and we know that B is skilful because of the very fact that A occurred.

To put this more concretely, the same political gambit which succeeds for one leader can fail miserably for another. The former's skill, according to conventional standards, is the ability to judge when 'appropriate' circumstances were in evidence. But in virtually every such instance, the specific circumstances identified as decisive in influencing the timing of the gambit turn out to be highly ambiguous. They could as easily have been interpreted to support a different course of action.[1] In short, the gambit was skilful because it was successful, not the other way around. Politicians considered skilful are those who produce such outcomes with surprising frequency, though even this is rarely subjected to verification. But is someone who calls a coin-toss correctly 75 out of 100 times skilful or lucky? This question acquires particular salience

* Originally published as 'Political skills: introducing reform by stealth', in Rob Jenkins, *Democratic Politics and Economic Reform in India*, Cambridge, Cambridge University Press, 1999, pp. 172–207.

when, as in politics, an early lucky streak (say, three out of four) effectively generates better odds for future tosses by creating a power base which can act as a cushion for errors that would be fatal for politicians at earlier stages in their careers.

Indeed, in the literature on economic reform and democracy there is a good deal of support for a focus upon political skills. Guillermo O'Donnell has argued that if there is any hope of solving the prisoner's dilemmas that confound efforts to manage economic and political change simultaneously, 'it probably lies in finding areas...in which skilled action (particularly by the government) can lengthen the time horizons (and, consequently, the scope of solidarities) of crucial actors.'[2]

Neither the political incentives thrown up by economic reform nor the political institutions prevailing in India necessarily dictated the outcome of politically sustainable economic reform. They provided breathing space and conducive conditions for governing elites seeking to outmanoeuvre entrenched interests. But would-be reformers required distinct skills in order to exploit these openings. We have seen many of these on display—especially the ability to perform the complex utility calculations which are instrumental in the creation and maintenance of political networks and, ultimately, in the capacity to broker the agreements which underwrite policy change. But if we revisit the logic which underpinned the arguments about incentives and institutions, it is possible to see the need for a somewhat different, though complementary, type of skill.

One of the arguments was that, in responding to the uncertainties that arise when policy change is initiated, governing elites are able to rely upon the tendency of socio-economic elites to operate according to established patterns of interaction. Politicians were thus able to broker arrangements on this basis, while, crucially, retaining the capacity to deviate from the accepted norms when new incentives and constraints presented themselves. Accomplishing what in game-theoretical terms amounts to a disguised 'defection' requires mastery of a range of political skills, particularly those which democracy tends to breed in its practitioners. In particular, it depends upon a talent for obfuscation, the use of intentional ambiguity, and the exploitation of other politically expedient means in the pursuit of constantly shifting policy objectives.

These tactics disrupt and complicate the utility-calculating capacity of interest groups, which tends to disarm them, while the prospect of future rounds of negotiation means that the result is rarely open revolt. It also needs to be pointed out that interest groups themselves are not averse to misdirection and the use of clandestine lobbying. One study of reform to the intellectual property rights regime argued that the business association representing the largest transnational pharmaceutical companies operating in India 'has run a stealthy, behind-the-scenes campaign to convert the opinions of Indian policy elites regarding patent reform.'[3] This, it seems, was only fitting, given the government's approach to bringing Indian patent law into conformity with its treaty obligations, which one editorial referred to as reform 'by stealth'.[4]

The extent to which actually existing democracy appears to make the skilful use of such tactics essential calls into question the validity of rather more naive conceptions of democracy. Lest this be mistaken for a teleological form of reasoning, it is important to stress that democracy not only makes such skills *necessary*; it also makes their prevalence *possible*.[5] It does this, chiefly, by permitting governing elites to use the openness of the political system to assess continuously the relative worth of political backing from competing socio-economic groups. This, in turn, enables a better appreciation of which to accommodate, which to abandon, and which to leave in limbo. A studied ambiguity on policy, allowing relatively low-cost subsequent revisions, is vital to this process.

Political skills are, however, important to any political system, democratic or authoritarian. They are an adaptation to the prevailing political context. In India, a premium has been placed on the ability to blur conflicts of interest between social groups. Often this has been accomplished by allocating 'hidden' subsidies and holding out the promise of future rewards, particularly in the form of government posts. During this period of economic reform, however, the flexibility of India's political actors (including politicians and non-elected elites) has proven extremely helpful in taking advantage of the institutions which the specific nature of Indian democracy puts at their disposal. Indeed, it is a skill that has been honed through a prolonged exposure to an environment of fluid competitive politics, in which cultivating new groups without necessarily abandoning long-time supporters is a common practice. This is not circular reasoning of the 'political will' variety but an adaptation to an institutional constraint.

Attempting to divorce an analysis of institutions from an examination of the skills necessary to operate within them effectively—to say nothing of the skill involved in their creation and rejuvenation—is in some ways as artificial as distinctions between economic and political factors in the process of policy reform. But this problem is inherent in the study of any system. Separating the parts from the whole, or from each other, leads ultimately to distortions of meaning. The hope is that the analytical value of identifying the functional role played by each part outweighs the danger of misrepresenting the whole.

The remainder of this chapter examines the use of these tactics. The first section concerns the skill of governing elites at maintaining the appearance of essential continuity with the past, while simultaneously undermining the basis upon which previous institutions have operated. The second section focuses on the inverse of the first: disguising continuity as change.

CLOAKING CHANGE IN THE GUISE OF CONTINUITY

One of the skills which reforming governments must possess is the capacity to cloak change (which tends to cause anxiety among those privileged by the status quo) in the appearance of continuity. The need to find innovative ways of accomplishing this considerable feat was emphasized by Robert Packenham in his study of why reform became politically sustainable in Argentina under Menem. His argument was that Menem 'combined continuity and change in such a way that the symbols of continuity facilitated the changes rather than hindered them.'[6]

There would seem to be ample precedent for achieving such a transformation in India. According to Ashis Nandy,

the tradition in India is to alter the dominant culture from within, by showing dissent to be a part of orthodoxy or by reinterpreting orthodoxy in terms of the needs of dissent: This is especially true of ideological deviations or innovations, the type of challenge the society has repeatedly faced and become experienced at handling.[7]

This is what India's reformers have tried to achieve since at least 1991, if not longer. To the extent that economic reform was considered a non-issue in the general election campaigns of both 1996 and 1998 (despite the BJP's *swadeshi* rhetoric in the latter contest), they have for the time being succeeded.

While we are arguing that change can take place within a context which appears to favour continuity, we are not arguing for the rhetorical or visionary powers of India's politicians. Even sober World Bank economists can be seduced by the notion of politicians creating a 'vision' which enables them effectively to promote change. Other World Bank-funded research contains similar views. To the extent that such studies recognize the importance of creative leadership and the capacity to transcend transitory interest-group configurations, they correspond to much of what this thesis is arguing. For instance, Leila Frischtak, a World Bank consultant in the Private Sector Development Department, argues that in some developing countries,

[t]he continual need to anticipate society, to generate new realities that are not yet

under the control or on the agenda of powerful interests, becomes the primary means for not succumbing to the control of these interests, and for simultaneously resolving disputes among them.

So far so good. Frischtak, however, extends this logic to claim that a government possesses governance capacity 'only to the extent that it can achieve sufficient autonomy from society by articulating a vision of the future that is distinct from, and goes beyond the diverse interests of this society.'[8] We need not reject the notion that providing a 'meta goal or meta idea'[9] *can* be an important aspect of governance in order to state that, in India, politicians have relied far less on this positive form of vision-creation than they have on the ritual intonation of developmental shibboleths to conceal reform's radical implications and thereby reassure those groups who may be threatened by them. This approach has the advantage—for Indian politicians as well as for the plausibility of our argument here—of demanding far less impressive rhetorical skills. In fact, the few attempts of India's reformers to project encompassing visions of what liberalization means have involved tired clichés that emphasize continuity with the past. Narasimha Rao's orations, for instance, often returned to Gandhian themes of village self-reliance and their purported relevance to a market economy.[10] At other times they stressed the compatibility of nationalism and entrepreneurship, as he did on the occasion of the birth centenary of pioneering Indian industrialist G. D. Birla.[11] Most often, Narasimha Rao reaffirmed his commitment to social welfare. As he stated in a speech at the London Guildhall: 'No multinational will build a primary school in India, no foreign investor will set up a health centre. These are jobs for the government. Let the multinationals handle the top sector, we will manage the grassroots. This is the way forward as I see it.'[12]

Attempts to reinterpret past doctrines, such as Manmohan Singh's repeated claim that liberalization was simply an alternate means to the cherished goal of self-reliance, or that freeing the market was the culmination, rather than the abandonment, of Nehru's development vision, went largely ignored.[13] They did not capture anyone's imagination. At most, they may have served a limited goal of reinforcing a default impression of 'politics-almost-as-usual'.[14] Projecting such an image is more useful than standard accounts of visionary leadership allow. By lulling enemies of change into a false sense of security, obfuscatory tactics play a large role in supporting this sort of rhetoric, which on its own would serve little purpose.

Even the altered dynamics between the central and state governments illustrate the importance of both imperceptible change and the exploitation of power differentials rather than the consensus-generating capacities for which democracy is usually praised. In so far as reformers in New Delhi were able to rely upon state governments to perform many of the unpleasant tasks arising from adjustment, without openly acknowledging the coercive means by which their services were enlisted, this represents a relatively untransparent method of effecting sustainable policy reform. That triggering state government involvement in reform involved pitting states against one another, starving states of resources, and providing new opportunities for patronage and profiteering at the state level was, of course, never admitted. It was in many ways an opaque and gradual process which only revealed its radical consequences much later.

Indeed, the political benefits accruing from the conflictual relationship underlying this burden-transferring process even escaped the notice of S. Guhan, the commentator who illustrated the importance of state-level political arenas. Voicing the standard diagnosis of federalism's ills, Guhan pleaded for the tidy public-administration solutions of which good-government theorists are enamoured:

> the reforms cannot be approached in a dichotomous, segmented manner with the Centre playing its own narrowly conceived part, leaving the States to play theirs at the pace and manner determined by each of them. Quite clearly, the reform process will have to be conceived and pursued in a framework of *cooperative* federalism that takes into account the distribution not only of economic burdens and benefits between the two levels, but also of the political constraints.[15]

Yes, it *would* be nice if various levels of government worked in a coordinated fashion. But in reality politicians at different levels have different concerns and different interests, and they often represent different parties. Unloading thankless responsibilities on to others is part of the time-honoured tactic of shifting blame. An idealized notion of democracy should not blind us to its pervasiveness in the process of promoting policy change in democratic India. The *conflictual* nature of federalism provided some of the tools with which accomplished buck-passers in the central government were able to generate competition as a way of furthering their preferred agenda.

An examination of government policy in three areas will illuminate the existence and political function of this pattern of obfuscation. The first concerns aspects of anti-poverty policy; the second deals with subsidized credit; and the third involves policies relating to privatization and labour.

Economic Reform, Shell-Game Politics, and the Poor

Two examples from policy in the 'social sectors' are worth exploring. The first relates to food subsidies. The Government of India's approach to the food subsidy bill, according to one observer, is 'as close to shell game politics as you will find'.[16] The government has loudly trumpeted its steadfast refusal to comply with World Bank recommendations that it drastically curtail the Public Distribution System (PDS), through which rice, wheat, sugar, kerosene, and other essential commodities are sold at subsidized prices to 'ration card' holders. National leaders are able to portray this as a determined stand against attempts to undermine India's sovereignty.[17] It is held up as proof of their continued commitment to India's poor and downtrodden. Government officials make frequent mention of the fact that the budgetary allocation for the food subsidy has risen or remained constant in the years since liberalization began.

What this masks, however, is that this level of budgetary support for the food subsidy has not been sufficient to offset the steep rise in government support prices offered to cultivators of wheat and rice.[18] As a result, poor consumers have been forced to pay far higher prices. The fact is that it would have required *even higher* increases in the level of budgetary support in order to stabilize the price at which grains are sold to 'ration card' holders in the Public Distribution System's (PDS) 'fair-price shops'. While 'increasing the level of budgetary support' for the PDS, the government nevertheless made essential commodities more expensive for the poorest of the poor.[19] But that was not all. Through a deft display of political legerdemain, it transferred a substantial portion of the subsidy from consumers to farmers. This was deemed necessary to compensate for the government's failure to take other measures demanded by farmers. For instance, it did not increase fertilizer subsidies in line with the previous trend or extend the loan-waiver scheme initiated by the V.P. Singh government. The result was to change the way subsidies were delivered. It is significant that the government did not increase its commitments through *overt* subsidies. Instead, it handed out enormous increases in the form of 'price incentives' for farmers, while recouping as much of this outlay as possible from those who rely on subsidized foodgrains, namely, the poor. While maintaining the appearance of continuity (maintaining the food subsidy), the government effected a dramatic change (massive increases in the prices at which consumers bought them through the PDS).

It would be a mistake to consider this an isolated episode.[20] Moreover, the downstream implications are important if we are to comprehend the ways in which incentives, institutions, and skills can work together in support of change. This is because the opaque manner of bringing about a qualitative shift in the food subsidy—increasing need, while reducing outlays as a percentage of GDP—will influence the government's capacity to effect further reform in this area. The policy feedback effect requires a supportive institutional climate in order to produce results. It also relies upon the application of tactical skill. The rise in the prices at which foodgrains are sold through the PDS—the 'issue price'—shortened the distance between the 'subsidized' and market prices, leading to a very large decline in consumption through the PDS, from 20.8 million tonnes in 1990 to 14 million tonnes in 1994. This is because PDS issue prices during that period rose even faster than the consumer price indices for the groups most in need of subsidized foodgrains.[21]

Ashok Gulati and Shashanka Bhide, two economists specializing in subsidy issues, have argued that this policy of retaining an administrative network of subsidized fair price shops, while slowly removing incentives for people actually to use them by bringing their prices closer to market levels, was a strategic way of deferring open conflict on the issue. It was also, they argued, an extremely shrewd way of softening the introduction of a system better targeted towards the poor.

We cannot know whether this was, in fact, a 'calculated move', and any effort to ascribe such strategic genius to Indian reformers should rightly be greeted with suspicion. But the ability to respond skilfully to opportunities that arise from previous decisions is arguably something that democratic politics engenders in its practitioners. Gulati and Bhide's further point was that if rises in PDS issue prices were a prelude to a focus on greater targeting, it would be 'better for the government to come out openly with its policy and have the courage to announce the withdrawal of the untargeted PDS.'[22] This, of course, it did not do. After roughly a five-year delay, during which many pro-poor activist groups had been thrown on the defensive, the United Front coalition which succeeded Narasimha Rao's government did continue the process of PDS reform in the way predicted by Gulati and Bhide's account: the concept of targeting became further entrenched with the introduction of the Targeted PDS (TPDS).

Imploring reformers to avoid taking paths of lesser political resistance is a favourite pastime of neo-liberal economists,[23] though if anyone should know that such pleas will fall on deaf ears, it should be neo-liberal economists themselves. They would do better to probe the additional political implications of the central government's de facto retreat from food subsidies to the poor. One reason why it was able to get away with such sins of omission is that it is state governments, the first line of political defence, who must face the irate public. Electorates vent their frustrations at the most accessible level of government, not necessarily the one most responsible for their problems. This may be unfair, but so is the abuse hurled at ticket clerks when trains are late or cancelled. The laying of blame is a political process, one that by no means follows strict rationality.

Faced with protests, and the futility of blaming New Delhi, many state governments in India were, in effect, forced to substitute their own food subsidies to offset what the central government had withdrawn. The most notable example was the highly expensive Rs 2 per kg rice scheme in Andhra Pradesh, which emerged as a result of a campaign promise during the 1994 assembly elections. In that case, not only was the newly installed non-Congress state government forced to clean up the mess created by the central government's PDS price increases, it was also blamed for its lack of fiscal prudence when it had done so. With a good deal of the responsibility firmly laid upon its shoulders, honouring this commitment at the lowest possible cost by cutting corners became a major preoccupation of the state government. Obfuscation at the centre begat more obfuscation in the states.

Andhra Pradesh had the most expensive subsidy scheme, but others took similar actions, and for similar reasons. In Karnataka, the Congress government of Veerappa Moily in 1994 reduced the prices at which PDS outlets in the state sold rice and wheat. This cost the state's exchequer Rs 420 million. As a newspaper editorial noted:

> The decision to reduce the end prices of grains also represents the additional financial burden that the states are forced to carry on account of the Centre's fiscal stabilization programme. While the Centre raised issue prices to contain food subsidies, Mr Moily reduced it to ensure demand among the weaker sections.[24]

If we recognize that only *some* states found it necessary to cushion the blow of the central government's PDS price rises, it is possible to gain an even greater perspective on the extent to which the politically unpalatable consequences of underhanded tactics are masked by the veneer of continuity. Slowly emerging in India is a system in which the states with the most assertive populations—not necessarily the most deserving—take remedial action. In practice, the distribution of public resources thus takes a *politically* more efficient form: it apportions the price rises in accordance with regional, rather than national, thresholds at which such hardships translate into widespread political discontent. After all, poorer groups are not as politically assertive in Rajasthan and Orissa as they are in Karnataka and Andhra Pradesh. In this sense, it is valid to ask, as Mick Moore's study of the politics of adjustment in Sri Lanka did, whether one unintended consequence of how liberalization has been implemented in India has been to 'remedy an historic "weakness" of the...political system: the relatively indiscriminate and inefficient distribution of relatively large volumes of material patronage such that they purchase little lasting support for the party in power.'[25] To whatever extent this has taken place, it has not been advertised.

The second example of shell-game politics is the proliferation of employment-generation schemes, which have been among the major 'safety net' programmes during the period of economic reform. The massive expansion of such schemes was an attempt to enhance the government's pro-poor credentials (or at least curtail their erosion), while still finding ways to benefit groups whose clout might pose a serious threat to reform. This was possible because employment-generation programmes in India have been prone to leakages, benefiting individuals outside the official target groups.

The national schemes which have been so much more in evidence during the reform period are modelled on Maharashtra's Employment Generation Scheme (EGS), which continues as a separate programme. Both the EGS and the national Jawahar Rozgar Yojana (JRY) guarantee—in theory, and for the most part in practice as well—daily wage employment to citizens willing to contribute their labour. Because the work is physically demanding, and the pay minimal, the EGS (and to a lesser extent the JRY) is widely considered extremely well targeted at the poorest of the poor. But the nature of the programme has encouraged the formation of a considerably more broad-based constituency to support its continuation, and indeed expansion.[26] The rationale of both the EGS and JRY is not only to put people to work, but also to enhance the value of rural public assets, such as roads and irrigation canals. But, in reality, the work that is performed by poor labourers, paid from public funds, is often used to upgrade facilities used primarily by prosperous and middle-class land-owners who otherwise despair of having canals desilted or roads maintained. In some cases, much of the work carried out under the EGS actually 'turns out to be land improvements…on land belonging to richer rural households'.[27] The JRY, as it evolved as a national programme administered by state and local governments, followed a similar pattern.[28] Both the JRY and EGS also provide opportunities for local politicians and bureaucrats to intervene in the selection of works projects and the recruitment of labourers.[29]

If politically sustainable adjustment requires continued commitment to poverty alleviation programmes—and if such commitment is likely to arise only when a solid constituency remains to support it—then the emergence of the 'targeted-yet-leaky'[30] JRY as a major plank of the Indian social safety net must be viewed as an important contributor to the political sustainability of economic reform. It may not represent the most economically efficient allocation of resources, or the most equitable means for helping the poor.[31] But given Indian realities it is remarkably well adapted to the need for satisfying groups other than the poor, as well as the need for a concealing mechanism to mask this fact.

Shifting Priorities But Not Official Policy

The government's approach to the issue of 'priority-sector' lending also relied upon tactical skill. Banking regulations stipulate that 40 per cent of financial institutions' total outstanding credit must be allocated to priority sectors, mainly agriculture and small-scale trade and industry. Rather than taking a stand that 'directed credit programmes' lead to allocative inefficiencies, and then 'selling' this reform by persuading farmers and small-scale industrialists that they will be more than compensated by other fiscal and regulatory reforms,[32] the government decided to proceed quietly. Officials of the finance, agriculture, and industry ministries loudly proclaimed at every opportunity their undying commitment to priority-sector quotas and their determination not to cave in to World Bank and IMF pressure on this issue.

Unofficially, banks were consistently permitted to fall short of the stipulated targets—a phenomenon that the erring bank officers themselves admit is largely caused by liberalization. A general manager at the Bank of Baroda in charge of priority-sector lending said: 'After the government kicked off its liberalization drive, a lot of credit is being pumped into export finance. So banks have been finding it rather difficult to maintain the level of agricultural disbursements.'[33] This was also partly because the banking sector had been exposed to competitive pressures. As another bank executive admitted, 'At a time when we have to worry about staying afloat, we are just not prepared to take such risky assets in our books.'[34] In fact, 22 of the 28 nationalized banks failed to meet their targets in 1993.[35] As of March 1993, only 33 per cent of gross bank credit was directed to priority sectors, considerably less than the target of 40 per cent.[36] No action was taken against the banks.

The Reserve Bank of India, the agency responsible for setting targets and monitoring compliance, was aware that slippage on priority-sector lending would take place. According to one official, this was tacitly permitted because the banks had already been subjected to considerable shocks that year as a result of new accounting procedures instituted to prepare Indian banking for a more open-market economy.[37] In order not to upset the banks too greatly, it was decided to allow them, temporarily, to reduce their commitment to 'directed credit'. The calculation was that changes then being made to the definition of 'small-scale industry'—allowing larger firms to qualify—would in future years make it possible for banks to increase lending to this 'priority sector'. In other words, a behind-the-scenes compromise permitted one interest group (banks) to withstand the costs of policy reform at the cost of another (the small-scale sector), until such time as the latter could be redefined in ways that would privilege yet another group (slightly larger firms). Through such means was the charade of continuity maintained.

In fact, several changes to the priority-sector guidelines were quietly introduced. New banks were exempted from priority-sector quotas for their first three years in business. For the first time, a firm's export-orientation made it eligible for priority status, thereby increasing the size of the 'target' group for directed credit and making it easier for banks to meet their quotas. The rules regarding which housing loans would qualify as priority-sector lending were also relaxed. Previously, only housing loans of Rs 5000 or less made to members of scheduled castes or scheduled tribes counted under the priority-sector heading. The limit was raised to Rs 200000 per loan, and the restriction to scheduled castes and tribes was withdrawn.[38] 'Indirect lending' was also permitted to count towards meeting the banks' quotas, meaning that loans to state electricity boards for rural electrification projects,[39] for instance, could be treated as agricultural loans, as could lending for high-tech agricultural activities such as tissue culture and greenhouse-based floriculture.[40] Retail trading, usually considered less deserving than other sectors, increased its share of priority-sector lending substantially between 1990 and 1994.[41] This was unsurprising, given that the ceiling for qualification was hiked from Rs 25000 to Rs 200000.[42] The government permitted some commercial banks to close loss-making branches,[43] and private domestic and foreign banks were allowed to meet priority-sector obligations by parking funds with the National Bank for Agriculture and Rural Development (NABARD). Even with these crucial (unpublicized) concessions, priority-sector lending as a percentage of net bank credit fell from 42.4 per cent in 1990 to 35.3 per cent in 1994.[44] The priorities changed—especially as banks began to focus their efforts on loans above Rs 200,000—but the official commitment to directed credit remained untouched.[45]

This division was mirrored institutionally in the RBI's bureaucracy: the department of rural planning and credit would publicly prod the banks to increase lending to agriculture and the small-scale sector, while the department of banking operations and development was itself encouraging the scaling back of such lending practices.[46]

Through the Back Door: Indirect Approaches to State-owned Firms and Labour

The approach to reforming state-owned firms and the industrial relations regime has relied upon similarly indirect methods. Even some foreign observers have begun to recognize that the government has not only faced political constraints but has also attempted to overcome them through relatively unconfrontational tactics. As one put it:

It would be nice if privatization were speeded up, but the government is allowing companies to compete against state-owned companies, and that's a back-door way of doing it. China has followed a similar policy of ignoring some very tricky issues, and concentrated on getting private investment to increase.[47]

In fact, compared to some of the other means the government has employed, subjecting public-sector firms to competition is a relatively above-board approach. Automobile manufacturer Maruti, for instance, has remained nominally a government enterprise, though the Japanese firm Suzuki has slowly been permitted to increase its joint-venture equity participation from 26 per cent, to 40 per cent, and then to a controlling 50.2 per cent. Former finance minister Madhu Dandavate termed this 'back door' privatization, and considered it consistent with the government's general policy of 'double-faced liberalization'. That he is right is less significant than the fact that protests such as his failed to generate the political backlash that he and others clearly expected.[48]

Another example of the skill with which Indian politicians have practised reform by stealth is the coal sector. The long history of trade-union militancy in this sector has made governments particularly wary of taking decisive action. Disruption in the supply of this vital input has the capacity to cause serious economic disorder. The existence of powerful political patrons behind the monopoly supplier, state-owned Coal India Limited (CIL), added an extra measure of caution to the statements of reformers and political managers in Narasimha Rao's circle.[49] Diverting coal supplies to clients willing to pay a premium above the state price was over the years a lucrative source of illegal income for politicians with connections at various levels of CIL's operational hierarchy.[50] During the first four years of reform, the result was a spate of government denials that the coal sector would be thrown open to the private sector.[51] Even limited disinvestment of CIL's shares to raise resources was deemed too sensitive to risk.

Nevertheless, a quiet start was made towards deregulation. It began with a bidding process that resulted in 20 private firms being short-listed to set up coal washeries. The most significant move, however, was the decision in 1994 to allow firms investing in power generation, steel, and cement projects to establish 'captive' coal mines—a step which was the result of intense lobbying by a group of firms that ultimately included those bidding for the coal washery projects.[52]

Permission was to be granted only to those firms which could justify the need for a captive supply on the basis of projected productivity gains from vertical integration. According to Pranab Bardhan, the process of 'indirect' liberalization in the coal sector subsequently took other forms consistent with this logic. CIL had its monopoly further undermined when the Government of India permitted certain businesses to import coal if the supply from CIL was 'erratic', which it almost always was. This is another means of building a constituency for future policy reform.[53]

This type of policy modification has three important implications. First, the criteria in such ad hoc policies are notoriously imprecise, leading to decisions being made on a discretionary basis. This allows a new source of corrupt income to emerge. Second, because this happens at the same time as the old system of CIL favouritism is still relatively intact, a period of overlapping patronage defuses opposition from within the political and bureaucratic elite.[54] Third, and most important, the overlap period helps to nurture an actual, concrete 'proto-constituency'—the firms with captive mines–capable of contributing to the battle for more direct forms of reform at a later stage. It is a process which relies on systematic obfuscation about future intentions, if not outright deceit.

This state of affairs is also very significant for our understanding of why traditional approaches to modelling the political economy of economic reform do not produce the expected results. Most models envision the substitution of a constituency of 'winners' from reform for those groups who 'lose' in the redistributive process. Yet this often—perhaps even in a majority of cases—does not take place. To reiterate, the reason is that the winners are always *potential* winners, most likely dispersed and poorly organized because of the extreme uncertainty that they will actually reap the promised benefits. The costs to the usually well-organized losers, on the other hand, appear very real indeed. When, as in the case of the coal sector in India, the winners have been able to taste some of the rewards, they are a more potent source of support to reformers, who likewise are that much more inclined to believe that they can effect a relatively costless substitution of their support base. The potential losers, for their part, are more likely to have been lulled into a false sense of complacency as a result of their apparent ability to prevent the government from taking the most serious steps towards reform.

The result of this strategy of 'back door reform', then, is to strengthen the government's political position when the economic logic reaches its ultimate conclusion and a decision on more substantial deregulation and privatization becomes unavoidable. As the Economist Intelligence Unit put it: 'The question must inevitably be raised soon as to why the nationalized company is needed at all and why prices should be set administratively.'[55] Allaying the apprehensions of powerful figures about what the future might hold for the sectors in which they have interests is not easy. An economist who has served on the boards of several public-sector firms argued that it requires 'an approach reeking of business as usual'.[56]

It bears reminding that this capacity can rely substantially on tactics of obfuscation. Even the sale of shares in public-sector firms 'is a kind of privatisation by stealth.'[57] With most of the attention focused at the national level, state governments have seized the limited opportunities to take action. By early 1995, for instance, Orissa, Meghalaya and other states were 'quietly selling off state electricity distributors and generators'.[58] The communist-controlled government of West Bengal also preferred 'to privatize quietly, often through under-the-table deals'.[59] The West Bengal State Electricity Board's Kasba gas turbine, for instance, was effectively sold to the R.P. Goenka industrial group in the guise of a leasing arrangement. In this and other instances, chief minister Jyoti Basu has used his personal popularity with the electorate as a lever with which to pressure the leaders of his party's affiliated trade union to take a more 'pragmatic' approach to foreign investment, privatization, and tax reform.[60]

Perhaps the best example of reform by stealth is in the area of industrial-relations policy. State governments have been waging a guerrilla war on this front, taking action in isolated incidents and sapping the power of unions to resist encroachments upon their rights. This has taken place without alterations to official policy. The central government can claim to have left India's labour-relations regime intact. Indeed, India still has some of the most pro-worker labour laws in the world. Implementation is another matter.

Several means have been employed for bringing about the sort of flexible labour environment that a market economy is deemed to require. Voluntary retirement schemes (VRSs) have been among the most popular. The government originally devised the VRS framework as an integrated programme for redeploying surplus labour, and one or two retraining centres were opened with great fanfare. Companies opting for the VRS route are officially required to abide by specified procedures, including extensive consultation with unions. These are routinely ignored. By September 1996, 85,000 workers in state-owned firms had been retrenched through one or another VRS—there were many more in the private sector—but only 2,000 had been given retraining. The number actually redeployed through the VRS machinery is anyone's guess.[61]

The strong sense of complicity between government and employers has contributed to an atmosphere in which trade unions perceive few options other than to make massive concessions. Even business leaders recognize the change of attitude. P.K. Dutt, vice-president of the West Bengal Chamber of Commerce and Industry, stated in 1994 that 'without a shade of doubt, the attitude of the unions and politicians has turned around.'[62] While the increasing willingness of workers to opt for VRSs is cited by industrialists as evidence that labour has woken up to business realities, trade-union leaders argue that it is the 'uncertainty' created by government betrayals that causes workers to lose hope and take what they can get.[63] The point is that even a 'non-policy' can generate results by creating an impression that unofficial continuity might be worse than official change.[64] This is especially true in a climate in which unions have been subjected to divide-and-rule tactics by both national and state governments.[65] Moreover, the tendency for union leaders to be secretly in league with governments has led to divisions between rank-and-file members and their representatives.[66] Government decisions which discriminate arbitrarily among different classes of employee have even served to sow discord among workers within firms which have initiated a VRS.[67]

Another way in which governments made progress on 'back door' labour reform without having actually to reform labour legislation was by allowing firms to substitute their regular employees with contract employees. As one account put it, '[w]hen it became clear that there may be no legal Exit Policy, contract employment ballooned'.[68] While the law states that employers are permitted to hire workers on a contract basis only in certain types of seasonal jobs, governments have turned a blind eye to the abuse of this provision.[69] The contract labour approach is complemented by the corporate restructuring techniques used by many firms to skirt labour laws.[70] A study conducted by the All-India Management Association found that the absence of labour-market reform had not prevented firms from using restructuring as a way of closing unviable production units.[71]

With the assistance provided by cooperative state governments and trade unions affiliated to state-level ruling parties, companies have become skilled at combining this array of indirect tactics. It is worth citing one such case to provide a taste of the possibilities that have been opened up by governments which nevertheless refuse to take concrete action on labour-market reform. Industrial giant Hindustan Lever Ltd. (HLL) decided to close down Indian Perfumes Ltd. after acquiring the firm as part of a large corporate merger. Since industrial-relations laws presented an obstacle, it was decided that taking action on the grounds of health, safety, and environmental problems at the plant would suffice. The state government regulators, on orders from their political bosses, were willing to oblige. Still, labour regulations required that scheduled output not be stopped, so production was shifted to a new site where sub-contracting was used to lower costs. But since there were still more than 100 salaried workers in the unit—the minimum required for the no-closure provisions to apply—HLL offered workers VRS packages, 85 of whom accepted, fearing that waiting might get them nothing, given the state government's clearly pro-management stance. This pushed the workforce well below 100, freeing the firm from the shackles of India's officially tough, but unofficially malleable, labour-relations regime.[72]

Given such de facto labour reform, it is perhaps no surprise that the World Bank's Country Economic Memorandum for 1996 and its Country Study for 1997 made less noise than usual about the need to reform labour legislation. In September 1996, a western diplomat remarked that foreign investors visiting India no longer considered labour-market reform a top-priority issue.[73] The government's sins of omission had, for the time being, begun to produce the intended results by other means.

THE MIRROR IMAGE:
CONTINUITY MASQUERADING AS CHANGE

The types of skills that support the tactics outlined above have been practised by ruling parties in India from across the ideological spectrum. But the task of managing the politics of economic reform was (and is) considerably more difficult for those non-Congress governments, at the centre and in the states, which campaigned on an anti-liberalization platform. They must effect new reforms while simultaneously undertaking efforts to undo some of the reforms introduced under Congress rule, or at least *appear to be doing so*. In this sense, they must cloak continuity (with earlier liberalizing policies) in the garb of change (reverting to illiberal policies).

Policy Decoys and Political Camouflage

One way that such governments reduce their vulnerability to charges of betrayal by their supporters is by pursuing 'decoy' policy measures which can be portrayed as evidence of their commitment to resisting reform. These help to make the overall thrust of policy reform more ambiguous. The cancellation of the Enron power project by Maharashtra's incoming Shiv Sena–BJP government in 1995 is a good example of a high-profile symbolic issue which arguably helped to distract attention from the many liberalizing steps taken by its ministers.[74]

While such decoys are useful, some policies require additional political camouflage. In Maharashtra, one of the most controversial concerned land reform. The preceding Congress government under Sharad Pawar had pushed through an amendment to existing legislation to raise the ceiling on individual holdings, and relax norms on the transfer of agricultural land to corporations. While it is in no party's political interest to press too hard for the repeal of legislation prohibiting the sale of agricultural lands to corporations, the Shiv Sena–BJP government in Maharashtra nevertheless wanted to pursue this option. Again demonstrating the federal learning effect, it stole a page from the playbook of its Congress counterpart in Madhya Pradesh, which had found creative ways of facilitating corporate farming without subjecting itself to the bruising political battle that would have accompanied an attempt to amend existing legislation. In June 1995, the Madhya Pradesh government, on an ad hoc basis, began awarding exemptions from the land-ceiling laws for contract farming and agro-development projects.[75] In the process it found a new role for a troubled public-sector firm, using the Madhya Pradesh State Agro-Industrial Corporation, which owns vast tracts of land, as a joint-venture partner for private-sector investors.

While continuing its public denunciations of the Pawar government's land-reform amendments, which had yet to become law because they were still awaiting the assent of the President of India, the Maharashtra government proceeded in the same way that Pawar had, by acting quietly to circumvent the existing legislation. It even went a step further than Madhya Pradesh's government, allowing individual company directors to buy plots within the land-ceiling limits. The plots were then sold to individual investors, such that no individual held more than the law allowed. Maxworth Orchards (India) Ltd. used this method for developing 15,000 acres of land. The land is owned by individuals, but managed by the company. Both states were thus able to skirt the spirit of the law, and avoid opening themselves up to damaging public debates over the propriety of corporate farming. 'Selling' the benefits of this type of reform to the rural electorate is not considered smart politics.[76]

Part of the skill in performing this delicate balancing act comes from choosing issues that can be portrayed as evidence of a commitment to economic nationalism but will not unduly constrain future policy choice. During the last year of the Narasimha Rao government, the commerce and finance ministries studied the feasibility of introducing more stringent 'local content' regulations for manufactured products—rules which would require specific product sectors to contain a stipulated percentage of locally produced parts. One reason why this particular policy appealed to astute political managers was that it would have had little impact.[77] It was designed as window-dressing. In the automotive industry, the targeted sector, a marked move in the direction of increased local content was already being propelled by economic exigencies. The decline of the rupee's value against the dollar (down by more than 16 per cent between mid-1995 and early 1996) had inclined many joint ventures to increase the indigenous content of their assembled products as a way of reducing production costs. DCM Daewoo Motors Ltd., for instance, was pressing towards total in-house production. It hoped to have 90 per cent of its components (in value terms) produced locally by 1997–8.[78]

Such politically low-cost 'indigenization' strategies were followed by both United Front and BJP economic strategists, allowing both governments to make good on their economic nationalist rhetoric without taking difficult decisions. This is in the tradition of the Narasimha Rao government, which preferred to introduce reform measures by stealth rather than trumpet them loudly. In fact, it is the mirror image: the tactic is to accentuate fairly insignificant areas of governmental resistance to the neo-liberal agenda, even as market forces are heading inexorably in the same direction. It is wrapping the logical culmination of existing economic trends in the garb of deliberate policy change.

The objective of such manoeuvres is to find policy solutions with an optimal political cost-benefit ratio, which, given the complexity of the constraints facing India's reformers, is not an easy task. Proponents of the local-content strategy, for instance, had to calculate whether the rupee's slow decline against other major currencies was likely to continue. They were swayed by the fact that gradual slippage suits increasingly powerful economic lobbies: a cheap rupee means that exporters will find their products easier to sell in foreign markets, while firms producing for the local market will find greater protection from competing imports, provided they are not too reliant on imported production inputs. Moreover, all this can be done without antagonizing the multilateral lending institutions, since it implies neither an explicit subsidy to exporters (a major drain on the budget in the pre-reform days) nor higher direct tariff barriers against foreign imports. These kinds of creative (and undeniably sly) solutions to the political difficulties associated with implementing economic liberalization are a speciality of India's politicians.

The Impure Motivations of Opposition Politics

A decided lack of transparency was also integral to the means by which the Shiv Sena–BJP government in Maharashtra went about systematically undermining the sugar cooperative sector. This refers primarily to a reversal of one of the means-ends relationships stressed in the first part of this chapter. Instead of using decidedly untransparent tactics of intimidation to threaten groups into supporting liberalization, the Shiv Sena–BJP government has used the language of liberalization to justify regulatory changes that it hopes will threaten a substantial segment of this Congress party bastion into joining its ranks. The key element in this still-unfolding plan is the government's standing threat to formalize a phenomenon that Sharad Pawar had merely, on occasion, turned a blind eye to—allowing sugar-cane farmers to sell their cane to cooperatives other than those of which they are members. The government claims that such a move would be consistent with the notion of fostering a free market that would benefit farmers. It also, of course, knows that it would mean the death of many cooperatives.

The threat to implement this proposal is combined with clandestine offers of financial support,[79] as well as protection from various environmental regulations and corruption investigations, for groups that lend backing to the ruling-party alliance. A prominent Congress MP from the sugar belt calls this strategy 'a classic carrot and stick approach. The [Shiv Sena-BJP] combine is trying to woo the belt with tickets [that is, party nominations for local, state, and national elections], licences, seed capital and, of course, punitive action.'[80] The Shiv Sena–BJP government's hand is strengthened in pursuing this strategy by the lack of sympathy for the sugar sector among the Maharashtra electorate at large. Moreover, Congress indignation at the government's tactics rings hollow, especially when most people regard the Shiv Sena–BJP offers of favouritism as little more than an extension of what Congress state governments have done for decades. As for the intimidation, we have seen that Sharad Pawar played that game, as did one of his predecessors. As chief minister in the mid-1980s, S.B. Chavan, who did not emerge into politics through the sugar-cooperative route, attempted to counter his rivals in the party by clamping down on corruption and irregularities in cooperative elections. Because he operated from within the Congress Party, Chavan's efforts were fairly easily thwarted.[81]

The logic of democratic competition has unleashed a more capable enemy in the form of the Shiv Sena–BJP government. It has, moreover, been able to cloak its political intentions in the guise of promoting economic efficiency. While some of its other tactics would not find a place in a World Bank manual on good government, the Manohar Joshi administration's attack on one of the main strongholds of its political enemies is, as a secondary effect, helping to introduce a greater degree of market orientation. This is certainly true in the case of the cooperative banking sector in Maharashtra.[82] Jayaprakash Mundada, minister for cooperatives, cited market-friendly motivations, rather than political self-interest, for the government's decision to split the state's Congress-dominated cooperative banking system by creating a state-level urban cooperative bank free from the predations of the rural banks:

We have only tried to bring about some competition which is both necessary and healthy. It will help streamline the functioning of the MSCB [Maharashtra State Cooperative Bank]. After the urban co-operatives' apex bank began to function, the MSCB hiked its interest rates on deposits from 12 to 15 per cent.[83]

Similar motivations underlie the Shiv Sena–BJP government's efforts to replace the Bombay Industrial Relations Act of 1948. The Maharashtra Harmonious Labour and Industrial Relations Bill is designed primarily to undermine the hegemony of the Congress-affiliated Rashtriya Mill Mazdoor Sangh in the textile industry, and to replace it with BJP and Shiv Sena unions.[84]

Economic Reform, Identity Politics, and Political Discontent

A political system's capacity to cope with issues which are not, strictly speaking, related to the politics of economic reform can nevertheless have a decisive impact on the political sustainability of adjustment programmes. A potent combination of economic dislocation and the assertion of identity politics, for instance, has the potential to disrupt political and economic life in any socially or ethnically heterogeneous state. As one commentator remarked, while 'China's super-charged economic growth and the spread of modern commercial communication and transportation links are widely supposed to be further integrating the country…this dynamism has the potential to fuel ethnic and linguistic divisions'.[85] As uneven capitalist development intensifies, the Chinese government's capacity to promote a 'unified multinational state' through official programmes aimed at fostering the economic development of its 55 'minority nationalities'—those not from the majority Han group—has come under severe strain.[86] Moreover, the burgeoning of cultural identity among different subsections within the Han grouping, which accounts for 91 per cent of the population, has at least part of its roots in the growth of voluntary associations that have arisen alongside private-sector initiative.[87]

A useful way to conceptualize the interaction between reform-related and identity-based politics is to assume that every government has its breaking point—as variable, uncertain, and self-defined as it may be. If this is true, then we cannot assume a clear division between reform-related strains and those stemming from other political pressures. This is not to say that the pressure emanating from different issues—such as economic reform and identity politics—can be plugged into a simple formula in which the reform-related stresses are added to identity-issue strains to arrive at a political-pressure quotient. In some cases, the salience of one type of issue diverts attention from the other. The destruction of a sixteenth-century mosque in December 1992 by Hindu nationalist extremists in the north Indian town of Ayodhya certainly stole some of the limelight from less dramatic reform-related events of that period, like changes to import-export regulations. But the 'distract-and-reform' process does not always unfold so neatly, and it is certainly not always a conscious strategy. Even the Ayodhya incident subsequently entered into the government's calculations of what new reform measures were possible. Referring to a failure to reduce the government's food-subsidy bill in 1993–4, the finance minister alluded to this issue:

There were extraordinary circumstances. Last year our country's energies had to be devoted to the more important issues, which came in the wake of Ayodhya, to see that this country's cohesion is not destroyed by the divisive forces which suddenly appeared much stronger than they later turned out to be. If we had let a cat loose among the pigeons in that atmosphere, it could have been misused by our opponents to strengthen themselves. I think there were valid political reasons, therefore, for raising procurement prices while a decision on issue prices was deferred.[88]

What is necessary is to avoid overload of the type that would undermine a government's willingness to gamble on its ability to contain the political disruption that might accompany further reform. This, in turn, requires an ability to assess when identity issues are additive (requiring a resort to stealthy means), divertive (furnishing an opportunity for major new reforms), or potentially overlapping (making them susceptible to an attempt at integration).

Indeed, the substantive divide between identity politics and economic reform is not always so great. The identification of many caste groups with traditional occupations provides a potent focal point for projecting resistance to reform. This is true among small traders, who often use caste associations to organize lobbying efforts and general strikes to protest against increases in sales tax. The large percentage of landless labourers who come from the 'scheduled', or ex-untouchable castes is another example of the power of social identity to infect the political struggles that emanate from changes in economic policy. As one analyst of the political fallout of the 1994–5 budget observed, '[p]olitical workers realize that it will be easier to convince a Harijan [scheduled caste] or a tribal about his own economic disabilities as a [low-caste] *chamar* rather than as an agricultural worker.'[89] Since Indian politicians generally conceive of electorates as mosaics of caste and community 'vote banks', this linkage between social and economic identity is a source of much worry.

An example of how these factors affect the political management of economic reform is the issue of 'reservations' in government employment for members of 'backward castes'. There is great concern among political representatives from these communities that the shrinkage of the state associated with liberalization will marginalize reservation policy as a tool of political mobilization. Some even suspect that one of the motivations behind the privatization of the economy is the desire among more privileged castes to remove decision-making from the public 'political' realm at precisely the moment when backward castes have begun to assume unprecedented state power.[90] In the two years prior to the initiation of the current programme of economic reform in 1991, India's two most populous states, Uttar Pradesh and Bihar, elected governments headed by backward caste chief ministers heading explicitly backward-caste-oriented parties.[91] In 1990 and 1991, the country had witnessed a serious backlash from upper-caste activists against the V.P. Singh government's attempts to broaden the scope of reservations for lower castes, the first substantial attempt to make this an issue of national scope.

Because of this deep suspicion among backward-caste political leaders, Indian reformers have been forced to guard against the possibility that 'reservation agitations' will be transformed into emotionally charged political movements against economic reform. Finance Minister Manmohan Singh told the annual session of the Confederation of Indian Industry that the process of reforms could be affected by the apprehension of the scheduled castes and tribes that their opportunities will shrink as the public sector diminishes, stating that '[i]f this thought acquires momentum, it will hurt the process of reforms.'[92]

Appealing to a shared sense of regional identity in order to justify politically difficult policy reversals has proved to be an effective tactic in other states as well. Rajasthan chief minister Bhairon Singh Shekhawat couches his government's embrace of market-oriented policies in terms of defending the state's people from nefarious forces outside the borders of Rajasthan. The New Mineral Policy of 1994, for instance, was required because 'the centre had left the states to fend for themselves.'[93] In addition, the Government of India's failure during the years of central planning to help set up industries in Rajasthan had made it an unattractive prospect for private investors as well. As a result, Rajasthan's 'indigenous entrepreneurs'—the Marwari community, members of which head some of India's best-known industrial houses—were forced to leave their 'homeland'. This has undermined the 'integrity and self-reliance of Rajasthan's culture', according to Shekhawat. Helping them to 'come home to Rajasthan' was how Shekhawat described his efforts at liberalization. This, he argued, was just one part of his larger effort to rebuild the people's pride in Rajasthan.[94] To understand the associations of regional pride in Rajasthan's current political climate, one must take into account the Rajasthan BJP's strategy of mobilizing religious identity around a regionalized form of Hindu nationalism, one which holds a special place for Rajasthan in the national Hindu reawakening and tends to emphasize the political dominance of the Rajput caste.[95] Regionalism, Rajput revivalism, and Hindu nationalism have become very closely intertwined. In such a climate, efforts to justify support for liberal economic reform with claims of restoring Rajasthani pride and the integrity of its indigenous culture—an appeal to regional identity—tap into a stream of associations that includes issues of religion- and caste-based mobilization. It deflects political criticism by, in Nandy's terms, 'showing dissent to be a part of orthodoxy'.

Pushing through reform measures involves a broad range of underhanded tactics, only a small sampling of which have been outlined in this chapter. It is important to emphasize that many of these would not be out of place in a western democracy. For instance, in April 1995, in an effort to rally votes to defeat an opposition-sponsored budget-related motion, which would have amounted to a vote of no confidence, Congress Party managers reminded first-time MPs who might be flirting with dissidence that they would lose their pensions if the government failed to complete four years in office.[96] The variations on this theme are almost endless. In the same month, it was revealed that, 'in a notable instance of lack of transparency', the Foreign Investment Promotion Board (FIPB) allowed Indian firms to circumvent a law which prevents royalty payments to multinational firms by permitting them to pay American and British wholly-owned subsidiaries what it termed an 'R&D access fee'.[97] The FIPB also signed agreements with two American firms for the extraction of methane gas from coal beds, though the government had not previously published guidelines or announced its intention to attract foreign investment in this sector.[98] In April 1994, representatives of service industries were outraged by the finance minister's authorization of an unpublicized circular by the Central Board of Direct Taxes which brought them into the tax net for the first time. When contacted by reporters for comments on this 'quiet' move, many service industry companies had not even heard of the circular. Those that had were amazed at the flouting of 'recognized norms of consultation', particularly as they had been involved in the pre- and post-budget discussions with the finance minister.

Most studies of democratic governance capacity, especially those preoccupied with the contrasts between new democracies and their authoritarian predecessors, fail to recognize the vital importance of these types of tactics in allowing adjustment to become politically 'consolidated'. The architects of the good-government agenda have instead advanced a vague, sanitized, and ultimately unconvincing version of how transparency (implicitly equated with formal democracy) will assist reformers by facilitating the 'selling' of reform to a vibrant, well-organized civil society. The sort of manipulative and obfuscatory tactics employed regularly in the implementation of reform are, however, a much truer representation of the political reality in India. Above all, they are an integral part of the democratic political process wherever liberal democracy is practised successfully, whether in the developed or developing world.

NOTES AND REFERENCES

1. An oft-cited case of 'successful' decision-making, based upon inherently ambiguous cues, and yet subsequently attributed to political skill, is the Cuban missile crisis. See Graham Allison, *Essence of Decision: Explaining the Cuban Missile Crisis* (Boston, Little, Brown, 1971).

2. Guillermo O'Donnell, 'On the State, Democratization and Some Conceptual Problems: A Latin American View with Glances at Some Postcommunist Countries', *World Development,* vol. 21, no. 8 (1993), p. 1376.

3. Michael W. Bollom, 'Capturing Ideas: Institutions, Interests and Intellectual Property Rights Reform in India', paper presented at the Annual Meeting of the American Political Science Association, Washington, DC, 28–31 August 1997.

4. 'In a premeditated ploy to bypass parliament, [the government] waited for parliament's winter session to end and then, just days later, took brazen recourse to ordinance raj to amend the patents and customs laws . . . [which were then] presented to the president for his signature at the very last moment.' See 'By Stealth', *Economic and Political Weekly,* 7 January 1995, p. 3.

5. Teleological reasoning, which is based upon the fallacy that the inevitability of a given end-state 'requires' the emergence of a corresponding process in order to facilitate its achievement, is not uncommon in political analysis. A good overview of this pitfall can be found in Jose Serra's critique of Guillermo

O'Donnell's attempt to 'explain' the rise of authoritarianism in Brazil with reference to the structural requirements of capitalist development. See Jose Serra, 'Three Mistaken Theses Regarding the Connection between Industrialization and Authoritarian Regimes', in David Collier (ed.), *The New Authoritarianism in Latin America* (Princeton, Princeton University Press, 1979), pp. 99–164. For another good example, see Theda Skocpol, 'Wallerstein's World Capitalist System: A Theoretical and Historical Critique', *American Journal of Sociology,* vol. 82, no. 5, March (1977).

6. Robert A. Packenham, 'The Politics of Economic Liberalization: Argentina and Brazil in Comparative Perspective', Working Paper No. 206, Kellogg Institute for International Studies, University of Notre Dame (April 1994), p. 9.

7. Ashis Nandy, *At the Edge of Psychology: Essays in Politics and Culture* (New Delhi, Oxford University Press, 1990), p. 51. This may not be a peculiarly Indian trait. It may, in fact, even have been reinforced by the encounter with the British. Eric Hobsbawm has argued that most of the major changes to British economic, social, and political life since 1750 involved a marked preference for maintaining the form of old institutions, but with a profoundly changed content. *Industry and Empire* (Harmondsworth: Penguin, 1968), p. 18.

8. Leila L. Frischtak, 'Governance Capacity and Economic Reform in Developing Countries', *World Bank Technical Paper No. 254* (Washington, DC: The World Bank, 1994), pp. 23, 24

9. Ibid., p. 25.

10. For instance, his speech to a seminar on 'Panchsheel and Global Diplomacy' in New Delhi in June 1994 *(Asian Age,* 28 June 1994).

11. *Hindustan Times,* 20 April 1994.

12. *Sunday,* 27 March–2 April 1994, p. 14. As one commentary pointed out, the emphasis on continuity, which Rao called 'the middle path', was much closer in style to Indira Gandhi's approach to reform in the early 1980s than to Rajiv Gandhi's brash attempts at liberalization in the second half of the decade. *Business India,* 11–25 April 1994, p. 51.

13. This was most forcefully articulated in his budget speech to parliament for fiscal year 1992–3. See *Times of India,* 1 and 2 March 1992. Singh also claimed in other speeches that liberalization would correct urban-biased development policies, and thus rectify the Nehruvian overemphasis on industrial development by bringing India closer to a Gandhian vision. See the report on his speech at the National Institute of Advanced Studies, *Asian Age,* 5 July 1994.

14. This phrase was suggested by Sanjaya Baru, editorial page editor of the *Times of India.* Interview, 29 April 1995, New Delhi.

15. S. Guhan, 'Centre and States in the Reform Process', in Robert Cassen and Vijay Joshi (eds), *India: The Future of Economic Reform* (New Delhi, Oxford University Press, 1995), p. 101 (emphasis added).

16. Interview with Narendar Pani, acting resident editor, *Economic Times* (Bangalore edition), 18 April 1995, Bangalore.

17. In order to quell speculation that India was considering the abolition of food subsidies in response to international pressure, Civil Supplies and Public Distribution Minister A.K. Antony told a press conference: 'Whatever may be the constraints, there is no question of reducing or abandoning the food subsidy because food security is as important as national security, if not more.' *Asian Age,* 9 July 1994.

18. It also masks the fact that much of this subsidy—indeed a rising proportion—goes to pay for storage costs, which have been increasing as rising prices have reduced offtake by consumers. According to Partha Pratim Mitra, Controller of Accounts in the central government's power ministry, while the 'total food subsidy between 1984–85 and 1994–95 grew at an annual average rate of 19.5 per cent...the consumer subsidy went up by about 9 per cent during this period.' See his 'Economics of Food Security: The Indian Context', *Social Action,* vol. 46, July–Sept. (1996), p. 281.

19. See 'Illusion of Plenty', *Economic and Political Weekly,* 15 October 1994, p. 2073.

20. For instance, another example of adjustment's burdens being shifted on to the poor involves the activities of the National Cooperative Development Corporation (NCDC). 'In the context of adjustment,' argues Raghav Gaiha, 'the level and pattern of assistance by NCDC...[indicates that] the share of cooperatives for the weaker sections in total assistance declined from about 10.5 per cent in 1991–92 to 7.5 per cent in 1992–93.' See his 'Structural Adjustment, Rural Institutions and the Poor in India: A Comparative Analysis of Andhra Pradesh, Maharashtra and Karnataka', paper prepared for the UN Food and Agricultural Organization, 27 September 1994, p. 78.

21. *Frontline, 26* January 1996, p. 79.

22. Ashok Gulati and Shashanka Bhide, 'What Do the Reformers Have for Agriculture?', *Economic and Political Weekly,* 6–13 May (1995), p. 1091.

23. Anne Krueger told an Indian journalist that, in the area of economic reform, 'the main thing...is for the government to make its intentions very clear'. While this might hold true if the only objective were to reassure 'entrepreneurs waiting to see if the reforms are there to stay' (ibid.), it ignores the political logic which must simultaneously inform policy implementation.

24. *Deccan Herald,* 24 March 1994.

25. Mick Moore, 'Economic Liberalisation versus Political Pluralism in Sri Lanka', *Modern Asian Studies,* vol. 24, no. 2 (1990), p. 352, fn. 20.

26. See Robert S. Jenkins, 'The Politics of Protecting the Poor During Economic Adjustment in India; The Case of Maharashtra', in Usha Thakkar and Mangesh Kulkarni (eds), *Politics in Maharashtra* (Bombay, Himalaya Publishing, 1995), pp. 195–212.

27. Harry W. Blair, 'Success and Failure in Rural Development: A Comparison of Maharashtra, Bihar and Bangladesh', paper presented at the annual meeting of the Association of South Asian Studies, San Francisco, 25–27 March 1988, p. 7.

28. Interviews with a senior IAS officer in the accounts and audits bureaucracy, 9 October 1993, New Delhi; and a middle-ranking IAS officer knowledgeable about the JRY in Maharashtra, 1 March 1994, Pune. See also *The Hindu*, 18 October 1995.

29. For example, see the study conducted by the Institute of Regional Analysis, reported in *India Today*, 15 February 1995, p. 98.

30. This was the phrase used by a middle-ranking IAS officer knowledgeable about the JRY in Maharashtra. Interview, 1 March 1994, Pune. This paradox was further confirmed in the report of the Comptroller and Auditor General of India for the financial year ending 31 March 1994. Though it criticized the Rajasthan state government for accounting irregularities and diversion of funds between programmes, the report also found that the level of employment generated exceeded programme targets. Even accounting for falsification— such as the inclusion of bogus names on employment registers—this was a considerable achievement, made possible in part by payment (in at least two districts) of wages lower than the prescribed minimum. That workers would nevertheless turn out in large numbers suggests that targeting works despite pervasive graft. See *Observer of Business and Politics*, 2 May 1995.

31. Two evaluations of the JRY conducted by central government ministries found that roughly one-third of village panchayats implementing JRY schemes did not possess a copy of the JRY guidelines. It is therefore not surprising that, even according to official records, 18 per cent of JRY workers in 1992–3 were from ineligible economic categories—that is, households with incomes exceeding the poverty line. *Economic Times*, 20 January 1998.

32. This was the recommendation of the Narasimham Committee report on financial-sector reform, which argued that fiscal policy was the least distorting means for achieving redistributive ends. Credit policy, on the other hand, was considered an unnecessarily blunt instrument.

33. *Business World*, 28 July–10 August 1993, p. 89.

34. *Business India*, 25 October–7 November 1993, p. 99.

35. Ibid.

36. 'Banking: Lost Priority', *Economic and Political Weekly*, 18 December 1993, p. 2756.

37. Interview with a senior RBI official, 11 April 1995, Bombay.

38. *Business Standard*, 25 March 1994.

39. *Business World*, 5–18 April 1995, p. 131.

40. 'A Matter of Priority', *Business India*, 3–16 June 1996, p. 106.

41. *Business Today,* 22 April–6 May 1995, p. 36.

42. *Business Standard,* 25 March 1994.

43. 'Monkeying with Rural Credit', *Economic and Political Weekly,* 18 September (1993), pp. 1959–60.

44. *Business World,* 5–18 April 1995, p. 131.

45. 'A Matter of Priority', *Business India,* 3–16 June 1996, p. 106

46. *Economic Times* (editorial), 24 November 1993.

47. This was the view of Malcom S. Forbes, Jr., president and editor-in-chief of *Forbes,* the US-based business magazine. *India Today,* 15 March 1995, p. 133.

48. See Madhu Dandavate, 'Patronage to Maruti: Government's Policy of Double-Faced Liberalisation', *Indian Express,* 1 December 1993.

49. One newspaper editorial argued that over-regulation had 'led to the emergence of unofficial premia on different grades of coal, which was usually realized by the coal mafia. Indeed, many people believe it is because of the mafia that it is difficult to dismantle the present system.' *Economic Times,* 15 January 1994.

50. In January 1997 the Central Bureau of Investigation arrested CIL's former director of finance, Suresh Jha, for misappropriation of public funds. *Asian Age, 8* January 1997.

51. For instance, *Financial Express,* 18 March 1993.

52. *Observer of Business and Politics,* 18 April 1994.

53. Seminar on 'The Politics of Liberalisation', Birkbeck College, University of London, 17 June 1998.

54. The nurturing of a transitionary constituency was also facilitated by the government's decision to allow downstream users of coal to resell it, which was part of a more market-oriented approach to distribution. *Economic Times,* 15 January 1994.

55. Economist Intelligence Unit, *Country Report—India,* 4th Quarter, 1994 (London, 1994), p. 32.

56. Interview, 26 November 1993, New Delhi.

57. Economist Intelligence Unit, *Country Report—India,* 2nd Quarter, 1995 (London, 1995), p. 22.

58. Ibid., p. 23.

59. 'If Government is Frank, PSUs [Public-Sector Undertakings] Only Mean Cash', *Asian Age,* 8 November 1994.

60. Interview with Jayanta Sarkar, correspondent for the *Far Eastern Economic Review,* 26 April 1995, Calcutta.

61. *Times of India,* 6 September 1996.

62. *International Herald Tribune,* 8 September 1994. See also, 'Rethinking Reform', *Business India,* 10–23 April 1995, p. 141, which analyses the AITUC's

questioning of its traditional hostility to economic reform; and 'Labour Turns its Back on Militancy', *Business World*, 1–14 July 1992, pp. 28–33. The secretary of the union at the Maharashtra government-owned MAFCO actually voiced his support for privatization of the company. *Business India*, 11–24 March 1996, p. 100. Perhaps the best example of this trend is the position taken by the union leaders of the public-sector engineering company Jessop, who argued that instead of immediately paying workers the three months' back wages owed them (even though the firm had just been given Rs 58.40 million from the central government), the company should use the funds to improve future business prospects—by buying raw material to keep production going, and taking employment preservation into account when choosing among future business strategies. *Economic Times*, 4 February 1998.

63. *Economic Times*, 17 March 1994.

64. A study by the Maniben Kara Institute reported that of workers who accepted VRS packages, 63 per cent did not do so voluntarily, but due to physical intimidation by hired thugs and employers' threats of illegal lockouts. Reported in Ernesto Noronha, 'Wages of Globalisation', *Humanscape*, March 1998, p. 12.

65. In 1994, for instance, the Maharashtra state government allegedly worked with the management of Otis Elevators to stoke inter-union rivalries at its Kandivli plant in Bombay. *Business India*, 14–27 March 1994, p. 131. At the national level, one faction of the National Federation of Indian Railwaymen deplored the 'blatant partisan attitude of the railway ministry in favour of the small minority group'. *Business Standard*, 25 January 1994.

66. *Business World*, 12–25 January 1994, p. 115.

67. This happened in the case of the public-sector Coffee Board. *Economic Times*, 17 April 1994.

68. Gurbir Singh, 'Who Needs an Exit Policy Anyway?', *Economic and Political Weekly*, 10 June (1995), p. 1360.

69. In fact, the Tamil Nadu state government itself, through its state electricity board, was eventually found by the Supreme Court to have been one of the worst violators of contract-labour regulations. *Business India*, 5–18 June 1995, p. 149. CITU general secretary M.K. Pandhe accused Coal India Ltd. (CIL) of pursuing a concerted strategy of increasing coal production through contract labour. He also criticized the central government for failing to take action against these malpractices, though he admitted that some trade union leaders had themselves become contract labour middlemen, under false names, supplying casual labour to CIL subsidiaries. *Economic Times*, 28 December 1994.

70. For instance, the B.K. Birla group, which planned to transfer a business unit that had experienced chronic labour unrest to a dormant subsidiary. *India Today*, 15 August 1992, p. 57. And in an effort to retrench workers in its

electronics division, Ceat's personnel manager claimed that there were in fact two separate business units, each with fewer than 100 workers, the minimum required for India's pro-labour laws to take effect. *Times of India,* 11 September 1996.

71. *Economic Times,* 1 December 1993. Bush India, to take one example, ceased operations and re-registered as a way of moving its workers on to contract status. *Economic Times,* 7 February 1994.

72. See Mahesh Gavaskar, 'Labouring Over a Capital Task', *Humanscape,* May 1997, pp. 17–19.

73. Interview, 7 September 1996, New Delhi. This was also the view of a senior executive of a major British multinational firm. Interview, 29 August 1996, New Delhi.

74. When the project was subsequently reinstated, the Shiv Sena chief minister claimed to have negotiated a better deal for the state's consumers than had his Congress predecessor.

75. *India Today,* 15 March 1996.

76. Interview with a bureaucrat who previously held senior posts in state agricultural agencies, 12 September 1996, Bombay.

77. This strategy was revealed in an interview with a former policy adviser to the Government of India, 5 September 1996, New Delhi.

78. *Times of India,* 25 February 1996.

79. Some of these inducements have borne fruit. The chairman and entire board of one sugar cooperative quit the Congress and joined the Shiv Sena in exchange for promises of financial support. *The Hindu,* 21 January 1996.

80. *Indian Express,* 24 February 1996.

81. B.S. Baviskar, 'Leadership, Democracy, and Development: Cooperatives in Kolhapur District', in B.S. Baviskar and Donald W. Attwood (eds), *Finding the Middle Path: The Political Economy of Cooperation in Rural India* (Boulder, Colo., Westview Press, 1995), pp. 157–75.

82. Interview with Mayank Bhatt, special correspondent for *Business India,* 9 September 1996, Bombay.

83. *Business India,* 23 September–6 October 1996, p. 132. See also *The Hindu,* 6 January and 24 February 1996.

84. *Indian Express,* 21 June 1996. The Shiv Sena–BJP government, like its Congress predecessor, has resolutely refused to announce a clear-cut policy on the selling of the valuable central-Bombay land owned by textile companies. As a result, a number of firms were permitted, without the announcement of any specific policy, to go into the property-development business themselves. As of April 1995, three major firms had taken this circuitous route, precisely because of 'the absence of a clear-cut policy' by the state government. *India Today,* 30 April 1995, p. 101. Many more had taken unauthorized, but unofficially

tolerated, action by early 1996. An activist working on behalf of displaced textile workers stressed the clandestine nature of what is taking place: 'The mill area is being destroyed quietly and systematically...Crores [tens of millions] of rupees are passing hands in the land deals of Girangaon, most of it in the black.' *Frontline*, 26 January 1996, p. 94.

85. D.C. Gladney, 'Unity vs. Diversity in China', *Asian Age*, 6 March 1995 (originally published in the *International Herald Tribune*).

86. For an analysis of the shifting nature of regional inequality during different phases of the reform period, see Tianlun Jian, Jeffrey D. Sachs and Andrew M. Warner, 'Trends in Regional Inequality in China', *Working Paper 5412* (Cambridge, Mass., National Bureau of Economic Research, January 1996).

87. Gordon White, 'Market Reforms and the Emergence of Civil Society in Post-Mao China', IDS Working Paper No. 6 (Brighton, Institute of Development Studies, 1994).

88. *Business World*, 9–22 March 1994, p. 39.

89. P. Raman, 'Political Fallout of the Budget', *Business Standard*, 7 March 1994.

90. A variation on this theme is the statement by Bihar chief minister Laloo Prasad Yadav, a major political leader of the backward castes: 'Brahminism in this country has been conspiring with US imperialism in implementing the Dunkel [GATT] proposals and reducing the backward classes to slaves.' *Sunday*, 13–19 March 1994, p. 7.

91. Mulayam Singh Yadav became the chief minister of Uttar Pradesh in 1989, and Laloo Prasad Yadav took power in Bihar in 1990. After a period of BJP rule from 1991–2, and a subsequent year of centrally imposed president's rule, Mulayam regained power in December 1993, only to lose it again in 1995. In Bihar, Laloo Prasad Yadav's government served its full five-year term, and was re-elected in 1995.

92. *Economic Times*, 20 April 1994.

93. *The Hindu*, 17 August 1994.

94. Interview with Bhairon Singh Shekhawat, 20 April 1994, Jaipur.

95. This idea has been developed in greater depth in Rob Jenkins, 'Rajput Hindutva: Caste Politics, Regional Identity, and Hindu Nationalism in Contemporary Rajasthan', in Christophe Jaffrelot and Thomas Blom Hansen (eds), *The BJP and the Compulsions of Politics in India* (New Delhi, Oxford University Press, 1998).

96. *The Telegraph* (Calcutta), 25 April 1995.

97. *Financial Express*, 27 April 1995.

98. *Indian Express*, 27 April 1995.

7

The Limits of Economic Nationalism in India
Economic Reforms under the BJP-led Government, 1998–9[*]

BALDEV RAJ NAYAR

One of the more stunning political developments of the 1990s in India has been the rapid rise of the Bharatiya Janata Party (BJP). Emerging as the largest single political party in the Lok Sabha in the middle of the decade, it assumed power at the centre in 1998, even if only at the head of a multi-party coalition. The BJP's rise to this position marked a political watershed: it had long been considered to lie outside the accepted value structure of the political system because of its links with the cadre-based, Hindu nationalist cultural organization, the Rashtriya Swayamsevak Sangh (RSS).[1]

The BJP has regarded itself as a distinctive party—'the party with a difference'—since it rejects the larger normative consensus among India's political parties regarding secularism, viewing it pejoratively as pseudo-secularism designed to appease the minorities.[2] The party avers itself to be particularly different from other, presumably soft-minded, political parties in the arena of national security as well, where it is single-mindedly dedicated to building a strong India. Significantly, the BJP also considers itself distinctive in economic affairs. It rejects the developmental models followed by the Congress Party, whether the earlier Nehruvian one that invested the state with the commanding heights over

* Originally published as 'The Limits of Economic Nationalism in India: Economic Reforms under the BJP-led Government, 1998–1999', in *Asian Survey*, XL (5), September/October, 2000, pp. 792–815.

the economy or the more recent one (since 1991) of Narasimha Rao that drastically shifted the emphasis from the state to the market. More broadly, the BJP rejects both communism and capitalism, perceiving their foreign origins as rendering them out of harmony with India's cultural traditions. Instead, it opts forthrightly for *swadeshi*, which it equates with 'economic nationalism'. In my view, it should also be understood as standing, beyond protection for local industry, for an organic model of a well-integrated economy and society rooted in indigenous (Hindu) cultural values, including restraint on Western-style consumption patterns.

The question that emerges as being of interest here is whether there has been in actual practice anything distinctive about the BJP's economic policy in contrast to that of the Congress Party's. To some extent, the question may not yet have a definitive answer, for the BJP was in power for a bare 13 months and that, too, as part of a coalition. However, that it was in power through the mechanism of a multi-party coalition and was that coalition's dominant partner are facts in themselves highly significant in that they evidence both the limits and the possibilities of implementing the BJP's economic programme. The BJP's period in office, even if brief, nonetheless provides an opportunity to assess its policy behaviour against its stated ideology.

The empirical proposition that emerges from a review of the actual record of the BJP during its first term in office, as against its stated ideology, is that there is nothing really distinctive about the BJP governance in relation to economic policy. This finding is significant in view of the BJP's emphatic perception of itself as a distinctive party, which is also how it is characterized by its antagonists. This raises the important question as to why there should be little to differentiate the BJP in office from the Congress Party or from the United Front. The explanation for the phenomenon of similarity in economic approach during governance seems to be twofold. First, it lies *internally*, in the centrist tendency of Indian politics in the context of the country's immense social diversity and the considerably institutionalized nature of its political framework of democracy. Second, it lies *externally*, in the nature of the modern international system, primarily in terms of the substantial incentives to participation in a highly, though asymmetrically, interdependent world economy. It also lies in the pressures of realpolitik. The empirical proposition and the explanation are elaborated below; the analysis reverses the usual order of description followed by explanation, so as to provide a better comprehension of the dynamics of politics and policy-making under the BJP-led government.

THE CENTRIST TENDENCY IN INDIAN POLITICS AND
THE INTERNATIONAL SYSTEM AS EXPLANATION

Certainly, the most impressive fact about the Indian polity among the larger developing countries is its uniqueness in sustaining a democratic political framework for more than a half-century, justifying claims to Indian exceptionalism.[3] Over this period, political groups in India have thus confronted a political system in which the ballot box is the final arbiter in their quest for power. Despite the deterioration in the level of its institutionalization after the first quarter-century following Independence, India's political system has still proven sturdy and resilient enough to bar seizure of power through violence or the possession of the means of violence; putschist politics has simply not been possible. The mainline communist parties have since the early 1950s had to conform to the political requirements of the overarching democratic framework, while no Hindu nationalist group has ever contemplated seizure of power through violent means.

Coalition building is an integral part of the process of acquiring state power within a democracy. Narrowly based political groups are likely to make for extreme positions in politics, whether in regard to ideology and policy or intergroup relations. On the other hand, coalition building for a winning majority, whether in national politics or in the legislature, is likely to make for moderation in politics and policy. That tendency is strengthened by India's immense social diversity, which renders every group in practical terms into a minority. More than 200 years ago, James Madison (in the *Federalist Paper*, No. 10) had recommended extending the size of a political unit as a means, through encompassing greater diversity, to achieving the aim of moderation in politics and policy. What Madison intended to accomplish through political engineering has, however, been structurally given in India, especially for the centre, by its vast diversity. Interestingly, even the Hindu nationalists recognize the impact of India's diversity in advancing moderation. Lal Krishna Advani, the BJP's pre-eminent party organizer and theoretician, in 1980 underlined that in India, 'a party based on ideology can at the most come to power in a small area. It cannot win the confidence of the entire country—neither the Communist Party nor the Jana Sangh in its original form.'[4]

Functional as diversity may be in some respects, it can also have adverse consequences for politics, aggravating tensions and conflict in society as a result of the appeals by political parties to ethnic groups. Diversity thus sets in motion two opposing processes: ethnic mobilization and coalition building. No party is immune to either process, and all have to develop strategies to cope with both, even if at different levels of the political system. The situation is simultaneously pregnant with tension for relations within political parties, principally between the parliamentary or government wing and the organizational wing along with its associated interest groups. The parliamentary wing is likely to be oriented to the wider political environment, with the aim of acquisition of power within its constraints, while the organizational wing is likely to be more oriented to the interests, material and ideal, of its membership and related interest groups. Take, for instance, the relationship between the RSS as the sun or mother, as it were, and the BJP as the satellite or child, with cadres from the former constituting a large part of the membership of the latter. The RSS as a cultural organization is exclusionary in its membership and approach, intent on advancing the interests of the Hindus as a nation. On the other hand, politics and the quest for power in the context of a diverse and divided society demand that the BJP as a political party be inclusionary and compel it to seek coalitions with other political groups. The compulsion to be inclusionary and to form coalitions is likely to make for internal differences over policy and for compromise to overcome them. It may also give rise as a result to occasions where divergence emerges in strategy and policy between the BJP and the RSS. How to resolve the resulting tension between the BJP and the RSS, and within the BJP between its parliamentary and organizational wings, is the most formidable challenge for the BJP leadership.

In brief, India's institutionalized political structure dictates that power can be acquired only through the democratic process. That process, particularly as reinforced by India's social diversity, further dictates that political groups engage in coalition building. In turn, coalition building requires compromise among narrowly based political groups and the moderation of their narrow and extreme political positions toward a centrist stance. The BJP cannot be and is not immune to that process, at least over the longer run.

The Incentives to Globalization and Liberalization

Even though at one time an anathema in Indian politics, economic liberalization—incrementally, if not rapidly—has in the contemporary era of globalization become an aspect of the centrist position in the area of economic policy. Since the 1980s, national decision-makers have recognized the need to open the economy more widely. This has resulted from the awareness that, although the gains from participation in the world economy are unequally distributed in favour of the developed countries, shrinking away from active participation in it carries penalties by way of slower economic growth. It is precisely this awareness that lay behind the United Front coalition government (1996–8), most of whose constituents had earlier opposed liberalization, coming around to accepting its necessity. That behaviour of the coalition government was testimony to a changed mind-set. The attractiveness of a more open economy was reinforced—negatively by the failure of the contrasting closed economy model through the economic collapse of the Soviet bloc, and positively by the high-growth experience of the East Asian economies. As a consequence, there are powerful incentives for national decision-makers to follow similar policies in respect of liberalization and globalization. The BJP in office is no more immune to these incentives than are other governments.

Realpolitik and Economic Policy

The process of liberalization has at times been pushed forward also by the application of coercive pressures by the developed countries—directly and through the various international financial institutions—in order to advance their interests. I think that a country's economic actions may additionally spring from strategic impulses. Particular countries may adopt more open policies that accommodate the economic demands of one or more developed countries as side payments to bridge or smooth over strategic differences. The BJP as a ruling party is not immune to either coercive pressures or political calculation.

THE CENTRIST TENDENCY IN THE BJP'S LONG MARCH TO POWER

Because of the BJP's continued linkage to the RSS, through the party's considerable reliance on the RSS cadres in political mobilization, discussions about it often bristle with characterizations such as communal and sectarian, fascist and semi-fascist, and with accusations of having a hidden agenda to convert India into an authoritarian and theocratic Hindu state. For long, most other political parties treated the BJP as a political pariah even as they readily used, when convenient, its political support in their own drive to power.

In the most thorough and insightful treatment to date on the politics of Hindu nationalism, Christophe Jaffrelot[5] takes a somewhat different view of the BJP. He interprets its development in terms of oscillation between a strategy of ethnic mobilization and a strategy of moderation and alliance building. The oscillation theory is an attractive one, but it still tends to place the dynamic for change in the internal structure of the party, where the cadres are oriented toward the RSS and the party leadership is oriented toward the larger political system. I take a different reading of the historical material here. I suggest a unilinear direction in change in party strategy towards moderation and coalition-building—under the external stimulus of the structural features of India's democratic framework and social diversity—but one which was seriously interrupted, and partly disrupted, by antagonist political forces external to the party. In determining the longer-run direction of the BJP, it tends to downplay somewhat the within-party tension in favour of the structural features.

This different reading is indicated here in only the briefest of outlines in order to avoid diversion from the principal concern of the analysis with recent economic policy. As the BJP's predecessor, the Jana Sangh, founded in 1951, took part in the country's political process, it came to moderate its political stance and engage in forming alliances with other political parties. Eventually, in 1977, it merged itself into the hastily created Janata Party, which came to power at the centre in that year following the electoral defeat of the Congress Party. The Janata coalition collapsed in 1979. The former Jana Sangh leaders were not the cause of the collapse, even though they were made the pretext for it in the factional infighting; indeed, they tried hard to have the party stay united.

The bitter and humiliating experience at the hands of some of the coalition partners resulted in the revival of the Jana Sangh in 1980 in the new incarnation of the Bharatiya Janata Party, but on the moderate platform of secularism and Gandhian socialism. The BJP's moderate path was disrupted in the 1980s by forces external to the BJP rather than from within. Faced with threats to national unity on the part of religion-based movements, the Congress Party had turned to a softer position on Hindu nationalism in order to attract political support for itself. At that point, the BJP took to a militant course to prevent the erosion of its exclusive constituency. However, this course was soon exhausted, while the political process drove home the lesson that power at the centre, or even in the states, could not be obtained or retained except on a wider and more inclusive political base. By the mid-1990s, the BJP had moderated its position and turned to an alliance-building strategy. It is noteworthy that, when the BJP finally succeeded in achieving power at the center in 1998, it did so as part of an 18-party coalition. Significantly, to arrive at this coalition arrangement, the BJP placed a moratorium on the core issues of its agenda in order to create a common platform for the coalition.

THE BJP'S ECONOMIC AGENDA AND THE CENTRALITY OF THE NATIONAL INTEREST

Since the BJP is often identified as a revivalist party of the Hindus, whose religion predates the Christian era, there is a tendency to assume that its economic programme must represent a reversion to some archaic, antediluvian form of economic thinking. While its prescriptions may be presented under traditional nomenclature and one may not necessarily agree with them, they represent, in fact, an intellectually cogent and balanced, rather than ideological, position. I believe that they have honourable intellectual precursors in the mercantilism of Alexander Hamilton, Friedrich List, the advocates of managed trade in the West, and the contemporary practitioners of preferential trading blocs in free-trade areas.

The Congress Party government under Prime Minister Narasimha Rao initiated the acceleration of economic liberalization in 1991. In response, the BJP began to develop a more coherent economic programme of its own. The first outcome of this effort was an elaborate 54-page Economic Policy Statement in 1992. After that, the party's economic proposals were embodied in the electoral manifestos of 1996 and 1998. The election manifesto for 1998 remains the latest statement of the BJP's economic programme, since the party decided to forego a separate manifesto for the 1999 elections in favour of a single manifesto for the BJP-led National Democratic Alliance. This manifesto is the more relevant document for consideration, since it immediately precedes the formation of the BJP-led government in 1998. It is the most elaborate among the manifestos of all the parties and has the most coherent viewpoint underlying its various chapters.

The starting point for the BJP's thinking on economic policy is that the solution to the country's economic problems lies not in foreign models but rather within the country itself. Rejecting both communism and capitalism, the BJP offers a community-based approach that is stated to be derived from India's national heritage. Rhetorical homage to a model supposedly derived from tradition aside, the key impulse that underlies the BJP's economic programme is really 'the vision of every patriotic Indian to see our beloved country emerge as a strong, prosperous and confident nation, occupying her rightful place in the international community.'[6] That vision, no doubt, mandates freedom from hunger, unemployment, fear, and corruption, but also, importantly, 'to see India, the world's oldest cradle of civilization, transform itself yet again into a benign global power.' Toward the end of assuring a strong and prosperous

nation, the BJP wants to build a modern economy—not restore some traditional
subsistence economy based on old technology—and endorses rapid economic
development. The guiding principle that is central to the BJP in determining
economic policy is not dogma but entirely 'considerations of *national interest*
and what is appropriate for us.' Older technology may be more appropriate for
a labour-surplus economy, but the attraction lies in its functionality, not in
its age.

In underlining national interest as the guiding principle for economic
policy-making, the BJP is motivated by the strong belief that that is what all
nations, in fact, do: 'Every nation advocates free trade in all global fora but, in
practice, they compulsively resort to quotas, tariffs and anti-dumping measures
to protect their national interests....While the declared agenda is free trade, the
undeclared, but actual, agenda is economic nationalism.' Accordingly, 'India,
too, must follow its own national agenda,' and 'the broad agenda of the BJP will
be guided by Swadeshi or economic nationalism.' To the BJP, 'Swadeshi simply
means "India First". This is the governing principle of all nations.' The concept
is not to be understood simply in the narrow sense of protectionism: 'By
Swadeshi one means that the local resources and talents have the full *scope* for
development in national interest and the benefits therefrom should primarily
flow to the people. Integration into a global economy should not mean oblitera-
tion of national identity and predominant sway of powerful economic forces
from the outside.'[7]

The BJP as well as its predecessor, the Jana Sangh, had for long been against
the excessive state intervention in the economy characteristic of the Nehru
model. While 'urging a liberal economic regime in which the full creative genius
of the Indian people could flower,' the BJP indicted the Nehru model rather
severely for having given rise to centralization, economic inefficiency, suppression
of entrepreneurship, and corruption. With the reforms undertaken by the
Narasimha Rao government in 1991, the Congress Party had snatched the
BJP's liberalization plank away, as it were. However, the pre-empting of the
liberalization model by the Congress Party did not leave the BJP without a line
of attack. That line, while accepting the general direction of the policy of
liberalization, set out a distinctive path that was consistent with BJP's
philosophical position. Rejecting the conception of liberalization as a single
homogeneous policy, the BJP distinguished between 'internal liberalization'
and 'external liberalization' or globalization. The central question then became
one of sequencing. Its principal critique against the Congress government was
that it had opened up India to ruthless foreign competition without first

making sure that Indian firms were competitive. In its view, India should have first allowed local firms, which had been throttled for nearly four decades by state controls, to learn to compete among themselves over a period of ten to fifteen years before forcing them to confront foreign competition. In not doing so, the Congress government had undermined the national economy by facilitating its being overwhelmed by foreign multinationals. Instead, the BJP would have followed a policy of internal liberalization first. This policy would then have been followed by external liberalization. The overall prescription by the BJP was to

evolve a consensus on the time span required to enable our industries to adjust to the exacting demands of international competition. It means rapid, large-scale internal liberalization, but calibrated globalization so that the Indian industry gets a period of seven to ten years for substantial integration with the global economy....India must move carefully and gradually towards integration with the global economy and even as it so does [sic], it must act in a manner that suits its national interest. This strategy recognizes that Indian industry needs a period of transition before it can compete with global players. All policies of tariff reduction and lifting of quantitative restrictions will be formulated taking the above facts into account, but the objective will be to protect the national economy and national interest like all nations do and not to indulge in economic isolationism.[8]

The BJP is neither in favour of economic isolation nor opposed to foreign investment. Instead, the BJP is guided in its position by what it considers to be in the national interest. It believes that economic development in India has been and should continue to be financed primarily by local capital, with foreign capital playing only a supplementary role. Accordingly, the 1998 BJP manifesto suggested that a BJP government would

ensure that FDI [foreign direct investment] flows into such priority areas and not in areas where the domestic industry is functioning well. The BJP Government will frame policies to restrict FDI in non-priority areas. FDI will be encouraged to promote exports rather than target the domestic market. FDI is welcome in a non-predatory role in joint ventures rather than in 100% subsidiaries.

While eager to open the insurance sector to competition 'by involving [the] Indian private sector in the insurance business', the BJP was averse to opening it to foreign companies. It also wanted foreign companies to stay out of the consumer goods sector and to focus instead on high-technology areas and infrastructure ('computer chips yes, potato chips no'). In regard to foreign trade and patents, it was highly critical of WTO: 'The major task facing our country in the economic sphere is the preservation of a measure of autonomy in the management of the national economy, which the Congress Government surrendered meekly by accepting without resistance the highly prejudicial WTO conditionalities.'[9] In order to preserve national autonomy, it promised a restrictive national regime of licensing in respect to patents and services.

The BJP's outlook on the world economy is embedded in a broader economic approach that accords special importance to the interdependence of industry and agriculture in the national economy and gives a critical role to small-scale industry. The BJP promises 'to reverse the process of economic, social and political marginalization of India's rural population and effectively fight the elitist, anti-kisan [farmer] Congress mind-set,' and to that end 'earmark 60% of Plan funds in the budget for agricultural and rural development.'[10] It sees housing construction as a critical social need and a means for generating employment. In line with its nationalist posture, but contrary to policy projections based on its allegedly high-caste middle-class social base, the BJP makes rapid advance in health and education a key aim. It commits a future BJP government to providing potable drinking water to all villages and slums, increasing state spending on education to 6 per cent or more of GNP in five years, and giving priority to free primary education.

Even though in the working out of the joint 'National Agenda for Governance' with its allies the BJP gave up what were regarded as contentious issues or extremist measures, its economic platform on India's relationship with the world economy seems to have been largely acceptable to its allies. In other words, there was little difficulty in arriving at a consensus on economic nationalism. Besides promising primacy for removal of unemployment, high priority for infrastructure, allocation of 60 per cent of plan investment to agriculture in order to increase the purchasing power of the people, accelerated investment in the social sectors, particularly housing and education, the brief document on the joint agenda summarily stated:

We will continue with the reform process, give it a strong Swadeshi thrust to ensure that the national economy grows on the principle that 'India shall be built by Indians.' We will carefully analyze the effects of globalization, calibrate its process by devising a timetable to suit our national conditions and requirements so as not to undermine but strengthen the national economy, the indigenous industrial base and the financial and services sectors.[11]

Despite the claims to novelty about the BJP's economic policy, on the basis of a philosophy based on India's national heritage, not much credence need be placed on them. Protectionism is not the domain of any given ideology. Peter Burnell, an authority on the subject of protectionism, points out that economic nationalism is 'in some versions and some accounts actually subsumed under socialism'.[12] Indeed, while economic nationalism initially developed in India as part and parcel of the struggle against colonialism, in the post-Independence period economic nationalism had progressive origins insofar as it formed the central thrust of economic planning launched by Nehru in his vision of India's march toward a socialist society. Interestingly, Nehru aimed to build a largely autarkic economy through self-sufficiency in heavy Industries. Significantly, the underlying aim of Nehru's economic strategy was precisely the same as that of the BJP—to make India into a great power. Essentially, what seems to have happened is that the BJP snatched away the flag of nationalism, including economic nationalism, from the Congress Party when the latter tended to lose sight of Nehru's national vision amidst widespread corruption and the pressures of the great powers.

Since both the BJP and the Congress Party after 1991 largely agreed on internal liberalization, the real test of BJP's performance in relation to its claims to a distinctive economic policy pertains to external liberalization. To be sure, the BJP also places greater emphasis on agriculture and the informal sector, and on an accelerated privatization of the public sector, but these aspects can be easily accommodated within the economic agenda of the Congress Party. Briefly, from the stated position of the BJP, one would expect it to be more restrictive than the Congress Party had been in relation to trade policy, foreign direct investment, the opening of the insurance sector to foreign companies, and patents policy.

ECONOMIC POLICY REFORMS UNDER THE BJP–LED GOVERNMENT

Any assessment of the performance of the BJP-led government must take into account the fact that the government was in power for only a short time, just 13 months. Even over this short period, its record was not spread evenly. The period can be divided into two phases: the first lasted eight months and proved to be an absolute disaster in terms of the management of the economy, while the second demonstrated a great deal of movement and showed considerable promise that was not fulfilled.

Legislative and Economic Mismanagement and the Steep Learning Curve

During the first phase, especially its first four months, the economy, which had been on a downslide for nearly two years, was allowed to drift, with serious consequences for the reputation of the government and therefore doubts about its continuance in power. Three important factors underlay the dismal performance. The first of these concerned the nuclear tests in May 1998 after the government had been in power for hardly two months. The nuclear tests had a twofold effect on the economy and economic policy. On the one hand, the government perforce became completely preoccupied with the diplomatic fallout of the nuclear-tests, as the Western coalition under the leadership of the US sought to isolate India politically and to punish it economically. On the other hand, while the tests were overwhelmingly popular with the public, they made the government politically vulnerable. The economic sanctions and the diplomatic isolation aggravated an already deteriorating economy, and escalated economic uncertainty. Meanwhile, the razor-thin majority of the government made it risk-averse and reluctant to undertake any important, and therefore controversial, economic initiatives.

The second factor, which deepened fears about political instability, had to do with the perils of coalition-management in a government comprising 18 partners, especially from the exceedingly recalcitrant and obstreperous J. Jayalalitha, who eventually defected and brought about the downfall of the government. Until then, the government remained preoccupied with the constant pulls of allies. With survival as its paramount concern, major economic initiatives were precluded. The allies were not the only source of problems. At the very beginning, the RSS vetoed Vajpayee's initial selection of Jaswant Singh as finance minister because of his more favourable attitude toward multinationals. To some extent, the RSS veto served to undermine Vajpayee's capacity to manage the government by showing him up to be a weak leader who could not stand up to the RSS bosses.

A third factor that affected the functioning of the central government adversely was the lack of experience on the part of most of its ministers. This feature resulted in making them dependent on the bureaucracy; but the bureaucrats, long used to working with the Congress and expecting it to return to power soon, were not inclined to be very cooperative. The consequence was incapacity on the part of the government to push through new initiatives during its honeymoon period.

The Fiasco of the First Budget

The annual budget is the most important statement of the government's economic policy, but the reception of the budget by the public and economic actors depends on their prior expectations. In the case of the budget for 1998–9, the finance minister's task was a formidable one in view of the state of the inherited economy and the excessive expectations over the budget. Especially since mid-1996, the economy had been on a severe downturn. It was in tatters before Yashwant Sinha took over as finance minister. The gravity of this economic situation was compounded by the economic sanctions that followed the 1998 nuclear tests. For instance, World Bank loans were no longer available to the Government of India except for humanitarian projects. There was also a notable drop in foreign investment. Foreign investment had already seen a considerable decline since 1996–7; after the nuclear tests, it fell further. Foreign portfolio investors, rather than bringing in money, were selling off their holdings; in the process, they hammered down the stock markets.

It was in the midst of a growing economic crisis that Finance Minister Sinha had to develop his first budget. The challenge for him was how to get the economy out of its depressed state and how to overcome the decline in foreign aid and loans as a result of the economic sanctions. The expectation was that Sinha would present a tough budget that would show the world that India meant business in the post-nuclear period. Some counted on major reforms in the budget that would, under the pressure of the economic sanctions and the country's political isolation, suddenly reject the BJP's platform of economic nationalism and make a giant leap to globalization.

The budget came as a major disappointment to investors, especially foreign investors, though Indian industry gave it a warm welcome. The immediate epithet that was applied to it by the usually liberal-oriented financial press and journals was that it was a *swadeshi* budget. The reason for the choice of that epithet was that Sinha did not extend any special welcome to foreign investors, believing that the existing incentives were sufficient. He shrugged off the sanctions as of little consequence for the Indian economy, and therefore not deserving of any extraordinary counter-measures. More significantly, the budget manifested a deeper sentiment for reliance for investment on local business and non-resident Indians (NRIs) in the belief that they were more loyal to India and more sensitive to its needs. To overcome the temporary constraint on the inflow of foreign funds to the Indian government, the finance minister launched the Resurgent India Bonds. These bonds were designed specifically for purchase by NRIs. Contrary to the initial doubts of most observers, the bonds turned out to be highly successful, yielding $4.3 billion. I interpret this outcome as a symbol of the country thumbing its nose at the economic sanctions. Further, the finance minister, in order to assure Indian business a level playing field, placed a special additional duty on imports. Most analysts, however, were critical of the huge increases of the order of 19 per cent in the plan allocations for investment with a view to kick-start the economy, fearing that they would lead to double-digit inflation.

Beyond these aspects of the budget, what emerged as really disturbing was the management of the budget after its presentation. One day hefty increases in petrol prices were announced, and the very next day were largely rolled back in the face of public outrage. Similarly, the government raised the price of fertilizer but opposition from allies and adversaries forced it to withdraw the increase. Again, the finance minister imposed a special additional duty of 8 per cent on imports to provide Indian industry a level playing field, but then, in response to attacks from different quarters, cut it to half. These frequent changes showed the weakness of the BJP vis-à-vis its allies. Critics in parliament and outside began referring to the finance minister mockingly as 'Rollback Sinha'. The government appeared bewildered and, in the context of the frequent changes made to the budget, the pertinent question seemed to be not whether the BJP had a hidden agenda, as often charged, but whether it had any agenda at all.

The question arises whether the Sinha budget was really *swadeshi,* notwithstanding the consensus about that characterization among the liberal-oriented financial press and the partisan political opposition. Actually, it would seem, there was little basis for such a characterization of the budget, particularly as it was finally passed. There were really slim pickings for the *swadeshi* lobby. The special additional duty was halved when a part of the industry protested against it. Even with this extra duty, India remained fully compliant with its commitments to the WTO. The additional duty was simply a countervailing one aiming to net out the effects of local taxes. It was really no different in its impact from the special import duty of 5 per cent imposed by the United Front government the previous year. Moreover, the Resurgent India Bonds were not an innovation by Sinha. Congress Party governments in 1988 and 1991 launched similar bond schemes for the mobilization of funds from abroad. It seems that the charge of *swadeshi* was made against Sinha because he had refused to hurriedly lay out the red carpet to foreign investors with new incentives, which the advocates of globalization wanted. It was really excessive expectations, and not substance, that led to the budget being described as *swadeshi.*

In the final analysis, the budget was *swadeshi* not for its content but simply for having been presented by the BJP. Nothing had been taken away from foreign investors; indeed, the finance minister intended to double FDI in the next two years while foreign institutional investors (FIIs) were now allowed to invest in unlisted debt. Significantly, there was no increase in taxes on domestic or foreign companies. However, the frequent changes in the budget resulted in the BJP-led government being stuck with the label of ineptitude in the legislative management of the budget, which it could not shake off. In the end, the budgetary process proved to be a disaster area for the BJP and its reputation in governance.

In the midst of the perception of ineptitude, some of the positive aspects of the budget were ignored. The BJP's determination to deepen reforms was manifest in the bold decision to open up the insurance sector to private enterprise, albeit by allowing only Indian entrants. Insurance reform signalled a moderate increase in liberalization. In so doing, the BJP went further than any earlier government. Also radically different was the increase in the plan allocation for agriculture, of the order of 58 per cent (as against the cut of 12 per cent in the previous year's budget). The hefty increase was based on the government's belief that a healthy rural economy is good for the long-term health of the national economy. The budget also increased the allocation for education by 50 per cent; this was in part-fulfilment of the determination to take expenditures on education to 6 per cent of GDP. Again, the budget embodied a radical decision by the government to bring its share in the equity of non-strategic public sector enterprises down to 26 per cent, besides the delicensing of coal, lignite, and petroleum. In the light of these initiatives, Sinha objected to the charge that his budget showed no vision, no big ideas, and that it was merely inclined to tinkering. He was correct in claiming that he had taken a balanced approach rather than grandly emphasizing one or two issues to the exclusion of others.

Deepening of the Economic Crisis and the Electoral Shocks

It was Sinha's misfortune that he had to present his budget in the context of enormous turbulence in the world economy, particularly in East and Southeast Asia, and a decline in India's agricultural production during the preceding year. After the presentation of the budget, the financial markets were in continuous turmoil. The rupee also continued to depreciate. Some critics predicted an economic meltdown. It may not have been the case that the budget caused the fall in the stock markets, but it undoubtedly failed to reverse the free-fall resulting from change in market sentiment under the impact of the economic sanctions, the contagion of the Asian economic crisis, and political uncertainty.

Prices rose sharply; the rate of inflation based on the consumer price index for industrial workers more than doubled from 8.2 per cent in April to 19.7 per cent in November 1998; while that based on the index for agricultural labourers more than quadrupled from 4.6 per cent to 18.3 per cent.[13] However, the impact of the price rise was especially marked in particular sectors. Weather-inflicted misfortune led to the shooting up of prices of vegetables, especially onions. Power outages for extended periods and shortage of water supply angered the public in the capital. The rise in crime deepened the image of the BJP as incompetent and ineffective in governance. The problem was not so much the authoritarianism or fascism of the BJP, as had been predicted, but rather its inability to exercise authority at all. The management of the economy turned out to be another disaster area for the BJP. The resulting public alien-ation spilled over into several state elections.

The victory of the Congress Party in the elections to state legislatures in November 1998 in the three important states of Delhi, Rajasthan, and Madhya Pradesh came as a stunning blow to the BJP. The debacle in these elections was not simply a judgement on the performance of the state governments ruled by the BJP in Delhi and Rajasthan; rather, in what amounted to a semi-national election, the comprehensive sweep of all the three states by the Congress Party was a resounding pronouncement on the performance of the BJP government at the centre. The election results signalled a resurgence of the Congress, leading to the belief that the BJP-led government's days were numbered, as the coalition would soon disintegrate. The elections underlined that ideology was not enough, and that performance in governance mattered to the electorate, even in the BJP's citadel in the capital. In the view of the public, governance was another disaster area for the BJP.

BJP's Conversion to the Globalization Paradigm

After the fiasco of the first budget of the BJP-led government, Vajpayee became concerned about the public image of the government as a doddering coalition and, more substantively, about the continuing decline and turbulence in the economy. He became determined therefore to take a direct hand in economic management and economic reforms. However, it would be a mistake to think that until then the government had done nothing in that direction. In fact, quite a few initiatives had been undertaken in different areas, with individual ministers eager to establish a record for themselves.

Liberalization Before the Budget

Several ministers were particularly active in the area of economic policy reform. Indeed, it would seem that the liberalizing face of the BJP was already manifest;

only it had been overshadowed by the caricaturing of the budget as *swadeshi* and by the foreign criticism of the nationalism evident in the nuclear tests. Soon after taking charge as finance minister, Sinha declared that the 1991 reforms had been 'a step in the right direction', assured multinationals that they 'have nothing to fear' from BJP's policy of economic nationalism, and vowed to 'deepen, broaden and accelerate' reforms.[14] In what was the first major economic policy pronouncement of the BJP-led government, Commerce Minister Ramakrishna Hegde inaugurated the second generation of reforms in April 1998 by boldly moving faster than required by India's commitments to WTO on phasing out quantitative restrictions on imports, including consumer goods, and hastening the process of integrating the economy with the global economy.

Hegde's bold move did not go unnoticed. An editorial in the *Times of India,* arguably the most influential newspaper in India, observed: 'For all its *swadeshi* rhetoric, the BJP-led government has shown itself in practice to be eminently pragmatic and progressive.'[15] Another editorial also agreed, commenting that Hegde 'has risen above the pettiness *of swadeshi* and pushed for a more liberal trade regime.'[16] An economics reporter for *India Today* thought that Hegde's dramatic move 'might embarrass those who had written off a BJP-led Government as *swadeshi* fanatics.'[17]

A similar trend was obvious in industry, where the government early on decided against the BJP's long-standing commitment to institute a 'negative list' of non-priority areas, especially consumer goods, from which foreign investors would be barred. India's premier financial newspaper viewed the decision as evidence that 'the sobering realities of governance have overtaken *swadeshi*.'[18] Paradoxically, the assertion of nationalism through the nuclear tests quickened the pace of government approval of foreign investment proposals in an endeavour to compensate for the fall in official aid flows and to strengthen the business lobby abroad against the sanctions. The effort drew the editorial comment that 'one of the first casualties of Shakti [code name for the nuclear tests] has been *swadeshi*.'[19] As a signal to foreign investors, Industry Minister Sikandar Bakht also amicably resolved the dispute, inherited from the previous government, between Suzuki and the government over management control in the automobile giant Maruti. The government also quickly signed counter-guarantees for several power projects.

In perhaps the most important piece of economic reform legislation brought forward until then by the BJP-led government, Power Minister P.R. Kumaramangalam introduced a bill in parliament in June 1998 to convert the state electricity boards into independent state electricity commissions in order to rescue them from their bankrupt position. The bill was an indicator of the reformist intent of the government. The effort was hampered in the face of strident opposition from some of the coalition partners. In another area, Housing Minister Ram Jethmalani brought considerable dynamism to his ministry; with determination, he pushed for the repeal of the Urban Land (Ceiling and Regulation) Act, a deterrent to investment in housing, even though success came only in the next year. In sum, the reformist inclinations of the BJP-led government were already manifest.

Liberalization After the First Budget

Placed on the defensive by the nuclear tests and the experience of the budget, the government's drive for reforms had stalled. Recovering its balance after the passage of the budget in July, but fearing that it may face a no-confidence motion during the coming winter session in November, the government entered a more assertive phase. The continuing economic slowdown created pressure on the government to move decisively in the economic arena. Like Narasimha Rao, Vajpayee made the economy his priority. According to T.T. Ram Mohan, Vajpayee's cabinet reviewed ways 'to launch a steady stream of policies and initiatives that would enable the ruling coalition to drastically improve its image, and prepare it for the polls if necessary.'[20] The coming independence anniversary also provided a stimulus for new policy initiatives. The government then unveiled a far-reaching time-bound plan for the information technology sector, which was received with enthusiasm by the computer industry. A definite indication of the government's determination to move forward along a broader front came with a major bureaucratic shuffle and the strengthening of the Prime Minister's Office.

There then followed the appointment of two blue-ribbon advisory councils, one consisting of eminent economists and the other of top business leaders, to advise the prime minister on economic policy. This caused some bitterness in the BJP because the members appointed to these councils could as well have all been appointed by the Congress Party. Two of the BJP's resident economists, known for their enthusiasm for economic nationalism—Jay Dubashi and Jagdish Shettigar—were excluded because they were considered too ideological. Also ignored was Rahul Bajaj, the foremost exponent of economic nationalism in Indian business and a charter member of the Bombay Club. Later, a series of policy moves by the government cumulatively added to the BJP shifting its centre of gravity to the globalization agenda of the previous governments of the Congress Party and the United Front. The government delicensed the sugar industry, and decided to join the Paris Convention on intellectual property rights.

In its determination to signal that the BJP government had an outward-looking orientation, the cabinet decided to bring forward two pieces of highly important legislation. These pieces of legislation had been approved earlier by the previous governments but had not received legislative approval. These controversial bills included the Patents Bill and the Insurance Regulatory Authority Bill (IRA). The BJP's decision to make the IRA bill its own was momentous for two reasons. First, the BJP had prevented the introduction of the bill by the United Front government the previous year when it was in the opposition. Second, unlike the draft of the United Front government that only provided for the appointment of an insurance regulatory authority, though with the unstated intent of subsequently opening up the insurance industry to private competition, the BJP's amended bill was far more radical in that it allowed foreign companies to invest and did so at the high level of 40 per cent of equity (including 14 per cent by NRIs). This represented a remarkable somersault in the BJP posture on globalization, even though the passage of such a bill remained a questionable proposition.

The electoral setbacks in the state elections did not deter the BJP-led government from proceeding with the new globalization agenda but only added to its determination to persevere. Apparently, the government was convinced that, if it eventually had to go, it had better go out with a record of performance behind it, rather than remain paralysed. However, for some from the BJP it was a moment of truth, for their world had just been turned around. Initially, Human Resources Minister Murli Manohar Joshi, a former BJP president, had taken a hard-line position against the opening up of the economy but finally came around. On the other hand, Home Minister Advani, deemed to be close to the RSS, forthrightly accepted the new line. With his usual no-nonsense pragmatism, he took the stance that one cannot just keep on holding to old positions and that being in charge of government made a difference: 'When we were not in the government, we felt that opening up of the insurance sector to Indian private entrepreneurs would suffice. But in government, with a determination to make as much progress as we can in the field of infrastructure, we felt that a different approach was called for.' More broadly, he added: 'No economic philosophy should become a dogma. The BJP believes in *swadeshi*, which in essence means that India has to develop on its own. It certainly does not mean xenophobia or belief that everything foreign is bad.'[21] Similarly, Sinha realized: 'There's a big difference between being in the government and outside the government. In government, you have access to a great wealth of information which could change your opinion. I don't see why ideas should not be changed and modified over the years?'[22]

For most BJP ministers in the cabinet, the opening up of the insurance sector was no longer considered antithetical to *swadeshi*. Indeed, *swadeshi* was now given a new interpretation to make it consistent with globalization, with Finance Minister Sinha maintaining: 'Swadeshi actually means competition, going out to the world and winning.'[23] Subsequently, in a long interview, Sinha elaborated on this sentiment, in the process making globalization the best means to swadeshi:

I understand *swadeshi* basically as a concept which will make India great. And India can be great only when we become an economic superpower....We can be great by being able to compete. I think competition is the essence. I am a great believer in competition. We are willing to face it abroad and here. After the nuclear tests, to think that we will go the East India Company way, or that transnationals will come in and take over, or that they will exercise undue influence, that foreign investment should be resisted—these are all concepts which are not valid any more. And therefore, *swadeshi*, globalizer, and liberalizer are not contradictions in terms. I personally think that globalization is the best way of being *swadeshi*.[24]

It is unclear whether Sinha may earlier have been fully in favour of liberalization, but Vajpayee has all along been the liberal face of the BJP. However, neither Sinha nor Vajpayee could have single-handedly persuaded all of the BJP ministers on the merits of economic reform. What the episode disclosed was that there was, indeed, always a substantial liberal wing in the BJP that had now taken charge of the government, and that it had been responding to the requirements of coalition-making in the Indian situation. The eminent economic columnist Swaminathan Aiyar relates his experience with Vajpayee during the 1998 elections when Vajpayee seemed to him to be distancing himself from what Aiyar thought was the historical position of the BJP:

I asked you at the time, is this not dilution of policy? Not at all, you replied. When the Jana Sangh started, it had to cater to the aspirations of a small section of society. As the party grew and grew, it had to cater to the aspirations of several other sections of society. This, you declared, was not dilution but evolution.'[25]

However, such an evolution in a centrist direction and in joining the mainstream was not acceptable to all in the Hindutva family.

The Hindutva Empire Strikes Back

The reaction to the shift by the government on globalization was not too long in coming, and it came from the RSS and its other affiliates as well as from the

BJP organizational wing and a segment of its parliamentary wing. The most strident assault on the government's position came from the Swadeshi Jagran Manch (SJM) (Front for the mass awakening of economic nationalism)—and it was quickly echoed by other RSS affiliates. The special clout of the SJM derived from the presence on its steering committee of K.S. Sudarshan, a top functionary of the RSS who later became the supreme leader of the RSS, and Dattopant Thengadi, a highly regarded aging RSS leader who had founded the SJM and the trade-union arm Bharatiya Mazdoor Sangh (BMS). That lent SJM's pronouncements the imprimatur of the RSS itself.

Normally, the expectation would have been that the entire RSS family would discuss things quietly and privately and bring the government into line. But the government did not seem to be amenable, for a two-day meeting of the SJM's steering committee at August-end in 1998 brought the dispute definitively into the open, with a stinging resolution warning the government 'not to give in to vested interests and business lobbyists' and 'not compromise with national interests.' It urged the government 'to refrain from allowing FDI directly or indirectly in the insurance sector.' Its attack was wide-ranging, raising serious objection to retaining bureaucrats 'who are habituated to compromise national interests' and appointing persons on advisory committees 'who are hostile to the very idea of *swadeshi*.'[26] The SJM moderated its stand for a while, but then charged into the government with renewed vigour after the BJP's losses in the state elections, which were attributed to the government having gone back on its swadeshi platform. By the end of November, 25,000 BMS workers from all over India protested in front of parliament against the government's economic policies. There, Thengadi accused the government of proposing the insurance bill under American pressure and asked it to 'desist from taking an anti-national course'.[27] Interestingly, the left parties welcomed the SJM's resistance to the opening up of the insurance sector to foreign investors.

Soon, the SJM was joined in its opposition by the BJP organizational wing. BJP president Kushabhau Thakre underlined the contradiction between the party's rhetoric and the government's plan on insurance, complaining: 'The party was given no indication that this was in the offing. Till yesterday, we were saying something, and now our government is doing just the opposite.'[28] In similar vein, Jay Dubashi, member of the BJP national executive, underlined in an open letter to the BJP president:

the government has suddenly made an about-turn and is now following an agenda of its own, which not only differs markedly from ours but is in many respects diametrically opposed to it...[T]he government's stand is diametrically opposed to the party's long-standing position on these issues.'[29]

Several seasoned members of the BJP's parliamentary wing expressed their opposition to the government's plans. The attack on the government turned into an avalanche. Most critically, the RSS pitched in, after a rarely held study session, with a resolution strongly censuring the government's conduct in allowing FDI in insurance. RSS strongman Sudarshan held a veiled threat to the BJP and the government by declaring that the RSS had never aligned itself with any particular political party but that it only supported those parties that reflected its overall views.[30] 'There was evident in the RSS a sense of having been betrayed by the government, worry about the 'Congressization' of the BJP,[31] and its straying away from the RSS. The relations between the two had plummeted, and one commentator thought 'the scale of RSS attack this time is truly phenomenal.'[32]

Vajpayee and Government Stand Firm

Despite the rising tide of criticism and protest from the RSS and its other affiliates, Vajpayee refused to yield. This development was unlike the past when the political party would normally fall in line after being reprimanded by the RSS to mend its ways. It was also unlike the occasion at the beginning of the BJP-led government when Vajpayee let the RSS veto his appointment of Jaswant Singh as finance minister. Now, he inducted him as foreign minister, in sheer defiance of the RSS. Vajpayee also brought the BJP organizational wing into line with the government. At the meeting of the national executive of the BJP at Bangalore in early January 1999, which was a turning point in the relations between the government and the BJP, Vajpayee stood firm and refused to subordinate himself to the party organization, asserting the primacy of the prime minister and government: '[W]idest consultations are desirable, but decisions of the government are final' Vajpayee seemed determined to disengage the BJP from the RSS. Eventually, the party had to accept the position that 'government knows best.'[33]

Nor would Vajpayee concede specifically on his economic policy reforms, and he considered it an embarrassment that the party instead of being supportive was adding to the government's problems. The party finally had to give in; the economic resolution, as one newspaper editorial put it, 'all but disavowed the mind-set of economic nationalism,' aiming 'to silence the strident *swadeshi* lobbies among the Sangh Parivar.[34] After the Bangalore meeting, the BJP rallied to the defence of government policies against the attacks of the SJM and its allies. This definitely marked a change in the relationship of the BJP to the RSS; the equations within the family seemed changed and it was the party that appeared to have acquired primacy. The resulting consequences for policy covered a wide arena, including treatment of minorities. In due course, a sort of truce developed within the family in view of the threat to the stability of the government from the Congress and other parties, but significantly the truce was on the BJP's terms.

Vajpayee and his government pushed forward with economic policy reform. However, its success depended on cooperation from the Congress Party, since the government lacked a majority in the upper house (Rajya Sabha). Such cooperation was forthcoming only for the Patents Bill, apparently since the Congress Party was the one to have made the international commitments for it when in office. However, the IRA bill was a different story. The Congress Party proved to be devious about extending support, since the credit for the most important globalization measure since the reforms of 1991 would then have gone to the BJP. Indeed, the Congress Party became desperate to oust the government precisely when it saw the BJP finally getting its act together along a wide front, including foreign relations, and becoming adept at governance. Even as it failed to get the IRA bill and other measures enacted because of the non-cooperation of the Congress Party and the blocking tactics of the other opposition parties in parliament, the BJP had by its actions before its downfall made abundantly clear the shift in its outlook on globalization.

Beyond economic policy reform, which was also manifest in other areas—such as buy-back of shares, innovatively amending telecommunications policy, opening internet services to the private sector, moving more boldly on phasing out quantitative restrictions on imports—the government had learned to manage the economy better, with some help from nature. The government's second market-friendly budget for 1999–2000 was marketed better and it triggered a boom on the stock market to reach record levels: there were no rollbacks this time. Meanwhile, the GDP growth rate for 1998–9 increased to near 7 per cent, agricultural production reached record levels, industrial recovery was underway, and inflation was at its lowest in some two decades. Subsequently, despite the war-like conflict with Pakistan over Kargil, which added immensely to Vajpayee's stature as a mature and responsible statesman, inflation remained low and the stock markets remained largely stable. The BJP's continued commitment to reform was manifest after the return of the coalition to power following the 1999 elections.

CONCLUSION

India's immense social diversity and the considerable institutionalization of its democratic political framework have had a significant impact on the party system. This social heterogeneity has made reaching concrete policy decisions difficult. However, under its impact India's political parties have tended to become centrist. More recently, they have tended to enter into alliance building. Therefore, coalition building has moderated the extreme ideological positions of individual parties. Social diversity has had a double effect. In the arena of political mobilization, it has accentuated appeals to ethnic identities. At the same time, it has attenuated tension by advancing a centrist agenda. No national party appears to be immune from either tendency.

The centrist tendency of Indian political parties as manifested by the BJP was apparent earlier in its precursor, the Jana Sangh. It was apparent, again, in the early years of the BJP. The tendency was disrupted, not by forces internal to the BJP, but forces external to it. As the Congress Party oriented itself favourably towards Hindu communal forces in the context of threats to national unity on the part of religion-based movements, the BJP changed direction to reclaim and protect an earlier exclusive constituency. But the compulsions of power-seeking made the BJP once again moderate its position and launch an alliance-building strategy. It is significant that the BJP came into power as part of a larger coalition, in the course of the formation of which the BJP had to give up its extremist planks. The experience of the BJP, if sustained, would not be unique; similar changes have been commonplace in other democracies.

The learning experience as a result of being in charge of a multi-party coalition government has further induced moderation in the BJP. Once in power, the BJP pursued a moderate economic agenda. The BJP's earlier strident position on economic nationalism (swadeshi) has been discarded in favour of a stance that is convergent with that of the Congress Party and the United Front. This article concludes that the centrist tendency generated by India's political system is the principal explanation for the change in the BJP's moderate economic policy. In an era of economic globalization, the acceptance of economic liberalization is a manifestation of the centrist tendency in Indian politics.

NOTES AND REFERENCES

1. On the RSS, see Walter K. Andersen and Shridhar D. Damle, *The Brotherhood in Saffron: The Rashtriya Swayamsevak Sangh and Hindu Revivalism*

(Boulder, Colo., Westview Press, 1987). Fundamentally, in its organization and ideology, the RSS has been, in part, reflective of an emulative strategy of 'semitization' of Hinduism through selectively borrowing from those whom it perceived as its adversaries—Muslims and Christians—such features as it believed to have contributed to their power and enabled them to conquer India and dominate the much more numerous Hindus. See Christophe Jaffrelot, *The Hindu Nationalist Movement in India* (New York, Columbia University Press, 1996), pp. 51, 76, 78. In this sense, the RSS is only a copy; Islam and Christianity are the original models.

2. The various contending versions of nationalism in India share with nationalism in the developing countries the generic features of 'imagined community' and 'derivative discourse'; however, they differ in respect of the contours of the imagined community. On the concept, see Benedict Anderson, *Imagined Communities: Reflections on the Origins and Spread of Nationalism* (London, Verso, 1983) and Partha Chatterjee, *Nationalist Thought and the Colonial World: A Derivative Discourse?* (London, Zed Books, 1986).

3. See Myron Weiner, *The Indian Paradox: Essays in Indian Politics* (New Delhi, Sage, 1989).

4. Cited in Jaffrelot, *The Hindu Nationalist Movement in India*, p. 314.

5. Ibid.

6. Unless otherwise indicated, citations in this section are from BJP, 'Vote BJP, Vote for a Stable Government, Vote for an Able Prime Minister: Election Manifesto 1998' (New Delhi, 1998).

7. Ibid.

8. Ibid.

9. Ibid.

10. Ibid.

11. The NDA manifesto is reprinted in C. P. Bhambhri, *Indian Politics Since Independence* (New Delhi, Shipra Publications, 1999), pp. 224–30.

12. Peter J. Burnell, *Economic Nationalism in the Third World* (Brighton, Sussex, UK, Wheatsheaf Books, 1986), p. 78.

13. Government of India, *Economic Survey 1998–99* (New Delhi, Ministry of Finance, 1999), p. 66.

14. 'MNCs Have Nothing to Fear, Says Sinha', *The Times of India*, 21 March 1998, and 'Reform Process Will Be Accelerated, Broadened', *The Times of India*, 26 March 1998.

15. 'Swadeshi Liberalism', *The Times of India*, 15 April 1998.

16. 'Reassuringly Boring', *Economic Times*, 14 April 1998.

17. Shefali Rekhi, 'Blow to Saffronomics', *India Today International,* 27 April 1998, pp. 30–1.

18. 'Sense on FDI', *Economic Times,* 4 April 1998.

19. 'Open for Business', *The Times of India,* 19 May 1998.

20. T.T. Ram Mohan, 'Steady as She Goes', *Economic Times,* 3 September 1998, and Anupam Goswami, 'Powered Shift', *Business India,* 24 August–6 September 1998, pp. 50–5.

21. 'Advani Guides Party Back to Insurance Reform Path', *Economic Times,* 9 December 1998.

22. Yashwant Sinha, 'We've Revived Confidence', *India Today,* 23 August 1999.

23. 'Swadeshi Is Competition, Not Return to Dark Ages', *Economic Times,* 11 September 1998.

24. Yashwant Sinha, 'Globalization Is the Best Form of Swadeshi', *Business Today,* 22 January 1999, pp. 98–101.

25. See Swaminathan S. Anklesaria Aiyar, 'Swaminomics', *The Times of India,* 10 January 1999.

26. 'Sangh Parivar Assails Govt.'s Economic Policy', *Times of India,* 1 September 1998, and 'Swadeshi Jagran Manch Expresses Concern at Some Policy Decisions of the Government', *Organizer,* 50:7, 13 September (1998), p. II.

27. 'SJM Reads Between the Lines, Softens Stand on Govt.', *Economic Times,* 11 September 1998, and 'BMS Cautions Vajpayee Government', *Organizer* 50:20, 3 December (1998), p. 3.

28. 'BJP's Divide on Insurance Deepens', *Economic Times,* 7 December 1998.

29. Jay Dubashi, 'Open Letter to Kushabhau Thakre,' *Economic Times,* 26 February 1999.

30. 'RSS Censures Govt. on Economic Policies', *Economic Times,* 15 December 1998.

31. P.R. Ramesh, 'PM versus the Parivar', *Economic Times,* 10 January 1999.

32. Vidya Subrahmaniam, 'RSS-BJP Standoff: Straining at the Umbilical Leash', *The Times of India,* 12 January 1999.

33. Ramesh, 'PM versus the Parivar'.

34. 'Quietus to Swadeshi', *Hindu,* 6 January 1999.

ECONOMIC REFORMS
AND THE POLITICAL ECONOMY

8

Iconization of Chandrababu
Sharing Sovereignty in India's Federal Market Economy*

Lᴌᴏʏᴅ I. Rᴜᴅᴏʟᴘʜ ᴀɴᴅ Sᴜsᴀɴɴᴇ Hᴏᴇʙᴇʀ Rᴜᴅᴏʟᴘʜ

The dawn of liberalization in the early 1990s saw the gradual emergence of a federal market economy, with decision-making powers shared between the centre and states. A measure of economic sovereignty and decentralization has now placed the onus on state chief ministers to effect economic growth in their respective states. Not only do they need to negotiate a path that avoids undue capitulation to populist pressures; to invite private investment, they must work in consonance with the centre's new role as a regulator and fiscal disciplinarian and deal with the hard-budget constraints demanded by the faceless, international credit-rating agencies.

In this chapter we try to explain how in the 1990s India moved from a command economy to a federal market economy. Under conditions of a federal market economy, the states command a larger share of economic sovereignty than they did under the conditions of a centrally planned economy. Whether they do well or badly economically depends more on what they do for themselves. States can act in ways that transform their initial economic situation; agency can modify structure.

We argue that a necessary condition of a shift from a command to a federal market economy has been the economic liberalization policy launched in 1991 by the Narasimha Rao Congress government. Its sufficient condition, we argue, is the displacement of public investment by private investment as the engine of economic growth. The states have become the principal arena for private investment. Their competition for private investment has generated races to the

* Originally published as 'Iconisation of Chandrababu: Sharing Sovereignty in India's Federal Market Economy', in *Economic and Political Weekly*, 5 May 2001, pp. 1541–52.

bottom and to the top. States seem to be learning that it is better for them to forego short-term benefits and to adopt the mutually advantageous benefits of cooperation over the longer term. At the same time that the states of the federal system are learning that it is better for them to cooperate than to defect, the union government in New Delhi is transforming itself from the interventionist, tutelary state of a centrally planned economy and the permit-licence raj to the regulatory state of a federal market economy that tries to enforce fiscal discipline and to ensure transparency and accountability in market and federal processes.

CHIEF MINISTERS AS ENTREPRENEURS

Ben Anderson gave us nations as 'imagined communities', Satish Deshpande gave us 'imagined economies' and Tim Mitchell gave us the 'national economy...as a representation'.[1] Economies like nations can be understood as constructions, products of symbols and rhetoric as well as of theorists' and practitioners' concepts and categories. This chapter starts with the contrast between how India's economy was imagined in Jawaharlal Nehru's day and how it has come to be imagined in the post-liberalization era, a centralized planned economy in the 1960s and a federal market economy[2] in the 1990s. Commonly understood as sites for 'truck, barter and exchange' and getting the prices right, economies are also sites for symbolic dramas. In the symbolic politics of imagined economies, actors appear on a public stage. They speak from scripts that go beyond the positivist world of the professional economist, beyond the interests and preferences of capital and labour, consumers and producers, buyers and sellers. The federal market economy is populated by persons, places and relationships that constitute a coherent symbolic world.

In the 1950s and 1960s, the heyday of India's five-year plans, Prime Minister Jawaharlal Nehru cut a heroic figure as chairman of the Planning Commission that he put at the centre of India's industrial modernization. The Indian state would occupy the commanding heights of the economy. Nehru imagined big dams as temples for a powerful Indian nation. As the new millennium opens, the heroic age of centralized planning has become a fading memory. In the 1990s drama of economic liberalization, state chief ministers play leading roles in India's emergent federal market economy. They are seen on front pages, the covers of news magazines and television screens, making and breaking coalition governments, welcoming foreign statesmen and investors, dealing with natural disasters and domestic violence. By March 1995 a perceptive Raja Chelliah could observe:

The relative spheres of activities of the two levels of the government have been thrown into a flux. The scope for real decentralisation of economic power has been greatly increased and new vistas have opened up for creative and innovative activities by the subnational level governments.[3]

By the end of the 1990s, state chief ministers became the marquee players in India's federal market economy.

What has attracted media and policy attention in recent years is the competition among the states for international attention and for domestic and foreign private investment. State chief ministers and their finance and industries secretaries have gone abroad to the US, western Europe, Japan, in search of private investors, including NRIs. As the new millennium opened, India's state capitals were attracting world leaders: Bill Gates and Bill Clinton in Hyderabad; Yoshiro Mori and Li Peng in Bangalore. Clinton's visit capped Andhra Pradesh chief minister Chandrababu Naidu's relentless efforts to be known as India's most successful chief minister. From Dallas to Davos, he promoted his ambitious plans to transform Andhra Pradesh from a middle-rank into a top-rank state.[4] As a leader of one of the growing number of politically successful state parties, the Telugu Desam, his efforts to promote and use information technology caught the national imagination. Earlier, counter-intuitively, it had been Jyoti Basu, the long-serving Communist chief minister of Bengal, who took the lead in aggressively wooing job- and revenue-generating capital.[5] By mid-2000 it was S.M. Krishna, Karnataka's Congress chief minister, who appeared to be showing India its economic future. As *Outlook* magazine put it, 'Watch out, Naidu. S.M. Krishna is winning both panchayat polls and investors.'[6] In a world of federal competition in which some observers fear that a race to the bottom will make all the states worse off, Naidu and Krishna seem to be pursuing a race to the top that could make both better off.

The defining event that shifted attention to the states as arenas of economic decision-making occurred in 1993 when the government of Maharashtra (GoM), India's most industrialized state and home of India's pre-eminent global city, Mumbai, began negotiations with the Texas energy giant, Enron, to build a $3.5 billion, 2000 megawatt power plant. The negotiations revealed the downside as well as the upside of autonomy. States can seize the opportunity provided by the centre's diminished influence and resources to shape, for better or worse, their own fates. On 8 December 1993 the GoM and the Maharashtra State Electricity Board (MSEB),[7] signed a Power Purchase Agreement (PPA) with Dabhol Power Company, Enron's Indian subsidiary, for the supply of about 2000 MW of power. Described as 'one of the largest contracts (civilian or military) in world history, and the single largest contract in (India's) history,' it involved total energy investment of $3.5 billion over the life of the 20-year contract and, as estimated in 1996 on the basis of then prevailing indexed fuel costs, $34 billion over the same period to be paid by the MSEB to Dabhol/ Enron.

What matters about this event for our story is that the government of India (GoI) played at best a supporting role. In September 1994, it provided a sovereign counter-guarantee, a decision it came to regret. The GoI's agents—for example, a cabinet committee, the finance minister and the Central Electricity Authority (CEA) —opposed the project. So did the World Bank. The GoI was cajoled, bullied, and, for all practical purposes, pushed aside by the Government of Maharashtra (GoM), whose actions some have called shady, foolhardy or illegal. More recent reflections indict the project and its failure to use competitive bidding instead of non-transparently negotiated 'memos of understanding', as 'a perpetuation of old command-and-control habits' and an invitation to corruption rather than an instance of liberalization.[8] The actions were also potentially disastrous for the GoM and possibly for New Delhi, whose sovereign guarantee could make it financially liable if the GoM/MSEB finds it cannot pay its bills for the high-cost electric power it is committed to purchase over the 20 years of the contract.[9]

As we write in 2001, eight years later, the financial and political ups and downs of the Enron deal continue to rivet the country's attention on state-level economic decision-making. It suggests that sharing economic sovereignty and economic decentralization carry hazards as well as opportunities.

Our use of the term 'federal market economy' is meant to draw attention to the fact that the new imagined economy evokes not only the decentralization of the market, but also new patterns of shared sovereignty between the states and the centre for economic and financial decision-making. This increased sharing shifts India's federal system well beyond the economic provisions of its formal constitution. Over the last decade it has become clear that if economic liberalization is to prevail, it is the state governments and their chief ministers that can and must break the bottlenecks holding back economic growth. Can they and their governments negotiate a path that avoids surrender to populist pressures and yet effectively responds to the inequalities generated by market solutions?[10]

If state chief ministers have become marquee players in the drama of the federal market economy, business leaders, economic regulators and a new breed of policy intellectuals can be found in conspicuous supportive roles. They overshadow the actors whose predecessors in Nehru's time shared the limelight focused on the centrally planned economy: the able but now almost invisible deputy chairman of the Planning Commission in New Delhi's Yojana Bhavan, K.C. Pant; the more visible union finance minister, Yashwant Sinha; and other economic ministers and secretaries to government. As profit has come to be seen as a measure of productivity rather than as a symbol of greed and of anti-social gain,[11] the media increasingly depict India's businessmen (there are still few women) as persons to respect and emulate. Kumaramangalam Birla, Ratan Tata, Dhirubhai Ambani,[12] the young heirs of old business houses and the energetic builders of new; the IT entrepreneurs such as Wipro's Azim Premji and Infosys' S. Narayana Murthy—these are the persons with whom state chief ministers do business, the entrepreneurs and managers who are said to make things happen and make the economy grow. As India moves from a centrally planned, state-dominated economy to a decentralized federal market economy, the economic views, philosophies of life and ways of living of India's successful business men have come to attract some of the respect and admiration earlier enjoyed by the sentinels guarding the economy's commanding heights.

Also overshadowing the images of an increasingly obsolescent Nehruvian interventionist state dominated are the administrators and policy intellectuals of India's emergent 'regulatory state',[13] persons such as Reserve Bank of India (RBI) chairman Bimal Jalan, Securities and Exchange Board of India (SEBI) chairman D.R. Mehta, former National Council of Economic Research (NCAER) director-general, Rakesh Mohan (now economic adviser to government), and Confederation of Indian Industries (CII) director-general, Tarun Das.

THE FEDERAL MARKET ECONOMY: CAUSES AND REASONS

Economic liberalization, the dismantling of the 'permit-licence raj' and an increasing reliance on markets, proved to be an enabling factor for the emergence of the federal market economy. The dismantling of controls provided a window of opportunity for enterprising state governments. But economic liberalization tells only part of the story of the emergence of a federal market economy. It was a necessary but not a sufficient condition. Equally important was the marked decline in public investment and, as a consequence, of the centre's financial leverage. Capital expenditure of both centre and states as a ratio of total government expenditure declined from 31.2 per cent in 1980–1 to 14.62 per cent in 1995–6.[14] The central government no longer had the resources to finance large capital investments on its own. Further borrowing is constrained by large external and internal deficits[15] and by rising interest rates that increase the cost of carrying new debt and of rolling over old debts.[16] In 1998–9 interest payments as a ratio of the centre's revenue receipts were 52 per cent.[17] The centre's deficit and the interest payments it entailed made it increasingly difficult for the centre to help the states with investment funds or bail-outs. The centre's gross assistance to states' capital formation declined from 23 per cent of the centre's revenue expenditure in 1990–1 to 12 per cent in 1998–9.[18] This sharp decline proved to be an incentive for some states prepared to take advantage of the economic liberalization climate to pursue private investment.

But economic forces were not alone in moving India from a centralized planned economy to a federal market economy. Political forces were equally important.

The movement from a command economy to a federal market economy is as much due to changes in the party system as it is to transformations of economic ideology and practice. Independent causal chains may have resulted in economic liberalization and the transformation of the party system during the 1990s but, once in place, the two phenomena began to interact in ways that proved mutually reinforcing. The dominant party system of the Nehru-Gandhi era that enabled Congress Party governments to engage in centralized planned investment gave way from 1989 onwards to a regionalized multi-party system and coalition governments in which state parties play a decisive role.

Since the ninth national election in 1989 returned a hung parliament, coalition governments have given ample scope to state parties. Atal Behari

Figure 8.1: Rise of state parties percentage of votes

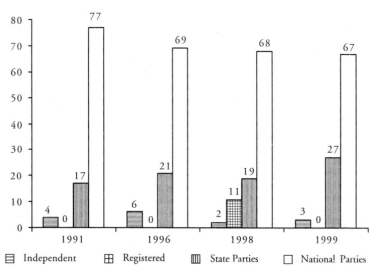

Figure 8.2: Rise of state parties percentage of seats

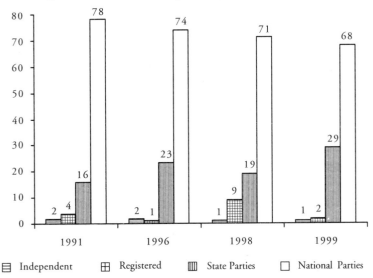

Vajpayee's 1999 majority included 120 MPs from single-state parties.[19] His National Democratic Alliance (NDA) government can be understood as a federalized coalition. Economic and political decentralization were working in tandem.

As shown in the accompanying Figures 8.1 and 8.2,[20] between the tenth national election in 1991 when economic liberalization began and the 13th national election in 1999, the votes and seats of national parties have declined 10 per cent each, from 77 and 78 per cent to 67 and 68 per cent respectively. The votes and seats of state parties, by contrast, have risen 10 and 13 per cent respectively, from 17 and 16 per cent to 27 and 29 per cent respectively. Regional parties now play a pivotal role not only in a multi-party system and in the formation and conduct of coalition governments, but also in the dynamics of the federal market system.

FROM PUBLIC TO PRIVATE INVESTMENT IN STATES

Our story of the emergence of a federal market economy that gives states greatly increased scope to shape their economic fate begins with a paradox. As we have already suggested, India's deficits, both at the centre and in the states, seemed to be mounting and intractable. Both centre and states had bankrupted themselves by borrowing to pay for things they could not afford. It was this desperate condition, the foreign exchange crisis of 1991, which precipitated the reforms. Sachs, Varshney and Bajpai put it this way:

> The foreign exchange crisis of July, 1991 not only gave the IMF and World Bank an opportunity to insist on policy change, but also reform-oriented bureaucrats inside the government to pursue their long cherished agenda. A possibility of financial collapse led to a new resolve at the governmental level.[21]

At the centre, the downward slide to deficit financing began with borrowing to pay for Rajiv Gandhi's extraordinary mid-80s military modernization programme. For two years running India spent more per annum on weapons purchases (over $4 bn each year) than any other country.[22] In the Rajiv Gandhi era, the GoI abandoned the fiscal conservatism which it had inherited from the raj and continued to practice for almost four decades. Like other developing countries in the 1980s, its debt mounted as a result, inter alia, of annual budget deficits and succumbing to the temptations offered by commercial banks. In the states, deficits were the consequence of populist exploitation of soft budget constraints such as subsidies,[23] administrative pricing, and labour redundancy. The single largest source of state deficits has been state electricity boards (SEBs). State governments so far have proved unwilling to levy or unable to collect adequate user charges for piped water, irrigation, and electricity. Some states have provided free electricity to cultivators, others charge nominal prices. A lot of electricity is unmetered or stolen; the late Power Minister, Mohan Kumaramangalam, thought the amount might be as high as 40 per cent.

The reluctance of states to collect user charges is the fruit of a long-term secular political trend, the political hegemony in the 73 per cent of the population still classified as rural[24] of those we have elsewhere called 'bullock capitalists', small to medium-sized self-employed independent agricultural producers.[25] They overlap with other backward classes (OBC), less privileged classes such as Yadavs. Together bullock capitalists and OBCs constitute the largest and among the best organized voting constituency in most states. Their emergence into political power roughly coincides with decline in the 1980s of financial discipline.[26] As bullock capitalist/OBC cultivators consumed more and more electricity to irrigate second, third, and even fourth crops, they used their votes to resist efforts to collect user charges. No amount of proof that cheap or free electricity disproportionately benefited better-off farmers altered the perception that increased user charges is an anti-poor policy. In 1996–7 the commercial losses of SEBs were estimated to be over Rs 9,000 crore[27] By 2001–2 the power subsidy burden is expected to be a staggering Rs 41,238 crore (almost $ 10 billion), with Rs 29,461 crore (over $ 6 billion) attributable to agriculture.[28] Who will bell the bullock capitalist/OBC cat?

Ahluwalia uses more discreet language to characterize India's deficit crisis:

Over the years, both the centre and the states have seen a burgeoning of non-Plan expenditure in the face of inadequate buoyancy of revenues. They have responded by resorting to larger and larger volumes of borrowing. The process has led to a steady build up of debt, which in turn has generated a rising interest burden.[29]

Ahluwalia's Table 10, 'Interest Payment as Percentage of Total Revenue' (in India's 14 largest states) shows that the ratio of interest payments to tax revenues has increased from 7.7 percent in 1980–1 to 13.1 in 1990–1 and to 17.6 per cent in 1996–7. The 10 per cent increase over 17 years has radically reduced the capacity of states to finance development expenditures from current revenues and made them more dependent on borrowing. Interest payments as a percentage of total revenue in two of India's poorest states—Uttar Pradesh and Orissa—as measured in per capita income have increased by 17 per cent in 17 years. Surprisingly, in Bihar, the poorest state, the percentage increase is much less, but for an unattractive reason. Bihar has borrowed proportionately less because it substantially reduced its level of Plan or development expenditure. Better off states with low percentages of interest payment to total revenues in 1996–7 are Haryana (11.83), Tamil Nadu (12.33), Karnataka (12.55), Maharashtra (12.70), and Madhya Pradesh (13.74).

The large current deficits in the states are recent and not entirely of their own doing. They are victims of the union government in New Delhi. The Government of India, in the form of I.K. Gujral's United Front government, made the profligate decision in 1997 to further increase the Fifth Pay Commission's budget- and inflation-busting recommendation of a threefold increase in central government employees basic pay; under severe pressure, state governments soon followed suit.[30]

So runs the story, of defeat. What is the story about snatching a partial victory from the jaws of defeat? As public expenditure in India's federal states has declined, private investment in many states has come to the rescue. Surprisingly, even though the centre's and the states' mounting deficits have led to a decline in the scale of public or planned investment for growth, there is 'no statistically significant relationship between state plan expenditure as percentage of SDP (state domestic product) and growth performance across states in either...' the 1980s or 1990s.[31] The lack of correlation between state plan expenditure and the growth performance should not surprise us, Ahluwalia argues, because it is total investment which affects growth and almost three fourths of the gross fixed investment at the national level comes from the private sector, private corporate investment accounting for 38 per cent and private household investment accounting for 33 per cent.[32]

This brings us to the heart of our argument about India's emergent federal market economy: the decline of central public investment and growth of private investment gives the federal states, the immediate sites of private investment, a greatly expanded role in economic liberalization and in promoting investment and growth. They do so in highly variable ways that are as contingent on agency—that is, policy initiatives, leadership, good governance—as on structure, for example, previous economic position. Ahluwalia enumerates the elements affecting growth: it would be

simplistic...to focus on investment as the critical determinant of growth...efficiency of resource use (i.e., its productivity as measured by ICOR[33]—incremental capital output ratio—the number of investment dollars needed to produce one more dollar of real GDP, a ratio that depends in part on technological innovation) is at least as important as the level of investment. Efficiency in turn depends upon many other factors such as the level of human resource development, the quality of infrastructure, (and) the economic policy environment...[34]

We would argue that two factors that make for efficiency of resource use—the level of human resource development and the quality of infrastructure—are investment-dependent. While human resource development—a low public priority in India—remains primarily if not exclusively the domain of public investment,[35] attracting private investment in infrastructure has become an arena of intense competition among states.

Success in attracting private investment in infrastructure depends on the boldness, imagination and tactical and strategic skill of civil servants and politicians at the state level, not least state chief ministers.[36] The economic policy environment and quality of governance[37] are distinctly in the political domain too. Rob Jenkins persuasively shows that under conditions of democratic politics that open the way for vested interests to stymie economic liberalization, politicians have to be able to 'succeed by stealth', conceding form to gain substance, going around rather than confronting obstacles, invoking continuity to bring about change.[38]

CHANGING RANK: ACCELERATING AND DECELERATING GROWTH

Over the past two decades, the 1980s and 1990s, variable growth among India's states has produced marked disparities. Some have argued that the effect of liberalization on the federal system is to make better-off states richer and worse off states poorer. This is not an adequate summary of the problem. The propensity of some states to grow did not coincide with their per capita income ranking or their ranking on a poverty index. Thus, of India's 14 largest states, the first and third highest with respect to per capita income (Punjab and Haryana) and the second and third lowest with respect to per capita income (UP and Bihar) experienced declining growth rates between the pre-liberalization 1980s and the post-liberalization 1990s. The rest of the 14 largest states increased their growth rates, some markedly more than others. This suggests that as the states have been forced to rely on themselves financially and politically, they have had, perforce, to take responsibility for their economic fate.

Examining the rank of states over time as measured by per capita domestic product indicates movement in the middle ranges but stability at the top and bottom (see Table 8.1, State Rankings by Per Capita Domestic Product, 1980–

Table 8.1: State rankings by per capita domestic product

State	1980–1	1990–1	1997–8	+Higher/– Lower Rank (between 1980–1 and 1997–8)
Andhra Pradesh	9	8	9	0
Bihar	14	14	14	0
Gujarat	4	4	4	0
Haryana	3	2	3	0
Karnataka	6	7	7	−1
Kerala	7	9	6	+1
Madhya Pradesh	10	11	11	−1
Maharashtra	2	3	2	0
Orissa	11	13	13	−2
Punjab	1	1	1	0
Rajasthan	13	10	10	+2
Tamil Nadu	8	5	5	+3
Uttar Pradesh	12	12	12	0
West Bengal	5	6	8	−3

1, 1990–1, 1997–8.) West Bengal dropped by three positions and Orissa by two. Rajasthan and Tamil Nadu climbed by three, and several others moved up or down by one position except for Punjab. Maharashtra and Haryana remained in the top three positions and Bihar, UP and Orissa continued to make up the bottom three.

Growth in SDP depends to a considerable extent on investment. We can learn a lot about relative success and failure by studying how investment in individual states has been doing over the past two decades: one decade pre-liberalization and the other post-liberalization. As Ahluwalia put it,

the economic performance of the individual states...has received less attention than it deserves in the public debate on economic policy...there is very little analysis of how individual states have performed over time and the role of state government policy (and, we would add, leadership) in determining state level performance...[39]

Unfortunately, there is no reliable information about which can be taken to be the principal cause of variation—the total level of investment or gross fixed capital formation in individual states. Precisely specifying the causes of investment variation awaits better state-level data.

The degree of dispersion in growth rates across states increased significantly in the post-liberalization decade. In the 1980s the range of variation in the growth rate of SDP was from a low of 3.6 per cent per year in Kerala to a high of 6.6 percent in Rajasthan, a state at that time near the bottom in per capita SDP. The spread between low and high was less than a factor of two. Post-liberalization, in the 1990s, the variation was much larger, from a low of 2.7 per cent per year for Bihar to a high of 9.6 per cent per year for Gujarat, a factor exceeding 3.5.

When differences in the rates of growth of population are taken into account and we judge the states in terms of growth rate per capita, the disparities in performance across states become even more marked.[40] In the 1980s, the variation in growth rates per capita ranged from 2.1 per cent in Madhya Pradesh to a high of 4 per cent in Rajasthan, a ratio of 1:2. Post-liberalization in the 1990s, the difference between the highest and the lowest per capita growth rates increased to a ratio of 1:7, with Bihar and UP barely growing at 1.1 per cent and 1.2 per cent respectively and Gujarat and Maharasthra surging ahead at 7.6 per cent and 6.1 per cent respectively.

Nationally, although growth per capita accelerated in the 1990s, it decelerated in the three poorest states: Bihar, UP, and Orissa. Growth in per capita SDP also decelerated in the two richest states per capita—Haryana and Punjab—but their deceleration, unlike that of the three poorest states, was from a relatively high level of growth in the 1980s.

High growth performance was both geographically and politically dispersed, a finding that seems to undermine theories about backward and dynamic regions or unsuitable and facilitative party ideologies. The six states whose SDP grew by more than 6 per cent in the 1990s included Gujarat (9.6 per cent—west, BJP), Maharashtra (8 per cent—west, Congress, then Shiv Sena–BJP), West Bengal (6.9 per cent—east, CPI(M)), Tamil Nadu (6.22 per cent—south, AIADMK, then DMK), Madhya Pradesh (6.17—north, Congress), and Rajasthan (6.54—west, BJP, then Congress).

The 'BIMARU' states (Bihar, Madhya Pradesh, Rajasthan and UP), which Ashish Bose grouped under this acronymic pun because they allegedly shared 'sick' demographic characteristics such as high fertility rates and low female literacy, have been stereotyped as the backward India that is dragging down an economically progressive India. They are not, however, homogenous as far as economic performance is concerned. Bihar and UP performed poorly in the 1980s and performed even worse in the 1990s. But Rajasthan and Madhya Pradesh have done fairly well. Indeed, in the 1980s Rajasthan was India's fastest-growing state (6.6 per cent) and in the 1990s it was among the half dozen states that grew at over 6 per cent (6.54 per cent). MP's growth in the 1980s at 4.56 per cent was below the national average of 5.24 per cent, but in the 1990s it joined the top performers by accelerating to 6.17 per cent.

The surging growth of several poor states such as Rajasthan and Madhya Pradesh and the lagging growth of some rich states such as Punjab and Haryana suggests that poverty is not a trap and wealth no guarantee. States can act in ways that transform their initial economic situation.

RACE TO THE TOP VS RACE TO THE BOTTOM

It is both a virtue and a vice of federal systems that they generate interstate competition. Such competition can take the virtuous form of a race to the top or the vicious form of a race to the bottom. The race to the top takes the form of attracting private investment by providing a skilled and committed labour force and a good work culture; good infrastructure, especially power, transport and communication; and good governance.

The race to the bottom is driven by competition to provide a variety of concessions that, allegedly, will attract private investment, but that force the state to forego needed revenues. R. Venkatesan and Sonalika Varma note in their

244 INDIA'S ECONOMIC TRANSITION

NCAER study (1998) of policy competition among the states that offering incentives to attract direct investment 'is akin to a "prisoner's dilemma" in that it is collectively rational not to give incentives to attract direct investment, while at the same time it is individually rational to provide incentives.'[41] According to their study, such concessions can be categorized as financial, where a state government provides funds for investment; fiscal, where a government reduces the tax burden for the incoming industry; and others such as power tariff concessions and assistance with project analysis and design.[42]

Before turning to the consequences of using incentives to attract direct investment, let us explore the question: do the incentives which trigger the race to the bottom matter? Do they do the trick? One answer is provided by the results of a survey of managers 'based largely in north India' but including the southern state of Tamil Nadu. The results show that 'the top ranking factors influencing the decision to invest are related to infrastructure (namely, transport, energy, telecommunications and water).' According to the survey, 'neither financial nor fiscal incentives are important, but good quality infrastructure that investors rank as the most important factor in investment decisions [is].'[43] Venkatesan and Varma add to this generalization that 'surveys and statistical analysis on the relative importance of incentives over other determinants reveal that incentives play a limited role in the FDI locational decision.' There is 'a relatively weak but somewhat positive relationship between incentives and investment....[But] it would wrong to assume that incentives offered by states are irrelevant as a source of attracting FDI. When fundamental determinants across states are similar, incentives help the foreign investors towards making a particular locational decision.'[44]

Rob Jenkins (2000) argues that concessions to attract direct investment, and, more broadly, tax competition among states 'further de-link states' economic fates from one another—contributing to the pattern of provincial Darwinism that...has reduced the effectiveness of resistance among state-level elites.' In a footnote to this sentence he qualifies this race-to-the-bottom view of interstate competition by observing that 'there have been some moves to counter this trend...At a CII summit in January 1995 West Bengal chief minister Jyoti Basu strongly emphasized the need to end the interstate taxation war and incentive war to woo investors because it would ultimately be of 'zero gain to the states and result in loss in revenue.'[45]

By early 2001, Jyoti Basu's view that the states should avoid a beggar-your-neighbour interstate competition was gaining.[46] The finance ministers and secretaries of the states had joined together to get the centre to promote a uniform system of sales taxes among the states and to 'do away with tax incentives wars'. By January 2000, implementation had progressed in most states. By February 2001, state finance ministers had agreed that on 1 April 2002 the states would adopt a uniform CENVAT (central value added tax) as the country's principal excise tax.[47] If incentives and state sales tax competition create a prisoner's dilemma situation, it is also true of such situations that iteration, communication, and learning can lead to cooperation rather than defection. This seems to be what is happening to moderate if not eliminate the race to the bottom.

THE REGULATORY STATE AS CONSTRAINT ON AUTONOMY

We have argued that a federal market economy is fast replacing a Nehruvian centralized command economy in the country's economic imagination and practice. The centre's hazardous financial condition[48] and the decline of central planning[49] and of public investment that accompanied it have forced the states to become more self-reliant. But there is a paradox. Even as the centre becomes less able to intervene through its control of public investment, permits, and licences, it assumes a new role as a regulator concerned with market imperfections and state fiscal discipline. As the centre's role as an interventionist state has faded, its role as a regulatory state has grown. The centre has attempted to impose hard budget constraints on the states. So too have market-oriented international and domestic credit-rating agencies. Such agencies evaluate 'economies' by assigning grades such as A, B and C that affect interest rates and thus the cost of capital.[50] Financially strapped states cannot borrow at viable rates to build the infrastructure that promises growth—and, sometimes, to meet current expenditures—unless they can demonstrate that they command the income streams to pay back the loans. As bonds become a larger component of public finance, credit rating agencies loom ever larger as the market's guardians of hard-budget constraints.[51]

India's states are also being exposed to the discipline of international lenders such as the World Bank and the Asian Development Bank, Andhra Pradesh chief minister Chandrababu Naidu led the way by negotiating the first state level World Bank development loan. By mid-year 2000 five more states had followed Andhra's lead. States that want development loans are being obliged to observe a third form of conditionality in addition to that of the centre and the credit-raters: namely, the discipline that demonstrates to the WB, the ADB, and other international lenders that they are credit worthy.

Why the need to impose and monitor hard-budget constraints? To a greater or lesser degree India's states are deeply in debt. For years their politicians have competed by offering voters give-away populist measures. Especially prominent among them are subsidies for agricultural inputs, for example, subsidies for irrigation, fertilizer, and, most prominent, electricity. Agricultural subsidies are directed to the single largest block of voters, the enormous constituency of agricultural producers.[52] Students pay a purely notional amount for a college, professional, or postgraduate education. Public utilities do not come close to recouping their costs, let alone generate income for maintenance or investment in improved technology or expansion. State public corporations do not generate profits and default regularly on the loans for covering their losses.[53]

At the end of December 1999 Nirupam Bajpai and Jeffrey Sachs were noting with alarm the state of the states' finances:

the revenue expenditure under non-developmental heads is expected to rise (in 1997–98) by about 20 per cent over an increase of 14.8 per cent in 1996–97; interest payments and administrative services would account for over 60 per cent of the total increase in revenue expenditure in 1997–98...the revenue deficits of the state governments have, been rising since 1997–98. Large and persistent revenue deficits have implied a diversion of high-cost borrowings for consumption purposes, leading to a declining share of investment expenditures...the investment outlays of the states as a ratio of the GDP declined from 2.8 percent in 1990–91 to...2.2 per cent in 1997–98. An expenditure pattern of this type has had...wide ranging implications such as for the adequacy and quality of infrastructure.[54]

The states have been in the habit of covering shortfalls occasioned by their failure to recover the cost of services through overdrafts on the centre, a practice referred to by government financial bodies as 'gap-filling'. One can imagine the softness of soft-budget constraints in India when one considers that until the Tenth Finance Commission, 'successive finance commissions established a tradition of unconditional debt forgiveness... These developments built expectations that the states need not be overly concerned with mobilizing resources since ever-expanding and politically more expedient financing would be forthcoming.'[55] By the late 1980s and certainly by the time the Narasimha Rao government launched economic liberalization in 1991, the centre lost the capacity routinely to bail out state governments. Faced with mounting deficits that drove up interest rates, it found it increasingly difficult to borrow for investment in economic growth, much less to finance state government deficits. Faced with the consequences of its own imprudence, the centre has become an advocate for and enforcer of fiscal discipline on the states. To that end, and to cope with state deficits' debilitating effect on the centre's fiscal deficit, Prime Minister A B Vajpayee, Finance Minister Yashwant Sinha, Power Minister Suresh Prabhu and Planning Commission Deputy Chairman K.C. Pant called on state chief ministers assembled in New Delhi to agree to a time-bound one time settlement of the states' Rs 26,000 crore power arrears. The finance minister suggested that 'we could think of issuing bonds and hold them till such time that the SEBs are in a position to pay', and the prime minister called on the states 'to revise agriculture tariff to raise it to at least 50 per cent of the average cost in three years.'[56]

The centre is not without means for enforcing fiscal discipline on the states. Under the constitution states must solicit and receive central government permission for all foreign borrowing and, de facto, for domestic borrowing as well.[57] The centre exercises significant influence over lending institutions.[58] It can also use the substantial energy supplies it controls through its ownership of the large thermal and hydel projects operated by the National Thermal Power Corporation (NTPC) and the National Hydel Power Corporation (NHPC) to enforce fiscal discipline on state electricity boards. Like California's reliance on states in the north-west in the US, many Indian states rely on the centre for the viability of their power supply. The NTPC, the NHPC and Coal India can and sometimes do use their control of power to deny supplies to defaulting states.[59] Despite the demise of the 'permit-licence raj' the centre still reviews large foreign and domestic investment proposals.

Whether the constitutionally mandated finance commissions, appointed every five years to recommend allocation of certain centrally collected taxes between centre and states and among the states,[60] are agents of profligacy or discipline is subject to heated political debate. Southern and western state politicians and civil servants think they see a protector of fiscally irresponsible and incompetent northern states.[61] Traditionally, as heirs of the redistributive philosophy of the founding generation, the commission was seen as the rectifier of unacceptable disparities among the federal states.[62] The Eighth, Ninth and Tenth Commission recommendations down to the year 2000 tilted central tax devolution markedly toward equalising the financial condition of the states rather than encouraging effort and effectiveness. After states began routinely to operate in deficit in the 1980s, finance commissions equally routinely, but without incentives or consequence, preached deficit reduction.[63] The Tenth Finance Commission, recommending for the period 1995–2000, rewarded indices of backwardness (large population, low per capita income) to the extent of 85 per cent while rewarding effort and initiative, such as infrastructure building and tax mobilization by a meagre 15 per cent.[64] The Eleventh Finance Commission Report (2000), which reduced the percentage high-income states would receive in the total tax devolved by the centre to the states from 13.14 per cent to 9.75 per cent, also reduced the share of the middle-level states. In the wake of that report, Naidu, the Andhra CM and supremo of the Telugu Desam Party (TDP), a key component of the governing National Democratic Alliance (NDA) coalition, declared war on the commission. In August 2000, he publicly led a revolt of eight high- and middle-level states. They challenged the traditional role of the finance commission as federal equalizer, and condemned it for encouraging fiscal and reproductive profligacy.[65] The call led to a marginal adaptation by the commission in a supplementary report. Whether finance commissions are competent under the Constitution, as the Eleventh Commission claims to be, to make their grants conditional on fiscal discipline is being debated.[66]

The centre also can pass defining legislation from a constitutionally enumerated list of current subjects on which both the centre and the states may legislate.[67] One of those subjects is electricity. The Electricity Act, 2000, a centre-initiated piece of legislation, places the central electricity authority and newly established central and state electricity regulatory authorities in a dominant position with respect to state electricity planning and management.[68]

In recent years, the centre has increasingly asked states to accept conditionalities in return for permissions and resources. In May 2000 Prime Minister Vajpayee told the country's chief ministers assembled for a rare meeting of the interstate council that 'the union government has taken some difficult decisions to contain subsidies at the centre. The states would be well advised to do the same.' There was no alternative, he added, to the 'new viable sustainable paradigm of a financial regime'.[69] No power supplements would be available to states unless they impose user fees on electricity and show that the fees provide a reliable income stream for payments to the centre for the energy supplied. In a constitutionally controversial move, he also told the chief ministers that there would be no release of funds allocated by the finance commission until a state shows credible evidence that it will mobilize the resources needed to meet the requirement of its own budget, and that there would be no loans from the centre without establishing an escrow account based on revenue income or user fees that guarantees the repayment of the loan. While in all of these assertions the bite has routinely fallen short of the bark, and intent fallen victim to postponement, they do reflect the new regulatory role of the centre.

It would be wrong to suggest that the states regard the new fiscal discipline entirely as a burden. It also is way to establish and defend the state governments' autonomy from local political pressures. 'It is not your friendly state governments who are making these oppressive demands. Our hands are tied by central interference and control.' Something analogous happened at the national level at the outset of liberalization in 1991. Prime Minister Narasimha Rao and Finance Minister Manmohan Singh were able to shelter their fledgling hard budget-constrained liberalization measures against political attack by pleading that without such measures international lenders would not help India avoid default. Similarly, state chief ministers can now blame the imposition of user charges for services on the centre, even while benefiting from the financial and political independence they make possible. It remains to be seen whether politicians can supply firm power for most of the working day and, if they can, whether, when they levy and collect user charges for it, they will be re-elected.

But the centre as regulator and fiscal disciplinarian is not the only constraint with which states have to deal as the price of their newfound autonomy. They also have to deal with the hard-budget constraints required by faceless, apolitical credit-rating agencies. With fewer and fewer public investment funds available for infrastructure investment in power plants, bridges, roads, ports and telecommunications, states have increasingly turned to private borrowing, usually in the form of bonds. Their capacity to borrow at a reasonable cost in terms of the interest rate to be paid depends on their ranking by credit-rating information systems of India: CRISIL and CARE, the two major domestic credit-rating agencies. CRISIL downgraded Maharashtra's credit rating in October 1999 just as the state was about to issue bonds to fund four irrigation projects. CRISIL pointed to the deterioration in the fiscal situation of India's richest state after it matched the centre's pay raises for government employees.[70] Foreign private investors, like domestic ones, make their investment and interest-rate decisions in the light of credit ratings, but foreign investors pay attention to international raters such as Standard and Poor's.[71] Working for and achieving favourable credit ratings has increasingly become a powerful incentive for states to practise fiscal discipline and implement hard-budget constraints. The market has, like the centre, begun to regulate state economic thinking and conduct.

What are the implications for a federal market economy of coalition governments based on one national party such as the BJP and several politically decisive state parties? Is a BJP-led central government prepared to tighten the fiscal screws on a BJP-controlled state government? Would it be tempted to use central government discretion and resources to help woo voters in a state assembly election where its candidates are fighting from behind? Would it want to tighten fiscal discipline on a laggardly UP where its government was already in deep trouble politically? Would a coalition government be prepared to resist demands by key state parties in its coalition? Will one result of state parties playing a more important role in national politics be to compromise the centre's role as market regulator and guardian of fiscal discipline?[72] Such a tendency will be countered by the depth and seriousness of the centre's and the states' fiscal deficits, and by pressure from coalition partners and departmental bureaucrats to observe some appearance of even-handedness. To address deficits, India's states will have to be able to collect user fees for services provided and to attract private investment, both foreign and domestic, to upgrade and expand not only their physical infrastructure but also their education and health services.

CONCLUSION

The emergence in the 1990s of a federal market economy that replaced a Nehruvian permit-licence raj and centrally planned economy followed the launching of economic liberalization in 1991. The market economy it fostered was a necessary but not sufficient condition for the formation of a federal market economy. The sufficient condition was the transformation of India's party and government system from a one-party-dominant-majority party system to a regionalized multi-party coalition government system. The economic and political causal chains proceeded more or less independently until 1989–1991 when they intersected. The result of that intersection was a mutually reinforcing relationship that helps to account for the formation of a federal market economy. The states in India's federal system command more economic and political sovereignty than they did under a Nehruvian planned economy; their voices matter more in economic and political decisions. States are challenged to be more self-reliant; increasingly, they have to navigate as tubs on their own bottoms. But they are also faced with new restraints on their enhanced autonomy. As the centre's interventionist and tutelary role has faded, its role as regulatory state has expanded. The states have found that the price of more freedom is more responsibility for growth and fiscal discipline.

NOTES AND REFERENCES

1. Benedict Anderson, *Imagined Communities: Reflections on the Origin and Spread of Nationalism* (London, Verso, 1983). 'Communities are to be distinguished, not by their falsity/genuineness, but by the style in which they are imagined' (ibid., p. 15).

The phrase 'imagined economies' is taken from Tim Mitchell's paper, 'At the Edge of the Economy', presented at the South Asia and Middle East (SAME) workshop. University of Chicago, 2 February 1995. The argument about the recent invention of the idea of the economy is also made in Mitchell's 'Fixing the Economy', *Cultural Studies*, 12, 1 (1982), pp. 82–101.

Satish Deshpande, 'Imagined Economies; Styles of Nation-Building in Twentieth Century India', *Journal of Arts and Ideas,* 25–26 December (1993), pp. 5–35. 'If nations are indeed "imagined communities" as Benedict Anderson has so persuasively suggested, then I would argue that one of the dominant modes in which the Indian nation has been imagined is a community of producers, as an economy...' (ibid., pp. 5–6).

2. We distinguish Barry Weingast's deductive use of a model—'market preserving federalism' (MPF)—to assess and judge Indian federalism from our use of a Weberian-style ideal type, a federal market economy, that enables us to organize our inductive analysis of ideas and practices in India. Sunita Parikh and Barry Weingast conclude that 'the Indian case far better illustrates what occurs in the absence of market-preserving federalism...India's federalism retains the hierarchy of federalism but eliminates the main mechanisms that sustain strong markets. States are not free to set their own economic policies. Nor can they capture the gains from policies that foster economic growth.' Sunita Parikh and Barry R. Weingast, 'Response to Jonathan Rodden and Susan Rose-Ackerman, "Does Federalism Preserve Markets?"', and Ronald I. McKinnon and Daniel Rubinfield, 'Commentaries', *Virginia Law Review,* 83, 7, October (1997), p. 1611.

As will become clear from our analysis below, we come to quite different conclusions. See also Barry R. Weingast, 'The Economic Role of Political Institutions: Market-Preserving Federalism and Economic Growth', *Journal of Law, Economics and Organisation,* 11, Spring (1995).

3. Raja Chelliah (ed.), *Towards Sustainable Growth: Essays in Fiscal and Financial Sector Reforms in India* (New Delhi, Oxford University Press, 1996), p. 19.

4. In the annual ranking of states compiled by *Business Today*, which ranks 26 states according to the perceptions of CEOs about states as investment destinations, Andhra went up from 22nd in 1995 to third in 1999. 'State of the States', *Business Standard,* 29 December 1999. Insofar as perceptions as much as 'objective conditions' shape investment behaviour, this is a consequential measure.

5. See Aseema Sinha's case studies of Bengal, Gujarat, and Tamil Nadu in 'From State to Market—via the State Governments: Horizontal Competition after 1991 in India', paper presented at the Association of Asian Studies Annual Meeting, Boston, 11–14 March 1999.

6. *Outlook*, 25 June 2000, pp. 16–18.

7. Our account of the Enron episode is largely based on the carefully researched, highly critical book by Abhay Mehta, *Power Play: A Study of the Enron Project* (New Delhi, Orient Longman, 1999).

Also useful is Sidharth Sinha, 'Private Participation in Power: Dabhol Power Company—A Case Study', and Sidharth Sinha, 'Appropriate Return to Equity in Private Power Projects: Dabhol Power Project Company—A Case Study' in G. Raghuram, Rekha Jain, Sidharth Sinha, Prem Pangotra and Sebastian Morris (eds), *Infrastructure Development and Financing: Towards a Public-Private Partnership* (New Delhi, Macmillan, 1999) pp. 122–60 and 161–9.

8. Amulya Reddy, 'Lessons from Enron', *The Hindu*, 6 January 2001.

9. In early 2001, Enron did indeed invoke the government of India's sovereign guarantee, when MSEB appeared unable to meet its payments for November and December 2000. According to state power minister Padmasinh Patil, this was no freebie for the GoM, as GoI 'will, in turn, recover it from funds allocated to the state government.' *Business Line,* 7 February 2001.

10. We are not alone in attending to the federal dimension of economic reform and decision-making. Rob Jenkins breaks new conceptual and empirical ground in *Democratic Politics and Economic Reform in India* (Cambridge, Cambridge University Press, 1999). It goes beyond previous work on economic reform in India. Chapter 5 of this book, 'Political institutions: Federalism, informal networks, and the management of dissent' (pp. 119–71) offers strong evidence for the existence of an emergent 'federal market economy'.

See also Aseema Sinha, 'From State to Market: India and the Theory of Market Preserving Federalism', paper presented at the APSA annual meeting, Washington, DC, 31 August–4 September 2000, and Aseema Sinha, *The Regional Roots of Developmental Politics in India: A Divided Leviathan* (Bloomington: Indiana University Press, 2005).

We have benefited as well from John Echeverri-Gent's work on a 'decentered polity'. It theorizes and explains the economic decision-making and party system transformations of India's federal system and relates them to the shift in the 1990s from an interventionist to a regulatory state. See his 'Politics in India's Decentred Polity', in Marshall Bouton and Philip Oldenburg (eds), *Asia Briefing 2002* (forthcoming). Echeverri-Gent developed his conceptual distinction between an interventionist and a regulatory state in his work on SEBI's regulation of the Bombay Stock Exchange. He calls SEBI India's first independent regulatory agency in 'Governance Structures and Market-Making: Regulating India's Equity Markets in a Globalising World', paper presented at the University of California, Santa Cruz, November 1998.

The Observer Research Foundation's *Economic Reforms: The Role of the States and the Future of Centre-State Relations,* Observer Research Foundation, New

Delhi, 1996, is written from the perspective of an earlier paradigm in the study of federalism and centre-states relations in India, see, for example, Balveer Arora's essay, 'India's Federalism and the Demands of Pluralism'. Lawrence Saez examines many of the federal issues in 'Federalism Without a Centre: The Impact of Political Reform and Economic Liberalisation on India's Federal System', Ph.D. dissertation, Political Science Department, University of Chicago (1999).

The government of Rajasthan provides an example of the entrepreneurial breaking of bottlenecks that can characterize the use of, in Rob Jenkins' phrase, 'stealth' in the sharing of sovereignty or decentering of the polity. Blocked by the provisions of the obsolete Telegraph Act, 1885, and the Wireless Telegraphy Act, 1933, from attracting investment to upgrade telecommunications in Rajasthan, including new developments in information technology, the government contracted for project designs for laying a fibre optic cable or 'spine' throughout Rajasthan and sought investors to implement it. The cable would not violate the two acts, which barred private companies from transmitting voice messages on telephone ground lines. The acts did not bar transmitting data or digital information. Personal Communication, Arvind Mayaram, Secretary to Government for Industries, December 1999.

11. For a discussion of profit and the profit motive in pre-liberalization India, see Lloyd I. Rudolph and Susanne Hoeber Rudolph, *In Pursuit of Lakshmi* (Chicago, University of Chicago Press, 1987), pp. 26–7. See also Jeffrey D. Sachs, Ashutosh Varshney and Nirupam Bajpai (eds), *India in the Era of Economic Reforms* (New Delhi, Oxford University Press, 1999), pp. 21–2.

12. See Hamish McDonald's serious biographical and analytical economic history, *The Polyester Prince: The Rise of Dhirubhai Ambani* (Sydney, Allen and Unwin, 1998). Through summer 2000 Ambani succeeded in preventing the sale of the book.

13. Lloyd I. Rudolph and Susanne Hoeber Rudolph, 'Redoing the Constitutional Design: From an Interventionist to a Regulatory State' in Atul Kohli (ed.), *The Success of India's Democracy* (Cambridge, Cambridge University Press, 2001).

14. D.K. Srivastava, 'Emerging Fiscal and Economic Issues', *Seminar,* 459, November (1997), p. 50.

15. Keeping in mind that to be eligible to join the European Union's monetary community (the Euro) states had to bring down their fiscal deficits to 4 per cent of GDP provides a comparison with the Indian situation. It has been hard-pressed since liberalization began in 1991 to keep the domestic deficit below 6 per cent of GDP. Manmohan Singh as finance minister in the Narasimha Rao government from 1991–6 brought the deficit down from 8.3 per cent in 1990–1 to 5.7 per cent in 1992–3. Subsequently it fluctuated: 7.4 per cent in 1993–4, 6.1 in 1994–5 and 5 in 1998–9. Government of India, Ministry of

Finance, Economic Division, *Economic Survey, 1996–97* (New Delhi, Ministry of Finance, 1997), Table 2.2, 'Components of Gross Fiscal Deficit of the Central Government', p. 19; and Government of India, Ministry of Finance, Economic Division, *Economic Survey 1999–2000* ((New Delhi, Ministry of Finance, 2000), Table 2.1, 'Trends in Parameters of Deficit of Central Government', p. 27.

India's external debt stood at $33.8 billion when Rajiv Gandhi took over as prime minister in 1984–5; rose to $60.6 billion by the end of his term in 1988–9; had risen further to $85.5 billion in 1991–2 and to $101.1 billion in 1994–5, but declined to $93.7 billion in 1995–6, and had risen only slightly to $97.7 billion in 1998–9. World Bank, India, *Sustaining Rapid Economic Growth* (Washington, DC, World Bank, 1997), Table A3.1(a), p. 78 and Government of India, *Economic Survey 1999–2000*, Table 6.12, 'India's External Debt Outstanding', p. 110.

16. Government of India, *Economic Survey 1996–97*, p. 26.

17. Government of India, *Economic Survey, 1999–2000*, Table 2.2, 'Receipts and Expenditures of Central Government', p. 8.

18. Government of India, *Economic Survey, 1999–2000,* Table 7.l, 'Gross Capital Formation from Budgetary Resources of the Central Government', Appendix, s38.

19. Kewal Varma counted the BJP, Congress, CPI and CPM as national. *Business Standard,* 29 October 1999.

20. The data found in the Table 8.1 have been compiled from Election Commission of India. *Elections in India: Major Events and New Initiatives 1996–2000* (New Delhi, Election Commission of India, 2000); 'Lok Sabha Poll: An AIR Analysis', News Service Division, All India Radio, Government of India, New Delhi (1991); Election Commission of India, *Statistical Report on General Elections, 1996, to the Eleventh Lok Sabha, Volume I (National and State Abstracts)* (Election Commission of India, New Delhi, 1996); ibid. for 1998 and for 1999; URL for the Election Commission of India: http://www.eci.gov.in, where data for the 1996, 1998 and 1999 elections are available on-line. The data on votes and seats are presented according to Election Commission definitions for national party, state party, registered party and independents.

21. Sachs et al., *India in the Era of Economic Reforms.*

22. For details see Lloyd I. Rudolph, 'The Faltering Novitiate: Rajiv Gandhi at Home and Abroad', in Marshall M. Bouton and Philip K. Oldenburg (eds), *India Briefing 1939* (Boulder, CO/New York, Westview Press, The Asia Society, 1989).

23. According to Rakesh Mohan, subsidies accounted for 14.7 per cent of GDP in 1998–9. Of this amount, only 4 to 6 per cent were 'justified'—that is, help the poor for whom subsidies are intended. India has gotten away from

pricing public goods, Rakesh Mohan told the 16–18 December 1999 Confederation of Indian Industries-sponsored conference on infrastructure development. When public utilities such as electricity were private, they covered their costs and made money or they went bankrupt. He noted that 50 per cent of rural households have no electricity connections, with the consequence that the subsidized price benefits the relatively better-off who have connections, not the poorest. Because power does not pay for itself, and hence generates no money for investment, expansion has to come from money borrowed at 12–14 per cent. Paying for expansion this way becomes one of the major components of subsidies. Notes on Rakesh Mohan remarks. 16 December 1999.

24. Government of India, *Economic Survey 1999–2000*, Table 9.1 'Population of India – 1991', p. s–114.

25. Rudolph and Rudolph, *In Pursuit of Lakshmi*, p. 50.

26. Interview, K.C. Pant, Deputy Chairman, Planning Commission, February 2000.

27. Confederation of Indian Industry, 'An Overview of the Challenges for Infrastructure Development in India: Background Paper for Infranet '99', paper prepared by Pricewaterhouse Coopers, CII, New Delhi (1999), p. 21. For data on electricity charges as of 1998 by state and category (that is, domestic, commercial, etc.), see Central Electricity Authority, *Average Electric Rates and Duties in India* (New Delhi, Government of India, Central Electricity Authority, April 1998). The CEA's structure and functions are described in Central Elecrticity Authority, *Central Electric Authority and Indian Power Sector* (New Delhi, CEA, October 1996).

28. Government of India, *Economic Survey, 2000–2001*, Table 9.4, p. 176. For the overall picture with regard to power, see pp. 174–7.

The Economic Times, 23 February 2001, reporting on the recently released *Economic Survey, 2000–2001* commented with regard to the Rs 41,238 crore: 'That's enough money to add 8,000 MW of new capacity to the national grid. Which, by the way, is almost half of National Thermal Power Corporation's (NTPC's) total capacity built over the last 50 years.'

'The hidden subsidy for agriculture and domestic sectors', *The Economic Times* continued, '...which was at a modest Rs 7,449 crore in 1991–92 (accounting for 1.1 per cent of GDP) has been increasing at an alarming rate. It currently accounts for 36 per cent of gross fiscal deficit of state governments.'

The subsidy bill of the power sector includes losses incurred by the state electricity boards from transmission and distribution. Such losses included theft and non- and poor metering. Transmission and distribution (T&D) losses for 2001–2 are estimated by the *Economic Survey, 2000–2001* at Rs 25,000 crore.

29. Montek Singh Ahluwalia, *The Economic Performance of the States in the Post Reforms Period* (New Delhi, NCAER, 2000), pp. 33–4. See also Reserve

Bank of India, *State Finances: A Study of Budgets, 1999–2000* (Mumbai, Reserve Bank of India, January 2000). Some of Ahluwalia's tables draw on this document, as do we for some of our arguments.

30. Nirupam Bajpai and Jeffrey Sachs, 'The State of State Government Finances', *The Hindu*, 6 December 1999. For more details on the Fifth Pay Commission, see Nirupam Bajpai and Jeffrey Sachs, 'Fiscal Policy in India's Economic Reforms' in Sachs, et al., *Era of Economic Reforms*, pp. 96–7.

31. See Ahluwalia. *Economic Performance*, section on 'Investment and Growth in Individual States', pp. 20–5, including his discussion of Table 8, 'Plan Expenditures a Percentage of SDP (state domestic product as). In the 14 largest states that Ahluwalia analyses, the ratio of state plan expenditure to SDP declined from an average of 5.7 per cent in the 1980s to 4.5 per cent in the 1990s. 'The decline of 1.2 percentage points in state plan expenditures almost certainly hides an even larger decline in investment for new capacity, because of the increase in the revenue component of the Plan...There is considerable variation across states in the ratio of state plan expenditure to SDP...[but] there is no statistically significant relationship between state plan expenditure as a percentage of SDP and growth performance across states...in the 1980s or the 1990s' (ibid., p. 21).

32. 'Public sector investment at the national level is only about 28 per cent of total investment and this includes both the centre and the states.' Three-fourths of national-level gross fixed investment comes from the private sector, 38 per cent from private corporate investment, and 33 per cent from private household investment. At 28 per cent of total investment, public investment by the centre and the states accounts for about 6.8 per cent of GDP, of which state plans account for only a third. Ahluwalia, *Economic Performance*, p. 22.

33. Paul Krugman elucidates the role of ICOR with illustrations from 'Asian' economies and from the former Soviet Union. 'The debate over Asian productivity still rages [in 1999]...Asia achieved remarkable rates of economic growth without correspondingly remarkable increases in productivity. Its growth was the product of resource mobilization rather than efficiency...As in the case of the Soviet Union...given the lack of rapid productivity growth, Asia was bound to run into diminishing return. By 1997 Malaysia was investing more than 40 per cent of GDP, twice its share in 1970; Singapore was investing half its income. These rates of investment sure could not be pushed much higher, and merely maintaining them would not be enough to sustain growth...Given rising ICORs, growth could be sustained only via an ever-increasing investment rate, and that just wasn't going to happen.' Paul Krugman, *The Return of Depression Economics* (New York, W.W. Norton, 1999), pp. 33–4.

34. These factors can reinforce or contradict each other; they cannot be read in mutual isolation. For example, Ahluwalia points out that Kerala ranks high in

'human resource development' where literacy is taken as the best available proxy measurement but low in 'economic policy environment'. This can help to explain why Kerala, which ranked as the most literate state in 1981, 1991, and 1997, remained in the middle ranks over those years in 'Annual Rates of Growth of Per Capita Gross State Domestic Product' (see his Tables 2 and 5). He also points out that although the levels of literacy in the 'slow growing states' of Bihar, UP and Orissa are distinctly lower than the average for all states (see his *Economic Performance*, Table 9, 'Total Literacy Rate', p. 50), there is no statistically significant correlation between growth of SDP and the level of literacy. Ahluwalia, *Economic Performance*, p. 19.

35. We say primarily but not exclusively, because both education and health, hitherto arenas for public investment, are under increasing pressure to recoup larger proportions of their running and capital, expenses from hitherto nominal 'user charges'.

36. For a recent overview of investment opportunities in infrastructure, see Cabinet Secretariat, Government of India and National Council of Economic Research with assistance from Arthur Andersen, *India's Infrastructure: Investment Opportunities* (New Delhi, GoI and NCAER, 1997). The publication deals with investment opportunities in power, oil and natural gas, coal, mining, roads, urban infrastructure, telecommunications, civil aviation, and ports.

37. On the importance of good governance for attracting private investment see The World Bank, *The State in a Changing World: The World Development Report, 1997* (New York, New Delhi, Published for the World Bank by the Oxford University Press, 1997). According to the Bank, private investors are more likely to invest when they perceive 'predictability of rulemaking, political stability, security with respect to crimes against persons and property, reliable judicial enforcement and freedom from corruption'. Figure 2.4, p. 37, shows three scatter-grams that indicate a close relationship between 'credibility' (reliable state institutions as specified above) and economic performance (pp. 34–8).

38. See Rob Jenkins, *Democratic Politics,* p. 176, where he observes: 'One of the skills which reforming governments must possess is the capacity to cloak change, which tends to cause anxiety among those privileged by the status quo, in the appearance of continuity'. In our reckoning, leadership includes not only chief ministers and their cabinet colleagues but also entrepreneurial civil servants.

39. 'The Plan document...is not disaggregated into targets for the growth of State Domestic Product in individual states, nor does it report the growth performance of different states in the past, nor analyse the reasons for differences in performance across states. The Annual Economic Survey brought out by the finance ministry is also silent on these issues.' Ahluwalia, *Economic Performance*, p. 1.

40. See ibid., Table 2, 'Annual Rates of Growth Per Capita Gross Domestic Product', p. 44.

41. R. Venkatesan and Sonalika Varma, *Study on Policy, Competition Among States in India for Attracting Direct Investment,* (New Delhi, NCAER, October 1998), p. 59. The authors go on to say that investment decisions are 'a function of a wide range of factors...(such as) political stability, infrastructure availability, extent of labour unrest, presence of good backward and forward linkages, incentives provided [sic!], attitude of the bureaucracy towards the investors, etc.'

42. Financial incentives are 'defined as those where the government is directly involved in the financing of the projects and comprise: provisions of funds for financing investment operations; government involvement in fixed capital investment for new industrial units; financing and other assistance in setting up, technologically pioneering and prestigious units; expansion and diversification of existing units.' Fiscal incentives—'mainly aim at reducing the tax burden and (or providing subsidies) to an investor. These include: provisions for various sales tax exemptions: deferment of tax schemes; octroi exemptions (an indirect tax); reductions and exemptions of other taxes such as property taxes; other incentives, such as export based incentives.' Other incentives—'many other incentives are also provided to help in the setting up of projects. These include: help in formulating project analysis; allowances for subsidising services like generating sets; feasibility reports; incentives for modernization schemes, special incentives and all other incentives that cannot be classified under a common head but basically which increase the economic viability of a foreign unit by non-financial means'. *Study on Policy,* p. 45.

43. Ibid., p. 49.

44. Ibid., pp. 50–1.

45. The Rob Jenkins (2000) gloss and quote are from his *Democratic Politics,* pp. 132–3. The Jyoti Basu quote is from *Asian Age,* 6 January 1995, as cited by Jenkins, fn. 34, p. 133.

Chief ministers and finance ministers met in conference on 16 November 1999 and decided on unified floor rates for sales tax. Government of India, *Economic Survey, 1999–2000,* Box 2.5, p. 38 reported 'implementation of uniform floor rates of sales tax by states and union territories from January 1, 2000'.

An interview with Mahesh Purohit, professor at the National Institute of Public Finance and member-secretary of the empowered committee of state finance ministers to monitor sales tax reform, stated, in an interview in *Business Line,* 13 February 2001, that he was confident about VAT being introduced by 1 April 2002. Its introduction would be accompanied by reduction of a, by then, uniform Central Sales Tax (CST) from 4 to 3 per cent by 1 April and then to 1 per cent by 1 April 2003. Purohit said that the CST at 4 per cent as of

2000–1 yielded about Rs 9,000 crore. 'We are considering,' Purohit said, 'three rates of value added tax—a low tax rate for some necessary items, a high rate for luxury items and a general rate for all other products. What this general rate would be—which will be the floor rate—is the crucial question, and we are working on it now.'

Purohit also said that two additional interstate committees were assisting the empowered committee of state finance minister to monitor sales tax reforms, the committee of finance secretaries and a committee of state commissioners of tax. *Business Line*, 13 February 2001.

46. Interview with P.V. Rajaraman, secretary, finance, government of Tamil Nadu, 4 February 2000, Fort St. George. Rajaraman told us that Tamil Nadu and Maharashtra over five years made competitive offers with respect to free-hold land and infrastructure. Continuing this way for five years caused serious revenue loss. The race to the bottom was halted by cooperative efforts by the states to institute a common sales tax. The finance ministers were said to be influenced by a speech by Raja Chelliah on the need for tax reform.

47. The 'first decisive steps' towards replacing the existing sales tax regime and replacing it with a system of value added tax, a VAT or, in this case, a CENVAT, were taken on 16 November 1999 when the finance ministers of the various states met in New Delhi. Mahesh Purohit, Professor, National Institute of Public Finance, and member-secretary of the empowered committee of state finance ministers to monitor sales tax reform, said on 12 February 2001 that, having pushed the zero date back one year, from 1 April 2001 to 1 April 2002, he was 'fully confident that by that date VAT would be introduced by in all the major states.' *Business Line*, 13 February 2001.

Earlier a *Business Standard* headline on 11 January 2000 announced 'January 15 deadline for uniform sales tax'. The story read in part: 'Penal action is being contemplated against states not implementing the decision to adhere lo uniform sales tax floor rates and to phase out sales-tax related incentive schemes by 15 January. This was decided at the meeting of the standing committee of state finance ministers which asked the 13 states which had not implemented the decision to do so by the stipulated date. During their meeting in November, states and union territories agreed to implement uniform sales tax floor rates and to do away with tax incentives war from 1 January. West Bengal finance minister, Asim Das Gupta, the convener of the meeting...told reporters that Maharashtra, West Bengal, Gujarat, Andhra Pradesh, Kerala, Assam and Tripura had already implemented the decision. He said Delhi and Uttar Pradesh, which had partly implemented the decision, had agreed to do so in toto. With respect to the union territories...Yashwant Sinha [the union finance minister] assured the meeting that necessary steps would be taken so that same compliance is reached by them.'

For an overview of tax reform challenges and proposals, see Chelliah's 'An Agenda for Comprehensive Tax Reform' in Raja Chelliah (ed.), *Towards Sustainable Growth: Essays in Fiscal and Financial Sector Reforms in India* (New Delhi, Oxford University Press, 1996), pp. 138–59.

In the meanwhile, just under the wire, the Tamil Nadu government announced on 27 October 1999 that Ford India, which had recently established a $450 manufacturing plant in the state, had been granted a concessional 1 per cent ad valorem sales tax rate for vehicles and parts manufactured in the state and sold interstate to registered dealers or governments. This concession would be valid for 14 years from 1 November 1999. *The Hindu,* 28 October 1999.

48. In early 2000, the centre's fiscal deficit was hovering at 5.6 per cent despite persistent efforts to bring it down to the 4 per cent-level that has become something of a world standard. Interest payments on the deficit had risen to an alarming 50 per cent of central revenue. *The Hindu,* 14 March 2000.

49. The Planning Commission, 'finding itself somewhat marginalized in the decision-making mechanism of the central government,' prepared a confidential internal note in April 2000 urging that it be given a much larger coordinating role in the federal system. 'In the domestic sector the commission feels that it should be allowed to play the role of an arbitrator whenever there is "lack of harmonisation" of policy between various tiers of government and also between regions in the country.' It seems clear that the Commission was seeking to define a new regulatory role for itself in the federal market economy. *The Hindu,* 11 April 2000.

50. In February 2001 CRISIL downgraded a Maharashtra state government-supported bond issue, explaining it had done so because of the GoM's non-payment of monthly dues to Dabhol Power Corporation, the Enron affiliate. *The Economic Times,* 6 February 2001.

51. Thomas L Friedman has popularized the relationship between credit-rating agencies and the hard-budget constraints of market competition in *The Lexus and the Olive Tree* (New York, Anchor Books, Random House, 1999, 2000), p. 109, with his terms, the 'golden straitjacket' and the 'electronic herd' of 'faceless stock, bond and currency traders sitting behind computer screens all over the globe...and big multinational corporations...This herd...is beginning to replace governments as the primary source of capital for both companies and countries to grow.'

For hard- (and soft-) budget constraints see Janos Kornai, *Vision and Reality. Market and State: Contradictions and Dilemmas Revisited* (New York Routledge, 1990).

52. The importance of subsidies for agricultural inputs has to be imagined in the context of the 65 per cent of the workforce located in the agriculture sector and the almost 70 per cent of the population that live in what are classified as rural or town areas.

Bal Thackeray, leader of the Shiv Sena, a Maharashtra-based regional party, promised farmers free electricity in October 1997, while out of power. In 1999, when the Shiv Sena formed the state government in coalition with the BJP, the BJP leader, Gopinath Munde, announced that this promise was not viable. By that time, the earlier promise had seriously affected payment of electricity charges. *The Economic Times,* 13 January 1999. Punjab too supplied free electricity to farmers. *Outlook,* 28 December 1998.

Until recently, agricultural/rural electricity consumers have been subsidized by industrial consumers, whose rates are four to five limes higher than those paid by agriculturalists. As the agricultural sector's consumption of electricity in particular states mounted (in Rajasthan over the past 10 years it jumped from 10 to 40 per cent of an expanding total supply, so that in 1999–2000 it equalled industry's proportion), the system of cross-subsidization from industry to agriculture broke down, opening the way in 2000 to raise user charges for the agricultural economy.

53. Loan defaults by state corporations, especially electricity and roadways corporations, are heavily implicated in the very high level of non-performing assets of public sector banks. Frequently such loans are backed by state government guarantees. State industrial, commercial, and service corporations have been 'notorious for defaulting on their debt and their (respective state) governments had earlier shown no interest to honour their obligations.' 'Double Whammy: As State Corporations' Finances Worsen, States are Dragged Down', *Business Standard,* 21 October 1999.

54. Nirupam Bajpai and Jeffrey Sachs, *The Hindu,* 6 December 1999.

55. World Bank, *India: Sustaining Rapid Economic Growth* (Washington DC, World Bank, 1997), p. 21.

56. See front page story in *The Economic Times,* 4 March 2001, 'One-Time Settlement for SEBs Mooted: Centre to Power Reforms'.

57. Article 293 (1) restricts state borrowing to domestic lenders: 'the executive power of a state extends to borrowing within the territory of India upon the security of the consolidated Fund of the state...' Equally decisive for the centre's enforcement for fiscal discipline is Article 293 (3). It requires states that owe money to the centre to obtain the centre's consent to borrow. 'A state may not without the consent of the government of India raise any loan if there is still outstanding any part of a loan which has been made to the state by the government of India.' Since all states owe money to the GoI, the condition applies to all states. Borrowing by state corporations often avoids this permission.

World Bank loans to state governments involve intensive negotiations between individual states and the Bank, but, because they are foreign loans, they have to be processed and cleared by the central government. World Bank loans reach particular states as 70 per cent loan, 30 per cent grant. In fact the centre, in return for additions to its foreign exchange balance, lowers the interest rate that states pay and absorbs the risk of variable foreign exchange rates.

58. The Power Finance Corporation (PFC), for example, has used its leverage to nudge states to set up state electricity regulatory boards, devices to move the setting of electricity rates out of the hands of politicians and into a cost-recouping process. In 1999 the PFC was offering a 5 per cent subsidy on loans taken where states set up such boards. Since then, central loans are threatened to be withheld where states do not take such steps. *The Economic Times*, 5 January 1999.

In October, 1999, when the financial standing of many public sector banks was in jeopardy as a result of heavy exposure to the non-performing assets of state-level corporations, observers thought that the 'Reserve Bank of India (RBI) might come out with a list of criteria regarding such issues. This could include a limiting amount for such corporations as well as compulsory rating for them.' 'State Corps May be Told to Adhere to Specific Norms', *Business Standard*, 27 October 1999.

59. 'Recently, the central public enterprises have been instructed by the central government to discontinue supplies to states in arrears. Thus Coal India has implemented a 'cash and carry' policy for supplies to the State Electricity Boards (SEBs) in arrears, and the National Thermal Power Corporation has, at times, cut power supplies'. World Bank, *India: Sustaining Rapid Economic Growth*, p. 21.

60. See Constitutional Articles 280 and 281, which deal with the Finance Commission. Finance Commissions (FCs) make recommendations to government and the government places its version of the FC's recommendations before parliament for its approval. FC recommendations are generally accepted with minor modifications. For exceptions, see 'Don't Shoot the Commission', *Economic and Political Weekly*, 23 September 2000, pp. 3451–2.

Finance Commission awards during the Nehru-Gandhi era were sometimes encroached upon by the Planning Commission, which in its heyday and even now makes developmental grants which cannot always be distinguished from grants-in-aid of revenue.

Made up of a chairman and four members appointed by the President of India from among knowledgeable and distinguished persons, commissions are asked to 'determine what proportion of the receipts from designated taxes collected by the union government must be passed on to the states and how much in addition must be provided as grants-in-aid to states in need of such assistance after taking account of the amounts likely to accrue to them by way of tax devolution.' 'Don't Shoot the Commission', *Economic and Political Weekly*.

61. Interviews with chief secretaries, finance secretaries, and industry secretaries in Maharashtra. Andhra Pradesh, and Tamil Nadu in February 2000.

62. 'Under the aegis of national planning, it has been the declared policy to ensure balanced development of all regions...' Chelliah, *Sustainable Growth*, p. 25. Like other observers, Chelliah notes that intention to the contrary notwithstanding, 'interstate disparities have...increased.'

63. Madhav Godbole, 'Finance Commissions in a Cul-de-sac', *Economic and Political Weekly*, XXXVI, 1, 6 January (2001), pp. 29–30.

64. M.M. Sury, *Fiscal Federalism in India* (Delhi, Indian Tax Institute, 1998), pp. 81, 181.

65. The criticisms and calls for redress of the Eleventh Finance Commission awards were initiated by Andhra Pradesh's chief minister, Chandrababu Naidu. He implied that the commission was using a formula that rewarded feckless high population growth, low-economic growth states such as Bihar and Uttar Pradesh, and penalized successful low-population growth, high-economic growth states such as Andhra Pradesh and the seven other states who joined Chandrababu's campaign. The campaign did not succeed in changing the overall framework of the Eleventh Finance Commission's award, but did succeed in having Rs 53 billion additional funds allocated to the low-population growth, high-economic growth states.

The *Economic and Political Weekly*, in its issue of 23 September 2000, pp. 3451–2, editorialized in alarm that 'never until the Eleventh Finance Commission has the report of any commission been subject to the kind of attacks and charges that have followed the publication of the report of this commission...' At the same time it admitted that 'the task of allocating funds...is undoubtedly a formidable one, especially when the goals to be achieved happen to embody fundamental conflicts between equity and efficiency'.

66. Commissioner Amaresh Bagchi dissented from the Eleventh Finance Commission's conditionalities on this ground.

67. Constitution of India, List III, Concurrent, item 38.

68. See memorandum by Pramod Deo, Principal Secretary, Energy, Government of Maharashtra, 'The Electricity Bill 2000: A Critical Appraisal', no date, ca. May 2000, which provides a history of the legislation and suggests the ways in which states can shape their own energy regime if their legislation precedes the passage of the central act.

69. 'Share the Burden of Hard Decisions: PM', *The Hindu*, 21 May 2000. Not that the chief ministers acquiesced supinely. 'There is no reason,' said Maharashtra chief minister Vilas Rao Deshmukh, 'why the centre should take decisions which affect millions of families across the country on its own without taking popular governments in the states into confidence.'

70. When CRISIL downgraded bonds of four state corporations charged with Konkan irrigation, Krishna valley development, Tapi irrigation, and Vidarbha irrigation, it blamed the 'persistent rise in [Maharashtra's]...revenue

and fiscal deficit to higher levels' on the 'revision in pay scales of state employees following recommendations of the Fifth Pay Commission.' 'Fiscal recovery in the long run,' CRISIL wrote, 'would be contingent on the state government's willingness to speedily implement significant revenue augmentation and fiscal reform measures.' *Business Standard*, 7 October 1999. CARE, another major domestic credit-rating agency, came in with a more favourable rating earlier in the year for a bond issue to support a Godavari project. *The Economic Times*, 8 January 1999.

71. Indian papers regularly carry the credit ratings of international and domestic credit-rating agencies such as Standard and Poor's and CRISIL. See, for example, the report by Standard and Poor's in March 2000, affirming its triple-B/A-3 local currency sovereign credit rating and its double-B/single-B foreign currency sovereign credit ratings for the Republic of India. *Hindustan Times*, 22 March 2000.

72. Kewal Varma argued in October 1999 that as 120 of the 300 members of the governing coalition in parliament were from single-state parties (he counted the BJP, Congress, CPI and CPI [M] as national), the state voice at the centre had grown. He also argued: 'Increased regional influence at the centre means that the fiscal deficit will not be contained.' 'Globalisation versus Localisation', *Business Standard*, 29 October 1999.

9

Economic Reform, Federal Politics, and External Assistance
Understanding New Delhi's Perspective on the World Bank's State-Level Loans[*]

JASON A. KIRK[1]

Since the mid-1990s, international aid providers to India have been evolving new assistance strategies that seek to reshape development policies in the country's states. The World Bank lending agencies,[2] as well as the Asian Development Bank (ADB) and Britain's Department for International Development (DFID), are selectively channelling resources toward states that demonstrate commitment to a broad range of fiscal and governance reforms. While the lenders' emphases differ somewhat and their programmes with particular states vary in the details, the main thrust of policy-based assistance has been to encourage states to adopt an overall framework of fiscal contraction, and within this to restructure their expenditures to increase education, health, and physical infrastructure investments, while reforming or privatizing unprofitable state-owned enterprises (SOEs), reducing outlays for salaries and other administrative costs, and narrowing the provision of consumption subsidies and other welfare expenditures to households below strictly defined poverty lines. The general approach, variously called a 'focus states' or 'partner states' strategy, seeks to encourage economic growth and targeted poverty reduction in reform-committed states, and thus to promote them as models for the rest of the country.[3]

This chapter examines the turn toward sub-national policy-based lending by the World Bank—the largest and most high-profile of the aid providers—

* This paper was commissioned for this volume.

and suggests what this change signifies with respect to India's external economic relations and domestic federal politics. Historically, India has sought to retain maximum policy autonomy vis-à-vis the international financial institutions (IFIs), especially the World Bank (hereafter 'the Bank') and International Monetary Fund (IMF). At the same time, the central government in New Delhi has used constitutional provisions, the planning apparatus, and intergovernmental fiscal institutions to exercise careful control over state finances and the distribution of investment across the states, in an attempt to influence their developmental policies.

Against this backdrop, the Centre's support for selective state lending and conditionality by the Bank presents an intriguing puzzle. It might be tempting to surmise that the Centre has bowed to pressure from the Bank, the states, or both—that the new lending approach reflects a diminishment of the Centre's autonomy vis-à-vis the Bank and/or its authority vis-à-vis the states.[4]

However, this chapter will show that this 'diminished central capacity' thesis certainly does not accurately describe the Centre–Bank dimension of the tripartite interaction that is sub-national adjustment lending. On the contrary, the Bank proposed its focus-states strategy in 1996 as a response to what its own staff perceived as its longstanding *lack* of policy influence in India—stemming both from India's generally low reliance on aid, and from India's traditionally vigorous defence of its sovereignty in all aspects of its international relations. India was not compelled to accept the Bank's sub-national loans and conditionality from a resource-needs standpoint, and as the strategy has continued to evolve, the country's foreign exchange holdings have increased manifold and its overall external borrowing has actually decreased. Simply put, the Centre has supported the Bank's proposal not because it has had to do so, but because it has actively chosen to.

Turning to the Centre–states dimension, we might expect to find greater support for a diminished central capacity hypothesis. As many observers have noted and as this chapter will make clear, the evolution underway in India's party system and Centre-state relations—and in particular, the trend toward central coalition governments in which state-based parties can wield pivotal clout—*is* constraining the ability of central authorities to push the country's states to undertake politically difficult fiscal and governance reforms. Many of the so-called 'second generation reforms' needed to consolidate the national economic liberalization programme launched in 1991 lie within the purview of the state governments, whose commitment to liberalization remains highly uneven. When the Bank in 1996 proposed the new assistance strategy, central policy-makers therefore embraced the scheme in the view that it would enhance their own leverage over state policies. The Centre[5]—more specifically, the Ministry of Finance and its Department of Economic Affairs (DEA)[6]—reasoned that Bank-sponsored programmes in select states would serve as the necessary catalyst to a transformation in state policies (and, correspondingly, in India's intergovernmental fiscal institutions) that central reformers were already eager to bring about, but that they themselves could not push beyond the constraints of federal coalition politics.

Readers familiar with the theoretical literature in international relations might recognize this motivation as an example of what has been called a 'two-level game', following a seminal 1988 article by Robert Putnam. Putnam actually refers to two distinct scenarios: one in which national-level authorities strategically use domestic political constraints to 'tie their own hands' and thus strengthen their bargaining position in international negotiations, and another in which they enter into international agreements in order to achieve domestic objectives that they would not be able to realize on their own—thus effectively thrusting domestic policy conflicts into the international arena in an effort to render them subject to third-party authority.[7] It is the latter perspective that is most relevant to the strategic interaction between the Centre, the Bank, and the states, and the use of Putnam's framework as a departure point for analysis might encourage us to focus on the domestically compromised authority of the Centre that has led it to invoke such a mechanism.

However, a more nuanced way to look at the Centre's embrace of subnational adjustment lending is that it signifies the Centre's ability to adapt to the new political environment of coalition government, and to devise novel ways of achieving its economic reform goals in spite of the states' greater capacity to resist New Delhi's pressure. The selected 'focus states' may be enjoying a sense of independence that comes with greater access to the Bank's resources and a more direct policy dialogue with Bank officials, but the Centre effectively retains ultimate (if arm's length) discretion over their relationships with the Bank, and it still exerts considerable control over the overall distribution of external assistance across states. In other words, it is misleading to argue (as one analyst has) that the Centre has 'taken itself out of the picture' by lending the Bank engage in policy-based lending to states.[8] It is still very much the final authority in all matters of external lending to states, though for its two-level game strategy to work, it must encourage the *impression* that the Bank is independent in evaluating states' commitments to reforms as a pre-condition for assistance.

And yet, as this chapter will also suggest, in its implementation the 'focus states' strategy has so far fallen short of the high hopes its Bank and Indian architects had set for it. Fiscal indicators in the Bank's group of states have moved toward the targets set forth in their fiscal frameworks for reform, though the progress that has been made cannot necessarily be attributed to the Bank's involvement, for reasons discussed below. For the states as a whole, however, deficits have continued to climb to a level that has led some analysts (including the Bank) to express concern. The central government shares some of the responsibility for this, since its own fiscal policies at times have sent mixed signals and placed pressure on the states to maintain high current spending, particularly on salaries.

Thus, whatever limited progress has been made in the Bank's focus states themselves, the hoped-for broader 'demonstration effects' of the assistance strategy are yet to materialize. Though there are surely many reasons why other states might be reluctant to imitate the reforms of the focus states, one factor that should give pause both to the Bank and to the Centre is an oft-expressed cynicism about why the original focus states were selected: in the absence of transparent selection procedures, many observers have surmised that states were chosen on the basis of what might be called 'good politics' rather than 'good policies'.

There is some truth to this; as we shall see, partisan political factors *have* indeed figured in state selection to some extent, though neither as prominently nor as consistently as is often assumed. What observers may not realize is that when states have been chosen for political reasons, the impetus for this has come more proximately from *the Bank*, and only indirectly from the Centre. Ironically, the very control that the Centre continues to exercise over states' borrowing from the Bank diminishes the latter's ability to act in a politically disinterested manner—the very essence of the two-level game stratagem. The Bank, concerned that the Centre might at any moment rescind its support for the focus-states strategy, felt compelled to seek 'protection' against this eventuality by selecting as the major recipient of selective aid the state of Andhra Pradesh (AP), whose governing Telugu Desam Party (TDP) just happened to occupy prominent positions in successive central coalition governments from 1996 to 2004 (the logic behind the selection of Karnataka and Uttar Pradesh was different, but it is AP that has attracted the most money and therefore the most attention). Thus, the Bank's own predicament in India has somewhat diminished its ability to remain 'above the fray' of domestic politics and to calibrate its stance toward state governments solely on the basis of objective policy criteria.

This study proceeds as follows. The first section provides brief historical background to explain the Bank's motives for proposing a new lending strategy in the mid-1990s focused on state-level reforms. This side of the story—the 'supply side' explanation for sub-national lending—concerns the Bank's long-standing frustration at its relatively weak leverage over India's economic policies, and its belief that concentrated lending to a few states would increase its policy influence throughout the country. The second section turns to the more puzzling question of why India's central government, against its traditionally strong defence of economic sovereignty, decided in 1996 to support the approach. It briefly reviews the two-level-games literature and suggests how this framework applies in the context of economic reform under India's federal political system—thus offering a 'demand side' explanation for the Centre's support. Turning from the genesis of the approach to its implementation, the third section (tentatively and partially) assesses the extent to which the focus-states strategy has succeeded so far, especially in terms of its own major objective of fiscal reform. The conclusion draws implications for India's external economic relations, and for the internal challenges to economic reform created by its evolving Centre-state politics.

THE 'SUPPLY SIDE': WHY IS THE WORLD BANK GOING SUB-NATIONAL IN INDIA?

Though sub-national adjustment lending could not have been launched without the express support of India's central government, the story behind the strategy begins at the Bank rather than at the Centre—and within the Bank, at the level of the India country team. While consistent with a growing conventional wisdom and international trend in favour of decentralized fiscal and governance institutions, the Bank's sub-national shift in India was not the product of a top-down directive by its senior management or pressure from its donor governments. Rather, it represents a bottom-up response by the Bank's India team to particular challenges of lending to a large, proud, and relatively self-sufficient borrower. What is striking to note, however, is that other country departments within the Bank—working with other federal and quasi-federal borrower governments—have also developed selective sub-national lending approaches in recent years.

A Cross-national Trend Rooted in Specific National Experiences

The Bank first introduced sub-national conditionality in 1994 in Brazil, in response to a request by federal authorities there concerned with burgeoning state budget deficits and debt. In 1995–6, while the Bank's India department was beginning to formulate a sub-national strategy, Bank staff and Argentinean authorities were negotiating adjustment loans for a set of that country's provinces. At the time, however, the India team was 'barely aware' of its counterparts' experiments in Latin America.[9] More recently, the Bank has introduced sub-national reform lending in Mexico (2000) and Pakistan (2002), and a similar programme for Nigeria appears to be in the works. Only *after* all these programmes were initiated did the Bank begin to encourage any systematic dialogue on the selective sub-national approach across country departments for all these borrowers.[10] Constitutional and political differences among countries create important variations in lending arrangements: for example, Brazil's states may borrow from external lenders directly, whereas in India the Bank lends to the central government, which transfers the funds under an on-lending formula as part of the states' Plan assistance.[11]

The differences between the focus-states approach and the traditional relationship among the Bank, the Centre, and the states are represented in a simple visual schematic in Figure 9.1. Interaction between the Bank and India's states is not new, but the focus-states strategy has departed from the traditional approach in two important ways. First, in the past the Bank made no deliberate attempt to determine how its loan resources would be allocated among the states. Second, to the extent that the Bank engaged in policy dialogue with India, it was basically confined to the central government level. The Bank invested in particular development projects in the states—in infrastructure, in education and health, in rural development, and so on—but left it to central officials to determine how projects would be dealt out among the states as implementing agencies.

Under the focus-states approach, the Bank has taken the view that the overall policy environment in some states is much more conducive to economic growth and poverty reduction than in others. The Bank aims to 'maximize the developmental impact' of its assistance by 'focusing' it in states with good policies, in hopes that their strong developmental achievements will encourage other states to undertake similar reforms. India's central government has formally agreed to pass on the rupee equivalent of the Bank's dollar-denominated

Figure 9.1: World Bank assistance to India and its states: Traditional and 'focus states' approaches

Traditional Approach

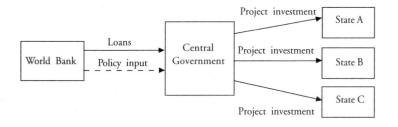

'Focus States' Approach

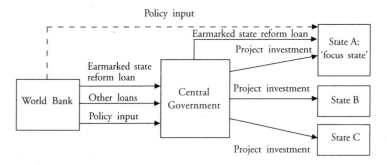

Note: For earmarked 'focus states' loans, the Centre is the borrower. It agrees to on-lend the rupee equivalent of the World Bank's dollar loans to the state government (the loan 'beneficiary').

Source: Author's conceptualization, based on official documents and interviews.

loans/credits to the designated state governments that are listed as 'beneficiary' on the official loan documents (the Centre itself is the 'borrower').[12] Summing up the contrast between the traditional and new approaches, one Bank official put it this way: 'We've gone from investing in a sort of all-India "mutual fund" to picking individual "stocks".'[13] Extending the analogy, if under the earlier set-up the Bank let the Centre act as 'fund manager', it is now actively managing its own state-wise investment portfolio.

The World Bank and India: A Special Relationship and a Long-standing Frustration

In India, the Bank's sub-national interest evolved out of the staff's frustration with its limited influence over the country's policies. India is one of the Bank's largest annual borrowers—in cumulative terms, *the* largest borrower—and the Bank assigns a great deal of importance to it. Invoking the title of Paul Scott's classic novel, a staff member interviewed in the mid-1990s called India 'the "Jewel in the Crown" of the World Bank', and said often the Bank's reputation has 'tended to be measured in terms of what it could do for India.'[14] Historically, however, the Bank has had only limited success in influencing India's policies. Despite the high absolute lending volume, India is relatively much less dependent on aid than are most other countries of a similar per-capita income level, and it has often resisted external advice that does not reflect the consensus of its senior policy-makers. Bank lending to India has carried major policy conditionality only during major economic crises such as in 1966 and 1990–1, which rendered the country desperate for the foreign exchange that external assistance could provide. At both these junctures, the senior leadership in India contained a contingent strongly in favour of liberalization, but only after the latter crisis was serious reform sustained.

In the crisis of 1966, a new government led by Indira Gandhi backed away from further implementation of a major Bank-sponsored reform programme when it encountered a torrent of domestic criticism—especially by state-level leaders from Mrs. Gandhi's own Congress Party—following the first devaluation of the rupee since India's independence.[15] Critics accused Mrs. Gandhi of surrendering to imperialist pressure, particularly from the US. In the years following the crisis, her government quickly amassed a foreign exchange cushion so as never to be so 'vulnerably dependent' on foreign aid again.[16] The episode affected the Bank's relations with India for long afterward. Though Bank lending to India increased significantly during the 1970s, almost all of it took the form of loans for specific projects, which did not carry major economic policy conditions. The Bank's avoidance of conditionality continued right through the 1980s, putting its policy toward India out of step with its operations in many other countries during the 'decade of structural adjustment.'

In 1990–1, India underwent another economic crisis, proximately triggered by the Gulf War but stemming more fundamentally from unsustainable macroeconomic policies during the 1980s, especially heavy deficit spending by the Centre and states. Famously, at the peak of the crisis, India's foreign exchange reserves fell to a mere two weeks' worth of import finance. This time, India's senior leadership stood more united in favour of liberalization and sought to sell the reforms domestically by saying they were necessary in order to claim India's rightful status as a global power.[17] This coherence was remarkable in that the government was new and the Congress Party did not initially hold a parliamentary majority, though members of the central elite such as Finance Minister Manmohan Singh, Commerce Minister Palaniappan Chidambaram, and Commerce Secretary Montek Singh Ahluwalia had long advocated liberalization and used the economic crisis as an opportunity to advance a reform agenda. Further, at the international level, the collapse of the Soviet planning model and the economic ascendancy of past adversary China under its reform programme were key factors in inciting liberalization. India accepted an IMF stabilization package worth US $2.3 billion and a US $500 million structural adjustment loan from the Bank, and moved quickly to initiate sweeping policy changes. The contrast with earlier aborted liberalization efforts created excitement: *The Economist*, for example, proclaimed India a 'tiger uncaged' at last.[18]

Exuberance, however, soon gave way to a more sober assessment of the tasks ahead. Whereas the initial phase of liberalization was largely within the purview of the senior central policy elite, it became clear that the 'second generation of reforms' would require fundamental institutional changes—particularly in the states—that were more complex and long-term in nature.[19] Since the Bank's limited policy input was essentially confined to New Delhi, it worried that it would become disengaged from the adjustment process. When disbursement of its national-level adjustment loan was completed, project loans again began to dominate its India portfolio. By 1993, Bank staff began to lament that their 'assistance strategy' was not really a strategy at all, but rather a sundry assortment of disconnected projects.[20] More fundamentally, they suspected that the 1991 adjustment loan had been 'an accident' made possible only by the crisis, and that without careful planning the Bank again might forfeit the opportunity to meaningfully influence the shape of economic policy in India.[21]

A New Country Director and a New Approach: 'Let a Few Get Rich First'

Significantly, in 1996 the Bank appointed a new Country Director for India. Edwin Lim had served as Chief of Resident Mission at the Bank's Beijing office from 1985 to 1990, and he drew lessons from China's rapid growth experience. Noting that the Chinese economic miracle had benefited some of its provinces much more than others, Lim invoked Deng Xiaoping's dictum, 'Let a few get rich first.' He proposed a new Bank strategy for India: it should be deliberately anti-egalitarian in lending to the states, and should lend heavily to the most reform-committed among them to encourage them to achieve their full growth potential. Their success, he suggested, would present 'demonstration effects' to the rest of the country that would be more influential than any financial amount the Bank could set forth. By practicing 'selectivity' and concentrating lending in a handful of states, Lim argued, the Bank could leverage greater policy influence throughout India.[22] Even before Lim arrived at the Bank, there had been some discussion of policy-based lending at the state level (as noted later in this chapter), but the new Country Director placed a distinctive stamp on this previously nebulous notion by arguing that the Bank should lend heavily and visibly to the most reform-oriented states.

However, the Bank would have to secure the support of India's central government for the strategy. The proposal stood in sharp contrast to India's traditional norm (in theory, if not always in practice) of distributing public investment across the states in pursuit of regionally balanced development— though some central policy-makers too were beginning to doubt the usefulness of this approach. More fundamentally, the Bank's proposal could have been interpreted as an affront to India's economic sovereignty. But central officials did not see it that way in 1996. As the next section demonstrates, key reform enthusiasts in New Delhi were more than happy to permit the Bank to establish adjustment programmes in select states, and saw external conditionality as a helpful boost to their own efforts to bring about reforms in state-level and intergovernmental institutions.

THE 'DEMAND SIDE': WHY DID NEW DELHI SUPPORT SELECTIVE STATE–LEVEL LENDING?

In the fall of 1996, just after India's first national election since 1991 and shortly after his own appointment as Country Director, Lim called on new Finance Minister P. Chidambaram to secure his approval of the Bank's focus-states strategy. Lim offered the 'demonstration effects' rationale, and sweetened the proposal by suggesting that state-level adjustment lending could become a vehicle for expansion of the Bank's total assistance to India, from an annual mid-1990s average of US $1.5 billion to US $3 billion.[23]

What led Chidambaram to embrace such a significant change in India's relationship with the Bank? Given the possibility of doubled Bank lending, it might be tempting to conclude that the motivation was simply financial.

However, by the mid-1990s India had returned to a more comfortable foreign exchange position (about US $60 billion), and the dollar incentive that had accompanied its acceptance of Bank conditionality in 1966 and 1991 was not a major factor. Moreover, with the benefit of hindsight, we can even more firmly reject a resource-needs explanation. While subsequent central governments (until recently) have continued to endorse the focus-states approach, India's foreign exchange reserves have climbed toward US $100 billion and its leadership has become increasingly assertive about the terms under which it will accept aid—even manoeuvring to symbolically redefine itself as an aid provider and not just a recipient. In 2002–3, India paid US $3 billion in IMF and World Bank debt ahead of schedule, informed 22 donor countries that it will longer accept their aid on a bilateral basis once existing programmes are completed, and announced plans to double its own annual aid budget (to US $1.2–1.4 billion) to assist countries in Africa and elsewhere in Asia.[24]

The Domestic 'Two-Level Game': Theory and Comparative Findings

The 'two-level games' framework provides the explanation for India's acceptance of the Bank's focus-states strategy that material-resource considerations cannot account for. While the original impetus came from the Bank, the Centre authorized and embraced the strategy with a view to strengthening its own leverage over state finances and policies. A key premise of Putnam's framework is that 'international negotiations sometimes enable government leaders to do what they privately wish to do, but are powerless to do domestically.' Putnam contends that IMF programmes, for example, are often misleadingly criticized as externally imposed, when in fact domestic authorities sometimes 'exploit IMF pressure to facilitate policy moves that are otherwise infeasible internally.'[25]

Following Putnam's original 1988 article, there has been a growth in studies of this phenomenon in recent years. Judith Goldstein, for example, shows how the US president used the 1988 Canadian-US Free Trade Agreement and later the North American Free Trade Agreement (NAFTA) to overcome bureaucratic and congressional opposition to trade liberalization.[26] Robert Paarlberg examines US and EU uses of General Agreement on Tariffs and Trade (GATT) negotiations to achieve politically difficult agricultural reforms in their respective domestic arenas.[27] And echoing Putnam's claims about the IMF, James Vreeland argues that governments enter IMF agreements to achieve politically unpopular goals such as fiscal austerity and the upward redistribution of income.[28]

A few scholars have sought to clarify the mechanisms through which international organizations enhance the leverage of particular domestic actors. For example, Jon Pevehouse and Daniel Drezner both argue that international organizations (IOs) influence domestic political outcomes through a combination of formal and informal mechanisms. Pevehouse sees IOs as engaging in both 'hand-tying'—applying direct pressure for certain policies through formal membership requirements and conditions—and 'socializing' of national elites who fear policy change.[29] Drezner draws a distinction between domestic 'policy initiators' and 'policy ratifiers', and suggests that leaders, particularly in highly decentralized countries, face more potential roadblocks to policy implementation, and thus have incentives to 'use the resources of international organizations to force acquiescence from domestic ratifiers.' He too sees IOs as acting to influence countries' domestic politics through both formal and informal means, with the latter including sparking changes in domestic actors' preferences by providing an arena for 'new modes of inter-subjective understanding'.[30] Further in this chapter, we will consider what mechanisms of external influence apply in the context of the Bank's sub-national reform loans in India.

The 'Second Stage' of Structural Adjustment in India: The Role of State Finances

As a key member of the economic team that launched India's adjustment programme in 1991, Chidambaram was deeply committed to liberalization.[31] Like other reform advocates, he understood by the mid-1990s that for India to proceed beyond the first stage of reforms, the state governments would have to effectively 'ratify' the Centre's adjustment initiatives by committing to complementary measures. Many key areas of economic policy—including important aspects of rural development, education, health, industrial policy, the provision of physical infrastructure, and tax policy—are subjects in which the states hold important powers, either by constitutional writ or by historical convention.

Moreover, many of the most politically difficult reforms would have to transpire at the state level. Since the early 1980s, increasingly competitive electoral politics in many states has encouraged the abandonment of what had until then been a fairly consistent tradition of fiscal prudence; by the mid-1990s, sustainable fiscal deficit reduction would require that the states cut popular consumption subsidies, reduce government payrolls, painstakingly restructure or privatize inefficient SOEs, and mobilize additional revenues. The political challenges presented by such a reform agenda were daunting. For example, farmers—a key constituency in many states—were not likely to back a

Figure 9.2: Key trends in state governments' expenditures

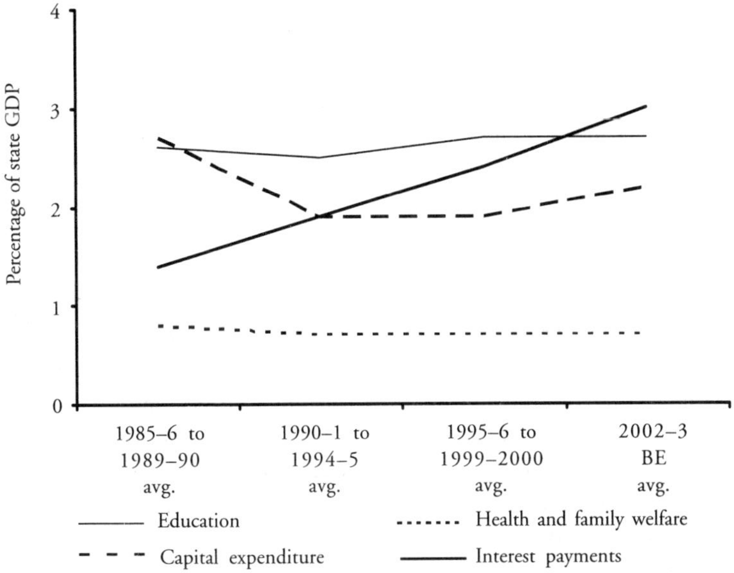

Note: BE = Budget Estimates.
Source: Reserve Bank of India bulletin (various issues).

state government that rescinded cut-rate power, fertilizer, and irrigation provision. Nor would many middle-class voters support an end to price ceilings on food staples such as rice or the introduction of new user charges for state services; state employees' unions could be expected to oppose bureaucratic downsizing and reform of the money-losing SOEs such as the state electricity boards (SEBs); and so on.[32]

Reform advocates contended that, however difficult they may be, such measures were necessary since the growing proportion of the states' revenue expenditure devoted to interest payments—for loans taken to finance what had become structural deficits—was consuming funds needed for developmental investments, especially in such areas as education and health, and for capital expenditure designed to expand economic capacity (see Figure 9.2).

Centre–State Fiscal Transfers: 'Soft–Budget Constraints' and Perverse Incentives

Along with the internal electoral compulsions leading states to maintain large budget deficits, federal political factors and the states' structural position as sub-national entities in a revenue top-heavy federal system undermined their incentives for fiscal discipline. Recent comparative work on public finance in multi-level government settings points toward the common problem of *soft-budget constraints*, which exists when sub-national governments expect that the central government can be made to 'accommodate and share in excess expenditures' through fiscal transfers and bail-outs.[33] According to this perspective, sub-national governments place their own electoral self-interests (put more charitably, their constituents' interests) before the interests of the country as a whole. This entices them to run budget deficits with the expectation that they can shift the cost burden to the central government. For a variety of reasons, ranging from explicit legal obligations to less formal considerations of dependence on sub-national allies for political support, the central government may find it impossible to commit *not* to share in expenditures or to save a sub-national government from the consequences of its own profligate spending—especially when a localized fiscal crisis could create trouble for the whole country. Case studies on a wide range of countries provide evidence of this pattern.[34]

In India, as in other federal countries, the soft-budget constraints of sub-national governments present challenges for central policy-makers. In fact, the issue is particularly significant in the Indian context, where central transfers fund a relatively high share of state government expenditures. India exhibits a high *vertical fiscal imbalance* compared to many other federal countries—meaning there is a significant asymmetry between the assignment of revenues and expenditures between the Centre and the states. India's states in the 1990s accounted for between 55–60 per cent of total government expenditures, but only about a little more than one third of total revenues.[35] This exacerbates the states' incentives to spend on electorally popular but fiscally imprudent budget items, since it is generally the Centre that is concerned with raising the revenues to pay for them.

Moreover, apart from the generic problem of soft-state-budget constraints, India's system of fiscal federalism exhibits particular features that further undermine the states' incentives for fiscal discipline. A detailed description of the complex Centre-states fiscal transfer regime is beyond the scope of this chapter, though its most relevant features can be summarized.[36] It encompasses three principal entities: first, the constitutionally mandated Finance Commission, an independent body of technical specialists which convenes every five years to set rules for the devolution of certain central revenues to the state governments; second, the extra-constitutional Planning Commission, a quasi-independent entity which coordinates development plans between the Centre and states;

and third, the various central government ministries that control the budgets of what are known as 'centrally sponsored schemes'.

While devolution formulae change somewhat from one Finance Commission to another, they have generally followed a 'gap-filling' methodology to meeting shortfalls in state budgets, which some analysts suggest reduces the states' tax efforts and may even encourage them to inflate budgetary projections and incur strategic deficits.[37] As one scholar put it, 'The allocation is based on measures of policy failure more than on success.'[38]

Other aspects of the federal fiscal system give central officials significant discretion over resource transfers—raising the possibility that allocation decisions are susceptible to partisan political influences. Central ministry transfers are generally the area of least transparency, but the Planning Commission too holds enough discretionary powers to allow political factors to influence its allocation decisions at the margin—especially since its transfer criteria are subject to review by the National Development Council (NDC), which is chaired by the prime minister and includes all central cabinet ministers and the states' chief ministers. Partisan resource allocation can act as a further disincentive to fiscal prudence on the part of state governments, which recognize opportunities for political shortcuts around responsible budget practices.

The Reform Game: Pushing State-Level Reforms, Tying Central Hands

By the time of Lim's 1996 visit, Chidambaram and other central reform advocates recognized that in order for the states to adopt the reforms necessary to consolidate structural adjustment, the Centre would have to transform India's fiscal federalism from a labyrinth of soft-budget constraints, perverse incentives, and favoured resource access for states with important political connections at the Centre into a more performance-based allocation regime. Not only would this require reordering the system's formal aspects to reward responsible budget practices, but the Centre would also have to tie its own hands to prevent political resource allocation from undermining the principle of holding states accountable for their fiscal policies.

Chidambaram told Lim that he and other central officials believed that India's fiscal federalism was in need of major reform, but that Centre-state politics in the context of coalition government constrained this course of action.[39] The Centre was in a particularly poor position to try to enforce state fiscal discipline following the 1996 election, in which the Congress Party lost power and the motley United Front (UF) coalesced to form the central government.[40] The UF coalition depended on support from a number of state-based parties, whose defection could bring down the government. This made it especially difficult for New Delhi to credibly commit to refrain from funding states' budget deficits in order to compel them to reform.

As an interesting counterfactual, we might wonder if a central government under the control of a single majority party, such as the Congress, would have shown as much enthusiasm for the Bank's state-lending proposal. The evidence bearing on this question is not entirely clear. Cross-national analysis shows that in countries where the party of the national government also controls a large proportion of sub-national governments, aggregate deficits and inflation tend to be lower than in federations with fragmented party systems, suggesting that central elites may be able to rely on informal party networks (and a sub-national government's knowledge that its own electoral fate may be tied to the achievements of central reformers) to enforce sub-national fiscal discipline.[41] In the Indian case, however, this finding may not hold true: one pair of recent studies shows that during the era of Congress dominance, deficits tended to be *higher* in Congress-ruled states than in non-Congress states, apparently funded by partisan central transfers.[42] But this finding does not discount the possibility that a Congress central government committed to economic reform might have *believed* that it could now promote fiscal discipline in the states, and therefore did not need the Bank's help as a kind of third-party enforcer. It is precisely such beliefs held by central policy-makers—beliefs formed in the context of incomplete information and uncertainty—that we must try to understand.[43]

We cannot know for certain whether a stronger central government would have granted the same approval to sub-national adjustment lending as Chidambaram did in 1996, but interview evidence suggests that a similar Bank overture to his predecessor just one year earlier met with little enthusiasm. In September 1995, at the annual Bank-IMF meeting in Madrid, Bank officials intimated to Indian officials that they wished to establish policy-based lending to select states, but Finance Minister Manmohan Singh did not pursue the idea despite his commitment to liberalization. It is unclear whether Singh—a major architect of the 1991 liberalization—actively opposed such lending by the Bank, whether the central Congress government's greater strength at the time led him to assess that it might be positioned to encourage state-level reforms on its own, or whether the Bank's still-nascent proposal simply failed to spark interest.[44]

Whatever the judgments of the preceding dispensation, Chidambaram's finance ministry apparently did not believe it could achieve the desired state-level adjustment without the involvement of the Bank, given the fragility of the

UF coalition. Chidambaram may not have conceived of the precise mechanism through which the Bank's involvement would strengthen central efforts to promote state-level reforms: in an interview with the author, he simply said he thought it would 'do the states some good to expose them to the conditionalities of external lenders.'[45] But a statement he made to Lim offers some insight into how he perceived the relationship among the Centre, the Bank, and the states. Chidambaram told the Bank's country director that he considered Bank loans to be a resource of the Centre: 'I consider your money to be my money,' he said.[46] Clearly, in Chidambaram's scheme of things, the Centre was hardly 'removing itself from the picture'.

The states did not necessarily have to see it that way, however. If we apply the two-level-games framework, we can deduce the basic means through which the Bank's involvement might assist central reformers. The Centre could maintain the existing fiscal transfer system, and selective Bank loans could be used to give reforming states access to additional funds on top of their normal Plan allocations.[47] This would frame inter-state competition for resource transfers in positive-sum rather than zero-sum terms, since the Centre would not be 'taking away' resources that non-reforming states viewed as entitlements. Moreover, if some states did complain about lack of access to Bank loans, the Centre could plead (however disingenuously) that its own hands were tied: it was the Bank's prerogative to stipulate policy conditions for focus-states assistance, and if states did not like the arrangement, they could take their complaint to the Bank. And since, unlike the Centre, the Bank did not depend on state parties for political support, it would be in a better position to enforce fiscal discipline and hold state governments to their reform commitments. In short, the Bank's position as an external actor might enable it to impose not only reform conditions that the Centre could not impose on the states but also constraints regarding resource transfer decisions that the Centre could not credibly impose on itself.

Over the longer term, if enough states became socialized in the Bank's standards of fiscal discipline and began to identify their economic and electoral interests with reform rather than continued profligacy, it might even create political space for the Centre to restructure the transfer regime to offer better performance incentives. Sub-national conditionality by an external lender would thus serve as a catalyst to the broader reforms in state policies and fiscal federalism that central reformers such as Chidambaram strongly desired but did not believe they could achieve on their own.

However, from the central government's perspective, the strategy depended on a sleight-of-hand feat. The Centre had to convince the states that it was bound by the Bank's conditionality in awarding them access to loans. At the same time, however, the Centre presumably would wish to remain confident of its ultimate control over state borrowing and inter-state resource allocation, so as not to be sidelined by direct dealings between the Bank and state governments, whose electoral and financial self-interests might undermine national economic goals. Reconciling these imperatives would be a delicate balancing act. The remainder of this chapter will evaluate the extent to which the Centre has succeeded in this, and whether the focus-states strategy has lived up to its architects' expectations.

THE IMPLEMENTATION AND ACHIEVEMENTS OF FOCUS-STATES LENDING: A MIXED RECORD

This chapter's primary concerns so far have been to explain why the Bank proposed a strategy of selective sub-national adjustment lending in India and why the Centre's support for the strategy was so forthcoming. Since the strategy has by now been in place for more than half a decade, however, it is also possible to offer some tentative observations regarding its implementation. The purpose of this exercise is not only to offer preliminary evidence of whether or not sub-national adjustment lending 'works,' but also to suggest what its implementation tells us about both continuity and change in India's relations with the Bank, and, within India, about the Centre's relations with the states.

The Fiscal Story So Far: Isolated Improvements amid General Slippage

A detailed assessment of the Bank's multifaceted reform programmes is beyond the scope of this chapter. The focus here will only be on some general evidence related to the core objectives of fiscal restructuring and deficit reduction. The evidence so far should be interpreted as preliminary and indicative only, and, given all the other political, economic, and environmental 'noise' that might influence states' finances, we must be cautious in assuming that there is a causal connection between the Bank's conditionality and the states' fiscal indicators. There is, for one thing, the problem of possible selection bias: government leaders in the focus states might have been inclined to initiate adjustment anyway, even in the absence of conditional Bank assistance. Indeed, the states were ostensibly selected on the basis of 'demonstrated reform commitment'.

With this caveat in mind, the Bank's own data suggest that its three focus states have modestly outperformed a representative sample of other states in

Figure 9.3: Selected fiscal indicators for World Bank focus states
and other states

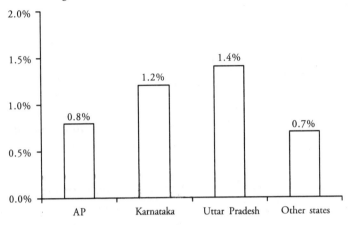

Change in Own Tax/GSDP Ratio Between 1998–9 and 2001–2 LE

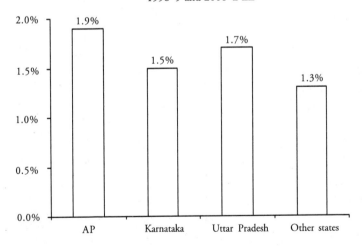

Change in Average Capital Outlays/GSDP Ratio between
1998–9 and 2001–2 LE

Notes: GSDP = Gross State Domestic Product.
LE = Latest Estimate.
Other States = Bihar, Gujarat, Haryana, Kerala, Madhya Pradesh, Orissa, Punjab, Rajasthan, Tamil Nadu, and West Bengal.
Source: World Bank, Country Assistance Strategy Progress Report (Washington, DC: World Bank, 2003).

increasing their capital investments and mobilizing additional revenue (see Figure 9.3). There is considerable variation within the focus states group, however. Karnataka and UP significantly outperformed the average for other states on revenue mobilization, but in AP—the state with the longest history of Bank borrowing and the biggest increase in capital spending—revenue mobilization only slightly exceeds the average for other states. New spending in AP is being financed mainly by borrowing, much of which is accounted for by the Bank loans themselves. Some commentators have expressed concern that, by its very financial support, the Bank is creating the possibility of a debt trap in AP. However, AP's approach may prove sound *if* it continues to use the Bank's relatively low-interest loans to make capital investments, and *if* these contribute to a future rate of economic growth that outstrips the state's future debt-service obligations.

Table 9.1: Fiscal trends in Andhra Pradesh, Karnataka, and Uttar Pradesh, 2000-1 to 2004-5

				(percentage of GSDP at current prices)	
	2000–1	*2001–2*	*2002–3*	*2003–4 (RE)*	*2004–5 (BE)*
Andhra Pradesh					
Revenue Deficit	2.5	1.8	1.8	1.5	0.9
Fiscal Deficit	5.1	4.2	4.4	3.8	3.4
Total Debt	28.2	30.0	31.6	31.8	31.7
Karnataka					
Revenue Deficit	1.7	2.8	2.1	0.9	+ 0.1 (surplus)
Fiscal Deficit	3.8	5.1	4.2	4.0	2.7
Total Debt	24.0	28.1	30.0	30.6	30.3
Uttar Pradesh					
Revenue Deficit	3.6	3.3	2.5	8.9	2.3
Fiscal Deficit	5.9	5.2	4.7	9.1	4.3
Total Debt	45.8	49.0	50.1	55.1	54.6

Notes: GSDP = gross state domestic product. RE = Revised Estimate. BE = Budget Estimate.

'Total Debt' means total outstanding liabilities, borrowings (internal debt, central loans, Provident Fund, etc.), and others (Reserve Funds, deposits).

Source: Government of India, 12th Finance Commission, *Fiscal Profiles of States* (Website: http://fincomindia.nic.in).

With respect to broader revenue deficit, fiscal deficit,[48] and debt-stock trends, the record of the Bank's focus state group is also mixed (see Table 9.1). UP clearly presents a far different picture from AP and Karnataka: its deficits remain considerably higher, and its debt has reached an alarmingly high level of more than 50 per cent of Gross State Domestic Product (GSDP). AP and Karnataka started out with smaller deficits and have been more consistent in their progress on further reduction; on the revenue account, Karnataka is even estimated to have achieved a modest surplus in 2004–5. Interestingly, though AP has received more money and public emphasis from the Bank, Karnataka has quietly maintained a somewhat stronger fiscal performance record.

For India's states as a whole, fiscal deficits have continued to climb since the beginning of Bank lending for selective sub-national adjustment in the mid-1990s. The states' combined gross fiscal deficits rose from 2.6 per cent of India's GDP during the Eighth Plan period (1990–1 to 1994–5) to 4.2 per cent

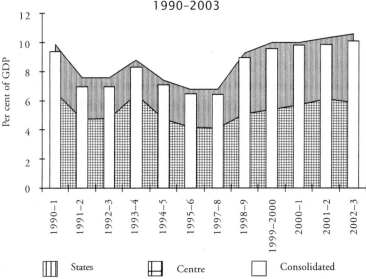

Figure 9.4: Centre, states, and consolidated fiscal deficits, 1990–2003

Notes: Consolidated deficit indicators net out the inter-governmental transactions between the Centre and states, and thus do not equal to the sum of the Centre's and states' deficits (1990s Centre figures also exclude 'small savings' allocated to states).

Source: Adapted from Nirvikar Singh and T.N. Srinivasan, 'Fiscal Policy in India: Lessons and Priorities', Paper presented at the International Monetary Fund/National Institute of Public Finance and Policy Conference on Fiscal Policy in India, New Delhi, 16–17 January 2004.

during the Ninth Plan period (1995–6 to 1999–2000) and 4.7 per cent in fiscal year 2002–3 budget estimates. Together, state fiscal deficits account for more than 40 per cent of the consolidated fiscal deficit, which has averaged more than 9 per cent of India's GDP since the mid-1990s and risen further to more than 10 per cent in 2002–3 (see Figure 9.4).

While the states are ultimately responsible for their own policy choices, it must be acknowledged that the central government has not always shown consistent fiscal prudence in its own policies and accompanying signals for state finances. For example, in 1997, just months after Chidambaram's finance ministry accepted the Bank's focus-state proposal, new Prime Minister I.K. Gujral ordered a 35 per cent increase in pay for central employees based on the recommendation of the Fifth Pay Commission, which placed informal pressure on state governments to raise pay for their own employees.

There is some debate in India over whether these continued high fiscal deficits are a serious problem. At least in the short run, in view of its strong current account position, India does not appear to be vulnerable to the kind of major crisis that struck Argentina in 2002. Nevertheless, in late 2003 the World Bank issued a report expressing its concern.[49] This prompted Finance Ministry and Planning Commission officials to issue public statements criticizing the Bank's criticism (which were later partially retracted).[50] This minor commotion suggests that, their appreciation of the Bank's sub-national conditionality notwithstanding, there is still some sensitivity among Indian officials when it comes to external policy advice.

This much is clear, however: the wider 'demonstration effects' that were supposed to follow from the Bank's select state adjustment programmes are yet to materialize. In part, this may reflect non-reforming states' perception that the selection of focus states (as with the allocation of other central transfers) reflects not the quality of a state government's economic policies, but rather the extent of its political influence.

The Political Economy of 'Selectivity': Reform Commitment, Political Clout, or Both?

Initially, the process through which the Centre and the Bank selected focus states lacked transparency, a situation for which both India and the Bank bear responsibility. With all sides preferring flexibility to rigid criteria, for nearly half a decade there were no formal guidelines stipulating the steps that states had to take in order to demonstrate the 'clear reform commitment' that was required for entry to the focus-states club.

This procedural murkiness engendered a commonly held impression that permission to borrow from the Bank is a special privilege awarded to states that wield particular kinds of political leverage in New Delhi owing to their special importance to the central government. This view reflects a broader cynicism about the influence of politics in Indian fiscal federalism, and may at least in part help explain why other states have not rushed to emulate the policies of the focus states.

Political factors have indeed played some part in the selection of focus states, though it must also be acknowledged that the governments of AP, Karnataka, and UP each showed prior inclination to reform. On balance, it seems fair to say that *both* special political significance *and* genuine reform commitment appear to have determined the selection of states so far. For the sake of brevity, the following discussion will not attempt to arbitrate between these factors for each of the three focus states, but rather will focus on the case of Andhra Pradesh, whose programme with the Bank has been most responsible for creating the impression of a politicized process. Insider connections and coalition politics did play some role in the selection of AP as the first Bank focus state, though under the leadership of Chief Minister N. Chandrababu Naidu (1995–2004), it also demonstrated a willingness to reform well above the Indian average. And the Bank has hardly been alone in praising it: for example, a study for *India Today* magazine by economists Bibek Debroy and Laveesh Bhandari called AP India's 'fastest mover' in improving indicators across a range of fiscal, economic, and social dimensions between 1991 and 2001.[51]

Within weeks of the central finance ministry's approval of the new lending strategy in the fall of 1996, World Bank President James Wolfensohn made his first official visit to India, and Naidu flew to New Delhi to meet him. Naidu, who had served as AP's finance minister before ousting his own father-in-law to become chief minister in 1995, relied on personal connections in the central Finance Ministry to facilitate the unusual direct meeting with Wolfensohn.[52] Moreover, Naidu's newfound political clout, by virtue of his Telugu Desam Party's (TDP) key membership in the fragile UF coalition, suggested that his pitch for Bank assistance would get a sympathetic hearing from the central government. As central officials looked on, Naidu displayed a PowerPoint presentation to Wolfensohn describing plans for economic and governance reforms. The Bank chief was suitably impressed, and by December Lim was in Hyderabad with a deputation of Bank staff and an offer to lend AP up to US $3 billion in coming years.[53]

Some observers have seized on AP's selection as proof of the Centre's political captivity to state-level allies in the new era of coalition politics, and assumed that the Centre, bowing to Naidu's demands, simply instructed the Bank to favour AP. True, they said, Naidu presented himself as a visionary liberalization advocate, and as CM he had already taken a few small steps to correct AP's severe fiscal imbalances, issuing a frank White Paper about state finances, reducing AP's heavy subsidy on rice consumption, and raising power tariffs. But as one critic put it, 'other states had not gone as far down the populist road to begin with.'[54] In the absence of objective criteria as a basis for measurement, the extent of Naidu's 'reform commitment' essentially lay in the eye of the beholder. While some viewed the self-described 'CEO of Andhra Pradesh' as a genuine reformer with a sound understanding of the state's economic problems, others saw him as a master of illusion, wedded to political expediency and with no real commitment to liberalization.

Ironically, the premise behind the Centre's 'two-level-game' support for the Bank's focus-state lending was that the Bank's position as an external actor would facilitate a more objective and performance-based resource allocation to encourage state reforms; it was 'above politics' in a way that the Centre could not afford to be in the context of a tenuous coalition government. But since the Bank had its own motivations for the strategy and feared that the Centre might rescind its support, it found AP's political stature to be a major asset at this early stage of focus-state lending. According to Lim, Naidu's clout in New Delhi offered 'protection' for the Bank in the event that central officials had second thoughts about the strategy.[55]

Naidu, for his part, never attempted to hide his political influence at the Centre; rather, he wore it like a badge of honour.[56] In a book published in 2000, he boasted of his state's changing fortunes in the era of central coalition government, saying that 'the TDP's role in the UF government…led to the flow of a record quantum of funds under various sectors to Andhra Pradesh.'[57] Reports in the Indian media noted Naidu's ability to corner a disproportionate share of several different kinds of centrally managed resources for AP, including large supplies of food aid during the severe drought of 2002. For many observers, the state's high share of Bank assistance has been part of the same profile. AP accounted for more than 12 per cent of all Bank lending to India between 1998 and 2002 (whereas the state contains only 7 per cent of India's population).

But Naidu's attempts to court central favour were not always successful. In fact, when at least one of his requests for Bank assistance was deemed excessive, the Centre rebuffed him. In 2002, AP proposed new Bank borrowing that would have accounted for more than one-fourth of all aid to India for the year. Finance Ministry officials decided that the state had overreached, and sat on its application—forcing the AP government to increase market borrowing to make up for non-receipt of the Bank assistance that it had already budgeted for, on the assumption that the Centre's approval would be a foregone conclusion.[58] At least in this case, appeals by Naidu to the offices of the finance minister and even the prime minister did not change the outcome. In a reassertion of the Centre's ultimate authority over the relationship between the Bank and the state, when the Centre finally did agree to support AP's loan application, DEA Secretary C.M. Vasudev wrote to Wolfensohn that future allocation of state structural adjustment loans 'would be decided annually after discussions between World Bank and Government of India.'[59] But since all these decisions transpired behind closed doors, the details that might have led outside observers to a more nuanced assessment of the role of politics in the state selection process were simply not available.

Recent Developments

Since 2002, India's Finance Ministry has taken steps to make the selection of states for structural adjustment loans subject to more uniform and transparent criteria, ostensibly to reduce the risk that states would use the loans as temporary respite from their fiscal difficulties and would avoid taking tough reform decisions. It is also increasingly apparent that the Centre is concerned with reasserting its authority with respect to external assistance to the states.

In December 2002, Finance Minister Jaswant Singh announced that whereas 'in the past there has been no uniformity in the structural adjustment loans being taken up by the different states,' the Bank and other lenders were now 'being advised to ensure certain common criteria.' Selection, he said, would be based on a state's commitment to: first, generating revenue surplus and limiting its fiscal deficit to less than 3 per cent of GSDP within three to five years; second, eliminating or containing subsidies, especially in the power sector; third, raising user charges for services; and, fourth, improving governance and reducing administrative costs.[60] Singh further stated that state adjustment loans would comprise not more than 30 per cent of total annual World Bank lending to India (which essentially preserved the existing ratio, though the Bank had been pressing for a level closer to 40 per cent).

Following the announcement, Maharashtra, Orissa, and Tamil Nadu indicated plans to apply for Bank adjustment loans.[61] But as of this writing, only Orissa had seen its application forwarded by the Centre and approved by the

Bank's Executive Board (in November 2004). Thus, if it seemed at first that the Centre's announcement of formal state selection criteria would usher in a new phase of focus-states lending, with additional states vying for adjustment loans on the basis of more transparent performance benchmarks, the subsequent course of events has suggested otherwise.

In fact, the Bank's most recent Country Assistance Strategy (CAS) for India—a document prepared in close consultation with the Indian government—suggests that the Centre is going beyond mere efforts to normalize state selection, to a much more fundamental reassessment of the desirability of permitting the Bank to operate 'selectively' in the states. In one particularly revealing passage, the new CAS makes clear that the approach to state lending is undergoing revision:

Some important changes are…being implemented in the Bank Group approach to the States. Since 1997, the CAS has included a focus on States undertaking comprehensive reforms, in order to support the leaders of change and serve as a catalyst to the State-level reform process. With the widening gulf between the reforming and non-reforming States in India, leading to a concentration of poverty and poor social indicators in just a few States, some shifts in this approach are warranted. *Though the Bank Group strategy will retain an essentially reform and performance-based approach to the States, it will also change in ways that are intended to go as far as possible in opening up new opportunities for engagement with [the] largest and poorest States.*[62]

The best way for the Bank to help poor, non-reforming states, the original strategy held, would be for it to encourage them to help themselves: the success of the Bank's focus states would encourage policy emulation in others, even in the absence of loans. Under the new CAS, the emphasis is much less on states at the front of the pack, and much more on those at the very rear. 'Maximizing impact' now seems to mean directing more money (in the form of project and sectoral loans, if not general budgetary assistance) and policy dialogue toward states that exhibit the *worst* developmental indicators, in an effort to turn them around so they stop exerting a drag on the country as a whole.

In sum, the changes in the new CAS suggest that following the Centre's initial enthusiasm about the Bank's strategy of lending selectively to the most reform-committed states, an ambivalence or even antagonism toward the approach has more recently taken hold in New Delhi. Based on interviews by the author with both Indian and Bank officials in late 2003, it was clear that the impetus for rethinking the focus-states strategy had come from the former rather than the latter. This could reflect several factors: unresolved attitudes at the Centre about the principles that should more broadly govern inter-state resource allocation; a lingering mindset among some central officials that the Bank represents an intrusive rather than constructive influence in India's economic policies; and, possibly related to this, a change in the political leadership at the Finance Ministry after Chidambaram's initial approval of the strategy. The most recent CAS was drafted during Jaswant Singh's tenure—though in mid-2004 Chidambaram returned to his old post, and it will be interesting to see if he resurrects an interest in using Bank loans to favour strongly performing states. But irrespective of the particular personages at the top echelons of economic policy in India, the dilemma between allowing the high-growth states to achieve their full potential, while at the same time not wanting to let the poorest states fall even further behind, with disastrous consequences for human development, is one that will probably only intensify in the coming years.

CONCLUSION

Though the impetus for sub-national adjustment lending in India originally came from the World Bank as a response to its long-standing frustration at its limited policy influence in the country, the brief history of the strategy's implementation turns out be more India's story than the Bank's. India held the power to accept or reject the Bank's proposal. It accepted it because it conformed to goals its central policy-makers already held for state-level reforms, but could not achieve on their own owing to their dependence on state-level political allies for coalition support.

The two-level-games perspective, which straddles the intersection of the international relations and comparative politics literatures in political science, provides a useful point of departure for understanding the orientation of India's central government toward the Bank's focus-states loans, by offering the simple insight that internationalized policy commitments are sometimes used to address domestic political challenges. But the deficiency of this perspective is that it does not, on its own terms of focusing on decision-making by national-level policy elites, alert us to all of the factors at either the international or domestic level that may be relevant for understanding why such strategies arise—and why they might not work. At the international level, the perspective risks reverting to the traditional neoreolist and neoliberal perspectives on international organizations (IOs) as mere instruments of nation-states, without recognizing that IOs may have their own reasons for playing in a two-level game, and these might not conform to domestic authorities' reasons in every respect. In

India, the Bank's own concern with increasing its policy influence has led it to treat focus-state lending almost as an end in itself, and to allow political factors to influence the state selection process somewhat, with a view to encouraging the Centre to remain committed to the strategy.

In describing some of the challenges that a federal India faces as it endeavours to liberalize its economy, and its evolving relationship with the World Bank, this chapter makes a modest contribution to the broader literature on the nation-state in an era of globalization. Sub-national adjustment lending by the World Bank does *not* indicate a besiegement or impending demise of the Indian national state. India's leaders chose to embark on a course of liberalization in 1991 because they believed it offered better prospects than the central planning approach for achieving national developmental goals and international great power aspirations, and it was this same orientation that led India's reformist finance minister to endorse state-level reform lending by the Bank five years later.

We should be careful not to overstate this defence of the autonomous capacity of the Indian nation-state, however. As noted in the introduction, the view by Kripa Sridharan, that India's central government has 'taken itself out of the picture', by giving the Bank a direct policy line to the states, is surely misleading. But it is also possible to overstate the opposing perspective, as Rob Jenkins comes close to doing, when he asserts with respect to the Bank's state-level loans that 'In the end, the central government sees its will prevail, and need not fund the necessary [state-reform] programmes from its share of revenues.'[63] Nearly seven years after the first World Bank state-reform loan opened in AP, the central government can hardly be said to have 'seen its will prevail' with respect to state fiscal and governance reforms. Reform achievements in the Bank's focus states have been modest, and both fiscal and social conditions in the largest and poorest state, UP, remain dire. AP and Karnataka have fared better, but for the states overall, fiscal indicators have worsened rather than improved in recent years.

Nearly two decades ago, Lloyd and Susanne Rudolph described India as a 'weak-strong' state, a paradox that arises from its location 'on a shifting continuum between constrained and autonomous' vis-à-vis India's multifaceted and politically mobilized society. 'The international environment,' they argued, 'is far less salient for explaining Indian economic or political development than is the case for other Third World countries, unless it is salient in a negative sense, as an environment to exclude or keep at bay.'[64] Much has changed since they offered this appraisal, not least of all the opening of the Indian economy and the emergence of successive multiparty coalition governments to replace single party dominance at the Centre. It is also a remarkable turnabout that the Centre was willing, at least for several years, to regard the Bank as a helpmate in encouraging fiscal prudence rather than a threat to its own authority vis-à-vis the states.

Still, the characterization of India as a 'weak-strong' state remains apt in important respects, as this chapter has suggested. The Indian national state is strong enough to define its relations with external actors like the World Bank on its own terms, but it is weak in its capacity to marshal the internal coordination needed at multiple levels of government to consolidate the new economic policies favoured by the national leadership. This makes the 'second stage' of reform protracted and difficult, and may continue to give rise to the need for inter-party compromises that limit India's achievement of its full economic growth potential.

Yet India has defied pessimistic predictions in the past. If India *does* somehow gradually achieve the sub-national and intergovernmental institutional reforms necessary to consolidate its economic liberalization, and balances the achievement of a higher rate of growth with further reductions in poverty, New Delhi might decide that it can dispense with the World Bank's loans altogether, as it has recently done with many bilateral sources of aid. That would be a very good outcome for India's more than one billion people, and even—from the standpoint of seeing its policy advice succeed—for the World Bank.

NOTES AND REFERENCES

1. Research Specialist, Center for the Advanced Study of India, University of Pennsylvania, Philadelphia, USA. This essay draws on original research from a doctoral dissertation on the World Bank's sub-national structural adjustment loans in India. The author would like to thank the following for their comments on earlier versions of this work: Thomas Callaghy, John Echeverri-Gent, Francine Frankel, Rajen Harshe, Sunila Kale, Edward Mansfield, Rahul Mukherji, Rudra Sil, Douglas Verney, Ming Xia, and Vikash Yadav. Responsibility for any errors rests with the author alone, who can be contacted at jkirk@sas.upenn.edu.

2. The two primary lending arms of the World Bank group are the International Bank for Reconstruction and Development (IBRD) and the International Development Association (IDA). Whereas the lending resources of the former come largely from the sale of AAA-rated bonds in international capital markets, the IDA is funded by periodic capital contributions from the Bank's member countries, and its 'credits' carry significantly lower interest rates, longer maturities, and more generous grace periods than IBRD loans, and are intended for countries with relatively low per capita incomes. Since an extremely large

low-income country such as India could well absorb IDA's entire lending budget in any given year, it falls into a category of countries eligible for a blend of IDA-IBRD assistance.

3. The World Bank's original focus states—Andhra Pradesh (AP), Karnataka, and Uttar Pradesh (UP)—together accounted for about one-third of nearly US $10 billion in new Bank commitments to India from 1998 to 2002. A fourth state, Orissa, received support for reforms in its power sector, and its application for broader adjustment support was approved by the Bank's Executive Board in late 2004. The ADB's reform-based lending relationships are with Gujarat, Kerala, and Madhya Pradesh (MP), and DFID's are with AP, Orissa, West Bengal, and MP. See World Bank, *India Country Assistance Strategy 2001.* (http://lnweb18.worldbank.org/sar/sa.nsf/Countries/India/325408102115 C21585256B20002D6697?Open Document); Asian Development Bank, *India Country Assistance Plan 2000-02* (http://www.adb.org/Documents/CAPs/ IND/default.asp); Department for International Development, *India Country Strategy Paper 1999* (http://www.dfid.gov.uk /Pubs/files/india_csp.pdf).

4. Such an argument is broadly set forth in Kripa Sridharan, 'Federalism and Foreign Relations: The Nascent Role of the Indian States', *Asian Studies Review* 27, December (2003), pp. 463–89.

5. This study's use of shorthand terms such as 'the Centre' and 'New Delhi' to refer collectively to policy-makers in the Government of India is not meant to suggest any theoretical assumption of a unitary, rational actor. Central government policies can be inconsistent—reflecting differences among and between central officials and central politicians—and have at times significantly compromised efforts to promote greater fiscal discipline in the states.

6. Civil servants in the DEA manage relations with external lenders on a day-to-day basis: for example, the 'Fund-Bank Division' is responsible for routine interlocution with the IMF and World Bank. However, major policy decisions, such as authorization of the Bank and other lenders to introduce state-level adjustment lending, require approval by the finance minister.

7. Robert Putnam, 'Diplomacy and Domestic Politics: The Logic of Two-level Games', *International Organization,* 42, Summer (1988). For recent examples of this kind of analysis, see the contributions to Daniel Drezner (ed.), *Locating the Proper Authorities: The Interaction of Domestic and International Institutions* (Ann Arbor, University of Michigan Press, 2003). In recent work on India's states' interactions with the World Bank and the World Trade Organization (WTO), Rob Jenkins makes a similar point, without explicitly acknowledging the Putnam framework: '...The agreements reached between state governments and the World Bank commit many of these states to fiscal and expenditure management programmes that conform to what the central government had wanted to impose anyway, but had proven unable to get

implemented.' See Rob Jenkins, 'India's States and the Making of Foreign Economic Policy: The Limits of the Constituent Diplomacy Paradigm', *Publius: The Journal of Federalism*, vol. 33, no. 4, Fall (2003), pp. 63–82; p. 73.

8. Sridharan, 'Federalism and Foreign Relations'.

9. Author's interview with N. Roberto Zagha, Sector Director, South Asia Poverty Reduction and Economic Management Unit, World Bank, Washington DC, 26 September 2002. For a cross-national perspective, see World Bank, *Adjustment Lending Retrospective: Final Report* (Washington, DC, World Bank, 2001), annex A. While the 'sub-national adjustment loan' (SNAL) as a formal instrument was only approved by the Bank's Executive Board for use after fiscal year 1998–9, in effect the regional department staffs had already introduced such lending under various guises. In India, for example, the first formal SNAL went to UP in 2000–1, but a 1998–9 set of loans to AP introduced significant reform conditions through a multi-sector 'project loan' package. To avoid confusion, this chapter does not use the SNAL acronym. At least in the Indian case, the technical differences between the first AP and UP loans are less important than their similarities as part of the broader state-focused lending strategy.

10. Publication of the first comparative set of working papers on sub-national adjustment lending was expected in 2004 or 2005. Author's email correspondence with a senior economist at the World Bank, November 2003.

11. The central Planning Commission passes on external assistance to the states according to a 70 per cent loan/30 per cent grant formula, which is a subject of some dissatisfaction on the part of the states since the grant component (that is, International Development Association credits) of World Bank assistance is often higher than 30 per cent. Thus, states have claimed that New Delhi is profiteering from its intermediary role. The Centre argues that the practice is fair since it bears the foreign-exchange risk: it borrows from the Bank in dollars and eventually will have to repay it in dollars, whereas it on-lends to the states in rupees and will receive repayment in rupees, whose value against the dollar has in the past tended to decline over time.

12. This is a country-specific arrangement reflecting the Indian central government's preference for control over foreign loans to states. In contrast, in Brazil, where state governments enjoy more liberal borrowing privileges, they can be the 'borrower' on World Bank loans so long as the federal government in Brasilia provides a sovereign guarantee (required by the Bank's Articles of Agreement). Article 293, Clause 3 of the Constitution of India asserts the Centre's control over states' international borrowing: 'A state may not without the consent of the Government of India raise any loan if there is still outstanding any part of a loan which has been made to the state by the Government of India or its predecessor Government, or in respect of which a guarantee has been given by the Government of India or by its predecessor Government.'

Since all states have outstanding debt to the Centre, in practice this clause means they must seek its express permission to borrow from outside the territory of India.

13. Author's interview with Sumir Lal, World Bank External Affairs Officer, New Delhi, 11 August 2003.

14. Quoted in Catherine Caufield, *Masters of Illusion: The World Bank and the Poverty of Nations* (New York, Henry Holt & Company, 1996), p. 23.

15. For good summaries, see Jørgen Dige Pedersen, 'The Complexities of Conditionality: The Case of India'. in Georg Sørenson (ed.), *Political Conditionality* (Portland, OR, Frank Cass, 1993); and Rahul Mukherji, 'India's Aborted Liberalization—1966', *Pacific Affairs,* vol. 73, no. 3 (2000). On the broader conflict between Mrs. Gandhi and state-level Congress Party leaders, see Francine R. Frankel, *India's Political Economy, 1947–1977: The Gradual Revolution* (Princeton, Princeton University Press, 1978), chaps. 7 and 8.

16. John P. Lewis, *India's Political Economy: Governance and Reform* (New Delhi, Oxford University Press, 1995), pp. 139, 182.

17. See Jalal Alamgir, 'Managing Openness in India: The Social Construction of a Globalist Narrative', in Linda Weiss (ed.), *States in the Global Economy: Bringing Domestic Institutions Back In* (Cambridge, Cambridge University Press, 2003).

18. Cited in Gurcharan Das, *India Unbound: From Independence to the Global Information Age,* Revised Edition (New Delhi, Penguin Books India, 2002), p. 213.

19. On the general distinction between first- and second-stage reforms in economic adjustment, see Moisés Naím, 'Latin America: The Second Stage of Reform', in Larry Diamond and Marc F. Plattner (eds.), *Economic Reform and Democracy* (Baltimore, Johns Hopkins University Press, 1995), pp. 28–44.

20. Author's interview with Joëlle Chassard, India Country Coordinator, World Bank, Washington, DC, 17 July 2002.

21. Author's interview with N. Roberto Zagha.

22. Author's interview with Edwin Lim, Country Director for India (1996–2002), World Bank, Osterville, MA, 14 July 2003.

23. Author's interview with Joëlle Chassard.

24. *The Economist*, 21 June 2003; *Business Standard*, 6 June 2003. India has said it will retain bilateral aid ties only with the EU, Germany, Japan, the UK, and the US. As noted above, the UK's DFID has focused its efforts in select states in recent years. India's retention of this relationship, when it has severed many other bilateral aid ties, is further evidence that its policy-makers value selective sub-national aid.

25. Putnam, 'Diplomacy and Domestic Politics', p. 457.

26. Judith Golstein, 'International Law and Domestic Institutions:

Reconciling North American "Unfair" Trade Laws', *International Organization* 50, Autumn (1996), pp. 541–64.

27. Robert Paarlberg, 'Agricultural Policy Reform and the Uruguay Round: Synergistic Linkage in a Two-Level Game?' *International Organization*, 51, Summer (1997), pp. 413–44.

28. James Raymond Vreeland, *The IMF and Economic Development* (New York, Cambridge University Press, 2003).

29. Jon Pevehouse, 'Democracy from the Outside-In? International Organizations and Democratization', *International Organization* 63, Summer (2002), pp. 515–49.

30. Drezner, *Locating the Proper Authorities,* p. 16.

31. Chidambaram had served as commerce minister in the preceding government.

32. Policies varied by state. Cheap inputs for farmers were especially prominent in Punjab. AP exemplified how food subsidies ostensibly intended for the poor could be captured by others: by the mid-1990s, its rice subsidy covered 85 per cent of the population. See World Bank, 'Andhra Pradesh: Agenda for Economic Reforms', Report no. 15901-IN (Washington, DC: World Bank, 1997).

33. Jonathan Rodden, Gunnar S. Eskeland, and Jennie Litvack (eds), *Fiscal Decentralization and the Challenge of Soft Budget Constraints* (Cambridge, MIT Press, 2003), p. 6.

34. See chapters on Argentina, Brazil, Canada, China, Germany, Hungary, India, Norway, South Africa, the Ukraine, and the US, in Rodden et al. (eds), *Fiscal Decentralization.*

35. William J. McCarten, 'The Challenge of Fiscal Discipline in the Indian States', in Rodden et al. (eds), *Fiscal Decentralization,* p. 251.

36. For a comprehensive treatment, see B.P.R. Vithal and M.L. Sastry, *Fiscal Federalism in India* (New Delhi, Oxford University Press, 2001).

37. S. Gurumurthi, *Fiscal Federalism in India* (New Delhi, Vikas Publishing House, 1995), p. 35; cited in McCarten, 'The Challenge of Fiscal Discipline in the Indian States', p. 257.

38. Joydeep Mukherji, 'The Indian Economy: Pushing Ahead and Pulling Apart,' in Alyssa Ayres and Philip Oldenburg (eds), *India Briefing: Quickening the Pace of Change* (Armonk, NY, M.E. Sharpe for the Asia Society, 2002), pp. 55–90.

39. Author's interview with Edwin Lim. Besides Chidambaram, key like-minded central officials included Finance Secretary Montek Ahluwalia (his former commerce ministry colleague), senior economic advisors Shankar Acharya (a former World Bank official) and Jairam Ramesh, and DEA secretary V. Govindarajan.

40. Congress's defeat did not stem from public opposition to liberalization; in fact, opinion polls show that most voters were not particularly aware of changes during the initial phase of adjustment. The party's decline is a secular trend dating from 1967, owing to 'shifts in party organizational strength and support bases at the state level'. See E. Sridharan, 'The Fragmentation of the Indian Party System, 1952–1999', in Zoya Hasan (ed.), *Parties and Party Politics in India* (New Delhi, Oxford University Press, 2002), pp. 475–503. The 1984 and 1991 elections were exceptional in that they followed the assassinations of Indira and Rajiv Gandhi, which produced outpourings of voter sympathy for the party.

41. Though the authors caution that the effects of party ties on sub-national fiscal performance ultimately depend on a country's particular institutions. See Jonathan Rodden and Erik Wibbels, 'Beyond the Fiction of Federalism: Macro-economic Management in Multitiered Systems', *World Politics* 54, July (2002), pp.494–531.

42. See Stuti Khemani, 'Federal Politics and Budget Deficits: Evidence from the States of India', Policy Research Working Paper 2915 (Washington, DC, World Bank, 2002); and Stuti Khemani, 'Partisan Politics and Intergovernmental Transfers in India', Policy Research Working Paper 3016 (Washington, DC, World Bank, 2003).

43. On the importance of policy-makers' subjective understanding of the political economy environment in which they operate, see Merilee S. Grindle and John W. Thomas, *Public Choices and Policy Change: The Political Economy of Reform in Developing Countries* (Baltimore, Johns Hopkins University Press, 1991).

44. A former advisor stated that the Singh was opposed to selective state lending by the Bank, though Singh himself said that he barely recalled the Bank's 1995 proposal, which in any case did not seem fully formed at the time. Author's interview with Jairam Ramesh, 21 August 2002, New Delhi; author's interview with Manmohan Singh, 10 August 2003, New Delhi.

45. Author's interview with P. Chidambaram, 10 August 2003, New Delhi.

46. Author's interview with Edwin Lim.

47. I am indebted to Professor D.K. Srivastava, National Institute of Public Finance and Policy (NIPFP), New Delhi, for making this point clear.

48. The revenue deficit equals only the state government's current (non-capital) expenditure minus its tax revenues; the fiscal deficit equals total (current and capital) expenditure minus total revenue (tax and non-tax).

49. World Bank, 'India: Sustaining Reform, Reducing Poverty', Report No. 25797 (Washington, DC, World Bank, 2003).

50. *Business Line,* 24 July 2003.

51. *India Today,* 19 May 2003.

52. Senior DEA secretary and former AP administrative officer V. Govindarajan arranged the encounter; author's interview with a former senior DEA official, New Delhi, August 2002.

53. Author's interview with Joëlle Chassard.

54. Author's interview with Mohan Guruswamy, Economic Advisor, Ministry of Finance (1998–9), 19 August 2002, New Delhi.

55. Author's interview with Edwin Lim.

56. Since the early 1980s, a key element of the TDP's political rhetoric is that state politics has been subject to undue interference from the Congress-dominated Centre.

57. N. Chandrababu Naidu and Sevanti Ninan, *Plain Speaking* (New Delhi. Viking, 2000), p. 33.

58. Government of Andhra Pradesh, *Annual Fiscal Framework 2003–04* (Hyderabad: Finance Department, Government of Andhra Pradesh, 22 January 2003), p. 14.

59. Letter from C.M. Vasudev to James D. Wolfensohn; in World Bank, 'Report and Recommendation of the President of the World Bank on a Loan and Credit to India for the Andhra Pradesh Economic Reform Programme', Report No. P7508-IN 15 February 2002, annex A.

60. Letter from Finance Minister Jaswant Singh to State Chief Ministers; cited in *Jal News,* 11 December 2002 (http://www. angelfire.com/in/jalnews/ 2002/ 11122.htm).

61. *The Hindu*, 27 March 2003.

62. World Bank, *India: Country Assistance Strategy 2005–08* (draft version), p. 17; emphasis in original.

63. Jenkins, 'India's States and the Making of Foreign Economic Policy', p. 74.

64. Lloyd Rudolph and Susanne Hoeber Rudolph, *In Pursuit of Lakshmi: The Political Economy of the Indian State* (Chicago, The University of Chicago Press, 1987), pp. 1, 13, 3.

10

Managing Competition
Politics and the Building of Independent
Regulatory Institutions[*]

RAHUL MUKHERJI[1]

Why has India's telecom regulator been more successful than its power sector regulator in managing competition and reducing tariffs? Both were infrastructure sectors that required foreign investment for development in the context of capital scarcity. The regulator was supposed to stand as a neutral umpire between private and state capital, creating a level playing field for private capital in sectors that had been dominated by the state. Private capital, both foreign and domestic, was also to contribute to developing these sectors by increasing the level of competition and efficiency, resulting in lower tariffs to the consumer.

This chapter argues that while reforming power tariffs presented more political obstacles than did regulating telecom pricing, this does not fully explain the divergent outcomes in the two sectors. Instead, two other factors were important: (1) the role (and origin) of ideas in policy-making, and (2) the federal institutional structure.

The Telecom Regulatory Authority of India (TRAI) emerged as a result of ideational changes within the Prime Minister's Office (PMO) that favoured regulated competition. There was a consensus among key technocrats that private participation was essential in order to develop the robust telecom infrastructure required for promoting India's competitiveness in the global market. Much less was achieved in the power sector in terms of promoting competition prior to the balance of payments crisis in 1991.[2] The World Bank's initiative and guidance were more important in this sector.

* Originally published as 'Managing Competition: Politics and the Building of Independent Regulatory Institutions', in *India Review*, 3 (4), October 2004, pp. 278–305.

Second, unlike telecommunications, the management of which is controlled by the central government, power is a sector for which both states as well as the centre hold joint responsibility. (These responsibilities are delineated by the 'lists' framed in the Constitution, in which telecommunications is on the central list, while power is on the 'concurrent' list). This ensured that state governments and their electricity boards, which managed the generation and distribution of electricity within their jurisdictions, undermined the role of the central government in the management of the power sector. The telecom regulator could suggest national-level policies with greater ease, and had only the department of telecommunications (DOT) within the ministry of communications to struggle against. In the power sector, each state-level regulator had to contend with its state electricity board (SEB), and the central electricity regulatory commission had to deal with the ministry of power and the central public sector undertakings. In the power sector, there were too many regulators trying to discipline too many incumbents.

The crisis of 1991 and India's attempt to steer its policy toward trade orientation and regulated competition helped both sectors to liberalize. But changes in technocratic orientation favouring telecommunications privatization, especially at the level of the PMO, and dating back to Rajiv Gandhi's tenure, helped to create a more flexible telecom policy. The TRAI had a more robust learning experience and was thus better able to contest the government's monopoly than was the CERC or the individual state-level electricity regulatory commissions. This chapter suggests that reforms which are homegrown, with ideational changes that take root in key bureaucratic niches over a course of years before policy change is effected, are more likely to succeed.

TELECOM REGULATION

This section describes the importance of changes in the technocratic orientation within the PMO, which was the primary driver of change favouring private sector participation in telecommunications. Telecommunications became a major development priority in the Seventh Five-Year Plan (1985–90). There was a constant tussle between the PMO and the Ministry of Communications regarding the entry of private players. The PMO wanted to usher in competition; the ministry resisted it. This struggle continued even after the balance of payments crisis of 1991, when the pace of reforms was accelerated. TRAI was born long after private enterprise had been permitted in the telecom sector, and owed its existence to the chaotic situation that unregulated privatization had created.

Changes in Policy Orientation Before 1991

As reflected in numerous government reports, the late 1970s and the early 1980s were a period characterized by a review of India's import substitution industrialization policy. The government was keenly watching China's move toward export-oriented growth through the special economic zones, an idea it tried to implement in India. During her second period in office in the early 1980s, Prime Minister Indira Gandhi noted that the moves toward economic decentralization undertaken by the Janata government that had held office during the late 1970s had produced robust industrial growth.[3] Mrs Gandhi's tenure as prime minister after 1980 witnessed a significantly greater emphasis on telecommunications. Private sector involvement and the liberalization of imports were encouraged. A significant contribution of the Sarin Committee Report of 1981 was to recommend splitting up of posts and telegraphs into separate departments. This was to facilitate greater emphasis on telecommunications within the Ministry of Posts and Telegraphs. The mood within the government was to bring telecommunications out of the infrastructure of the postal system, and to give it greater importance. Electronics and telecommunications were viewed as being strategic assets for India's development. The principle of private-public partnership was accepted in deals with Alcatel of France. This included the setting up of 500,000 lines per year, research and development assistance to the telecommunications research centre, and 200,000 lines of finished equipment.[4]

In 1984, domestic private production of terminal equipment was permitted for the first time. The public sector lobby opposed this move, and the conflict was referred to the Cabinet. In 1985, conflicting ideas about the role of private capital, small-scale industry, and foreign capital were circulating within various parts of the government. Many domestic business houses seemed interested in participating in the telecom sector. Thanks to the Alcatel precedent, foreign firms were showing interest as well.

Rajiv Gandhi's prime ministership increased the momentum toward internal reorganization, privatization, and indigenous technological development—inspired by the South Korean experience.[5] The PMO took a direct interest in telecom restructuring by creating a department of telecommunications (DOT), a telecommunications commission, and the Center for the Development of Telematics. Rajiv Gandhi's premiership is known for the six technology missions dedicated to development. The telecom mission emphasized both the quality of service and its universal reach to rural areas.

The creation of the DOT within the ministry of communications in 1985 led to the formal separation of telecommunications from the department of posts. Parts of the DOT were significantly corporatized, despite fierce resistance from the bureaucracy and the unions. In 1986, the semi-corporatized Mahanagar Telephone Nigam Limited (MTNL) and Videsh Sanchar Nigam Limited (VSNL) were created to serve the metropolitan areas of Delhi and Mumbai, and to provide long-distance services. The government owned 67 per cent and 33 per cent of the shares in MTNL and VSNL respectively.

A powerful telecom commission was established in 1989 for policy guidance. The idea was to create a semi-autonomous policy-cum-regulatory authority as a check against the old-fashioned thinking within the DOT. It tried to reason with trade unions, and succeeded in some workforce reductions. Unfortunately, the commission's policy autonomy lasted less than a year, ending when V.P. Singh became prime minister.

Such major changes in policy needed to overcome opposition from the incumbents within both the ministry of posts and telegraphs and the department of telecommunications. The idea that MTNL, serving the metropolitan areas, would be financially more viable than the DOT was fiercely resisted by the latter. When MTNL decided to give a performance bonus to its 70,000 employees in 1990, the 380,000 remaining DOT employees opposed the move. This resistance was the jolt that led to the establishment, thanks to the initiative of Prime Minister Chandra Shekhar, who succeeded V.P. Singh in 1990, of the telecom restructuring committee, better known as the Athreya committee.

By the late 1980s and the early 1990s, both domestic and foreign business users began to demand more competitive prices and efficient service provision. The Federation of Indian Chambers of Commerce and Industry (FICCI) desired better provision of long-distance data communication. FICCI, the Confederation of Indian Industry, and the Associated Chambers of Commerce all advocated cost-based pricing.[6]

Developments within the WTO signalled the acceptance of telecommunications liberalization at the multilateral level. The annex on telecommunications within the General Agreement on Trade in Services achieved more than other sectors. The bulk of the negotiations favouring competition in the telecom sector occurred between 1989 and 1997. This international political climate favouring telecom deregulation in India was clearly evident when the US negotiating team tabled complaints against India's telecommunications policy in 1990.[7]

In setting up the Athreya committee, the Chandra Shekhar government sought an independent opinion on whether the DOT's recommendation to absorb MTNL was appropriate. The PMO had first approached Citibank for advice. Citibank recommended M.B. Athreya, an academic and business consultant with a PhD from the Harvard Business School, to chair the committee. That Chandra Shekhar, who had ideological differences with Rajiv Gandhi, turned for independent opinion to Citibank and to Athreya showed that the PMO was willing to take a broader view of policy after consulting a variety of players. The Athreya committee report was available in March 1991, just before India's new conditionally based loan agreement with the IMF was signed in June 1991.

The Athreya committee argued that telecommunications in India needed three kinds of institutions. It needed policy-making, regulatory, and field-oriented institutions. The telecom commission could perform the policy role, an independent regulator was needed to promote competition, and the field role within the government could be played by the DOT. The Athreya report suggested opening up the manufacturing of special rugged telecommunications switches, currently produced solely by the government, to the Indian private sector. It recommended corporatization of the DOT and sequenced liberalization of cellular and value-added services, followed by the liberalization of basic services—local, long-distance, and international.[8]

In other words, much had been achieved before the advent of the balance of payments crisis in 1991. The private sector was manufacturing customer premises' end-use equipment, including telephones and electronic multi-line phone switching systems such as EPABX. The self-employed and small shopkeepers could open public call offices. MTNL and VSNL were allowed to operate as semi-corporatized entities. Most importantly, the Athreya committee had provided India the blueprint for reforms, which would turn out to be prophetic in the years to come.

From 1991 to 1997: Evolution of the Regulator

The period between 1991 and 1997—when an Indian telecom regulator was created—was a period of intense tussle between, on the one hand, a technocratic consensus in favour of competition, and, on the other, the DOT, which was creating obstacles to independent regulation. The foreign-exchange crisis aided the implementation of the bold pro-competition measures suggested by the Athreya committee report, despite opposition from the DOT.

The DOT bureaucracy was opposed to any initiatives favouring competition.

The communications secretary in the post-1991 period was not a committed reformer. According to an expert opinion, the technical staff within the DOT management was fiercely opposed to liberalization. The Indian Administrative Service (IAS) officers, on the other hand, tended to be more in favour of competition and modernization.

The government telecommunications sector, employing about 450,000 workers, opposed competition after the bidding for cellular licenses began in 1992. The process gained momentum after the National Telecom Policy of 1994. Workers also opposed the corporatization of the DOT recommended by the Athreya committee. The National Telecom Policy inspired strike threats from the major unions in the telecom sector.

The corporatization of the DOT as envisaged by the National Telecom Policy failed. The only recourse was to allow the private sector to compete with the DOT. In May 1995, employees of the public sector Indian Telephone Industries (ITI) in Bangalore tried to block the bidding process by arguing in the Guwahati High Court that this would contravene the universal service obligation and threaten national security. The court ordered a 'stay' on the tendering process. The stay order was overruled by the Supreme Court, which opined that it was not the judiciary's job to decide whether a particular policy was bad. Responding to growing worker discontent, the communications minister promised funds for upgrading DOT workers, to be raised through the bidding process.[9]

To give momentum to the liberalization process, the government selected N. Vittal, an IAS officer with impeccable pro-reform credentials, in 1993. Vittal had done pioneering work within the department of electronics, had been an ex-officio member of the telecom commission, and had also been a member of the Athreya committee. Vittal boosted the bidding process for cell phone and basic telephone licenses.

Subsequently, Vittal and A.N. Verma, the director of the Foreign Investment Promotion Board, had tried to convince Communications Minister Sukh Ram that the foreign equity limit needed to be raised to 51 per cent. Other proposals had suggested capping foreign equity at 40 per cent of the shares for national security reasons. Even the US restricted foreign companies to a minority share. Sukh Ram and Prime Minister P.V. Narasimha Rao took a middle position, capping foreign equity at 49 per cent.

In the initial stages, the PMO and the telecom commission headed by Vittal spearheaded the reform process, often in opposition to the communications minister. The communications minister, pressured by domestic lobbies, wanted to go slowly on liberalization. Vittal was removed in September 1994, after less than a year in the job.[10]

Opposition parties like the Bharatiya Janata Party (BJP) were criticizing the Congress for its elitist reform agenda. The BJP won elections in two southern states in November 1994. In February 1995, the Congress lost elections in Maharashtra and Gujarat. BJP general secretary Pramod Mahajan accused the Congress of opening telecommunications to private sector participation just before the elections, allegedly in order to obtain illicit kickbacks to help the Congress fund its election campaign. Ironically, when the BJP came to power the same minister would become the pro-reform champion for the telecom sector.[11]

What kind of regulated competition did India's political economy support between 1994 and 1997? Until 1997, the DOT was service provider and regulator all rolled into one. Privatization and competition arrived before the regulator. This was despite the recommendation of the telecom restructuring committee. The DOT exploited its regulatory position to secure its monopoly. Yet the DOT did such a shoddy job of introducing competition, promoting only companies of its choice through an opaque process of accepting private players, that the need for an independent regulator became more apparent than ever.

The regulatory process leading up to the 1994 National Telecom Policy had the following salient characteristics: one private operator would be licensed along with the DOT for basic telecom and paging services; the country was divided into 20 circles, or regions, and two private operators would be licensed for cellular services in each circle. The DOT did not show much interest in the cellular business because it was considered a luxury service where the business potential had not become apparent. There needed to be a foreign partner fulfilling a tough operating experience criterion and holding a minimum of 10 per cent equity. The tender process was heavily weighted (72 per cent) in favour of the company that would pay the highest license fee. There were also weightings for network rollout (10 per cent), local equipment (3 per cent), and rural services (15 per cent), which were less onerous.

The DOT secured the regulatory advantages for itself in a number of ways. First, the DOT did not state the weightings for the criteria mentioned above (though the selection criteria were eventually announced in May 1995).

Second, the DOT took full advantage of its licensing powers under the Indian Telegraph Act of 1885 to diverge from the terms of tender. In many circles the DOT opined that the highest bids were less than what the tender evaluation committee thought was a reasonable levy—but the criteria of reasonable levy in relation to the profits that the business was expected to make were not specified before the bidding process. Lack of transparency in the tender process and uncertainty about the DOT's commitment to a tender document (the contract between the DOT and the private player) raised the costs of reaching an agreement. This was especially true for foreign companies. Many international firms that had placed bids in the first round did not bid in the second. Eight regions failed to receive any bids and the DOT was forced to reduce the MRP (maximum retail price) by 30 per cent. By 1999, there were only two operators for basic services, and cellular operators had signed only one million subscribers.

Third, the enormous weight of the highest license fee for evaluating the success of a bid gave the DOT a substantial edge over whatever private producers ultimately won the tenders, because they would then be competing in the market against the DOT, which would not have to pay such a license fee. Private players made huge bids for licenses anyway. The private telephone companies owed the government $873 million toward their outstanding license fees in 1999. A level playing field would have demanded corporatization of the DOT and its being subjected to similar conditions for entering into business.

The revenues derived from the bidding process were used by the finance ministry to reduce the budget deficit, not by the DOT for improving the quality of telecom infrastructure. The finance ministry thus had an even greater incentive than the DOT to extract the highest license fee.

Fourth, the government opened up basic services before privatizing long-distance services. Basic services are less profitable in the short run. The VSNL could make profits on its long-distance services and subsidize basic services provided by the DOT. The private sector has therefore been a firm advocate of tariff rebalancing within the DOT, which would ensure that the DOT's basic tariffs are cost-based rather than cross-subsidized by VSNL's profitability. The World Bank was opposed to opening up basic services without opening up long-distance services, and many US-based companies stayed away from the bidding process because the short-term profitability of the licenses for basic services was not apparent.

Last but not least, political patronage increased the uncertainty regarding the bidding process. With a turnover of just Rs 2 billion ($44.4 million), Himachal Futuristic Corporation Limited bid Rs 8.5 billion ($188.8 million) for cell phone licenses for nine telecom regions. The tender evaluation committee decided to place a cap of three regions per company, but allowed Himachal

Futuristic to choose, rather than award it the three in which it had made the highest bids. Moreover, rather than rewarding the six remaining licenses according to the ranking of the bids, fresh bids were invited in January 1996. The privileged treatment for Himachal Futuristic led to charges of corruption against then communications minister Sukh Ram. This case was challenged in the courts.[12]

The problems leading to the birth of TRAI, which was conceived in 1994 and first suggested in 1991, highlighted the power of the government's service provider, the DOT. The Congress Party had delayed the implementation of a cabinet decision taken in May 1995. In December 1995, two public interest litigations were filed in the Supreme Court questioning privatization without regulation. The court dismissed these petitions in February 1996 after assurances from the government that such authority would be formed through a presidential ordinance.

TRAI became essential because of the mess that unregulated privatization had created in India. Parliament witnessed heated debates over the propriety of the tendering and licensing process. The Rajya Sabha (the upper chamber) blocked the TRAI bill, even after it was passed by the Lok Sabha (the lower chamber). TRAI was born with the help of a presidential ordinance in 1996, which lapsed after six months; parliament finally passed the TRAI bill in February 1997. The difficulty in setting up TRAI shows the difficulty of institutionalizing checks to the government's monopolistic tendencies.[13]

TRAI versus DOT 1997–99: Regulatory Mess

The initial TRAI constitution gave birth to a regulator with very few powers to ensure compliance from the DOT. First, it did not have jurisdiction over the Monopolies and Restrictive Trade Practices Act of 1969. This meant that anti-competitive behaviour on the part of DOT fell under the jurisdiction of the Monopolies Act rather than TRAI. Since the jurisdiction of the Monopolies Act with respect to government departments had not been settled, no clear mechanisms were devised against the government's own anti-competitive behaviour. Second, TRAI could resolve disputes between service providers but not between the licensor and the service provider. It had jurisdiction over the DOT as a service provider but not as a policy-maker. Third, TRAI had no powers to issue or cancel licenses or to allocate the radio frequency. The Indian Telegraph Act of 1885 gave this exclusive right to the DOT. Since the Telegraph Act was legislated in the age of national monopolies, there had been no perceived problem with the government being both a licensor and service provider. But in an age where a consensus on efficiency through private competition was being institutionalized, the DOT's role as both licensor and service provider conflicted with the objective of promoting competitiveness. Fourth, while TRAI could clarify the technical aspects of the bid, this power was meaningless, as it was constituted after three rounds of bids were over. Fifth, TRAI had the power to settle disputes related to interconnection agreements among service providers, but would be absent at the stage when the agreement was being negotiated. The market power of the incumbent, in this case the government monopoly DOT, gave it much leverage to arrive at agreements to its benefit. The private operators accepted agreements with the DOT only after it was clarified that such an agreement would be subject to adjudication by TRAI retroactively. This was the only area where TRAI recorded some success.[14]

TRAI was challenged in a controversy with the DOT over the issuance of licenses to MTNL for cellular and internet services. TRAI's failure to curb the DOT's unilateral behavior reflected the weaknesses in the TRAI constitution. In December 1998, MTNL announced its intention to enter the cellular services market. It was looking to tie up with one among 20 global companies, which could take up to 49 per cent equity in its cellular venture. The Cellular Operators Association of India was opposed to this decision. It argued, among other things, that the MTNL should pay a license fee at the level paid by other corporations. Two private operators also challenged the DOT's decision to allow MTNL into the market without seeking the recommendation of TRAI. TRAI's two-member bench ruled that even though the DOT was the licensing authority, it was necessary for it to request TRAI's recommendation before allowing MTNL into the cellular services market.

TRAI was concerned with maintaining investor interest in this sector so as to promote competition, which required checking the DOT's unilateral behavior. According to industry sources, the paging industry was losing $5 million per day. Cellular operators were in bad shape. Some companies had paid 1.6 times their investment in the network as license fees. Unable to pay license fees to the government, one company cancelled its plan to build a 2000-kilometer fibre-optic backbone across the southern states of Karnataka and Andhra Pradesh. TRAI viewed MTNL entry into the cell market without paying a license fee as being detrimental to cell phone operators in financial distress.

The tussle between the regulator and the DOT elicited an intervention from the PMO, which faced a choice between supporting the DOT and backing TRAI chairman S.S. Sodhi. The PMO was not willing to displease either side. Such regulatory confusion led to a resolution of the issue by the Delhi High

Court, as the DOT had appealed to the Delhi High Court after the adverse judgment from TRAI.

Ruling against TRAI, Justice Usha Mehra stated that it would be 'unimaginable that the power to grant license rests with the government but would be subject to the discretion of another Authority.'[15] Granting licensing powers to TRAI, the court argued, would make the DOT's power under the Indian Telegraph Act of 1885 redundant. TRAI's recommendations were non-binding. Thus TRAI's role was not to settle disputes between the DOT and the private operators. On appeal, the division bench of the Delhi High Court upheld the decision, making TRAI's role redundant. Disillusioned with this result, several multinational companies began to pull back. The telecom sector had brought in foreign investment worth $5 billion, among the highest of any sector in India.[16]

TRAI 1999 and Beyond: Getting out of the Mess

In early 1999, a high-powered group on telecommunications was set up to recommend the way out of this regulatory mess. The deputy chairman of the planning commission and foreign minister Jaswant Singh chaired the group, and it included, among others, two senior officials from the PMO. This signalled an inclination within the PMO to back the pro-competition elements within the government after giving due consideration to the communications ministry.[17]

The New Telecom Policy of March 1999 shifted the balance of power in favour of TRAI. First, the old license fee regime was changed to one that included a reduced license fee plus revenue share. Private operators were bailed out of the financial predicament caused by the old license-fee regime. This bailout package cost the government $900 million. Communications minister Jagmohan was single-mindedly averse to the bailout package. He was keen to cash the bank guarantees that would result from the default of various private operators.

Opposition leaders supported the new regime based on revenue sharing, which largely helped domestic private operators. It was rumoured that Reliance Telecom was behind this design. For example, Somnath Chatterjee of the Communist Party of India (Marxist) asserted that this move was essential to ensure that Indian capital would not get swept away by foreign capital in this sector.[18] Second, the DOT was allowed to become the third operator in all the circles. This was a decision favourable to the DOT. Third, TRAI was given arbitration powers to settle disputes between the service provider and the government. A telecom dispute settlement appellate tribunal was set up as an arm within TRAI, and given the status of a High Court. Fourth, TRAI's recommendations would be sought on the number and timing of new licenses, but the DOT would be the policy-maker and the licensing authority. Fifth, Bharat Sanchar Nigam Limited (the DOT arm providing basic services), along with the MTNL, would be corporatized by 2001. It would pay a license fee after 2001, which would be subsidized by the budget for its commitment to national and social obligations. Domestic and international long distance services would be opened to competition in January 2000.[19]

This opening up of basic services was ostensibly for letting private capital into a less profitable sector, which involved a universal service commitment. They were to pay a lower license fee. The 1999 telecom policy allowed basic operators to use CDMA technology with a 'wireless in local loop' facility, which allowed roaming facility within a short-distance charging area to these fixed operators. The wireless facility therefore threatened some of the local business of the cell operators. Private operators used the wireless facility to make their basic operations highly profitable, to the detriment of cell operators. This increased competition finally reduced cell phone charges, leading to an explosion of the customer base.

Cell phone operators opposed the wireless facility. This regulatory change increased competition for cellular service providers, lowered prices for the consumer, and benefited both private and public operators of fixed telephone services.

The wireless/CDMA technology allowed these phone companies to perform cell phone-type functions within a limited area while escaping termination charges that cell operators had to pay to the fixed telephone operators for interconnection. In January 2001 the DOT accepted TRAI's recommendations and issued guidelines for basic service licenses. Meanwhile, the telecom appellate tribunal dismissed a petition filed by cellular operators that sought to prevent fixed line operators from using limited mobility. The tribunal reminded the cellular companies that the telecom policy of 1999 had recommended limited mobility. The allocation of the radio spectrum was to be free and on a 'first come first served' basis. The cellular operators association urged the PMO to take action to stop this.

The government tried to compensate the cell operators for this disadvantage. First, it reduced the government's share of cellular revenues from 17 per cent to 12 per cent. In the past, the government had bailed out cellular operators by shifting them from a fixed license fee regime to a revenue sharing regime. Second, the government announced unlimited competition in basic services. If some basic operators had benefited, all the cellular operators could benefit too. It announced a license-fee-plus-revenue-sharing regime. In February 2001, letters of intent were issued to 40 out of 132 applications. On hearing about an alleged Rs 1.3 billion ($28.8 million) scam favouring basic service operators, opposition parties forced the prime minister to persuade the DOT to refrain from issuing more letters of intent. Ultimately, the free allocation of spectrum was permitted, but detailed conditions for spectrum allocation were laid out.

The new policy led to accusations that the government favoured one particular operator (Reliance), which could exploit economies of scale. Reliance had used the limited mobility technology to provide substantial mobility by handing over the calls from one short distance charging area to another. The wireless loop technology had been successfully used to make calls beyond the limited area for which Reliance had received a basic service with limited mobility license.

Noting the problem of separate licenses, the government finally decided to *merge basic and cellular licenses* into one in October 2003. It was opined that there should be one license that included domestic long-distance, international long-distance, and internet services as well. Basic services operators could launch mobile services upon the payment of an additional fee.

Despite these regulatory setbacks, TRAI recorded significant achievements. MTNL, the government operator serving the metropolitan areas, was corporatized. BSNL, the government service provider for the rest of the country was also converted into a corporation. In 2003–4, mobile tariffs came down by 74 per cent, the number of subscribers increased from 13 million to 35 million, and the total number of mobile subscribers increased by 20.72 million—more than triple the figure for the previous year. In April 2004 alone, 1.65 million subscribers were added for fixed and mobile telephony. In recognition of this success, the TRAI was named Asia Pacific Regulator of the Year in 2004.[20]

THE POWER SECTOR

The story of regulation in the power sector contrasts sharply with what we have seen of regulatory reform in the telecom sector. There are three main reasons for this divergence. First, privatization has not yielded any significant results in the power sector. The political economy bias in favour of the status quo was far more entrenched in this sector. Second, in addition to problems caused by the inability of distribution companies to charge reasonable tariffs, especially from the agriculture sector, difficulties stemmed from the fact that the World Bank played a more direct role in setting policy agendas in the power sector, compared to its far less influential position in India's telecom reforms. The divergent outcomes across the two sectors highlights the absence, in the power sector, of a homegrown approach to institutional and policy reform, which had been so much in evidence in the telecom sector reforms. Third, since the power sector lay in the concurrent list of the Indian Constitution, much of the regulatory action was at the state level of India's federal system. Numerous state electricity regulatory commissions (SERCs) had a tough time fighting the politically entrenched state electricity boards (SEBs). Such has been the level of disillusionment with government monopolies at the state level that the World Bank has proposed that the power of the regulators be curbed and executive authority be enhanced, even as the Electricity Act of 2003 has enhanced the powers of the Central Electricity Regulatory Commission (CERC).

The inability of the power sector to collect revenues from the distribution of power has contributed significantly to India's fiscal deficit. In 2002–3 the aggregate fiscal deficit of the states was 4.7 per cent of GDP. The losses of the state electricity boards, at Rs 2.4 trillion ($53.3 billion) alone were equal to 1 per cent of India's GDP.[21] Between 1992–3 and 2001–2, the percentage of power supply costs recovered through the average tariff declined from 82.2 per cent to 68.6 per cent.[22] Pilferage accounted for about 40 per cent of the electricity generated.[23] The puzzle for generating competition in the power sector was how to involve the private sector in an area where a majority of customers were not used to paying tariffs.

The failure of north India's electricity grid in January 2001 highlighted the problem of the lack of coordination. With its Power Grid Corporation of India Limited, the government encouraged joint ventures to improve transmission facilities and avoid the loss of surplus power. An independent power transmission corporation was set up to encourage investment involving 100 per cent foreign equity in this sector.[24]

The World Bank spent close to $3.5 billion between 1970 and 1991 on the large thermal plants built by the National Thermal Power Corporation. Still, to meet its growing energy needs, India is seeking foreign and domestic private capital.[25]

The Politics of Power Tariffs

Why has it been difficult to impose cost-based tariffs for power in India? The politics of competitive party systems in India since 1967 generated a competition for subsidies. As the rural middle class grew, it demanded free power, fertilizer, and water, and the Indian state of the 1980s increasingly began to subsidize the politically mobilized agrarian sector.[26] According to one observer, the Congress party in the 1977 elections, in the immediate aftermath of the national Emergency, committed the original sin. The Emergency, imposed in 1975 by Indira Gandhi, was, according to some scholars, the product of the Congress' inability to keep its coalition intact. The Congress-led government in the state of Andhra Pradesh, for example, offered a flat rate for electricity based on the capacity of the pump rather than the amount of consumption. This was offered to farmers as a pre-election promise in return for getting elected. Politicians in others states—first Tamil Nadu, and then Maharashtra and Karnataka—followed suit. This was during a time (the early 1980s) when political movements among better-off farmers became the order of the day.[27]

Economic liberalization after 1991 made no impact on the politics of subsidies. The National Development Council's committee on power resolved that there would be a minimum agricultural tariff of half a rupee per kilowatt hour in 1996. The Tamil Nadu chief minister, who was party to the decision, rejected it as soon as she was back in her state's capital. Only nine states achieved the half-rupee-per-kilowatt-hour goal, and none achieved the other objective of recouping 50 per cent of the average cost of supplying power by 2001. The meetings of state chief ministers held in 2000 and in 2001 agreed on compulsory metering, energy audit, and upgrading electricity transmission and distribution. Progress on these fronts has been slow. In 2003, the Rajasthan government, which had set out to improve the power system in the state, lost the state elections. About a month before the May 2004 national elections in Tamil Nadu, the state's chief minister began reimbursing farmers what they had paid the SEB. Payments began reaching the farmers despite misgivings within the Tamil Nadu SEB itself.[28]

Some states offered a flat-rate tariff rather than free electricity. Meters were often removed and returned to the SEBs. The lack of proper meters posed a major threat to privatization of the distribution business, as it was difficult to measure the loss due to transmission and distribution. Often, electricity consumed by industries, municipalities, and friends of the power minister and SEB officials were recorded as theft by agriculturalists. If distribution companies, owned by the SEBs, had no way of knowing what their losses were, it would be tough to ensure the commercial viability of the entity.

The gravity of the situation led the ministry of power to recommend a set of incentives and disincentives for performing and non-performing states in 2001.

This advice closely resembled World Bank recommendations that conditioning future funding for cash-starved states on improvements in cost recovery could be one solution. This would require state-level leaders to convince key constituencies of the benefits of central help in return for reasonable tariffs.

A committee constituted to examine ways of allowing SEBs to clear their arrears to central public sector undertakings that supplied them with coal and other inputs recommended a conditionality-based system consisting of reform milestones such as the setting up of state electricity regulatory commissions and the metering of power supplies. There would be financial benefits for reformers, while non-reforming states that defaulted on payments to the public sector suppliers would experience a graded decline in power and coal from the same suppliers. If the default exceeded 90 days, the government would recover this amount against the central plan assistance.[29]

Encouraging Independent Power Producers

In October 1991, the Ministry of Power began to publish a series of notifications encouraging the entry of private power generating companies. These orders were enacted in the parliament as the Electricity Laws (Amendment) Act of 1991. The act permitted private entities to operate and maintain generating plants of any size. Other incentives included a guaranteed minimum 16 per cent return on equity investments that operated at their rated capacity for 6,000 hours in a year. There would be additional bonuses for better capacity utilization. There would be a five-year tax holiday, equity requirements of only 20 per cent, and there were selective counter-guarantees from the central government to cover payment default by SEBs. Armed with these incentives, the power minister travelled abroad in 1992 to woo investors.

This approach to power generation did not yield significant benefits, and the 1990s has been called the 'lost decade' for power generation in India. First, there were serious allegations of corruption. The Enron project in Maraslura was approved despite opposition from the central electricity agency, central and state bureaucrats, and the World Bank, and although the site had been earlier earmarked for a national thermal power plant. The memorandum of understanding (MOU) between the government of Maharashtra and Enron's subsidiary, the Dabhol Power Corporation, was signed with utmost secrecy.

Energy analysts and journalists revealed the astonishing complicity among officials that had helped to bend the laws in Enron's favor. Public interest litigation by Ajay Mehta and the Centre for Indian Trade Unions challenging the fraud was ignored, and the first phase of the project for a 690 MW plant was commissioned.

The result was disastrous. Such was the production cost of electricity in the state that by 1999 the Maharashtra State Electricity Board (MSEB), which was profitable in 1998–9, was running losses exceeding $300 million. The power generated by the Dabhol Power Project was about twice as expensive as the average cost of power in Maharashtra. The MSEB defaulted on its payment in December 1999 and in 2000. Maharashtra's electricity regulatory commission asked the state to purchase power from the lowest-cost producer. The default produced a credit downgrade for the Maharashtra government.

From a regulatory perspective, other questionable practices involved in the operation of this project deserve attention. Enron, for instance, preferred imported fuels, whose clearance had to come from the commerce ministry. The petroleum ministry allowed the use of naphtha as an interim fuel for gas-based short-gestation projects, founded on an overly optimistic estimate of the domestic availability of naphtha. There were complicated requirements for domestically produced and foreign-produced naphtha. The domestic availability of the fuel was found to be less than estimated. The high Enron tariffs depended to a large extent on the ill-fated choice of an expensive fuel. A regulator caring for consumer interests should have been quick to point this out.

Even so, industry associations and sections of the middle class supported the rapid move toward privatization. They resented the old-style bureaucratic malfunctioning of the state sector. The Ministry of Power firmly supported the reform effort. Indeed, the World Bank seemed to appreciate that India was bringing in private sector participation, though it was unhappy about the way in which this was being done.

There was also opposition within important sections of the bureaucracy. The central electricity authority caused the greatest delays in providing techno-economic and environmental clearances. Some senior finance ministry officials were opposed to the lopsided way in which the power purchasing agreements were being proposed. A few informed intellectuals and government officials complained that restructuring the SEBs to have greater autonomy from political masters was never explored as an option. They claimed that the government National Thermal Power Corporation was getting a raw deal. By the late 1990s there was a consensus within the bureaucracy that the policy on independent power producers was seriously flawed.[30]

The Era of Regulation

The policy favouring independent regulators was a brainchild of the World Bank, which it pursued with some tenacity. The Bank was dissatisfied that its approaches to power sector reforms had not met with the desired success in the 1980s. Throughout its substantial investments in the developing world, it had tried least-cost planning, marginal-cost pricing, promoting international accounting standards, and international competitive bidding. In 1991, power sector lending to the developing world, at $40 billion, accounted for approximately 15 per cent of the Bank's total lending. It noted the problem of unsatisfactory metering, billing and collection, low average tariffs, lack of a proper service orientation, and low rates of return on capital. These developments had occurred in the context of deteriorating macroeconomic conditions and an increased worldwide movement favouring competition.

The Bank fundamentally changed its power sector strategy and proposed an independent and transparent regulator. It noted the conflict of interest between the government as policy-maker and service provider, and wished to introduce a commercial orientation. It argued that the government should merely give policy direction, and not get overly involved with the production process. The regulator would hear the concerns of private investors, consumers, environmentalists, and other stakeholders. The Bank wanted to create an institution that would establish a legal framework to protect the interests of a variety of players affected by the production and consumption of power. To achieve these tasks it would encourage commercialization and corporatization of public sector assets and private sector participation. It declared that lending would be committed only to those who accepted the above principles.[31]

Orissa was the first Indian state to adopt the privatized regulation model in 1993. The Orissa model, with the longest history of state-level regulation, highlighted the extent to which the Bank got involved with the regulatory process in India. Orissa's selection was partly driven by the Haryana government's lack of appetite for bearing the short-term costs associated with reforms. Orissa's power sector was in bad shape, with plants being run at 36 per cent efficiency. Transmission and distribution losses amounted to 43 per cent of the electricity generated, and the proportion of bills collected was a miserable 17 per cent. There was no powerful agricultural lobby in Orissa and the sector consumed a paltry 5.7 per cent of the total electricity sales.

The dominant reason for the choice of Orissa was Chief Minister Biju Patnaik's strong support for entering into an agreement with the World Bank. The Bank's carrot—an offer to fund a hydroelectric power project in the state—was an important enticement for Patnaik. The chief minister also foresaw the impending bankruptcy of the SEB and thought that an external actor might help discipline the sector. The power restructuring project received $350 million from the Bank and another $110 million from the UK bilateral aid programme.

The project was anything but homegrown in Orissa. A major role was played by international consultants, who tended to impose their preferred strategies rather than build a consensus based at least in part on local knowledge of conditions in the state. The consultants decided on the single-buyer model. All generating companies were required to sell to the state-owned transmission company. Under these conditions, generating companies were unwilling to bear risk, which resulted in a resort to long-term power purchasing agreements as the preferred solution. These agreements, as in the Enron case, allowed for select private entities on an indicative basis, without competitive bidding. In a 'cost-plus' regime, where capital costs translated into tariffs, this could be viewed as being against the interests of the consumer. Moreover, the distribution companies had to buy power from the transmission companies, while the consumer could buy only from the distribution company in its area. And the transmission companies carried the unpaid bills of the distribution companies. The industry structure thus continued to be of a command and control type, unlike some more competitive models prevalent in the UK and Sweden. Under this system, the Orissa transmission company has accumulated overdue payments equivalent to Rs 150 billion, besides a total debt burden of Rs 300 billion ($3.3 billion and $6.6 billion respectively). This model was obviously neither sustainable nor likely to lead to an augmentation in generation capacity.

The consultants' view on the nature of the regulator was derived from a combination of the US and the UK traditions. In Latin American countries like Chile, the regulatory role is highly circumscribed and the policy directions are very detailed. Drawing from the UK and US experience, the Bank-led approach for India gave greater discretion on policy to the regulator, and the policy guidelines were of a more general nature. Such was the power of international consultants that several Indian policy analysts questioned their methods and the appropriateness of the model they deployed.

The Orissa Electricity Regulatory Commission (OERC) was born in 1996, following the Orissa State Electricity Reform Act of 1995. This was consistent with the Bank's advice. The OERC could play a limited though positive role, faced with tasks where it had to take on both the transmission company and the Bank. It forced the transmission company to reduce expenditures resulting from transmission and distribution losses, and restricted tariff increases. Second, it also rebuffed investor-friendly World Bank advice on tariff setting. The OERC has only been able to play a limited tariff-setting role. It could not effectively oppose power purchasing agreements or non-competitive bids, or make the industry structure less monopolistic.[32]

A 2001 committee criticized the astronomical cost at which international consultants were hired (Rs 30.6 billion, or $680 million), stating that judging by the state of the utilities for whose benefit the consultants were engaged, their advice could not be properly assimilated. The utilities, rather than gaining in strength from their advice, became heavily dependent on them. Moreover, the Bank's staff appraisal report was highly optimistic about the rise in demand for power in the state. In fact, industrial power did not grow as expected, and transmission and distribution efficiency, not to mention billing and collection efficiency, worsened with privatization.[33]

Other regulators also faced problems encountering their respective electricity boards or government departments. First, sometimes regulators did not have adequate information on fuel prices before deciding tariffs, thanks to the negative approach of the government entity it was supposed to be regulating. For example, the central electricity regulatory commission was supposed to set tariffs for the Neyveli Lignite Corporation, which was a public sector undertaking. But Neyveli Lignite had captive coal mines whose transfer prices for coal could not be examined by the regulatory commission—so how could the commission set tariffs without this data?

Second, the regulatory commission tried to protect the SEBs against the tariffs of public sector undertakings, which were operating on a cost-plus basis, and were imposing an increasing return on equity on the SEBs during the 1990s. The electricity supply tariffs provided for accelerated depreciation, which made the SEBs pay their dues upfront. The regulatory commission took up the matter with the public sector undertakings, which then challenged the matter in the Supreme Court. The Court upheld the regulatory commission's orders.

Third, multi-year tariff setting for the regulatory commissions has been difficult in the absence of adequate data on the cost of fuels. Each ministry, such as coal or petroleum, fought for its own sphere of power and prerogatives. Durable multi-year tariffs, which were important for attracting investment, were not realized.

The power sector's location on the concurrent list of subjects under the Indian Constitution has led to regulatory conflicts between the highly politicized SEBs and the corresponding state regulatory commissions. Two examples highlight this conflict of interest. The Tamil Nadu regulatory commission was rendered ineffective because a chairperson was not appointed, and the Karnataka government suspended a tariff order of its commission. Moreover, the SEBs have tried to protect their monopoly position in the transmission and distribution of electricity within their respective states. They have opposed third-party sales to consumers by the distribution companies; denied private parties access to the transmission systems by charging unduly heavy wheeling charges; tried to impose obstacles to the entry and exit of private players; and placed restrictions on private captive generation. A private concern generating electricity would not be able to transmit the surplus to other parts of the state if the wheeling or transmission charges were unduly burdensome.

Collusion between the regulatory commissions and the SEBs was also a problem at times. The Andhra Pradesh commission imposed high wheeling charges that made large-scale private generation of electricity uneconomical. They tried to stop third-party sales, which were allowed by earlier contracts. The state high court reversed this decision. At other times, however, the courts undermined the regulators. The Punjab and Haryana High Court gave a stay order on the decision of the SERC to increase power tariffs for industry. This stay raised the issue of the appropriateness of judicial intervention in matters that fell within the purview of the regulators.

In some cases, however, the regulatory commissions also had a success story to tell. In Karnataka, it allowed third-party sales and made private power generation easy, while in Maharashtra the commission successfully imposed a heavy fine on the state electricity board in 2001 for non-compliance with its directives. The central electricity regulator also imposed a fine on the Madhya Pradesh Electricity Board for violation of the grid code, apart from successfully taking on the central public sector undertakings on the issue of unduly heavy financial burdens they imposed on the SEBs. State electricity regulators have increased public awareness of what ails the SEBs: they have sought to expose the political nature of power tariffs and the problem of transmission and distribution losses. A great deal of authentic and valuable data has been generated by their reports.[34]

The most recent controversy on electricity regulation concerns the World Bank's attempt to move from 'independent regulation' toward a 'regulatory contract'. This represents a move away from the Anglo-American approach (mentioned earlier), and toward the French approach, which gives less discretion to regulatory authorities and more to the political authority. Justifying its policy shift, the Bank argued that it had not realized that power tariffs were a politically charged exercise that required the intervention of the executive. The new model exists in many power-purchasing agreements around the world. Regulation by contract would involve detailed guidelines on tariff setting, on who would bear the costs of power theft, on guarding against foreign-exchange fluctuations, on the public service obligation, and on how to administer a dispute settlement mechanism. Tariff setting would thus largely become the prerogative of the executive, and it was argued that detailed data was needed for such an exercise. Above all, a regulatory contract had to be a contract backed by the country's highest political authorities.[35]

Given the influence of the Bank, states like Karnataka are moving toward new legislation that would guarantee multi-year tariffs without the availability of detailed baseline data. Their consultants have argued that the investors would only bear collection risks from metered consumers, theft risk limited to starting levels of theft, risk in respect of inaccurate meters, and operational management and capital expenditure management risk. The exercise is an attempt to downgrade regulators and to get the state directly involved in privatization.[36]

Such an approach will, of course, encounter the much-noted rent seeking propensities in the Indian political system, conspicuously present in the Enron case. The Enron story highlighted the ways in which political masters could reach deals with corporations without any regard for the consumer or the SEB. The central electricity authority, in the absence of a regulator, failed to curb these propensities, which were clearly driven by political and corporate considerations.

The French model might work if the Indian central government or states within India possessed a level of institutional autonomy closer to that found in France.[37] But under Indian conditions, it would appear that independent regulation, though imperfect, provides better safeguards against the excesses of a state highly penetrated by corporate actors. The Enron case taught India what unchecked executive authority could produce. The power purchasing agreement experiment generated unsustainable tariffs and decelerated electricity generation in India. At a time when independent regulation in the power sector is beginning to mature, it would be cruel to kill it.

The Electricity Act of 2003 helps to address many of the problems outlined in this section of the chapter. Moreover, it seeks to centralize the governance of electricity by giving powers to the central electricity regulators to lay down guidelines regarding transmission charges and the elimination of cross-subsidies. The central regulatory commission will have powers to enforce grid discipline over the national grid. Trading in power and increased competition in generation, transmission, and distribution are envisaged.

CONCLUSION: MANAGING COMPETITION IN THE TELECOM AND POWER SECTORS

India's power sector got locked into an inefficient institutional reform path to a much greater extent than did the telecom sector. Once an inefficient path gets entrenched, it becomes difficult to change course toward a more efficient equilibrium, because any mode of organization is premised on high start-up costs, learning and network externalities, and adaptive expectations.[38]

If the path toward equilibrium was to be a movement toward efficiency engendered by competition, my argument suggests that the politicization of power sector tariffs, which began with election pledges in the late 1970s and led to institutional and citizens' expectations favouring it, went far deeper than the politicization of telecom tariffs. The SEBs got used to running losses and consumers got accustomed to poor quality power at low or no prices. Cost-based pricing of power was politically tougher to implement than the competitive pricing of telecom services. The challenge for power sector reforms is to get out of this inefficient path of low or zero tariffs and to adopt cost-based competitive tariffs. The politics of SEB control and joint pledges by chief ministers have been unsuccessful. Governance under the guidance and authority of independent, powerful, and yet accountable regulators is the more promising way forward.

Second, telecom sector reforms were driven to a greater extent by initiatives emanating from ideational changes within the PMO. Such initiatives included the first joint venture with Alcatel, private manufacture of telecom equipment in India, allowing privatized basic and long-distance services, the birth of the telecom regulator, and moves to empower the toothless regulator to help gain self-confidence. The process was no doubt marred by confusion, political bickering, and rent seeking. But policy-makers found an effective way of dealing with the powerful incumbent by strengthening the regulator.

Power sector reforms, on the other hand, could not find ways of getting around SEB losses and political interference. Consequently, private capital investment in generation, transmission, and distribution suffered. Power purchasing agreements in the early 1990s failed to expand generation: the policy of encouraging them, consistent with the philosophy of market-driven structural adjustment in the immediate aftermath of the balance of payments crisis of 1991, seems to have been the brainchild of the ministry of power, with sections of the middle class and industry supporting it. It did not have the explicit guidance of the World Bank.

The World Bank strategy of independent regulators, with all its attendant problems, met with some success. It led to some bold tariff-related pronouncements against the incumbents, and the generation of valuable data. Once operational, regulators succeeded—sometimes despite, rather than because of, World Bank advice. The Orissa electricity regulatory commission, for example, opposed high tariffs proposed by the World Bank, much to the Bank's dismay. The central government's Electricity Act 2003—by further enabling private generation, transmission, and distribution—should strengthen the hand of the regulator. Noting that centralized regulation was more successful than state-level regulation in the telecom sector, the act has enhanced the powers of the central regulator in relation to those of the states.

The World Bank has recently advocated a return to the power purchasing agreement model and abandoning independent regulation in the power sector. This move should be opposed. First, the power purchasing model led to uncompetitive bidding, little augmentation in generation, and unreasonably high tariffs. One could argue that powerful independent regulators could have checked some of the excesses of that experience, which the central electricity authority within the ministry of power was ill equipped to handle. If independent regulators could increase their sphere of influence beyond mere tariff setting, and enter into questions of licensing under fair and equitable terms, this could improve the sector's performance. This has been the experience of the telecom sector. The experience of both the telecom and power sectors suggests that privatization without regulation generates legal and regulatory confusion that cannot be sustained for long.

A homegrown approach to managing competition, based on a reading of international experience, but adapted to local conditions, appears to have significant advantages over approaches that seek to break through political logjams by means of strong direction from outside donors and consultants. This is consistent with literature suggesting that the IMF needs to pursue country ownership of programmes.[39] The Orissa power sector story lends support to this view. The policy advice of the Bank and international consultants was in some respects inappropriate. And at other times, even when the advice of the independent regulators was sound, a conflict of interest developed between the Bank, which was out to safeguard the interests of investors, and the regulator, whose chief concern was the welfare of consumers. The confidence gained by regulators in telecommunications and power reflected more a process of institutional learning than blind obedience to external agencies and experts.

NOTES AND REFERENCES

1. The author thanks Sunil Khilnani, Rob Jenkins, Montek S. Ahluwalia, and Partha N. Mukherji. Interaction with S.L. Kao, Rajat Knthuria, and M.B. Athreya helped. Ajoy Lywait provided excellent research assistance and Anjali Mukherji chipped in with timely editorial advice. The shortcomings nevertheless rest with the author.

2. On the political economy of reforms beyond 1991, see Rob Jenkins, *Democratic Politics and Economic Reform in India* (Cambridge, Cambridge University Press, 1999); and Rahul Mukherji, 'A Path to Trade and Investment Liberalization' (New York, Columbia University, PhD Dissertation, 1999). See also Rahul Mukherji, 'Economic Transition in a Plural Polity: India', in Rahul Mukherji (ed.), *India's Economic Transition: The Politics of Reforms* (New Delhi, Oxford University Press, 2007).

3. For Indira Gandhi's policy orientation in the 1980s, see Mukherji, 'Trade and Investment Liberalization', chap. 4; also see Indira Gandhi, *Selected Speeches and Writings – Vol. 4* (New Delhi, Government of India–Publications Division, Ministry of Information and Broadcasting, 1985), p. 236. For Indira Gandhi's policy orientation in the 1960s, see Rahul Mukherji, 'India's Aborted Liberalization – 1966', *Pacific Affairs,* vol. 73, no. 3 (Fall 2000), p. 381.

4. On developments in telecom policy favouring competition during Indira Gandhi's tenure, see Stephen U. McDowell, *Globalization, Liberalization and Policy Change* (New York, St. Martin's Press, 1997), pp. 127–35; and J.P. Singh, *Leapfrogging Development: The Political Economy of Telecommunications Restructuring* (Albany, State University of New York Press, 1999), pp. 141–3.

5. For a description of Rajiv Gandhi's orientation and partial success with economic reforms, see Atul Kohli, *Democracy and Discontent* (New York, Cambridge University Press, 1990), chap. 11.

6. For other sources of telecom policy before the balance of payments crisis of 1991, see Ben A. Petrazzini, 'Telecommunications Policy in India: The Political Underpinnings of Reform', *Telecommunications Policy,* vol. 20, no. 1, January–February (1996), pp. 40–1; M.B. Athreya, 'India's Telecommunications Policy', *Telecommunications Policy,* vol. 20, no. 1, January–February, 1996, pp. 11–17; and Singh, *Leapfrogging Development,* pp. 141–63.

7. On the US problems with Indian policy, see McDowell, *Globalization,* pp. 142–4.

8. Athreya, 'India's Telecommunications Policy', pp. 16–17. Interview with M.B. Athreya, New Delhi, 8 May 2004.

9. Petrazzini, 'Telecommunications Policy in India', pp. 43–4.

10. Ibid; Athreya, 'India's Telecommunications', p. 19; and Nikhil Sinha,

'The Political Economy of India's Telecommunications Reform', *Telecommunications Policy*, vol. 20, no. 1, January–February (1996), p. 31.

11. Petrazzini, 'Telecommunications Policy in India', p. 44.

12. On the licensing process and its implications, see Anupama Dokeniya, 'Reforming the State: Telecom Liberalization in India', *Telecommunications Policy*, vol. 23, no. 2, March–April (1999), pp. 111–22; Sinha, 'Political Economy', pp. 32–5; Athreya, 'India's Telecommunications', pp. 20–1; Petrazinni, 'Telecommunications Policy in India', pp. 49–50; and Rajni Gupta, 'Telecommunication Liberalization; Critical Role of Legal and Regulatory Regime', *Economic and Political Weekly*, 27 April 2002, pp. 1679–80.

13. Dokeniya, 'Reforming,' pp.122–3. See also Gupta, 'Telecommunication Liberalization', pp. 1669–70; and Singh, *Leapfrogging*, pp. 180–1.

14. On TRAI's mandate, see Dokeniya, 'Reforming', pp. 123–5; T.H. Chowdary, 'Telecom Demonopolisation: Policy or Farce?', *Economic and Political Weekly*, 25 February 2000, pp. 438–9. On the first interconnection controversy between the DOT and TRAI, see Gupta, 'Telecommunication Liberalization', p. 1670.

15. Ibid.

16. On the TRAI–DOT conflict over TRAI's licensing powers, see ibid.. See also EIU ViewsWire, 'MTNL Plans Cellular Service in Delhi, Bombay', *The Economist Intelligence Unit* (London, 7 January 1998); EIU ViewsWire, 'More Telecoms Trouble', *The Economist Intelligence Unit* (London, 4 March 1998); and EIU ViewsWire, 'Telecoms Authority's Wings Clipped', *The Economist Intelligence Unit* (London, 5 August 1998), all via www.viewswire.com.

17. On the composition of the Group on Telecommunications, see EIU ViewsWire, 'New Telecoms Policy in Pipeline', *The Economist Intelligence Unit* (London, 13 January 1999), via www.viewswire.com.

18. On the politics and economics of the shift to revenue sharing, see EIU ViewsWire, 'A Telecom Truce is Called', *The Economist Intelligence Unit* (London, 30 June 1999); and EIU ViewsWire, 'Government Intent on Telecoms Bailout Package', *The Economist Intelligence Unit* (London, 23 July 1999), via www.viewswire.com.

19. On the gains to TRAI and DOT from the New Telecom Policy 1999, see Gupta, 'Telecommunication Liberalization', p. 1671.

20. See www.trai.gov.in.

21. Urjit R. Patel, 'Plug Power Financials – Now!', *Business Standard* (New Delhi), 10 March 2004.

22. Madhav Godbole, 'Electricity Act 2003: Questionable Wisdom', *Economic and Political Weekly*, 27 September 2003, p. 4104.

23. Gajendra Haldea, 'Whither Electricity Reforms?', *Economic and Political Weekly*, 28 April 2001, pp. 1389–91.

24. Government of India, Ministry of Power, *Blueprint for Power Sector Development* (New Delhi, Academic Foundation, 2003), pp. 49–52.

25. Government of India, *Blueprint*, pp. 20–22.

26. For the rise of the rural sector, see Ashutosh Varshney, *Democracy, Development and the Countryside* (Cambridge, Cambridge University Press, 1995), pp. 169–72; Lloyd I. Rudolph and Susanne Hoeber Rudolph, *In Pursuit of Lakshmi: The Political Economy of the Indian State* (Chicago and London, University of Chicago Press, 1987), Chapters 12–13; and Subrata K. Mitra, 'Room to Maneuver in the Middle: Local Elites, Political Action, and the State in India', *World Politics*, vol. 43, no. 3, April (1991), pp. 390–413.

27. Navroz Dubash and Sudhir C. Rajan, 'Power Politics: Process of Power Sector Reform in India', *Economic and Political Weekly*, 1 September 2001, pp. 3369–70.

28. Dubash and Rajan, 'Power Politics', pp. 3383–4; and S.L. Rao, 'Economic Reforms and the Political Economy', unpublished paper, 2004. I am grateful to Amit Ahuja of the University of Michigan for bringing to my notice the pre-election behaviour of the Tamil Nadu chief minister.

29. Government of India, *Blueprint*, pp. 62–4.

30. On the policy of introducing independent power producers, see Dubash and Rajan, 'Power Politics', pp. 3372–5; and K.P. Kannan and N. Vijaymohan Pillai, *Plight of the Power Sector in India: Inefficiency, Reform and Political Economy* (Thiruvanthapuram, Kerala, Centre for Development Studies, 2002), pp. 393–8, 410–24.

31. International Bank for Reconstruction and Development, *The World Bank's Role in the Electric Power Sector* (Washington, DC, IBRD, 1993), pp. 11–18.

32. On the Orissa experience, see Dubash and Rajan 'Power Politics', pp. 3375–9; Gajendra Haldea, 'Whither Electricity Reforms?', in Joel Ruet (ed.), *Against the Current: Organizational Restructuring of State Electricity Boards* (New Delhi: Manonar, 2003), pp. 40–6; Ministry of Power, *Distribution Policy Committee Report – 2001* (New Delhi, Academic Foundation, 2003), pp. 129–33; T.L. Shankar and Usha Ramachandran, 'Electricity Tariff Regulators: The Orissa Experience', *Economic and Political Weekly*, 27 May 2000; and K. Ramanathan and Shahid Hussain, *Privatization of Electricity Distribution: The Orissa Experience* (New Delhi, Tata Energy Research Institute, 2003).

33. Ministry of Power, *Distribution Policy – 2001*, pp. 185–97.

34. On regulatory issues, see Rao, 'Economic Reforms'; S.L. Rao, 'Political Economy of Power', *Economic and Political Weekly*, 17 August 2002, pp. 3441–3; Madhav Godbole, 'Power Sector Woes: No Easy Answers', *Economic and Political Weekly*, 6 September 2003, pp. 3782–3.

35. Tonci Bakovic, Bernard Tenenbaum, and Fiona Wolf, 'Regulation By Contract: A New Way to Privatize Electricity Distribution', World Bank Working Paper No. 14 (Washington, DC, World Bank, 2003), pp. 1–6.

36. Madhav Godbole, 'Electricity Act, 2003: Questionable Wisdom', *Economic and Political Weekly*, vol. 38, no. 39, 27 September 2003, pp. 4104–10.

37. For a comparison of levels of state autonomy in the developing world, see Peter Evans, *Embedded Autonomy: States and Industrial Transformation* (Princeton, NJ: Princeton University Press, 1995).

38. Paul Pierson,' Increasing Returns, Path Dependence, and the Study of Politics', *American Political Science Review* vol. 94, no. 2 (June 2000), pp. 251–67.

39. On the design of IMF programs emphasizing country ownership of programs, see Mohsin S. Khan, 'IMF Conditionality and Country Ownership of Programs' IMF Working Paper 01/142, (Washington, DC, IMF, 2001).

11

Politics of Market Micro-Structure
Towards a New Political Economy of India's Equity Market Reform[*]

Rent-seeking is one of the most seminal concept in political economy in the last 30 years.[2] It transformed most economists' approach to economic development. Its normative implications have revised our understanding of the appropriate role of the state in economic development. Policy-makers have used arguments about rent-seeking as the rationale for a wide range of neoliberal policy reforms. The concept of rent-seeking has also transformed our understanding of the politics of economic reform by explaining why demonstrably inefficient policies persist.

Most who have applied the concept of rent-seeking to development have identified it with a neoclassical understanding of markets.[3] James Buchanan defines rents as 'that part of the payment to an owner of resources over and above that which those resources could command in any alternative use', or, more elegantly, 'receipt in excess of opportunity cost'.[4] He distinguishes between rents that occur in a market context and those created through state intervention. Buchanan contends that rents occurring in a market context are essentially rewards for innovation that enhance social welfare by promoting economic growth and development. Because these rents occur in a neoclassical 'market', they quickly dissipate as competitors emulate the innovator. In contrast, rents created by state intervention diminish social welfare because the intervention establishes rights that redistribute resources exclusively to the beneficiary of these rights. These rights constitute barriers to economic

* This paper was commissioned for this volume.

competition, and they interfere with the dynamic that promotes growth and development in the market context. Even worse, they create a rent-seeking dynamic that destroys value because rent-seeking dissipates resources in an unproductive manner.

In this chapter, I argue that Buchanan's distinction between 'intervention rents' and 'innovation rents' elides a third type of rent: market microstructure rents. The trading rules and institutions that comprise a market microstructure create rents when they benefit particular market participants, who then resist change to alternative rules that would create more efficient markets. The basic premise of market microstructure rents is that alternative trading rules create a variety of market microstructures with a range of consequences for efficiency and the distribution of rewards from competition. In contrast to intervention rents, which are produced by state interventions that restrict competition, market microstructure rents are created by market rules that shape competition in the absence of state intervention. In contrast to innovation rents that are dissipated by competition, market microstructure rents are reinforced by competition because the winners use their rewards to perpetuate existing institutions through new rounds of competition.

Eliminating market microstructure rents requires more than 'saving capitalism from the capitalists'. Ever since Adam Smith, political economists have been concerned that collaboration among capitalists can subvert market competition. Smith famously complained, 'People of the same trade seldom meet together, even for merriment and diversion, but the conversation ends up in a conspiracy against the public, or in some contrivance to raise prices.'[5] Economists Raghuram G. Rajan and Luigi Zingales have expanded on Smith's contentions by arguing,

Capitalism's biggest political enemies are not the firebrand trade unionists spewing vitriol against the system but the executives in pin-striped suits extolling the virtues of competitive markets with every breath while attempting to extinguish them with every action....Unfortunately, all too often and in all too many countries, the conspiracy enlists the help of the state in enforcing limitations on competition.[6]

Market microstructure rents do not require capitalists to secure state intervention to limit competition. Instead, the winners of market competition often resist state initiatives to reform market microstructures.[7]

In this chapter, I contend that the politics of India's equity market microstructure created strong resistance to reform. Part of this resistance was a result of the monopoly rents that India's brokers gained from limiting access to the market. However, analytically distinct conflicts arose from the politics of market microstructure, extending at least as far back as the highly critical Gorwala

Committee Report in 1951.[8] The rapid technological change that characterized financial markets in the last three decades of the twentieth century exacerbated the conflict by increasing the opportunity costs of maintaining India's unreformed equity market microstructure.[9] The informatics revolution made it possible to replace the quote-driven trading system with order-driven, computerized systems that automatically matched buyers and sellers.[10] The new technologies enabled authorities to 'dematerialize' trading through electronic exchange of shareholder rights and payments and thereby banish trading in physical shares and cumbersome settlement rules. Finally, the capital market revolution was based on the development of new financial products. Equity trading was increasingly supplemented by trading in financial derivatives that enable traders to manage risk and speculate on future market trends.[11] India eventually adopted all these innovations, leapfrogging from archaic market institutions and practices in the early 1990s to international best practices at the beginning of the new millennium. But in an effort to defend their market microstructure rents, financial intermediaries and their allies resisted state-sponsored reforms every step of the way.

This chapter examines the politics of equity market microstructure in India. It argues that officials in the Ministry of Finance generated much of the impetus for reform. Three factors motivated these officials to become agents of change. First, their experience made them acutely aware that public sector resources were inadequate to meet India's developmental needs. Second, as the 1990s progressed they were increasingly aware of the global best practices that developed in the wake of technological change. Finally, the legal infrastructure that regulated Indian equity markets provided them tremendous authority over the exchanges. Under the Securities Contracts (Regulation Act) 1956, the Ministry of Finance enjoyed the power to grant or withdraw recognition to any stock exchange. It also had the power to direct the exchanges to make or amend their rules, supersede the governing body of any exchange, and suspend the business of an exchange.[12]

The main opponents to reform were those stockbrokers and their corporate allies whose speculative strategies took advantage of the opportunities presented by central institutions of India's equity market microstructure: account period settlement and *badla* finance.[13] The speculative brokers gained control of the governing board of the Bombay Stock Exchange from 1988 through most of the 1990s. The brokers resisted reforms promoted by the Ministry of Finance by claiming a monopoly over market expertise and articulating an anti-government regulation ideology. While the Ministry of Finance was encouraged to

POLITICS OF MARKET MICRO-STRUCTURE ◆ 331

reform by changes in the global economy and foreign actors such as the World Bank and the foreign institutional investors who came to India in growing numbers during the 1990s, it received very little domestic support for reform. Investors were too dispersed and disorganized. Their presence was felt only in times of crisis when the Ministry of Finance took action to pre-empt popular discontent. Corporations listed on the market were also not major supporters of reform because many of them allied with the brokers to exploit opportunities for speculation and price manipulation.

The situation represented the kind of collective action problem that often impedes economic development—a case where a relatively small group resists reforms that would bring widespread benefits to their society because the reforms would undercut their privileged position. Rajan and Zingales are right to point out that market efficiency represents a public good whose provision is made precarious by the collective action problems that pervade the political process. But the problem is not so much that under competitive markets 'no one in particular makes huge profits from keeping the system competitive and the playing field level. Thus, everyone has an incentives to take a free ride and let someone else defend the system.'[14] Rather, the collective action problem arises because those securing market microstructure rents form a concentrated group of beneficiaries who resist change.

This chapter will begin its investigation of the impact of market microstructure rents on the politics of India's equity market reform by demonstrating how these rents empowered a coalition of speculative brokers to gain control over the governance of the Mumbai Stock Exchange. Next, the chapter demonstrates how the resistance of the BSE ultimately incited the Ministry of Finance to sanction the creation of the National Stock Exchange. It then examines the creation of electronic depositories and dematerialized trading. Next, it analyses the reform of institutions that were at the heart of market microstructure rents: the badla or carry-forward system of finance and the account period settlement. It concludes by contending that the existence of market microstructure rents suggests the need for a more sophisticated understanding of the politics of economic institutions.

MARKET MICROSTRUCTURE RENTS AND POLITICS WITHIN THE BOMBAY STOCK EXCHANGE

Reforming the stock market required securing the cooperation of the brokers who managed India's stock exchanges. Although under the Securities Contract

(Regulation) Act, the Ministry of Finance exercised tremendous authority over the exchanges, it relied on the exchange management to ensure the smooth functioning of the markets, and many of the reforms proposed by the ministry would have to be implemented by the exchanges. The reforms were controversial among the brokers. Supporters tended to be those who were in a position to take advantage of the increasing trade volumes that were supposed to follow the reforms, especially from institutional traders. The opponents of reform were brokers whose business was based on the speculative opportunities provided by the market microstructure.

The speculative trading that thrived under India's equity market institutions not only made some brokers very wealthy, it was also a source of power in the politics of equity-market governance. Badla or 'carry-forward trading' provided brokers with financing to increase their trading volumes and magnify their returns from speculation. Since banks were prohibited from financing brokers, a small number of brokers specialized in providing badla finance. This placed them in central positions of power. Not only did other brokers depend on them for finance, but the badla brokers gained access to information about other brokers' strategies. Their control over finance and access to information put them in a position to assemble groups of brokers acting as bear or bull cartels. Payments crises further enhanced the power of these 'big brokers', because when speculations did not pan out and brokers had trouble making payments, they turned to them for financial help. Even the governing board of the exchanges would turn to the big brokers for assistance in bailing out brokers in order to resolve the payments crises that periodically occurred on the exchange.[15] The result of the big brokers' control over finance was that they were able to lead networks of brokers and form powerful alliances in the elections to the governing board of the exchange.

On 30 March 1987, Mahendra Kampani, the vice-chairman of India's largest private sector merchant banking house, was elected president of the BSE governing board. Kampani was a reformer who advocated modernizing the BSE. He planned to reform the trading rules and upgrade trading technology as part of a long-term plan to facilitate the growth of the exchange. Kampani declared, 'I expect market capitalization will grow four times from Rs 25,000 crores [250 billion rupees] today to Rs 1,00,000 crores [Rs 1 trillion] by 1995. To handle the increased business, it is important to streamline systems, introduce new technologies, increase training, and speed the settlement process.'[16]

Kampani initiated an array of reforms. He had advocated setting up a central depository since 1985.[17] As president of the governing board, he established a training institute for brokers. Kampani negotiated an arrangement with the Bank of India to develop 'a stockholding depository facility'. He established a counter for transactions in odd-lot shares to increase liquidity. He allocated special space for trading debentures, and he initiated the development of a new all-India stock index based on 100 pivotal scrips.[18] Under Kampani, the BSE staff was given the independence to run the exchange according to their managerial expertise.[19] In contrast to most brokers, Kampani favoured permitting India's financial institutions to set up their own brokerages.[20] He welcomed the establishment of an independent regulatory agency.[21] It was during Kampani's tenure as president that the BSE installed the Stockscan system that used a computerized display to report changing market prices. Kampani appointed Tandem, Arthur Anderson, and the Computer Maintenance Corporation to conduct studies on the viability of computerization. With BSE executive director M.R. Mayya, he was said to have gone as far as selecting the computer system that the BSE would purchase to computerize trading.[22]

Kampani's tenure as president was abruptly ended despite his impressive accomplishments. His ouster from the BSE governing board in the March 1988 elections was not only the rejection of a large merchant banker who was viewed as not having the interests of the brokers at heart; it was also a refutation of state intervention in the markets. Many brokers were apprehensive about the changes that Kampani advocated. His view that financial institutions should be permitted to establish their own brokerages was particularly unpopular. Kampani aroused vehement opposition when he acquiesced to a temporary ban on short-selling and speculative trading that the Ministry of Finance imposed in the spring of 1987 after the market suffered a precipitous decline. Brokers began calling him a 'chamcha [sycophant] of the Ministry of Finance'.[23] Trading plummeted, and business fell by two-thirds over the year. Later, Kampani ran afoul of a powerful cartel of brokers who were waging a bear campaign against Bombay Silk Mills, a textile firm that he served as a director. The company fought the bear attack by buying up its shares. When it asked for delivery, the over-committed brokers were unable to deliver. As was its practice at the time, the BSE governing board arranged for a settlement, but the terms were viewed as unfavourable to the brokers. Kampani got pinned with the blame, even though he had recused himself from the decisions made by the governing board.[24]

The ouster of Kampani was led by brokers who reaped immense benefits from the BSE's market microstructure rents. Manu Manek, the protypical 'badla king, led the opposition.'[25] This 'dalal of dalals' was reported to control as many as twelve membership cards on the Bombay Stock Exchange (BSE), and he had many other brokers who served as his agents in speculative strategies made possible by market institutions such as badla and account period settlements.[26] While Manek cultivated a range of contacts across India's parties and government bureaucracies, he was a quintessential businessman who kept a low profile and used his political contacts to advance his business aims. Manek's involvement in the politics of the BSE was intended to enforce his view that the operations of the stock market should be free of government interference. His laissez-faire views extended to the internal governance of the BSE, and he was known to oppose rental increases and what he considered exorbitant fines levied by the exchange. Manek also resisted computerized trading.[27] Prior to the 30 March 1988 governing board elections, Manek organized a dinner at which the brokers formed a slate of candidates in opposition to Mahendra Kampani. Though Manek himself did not run, his slate of candidates won control over the board, and he played a key role in selecting the president of the exchange.

Manek's influence at the BSE gradually waned in the years before his death in 1997. It was supplanted by that of M.G. Damani, who provided a very different type of leadership. Unlike Manek, who had traded for years on the exchange and whose business was his primary concern, M.G. Damani was never a big trader. In fact, he spent much of his early career managing textile mills. Damani was more interested in the politics of the BSE. He attempted to transform the BSE Sharebrokers Forum—an organization that had until then served as a liaison between brokers and the sharebrokers' staff union to address their labour relations—into the primary forum for representing the BSE brokers' interests. Unlike Manek, who was a non-partisan, Damani was known to attend various functions of the Bharatiya Janata Party (BJP), which shared Damani's aversion to government regulation and his suspicion of foreigners. During the early 1990s Damani built support among the brokers by vociferously opposing SEBI's efforts to register brokers and impose a hefty turnover tax. Despite the headlines he garnered, Damani could not win elections to the BSE governing board until 1993, when he reached an accommodation with Manu Manek who then allotted him a slot on his slate. Damani and his allies, Bhagirath Merchant and J.C. Parekh, served as presidents of the BSE from 1994 through March of 1999 with the exception of 1995–6 when Kamal Kabra presided over the office.[28] Under the leadership of Manek and Damani, the brokers' resistance to reforms initiated by SEBI and the Ministry of Finance was an important factor shaping the politics of reform.

COMPUTERIZED TRADING AND THE CREATION OF THE NATIONAL STOCK EXCHANGE

The leaders of the Bombay Stock Exchange had talked about computerizing its operations ever since 1979 when BSE chairman Jeejeebhoy raised the possibility. Computerization had been financially and technologically feasible in India for quite some time. Kanpur's computerized stock exchange was up and running in 1990. Yet the BSE, India's most prestigious exchange, only computerized its trading system in 1995. To explain why, we must examine how the forces within the BSE resisted the introduction of new trading technologies in order to protect their market microstructure rents.

Resistance to computerization at the BSE was particularly strong because computerization was perceived to be detrimental to the speculative brokers whose interests were safeguarded by the governing board. Computerized trading usually involves a shift from a quote-driven to an order-driven system. This shift eliminates the opportunities for brokers to make profits by serving as 'jobbers' quoting prices for purchases and sales.[29] Under the trading rules at the BSE, brokers were not required to inform investors of the exact time and price at which they transacted. This lack of accountability enabled brokers to take advantage of investors by overcharging them and by speculating with their shares or money. By replacing the manual entry of trades into the exchanges records, computerization would prevent the practice of illicit 'adjustment entries' made after transactions to the prices or number of shares traded in an effort to enhance their profits.[30] On-line trading would minimize opportunities to take advantage of price differentials among the exchanges by facilitating expeditious communication of trading at various exchanges. Computerization would create an easily accessible record of each transaction, thereby making it easier for the authorities to catch insider trading. Brokers were particularly unhappy with the fact that computerization would provide more detailed information about their trading activities to SEBI, the government regulator.[31]

The Ministry of Finance had long favoured the computerization of India's stock exchanges. It had been an important recommendation of the 1985 report of the High-Powered Committee on Stock Exchange Reform convened by the ministry.[32] Under Manmohan Singh, the Ministry of Finance pushed harder. In August 1991, it approved the recommendations of the Pherwani Committee to set up a computerized 'National Stock Market System' that would create a computer-network to integrate trading on India's 21 regional exchanges. In addition, the committee recommended the establishment of a National Clearing and Settlement Corporation and a Central Depository Trust. It suggested that public sector enterprises could be listed on the exchange as a first step towards privatization. The Pherwani Committee also urged that the National Stock Market System develop a debt market, especially for long-term, fixed income securities. Seventy-five per cent of the members of the new exchange were to be professionals meeting strict standards for their qualifications. Members of existing exchanges would be limited to 25 per cent of the seats on the new exchange. In an effort to assuage the concerns of the BSE, the Pherwani committee recommended that the National Stock Market System be restricted to medium-sized companies, and 'companies that are initially listed on the NMS would eventually graduate for listing on the BSE.'[33]

The BSE viewed the National Stock Market system as a threat. It responded in three ways. First, it gave the appearance of expediting the technological modernization of the exchange. BSE executive director M.R. Mayya declared, 'Our people have taken the implementation schedules for computerization of trading on a war footing...'[34] A reporter observed that the BSE was

panic-stricken at the thought that an outside agency...might decide what was best for the capital market...Modernization plans are being announced every day—so far, the BSE has unveiled plans to introduce screen-based trading by April 1992, have a separate trading floor/time for debentures and debt instruments, put in place a separate electronic exchange and introduce corporate membership with a single card.'[35]

At the same time that it offered plans to modernize its own operations, the BSE attempted to discredit the Pherwani Committee proposals by hiring Arthur Anderson to conduct a study that criticized their report.[36] Finally, the BSE approached Murli Deora, the Congress party member of parliament who represented Mumbai, to present their case to the government.[37]

'The NSE was created only because of the BSE's resistance to the changes being promoted by the MoF and SEBI,' observed G.B. Desai, who served as BSE President during this period.[38] Key actors in SEBI and the Ministry of Finance resisted the creation of the NSE through much of 1992. G.V. Ramakrishna, the chair of SEBI, withheld his support to the proposal for a computerized national exchange, instead hoping that he could use it to pressure the BSE to modernize.[39] In the Ministry of Finance, the file concerning the creation of a computerized national exchange remained with Ashok V. Desai, special advisor to the ministry.[40] Desai also was inclined to give the BSE the benefit of the doubt and wait for it to modernize. However, during the year following the Pherwani report, the brokers at the BSE defiantly resisted SEBI initiatives to register them and levy a turnover tax. The BSE became enmeshed in the Harshad Mehta scandal, the largest scam in India's history. As Desai's concerns about their plan to modernize grew, he decided to visit Mumbai to see for himself what was really happening. It soon became clear that the BSE board members had no idea what it meant to computerize, and there was little hope that the BSE would computerize on their own. It was then that he shifted his support to the creation of the National Stock Exchange.

There is an irony in the Government of India, the creator of one of the most regulated non-communist economies in the world, sponsoring the establishment of a new securities market. Yet there is also a certain consistency. If the Indian government could set up a financial system dominated by the public sector, why could it not establish a securities market? Officials from the Ministry of Finance met with executives of the public sector Industrial Development Bank of India (IDBI) at the end of 1992 to begin developing plans for the NSE. S.S. Nadkarni, chair of IDBI, placed R.H. Patil at the head of a small team of IDBI officials to plan for the NSE. The team enjoyed a great deal of autonomy for its project, in part because Nadkarni had enough clout within the government to protect it and in part because virtually everyone outside the government expected the project to fail. The team fashioned its project in a most ambitious manner nonetheless. It rejected the National Stock Market System model proposed in the Pherwani report because, in the words of Ravi Narain, who became managing director in 2000, 'It was a "patches and bandaids" approach. We wanted to create a new system.'[41] The team also might have built on the electronic trading system that was already being operated by the Over the Counter Exchange of India (OTCEI). However, the IDBI team viewed the OTCEI, which was managed by its rival, the Industrial Credit and Investment Corporation of India, as being, 'based on a narrow vision...It was purely a market maker's market...It had a small capital base. Its technological base was not good enough. We thought everything was small. We conceptualized the NSE at the other end.'[42]

The NSE model was created in reaction to the problems that pervaded the broker-dominated BSE. Unlike the BSE, which was a non-profit association of persons—as were virtually all other stock exchanges in the world at the time—the NSE is a publicly owned, for-profit corporation. In contrast to the BSE, where brokers, as partners of the association, elect the governing board that is responsible for managing the exchange, the NSE's management is autonomous from the brokers and is responsible to the owners of the exchange—primarily public sector financial institutions. The separation of management from the brokers served to minimize the conflicts of interest that have impeded the adoption of new technologies on the BSE. Difference in the governance of the BSE and NSE also shaped their approach to membership. Concern to maximize the value of the brokers' membership cards led the BSE management to resist expanding the exchange's membership. The NSE's management, in contrast, was eager to attract professionally qualified members across the country. While the BSE attempted to protect the interests of its proprietor-owned or partnership-based brokerage firms by limiting the membership of corporate-owned brokerages, the NSE encouraged corporate ownership. Corporations or individuals could become members at the NSE by making a Rs 10 million interest-free deposit with the exchange and agreeing to pay a fixed fee on their trading volume. The Rs 10 million deposit was substantially less than the price of a BSE membership card at the time. As of March 2004, 89 per cent of the NSE's 891 members were corporates.[43]

The IDBI team was under pressure from the Ministry of Finance to get the system up and running as quickly as possible, and they put together a system with remarkable speed.[44] They hired Hong Kong-based International Securities Consultancy to assist with the project. It decided to use the TCAM System that was developed in the United States for the Vancouver Stock Exchange as the basis for their trading system. It selected a consortium of software developers led by Tata Consultancy Services to adapt the system. To overcome the problems of India's poor telecommunications infrastructure, the NSE became the first stock exchange in the world to use satellite communications to enable trading across the country. The trading system that was developed, the National Exchange for Automated Trading (NEAT), permits participants across the nation to simultaneously view the full market on a real-time basis, greatly improving the access of investors outside Mumbai, who previously had to work through multiple intermediaries to gain access to the country's largest market. By adding investors outside traditional centres, NEAT improved the market's depth and liquidity. NEAT permits investors to see prices on a computer screen before trading, and it automatically matches orders on a strict price/time priority. In doing so, it increases the transparency of the market. It promotes the efficiency of price discovery, and it minimizes the inefficiencies resulting from the vagaries of the open-outcry system. By enabling market participants to trade anonymously, the NSE's trading system promotes equal market access and curbs insider trading. At the same time, NEAT provides an audit trail that helps to resolve disputes and facilitates regulatory enforcement.[45]

The first trading on the NSE took place in its wholesale debt market in June 1994. Trading in its capital market segment began in November 1994. Few, least of all the brokers of the BSE, expected the NSE to succeed. However, the advantages of the NSE's technological infrastructure along with the pent-up demand for trading in areas outside Mumbai—by 1996–7 almost 60 per cent of the NSE's trading came from outside Mumbai[46]—contributed to the NSE's remarkable rapid growth. By October 1995—less than a year after it opened for trading—the NSE became India's largest stock exchange. In 2003–4, the NSE accounted for 67 per cent of India's trading volume, substantially exceeding turnover at India's second largest exchange, the BSE, where 31 per cent of trading occurred.[47] In terms of the number of transactions, the NSE has been the third largest exchange in the world since 2002.[48] In 2005, trading on the NSE was conducted in 345 cities through 2829 VSAT terminals.[49]

The success of the NSE has established a competitive dynamic that has expedited equity market reform. In order to avoid losing out to the NSE, the BSE and other Indian exchanges have had to adopt similar innovations. Furthermore, the demonstration effect created by the NSE bolstered the commitment of the Ministry of Finance and SEBI to compel innovation at the other exchanges. After years of stonewalling, the BSE converted to electronic trading in March 1995. By the end of 1999, all 23 of India's stock exchanges had installed electronic trading systems. As the NSE and BSE have expanded their trading networks across the country, the share of trading on India's 21 regional exchanges has declined precipitously. In 2003–4, the NSE and BSE together accounted for 98 per cent of total turnover in value terms.[50]

The NSE's Transformation of Clearing and Counter-Party Risk

The NSE developed important institutional innovations for clearing and risk management. Settlement and clearing at the BSE and India's other exchanges involved significant counter-party risk since trading partners often did not live up to their commitments. Brokers at the BSE attempted to control counter-party risk in primitive ways. They intuitively sized up their trading partners and assessed their reputation. The BSE governing board dealt with failure to meet commitments by negotiating some form of accommodation to make the commitment good, even when negotiating arrangements delayed trading and forced the exchange to close. The system worked to the disadvantage of investors—who suffered from the trading delays—and brokers who were not well connected and therefore less likely to be awarded a favourable settlement. It also created moral hazard for speculative brokers, and it inadequately protected against systemic risk.

In 1996, the NSE established the National Securities Clearing Corporation Limited (NSCC) as a wholly owned subsidiary in an effort to alleviate these problems. The NSCC introduced clearing and risk management principles that were widely used outside India. It eliminated counter-party risk by becoming the legal counter-party to the obligations taken on by each party of a transaction. The NSCC made payments to the seller and then took payments from the buyer. It delivered shares to buyers and took delivery from the seller. It then managed this risk by building up a substantial Settlement Guarantee Fund from the contributions of brokers as well as by imposing a rigorous system of margins enforced by an innovative system of on-line position monitoring and automatic disablement. Since its establishment, the NSCC has never failed to make good on its fulfilment of trading obligations, and the NSE has consistently kept to its settlement schedule, not once suffering from the payments crises that have troubled other exchanges.[51]

Ending the Registration Bottleneck: From Physical Certificates to Electronic Depositories

Until the late 1990s, equity transactions were completed only after the transfer of ownership was recorded by the registrar of the company whose equity had been traded. Before they could enjoy ownership rights, new owners were required to send transfer documents along with the equity certificates to the company registrar in order to have their name entered into the company's records as shareowners. The procedure presented two sets of problems. One had to do with the share certificates. During the 1990s, forgery of share certificates became an increasingly serious problem.[52] In 1995 and 1996 duplicate share certificates for equity in Reliance Industries, India's largest private sector firm, created a major scandal.[53] There were also problems with *benami* shares, or floating share certificates that had not been properly registered. In 1995, the Income Tax Department reported that the value of improperly registered, *benami* shares was Rs 500 billion.[54] The second set of problems concerned the registration of new ownership with company registrars. Sending documents through the Indian postal service was a precarious proposition that often involved substantial delays. The problems of physically transferring share certificates became especially acute after 1992 when foreign institutional investors traded in unprecedented volumes. Part of the problem was simply the slothfulness of the companies' departments for share registration. Companies often used discrepancies in the documents such as minor differences in signatures as a pretext for returning the documents without approval. At times, they deliberately withheld shares from the market to raise share prices.

Having created a reliable and expeditious clearing system, the NSE was able to eliminate registration problems by introducing share transfers through electronic depositories. A depository, in effect, functions as an electronic bank with accounts that hold an investor's securities. Having registered their securities with the depository, investors no longer need physical certificates. Registration is 'dematerialized' in the sense that transfer of ownership is registered through entries into the investors' electronic accounts.

During the summer of 1996 Parliament passed the Depositories Act enabling the establishment of electronic depositories. In October 1996, the NSE joined with the Industrial Development Bank of India and the Unit Trust of India to inaugurate the country's first depository, the National Securities Depository Ltd. (NSDL). To give dematerialized trading through the depository a jumpstart, SEBI ordered all institutional investors to settle their trades through a depository for a limited number of scrips beginning 15 January 1998. It further promoted dematerialized trading by making it mandatory in an increasing number of stocks. By March 2004, 5216 companies had joined the NSDL and dematerialized securities are valued at Rs 9662 billion. 5.2 million investor accounts had been opened with the NSDL. The NSDL serviced investors through 214 depository participants in 1719 locations.[55] By the end of June 2001, dematerialized settlement accounted for more than 99 per cent of turnover settled by delivery.[56] India's rapid conversion to dematerialized trading through a depository is a remarkable success by international standards.

One of the issues debated during passage of the Depositories Act of 1996 was whether the act should permit the establishment of one or more depository. Some analysts contend that a depository is very much like a natural monopoly with considerable advantages derived from its scale of operations. The benefits derived from the scale of operations justify having only a single depository. This position, for instance, is the basis for the American financial system allowing only a single depository. Others have contended that the benefits that can be derived from competition justify having multiple depositories. Wishing to avoid being left behind by the NSE and eager for the profits that a depository can bring, supporters of the Bombay Stock Exchange joined with those advocating multiple depositories. In February 1999, SEBI authorized the BSE in conjunction with its clearinghouse BOI Shareholding Ltd to launch the Central

Depository for Securities Ltd (CDSL) under the chairmanship of M.G. Damani, who completed his final term as president of the BSE in March of 1998. SEBI's authorization reflected a remarkable exercise of persuasion by the BSE in light of the fact that it came in the midst of a widely publicized SEBI investigation of the exchange's management after a payments crisis in June 1998. Rajendra Banthia, vice-president of the BSE, had been forced to resign in November 1998, and within weeks of SEBI's approval for the CDSL, the regulator ordered the removal of BSE president J.C. Parekh and BSE executive director, R.C. Mathur. Despite the controversy that surrounded its early days, 4810 companies agreed to make their securities available in dematerialized form through the CDSL by March 2004. The depository had 211 depository participants with 441 branches to service investors; however, the CDSL had attracted only 629,159 investor accounts.[57]

Battle over Badla: The Politics of Introducing Derivatives and Rolling Settlement

Badla, or carry-forward trading and the ability to 'net' trades over extended account period settlements were central to the market microstructure rents that benefited many brokers at the BSE. The masters of badla won personal fortunes. They constructed networks of supporters to assist in their speculative plays, and they were able to translate their wealth and loyalty from brokers into influence over the governing boards of the exchanges. Two steps were required to effectively replace badla: reforms must offer alternative means for proper hedging, and they must replace account period settlements with a system that does not encourage excessive speculation.

The government had banned badla several times before the 1990s, but irresistible pressure always arose to restore it. After wild market gyrations, G.V. Ramakrishna, the controversial head of SEBI, imposed another ban on badla on 13 December 1993.[58] His successors S.S. Nadkarni and D.R. Mehta looked for a compromise that would reform badla to include safeguards to the market that were acceptable to the brokers. Restoring badla was such a top priority for Mehta that he convened the G.S. Patel Committee to consider the matter on the day after he assumed his post at SEBI. The Patel Committee took less than a month to issue its recommendations, and badla was reintroduced at most Indian exchanges on 19 January 1996. The National Stock Exchange initially refused to permit badla, but on 10 February 1999 it introduced its own carry-forward product, the Automatic Lending and Borrowing Mechanism (ALBM). The ALBM functioned very much like a computerized form of badla with the difference that the NSSC served as an intermediary for all transactions and the ALBM functioned only for dematerialized stocks.[59] On 22 January 2001, the BSE replaced the modified carry-forward system that had been introduced according to the Patel Committee recommendations in 1996 with the Borrowing and Lending Securities Scheme (BLESS). The introduction of BLESS was in part a consequence of the fact that the ALBM had been taking business away from the BSE. It was also motivated by the fact that BLESS relaxed the restrictions on badla that had been imposed by the modified carry-forward system.[60]

Exchange-traded derivatives provide an attractive alternative to badla. In essence, the weekly or fortnightly settlement system that prevailed in India until 2001 was a type of futures market. Traders enter into an agreement to buy or sell at an agreed upon price at the future settlement date. Traders do not have a facility for managing the risk between the date of their transaction and the settlement. Badla is at best only a very crude means of hedging. It only allows traders to manage their risk by postponing payment from one settlement to the next. And unlike derivatives, which are traded on a separate exchange, badla trading is mixed with the cash market and can therefore distort price discovery. In fact, this capacity to distort price discovery on the cash market is what makes badla attractive to speculators wishing to profit by creating false market signals.

The NSE has played a key role in bringing to India the revolution in risk management that follows the introduction of derivatives. The inherent difficulty of creating a liquid derivative market in a developing country and its sensitivity to the opposition of the BSE caused SEBI to treat the issue with extreme care. The NSE requested permission to begin trading in index futures as early as 14 December 1995. SEBI did not respond until November 1996 when it announced the formation of a committee headed by L.C. Gupta to make policy recommendations for derivatives trading. The Gupta committee included 24 members, an extraordinarily large size as such committees go, representing a broad range of opinion.[61] The unwieldy committee deliberated for a lengthy period. It announced its recommendations in March 1998. Even after 17 months of deliberation, the recommendations were surrounded with controversy because one member, M.G. Damani, the president of the Bombay Stock Exchange, charged that the committee issued its recommendations prematurely.[62] Damani added a lengthy dissenting note to the committee's recommendations, in which he vehemently expressed two concerns. First, he contended that the report did not prescribe the details of the regulatory framework for derivatives trading. He opposed the committee's decision to leave

344 ♦ INDIA'S ECONOMIC TRANSITION

this to SEBI and the exchanges, a position that contradicted his overall aversion to government regulation of stock exchanges. Second, Damani warned,

In the last two years, we have witnessed a new phenomenon in out [*sic*] stock markets which is FII's capacity to influence the movement of index...Our market may be bled white; instead of more foreign exchange coming in by way of FII portfolio invest-ment, much more foreign exchange will be drained out by way of repatriation of profits....Between the hedging demand of the FII's and interest of the nation, the latter is more important.[63]

Once an enabling amendment was passed to the Securities Contracts Regula-tion Act in November 1999, SEBI gave its authorization. In June 2000, the NSE and the BSE initiated derivatives trading in the form of index futures. Futures based on the NSE's Nifty Index also began to be traded on Singapore's Simex Exchange. Trading in index options was authorized in June 2001, and trading in options on individual securities was initiated in July 2001. Futures trading on individual stocks was introduced in November 2001. Derivatives trading has grown rapidly. Total trading volume increased from Rs 1038 billion in 2001–2, its first full year of trading, to more than Rs 21,422 billion in 2003–4.[64]

At the same time that derivative trading was being introduced, reforms were gradually moving India from its account period settlement to rolling settlement. Until 1994 when the settlement period was reduced to one week, India's stock exchanges operated on a two-week settlement system in which the period between a transaction and settlement could be as long as 14 days. During the interim, market participants could square off their trades and be responsible only for the net difference. The system promoted unhealthy speculation be-cause it provided traders with 'infinite leverage' in the sense that if market trends moved in the direction anticipated, traders need not put up any cash or equity at all since they could net their earlier trade and collect the profits.[65] Rolling settlements, in contrast, fix the net position of all traders after the daily trading session and require them to settle each daily position after a fixed period. Under a T+5 rolling settlement, a net position at the end of any day (T) must be settled on the fifth working day after T. Reducing the period for netting to a day greatly limits the scope for intra-settlement speculation. By doing so, rolling settlements effectively separate the cash market from the futures market. Since netting occurs at the end of each day on every exchange, rolling settlement reduces the opportunity for arbitrage between exchanges.

Proponents contend that by distinguishing the market for delivery from speculation, rolling settlement promotes greater transparency and improves price discovery. It is also said to promote better regulation and to reduce default and systemic risk. Finally, advocates point out that adopting rolling settlement moves India towards the international standard. India was one of the last major countries to adopt rolling settlements.[66]

Opponents of rolling settlement countered that rolling settlements would reduce liquidity in markets that can ill afford such reductions. They also contended that India's market infrastructure is not ready for rolling settlement, citing, for instance, the need for more bank branches with electronic fund transfer facilities.

Measures to move from account period to rolling settlement enmeshed the Ministry of Finance and SEBI in the rivalry between the BSE and the NSE. At its founding, the NSE declared that shortening the settlement period would be one of its main objectives.[67] However, adopting rolling settlement along with index-based derivatives threatened to undermine the badla system prevailing on the BSE. It would transform institutions of market microstructure that shape the field of competition between India's two largest markets in ways that disadvantaged the more speculative brokers at the BSE.

The Ministry of Finance has consistently pushed for the adoption of rolling settlement. Finance Minister Yashwant Sinha publicly voiced his support. Implementation of rolling settlement is, however, under the jurisdiction of SEBI, and the regulatory agency moved equivocally in the face of efforts by the BSE to salvage badla.

SEBI's deference to the interest of the BSE was apparent in the manner it attempted to implement rolling settlement while allowing the BSE to develop a compatible form of badla. SEBI's reluctance to transfer shares traded in the BSE's badla system to rolling settlement threatened the success of the new settlement system. As long as the market's most liquid stocks remained in the less restricted badla system, there was little incentive to trade in rolling settlement stocks: thus, the move to rolling settlement could fail due to lack of liquidity.

On 15 January 1998 SEBI initiated a T+5 rolling settlement on an optional basis for eight stocks with dematerialized trading. On 15 September 1999, SEBI released a list of 45 stocks to be moved to rolling settlement.[68] Fifteen were from the BSE's 'A group' of 200 stocks traded on the badla market. Including scrips from this group of prestigious stocks that account for 85 to 94 per cent of the trading volume on the BSE was arguably vital to the success of rolling settlement.[69] However, before rolling settlement could be expanded, SEBI reduced the number of stocks placed under rolling settlement to 10, none of which were on the BSE's A list.[70] By August 2000, SEBI had placed 153 additional scrips under rolling settlement, but the list still did not include stocks traded under the BSE's badla system.[71] The continued exclusion of 'A group' stocks placed SEBI in the position of appearing to protect the practice of badla to the detriment of rolling settlement.

SEBI had included 'A group' stocks in its list for rolling settlement with the hope that a modified badla system compatible with rolling settlement would be in place. The BSE had submitted a proposal for modified badla at the beginning of September 1999. However, snags delayed the implementation of the new system. In the last week of October, SEBI created a committee chaired by board member J.R. Varma to consider the transition to rolling settlement.[72] The committee recommended implementation of the modified badla system, but the similarity of the proposal with futures on individual stocks incited controversy at a SEBI board meeting on 25 January 2000, and SEBI delayed issuing its approval of the revised badla system until 14 June 2000.[73] At this time, SEBI announced that 'A group' scrips would be included in rolling settlement as soon as the exchanges could modify their software to operationalize modified badla. The BSE told SEBI that it would take three months to ready the software for modified badla.[74] After meeting with the stock exchanges on 23 August, SEBI announced that the software would be ready by the end of November.[75] On 21 November 2000 the BSE finally initiated a modified badla system for 15 stocks on an experimental basis.[76]

SEBI's approach to badla and rolling settlement changed dramatically with the securities scam that broke out in March 2001. Parliamentary debates put intense pressure on Finance Minister Yashwant Sinha to demonstrate that he was cleaning up the mess. SEBI itself was discredited by its failure to take measures to prevent the scam as well as by its initial measures to minimize its impact. The Ministry of Finance put intense pressure on SEBI to act, and SEBI was eager to oblige. On 13 March, Yashwant Sinha announced in the Rajya Sabha that rolling settlement would be extended to the 200 prestigious stocks that were under the ALBM/BLESS system. On 15 March, SEBI asked all stock exchanges to create the infrastructure necessary for rolling settlement in these stocks. On 26 April, a SEBI panel proposed that ALBM and BLESS be banned as of 2 July. The panel also urged that trading in futures and options be created for individual stocks. After SEBI head D.R. Mehta met with Finance Minister Sinha on 10 May to review the steps taken in the wake of the scam, the SEBI board met on 15 May and ratified the ban of ALBM and BLESS. On 2 July, the 200 'A list' stocks were moved to rolling settlement and ALBM and BLESS were banned.

The banning of ALBM and BLESS and the transfer of the badla stocks from account period to rolling settlement occurred at a time when brokers were financially hard pressed. Trading volumes had already declined by 80 per cent after the March 2001 securities scam, drastically curtailing the revenues of most brokers. The banning of the carry-forward systems imposed an additional decline of trading volumes and another blow to the viability of many brokers' businesses. Switching from badla to derivative trading required extra capital investment. Furthermore, in January 2001, the Supreme Court had decided against the brokers in a five-year old legal dispute over SEBI's right to impose a 0.01 per cent turnover tax, and now SEBI was insisting that brokers pay up their back taxes. All this took place in face of unfavourable long-term trends, especially for small and regional brokers. The spread of screen-based trading had increased competition and lowered brokerage fees. Internet trading, which the NSE had initiated in 2000, put further pressure on broker revenues. With the presence of foreign institutional investors and the growth of India's mutual fund sector, institutional trading accounted for a growing share of overall volumes. Smaller brokers were unlikely to get institutional business and were increasingly cut out of the action. The spread of the NSE and the BSE throughout the country meant that trading volumes at regional exchanges dried up, placing most regional brokers in unviable financial positions.

The brokers organized and protested against the changes imposed by the Ministry of Finance and SEBI. Brokers at the Ahmedabad and Kanpur stock exchanges began strikes at the beginning of July 2001. The Ahmedabad brokers were so incensed that they burned SEBI chair D.R. Mehta in effigy. Brokers in Mumbai marched on SEBI headquarters.[77] On 23 July, for the first time in history, brokers across India went on strike. They formed the Securities Industry Association of India (SIAI) and selected Deena Mehta, chairperson of the BSE Brokers Forum, as its spokesperson. The SIAI demanded the restoration of carry-forward trading, liberalization of finance to stockbrokers and investors, concessions from SEBI on the turnover tax issue, greater accountability of the regulator, and recognition of the brokers' domain of knowledge along with an end to 'broker bashing'.[78] The SIAI lobbied hard for its demands, meeting with regional strongman Sharad Pawar and Mumbai MPs Jaywantiben Mehta and Kirit Somaiya. On 27 August 2001 they met with Finance Minister Yashwant Sinha who sat patiently through the brokers' presentation but did not budge an inch.[79] Despite the brokers' demands, badla trading remained banned and rolling settlement moved forward. All remaining stocks were switched to rolling settlement on 31 December 2001. On 1 April 2002, the Indian markets moved from rolling settlement on a T+5 basis to a T+3 basis. The settlement cycle was accelerated to T+2 on 1 April 2003. In a matter of ten years, India transformed the settlement system from one of the most archaic in the world to one that is at the frontier of global best practices.

CONCLUDING REMARKS

By 2001, reforms brought India up to par with the global standards for virtually every aspect of its equity market microstructure. The 'open outcry' system that restricted trading to the floors of stock exchanges in India's metropolises was replaced by screen-based, electronic order-book systems that instantaneously linked traders across the country through the world's first satellite trading system. Virtually all trading took place on a dematerialized basis through a central depository. The deeply flawed account period settlement system was replaced by a T+2 rolling settlement that is one of the most efficient systems in the world, and badla or carry-forward trading gave way to a rapidly developing derivatives market. As a consequence of these changes, the total value of transactions in securities has grown dramatically over the last ten years from Rs 1.7 billion in 1994–5 to Rs 50.8 billion in 2003–4,[80] and in the wake of the implementation of rolling settlements, market liquidity has improved dramatically.[81] All this is not to suggest that no problems remain. The micromarket structure of the primary market (despite its revival since 2003–4, in part because of the introduction of a screen-based book-building system) is still in need of reform.[82] The share of household savings invested in securities is small and has declined since the early 1990s. The mutual fund industry remains underdeveloped, and the regulatory capacity of SEBI needs enhancement. Nonetheless, the transformation of Indian equity markets is a remarkably successful chapter in the story of India's economic reform.

Three factors help to explain this success. First, technological change in the form of electronic trading systems and the development of new financial products created substantial opportunity costs to maintaining the status quo. Second, in the context of India's balance of payments crisis in 1991, officials in the Ministry of Finance were motivated by their growing awareness of global best practices to use their authority to modernize India's capital market. Finally, India's politicians and reformers in the Ministry of Finance had a relatively low 'political cost-benefit ratio' for reforming equity markets.[83] Equity market reform promised to ease demands on India's budgetary resources and attract foreign investment. At the same time, the reformers were not confronted by strong public sector institutions with vested interests in the status quo (such as in the banking sector) or the opposition of powerful political constituencies. Political resistance came primarily from India's broker community. Changes in the 1980s and 1990s contributed to a differentiation of interests in the community. While a faction intent on resisting reforms gained control over the governance of the BSE and other exchanges, its ability to resist was diminished by financial scandals. The brokers' resistance was, however, not without consequences. Their adamant refusal to modernize the BSE led the Ministry of Finance to support the creation of the National Stock Exchange. The NSE became an important impetus for reform, and its success compelled the BSE to follow.

The capacity of market microstructure rents to perpetuate inefficient market institutions undercuts the neoliberal position that economic development can be promoted by minimizing state intervention and maximizing the role of the market. Actors attempting to perpetuate market microstructure rents differ from rent-seekers as depicted by neoliberals. The brokers who resisted reforms did not rely on government intervention to give them exclusive rights. The institution of badla was not established through state intervention; rather, it evolved from competitive practices on the market. Nor was it sustained by state intervention. On the contrary, the pre-eminence of the BSE was perpetuated by the natural monopoly that it achieved through its superior liquidity and the social networks that formed from its patterns of trade.[84] Badla could not be terminated by turning matters over to the market. Ending the practice of badla necessitated state action, not just to prohibit it but also to create new market institutions such as derivatives and rolling settlement to supplant it.

The criticism that the neoliberal approach to markets fails to account for the impact of variable market institutions provides grounds for criticizing recent trends in comparative political economy. In recent years, political economists have focused on the economic impact of political institutions to the neglect of political impact of economic institutions. Their silence regarding the politics of market microstructure has inadvertently supported neoliberal claims that markets are inherently apolitical and efficient. Economists, having become increasingly interested in the consequences of imperfect information, multiple equilibria, and Pareto suboptimality, are more aware of the market imperfections. Recent work by leading economists such as Douglass North and Elahan Helpman has noted the importance of proper economic institutions for promoting economic growth; however, they have not adequately analysed the political process by which these institutions are created or stifled.[85] This study suggests that political economy should analyse the politics of markets as well as the politics of states. Since politics shapes the evolution of market institutions, political analysis has an important contribution to make in explaining variations in market institutions and ultimate developmental outcomes.

NOTES AND REFERENCES

1. An earlier version of this paper was presented at the annual meeting of the American Political Science Association, Boston, MA, 28 August–30 September 2002. The author wishes to express his appreciation to Durgesh Kasbekar, Alex Toma, and Jerry Meyerle for their outstanding research assistance. Thanks to Herman Schwartz, Lloyd Rudolph, Susanne Rudolph, Rob Jenkins, Sugata Bhattacharya, and the members of Network on South Asian Politics and Political Economy for their comments on an earlier version of this paper. Very special thanks to Ajay Shah and Susan Thomas for their gracious help and in some cases co-participation in fieldwork as well as for their generous sharing of their ideas about India's equity markets.

2. Seminal contributions to this huge literature are Anne O. Krueger, 'The Political Economy of the Rent-Seeking Society', *American Economic Review* 64: 3, June (1974), pp. 291–303; and Jagdish N. Bhagwati, 'Directly Unproductive, Profit-seeking (DUP) Activities', *Journal of Political Economy* 80: 5 (1982), pp. 988–1002. For a seminal development of the idea of rent-seeking to developing countries, see Robert H. Bates, *Markets and States in Tropical Africa* (Berkeley, University of California Press, 1981). For an interesting application to India, see Prem Shankar Jha, *India: A Political Economy of Stagnation* (New Delhi, Oxford University Press, 1980).

3. Of course, the concept of rents preceded the development of neoclassical economics, having been developed by classical political economists.

4. James M. Buchanan, 'Rent-seeking and Profit-seeking', in James M. Buchanan, R.D. Tollison and Gordon Tullock (eds), *Toward a Theory of the Rent-seeking Society* (College Station, Texas A&M University Press, 1980), p. 3.

5. Adam Smith, *The Wealth of Nations* (London, Penguin Books, [1776] 1999), p. 232.

6. Raghuram G. Rajan and Luigi Zingales, *Saving Capitalism from the Capitalists* (New York, Crown Business, 2003), p. 276.

7. The approach is similar to that of Neil Fligstein, *The Architecture of Markets: An Economic Sociology of Twenty-First Century Capitalist States* (Princeton, Princeton University Press, 2001). However, the notion of market microstructure rents differs from Fligstein's assertion that efficiency is socially constructed since it is premised on the notion that we can apply some objective standard to discern the relative levels of efficiency of different market microstructures.

8. John Echeverri-Gent, 'Governance Regimes and Equity Market Development', unpublished manuscript, University of Virginia. 5 October 2004.

9. Accessible discussions of the dramatic transformation of financial markets include Patrick Young and Thomas Theys, *Capital Market Revolution* (London, Financial Times–Prentice Hall, 1999); and Peter L. Bernstein, *Against the Gods: The Remarkable Story of Risk* (New York, John Wiley and Sons, 1996).

10. In a quote-driven system, 'market makers' (sometimes called 'specialists,' or 'jobbers') intermediate between buyers and sellers by offering to buy or sell securities at particular prices. The 'market makers' are remunerated for their service by the 'spread' between the prices at which they buy and sell. In an order-driven system, orders to buy and sell are matched without a market maker.

11. A derivative is a financial instrument whose value is based on some underlying price. Derivatives are often traded on their own markets, usually in the form of futures or options. Futures are contracts to buy or sell a fixed quantity at an agreed upon price on a designated date. Options are contracts that gives the holder the discretionary right to buy or sell a given quantity at an agreed upon price at a designated date.

12. 'Securities Contracts (Regulation) Act, 1956', in *Companies Act With SEBI Rules/Regulations/Guidelines* (New Delhi, Taxmann, 1999), pp. 2.3–2.24. The Ministry of Finance shared these powers with SEBI.

13. Until the implementation of rolling settlement in 2001, transactions on Indian markets did not have to be settled until the end of an official settlement period which lasted either one or two weeks. Shares and payment for transactions agreed upon during the period were exchanged only after the end of the period. *Badlawalas,* brokers who had finance or shares available for lending, negotiated deals with traders who wanted to carry forward their position until the end of the next settlement. Traders who owed payment for shares would negotiate a deal with a badlawala, who would make the payment in return for interest and payment at the end of the next period. Traders who wanted to sell shares could use a badlawala's shares on a similar basis. Often traders used the badla system to postpone payment for many consecutive settlements.

14. Rajan and Zingales, *Saving Capitalism,* p. 276.

15. Interview with M.R. Mayya, Mumbai, 28 August 1999; interview with G.B. Desai, former President, BSE of the BSE, Mumbai, 30 July 1999; Interview with J.C. Parekh, former President BSE, Mumbai, 11 August 1999; Interview with Bhupen Dalal, Mumbai, 31 July 1999.

16. Basudev Das and S.N. Vasuki, 'Brokers' badla', *Business India* (18 April 1988), p. 56.

17. Mukarram Bagat, 'Urgent need to reform', *Update* (March 1985).

18. Das and Vasuki, 'Brokers' badla', pp. 50–6.

19. Interview with M.R. Mayya, Mumbai, 28 August 1999. According to

the Executive Director of the BSE from 1983–93, 'Mahendra Kampani was a model person. He was an expert in computerization. He never interfered with administration.'

20. Das and Vasuki, 'Brokers' badla', p. 56.

21. Shrish Nadkarni and Ajit Agharkar, 'Securities board – Taking over from the CCI?' *Sunday Observer*, 15 November 1987.

22. Sucheta Dalal, 'Setting the Agenda for Change in Indian Capital Market', *Economic and Political Weekly*, 4 September 1999, pp. 254–64; Das and Vasuki, 'Brokers' badla', p. 56; and interview with G.B. Desai, former president of the BSE, Mumbai, 30 July 1999.

23. Interview with G.B. Desai, Mumbai, 7 August 1999.

24. The best account of Kampani's ouster is Das and Vasuki, 'Brokers' badla'.

25. Manek was described to me in these terms by C. Kamdar, broker, BSE, Mumbai, 10 June 1999.

26. S.N. Vasuki, 'Manu matters', *Business India* 18 April 1988, p. 55.

27. Ibid.

28. Bhagirath Merchant and J.C. Parikh were also active in the Sharebrokers Forum. Interview with G.B. Desai, Mumbai, 7 August 1999. Bhagirath Merchant served as president of the BSE in 1994–5. J.C. Parikh served as vice-president of the exchange in 1991–2, prior to the election of Damani to the governing board and during Damani's two terms as president in 1996–7 and 1997–8. He served as president of the BSE in 1998–9. Rajendra Bhantia was another supporter of efforts to represent the interests of speculative brokers. Bhantia served as treasurer in 1997–8 and vice-president in 1998–9.

29. The early version of the trading system software used at the BSE attempted to protect the interests of jobbers by including a window that enabled them to offer quotes. However, this window was never widely used. Interview with L. Hariharan, Deputy General Manager, Research, Statistics & Publications, Bombay Stock Exchange, Mumbai, 18 May 1999.

30. According to a report by the Securities and Exchange Board of India, 20 to 30 per cent of all transactions at the BSE had to be adjusted after each trading session. See 'SEBI indicts BSE for glaring lapses', *The Economic Times*, 11 March 1993. In its response to the SEBI report, the BSE conceded that this had previously been the case, but it declared that it had since brought down the number of adjustments to 5–8 per cent of all transactions. See 'BSE refutes several SEBI charges', *The Economic Times*, 3 April 1993.

31. Daksesh Parikh, 'Why brokers resist computerisation', *The Independent*, 15 June 1990; Devina Dutt and Anand, 'Stock Exchange: Insider Information', *Sunday*, 22 November 1992, pp. 60–4; 'In December, you might see a different shape for the market,' *Sunday*, 10 September 1995, pp. 52–3; and

Sucheta Dalal, 'Parallel SE in Bombay favoured', *The Economic Times,* 15 July 1991.

32. More precisely, the *Report of the High Powered Committee on Stock Exchange Reforms* recommended, '...the present method of recording the transactions and prices by the stockbrokers only in sauda book and thereafter the prices being broadcast or written on the black-board should be replaced by an electronic system whereby there is an instantaneous record of transactions...' Government of India, New Delhi, Ministry of Finance, Department of Economic Affairs, p. 135. See also pp. 211–28.

33. High Powered Study Group on Establishment of New Stock Exchanges, *Summary of Recommendations,* Mimeo., 30 June 1991, pp. 3, 9, 10.

34. 'National stock market system: The onus is on the BSE', *The Independent,* 30 November 1991.

35. Sucheta Dalal, 'Committee after Committee', *The Economic Times,* 8 September 1991.

36. 'Consultant debunks national SE plan', *Business Standard,* 22 January 1992.

37. 'Proposed national stock exchange: Finance ministry calls for debate', *The Economic Times,* 28 August 1991.

38. Interview with G.B. Desai, Mumbai, 30 July 1999.

39. Interview with G.V. Ramakrishna, New Delhi, 19 July 1999. According to one report, Ramakrishna sent a letter to the Ministry of Finance in May 1992 advising it to go slow on creating the NSE. See Debashis Basu and Roshni Jayakar, 'Battle for the NSE', *Business Today,* 22 April 1993, pp. 38–42.

40. Interview with Ashok Desai, New Delhi, 22 July 1999. The importance of Desai's visit was also confirmed by G.B Desai, president of the BSE at the time, and M.R. Mayya, the executive director of the Bombay Stock Exchange at the time. See interviews with G.B. Desai, Mumbai, 30 July 1999 and M.R. Mayya, Mumbai, 28 August 1999.

41. Interview with Ravi Narain, Mumbai, 26 August 1999. From the founding of the NSE until 2001, Narain served as assistant managing director of the NSE.

42. Interview with Dr R.H. Patil, Mumbai, 18 August 1999. Dr Patil became the NSE's first managing director. His assessment concerning the drawbacks of the OTCEI's technological base was supported by Rafiq Dossani, who was a frequent trader on the exchange during the 1990s. Dossani says that the modem-based communication on the OTCEI was very slow, much slower than the VCAT technology of the NSE, and the OTCEI's software was also inferior. Telephone interview with Rafiq Dossani, 7 June 2002.

43. NSE, *Indian Securities Market, A Review – 2004* (Mumbai, National

Stock Exchange of India Ltd, 2004), p. 82. This document is available online at www.nse-india.com/archives/us/ismr/us_ismr2004.htm; and NSE, *Fact Book 2005* (Mumbai, National Stock Ex change of India Limited, 2001), p. 4. This volume is available on-line at www.nse-india.com.

44. Montek Ahluwalia said, 'We are pressing Nadkarni to get it going in around eight to ten months. We would like trading to begin in 1993–94—even if means starting the NSE on the vary last day of the financial year.' Basu and Jayakar, 'Battle for the NSE'.

45. Ajay Shah, 'Institutional Change in India's Capital Markets', *Economic and Political Weekly,* 16 January 1999, p. 188.

46. The actual percentage was 59.2. NSE, *Fact Book 2001* (Mumbai,: National Stock Exchange of India Limited, 2001), p. 40. This volume is available online at http://www.nseindia.com.archives/us/fact/usfactbook 2001.htm.

47. NSE, *Indian Securities Market, A Review – 2004,* p. 91.

48. Ministry of Finance, Government of India, *Economic Survey 2004–05,* as accessed from http://indiabudget.nic.in/es2004-05/esmain.htm on July 21, 2005.

49. NSE, *Fact Book 2005*, p. 6.

50. NSE, *Indian Securities Market, A Review – 2004* , p. 91. Regional bourses continue to exist despite lack of turnover because they still collect listing fees. Government regulations mandate that companies list at two exchanges, and prior to the establishment of the NSE, it was the norm for companies to list at the BSE and a local exchange. Listing fees amounted to some Rs 6 billion in 2001–2. Regional exchanges received Rs 4 billion. See P. Vaidyanhathan Iyer, 'Regional bourses: Listing to extinction', *Business Standard,* 14 May 2002.

51. Ajay Shah, 'India's National Stock Exchange (NSE) and India's Over the Counter Exchange (OTCEI)' (Mumbai, Indira Gandhi Institute for Development Research, working paper, c. 2000); and *Indian Securities Market: A Review* (Mumbai, National Stock Exchange of India Ltd, 2001), p. 26.

52. Dwijottam Bhattacharjee, 'Fake shares flood stock market', *Business Standard,* 12 January 1994; and Rahul Joshi, 'Fake share certificates available for a price', *Indian Express,* 26 April 1994.

53. For a concise summary of the scam, see Hamish McDonald, *The Polyester Prince: The Rise of Dhirubhai Ambani* (St. Leonards (Australia), Allen & Unwin, 1998), pp. 243–52.

54. 'Fear of the Week', *Sunday,* 18 June 1995, p. 59. Harshad Mehta is reported to have created benami shares worth billions of rupees in an attempt to conceal his trading activities during the 1992 scam. See Anand, 'A share of trouble', *Sunday,* 19 September 1993, p. 60.

55. Depository participants—usually banks, financial institutions, or certified brokerages—serve as agents of the depository by providing investors with access to the depository. This data was taken from NSE, *Indian Securities Market, A Review – 2004*, p. 88.

56. NSE, *Indian Securities Market: A Review* (Mumbai: National Stock Exchange of India Ltd, 2001), p. 25. This document is available online at www.nseindia.com.

57. NSE, *Indian Securities Market, A Review – 2004*, p. 88.

58. Interview with G.V. Ramakrishna, New Delhi, 19 July 1999.

59. For a description of how ALBM worked, see Krishnan Thiagarajan, 'Putting idle stocks to work', *Business Line*, 14 March 1999.

60. Specifically, BLESS offered the opportunity for brokers delivering finance to the system to withdraw securities by paying a 15–20 per cent margin. Ashok Jainani, 'SEBI may call for revamp of lending, borrowing system', *Business Line*, 26 January 2001; and Ashok Jainani, 'The Long and short of ALBM, BLESS', *Business Line,* 9 March 2001. According to Anand Rathi, president of the BSE, '…This is the same system which SEBI had banned. So we are back to the old days [pre-December 1992].' Lancelot Joseph, 'Completing full circle', *Business India*, 8 January 2001. The SEBI committee on risk management became concerned about the ability of financiers to withdraw securities and banned the practices at the beginning of March. See 'SEBI discontinues 2 lending schemes fearing misuse', *The Economic Times*, 2 March 2001. Its concerns about the reversion to this less restrictive system were borne out after the March 2001 stock scam when more than 400 investors complained that brokers at the BSE refused to return their investments in the BLESS system. Apparently, their funds had been taken out of the system and reinvested in the unregulated 'grey badla market' in Kolkata. See Ashok Jainani, 'Major badla abuse comes to light', *Business Line*, 15 May 2001.

61. Interview with L.C. Gupta, New Delhi, 21 July 1999.

62. For a description of delays caused by M.G. Damani and SEBI, see Vivek Law, 'L.C. Gupta committee members upset over delay in finalizing report', *Financial Express*, 14 February 1988.

63. M.G. Damani, 'Comments on the Report of the Committee on Derivatives', 26 December 1997, accessed at http://www.sebi.gov.in/news/dissent.html on 20 June 2002.

64. NSE, *Indian Securities Market, A Review –- 2004*, p. 10.

65. Ajay Shah and Susan Thomas, 'Developing the Indian Capital Market', in James A. Hanson and Sanjay Kathuria (eds), *India: A Financial Sector for the Twenty-first Century* (New Delhi, Oxford University Press, 1999), pp. 225–6.

66. For discussions of the benefits of rolling settlement, see Ajay Shah and

Susan Thomas, 'Policy issues in India's capital markets in 2000 AD', Indira Gandhi Institute for Development Research, Mumbai, 2000, pp. 2–5.

67. NSE, *Indian Securities Market: A Review*, p. 3.

68. The OCTEI adopted rolling settlement when it began operation in September 1992. In July 1997 the NSE established a rolling settlement for a set of dematerialized stocks. For early rolling settlement on the OTCEI and NSE, see S. Vaidyanathan, 'Rolling settlement: The next 'big development in market'', *Business Line*, 22 August 1999. A SEBI board meeting on 5 January 1998 decided that rolling settlement on a T+5 basis would be introduced for all scrips traded in the dematerialized segment of the stock exchanges with effect from 15 January 1998. SEBI press release accessed at http://www.sebi.gov.in/test/power search.p...press/9801.html&search=rolling+settlement on December 5, 2000.

At the annual meeting of stock exchanges on 9 August, SEBI announced that it was setting up a committee comprising representatives of various stock exchanges to draw up a plan for compulsory rolling settlement. The committee, which first met on 19 August, decided to introduce rolling settlement on a T+5 basis in about ten scrips that were not eligible for badla. Abhishek Bhuwalka, 'Rolling settlement – Regulating carry forward', *Financial Express,* 28 September 1999; and Abhishek Bhuwalka, 'India: Rolling to global standards', *Business Line,* 15 August 1999; 'Panel to name 10 scrips by Sept-end', *Business Standard*, 25 August 1999. On 15 September 1999 Pratip Kar, Executive Director, SEBI, stated that 45 scrips would be included in rolling settlement. See 'India: SEBI to introduce rolling settlement in 45 scrips', *Business Line*, 16 September 1999; and 'Roll on, cautiously', *The Economic Times*, 17 September 1999.

69. On the BSE's 'A' group see: 'India: SEBI must think forward', *Business Line*, 29 August 1999; 'Settlement in 45 scrips', *Business Line,* 16 September 1999; and 'Roll on, cautiously', *The Economic Times,* 17 September 1999.

70. These ten were originally supposed to be placed on rolling settlement during the first week of December; however, this was done only by 10 January 2000. 'Sebi approves 10 scrips for rolling settlement system from January 10', *The Economic Times*, 1 December 1999).

71. The initial plan was to add 156 more scrips to the rolling settlment by 26 June 2000. Janaki Krishnan, 'Stock Markets: Sebi adds 156 more scrips to the rolling settlement', *Financial Express*, 9 February 2000; and 'Sebi to shift 153 scrips to rolling settlement in phases', *The Economic Times*, 9 February 2000. But only a total of 163 scrips were reported to be under rolling settlement by the end of the summer of 2000. 'Rolling settlement from end-Nov', *Business Standard*, 24 August 2000.

72. Rajeshwari Adappa Thakur, 'Sebi sets up panel to study badla in rolling settlement', *The Economic Times*, 2 November 1999; and 'J R Varma committee to review badla mechanism', *The Economic Times,* 5 November 1999.

73. For the controversy at the SEBI meeting see Vivek Law, 'Rolling settlement in A group may be delayed', *Business Standard*, 5 April 2000. For the 14 June SEBI meeting that approved badla modified for rolling settlement, see 'India: Carry forward in rolling settlement cleared', *Business Line*, 15 June 2000; Janaki Krishnan, 'Stocks: Sebi puts A-group scrips under rolling mode', *Financial Express*, 15 June 2000; 'New badla system for rolling settlement', *Indian Express*, 15 June 2000.

74. Vivek Law, 'BSE told to hasten software for carryforward in rolling mode', *The Economic Times*, 24 June 2000.

75. 'India: 'Rolling settlement once facilities are in place', *Business Line*, 24 August 2000; and 'Rolling settlement from end-Nov', *Business Standard*, 24 August 2000.

76. Dheer Kothari and Rakesh P. Sharma, 'Common BSE, NSE "A" scrips list elusive', *Business Standard*, 8 November 2000.

77. 'Brokers take to street, submit memo to SEBI', *Business Line*, 13 July 2001.

78. 'Brokers resistance to market reforms', *The Hindu*, 2 August 2001.

79. Lancelot Joseph, 'Who's to blame?', *Business India*, 17 September 2001.

80. NSE, *Indian Securities Market, A Review – 2004*, p. 11.

81. Market liquidity is best measured in terms of a trades impact on prices with a declining impact reflecting improved liquidity. Since the implementation of rolling settlements, the impact cost of buying or selling Rs 0.5 crore of the Nifty index has steadily declined from 0.27 per cent in 2001 to 0.09 per cent in 2004. Ministry of Finance, *Economic Survey 2004–05*, p. 78.

82. The Securities March Infrastructure Leveraging Expert Committee estimates that it often takes even longer than the 15-day maximum to complete the allotment of an issue. It notes that this compares unfavorably with international standards and the T+ 2 settlement cycle of the secondary market. (See Securities Markets Infrastructure Leveraging Expert Task Force, *First Report* (Mumbai, Securities and Exchange Board of India, 25 August 2004). Accessed at http://www.sebi.gov.in on 22 July 2005.

83. For the concept of the 'political cost-benefit ratio' of a reform, see Dani Rodrik, 'The Rush to Free Trade in the Developing World: Why so Late? Why Now? Will it Last', in Stephan Haggard and Steven B. Webb (eds), *Voting For Reform* (New York, Oxford University Press, 1994), pp. 61–88. See also William B. Heller, Philip Keefer, and Mathew D. McCubbins, 'Political Structure and Economic Liberalization: Conditions and Cases from the Developing World', in Paul W. Drake and Mathew D. McCubbins (eds), *The Origins of Liberty and Economic Liberalization in the Modern World* (Princeton, Princeton University Press, 1998), pp. 146–78.

84.Ajay Shah and Susan Thomas, 'David and Goliath: Displacing a Primary Market', *Global Financial Markets*, Spring (2000), pp. 14–23.

85. Douglass C. North, *Understanding the Process of Economic Change*, Princeton, NJ, Princeton University Press, 2005; and Elahan Helpman, *The Mystery of Economic Growth* (Cambridge, MA, Harvard University Press, 2004).

12

Bangalore
The Silicon Valley of Asia?[*]

AnnaLee Saxenian[1]

Information technology (IT) has become the *mantra* of Indian politicians and
policy-makers. Soon after taking office in 1998, Prime Minister A.B. Vajpayee
announced the widely quoted goal of making India a 'global information
technology superpower' and a 'forerunner in the age of the information revolution'. India's software industry has grown so rapidly that it evokes frequent
comparisons between Bangalore, one of India's leading software-producing
regions, and Silicon Valley. Moreover, the achievements of Indian professionals
in leading-edge technology industries abroad have contributed to a growing
sense of confidence in India, confidence that did not exist before. This confidence has come largely because India and Indians have participated in the
information technology revolution. The performance of India's IT industry
during the 1990s has been impressive, particularly in contrast to other sectors of
the Indian economy. The sector's compound annual growth rate (CAGR) for
1994–9 exceeded 40 per cent, compared to only 7 per cent for the economy as
a whole.[2] This strong growth was led by the software industry, which in 1999
accounted for 65 per cent of India's total IT revenues and employed more than
200,000 workers. Total software revenues of $3.9 billion in 1999 were close to
four times those of IT hardware manufacturing and grew more than 55 per cent
per year in the late 1990s. Moreover, the software industry's growth was driven
primarily by exports. While the domestic market for software has grown in

* Originally published as 'Bangalore: The Silicon Valley of Asia?', in Anne O. Krueger
(ed.), *Economic Policy Reforms and the Indian Economy*, New Delhi, Oxford University
Press, 2002, pp. 169–93.

absolute terms, software exports account for a large and increasing share of total industry revenue (see Table 12.1). This export success is particularly striking for an industry that remained peripheral to world markets throughout most of the 1980s.

Table 12.1: The information technology industry in India, 1993-9

(US$ millions)

	1993–4	1994–5	1995–6	1996–7	1997–8	1998–9
Software						
Domestic	230	350	490	670	950	1,250
Exports	330	485	734	1,083	1,750	2,650
Total	560	835	1,224	1,753	2,700	3,900
Hardware						
Domestic	490	590	1,037	1,050	1,205	1,026
Exports	93	177	35	286	201	4
Total	583	767	1,027	1,336	1,406	1,030
Grand total	1,143	1,602	2,296	3,089	4,106	4,930

Source: NASSCOM (1999, 2000).

This chapter examines the growth and performance of India's IT industries, with particular attention to the role of policy in this process. It first reviews the evolution of the software industry, highlighting the policy departures that have contributed to its rapid emergence and growth over the past two decades. It then turns to the formation of the National Information Technology and Software Development Task Force in 1998 and its policy recommendations that aimed at making India the number-one provider of IT products in the world. The concluding section steps back to address the role of the IT industry in India more broadly. It suggests that comparisons between regions like Bangalore and Silicon Valley not only mislead, but also distract attention from the deeper challenges and opportunities that IT offers for the Indian economy. In particular, the range of actors and the scope of policy debates need to be expanded significantly to realize the full potential of the IT revolution in India.

It is important to begin by putting the performance of Indian IT in a global perspective. India's $4 billion in software revenues in 1998–9 represented a very small fraction of an estimated world software market of some $300–500 billion.[3] Despite the sector's rapid export expansion between 1985 and 1995, from $28 million to $481 million, India's share of total world IT exports remained stable at 0.5 per cent.[4] Moreover, India's 0.5 per cent share of world IT exports in 1995 was less than the country's 0.6 per cent share of world aggregate exports in the same year.[5] These figures suggest the need for skepticism about the more inflated claims currently circulating concerning India's IT industries.

The weakest link in the IT sector—hardware development and manufacturing—remains small and barely viable. The industry suffered tremendously from the protection provided by the high import duties as well as from very limited access to foreign technology after IBM left the country in 1978. Personal computers, components, and other IT products manufactured in India in the 1980s were both costly and technically backward, which limited demand and hence the volume of production. The inability to gain scale economies proved fatal in a highly capital-intensive industry and, over time, contributed to the industry's decline. By the 1990s, most of India's IT hardware companies were transformed into direct or indirect dealerships for foreign brand computers and related products.[6]

India's total hardware revenues amounted to $1.03 billion in 1998–9 (see Table 12.1). The sector has not grown in the past five years, and its exports are negligible. The reduction of import duties to zero by 2002, as recommended by the World Trade Organization (WTO), will put severe pressure on India's IT manufacturers, and it seems likely that only those that are able to develop higher value-added products are likely to survive. The remainder of this chapter focuses on the software industry, as it is the sector in which an innovative policy regime has stimulated a different developmental dynamic.

THE EVOLUTION OF THE INDIAN SOFTWARE INDUSTRY, 1984–98

Prior to 1984 the Indian software industry operated within the framework of a highly regulated, autarkic model of import-substitution-led industrialization (ISI) and the ideology of self-reliance that guided the Indian economy. This policy stifled entrepreneurs and isolated India from the global economy. As a result, efforts to promote software exports during the period never took off. Policies that permitted the import of state-of-the-art computers in exchange for a guarantee to export a certain amount of software were not enthusiastically received.[7] Import procedures were cumbersome, duties were high, and obtaining foreign exchange for business expenses was difficult.[8]

Policy Reform in Software

The election of Rajiv Gandhi as prime minister marked the turning point for policy reform in India's software and computer industries. Gandhi's administration was the first to emphasize new policies for electronics, software, telecommunications, and other emerging industries.[9] A computer policy announced in November 1984 recognized software as an 'industry', making it eligible for an investment allowance and other incentives. The policy also lowered import duties on software and personal computers (PCs) and permitted the import of computers in exchange for software exports at a special low duty.

The passage two years later of the 1986 Computer Software Export, Development, and Training Policy-marked an explicit rejection of Indian ISI and the idea of self-reliance in software. The policy was designed to promote the domestic software industry and facilitate a 'quantum jump' in software exports by providing Indian firms with liberal access to the latest technologies and software tools to enhance their global competitiveness and to encourage higher value-added exports. To that end, the import of software in any form was permitted and various procedures simplified. The policy also invited foreign investment and promised to make venture capital available to encourage new firm formation and export growth.

The 1984 and 1986 policies were championed by N. Seshagiri, additional secretary at the Department of Electronics (DoE), who had long argued that India's policies were too restrictive, its procedures too cumbersome, and its idea of self-reliance self-defeating.[10] He also argued that for India to become a major software exporter, it would have to begin with high volume, low value-added exports and move up the value chain. 'He believed that India's failure to follow such a strategy had left it far behind the East Asia NICs in hardware exports. Thus, the 1984 policy explicitly recognized bodyshopping — the provision of labor-intensive, low value-added programming services, such as coding and testing, at client sites overseas—as valid exports. In spite of some ambivalence within the government about promoting bodyshopping, which a few technologically conversant policy-makers regarded as 'intellectual coolieism'.[11] Seshagiri was able to push through his policy, but only because of misconceptions that prevailed about software among most policy-makers:

[I]f the administrators and some of the bureaucrats had too deep knowledge, they might have prevented bodyshopping or on site services. Software was seen as a glamorous high tech industry. So they said, alright, do it.[12]

If limited understanding of the software industry allowed Indian firms to begin bodyshopping, it also prevented policymakers from taking decisive steps to actively promote the software industry. The 1984 and 1986 policies merely removed barriers to its growth. Sen writes that 'until 1991–92, there was virtually no policy support at all for the software sector. Even the term "benign neglect" would be too positive a phrase to use in this connection.'[13]

The greatest challenge for Indian companies in the 1980s was the lack of the international telecommunication links that are the necessary infrastructure for software exports. While the export of data via satellite links was permitted, establishing an earth station was a protracted procedure requiring permission from multiple government departments. For example, when Texas Instruments set up the first earth station in Bangalore in 1986, the process involved removing or breaking twenty-five different government rules.[14] Without reliable telecommunications links, Indian firms had no alternative to providing contract programming on-site (at the customer's facilities), typically in the United States.[15]

The Software Technology Parks (STP) scheme introduced by the DoE in the early 1990s insured that the infrastructure and administrative support for exporting were available *in* India. An STP is like an export processing zone for software: It gives export-oriented software firms in designated zones tax exemptions for five years and guaranteed access to high-speed satellite links and reliable electricity. The DoE also provides basic infrastructure, including core computer facilities, reliable power, ready-to-use office space, and communications facilities including internet access and sixty-four kilobits per second data-lines. As in the predecessor programs for export-oriented units, firms in the STP are allowed to import all equipment without duty or import licenses, and 100 per cent foreign ownership is permitted in exchange for a sizable export obligation.[16]

STP firms are also allowed to freely repatriate capital investment, royalties, and dividends after paying the necessary taxes. Administratively, the STPs provide a decentralized, single window clearance mechanism for applications from potential investors. While STPs can be established by anybody anywhere in the country, the DoE announced the first three in 1990 in Bangalore, Pune, and Bhubaneshwar, and another four the following year. In June 1991, the Software Technology Parks of India (STPI) was registered as an autonomous agency, reflecting the desire of the DoE to avoid direct government involvement in the industry. The local directors of individual STPs have wide-ranging powers and are intended to serve as 'friend, philosopher, and guide' to the industry while also functioning as the eyes and ears of the DoE.[17] Inclusion of industry representatives on the boards and councils of the STPs was also meant to emphasize the industry-friendly approach of the scheme. By 1998 there were 25 STPs under various stages of planning and development in different parts of the country (in addition to those sponsored by the DoE). The Information Technology Park, Ltd, in Bangalore, for example, is a partnership between the Karnataka government, Tata Industries, and a consortium of Singapore firms.

The introduction of the STPs coincided with the initiation in 1991 of the economic liberalization process in India.[18] Software producers benefited from general policy changes such as the devaluation of the rupee and the growing openness to foreign direct investment. They also benefited from the exemption from income tax profits on software and other service exports and, most importantly, the 1992 removal of import licensing on equipment and industrial imports. This allowed Indian companies to import the computers that its clients used and to produce or modify software for them directly.

To summarize, the policy reforms of the 1980s facilitated the emergence of an export-oriented software industry in India. However, export growth in this period was based exclusively on bodyshopping on site (with Indian programmers working at the client site, typically in the United States). The shift to offshore production, allowing the programmers to work at facilities in India, was only possible following the reforms of the early 1990s, particularly the removal of licenses on imports of industrial equipment and the establishment of the STPs.

Even after the pace of liberalization slowed in the rest of the economy in the mid 1990s, the software industry continued to benefit from a series of sector-specific policy reforms. This was largely due to aggressive lobbying by the industry association, the National Association of Software and Service Companies (NASSCOM).[19] In 1997, for example, all import duties on software were eliminated, and software firms were allowed to invest in foreign joint ventures and wholly owned subsidiaries to a limited extent.[20] And in 1998, software firms were permitted to offer ADR/GDR-linked stock options to employees.[21]

The active role of the industry association, NASSCOM, in shaping policy distinguishes the software industry from the computer hardware and other older Indian industries. NASSCOM has been influential in shaping the DoE strategy of working with software companies to provide critical infrastructure, while explicitly avoiding more detailed regulation or intervention. This is evident, for example, in the decision to organize the STPI programme as an autonomous unit (and eventually to privatize it). The DoE thus represents a very different model for India from an older generation of 'strategic' ministries that sought to specify, develop, and directly regulate technology and industry structure.[22]

NASSCOM's leaders interact continually with politicians and policy-makers, and the association is represented on many influential committees of the government of India. It also sponsors high-profile conferences and studies, consults for state governments, and promotes the Indian software industry around the world through a very effective web site as well as through attendance at international trade shows and foreign visits.[23] NASSCOM is also the sole source of IT industry data in India. Its annual strategic review provides the only detailed and up-to-date figures on employment, revenues, exports, and market share for the software and other IT industries. This provides leverage for the association, but is not an optimal situation for policy-makers or scholars.[24]

Software Industry Growth and Transformation, 1984–98

The post-1984 policy changes were crucial to the growth of the Indian software industry because they allowed domestic producers to exploit domestic resources in global markets. India's greatest asset is a large, educated, English-speaking workforce that is willing to work at relatively low wages. In spite of widespread illiteracy, India boasts thousands of educated engineers who have remained either underemployed or unemployed for decades. Few countries can match India's combination of low-wage, highly skilled workers. In 1994, wages for software programmers and systems analysts in India were less than a tenth of those for their US counterparts, and lower even than those in other developing countries, such as Mexico (see Table 12.2).

Table 12.2: International wage rates, software industry, 1994

Country	Programmer (US$)	Programmer Index	Systems Analyst (US$)	Systems Analyst Index
India	4,002	100	5,444	100
United States	46,600	1,164	61,200	1,124
Japan	51,731	1,293	64,519	1,185
Germany	54,075	1,351	65,107	1,196
France	45,431	1,135	71,163	1,307
Britain	31,247	781	51,488	1,287
Hong Kong	34,615	865	63,462	1,166
Mexico	26,078	652	35,851	658

Source: Business India (1995, p. 199), as cited in Parthasarathy (2000a).

Indian programmers also had the unanticipated advantage of familiarity with the Unix operating system in the 1990s. The failure to develop a commercially viable computer following IBM's departure from the country meant that Indian users relied on imports of a wide range of models and vintages from different manufacturers. Indian programmers thus learned to work on a variety of platforms, which proved helpful in acquiring contracts for the maintenance of various legacy systems. More important, computer manufacturers in the 1980s had no alternative but to rely on Unix (the first portable, machine-independent, multi-user operating system), even though foreign companies were developing proprietary systems at the time. By the 1990s, however, when Unix became the system of choice for PCs and workstations, India's Unix programmers had a skill that was extremely scarce elsewhere in the world.

Indian producers entered the world market in the 1980s by exploiting their cost advantage in the most routine, low-value-added segments of software production, such as coding, testing, and maintenance. The vast majority of these exports derived from bodyshopping, which has been referred to as an 'input-less' export because it requires only an overseas contract, a minimal amount of finance, and names of local programmers.[25] In these contracts, the amount of software code is specified in advance, and revenue is earned per line of code. Indian engineers who work overseas are paid their salaries in rupees and provided with minimal allowances for housing and expenses. Some refer to this business as 'resume selling' because it is, in essence, a lucrative form of labour cost arbitrage—and India boasts ample resumes. Indian educational institutions and polytechnics train more than 67,000 computer science professionals annually. Another 200,000 individuals enrol annually in the private software training institutes that have mushroomed in India in the 1990s.[26]

The policy changes of the 1980s are typically credited with stimulating the accelerated growth of Indian software exports. However, it is worth noting that this growth, at least initially, was more impressive in rupee terms than in dollar terms. Using quarterly data, Sen (1994) shows that between 1987 and 1993 a significant portion of export growth was accounted for by the falling value of the rupee (see Table 12.3). The devaluation meant that the growth due to a lower exchange rate was almost as great as the real growth rate in dollars.

The introduction of the STPs facilitated a gradual shift away from on-site to offshore (in India) service provision during the 1990s.[27] While on-site production accounted for 90 per cent of Indian software exports in 1990, the share had fallen to 58 per cent by 1998.[28] One advantage of offshore production soon became apparent. The twelve-and-a-half-hour difference between Indian

Standard Time and Pacific Standard Time allowed Indian firms to perform maintenance and re-engineering tasks for US customers by accessing their computers after regular users had finished for the day. Combined with growing shortages of skilled labour in the West, this helps to explain why hundreds of US and European corporations increasingly outsourced routine, labour-intensive projects, such as coding, maintenance, and Y2K solutions to Indian software houses in the 1990s.

Table 12.3: Annual growth of Indian software exports, 1987–93

Period	Total Growth (%)	Real Growth (%)	Exchange Rate (%)
1987–93	46	28	18
1987–90	41	29	12
1990–3	52	28	24

Source: Sen, as cited in Parthasarathy (2000b).

A growing number of foreign companies followed the earlier model of Texas Instruments and Hewlett-Packard and located offshore development centres (ODCs) in India in the 1990s. They were motivated by the labour-cost difference, to be sure, but the availability of high-quality skills was essential to these decisions as well. According to one US employer in Bangalore, the low wages matter because they provide an attractive trade-off to working in an environment plagued by chronic infrastructure problems:

[W]e came here because of the skills. We expanded because of the skills. We were able to come to India because the risk of being 10,000 miles away, the risk of the satellite link and the telephones and the flights were offset by the costs.[29]

There is anecdotal evidence that in the late 1990s the ODCs began to take on more sophisticated design and programming projects, either jointly or independently, and often as equal partners with their parent organizations.[30] This underscores the potential for upgrading in India. The chief executive of one ODC explains why his company waited until the 1990s to move to Bangalore:

Now...the feeling is that high-tech, leading edge quality, timely, delivered, supported software will come out. That was not a risk you could have taken five years ago...[I]f they had asked me then, I would have said no. I would have said, 'do anything, bodyshopping, subcontracting, modular work, but don't give full dependability here [in India] because nobody's ever done it. It's not proven.'[31]

He compared the work done at his centre with that at the headquarters in Silicon Valley:

New products come from here, new versions of old products come from here...[P]roducts on a particular hardware platform come from here as opposed to an application for a customer...It's the same thing that they do over there. Technologically, there's zero difference.[32]

The growth of offshore facilities also allowed some established Indian companies to begin building a base of in-house knowledge and to develop internal training programmes, quality processes, and productivity tools. This has facilitated the upgrading of their capabilities. In December 1999, 137 Indian companies had obtained either ISO 9000 or SEI-CMM level two certification, and 10 companies were certified at level five (the highest level, at which only six US companies are certified). Quality certification serves as an important marketing device for Indian companies while also improving their ability to manage time and resources involved in large projects.[33]

Today, some of the largest Indian software houses, such as Wipro and Infosys, have track records that allow them to win bigger consulting contracts, often on a turnkey basis.[34] This allows them to take on a greater range of software development processes and managerial tasks (such as overall project scheduling, quality, and productivity) than are required in bodyshopping, and to begin charging higher rates for their work. Rather than compete on the basis of hourly productivity, they aim to accumulate intellectual property by converting the knowledge gained during a series of consulting projects into broadly applicable software components that can in turn be customized for clients with similar needs. Industry observers have suggested that India's share of the world market for customized, as opposed to packaged, software is significantly higher than the aggregate data suggest.[35]

Despite the evidence that a handful of Indian software companies are gradually moving up the value chain and gaining international recognition for their quality and performance, the industry as a whole remains significantly less productive than its global competitors. While the Indian software industry employed some 180,000 workers in 1998, the annual revenue per employee in India was $15,000–20,000. This compared to $100,000 per employee in other software-producing countries such as Israel and Ireland.[36]

Moreover, it appears that the software boom has exacerbated the 'brain drain'. Programmers in India are increasingly aware of the global demand for their skills and the substantially higher compensation available in more developed economies. Many thus aspire to work for foreign companies not only for the relatively high wages but also for the opportunity to be transferred overseas. The US has been a major beneficiary of this trend. A recent study of the H-1B visa, which grants temporary work authorization to highly skilled foreign persons, reports that the number of Indian H-1Bs grew steadily from 1989, clearly becoming the largest category in 1994, doubling in size by 1996, and quintupling by 1999. Indians accounted for nearly half of all visas issued in 1999 (47 per cent). This amounted to 55,047 Indian workers in 1999 alone, and a total of 195,083 between 1989 and 1999. The next largest groups of H-1B visa holders were from the United Kingdom and China, but each accounted for 6 per cent or less of the total visas granted.[37]

There is growing recognition among Indian policy-makers and software producers of the need to accelerate the industry's shift into higher-value-added activities for two different reasons. On one hand, the developmental potential of the current trajectory is quite limited. The provision of routine software services for export may be highly profitable for individual companies, but it provides few opportunities for longer-term technological learning and upgrading.[38]

Meanwhile, India's labour cost advantage is eroding, in spite of its sizable labour pool. The software industry association estimates that wages in the software industry rose 21 per cent per year in the late 1990s, albeit from a low base.[39] Some analysts report that shortages of IT professionals are constraining the industry's growth.[40] As a result, India's producers face increasing competition from other low-wage, human-capital-rich countries like the Philippines and China. In the words of Desai,[41] chairman and managing director of Mastek Ltd., a leading Indian software company:

Indian [software] corporations are at a crossroads, faced with growing globalization and competition....[I]t is becoming difficult for them to compete only on one differential—the cost advantage; and this forces them to move to higher value addition in their offerings.

THE IT ACTION PLAN

While the central government initiated India's economic liberalization in the early 1990s, the state governments have pioneered some of the most far-reaching policy innovations in the IT sector. The chief minister of Andhra Pradesh, Chandrababu Naidu, has drawn attention both in India and around the world for his entrepreneurial, high-profile attempts to attract technology investment to the state and to promote the use of IT in his administration. Naidu has effectively promoted the concept of 'e-governance' (the use of IT in delivering public services) as a way to ensure greater accountability, transparency, and efficiency in the government of Andhra Pradesh. Many of the state's departments—such as treasury, employment, commercial taxes, rural development, registration, irrigation, excise, and police—are being computerized in order to both reduce corruption and improve service delivery.[42]

Naidu's efforts have triggered escalating competition from neighbouring states. The recently elected government of Karnataka, for example, has laid out an ambitious plan for upgrading its overburdened roads and other infrastructure. The governments of Tamil Nadu and Kerala are also developing IT policies that include investing in infrastructure, computerization of government offices, single-window clearance for IT ventures, and IT-related education. Today Andhra Pradesh and the other southern states where the software industry is concentrated are well ahead of the Government of India in their implementation of e-governance and other IT reforms.[43]

Naidu has thus initiated a bottom-up process of policy reform in this historically centralized polity. He has been a vocal proponent of national policy reform as well. His recent book, *Plainly Speaking,* lays out his views on many issues related to governance and information technology in India. He calls, for example, for greater devolution of central tax revenues to state governments and greater flexibility in fiscal management. He also argues that there is an urgent need for administrative reform and for the removal of discretionary powers in a country where 'bloated governments have bled their exchequers dry.' And he claims that the IT-related initiatives undertaken by his government have helped to redefine the meaning and content of governance within the country. Naidu was also instrumental in raising the issue of IT at the national level.[44]

The prime minister's office responded in 1998 with the formation of the National Task Force on Information Technology and Software Development. The task force was a high-powered group that included senior representatives from the private sector, government, and universities. It included Naidu and Sheshagiri (currently director of the National Informatics Centre) as well as the executive director of NASSCOM, senior executives from Infosys and Wipro, and a range of other scientists, professionals, educators, and military officials. It was also seconded the secretaries of various government departments, including electronics, finance, commerce, and telecommunications.

The task force moved extremely quickly—far more so than is the norm in India — and released its 'Information Technology Action Plan' a year after the group was convened. The task force also developed an unusually open and transparent process for collecting information and formulating recommendations, a process that involved consultation with an unusually wide variety of public- and private-sector actors.[45] All the task force documents are available on the internet. In the words of one of the background reports:

This is the first time in India that representatives of so many ministries, departments, industry associations, business houses, educational institutions and State Governments have interacted so intensively and in such a short period of time to cover so many bottleneck and promotional areas...[46]

As a result, the IT Action Plan is the most ambitious IT-related policy proposal in India since the Computer Policy of 1984 and the Software Policy of 1986. The plan lists 108 recommendations of 'revisions and additions to the existing policy and procedures for removing bottlenecks and achieving a pre-eminent status for India'. Additionally, it sets $50 billion in software exports and 'IT penetration for all' as targets for 2008.

The report is wide-ranging in coverage and sober in its assessments of the current constraints on IT development, in spite of often hyperbolic (if laudable) goals. It reflects a clear understanding of the needs of the industry and of the limitations of the Indian business environment—an understanding that could only have grown through consultation with the private sector and other industry specialists. This collaborative process in itself reflects an important step forward in policy-making in India. However, the wide-ranging nature of the report raises concerns about the implementation process and what, if any, processes are in place to insure that the more politically difficult or longer-term reforms are carried through.[47]

The action plan addresses the two concerns that are most frequently articulated by software and other IT producers in India: (a) the inadequacy of the infrastructure: telecommunications in particular, but also roads, airports, and power supply; and (b) the cumbersome bureaucratic hurdles and regulatory red tape involved in doing business.[48] As we have seen, India's telecommunications, roads, and air transport infrastructures rank extremely poorly, in the bottom 10 per cent of ranked countries, on a global scale.[49] Note, for example, telecommunications: in 1997 there were only 18.6 telephone main lines per 1000 people in India, compared to 55.7 in China, and the wait for a new connection was 12.17 months, compared to China's 0.68 months.[50] The state of the infrastructure imposes significant direct and indirect costs on producers and undoubtedly constitutes a barrier to foreign investment.[51]

The processes of starting and running an IT business in India have been simplified and streamlined since 1984. However, the complex rules and lengthy procedures for transacting business remain a source of tremendous cost and frustration. The costs are especially severe for companies in globally competitive industries like software, where success depends critically on speed, or 'time to market'. In the recent words of Infosys chairman N.R. Narayana Murthy: 'If you want to be the first mover in India, please expect a lot of delays and trying times....[Al]though in absolute terms the country may have made substantial progress, on a relative scale we have slowed down.'[52]

The infrastructure section of the IT Action Plan calls for the liberalization of the telecommunications market, particularly in the area of data communications, and expanded access to the internet. It recognizes the bottleneck created by the power of the department of telecommunications, Mahanagar Telephone Nigam Ltd, and Videsh Sanchar Nigam Ltd. (VSNL) in this sector. The report recommends: (a) elimination of the license fee for internet service providers, (b) termination of the VSNL monopoly as international gateway for the internet, (c) removal of the DoT monopoly on the long-distance backbone to allow railways, state electricity boards, and others to host fibre-optic backbones, (d) provision of free permits for last-mile access, and (e) opening of a specified radio frequency band for public wireless usage.

The action plan also provides 39 recommendations calling for systematic rationalization of Indian duty structure and of the Companies Act. It proposes the exemption of public and private infrastructure providers from all import duties. It proposes phasing in the zero-duty regime earlier than was agreed to at the WTO Information Technology Agreement in 1996. The same section also recommends an overhaul of financial regulations to enable the accelerated expansion of IT. It designates IT as a priority sector in order to insure a greater flow of funds from banks into the industry, calls on banks to establish venture capital (VC) funds, and recommends the removal of regulatory constraints limiting the availability of venture capital. It also proposes expansion of the software industry definition to include IT-enabled service exports such as data entry, call centres, and other back-office operations, to ensure that these businesses benefit from the tax exemptions currently granted to software exports.

The section on 'IT for all by 2008' calls for development of e-commerce or cyber law; a campaign for universal computer literacy; schemes to insure provision of computers and the internet in all schools, colleges, and public hospitals by 2003; and a variety of IT programs in universities. This section also calls for IT in rural India, the use of Indian languages for computers, and the development of indigenous technologies. The final section recommends bringing IT into government by allocating 1–3 per cent of the budget of each ministry and department for IT applications.

This IT Action Plan has provided an impetus for change as well as an ambitious roadmap for India in the IT sphere. Prime Minister Vajpayee signalled his political support for the plan in late 1999 by creating a new Ministry of Information Technology to oversee its implementation. The newly appointed IT minister has in turn promised that all the recommendations will be implemented by 2001. Many, such as the development of cyber law and regulations concerning overseas investment in venture capital, have been acted on already.[53] Other sections of the plan will be significantly more difficult to implement for political or institutional reasons (e.g., because of resistance from bureaucrats who fear the loss of control) or because they are far too ambitious, at least in the short run.

A telling example of the challenges involved in achieving regulatory reform in India today is the recent efforts to facilitate the growth of the VC industry. The IT Action Plan recommends the promotion of VC, and most industry representatives and analysts agree that a dynamic venture capital industry will be critical to the long-term development of Indian IT. They argue that a healthy VC industry will stimulate new entrepreneurial entry, broaden the range of activities in the field, and accelerate the country's move into higher-value-added activities.

However, the supply of venture capital in India remains very small by international standards, largely because the industry is governed by a multiplicity of conflicting and often cumbersome regulations and discriminated against in a variety of ways. The industry is currently regulated by three different regulatory bodies: the Securities and Exchange Board of India (SEBI), the Ministry of Finance, and the Central Board of Direct Taxes (CBDT). In addition, foreign VC firms are also governed by the Foreign Investment Promotion Board (FIPB) and the Reserve Bank of India (RBI). As a result, there are now three different, mutually inconsistent, sets of regulations governing the industry. For example, each prescribes different investment criteria for VC funds. These statutes in turn compete with existing corporation, tax, and currency laws—many of which are extremely anachronistic (including some that predate India's independence).[54]

This helps account for the modest size of the VC industry in a financial system that boasts substantial domestic and foreign investment. In 1998 there were only 21 companies registered with the Indian Venture Capital Industry Association, with approximately $700 million available for investment. This compares to Israel's 100 firms with $4 billion investible funds (in 1999) and Taiwan's 100 funds with $ 1.32 billion investments. Moreover, most of India's

VC firms are funded either by the public sector or by multilateral funding agencies![55] These firms typically lack the expertise or contacts in the IT field, or the willingness to take risks, that would be essential to the sort of value-added financing that is associated with VC in places like Silicon Valley.

In an attempt to address these limitations, in 1999 SEBI convened a committee on venture capital, led by a successful non-resident Indian entrepreneur from Silicon Valley, K.B. Chandrasekhar, with the task of recommending steps to promote VC in India. The committee's report develops a comprehensive vision for the growth of India's VC industry, based on a survey of the global experience, and it proposes a series of regulatory and institutional reforms to achieve this goal.[56] The SEBI board adopted the report in January 2000, signalling the seriousness of the government's intentions to pursue its recommendations.

However, many of the committee's proposals require changes that go beyond SEBI's jurisdiction, so that the final outcome will depend on the report's acceptance by other parts of the government, particularly the CBDT, the FIPB, and the RBI. Thus the pace of change remains difficult to predict, in spite of the ongoing efforts at reform by the Ministry of Finance (which, for example, recently proposed exempting venture capital funds from direct taxation) and SEBI, as well as the support of the IT ministry for these reforms.

IT IN INDIAN DEVELOPMENT: THE NEED FOR A LARGER VISION

Comparisons between Indian regions like Bangalore—where future IT growth depends either on continued supplies of low-cost skill or on shifting into higher-value-added activities—and the world centre of technological innovation, Silicon Valley, remain premature at best. This is not to discount either India's achievements or its potential. India's large skill base is an important competitive asset in the knowledge-based economy, and the successes of Indian engineers in the United States demonstrate their technical and entrepreneurial capabilities when working in a supportive environment.

However, comparisons with Silicon Valley are misleading because they imply that India could, or should, seek to replicate the US model in information technology. There are compelling reasons that India will need to define its own pathway in the IT era. Silicon Valley emerged in the post-War US economy with the advantage of a large domestic market, a widely educated population, and well-functioning infrastructure and regulatory institutions. The same factors have facilitated the swift diffusion of information technology into the US economy and society—and supported a virtuous cycle of technological innovation to meet the needs of local producers and consumers.

In India, by contrast, a vast rural, as well as urban, population lives in poverty, lacking even minimal levels of education.[57] The nation's transportation and communications infrastructures remain woefully inadequate.[58] Furthermore, substantial bureaucratic and regulatory constraints continue to hinder the modernization of the private sector. In fact, a recent survey ranked India's bureaucracy as the worst in Asia in terms of efficiency and integrity.[59]

The current approach to IT policy in India addresses the immediate obstacles to growth identified by a small number of established, export-oriented software producers. This has proven successful: IT policy reforms, business confidence, and investment have become mutually reinforcing. This is reflected in the escalating valuations of technology companies on the Indian stock exchanges over the past year.[60] It is also reflected in the growing number of multinationals locating overseas development centres in the established IT regions. And this process of policy reform continues. The IT bill passed in mid-2000, for example, sets up a framework for electronic commerce in India. The growing political influence of the software industry means that much-needed regulatory reform, particularly in the telecommunications sector, is being initiated by the Government of India. Moreover, competition between state governments for IT investments should ensure improvements in transportation and communications infrastructure, at least in select urban areas.

However, there is need for a substantially broader perspective on policy than that determined by the immediate needs of the software industry. The current policy approach risks accelerating the growth of IT as a small, modern enclave in a poor and backward economy. The export earnings from IT are important to India's GDP growth and foreign exchange reserves, but they could be detrimental to the rest of the economy. Several observers have cautioned against the dangers of the 'Dutch Disease', in which dollars earned from a narrow sector like IT (which remains under 1 per cent of gross domestic product) sustain an increasingly strong Indian rupee and hurt the competitiveness of other less productive sectors of the economy.[61]

The concentration of the software industry in a small number of cities in the south has the potential to exacerbate the already disparate rates of growth across states and regions in India.[62] Software employment and investments are overwhelmingly concentrated in urban areas in the southern states of Karnataka (Bangalore), Andhra Pradesh (Hyderabad), and Tamil Nadu (Chennai), along with the western state of Maharashtra (Mumbai) and areas surrounding Delhi. The evidence from the United States suggests that such spatial agglomerations of IT production resist decentralization due to powerful supply-side externalities in the provision of skill, inputs, and technology.

Moreover, as incomes in the software sector increase, they will likely continue to diverge from those in other sectors. Professionals in IT enclaves could become better connected, both economically and socially, to distant regions than to the rest of the Indian economy. Already most IT development occurs in STPs that are insulated from the day-to-day challenges of doing business in India by dedicated communications links, private power sources, and liberal rules for investment and taxation. While the growing traffic of managers and policy-makers between India and Silicon Valley has obvious benefits for India, it risks creating an international technical community with diminishing ties to (or beneficial impacts on) the rest of the country.[63]

The task for policy-makers who aspire for IT to become more than an enclave in an otherwise backward economy is to develop a wider range of industries and institutions to support the economic and spatial diffusion of IT. This will require more far-reaching attention to development of the infrastructure and to education in rural as well as urban India. It will also require a sustained attack on the political and bureaucratic obstacles to the adoption of IT in both the public and private sectors. Indian workers today are contributing to the development of software to modernize foreign governments and corporations while their counterparts at home remain woefully backward.

While investment in IT grew rapidly in India during the 1990s, the country's use of IT remains extremely low by international standards. In 1996, spending on IT was only 0.5 per cent of GDP in India, compared to 2.8 per cent in the United States and 1.3 per cent in Malaysia. In 1997, India had only 2.1 PCs per thousand people, compared to 406.7 in the United States and 46.1 in Malaysia. Even China and the Philippines boasted higher rates of PC penetration, with 6.0 and 13.6 per thousand people respectively. Finally, in January 1999, India had only 0.13 internet hosts per 10,000 people, while Malaysia had 21.36 and the Philippines 1.21 (see Table 12.4).

This is by no means to suggest that India should pursue a policy of 'computers at all costs'. Indeed, we have seen that there are many other (often more pressing) needs in India, ranging from investments in basic infrastructure to improvements in the quality and accessibility of education. And it is possible that a place like Malaysia has, given its level of development, actually over-invested in IT. The disappointing performance of the Multimedia Super

Corridor, which has failed to attract private investments, suggests that the substantial resources devoted to its high-speed communications network and other twenty-first-century infrastructure might have been more wisely invested.

However, judicious investments in IT offer the opportunity to improve the productivity of many other sectors of the Indian economy. Applications could be developed to meet many of India's domestic needs, from revamping the education and health care systems to modernizing the retail and agricultural sectors. The state of Andhra Pradesh has been a leader and a model in public-sector adoption of IT. Naidu's administration has pioneered the computerization of land records, for example, which improves the efficiency of public service while also reducing opportunities for corruption (formerly ample). The challenge for India is to overcome the bureaucratic resistance motivated by fear of the loss of jobs—or of opportunities for graft.

Table 12.4: International reliance on information technology

Country	Ratio of spending on IT to GDP (1997)	PCs per 1,000 People (1997)	Internet hosts per 10,000 people (1999)
United States	2.8	406.7	1131.52
Singapore	1.9	399.5	210.02
South Korea	1.6	150.7	40.00
Ireland	1.3	241.3	148.70
Malaysia	1.3	46.1	21.36
Mexico	0.9	37.3	11.64
Brazil	0.9	26.3	12.88
Thailand	0.6	19.8	3.35
Philippines	0.5	13.6	1.21
China	0.5	6.0	0.14
India	0.5	2.1	0.13

Sources: IT/GDP: OECD (1997); PCs: World Development Indicators (1999–2000).

IT also offers potential efficiencies in a wide range of private-sector activities, from distribution and marketing to banking to agriculture. Farmers, for example, can use IT for managing their timetables, crop scheduling, soil testing, controlling insects and rodents, and for marketing and water management. Similarly innovative applications of IT can help develop local language software and local content that will allow the entire population of India to access the benefits of the internet. This, too, will require both the continuation of liberalization and regulatory reforms as well as incentives for investments in innovation to meet domestic needs.

Looking Ahead: Strategies for IT

The new communications technologies have generated important new opportunities for India that should not be overlooked, opportunities to expand remote services such as medical transcription or call centres. These IT-enabled services involve tasks that are too routine for western workers, but not so repetitive that they can be automated. Such remote services could ultimately provide more employment in India than the software services sector, because they depend not on engineers but on large numbers of people with English-language skills and the willingness to work for very low wages.[64]

In addition, most scenarios for the IT sector envision Indian software companies starting to develop innovative products and applications as well as continuing to provide low value-added services for export.[65] Yet they typically overlook the opportunities in India for a localized process of innovation. IT producers must typically work closely with customers to develop expertise and to define and test new products. However, as long as Indian software houses continue to rely primarily on exporting, they forego the opportunity to test and perfect products through interaction with end-users.

India has the technical skill needed to experiment with developing new products and services for the domestic market. In this scenario, IT products would be developed as a means to enable creative solutions to local problems. The prerequisites for such a strategy include continued deregulation in telecommunications, support for entrepreneurship, and the levelling of the playing field so that IT products and services sold domestically enjoy the same tax benefits as those currently enjoyed by software export units. This should allow the private sector to find economically viable ways to serve the domestic market.

This strategy involves a commitment to experimentation with technology appropriate to the Indian environment. Products developed in the West are typically too costly and provide more features than are needed by the vast majority of the Indian population. If products and services were developed that were affordable and reliable, they could transform what is now a potential market into a very sizeable customer base. Consider a product like an electronic pager. The pagers available in India today are produced in the West and sell for approximately Rs 22,000, well beyond the means of most of the Indian population. However, the technology is so simple that a pager could be developed and manufactured locally for only Rs 100. At this price it would be affordable to 20 per cent of the Indian population (which is a very large market, equal to the size of the market in the West). Such products would in turn be likely to have substantial export potential elsewhere in Asia, Latin America, and the rest of the developing world.[66]

The Simputer represents a model of innovation to meet domestic needs. The Simputer is a very low-cost mobile personal computer (priced at under Rs 9,000, or approximately US$ 200) that was developed by a Bangalore-based team of engineers. The team—which is drawn from the Department of Computer Science and Automation at the Indian Institute of Science (IISc) and a local design company, Encore Software—designed the product explicitly for the Indian market. While the Simputer is extremely low cost, it applies leading-edge technologies. It is based on free software (the Linux operating system), is designed to be open and modular, and offers multiple connectivity options. It also includes a SmartCard reader/writer, which provides a delivery vehicle for financial transactions on the internet and for e-commerce.

The Simputer project offers a model of collaboration for India, as well as an innovative product. The collaboration between the IISc and Encore, a public-sector university and a private-sector company, is rare in India, but offers a way to efficiently leverage local capabilities. Similarly, a team at the Indian Institute of Management, Bangalore, is conducting a study of the likely applications for such a device in rural and semi-urban areas. Some of the potential applications include using the Simputer as a platform for microbanking, for data collection, for internet access, for dissemination of agricultural information, and as a laboratory for experiments in rural schools.

India already has the design capabilities for developing such products. These capabilities are also evident in the growth of very large-scale integrated circuit design in the ODCs, as well as in the activities of some small indigenous firms like the Bangalore-based Silicon Automation Systems and Encore, which are currently developing the sophisticated intellectual property components for semi-conductor design. However, India lacks the environment needed to support experimentation with the application of these skills to new markets.

Policies to support innovation should facilitate new firm formation. While existing producers typically have resources and experience, as well as established reputations, entrepreneurial start-ups offer flexibility and focus without vested interests. This is why they are frequently the first movers in defining innovative products and services. In India, however, the ten largest firms account for more than 50 per cent of software exports at the same time that they represent a small proportion of the total firms in the sector.[67] A vibrant entrepreneurial sector could ideally generate innovative small firms that, over time, collaborate with established IT producers to take advantage of their respective strengths.

Venture capital is the first step toward encouraging entrepreneurship. If widely available, venture capital can support multiple experiments with new products, new services, and new applications. But venture capital alone is not sufficient. The greater challenge for India will be to create the social and institutional environments that support a decentralized process of experimentation and innovation. The lesson of Silicon Valley is clear: entrepreneurship is a collective, not an individual process. It depends upon a wider process of collective learning, typically within a localized community.[68] Such a technical community is built through collaborations of the sort that are rarely practiced in India today: collaborations between firms of all sizes, ages, and specializations, between firms and universities or research institutes, and between firms and financial institutions (especially venture capital). The Simputer project represents an important model that should be replicated across India.

Collaboration between IT start-ups and established producers with knowledge of particular domains could be especially important in the Indian context. A Bangalore company, Innomedia Technologies, for example, developed a low-cost technology for interactive television that uses existing cable-TV infrastructure to provide video on demand, interactive media, and online shopping. Once the technology was defined, the firm built an alliance with the large, established manufacturer, Reliance Industries, to undertake volume production and distribution.

Such collaborations can, of course, involve partners from other regions in India and even elsewhere in the world. The large NRI community in Silicon Valley could become an invaluable resource in identifying and coordinating such long distance partnerships. However, the pre-condition is the creation in India of the local networks that support the recombination of capital, skill, and technology into new ventures. Such an environment is emerging from an R&D group led by the Telecommunications & Computer Networks Group at the IIT Madras. This group includes university faculty and several small R&D companies formed by alumni, as well as distant collaborators. The group's mission is to make possible 25 million internet connections in India in less than ten years. It has strategic alliances with IC manufacturers abroad to develop wireless access, fibre access, and internet access systems specific to the needs of developing countries.[69]

Comparable networks can be created in other regions. Policy-makers (ideally state governments, since they are typically closer and more responsive to local needs) might provide incentives for collaborations between companies, or between companies and local universities or other research institutions. Or they might facilitate associational activities that bring together local producers, researchers, and service providers to seek solutions to shared problems such as the shortage of skilled labour or the need for better infrastructure. This process should facilitate the creation of cross-cutting social and technical networks that, over time, support information sharing and collective learning.

The independent, outwardly oriented companies and institutions that currently characterize the Indian scene have the potential to become localized technical communities with differing specializations related to their institutional and resource endowments. India's secretive public-sector units, such as the aerospace and defence research outfits in Bangalore, for example, could provide a rich source of technological opportunities if their boundaries were opened up and skill and know-how were allowed to flow more freely within the region. Similarly, venture capitalists and other service providers could, with time, become more knowledgeable about local capabilities, opportunities, and resources in order to play a growing role in coordinating and facilitating local experiments across India.

Finally, while the Indian Institutes of Technology produce among the best engineers in the world, their graduates still leave the country in large numbers. This group (or even a subset of them) could play a technological leadership role in India in the coming decades if more were to return to or stay in the country. As it stands now, however, too few remain or return or return to make an impact. By accelerating the deregulation of telecommunications and other key sectors, upgrading the physical infrastructure, and enhancing conditions for entrepreneurship, the government could create conditions under which more nonresident Indians (NRIs) would be willing to invest in the Indian economy. It is even possible that young Indian engineers would return in far greater numbers than in earlier generations if they saw viable economic opportunities at home. This could make a substantial difference to India's future.

CONCLUDING COMMENTS

The IT industry has brought a wide range of important and tangible improvements to India. It has provided the confidence that India has a future in the new economy, and it has generated jobs, wealth, and exports. Moreover, the pace of policy reform in the IT industry has been unprecedented. This reflects, at least in part, the opening up of the policy debates to include new actors. The industry association, NASSCOM, has accelerated the policy reform process through its aggressive lobbying while helping to define a minimally interventionist model of industrial promotion. Meanwhile, entrepreneurial state governments, spurred on by the example of Andhra Pradesh, have pioneered a potentially far-reaching, bottom-up process of policy reform.

However, there are also substantial dangers in the current fascination with IT in India. The challenge today is twofold. First, there is a need to be very realistic about the limits of software as a development strategy for India. Bangalore is not Silicon Valley, and IT is not going to solve all of India's problems. IT is still a very small piece of the Indian output and exports, and even if it grows rapidly it will remain only one among many sectors that contribute to Indian development in the coming decades.

This suggests the second challenge: the need to widen the range of participants in the policy debates and to broaden their scope still further. The alliance between the large software industry and the government has restricted the debate over IT policy. The goal should not be to simply meet the needs of a handful of producers, but rather to use IT as a means to strengthen the fabric of the entire economy and to enhance opportunities and living conditions for the whole Indian population.

NOTES AND REFERENCES

1. The author is especially indebted to Balaji Parthasarathy, now with the Indian Institute of Information Technology, Bangalore, and to the participants of the workshop on Equity, Diversity, and Information Technology held at the National Institute of Advanced Study, Bangalore, in December 1999. Their research and wisdom are reflected throughout this document. Any errors are the author's alone. The author devotes special thanks as well to Sajjid Chinoy and Suraj Jacob, who provided outstanding research assistance at very short notice.

2. NASSCOM, *The software industry in India: A strategic review* (New Delhi, NASSCOM, 2000); Ministry of Finance, *Economic Survey 1999–2000* (New Delhi, National Informatics Centre, Government of India, 2001).

3. Ashish Arora, V.S. Arunchalam, Jai Asundi and Ronald Fernandes, 'The Indian software services industry', Working Paper, Carnegie-Mellon University, Heinz School of Public Policy and Management.

4. Organization for Economic Cooperation and Development, 1997, *Information Technology Outlook* (Paris, OECD, 1997), p. 50.

5. Ministry of Finance, *Economic Survey 1999–2000.*

6. Remarks made by Ashok Jhunjhunwala at a conference on Equity,

Diversity, and Information Technology, National Institute of Advanced Study. 3–4 December 1999, Bangalore, India.

7. C.R. Subramanian, *India and the Computer: A Study of Planned Development* (New Delhi, Oxford University Press, 1992).

8. IBM's 1978 departure from India, after its refusal to comply with the requirements of the Foreign Exchange and Regulation Act, is indicative. For details, see Joseph M. Grieco, *Between Dependency and Autonomy: India's Experience with the International Computer Industry* (Berkeley, University of California Press, 1984).

9. Rajiv Gandhi's administration also initiated the computerization of the railway reservation system and several government processes. One of his most innovative contributions was the creation of the Centre for the Development of Telematics, which pioneered indigenous digital switching technology to facilitate India's shift from electromechanical to digital switching and transmission.

10. Eswaran Sridharan, *The Political Economy of Industrial Promotion: Indian, Brazilian, and Korean Electronics in Comparative Perspective 1969–1994* (Westport, Connecticut, Praeger, 1996).

11. Interview with N. Vittal, former secretary of the Department of Electronics, New Delhi, 25 June 1996, cited in Balaji Parthasarathy, 'Globalization and Agglomeration in Newly Industrializing Countries: The State and the Information Technology Industry in Bangalore, India', Ph.D. dissertation, University of California at Berkeley, 2000.

12. Quoted in Parthasarathy, 'Globalization and Agglomeration'.

13 Pronab Sen, 'Exports from India: A systemic analysis', *Electronics Information and Planning* 22 (2) (1994), pp. 55–63.

14. Parthasarathy, 'Globalization and Agglomeration'.

15. The terminology used in the Indian software industry can be confusing. Onsite services are those in which programmers work at the customer's facilities, while offshore services are performed in a remote location, in this case in India.

16. Firms have to earn a net amount equal to 150 per cent of the hardware imported within four years. They also have to earn a net amount equal to 150 per cent of their wage bill on an annual basis. Though the STP scheme was meant for 100 per cent export units, in January 1995 STP firms were allowed to sell 25 per cent of their output to the domestic tariff area. The figure was revised to 50 per cent in 1999. Balaji Parthasarathy, 'An Asian Silicon Valley in Bangalore? Evidence for the changing organization of production in the Indian computer software industry', unpublished manuscript (University of California at Berkeley, Department of City and Regional Planning, 2000).

17. Interview with S.K. Agarwal, director of STPI, New Delhi, 20 June 1996. Cited in Parthasarathy 'Globalization and Agglomeration'.

384 ● INDIA'S ECONOMIC TRANSITION

18. For further details on policy changes in 1991 and since, see Krueger and Chinoy..

19. NASSCOM was founded in 1988 with 38 members. By 1999 it had 464 members and accounted for 95 per cent of software industry revenues.

20. Firms were allowed to invest up to 50 per cent of their foreign exchange earnings in the previous three years, subject to a maximum of $25 million.

21. ADR/GDR: American/global depository receipts. The ADR is a certificate, issued by a US bank, that trades like a share on NASDAQ, allowing the US investor to invest in a foreign market without having to deal with the risk of currency transactions. ADRs represent a certain number of domestic shares of the firm deposited with the bank. GDRs are similar to ADRs, except that they are traded on international stock exchanges such as the London Stock Exchange. The Reserve Bank of India permits Indian employees to remit up to $50,000 in a block of five years to ADRs/GDRs.

22. For a detailed analysis of the telecommunications case, see Parthasarathy, 'An Asian Silicon Valley'.

23. See http://www.nasscom.org/.

24. NASSCOM's data includes only the numbers provided by its members and thus overlooks large numbers of smaller software and IT companies that are not part of the association. NASSCOM's goal of promoting software industry may tend to bias the data as well. Future policy reform would ideally include creation of a reliable, independent source of detailed industry data.

25. Richard Heeks, *India's Software Industry: State Policy, Liberalisation and Industrial Development* (New Delhi, Sage Publications, 1996).

26. National Association of Software and Service Companies (NASSCOM), 'Indian IT Strategies', Report prepared by McKinsey & Co. (New Delhi, NASSCOM, 1999)

27. By 1995, 435 companies were registered under the STP scheme, accounting for more than 16 per cent of exports. Software Technology Parks of India (STPI), *Directory of STP Units* (New Delhi, STPI, 1997).

28. Parthasarathy, 'Globalization and Agglomeration', p. 28.

29. Interview with industry representative. Bangalore, 30 July 1996, as cited by Parthasarathy, 'Globalization and Agglomeration'.

30. The engineers at the Texas Instruments development centre, for example, developed a new digital signal processing chip that has become a standard.

31. Parthasarathy, 'Globalization and Agglomeration'.

32. Ibid.

33. Ashish Arora, 'Quality Certification and the Economics of Contract Software Development: A Study of the Indian Software Industry', NBER

Working Paper No. W7260 (Cambridge, Mass., National Bureau of Economic Research, July 1999).

34. Five companies account for close to 50 per cent of software industry exports: Tata Consultancy Services, Infosys, Pentaflour, Tata Infotech, and Wipro.

35. Arora et al., 'The Indian Software Services Industry'.

36. Ibid.

37. B. Lindsay Lowell, 'H-1B Temporary Workers: Estimating the Population', unpublished manuscript (Georgetown University, Institute for the Study of International Migration, 2000).

38. Arora, 'Quality Certification'.

39. NASSCOM, 'Indian IT Strategies'.

40. 'India Hit by Shortage of IT Professionals', www.siliconindia.com, 21 May 2000.

41. Ashank Desai, 'The Domestic Software Industry in Perspective', *Times Computing Online*, 6 January (1999). Available at http://www.timescomputing. com/19990106/spkl.html.

42. One project will facilitate integrated delivery of eighteen services (such as payments for water, electricity, property taxes, etc.) from six different departments. Another, the Multipurpose Household Study, will develop records of all individuals in the state and provide uniform data for all of the departments. See http://www.andhrapradesh.com.

43. The IT industry is concentrated in Andhra Pradesh, Karnataka, and Tamil Nadu, largely because of their concentration of engineering manpower. Sixty per cent of India's computer science graduates come from these three states. Rafiq Dossani, 'Reforming Venture Capital in India: Creating the Enabling Environment', Working Paper, Stanford University, Asia/Pacific Research Center, 2000.

44. This summary is drawn from a review of Naidu's book on the official website of Andhra Pradesh at http://www.andhrapradesh.com.

45. The taskforce set up four working groups: IT research, design, and development; IT human resources development; citizen–IT interface; and content creation and content industry. These groups each had 12–16 members and drew in a still wider range of perspectives. The task force secretariat also reportedly received some 8,000 e-mail messages providing policy suggestions. See http://it-taskforce.pic.in.

46. National Taskforce on Information Technology and Software Development, 'IT Action Plan' (New Delhi, National Informatics Centre, 2000). Available at http://it-taskforce.nic.in/diary.htm.

47. Sheshagri claims that 80 per cent of the recommendations have already

been implemented, but there is no way to confirm this figure. Mohana Prabhakar, 'Cyber Laws will be in place: Dr. N. Seshagiri', *Itspace.com* (2000). Available at http://www.itspace.com/ItspaceAlpha/features/print/Itpolicy/seshagiri.asp.

48. See, for example, Ashank Desai, 'Problems Confronting the Software Entrepreneur,' *Times Computing Online,* 17 March (1999). Available at http://www.timescomputing.com/19990317/spk 1. html; and AnnaLee Saxenian, *Silicon Valley's New Immigrant Entrepreneurs.* (San Francisco: Public Policy Institute of California, 1999). Available at http://www.ppic.org/publications/PPIC120/ppic120.abstract.html.

49. Krueger and Chinoy.

50. International Telecommunications Union (ITU), *World Telecommunications Indicators Database* (Geneva, ITU, 1998).

51. It is worth repeating the McKinsey-NASSCOM estimate that as much as $23 billion in IT export revenues and 650,000 jobs fail to materialize over an eight-year period because of limitations of the telecommunications infrastructure. NASSCOM, 'Indian IT Strategies'.

52. Cited in C. Chitti Pantulu, 'Entrepreneurs Should Be Prepared for Delays, Says Narayana Murthy', *The Financial Express,* 6 February 2000.

53. Task force convenor Sheshagri claims that roughly 80 per cent of the recommendations have been implemented, but it is very difficult to assess this claim.

54. The discussion of India's venture capital industry draws from Rafiq Dossani and Lawrence Saez, 'Venture Capital in India', Working Paper (Stanford University, Asia/Pacific Research Center, 2000).

55. Ibid.

56. Securities and Exchange Board of India (SEBI), 'Report of K.B. Chandrasekhar committee on venture capital' (New Delhi, SEBI, 2000).

57. Anjini Kochar, 'Emerging Challenges for Indian Education Policy', in Anne O. Krueger (ed.), *Economic Policy Reforms and the Indian Economy* (New Delhi: Oxford University Press, 2002), pp. 303–28.

58. Anne O. Krueger and Sajjid Chinoy, 'The Indian Economy in Global Context', in Anne O. Krueger (ed.), *Economic Policy Reforms and the Indian Economy* (New Delhi: Oxford University Press, 2002), pp. 9–45.

59. Joydeep Mukherji, 'Information Technology in India: Yet another missed opportunity?', *Standard & Poor's Credit Week,* 12 July (2000), pp. 18–25.

60. Software and related IT services companies now comprise 20–25 per cent of India's total stock market capitalization.

61. Mukherji, 'Information Technology in India'.

62. Montek S. Ahluwalia, 'State-Level Performance under Economic Reforms in India', in Anne O. Krueger (ed.), *Economic Policy Reforms and the Indian Economy* (New Delhi: Oxford University Press, 2002), pp. 91–121.

63. Mukherji, 'Information Technology in India' describes historic examples of Indian breakthroughs in mathematics and metallurgy that largely bypassed the general population and economy, often providing benefits to outsiders.

64. See 'Indian Business: Spice Up Your Services, '*The Economist*', 16 January 1999.

65. NASSCOM, 'Indian IT Strategies'.

66. Remarks by Ashok Jhunjhunwala at conference on Equity, Diversity, and Information Technology, National Institute of Advanced Study, Bangalore, India, 3–4 December 1999.

67. NASSCOM, 'Indian IT Strategies', reports that there are 826 companies in India engaged in the business of software exports.

68. AnnaLee Saxenian, *Regional advantage: Culture and competition in Silicon Valley and Route 128* (Cambridge, Mass., Harvard University Press, 1994).

69. Ashok Jhunjhunwala, Bhaskar Ramamurthi and Timothy A. Gonsalves, 'The Role of Technology in Telecom Expansion in India', *IEEE Communication Magazine* 36 (11) (1998), pp. 88–94.

13

Public Sector Restructuring and Democracy
The State, Labour, and Trade Unions in India[*]

SUPRIYA ROYCHOWDHURY[1]

This chapter looks at ways in which marketization reforms affect the empowerment, ideological universes, and functioning limits of popular institutions. Under what circumstances do left-leaning trade unions accept job cuts and wage freezes? What are the boundaries of consent and dissent? Case studies of three public sector companies in Bangalore city in the southern state of Karnataka, India, indicate that labour rationalization has occurred with trade union acquiescence and support. However, as yet there is no broad institutional framework to handle social security, rehabilitation, and redeployment of displaced workers. Public sector workforce reduction is taking place in a general economic context where there has been little growth of employment in the organized manufacturing sector. Beneath unions' apparent acquiescence to rationalization processes, there are critical areas of dissent. This dissent, however, has not manifested itself in a critical alternative to the state's rationalization policies. Changing party—union relations, and shifts in the internal dynamics of unions affecting choice of leaders, union aspirations, and ideologies—underwritten by the broader economic changes wrought by the marketization process— partially explain the inability of the labour movement to shape a definitive challenge to the marketization process.

* Originally published as 'Public Sector Restructuring and Democracy: The State, Labour and Trade Unions in India', in *The Journal of Development Studies*, 39 (3), February 2003, pp. 29–50, published by Frank Cass, London.

INTRODUCTION

The relationship between economic development and political regimes—particularly the complex relationship between free market capitalism and political democracy—has been a long-standing concern in political science. Economic liberalization programmes, which began in a large number of developing countries from the mid-1980s onwards, brought a sharper edge to the capitalism–democracy question. In most developing country contexts, the rationale for a shift from a statist and closed model of economic development is no longer questioned. However, the inegalitarian implications of economic reforms—frequently fraught with the potential for societal discontent and political challenge—are also widely acknowledged. As such, the question of an appropriate political framework, which would allow reformists to push ahead with a market-oriented reform agenda, has obviously attracted a great deal of scholarly attention.

The following general points need to be made regarding the fairly large literature on the theme of politics of economic reforms. The focus in this literature has been particularly on countries that have experienced political democratization and economic opening up almost simultaneously (East Asia, Latin America). As such, the concern has been with contexts where democratic frameworks are new and fragile, possibly lacking in institutional capacities to handle an upsurge of popular distributional demands, and vulnerable to authoritarian comebacks.[2] The concern with fragile democracies has generated a shared sense that the politics of adjustment or reforms is essentially a function of political *management*. Scholars seem to be inclined to the view that some degree of centralization of executive authority may be needed to get the reforms in place.

Centralised executive authority is important for overcoming policy stalemates. The successful initiation of reform depends on rulers who have personal control over economic decision making, the security to recruit and back a cohesive 'reform team', and the political authority to override bureaucratic and political opposition to policy change.[3]

In general scholars agree that in the long run, democracy, through strategic coalitions and consensus building, would allow for a more sustained thrust in reforms than is possible under overtly repressive systems. There is, however, relatively little specific discussion in the literature as to what such a democracy might look like, in a context where large numbers of people do not stand to gain from a marketization policy regime. Some scholars have pointed to the need for building new coalitions—some groups to be favoured, building up support against other groups who may be potentially hurt by reforms; there has also been the suggestion that protests by disaffected groups can, over time, be ignored.[4]

A relatively neglected area is the arena of civil society, and the impact of reforms, particularly, on the politics and ideologies of popular organizations— that is, organizations that purport to represent interests of low-income groups or other disadvantaged sections. If indeed consensus-forming and coalition-building across strategic societal groups is key to successful economic reforms, it would be important to examine the effects of these strategies on popular institutions and organizations, in terms of their ideologies, rhetoric and politics.

One way to do this would be to ask, for example, what are the circumstances in which populist, left-leaning organizations, such as trade unions, accept a market oriented policy package, which may entail job cuts and a wage freeze? What strategies do they use to resist and/or reformulate, and disseminate such policies? Do political debates within these organizations generate alternative models of development? This perspective would enable us to locate the predominant tendencies in the economic reform-institution dynamics and identify whether and in what ways the transition to the market affects the empowerment of popular sectors and shapes the ideological universes and functioning limits of democratic institutions.

This chapter examines the politics of labour in India as a sub-narrative of the politics of economic reform, within the broader framework of the economic reform-democracy relationship. Given India's noisy democracy, and a long tradition of labour activism, the specific dimensions of economic reforms which potentially may have hurt labour—privatization, retrenchment, market-driven hiring and firing, or even an exit policy for inefficient firms—have not been pushed too much by reform-oriented policy-makers. This has led several observers to stress that organized labour has been one of a set of powerful interest groups (such as rich farmers, professionals, and the industrial bourgeoisie) which have effectively impacted upon the policy making process to limit the pace and scope of reforms.[5] However, specific dimensions of the state–labour relationship in the context of liberalization highlight tendencies that do not readily fit into broad generalizations regarding labour's power.

In my earlier work, on private sector textile and jute mills[6] I have pointed out that as a large number of firms have declined in these sectors, the complex process of decay and restructuring has been accompanied by the displacement of a large number of workers. Such displacement frequently occurs without severance payment, and pushes the worker into the uncertain world of the unorganized sector. In a large number of such cases, trade unions have been powerless to resist job losses, and governments have given tacit consent to illegal closures and worker displacement.[7]

Thus there are seemingly opposed tendencies at work—a legal framework that continues to protect labour, while political-economy realities underlie a certain disempowerment of organized labour. This paradox in fact highlights the cutting edge of economic reforms, where democracy and the market interface—that is, where labour, trade unions, the state, and private entrepreneurs interact, with a shifting developmental paradigm in the backdrop.

Where the public sector is concerned, the state has sought to contract its economic role in manufacturing and even in infrastructure and services, and increasingly to signal private enterprise, both national and foreign, as the engine of growth in these sectors. Secondly, within the public sector itself, it has sought to modify what are now perceived as mistakes of the past—the prioritization of employment and social welfare over profitability—by an increased emphasis on efficiency and competition. These shifts in approach have led to an implicit, sometimes explicit, redefinition, of the state's relationship with an erstwhile favoured client—namely, organized labour in the public sector. There is now a greater stress than there was earlier on efficiency, discipline, and productivity. The Indian state—given its location in a pluralistic democracy and its ideologically diverse, and more recently its coalitional, character—is pulled in many directions. Thus the trends outlined above represent emerging tendencies rather than a complete shift.

A popular impression is that Indian public sector enterprises—given their public ownership, welfare concerns, and powerful unions accustomed to a patron–client relationship with the state—would be highly resistant to change in matters affecting labour. In this chapter, case studies of three large public sector firms show that significant labour rationalization has taken place in these companies, and that too with trade union support. These cases, then, exemplify changes occurring in somewhat unlikely contexts and therefore highlight the dynamics of shifts occurring in labour institutions and ideologies.

However, the chapter also highlights that, beyond consent, there are areas of worker *discontent, dissent*, and resentment around ongoing rationalization processes. These often remain unexpressed or are expressed only unsystematically. Consent, therefore, possibly coexists with its opposite form, critique/dissent. What, then, are the factors underlying consent? What are the reasons why dissent remains inchoately expressed? While the lines between trade unions' acquiescence/consensus and critical dissent may be blurred, it is nevertheless important to locate those lines. For, it is in that undefined space that it may be possible to decipher the ways in which an emerging market structure and ideology have a transforming impact upon popular sector articulations and organizations, and whether and in what ways the latter respond in terms of new concepts, strategies, and institutions.

The empirical material used in this chapter draws on case studies relating to labour rationalization processes in three public sector enterprises (henceforth PSEs), owned by the central government, located in Bangalore city, the capital of Karnataka state in southern India. The companies are: Bharat Electronics Ltd. (BEL), Indian Telephone Industries (ITI), and Hindusthan Machine Tools Ltd. (HMT); while each of these have units in many parts of India, the case studies pertain only to the head offices which are located in Bangalore.

Bangalore city has a significant history and presence of PSEs, many of which have a long background of active unionization. A strike conducted jointly by four of the units during 1980–1 has been the longest lasting strike in the history of PSEs in India. The study of these firms in the phase of liberalization, starting in the mid-1980s, therefore provides a useful platform for examining the changing nature of trade union activities and of management-labour relations.

Section II of this chapter offers an outline of the debate over public sector reform. This provides a framework for examining, in the following sections, in what ways labour response to rationalization locates itself in the debate. Section III presents the case studies of three central PSEs. Section IV examines the ways in which labour rationalization and new industrial relations (henceforth IR) strategies impact upon worker opportunities and empowerment. Section V briefly outlines institutional factors: internal dynamics of unions and union–party relations. These factors—in the broad context of a changing economic scenario—partially explain unions' lack of response in terms of an alternative conceptual framework to challenge marketization reforms.

REFORM OF THE PUBLIC SECTOR

In the debate around public sector reform, the undisputed fact is that many PSEs chronically make losses. In 1992–3, 104 out of 237 central PSEs made losses (after interest); these losses amounted to Rs 3,951 million.[8] As is widely known, during the 1960s through the mid-1980s, a large number of loss-making private enterprises were nationalized, primarily with the objective of protecting employment. Government resources continued to be spent on these loss-making enterprises.

A critical approach to these facts has increasingly defined state policy towards the public sector. First, the Bureau for Industrial and Financial Reconstruction (BIFR), which was established in 1987 primarily to review cases of company decline, received references for 82 central PSEs as unsustainable enterprises. Of these, as on November 1998, as many as 10 were recommended for winding up, and for the rest a variety of rehabilitation schemes were recommended. Second, in 1996 a Disinvestment Commission was established, and 40 PSEs were referred to it. The Commission in its first report recommended disinvestment of 49 per cent and 74 per cent in the core and non-core sectors respectively. Third, the share of budgetary support in the plan investment of the public enterprises came down from 23.5 per cent in 1991–2 to 18.6 per cent in 1992–3 and then to 15 per cent where it has remained constant.[9] Finally, in many PSEs, managers have pursued policies of reduction and redeployment of manpower as well as bans on fresh recruitment. Employment in public sector manufacturing declined in absolute numbers from 1.87 million in 1990 to 1.75 million in 1995.[10]

The question of manpower redundancy has been central in the critique of PSEs. Protagonists of privatization and/or labour rationalization have noted the possibilities of reduction through severance compensation. They have in general taken an optimistic view of the impact of severance on workers, both in terms of workers being able to find new employment and the possibility of redundancy payments adding to national savings.[11]

On the other hand, a central element of the criticism of privatization/labour rationalization has derived from the general decline in employment, which has occurred in organized manufacturing in the economy as a whole. The rate of growth in organized sector employment declined from 2.48 per cent in 1978–83 to 1.38 per cent in 1983–8, 1.05 per cent in 1993–4. In urban areas the percentage of those engaged in regular salaried employment declined from 44.2 per cent in 1977–8 to 41.5 per cent in 1993–4, and the percentage of those engaged in casual wage employment increased from 15.5 per cent to 18.2 per cent during the same period.[12] Thus the overall economic situation in terms of employment is such that displacement from the public sector as a result of privatization/disinvestment and/or rationalization would inevitably mean displacement from the formal/organized manufacturing sector. On an average, in manufacturing and construction, those employed in the unorganized sector earn 50 per cent less than those employed in the formal sector. The possibility of economic dislocation has been one of the central points raised by critics of the official approach to public sector reform.

Defenders of the public enterprise system—trade unionists and left-leaning intellectuals—have pointed out that the government has opted for disinvestment and employment contraction in PSEs over other more appropriate methods of fiscal discipline (for example, withdrawal of subsidies to the agricultural sector, or pruning the over-manned civil service). Second, in absolute terms, of the 7.2 million workers added to organized employment in the period 1976–94, 6 million (or 85 per cent) were absorbed in the public sector.[13] On the other hand, there has occurred a total reduction of one million in public sector manufacturing between 1991–5.[14] Thus, as far as manpower reduction is concerned, the axe seems to have fallen on public sector manufacturing rather than on the public sector as a whole. Finally, the wage revision for central government employees through the Fifth Pay Commission recommendations, implemented from the mid-1990s, does not cover PSEs. This has naturally led to much criticism from PSE employees.

While the need for restructuring is not denied, the debate is more over the way in which restructuring is to be defined and on the specific modalities of public sector reform. Even within the economic bureaucracy, which is by and large pro-liberalization, dissenting voices have indicated that the public sector needs to be restructured qua public sector—for example, by linking up public sector enterprises through a process of mutual demand generation and supply support.[15]

In the context of economic reforms, labour is under an overall threat. The spread of outsourcing, contracting, part-time labour, and a general trend towards capital-intensive technologies tend to leave labour outside the margins of organized employment. In such a context, the public sector provides, in a sense, the last citadel of protection for labour. The discussion in the following sections highlights in what ways unions and labour have responded, in general, to the debate over PSE reform, and more specifically, to the imperatives of rationalization within firms, as also how both the debate and the processes of restructuring have shaped the trade union movement.

CASE STUDIES

Each of the three central PSEs studied here[16]—Bharat Electronics Ltd (BEL), Hindustan Machine Tools (HMT), and Indian Telephone Industries (ITI)—were established in the period 1948–53, for the production, respectively, of defence electronics, machine tools, and telephone transmissions. With head offices in Bangalore, all three have several units in other parts of the country, and are considered to be amongst the flagships of India's large public sector system. Each of the three is set amidst sprawling acres of land, which have a township character, providing housing, schools, hospitals, subsidized meals, and transport.

From the mid-1980s onwards, however, this idyllic environ has given way to an increasing stress on efficiency and declining budgetary support, and a disciplinarian approach to labour has subtly replaced the welfaristic approach of the pre-reform era. We discuss two elements of restructuring in so far as these particularly affect labour: manpower reduction and redeployment, and, more briefly, wages.

Labour Reduction and Redeployment

The specific context to the adoption of labour rationalization programmes varied in the three cases. Import liberalization and competition from multinationals—both a result of the government's economic liberalization programme—affected HMT and ITI. At BEL, changes in production technology as well as competition from the private sector in the production of consumer electronics parts underlined the need for rationalization. In all three companies, the Voluntary Retirement Scheme (VRS) was adopted, from the mid-1980s onwards, as a means to ease out workers who are perceived to be redundant. The compensation scheme varies from company to company. Typically, those aged 40 and above, with a record of a minimum ten years of service, are offered a package of one month's salary for each completed year of service, combined with all other retirement benefits such as provident fund, gratuity, and so on. On an average, workers above the age of 45 rather than younger workers seem to opt for the VRS.

Bharat Electronics Ltd. (BEL) was set up in 1952 for the production of defence electronics, and later diversified to the production of parts used for consumer electronics. At present, one third of BEL's sales are to the private sector. Labour rationalization was introduced in BEL in response to changing technology of production. The use of plastic had rendered certain activities redundant, such as painting, chrome-plating, fitting, and welding. In these circumstances, the mid-1980s saw the company facing a problem of around 2000 surplus workers. The VRS has been adopted in three phases from 1987 to 1999 to ease out redundant workers. As part of the ongoing process of restructuring, the Receiving Valves Division and a plant manufacturing black and white television tubes were closed down (in 1982 and 1992 respectively) and the unit for the production of semi-conductors and capacitors was sold. Workers from these plants were redeployed within the company.

HMT was established in 1953 as a producer of machine tools. The company subsequently diversified into manufacturing watches and other engineering products. At HMT, import liberalization led to a declining share in the market for capital goods. Competition from multinationals like Titan generated a loss in market share in watches. Liberalization also saw the tightening of budgetary support for the company. In this general climate of crisis, workforce reduction was undertaken through the VRS from 1992 onwards. Subsequently, there surfaced a shortage of skilled manpower directly engaged in the production process. Given a ban on recruitment during a period when the company was implementing the VRS, management resorted to the strategies of reskilling and redeployment from redundant functions to essential functions. This strategy has meant transfers of jobs not only from one function to another but even in different geographical locations. In 1997, for example, the lamps production unit of the company in Hyderabad City was closed down and about 80 workers were transferred to the Machine Tools unit in Bangalore. Thus a combination of reduction and redeployment has been adopted.

ITI was founded in 1948. In the 1960s, the production of telephone transmission lines was started; in 1964, a collaboration with Bell of Belgium began. In 1987 a model plant was set up at the Electronics City unit with a 40,000-line exchange, and the technology shifted from electromechanical to electronic.

In the mid-1990s, ITI confronted a serious financial crisis. The backdrop to the crisis was the government's liberalization reforms in general and the National Telecom Policy (NTP) of 1994 in particular. Earlier ITI had a virtual monopoly over the market, and the company's pricing system was on a cost-plus basis. With the NTP 1994, multinationals such as Modi Alcatel, Ericsson, Fujitsu, and Siemens came into the market and the tender system was introduced. Multinationals quoted lower prices. Tenders determined orders. ITI faced a situation where orders declined dramatically. ITI's profits plunged from Rs 8,435 million in 1993–4 to a loss of Rs 8, 191 million in 1994–5. Losses continued in the following two years, until there was finally a turnaround in 1997–8.

Manpower rationalization, particularly through the VRS, was one of the most important elements in ITI's restructuring process. There have been two factors underlying the need for VRS: first, phasing out of old electromechanical devices and a shift towards digital technology (that is, change of technology); and second, opening up of the telecom sector to the private sector. The VRS has been implemented in different phases during the years 1991 to 1999.

Table 13.1 provides data on number of workers reduced and redeployed in the three companies, over the period 1987–99.

Table 13.1: Labour reduction through VRS in three public sector units

Name of company	Years of VRS implementation	Number of workers reduced	Total reduction (workers, clerks, managers)	Number of workers redeployed
BEL	1987–99	2773	3541	1378
HMT	1992–7	6000	NA	180
ITI	1991–9	3919	5000	4500

Source: Data collected from interviews with personnel managers in the companies concerned.

The Dynamics of Rationalization: Changing Industrial Relations Practices

PSE employees have traditionally seen themselves as lifetime clients of the state, their interests protected by institutionalized wage adjustments, job security, and many other attendant benefits. The removal of aging or redundant employees, closures, and transfers are all difficult rationalization schemes in the public sector context in India. What mechanisms, then, have served to accomplish these objectives?

In all three companies, management stated—and trade union leaders acknowledged—that a general change had taken place in the philosophy of industrial relations, from a 'management versus worker' approach to a 'we versus the problem' approach.[17] The underlying theme of this shift was recognition of the critical need to share information regarding the company with trade unionists and, through them, with the general body of workers. This recognition was institutionalized through certain structures of information sharing and employee participation at different levels.

From 1985 onwards, each of the three central public sector firms initiated the formation of joint committees, composed of representatives from management and from trade unions, which were designed to enact, coordinate and implement critical restructuring decisions.

In BEL a joint committee was set up in early 1992, composed of four members of management and four from the two negotiating unions. Initially the proposal to close a plant manufacturing TV tubes drew intense opposition from union representatives. Following this, all papers relating to the problems connected with the unit were handed over to the union representatives in an effort to communicate to them the urgency of the problem. In subsequent meetings, the unions appeared to have accepted the logic of the closure and were prepared to negotiate the terms and conditions of redeployment. Both management and union leaders stated that the decision to close the division was arrived at through a process of consensus building between management and the negotiating unions, with a collaborative problem-solving approach.

At HMT, the Bipartite Negotiating Committee (composed of management and union office-bearers) exists as the forum through which central issues facing the company are discussed and negotiated. Through the committee, the company's financial crisis and the urgency of downsizing was communicated to the workforce. A similar strategy of communication was adopted in the closure of the lamps production unit in Hyderabad City in 1997, whereby a large number of employees were transferred to a Bangalore unit.

Similarly, at ITI, unit-level and company-level joint committees hold meetings periodically where specific issues facing a unit, as well as those affecting the company as a whole, are discussed. At the company-level meetings, top management makes presentations on the general telecom scenario, and suggestions are invited from union leaders.

In addition to the committees which participate at the general policy level, each of the companies have instituted shop-floor-level and plant-level committees, composed of managers and trade union representatives, which handle problems and issues at the micro level. These issues are typically those of improving productivity, maintaining quality, and so on. The structures of participation at the shop-floor level give workers a chance to influence decisions which directly affect their day-to-day work lives, and are said to reinforce and strengthen the foundations of 'consensus', which is perceived by management as a critical instrument in company restructuring.

The new IR approach and structures outlined above are characteristic of a worldwide tendency in the last few decades towards creating more participatory and consensus-oriented management-worker relations.[18] In what ways can these structures be looked at within the framework of the question of worker empowerment? This question will be taken up in the last section of this chapter.

Trade Union Responses to Rationalization

The trade union system in PSEs provides a varying picture, but there are some emerging commonalties. In the public sector, firm-level trade unions have, typically and traditionally, been affiliated to the national trade union federations.

Federations such as the All India Trade Union Congress (AITUC), the Indian National Trade Union Congress (INTUC) the Bharatiya Mazdoor Sangh (BMS), the Centre of Indian Trade Unions (CITU) are in turn associated with major political parties.

From the 1980s, there has been an emerging tendency for firm-level unions to be independent of affiliations with the national federations. Of the three central PSEs examined, HMT and ITI have single, independent unions. At BEL, there are four unions, of which three are affiliated to central trade union federations, each directly linked to three of the largest political parties. At present the independent BEL Workers' Unity Forum is the largest union at BEL.

Trade union leaders at BEL were unanimous that employee reduction need not be a necessary feature of restructuring. In their perception, the basic problem at BEL stemmed from declining orders from the defence department and the failure of management to respond to this by diversifying the product portfolio. This failure had caused the need for employee reduction. In this context, each of the four unions had taken a similar stance: they neither actively supported nor opposed VRS.

At HMT, union leadership across the units appeared to be convinced of the inevitability of change, and their greatest challenge seems to have been to disseminate the logic of rationalization to the workforce. The closure of the lamps unit in Hyderabad and the consequent shifting out of workers to a unit in Bangalore involved the painful process of geographical transfer, separation from family, finding accommodation, and the like. Over these odds, the closure had been made effective by maintaining a sustained communication channel between leaders and workers, informing them of the need of the hour, and by insisting that the only option to transfer would be loss of service.[19]

The bottom-line to the new strategy adopted by both management and trade union leaders seemed to be that workers should see themselves as part of decisions, even though the decision may actually be opposed to their interests. An outstanding example of this at HMT, widely cited by management and union leaders, was the situation when, because of the company's financial difficulties, the 1992 revised wage structure could be implemented only in 1997. However, the company could not afford to pay the arrears in a lump sum. As such, a scheme was evolved whereby if a unit's production exceeds its set target, the compensation for that is adjusted with the arrears.

At ITI there is a single, independent union. The union leadership has not supported VRS openly, but has effectively provided tacit support to management implementing the VRS by not actively opposing it.[20]

In each of the companies, then, there were possibly two faces to trade unions' approach to rationalization. On the one hand, union leadership was critical of VRS as an instrument being used for displacing workers from secure employment. On the other hand, they responded to labour rationalization with pragmatism based on the awareness that the alternative to it would possibly be closure or privatization, both of which held out a deeper threat than labour reduction. This choice had become part of company jargon, handed down from management to union leaders, and thence to workers.

Wages

For these companies, wage revisions take place every three years, on the basis of individual company-level negotiations but within the broad parameters provided by the central government, and a general norm of parity is observed amongst central government owned PSUs. A fresh settlement had been due in January 1997. However, because of the financial crisis in companies like ITI and HMT, and in a context where the government was not willing to expand its budgetary support, the wage structure continued as in the previous settlement. An interim relief of 10 per cent of basic pay was granted (minimum of Rs 280 per month), which was to be adjusted with the arrears once a new settlement came into force.

The central government has been attempting to introduce a number of changes in the hitherto existing framework for collective bargaining. The government has proposed, first, that tenure of wage settlements should be increased from five to ten years. Second, the government has stipulated that negotiated wages should not come in conflict with the wage revision of officers and non-unionized supervisors of public sector enterprises. Additionally, the government has laid down that wage increases cannot be reflected in any price increase, and that no budgetary support will be available to fund any wage increase. At the company level, in order to keep demands at bay, management has stressed the idea that funding the pay revision is going to be a big challenge. As the current round of negotiations began, unions were told that they must suggest ways and means of funding any pay hike in the new settlement.

In general, wages of public sector workers have grown on an average by 7 to 10 per cent at every round of wage settlement. Nevertheless, the trends outlined above would indicate that the state is now engaged in wide-ranging efforts to alter the norms of collective bargaining in order to limit the scope of institution-alized negotiations for wage increase. Most union leaders stated that by stipulating the new conditions for wage bargaining the government is severely curtailing the collective bargaining space of unions.[21] On their part, unions have been inclined more towards structured negotiations than towards any combative form of collective bargaining such as strikes or work stoppages.

It is important to note that the present environment in which the current wage negotiations are being conducted is remarkably different from the combative approach adopted by public sector trade unions in Bangalore two decades earlier. At that time, negotiations over a wage settlement in each of the Bangalore PSEs broke down. This led to a joint strike by workers across the PSEs. Although the strike failed to obtain the workers' claims, its significance lies in the fact that it was the longest-lasting strike in the history of India's public sector and played a significant role in shaping the politics and discourse of the trade union movement in the country as a whole.[22]

BETWEEN CONSENT AND DISSENT: THE QUESTION OF EMPOWERMENT

The case studies contradict a widely held impression that labour in Indian PSEs frequently offers stiff resistance to rationalization. The findings reveal that labour rationalization programmes have in fact been implemented in these firms with trade union acquiescence. However, as outlined above, underlying acquiescence there also appeared a range of responses, from positive acceptance to reluctant support to critical dissent.

Given this range, it is possible that conflicting forces underlie the process of rationalization. In this section we take a closer look at two related pillars of current PSE restructuring strategies: first, new participatory structures, and, second, some institutional aspects of the VRS. This is done in order to highlight the ways in which a changing institutional context reflects on the system of worker opportunities and empowerment. In the interface of these forces we attempt to locate the dynamics of trade union responses to the onset of marketization.

As discussed earlier, new IR strategies have created greater worker awareness of the implications of technology changes as also of firms' financial situation. Additionally, through participation at different levels, workers attain a level of self-esteem as problem-solvers, and a sense of belonging to the organization. In this environment, difficult decisions such as transfers, redeployment, or reductions can be made to appear as the product of workers' own decisions. Thus the emphasis on creating consensus has certainly helped generate a sense of control for workers within the organization.[23]

Do these structures translate to workers' influence on decisions which affect their lives and futures? Can workers use these structures to challenge management's power over major decision-making processes? Many union office-bearers pointed out two areas in which they felt most powerless to affect decisions, despite the emergence of participatory IR structures. First, about 5–10 per cent of the workforce in the firms studied continued to belong to the category of contract labour, who work with a significantly inferior package of wages and benefits, and have subordinate status within the organizations. The new participatory IR norms and structures appear to coexist with, rather than challenge, the structural inequalities inherent in the contract labour system. Second, trade unions have by and large been unable to shape the modalities of VRS in a manner that would serve worker interests. A 1994 study on VRS in 12 Bangalore PSEs reveals that these companies had cut themselves off from the rationalized employees. Displaced workers who had opted for self-employment reported that they had been unable to get bank loans for starting up businesses.[24] Trade unions in these firms had put forward demands that the firms in question should adopt a more positive approach towards assisting VRS takers, by offering insurance, help in obtaining bank credit, and so on. However, the response from the companies towards former employees was largely negative.

In this context, it is particularly important to note that there has been hardly any growth in employment opportunities in the organized manufacturing sector in Bangalore, or in Karnataka as a whole. In the small-scale industry sector, for example, while there has been an absolute rise in the number of units, investment, and employment, the growth rate shows a decline on all these dimensions, as shown in Table 13.2. Further, employment per unit has declined from 9.14 in 1985 to 6.68 in 1994. A 1995 study which examined 50 industries across three zonal areas and across small, medium and large-scale sectors, showed declining trends in employment (see Table 13.3).

It was widely reported by union leaders that typically the capital gained through VRS is frittered away in unprofitable business ventures, personal loan repayment, dowry payment, or conspicuous consumption like celebration of a son's or daughter's marriage. VRS thus leads to loss of employment and a fall in living standards.

Finally, the National Renewal Fund (NRF) had been set up in 1993 to finance payment of compensation to workers taking the VRS—both in the public and private sectors—as also to provide for training of displaced workers in order to enable them to find new employment. It is now widely acknowledged that the NRF has been used only to support the payment of compensation to

VRS takers (and only in the public sector), and its effect on retraining and rehabilitation of workers has been insignificant.[25]

Thus the institutional structures to handle displaced workers—in terms of credit, counselling, retraining, or alternative employment opportunities—were not really in place. The point is not that all VRS takers are reduced to penury but that in a post-retirement context the large majority of VRS takers find themselves bereft of any institutional support. Trade unions had accepted the inevitability of workforce reduction, and had lent their support to VRS. But they had by and large been unable to shape the institutional context in which VRS was implemented in such a way as to ensure worker welfare.

Table 13.2: Declining growth rate in small-scale industries in Karnataka

	Growth Rates		
Years	Of unit	Of employment	Of investment
1971–80	15.66	13.21	15.05
1981–90	14.33	8.15	12.89
1991–4	12.83	7.92	14.09

Source: Rao and Inou, Industrial Development of Karnataka and New Industrial Policy (Institute of Developing Economics, Tokyo, Joint Research Programme, Series No. 112, 1995).

Table 13.3: Trends in industrial employment in Karnataka

	1990	1991	1992	1993
Total employment	69,749	71,728	69,132	57,249
Private sector	36,672	38,365	37,577	27,674
Public sector	33,077	33,363	3 1,555	29,575

Source: Rao and Inou, Industrial Development of Karnataka and New Industrial Policy (Institute of Developing Economics, Tokyo, Joint Research Programme, Series No. 112, 1995).

To summarize this section, the following tentative comments may be made. The new IR structures which seek to create space for worker participation are a product of management's strategic thinking and initiatives, not of the trade union movement or of worker initiatives. Such participatory practices as are produced by these structures are therefore largely controlled, that is, defined by management's broad interests. These structures generate a certain atmosphere of collaboration and have thus pre-empted management–worker conflict during a difficult period of adjustment. Such collaboration facilitates the process of production and the larger purpose of capital accumulation. Thus, in each of the cases studied, trade union and worker cooperation had been attained to support rationalization policies.

At the same time, there was a definite sense of worker discontent and of trade union leaderships' resentment and powerlessness, particularly over the negative impact of VRS on workers' lives, and over the shrinking opportunities for employment. The next section highlights some of the factors which underlie the complexity of unions' acquiescence/resentment over rationalization policies.

TRADE UNION POWERLESSNESS: ABSENCE OF A PARADIGM

Some scholars have used a broadly institutionalist framework of interpretation in order to explain trade union responses to economic liberalization and a certain diminishing of union leverage over states and employers.[26] In the analysis below I adopt a similar framework, looking broadly at both the changing equations in political party–union relationships and at the shifting internal dynamics of trade unions, reflecting worker interests, choice of leaders, and union objectives. These institutional changes are underwritten by shifts in the broader political economy, where both the numerical erosion of the organized sector of the workforce, and the worldwide shift in ideas, from statist welfarism to markets, has contributed to the diminishing political leverage of unions.

An interesting feature of the organized labour movement during the liberalization period has been a marked discrepancy between trade union politics at the national level and at local, firm levels. At the national level, most of the trade union federations have kept up a sustained critique of globalization's impact upon the workforce. This critique has been typically expressed over issues such as privatization, manpower reductions, imports and so on. Union reactions to the budget for 2001–2 provide a good example. The budget for 2001–2 proposed, for the first time, wide-ranging amendments to existing labour laws in order to facilitate more market-oriented hiring and firing, freer use of contract labour, and greater strictures on union formation within enterprises. These proposals evoked a critical response from the trade unions. A joint statement was issued by all the national trade union federations, including the Bharatiya Mazdoor Sangh (affiliated to the ruling Bharatiya Janata Party), criticising the proposed changes and committing themselves to a future course of protest activities.[27]

At the enterprise level, however, there is little evidence of percolation of this kind of protest or critique. Across the three PSUs examined, and across the unions in these enterprises, leaders made statements such as the following: 'The public sector is under attack; organized labour, particularly in the public sector, is being widely criticized for being pampered.'[28] One union office-bearer stated, 'Currently we are more defensive than offensive.' Another office-bearer said, 'The wind in the country has shifted; it is no longer in our favour; in Delhi trade union leaders are saying one thing; but when it comes to the unit we are told to do the opposite.'[29] This gap, between a critical rhetoric on the one hand and reluctant acquiescence to change on the other, was pointed out by a number of trade unionists.

The clue to this discrepancy may well lie in the fact that while critical of marketization, the trade union movement in general has not come up with an alternative formula which incorporates worker interests and also addresses the issue of industrial competitiveness and public sector performance. How does one ensure worker interests while at the same time making PSUs profitable in a competitive market? The trade union movement has not attempted to answer this question at a theoretical level. Trade unions' responses to the onset of marketization have been on a case-by-case basis. In practical terms, they have provided support—based partly on consensus, partly reluctantly—to restructuring schemes. At an ideological level, trade unions frequently voice critiques of economic reforms. But a policy alternative has not emerged from their critical discourse.

Given the absence of an alternative policy paradigm, trade unions are frequently helpless when faced with specific issues relating to enterprise restructuring and are compelled to accept labour rationalization as part of the official mode of restructuring. It is this vacuum which places trade unions perpetually on a defensive mode, and prevents the movement from being able to dialogue with management and government on the basis of a viable alternative. The disempowerment of trade unions in the present context, which was widely referred to by firm-level union activists and leaders, can possibly be traced to this situation where they are functioning without a paradigm.

There are a number of reasons for this faltering. The first set of reasons relates to changing ideas, interests, and preferences of workers at the enterprise level, and these, in turn, impact upon union leadership selection and leaders' ideologies and orientations. In an earlier era, union presidents were, almost invariably, external leaders, who were typically elected as presidents by virtue of their association with any of the national trade union federations as well as their local political bases. In contrast, union leadership now mostly goes to firm-level leaders rather than to external leaders. (In both ITI and in HMT, presidents of the unions are internal, that is, company employees.) This situation reflects a number of emerging tendencies. There is an increasing impatience, amongst younger workers in particular, with external leaders, who bring in political issues that have relatively little to do, in the perception of the average worker, with company issues. This change of perception has occurred largely because the issues themselves have become redefined in the eyes of the ordinary worker. The average worker is primarily concerned with individual welfare rather than with collective issues concerning the workforce as a whole. Thus many union office-bearers stated that they spend most of their time and energy on specific issues of worker benefits such as canteen services, transport services, medical benefits, individual worker problems with supervisors, and the like. This situation, obviously, enhances the importance of internal leaders relative to external leaders.

Union leaders thus do not see their see their role within the union as activists connected to a broader political agenda. They see themselves, rather, as professionals, with a given function defined within the limits of the company. Their success as trade union leaders is measured in terms of their ability and willingness to deal with firm-level issues rather than with broader issues of political economy. Concomitantly, there has been a loss of focus on issues outside the firm which pertain to the economy in general or to the public sector in particular. This partial depoliticization of trade union activities at the enterprise level has meant that unions at this level are, to some extent, conceptually and politically disconnected from the political-economy issues that are affecting their lives closely.

The second set of explanatory variables relates to the dynamics of the trade union–political party relationship. In a large number of so-called third world countries that embarked upon state-led economic development in the post-Second World War period, left-of-centre/social democracy-oriented political parties held political power for long periods or at least had a defining impact upon the choice of developmental models. Such political parties typically enjoyed large labour constituencies and trade union support. From the 1980s onwards, neoliberal marketization programmes, frequently initiated by these same parties, have put a strain on the erstwhile patron–client-like relationship between trade unions and labour-friendly political parties.[30]

In India market-oriented economic reforms are now being introduced and sustained by political parties across the spectrum, and across states. The most remarkable example of this of course is the Congress (I), long identified with a labour-friendly, left-of-centre, predominantly statist political position, and the first to initiate marketization reforms at the level of the central government. This trend is replicated in the case of other left-oriented parties. In West Bengal, the Left Front government under the Communist Party of India–Marxist (CPI-M) has long been engaged in the exercise of reining in the militancy of its constituent trade union, the CITU, in order to make the economic climate of West Bengal more attractive for private investors.[31] Similarly, the presently ruling National Democratic Alliance (led by the BJP), although a coalition of parties representing a broad ideological spectrum, has demonstrated a sustained bias in favour of marketization reforms. As mentioned above, the government's recently proposed major changes in labour laws have been jointly criticized by all the major trade unions, signalling an increasing standoff between market-oriented political parties and affiliated unions.

Across political parties, therefore, and regardless of their ideological hues, there seems to be a certain convergence over the issue of the need for labour rationalization in the context of marketization. This has obviously led to a certain alienation of the trade union movement from political parties and to their isolation from the political mainstream. A prominent Bangalore labour leader described the situation in the following words: 'Trade unions are no longer in the same wavelength as the government.'[32]

Finally, trade unions are not only distanced from increasingly market-oriented political parties but are also unable to connect—ideologically and organizationally—to other anti-marketization impulses, which have highly diverse constituencies and lack a common ideological/intellectual platform. The worldwide shift towards market-driven economic policies has created a general environment in which the efficiency/welfare duality is *most frequently weighed on the side of efficiency*. The faltering and undefined nature of trade union responses, in the specific context in which it was examined in this chapter, must also, at some level, be related to this generalized climate of weakening (in a global context) in which leftist and workers' organizations find themselves.

To this broadly institutionalist framework for explaining declining trade union leverage must be added what is an essentially economic-structural factor: the numerical shrinking of the organized workforce, mentioned at the outset. This factor has as much to do with India's specific political economy conditions —rigidity of labour laws leading employers to limit the number of employees— as with more recent trends associated with the liberalization process, sub-contracting, outsourcing, part-time work, and so on. These latter are processes over which the trade union movement appears to have little control, and has essentially had little scope to develop a paradigmatic response. But the disempowerment of the organized workforce appears to follow a logic whereby as the numerical weight of labour declines, so does their political leverage, thus creating a broader context where labour issues can be systematically sidelined.

To the extent that the disempowerment of trade unions is a function of declining numbers in the organized sector, it is also increasingly apparent that the trade union movement possibly needs to widen both its constituency and its discourse. Thus there is a need to move away from the partisan interests of a shrinking organized sector towards incorporating the interests of the informal sector, which now constitutes over 90 per cent of the workforce. A broad-based, workers' rights- and social security-oriented discourse could perhaps meaningfully replace the erstwhile exclusive engagement with the public sector.

NOTES AND REFERENCES

1. Research on this article was made possible by a grant from the Research Programme Committee of the Institute for Social and Economic Change, Bangalore, India. A briefer version was presented as a paper at a seminar at the Madras Institute of Development Studies in November 2000, and at the National Conference on 'Globalization, Democracy and Governance' at the Jawaharlal Nehru University, New Delhi, in September 2001. The author is grateful to participants at these two seminars for their comments. The author is particularly grateful to an anonymous referee for suggestions to strengthen the study.

2. This literature is fairly extensive. For a sampling, see Joan Nelson (ed.), *Fragile Coalitions, the Politics of Economic Adjustment* (New Brunswick, NJ, Transaction Books, 1989); Joan Nelson, *Democracy and Economic Reforms in Latin America* (Washington, DC, Overseas Development Council, 1994); Stephen Haggard, *Pathways from the Periphery: The Politics of Growth in Newly Industrializing Countries* (Ithaca, NY, Cornell University Press, 1990); Stephen Haggard, *The Political Feasibility of Adjustment in Developing Countries* (Paris, OECD, 1994); Stephen Haggard and Robert Kaufman (eds), *The Politics of Economic Adjustment* (Princeton, NJ, Princeton University Press, 1992); Stephen Haggard and Robert Kaufman, *The Political Economy of Democratic Transitions* (New Jersey, NJ, Princeton University Press, 1995); Adam Przeworski, Luis Bresser Pereira and Jose Maria Maraval, *Economic Reforms in New Democracies* (Cambridge, Cambridge University Press, 1993).

3. Haggard and Kaufman, 1995: 9.

4. See, for example, Marc Lindenberg, *Managing Winners and Losers: Assessing the Political Impact of Economic Strategies* (San Francisco, CA, International Center for Economic Growth, 1989); Haggard, *Political Feasibility.*

5. See, for example, Isher Ahluwalia, 'Reform of Public Enterprises', in Robert Cassen and Vijay Joshi (eds), *India: The Future of Economic Reforms* (New Delhi, Oxford University Press, 1996); James Manor, 'Political Dynamics of Economic Reforms', in Cassen and Joshi, *India: The Future.*

6. Supriya RoyChowdhury, 'Industrial Restructuring, Unions and the State: The Case of Ahmedabad Textile Labourers', *Economic and Political Weekly,* 24 February (1996), pp. L7–L8; Supriya RoyChowdhury, 'The State, Private Sector and Labour: Political Economy of Jute Industry Modernization, West Bengal, 1986–90', *Journal of the Indian School of Political Economy,* vol. 9, no. 1 (1997), pp. 126–7.

7. The decline of jute and textile industries was not directly the result of economic reforms. However, the onset of reforms, with the underlining of efficiency, competitiveness, and so on, provided the broader context in which the state as well as private employers could ignore the claims of workers in these sectors. This may not have been possible in an earlier era.

8. The decline of public sector enterprises is widely documented both in official and academic works. See, for example, Government of India, *Public Enterprise Survey, 1995–96,* Vol. 2 (New Delhi, GOI, 1996); Vijay Joshi and I.M.V. Little, *India's Economic Reforms, 1991–2001* (New Delhi: Oxford University Press, 1996).

9. Government of India, Ministry of Finance, *Economic Survey, 1998–99* (New Delhi, Ministry of Finance, 1999).

10. As quoted in Delhi Science Forum, 'Employment and Unemployment in the Indian Economy' in *Alternative Economic Survey, 1996–97* (New Delhi, Delhi Science Forum, 1997).

11. Joshi and Little, *India's Economic Reforms,* pp. 211–17.

12. Tables 6 and 3, Labour Statistics, *Indian Journal of Labour Economics,* vol. 40, nos. 1 and 2 (1997).

13. T.C.A. Anant and K. Sundaram, 'Wage Policy in India: A Review', *Indian Journal of Labour Economics,* Vol. 41, No. 4 (1998), pp. 815–34.

14. R.S. Ghuman and Lakhwinder Singh, 'Employment, Wages and Productivity in Public Sector Enterprises in India', *The Indian Journal Of Labour Economics,* vol. 41, no. 4 (1998), p. 924.

15. See, for example, Government of India, Economic Advisory Council (Chairman: Sukhamoy Chakravarty), *Public Enterprises in India: Some Current Issues* (New Delhi, Government of India, 1987).

16. The information in this section has been gained from interviews with personnel and industrial relations managers, trade union leaders and office-bearers in the three companies.

17. Industrial relations managers and trade union leaders in all three companies mentioned this shift. A manager at BEL used the exact phrase quoted in the text.

18. For a cross-national perspective, see Kirden Wever and Lowell Thomas (eds), *The Comparative Political Economy of Industrial Relations* (Madison, WI, University of Wisconsin, Industrial   Research Association, 1995); Frederick Deyo, 'Capital, Labour and State in Thai Industrial Restructuring: The Impact of Global Economic Transformations', in David Smith and Joseph Boroz (eds), *A New World Order: Global Transformations in the Late Twentieth Century* (Westport, CT: Greenwood Press, 1995); Maria Lorena Cook, Kevin J. Middlebrook and Juan M. Horcasitas (eds), *The Politics of Economic Restructuring: State–Society Relations and Regime Change in Mexico* (San Diego, CA, Center for US-Mexican Studies, 1994).

19. Interviews with trade union office-bearers at HMT, Bangalore, 6–10 February 1998.

20. Interview with Mr Michael Fernandes, President, ITI Employees Union, October 1998.

21. Interview with Mr Michael Fernandes, President, ITI Employees Union, October 1998.

22.   Dilip Subramanian, 'Bangalore Public Sector Strike, 1980–81: A Critical Appraisal', *Economic and Political Weekly*, 12 April 1997, p. 768.

23. Summarized from discussions with managers and trade union officers in the three companies.

24. Rameshwar Dubey, 'Implementation of Employee Assistance Programme Under NRF: A Case Study', *Manpower Journal*, Vol. 33, No. 4, January-March (1998), pp. 66–9.

25. See RoyChowdhury, 'Industrial Restructuring'; C.S. Venkataratnam, 'The Labour Adjustment Process', in S.L. Rao (ed.), *Reforming State Owned Enterprises* (New Delhi, National Council of Applied Economic Research, 1996).

26. See, for example, Katrina Burgess, 'Alliances Under Stress: Economic Reform and Party-Union Relations in Mexico, Spain and Venezuela', Ph.D. dissertation, Princeton University (1998); M. Victoria Murillo, 'From Populism to Neo Liberalism: Labour Unions and Market Reforms in Latin America', *World Politics,* vol. 52, no. 2, (2000), pp. 135–74; Miriam Golden and Jonas Pontusson (eds), *Bargaining for Change: Union Politics in North America and Europe* (Ithaca, NY, Cornell University Press, 1992).

27. Reported in *Frontline,* dated 14 April 2001.

28. Interview with General Secretary, BEL Employees Association, 12 May 1999.

29. Interviews with trade union office-bearers at BEL, Bangalore, 12–15 May, 1999.

30. For a good discussion of the political party–trade union rift in the Latin American context, see Murillo, 'From Populism to Neo Liberalism'.

31. Soon after the Left Front came to power consecutively for the sixth time in 2001, the new chief minister, who is a prominent leftist leader, explicitly underlined the need for a cooperative and non-militant workforce. 'Buddhadeb's Dig at Trade Unions', *Business Line,* 21 November 2001.

32. Interview with Mr Ananta Subramaniam, President, All India Trade Union Congress, AITUC office, Bangalore, June 1999.

14

Liberalization and Business Lobbying in India[*]

STANLEY A. KOCHANEK

The current trend toward economic liberalization is having a profound effect on business–government relations in the Third World.[1] Patterns of public policy play a major role in shaping interest group behaviour, determining channels of access, and conditioning the style of interest articulation. Interest groups not only attempt to shape public policy but are themselves shaped by the very public policy they seek to influence.[2] Following the parliamentary elections of 1991 in India, the new Congress-led government of Prime Minister P.V. Narasimha Rao was forced to make a dramatic break with the country's past economic policies in a desperate effort to ward off bankruptcy.[3] Encouraged by the International Monetary Fund (IMF), the government adopted a series of economic reforms designed to increase domestic competition, reduce direct government control of the economy, rely more extensively on market forces, open up the economy to global competition and foreign investment, and prepare Indian business to participate in the global economy. These dramatic changes in economic policy have fundamentally altered India's post-independence model of development and have had an especially dramatic effect on India's diverse business community. The reforms have significantly modified business strategies, lobbying styles and relationships to government.

In the years following independence, India created one of the most comprehensively controlled and regulated economies in the non-communist world. Its

* Originally published as 'Liberalisation and Business Lobbying in India', in *The Journal of Commonwealth & Comparative Politics*, 34 (3), November 1996, pp. 155–73, published by Frank Cass, London.

development model was based on a system of centralized planning, a mixed economy dominated by a hegemonic public sector and a private sector in which all basic management decisions involving investment, production, technology, location, prices, imports, exports, and foreign capital were controlled and regulated by the state. In theory, the model was designed to ensure that the economy would grow rapidly in a planned and self-reliant direction; that the private sector would invest only in high-priority industries approved by the government; that monopoly and concentration of economic power would be forestalled; that the state would come to control the commanding heights of the economy; and that steep tax rates for individuals and corporations would provide the resources for the plan, check the conspicuous consumption of the rich, and create a society based on social justice. In practice, however, the approach resulted in slow rates of growth, massive corruption, and an economy of shortages.

The creation and design of India's system of comprehensive control and regulation of private sector economic activity arose from a series of strategic choices made during the early years of the post-independence period from 1947 to 1951. These choices were based on a set of major political compromises which attempted to blend the experience of wartime planning and controls, domestic pressures for a policy of economic nationalism, and the liberal, Gandhian, and socialist ideological crosscurrents which existed within the nationalist movement. The policies which emerged from these compromises established a consensus in support of an Indian model of development based on a mixed economy in which the private sector would be controlled, regulated and protected by the state, and foreign capital would be permitted under highly restricted circumstances. Once created, the system grew incrementally from 1951 to 1969 as the result of a steady cumulative process of administrative development and elaboration, and was reinforced and supplemented by a wave of populist reform from 1969 to 1973, which added anti-monopoly legislation and tightened control over foreign capital.[4]

Once fully developed and matured, however, the regulatory system began to manifest a number of life-cycle rigidities in the 1970s, including a lack of speed in decision-making, a lack of innovation and a lack of flexibility. These rigidities combined to have a negative effect on private sector industrial growth and competitiveness. The period from 1973 to 1991 was therefore marked by a series of efforts to reduce the negative impact of regulatory policy while at the same time keeping the basic system in place. The result was a continuing process of liberalization designed to reduce delay, promote production, and encourage exports. The policy of liberalization was, however, never really coherent or based on a comprehensive evaluation of the regulatory system; rather, it was simply a series of ad hoc alterations or 'readjustments'. The objective was to accelerate production while leaving the fundamental outlines of the system untouched.[5] No real change in the basic policy structure was made until the July 1991 reforms of the Rao government.

BUSINESS AND COLLECTIVE ACTION

In response to the development policy of centralized planning and regulation of the private sector, the Indian business community developed a dual approach to dealing with the Government of India. At the collective level, business drew upon the wide array of well-organized and well-financed business associations that had grown up in the years preceding independence to deal with the British colonial government. These organizations included chambers of commerce, trade and industry associations, employers' associations, and two apex associations—the Federation of Indian Chambers of Commerce and Industry (FICCI), which represented indigenous capital, and the Associated Chambers of Commerce and Industry (Assocham), which represented foreign capital. Together these associations constituted the oldest, most organized and most politically autonomous structures of interest articulation in India capable of sustained collective action.[6]

At the individual level, the Indian business elite developed a highly sophisticated mode of discrete lobbying designed to achieve particularistic benefits from the new permit-licence quota raj. Each major business house established the equivalent of an industrial embassy in New Delhi, designed to act as a listening post, liaison office, and lobbying agency to deal with political and bureaucratic decision makers.[7] Because the leadership of specialized business associations was provided by the leaders of India's top 75 business houses, the two levels of lobbying were closely linked to each other and were capable of coordinated action.

While industrial embassies proved to be effective instruments in dealing with the new regulatory regime, the ability of business associations to influence basic economic and development policy was severely limited due to the relative autonomy of the state, the low status of the Indian business community, and the strong belief of political and bureaucratic decision makers in the efficacy of state intervention in the economy. According to M.S. Patwardhan, former President of the Bombay Chamber of Commerce Industry, chambers in India are hardly successful in influencing the direction of major government policy relating to industry, industrial licensing, monopolies legislation, taxation, pricing, industrial relations, etc. Their efforts are largely reactive rather than proactive. There is little rapport and mutual_confidence between the government and the chambers with the result that their interaction at annual general meetings, seminars etc. is either ritualistic with parties talking at each other from entrenched positions in words which are highly critical of each other or altogether emollient with the real problems swept under the carpet.[8]

Although Indian business associations were unable to influence major legislation or government economic policy, they were able to have a more limited impact on the detailed implementation of regulatory and distributive policies. Government control and regulation of the private sector placed vast discretionary powers in the hands of political and bureaucratic regulators, affecting every detail of private sector operations. Almost the entire time of business association secretariats was therefore consumed in preparing representations to government demanding changes and modifications in regulatory policies. The annual reports of Indian business associations are replete with copies of letters, memorandums, and petitions outlining the problems encountered by business in attempting to carry out day-to-day activities and demanding alteration or refinement of administrative policies, procedural changes, or removal of contradictions and anomalies inherent in the complex and overlapping system regulation. Specific demands include such things as the modification of working-capital norms set by the Reserve Bank, changes in company law rules, alteration of MRTP and FERA limits, changes in import policies, removal of tax anomalies, withdrawal of corporate tax surcharges, higher depreciation schedules and so on.[9]

The success of these demands was reflected in the large number of notes and modifications issued almost daily by the government reversing or modifying existing policies. For example, India's tax system became extremely complex due to a flood of tax notifications that provided special benefits to individuals and industries. As a result, a single item might carry five different duties for different purposes in different places.[10]

Although business was at times successful in securing minor alterations in regulatory policy, major changes in those policies were brought about not by business lobbying but by internal and external factors that were beyond the control of business. The liberalization policies of the late 1970s, for example, were largely due to the rise of Sanjay Gandhi as a political force. Sanjay had developed strong anti-bureaucratic attitudes in the process of trying to build a small car for the Indian market and therefore favoured a policy of deregulation.

Sanjay's pressure for change was reinforced by the 1973 and 1979 oil shocks and the 1981 conditionalities imposed by the International Monetary Fund as part of a major restructuring loan.[11] The same was true of the fundamental alteration of the Indian development model in July 1991, which was the result of the near bankruptcy of the state and the anticipated IMF demands that would accompany a new loan.

In short, the impact of the collective action by the Indian business community through its associations on government policy until 1991 was very limited. Peak associations representing business did not enjoy a high status and there was an absence of mutual cooperation, trust and respect between business and government. Government viewed business associations as grievance bodies, not partners.

BUSINESS HOUSES AND LOBBYING

Although the impact of collective action on government policy was limited, the regulatory and distributive character of the policy made the role of individual influence, connections, and particularistic demands by business houses the dominant factor in business-government relations. Businessmen in India were not without influence and power. They commanded large resources in the form of money, jobs, and productive assets, and they used these resources very effectively in the distributive realm of regulatory politics. The business–Congress Party relationship was multi-layered and complex. Despite the strong anti-business public rhetoric of politicians, members of the business elite enjoyed close and durable personal relationships with individual Congress politicians and ministers. These relationships had been developed during the freedom struggle when Indian businessmen supplied Congress leaders with money, hospitality, and political support and formed the basis of a well-established system of particularistic lobbying designed to secure individual benefits.[12]

The system of particularistic lobbying grew gradually as the regulatory framework matured and became increasingly complex. The development of the system passed through three distinct phases from 1951 to 1991. The first phase covered the period from 1951 to 1969 and marked the golden age of private sector development in India. The second phase, from 1969 to 1979, was characterized as the period of briefcase politics based on a mutual exchange of benefits among an iron triangle of businessmen, bureaucrats, and politicians. The third phase entailed an increasing externalization of corruption in the 1980s and 1990s, based on defence and infrastructure contracting with foreign suppliers.

Although business was initially frightened by Nehru's socialist rhetoric and talk of nationalization, the unlimited opportunities for industrial expansion in the 1950s and early 1960s resulted in business accommodation with the Nehru government. The new regulatory order proved to be more promotional than regulatory and opportunities for private sector investment expanded rapidly. Government actively encouraged business houses to undertake projects to meet plan targets, and business houses created industrial embassies to push projects though the regulatory clearance process. Gradually business learned how to make the system work in its favour and began to corner industrial licenses and secure monopoly control of various products.[13]

During the first decade and a half of planning, Indian businessmen were principally concerned with the expansion and growth of their own business empires and the protection of their individual interests. Each business house used the influence it acquired through patronage and individual contributions to Congress leaders to obtain benefits for its own family group. Although some collective benefits might incidentally accrue from policy changes, industrial embassies were designed primarily to secure licences, permits or quotas for individual business groups.

BRIEFCASE POLITICS: 1969 TO 1979

The pattern of business–government relations established by India's industrial embassies during the first two decades following independence underwent dramatic changes in the 1970s. The long-standing, intimate relationship between India's elite business families and Congress party leaders established during the struggle for independence was shattered as a result of the election of Indira Gandhi as prime minister and leader of the Congress in 1966 and the split in the party in 1969. Indira Gandhi's rise to power was accompanied by a shift to the left and a populist assault on the Indian business community. In an effort to undercut the Congress old guard's links with business and develop a populist appeal designed to attract the voles of the poor, Indira Gandhi nationalized private sector banks, enacted a whole array of new monopoly and regulatory legislation and introduced a ban on company contributions to political parties. These actions not only weakened her ties with business, but also left her Congress (I) party's coffers empty and eliminated the only legal mechanism for Indian business to contribute to political parties. As a result, noted a government committee, 'black money' became the main source of funds for political parties.[14] Black money or 'number two money' was accumulated by business via tax evasion, black-market operations and a whole array of mechanisms used to bypass and profit from government controls.

As a result of these changes, the period following the Congress split of 1969 was characterized by a member of the Indian Parliament as the era of 'briefcase polities',[15] a phrase used to describe the transfer of vast amounts of black money in the form of cash into the electoral coffers of the Congress (I) party. Prices for regulatory decisions involving permits, licences and quotas were assessed by Congress (I) ministers in terms of the number of briefcases required. Each briefcase held an estimated one million rupees. Initially, prices were set as a fixed fee but later they were levied as percentage of the benefits.[16] The politicization of the regulatory system was described by S.S. Marathe, former Industries Secretary, as follows:

After the Congress split in 1969 there was a marked increase in the number of decisions or clearances which were obtained by approaching the political level of decision making. In fact, it may not be a mere coincidence that there was a marked increase in the time taken for clearing applications...and the greater frequency with which these approvals were expedited by approaching the decision makers at the political level.[17]

The new strategy of using the regulatory system to raise large sums of money for election expenses for the Congress (I) was further developed and expanded by L.N. Mishra, Indira Gandhi's Minister of Foreign Trade. It was Mishra who was credited with creation of the politics of big money by combining the enormous leverage provided by the permit-licence, quota raj with the coercive powers of the state. In the words of one close observer,

Often representatives of trade and industry were called up by him to Delhi and asked to produce specified amounts. Those who declined were threatened with possible raids by people of the Revenue Intelligence and Enforcement Directorate, which were now operating under the Cabinet Secretariat. In Bombay financial circles stories started circulating of the amounts secured by the Foreign Trade Minister under such threats. Others who came forward willingly with whatever was asked for, received concessions, beyond their imagination, to expand their business and amass further resources. A number of new stars were born on the industrial firmament of India during this time.[18]

'Donations', according to Mrs Gandhi's biographer, Krishan Bhatia, had become more like extortions.[19] 'As elections grew more and more costly, and as the role of money in gathering votes became more important,' noted another observer, 'the government came more and more to resemble a bargain basement, where a rise in sugar prices, and increase in export subsidies, and an import licence for a scarce material, would be exchanged for cash donations to the party.'[20] A joke attributed to T.A. Pai, a former minister in Mrs Gandhi's government which reflected the atmosphere of the time noted: 'If a peon accepted money, it was called *bakshish;* if a clerk took it, it was *mamool* (custom); if an officer took it, it became a bribe; and if a minister look it, it was called party funds.'[21]

In this new atmosphere, businessmen willing to be cooperative had little difficulty in securing appropriate benefits. As Herdeck and Piramal have observed,

Newer industrialists who got their start in the 1960s and 1970s might have had a more instinctive appreciation for the possibilities of growth under a more regulated system. They grew quickly while older industrial families resisted the 'new politics' which required business to take a permanent genuflected posture before politicians.[22]

In an economy where government decisions counted as much as entrepreneurial skill, cultivating the right connections almost guaranteed success. Among the older industrial families that resisted the new politics were those located in South India. For South Indian business the 1960s were seen as a golden age. Business in the south grew rapidly and the region increasingly became the Detroit of India and a major textile centre. South Indian business houses, however, never really emerged as giants, as did business houses in Calcutta and Bombay. South Indian businessmen, especially the Chettiars, were much more conservative than their Marwari, Gujarati, and Parsi counterparts. They refused to invest outside their region, had a low tolerance for risk, and were very reluctant to borrow from government financial institutions out of fear of losing family control. Their growth in the 1960s was the result of strong encouragement from a state Congress government determined to develop local industry and the excellent connections they enjoyed with powerful Tamil Congress ministers in New Delhi.[23]

The development of South Indian business, however, slowed significantly in the 1970s as the local political climate turned hostile under the Dravida Munnetra Kazhagam (DMK) government and business lost its key Congress contacts in New Delhi following the split in the Congress. South Indian business was reluctant to become involved in the art of wheeling and dealing which became essential in the 1970s. They saw the 1970s 'as the dawning of an era of "fixing and bribing"'[24] and refused to engage in the required 'lobbying and manoeuvring' which became essential to success. They, therefore, found it difficult to manage the new political environment needed to secure projects and sanctions. 'Big projects necessarily mean big pay offs,' they noted and refused to engage in such practices.[25]

THE EXTERNALIZATION OF CORRUPTION

While the decade from 1969 to 1979 was characterized as the era of 'briefcase polities', the 1980s and early 1990s were marked by the externalization of corruption in India. Increasingly, by the late 1970s and early 1980s the exchange nexus that applied to industrial licensing, MRTP clearances, import/ export controls, and the entire regulatory system spread to large public sector civilian projects, military contracts, and infrastructure contracts with foreign companies. According to *India Today*,

it was a well-known fact in political circles that the Congress strategy since Sanjay Gandhi's time has been to eliminate the need for going hat in hand to Indian businessmen for donations to the party purse...much of the money now supposedly comes from foreign companies bidding for large contracts in India.[26]

The system had matured to the point that Rajiv Gandhi himself sadly proclaimed to the 100th anniversary celebration of the Congress party in December 1985 that 'corruption is not only tolerated but even regarded as the hallmark of our leadership.'[27] Rajiv promised to reform the system and was dubbed by many as 'Mr Clean'.

Unfortunately, Rajiv's Mr Clean image did not last very long. In early 1987 his Congress (I)-led government was rocked by a series of major scandals involving alleged favouritism to Congress business allies, illegal secret overseas bank accounts held by Congress supporters and huge kickbacks on government defence contracts involving a Rs 4.5 billion submarine deal with the West German company Howaldt Deutsche Werke (HDW) and the Rs 17.05 billion Bofors scandal involving the purchase of Swedish artillery pieces.[28] For the first time in post-independence Indian history, a prime minister had to assure Parliament publicly that neither he nor his family were involved in any illegal activity.

According to J.R.D. Tata, the externalization of corruption began in 1980 with the return to power of the Congress Party and Indira Gandhi. In a private meeting with R. Venkataraman, President of India, Tata told the President that 'since 1980 industrialists had not been approached for political contributions and that the general feeling among them was that the party was financed by commissions on deals.' In the case of Bofors and other defence deals, 'Tata said that though it was possible that neither Rajiv nor members of his family had received any consideration in the gun and 4 other defence deals, it would be difficult to deny the receipt of commissions by the Congress Party.'[29]

Tata's assessment of the shift in party funding was supported by the fact that Rajiv's restoration of the legal right of Indian companies to donate to political parties, which had been abolished by his mother, encountered such minimal resistance. 'We stopped fighting against corporate contributions to political parties,' noted one of its strongest advocates, 'because it was clear that they no longer counted.'[30] By the 1980s direct cash contributions to political parties by Indian business had ceased to be the dominant source of party funds.

Although the liberal economic reform policies of June–July 1991 weakened the old iron triangle of Indian businessmen, politicians, and bureaucrats, they have not significantly altered the system of public sector contracting. While the dismantling of major parts of the old permit-license, quota raj reduced the power of Indian bureaucratic and political regulators in the old economic ministries, the real action has shifted to the infrastructure ministries. 'The corridors of Udyog Bhavan (home of the Industries Ministry) may be empty after the dismantling of the "licence raj" in the manufacturing sector,' noted an industrial representative, 'but the crowd of industrialists, touts and agents has merely shifted to other ministries—power, telecommunications, surface transport, civil aviation and petroleum.'[31] 'The Prime Minister,' noted an editorial in the *Economic Times,*

goes abroad and invites investment. All our babus are taken care of, he assures foreign investors; the doors are open, there are no barriers...When the investors do come, they learn that they have been sold only half the story. The babus have been pushed behind; the politicians stand in front.[32]

The pervasiveness of the system is reflected in the persistent demand by the World Bank, the press, Indian business, and foreign investors for greater 'transparency' in government policy and procedures. In the words of Tarun Das, Secretary General of the Confederation of Indian Industry (CII), 'nowhere are the policies clear, transparent and provide for automatic clearance. Everything is done on a case-by-case basis; everything is non-transparent; everything has to be negotiated.'[33] Delay, discretionary action and kickbacks become the rule. 'The sums involved,' noted an editorial in *Business Standard,* 'are so large and the opportunities so many that no ordinary politician is able to resist the temptation to dip his fingers for a quick profit. The result is delay and confusion.'[34]

Because of the Government of India's financial difficulties a large number of infrastructure contracts have been opened up to foreign multinationals. This has generated considerable resentment and resistance from Indian business and has reinforced *Swadeshi* and anti-multinational sentiments. 'Thanks to corruption at the political level,' noted the *Business Standard,* 'even the domestic producer has not benefitted. While they are frozen out, the triumvirate of politicians, bureaucrats and foreign firms have had their pickings.'[35] The loss of lucrative contracts to foreign multinationals has thus resulted in sectors of Indian business joining with bureaucrats and Congress politicians opposed to reforms to block action. In the telecommunications sector, for example, Indian business has been seen as the chief force in getting the Home Ministry and security services to block action in the name of national security.[36] Indian business resents foreign interlopers taking their markets and their contracts.

The manipulation of infrastructure policy in India operates at two distinct levels. The first concerns the substance of the policy and the second involves the procedures adopted in translating the policy into action. In India, policy is made by a small group of decision-makers at the top of the system. The key players are the Prime Minister, the Prime Minister's Office (PMO), and the minister and the secretary of the ministry concerned. The policy is then passed down through the bureaucracy for implementation. Since the policy is usually very general, it requires the development of detailed guidelines. Those who are opposed to the policy will attempt to develop guidelines that will scuttle the policy. Others will use the process to their own advantage. 'Whenever policies are not comprehensive,' noted *India Today,* 'it becomes a reason for endless delay and administrative haggling, a way of asserting the discretionary power of the bureaucrat and an opportunity for bribes and corruption.'[37] The guidelines are kept secret from those affected so as to enhance discretionary power further.

Policy ambiguity is reinforced by procedural manipulation and decision making on a case-by-case basis. The case-by-case approach results in a highly complex process of collecting proposals, selecting those that fit the guidelines, comprehensive vetting of the proposals recommended, and a final decision based on the thorough review of each case. The process is open to delay and manipulation at each stage and has generated intense lobbying, court challenges, and repeated charges of a lack of transparency. In the power sector, for example, the government received proposals for 75 projects worth Rs 1.04 lakh crore for the generation of 32,662 MW of power.[38] All projects had to be cleared by the Cabinet Committee on Foreign Investment and by the government of the state in which the project was to be located. An initial group of fast-track projects were to be allocated on the basis of negotiations and not by the usual process of competitive bidding. Foreign companies have charged that the system lacked transparency and that decisions were taken solely on the basis of whims and fancies of the ministers and bureaucrats involved.[39]

The most notorious case cited involved the Rs 4,000 crore Krishnapatnam Thermal Project in the stale of Andhra. The original project called for building a 1,000 MW project. For some unknown reason, however, the project was split into two separate parts and contracts were awarded to two different companies. The formal selection procedure, moreover, called for the recommendation of a project consultant, vetting of the recommendation by an Investment Committee headed by the chief minister, and cabinet approval of the final decision. The award of one of the contracts to G.V.K. Industries, however, touched off a firestorm of criticism. G.V.K. Industries was a company which was known to be close to the chief minister and, it was charged, the award of the contract did not follow established procedures. Although the proposal was recommended by a consultant and approved by the investment committee, the chief minister immediately approved the recommendation and simply placed it before the cabinet as a fait accompli for formal ratification. The chief minister's action was met by an uproar from opposition political parties and even from members of his own cabinet. Opposition to the chief minister's initial decision grew even more intense when the second half of the contract was awarded to a relatively small American company represented in India by the chief minister's son-in-law. The chief minister was charged with nepotism, corruption, and insensitivity to democratic norms.[40] The charges against the Andhra chief minister were compounded by charges of similar indiscretions on other contracts.[41]

Charges of a lack of transparency involving infrastructure projects have also been levied at the national level. The most dramatic involved the $2.8 billion contract awarded to Enron, an American energy company based in Houston, Texas. Although an investigation failed to produce evidence of corruption, the contract was cancelled by the Maharashtra government. 'The difficulty,' noted *Business Standard,*

is that as long as the government is a major player, and as long as the imperatives of political funding remain what they are, transparency will always be at a discount. It would reduce the various ministers' room for maneuver too drastically. Whence the need for privatisation, because that would shift the costs of poor business judgement and graft to private sector rather than public sources.[42]

The problem of corruption has become so acute in India that a recent study by Transparency International ranked India as one of the most corrupt business environments in the world.[43] Real transparency in India, however, requires not only clear policy but also the development of alternative mechanisms for funding parties and elections.

Reforms and Collective Action

Although lobbying for particularistic benefits will continue to play some role, the economic reforms of 1991 have fundamentally altered the policy environment and business–government relations. The reforms have abolished a large number of instruments of control and regulation of the private sector and eliminated the need for repeated business visits to government offices to secure various permissions and clearances. As a result the preoccupation of businessmen and their associations with micro-level economic and regulatory policy has been replaced by a need to influence broad macro-level economic policies of the Government of India. This shift in focus has in turn required a totally different style of behaviour and lobbying. The pursuit of particularistic benefits has given way to a need for greater collective action and closer business–government cooperation and coordination.

The need for greater collective action has had a profound effect on the leadership, organization, and lobbying styles of Indian business associations. The decade of the 1980s was a period of turmoil for India's peak associations The decade saw a split in the elite-dominated FICCI, a reorganization and indigenization of Assocham, the rise of the Confederation of Indian Industry (CII), and a major fight among these apex associations for supremacy and proximity to government.[44] Historically, FICCI represented the voice of indigenous capital while Assocham spoke on behalf of foreign capital. Increasingly, however, they have become mirror images of each other and are seen by government officials as ineffective, grievance-oriented, ageing dowagers. In contrast, the CII, which came on the scene in the mid-1970s, has increasingly gained a reputation as a professionally run, outward-looking, pro-active organization with fresh ideas, a promotional style, and a developmental orientation.

The CII has developed a close rapport with the Government of India and has become the most effective and powerful lobbying organization in the country. Over the years the CII has systematically established deep roots in each of the major economic ministries, the Ministry of External Affairs, and the Prime Minister's Office (PMO). Its lobbying style is based on a more professional version of the principle of quiet diplomacy traditionally employed by Assocham and the techniques developed by the liaison men and lobbyists representing India's major business houses. The key to the CII's lobbying success is the development of a close working relationship with the bureaucracy—

India's permanent government—and an emphasis on the commonality of interests which stresses the joint objective of economic development. CII leaders and staff select key bureaucrats in critical economic ministries and attempt to build a trusting relationship with them. The process involves frequent informal personal contacts, providing up-to-date information, avoidance of public criticism, and working to help bureaucrats achieve their policy objectives without asking for a quid pro quo. Having established a close working relationship, demands are submitted in the form of carefully prepared briefs based on reliable data and well-reasoned arguments. Discussions are held in private and are based on a non-confrontational, constructive, cooperative, problem solving and bargaining style of negotiation. This style has given the CII a reputation within the bureaucracy of an organization that produces quality work and is highly professional, forward-looking and dynamic.[45]

Since the introduction of the 1991 reform programme, the CII has begun to play an increasingly influential role in shaping economic policy. They were credited, for example, with having lobbied successfully for reform of the Foreign Exchange Regulation Act (FERA),[46] and the Revenue Secretary of the Government of India went so far as to call the 1993–94 budget the 'Tarun Das Budget', a reference to the powerful Secretary General of the CII. As a result of its successes, the CII likes to refer to itself as the 'junior partner of the government'.[47] FICCI and Assocham, increasingly embittered by the growing visibility and influence of the CII, have begun to accuse the organization of being a handmaid and stooge of the government. At the same time, both organizations have embarked upon a major reorganization designed to enable them to compete more effectively with the CII.[48]

Although the business community has been the chief beneficiary of the 1991 economic reforms, the reforms have not enjoyed the unified support of the business elite or of India's apex business associations. While most industrialists and associations welcomed the move toward deregulation and decontrol of the domestic private sector 'as a dream come true',[49] they were far less enthusiastic about reducing tariff protection for Indian industry, the opening of the Indian economy to foreign trade and investment and globalization of the Indian economy. In the words of one industrialist, 'globalization is an attractive idea but it doesn't suit my pocket...It is a luxury I cannot afford.'[50]

Business resistance to economic reform crystallized in late 1993 as the immediate economic crisis began to ease. The initial attack came from members of the Bombay Club, an informal group of powerful elite families. The Bombay Club issued a public statement highly critical of the reform policies as unfair to domestic capital and failing to create a level playing field.[51] The statement demanded numerous changes in policy. First, the Bombay Club demanded that government focus upon a comprehensive series of internal reforms which would enable domestic producers to become more competitive and provide for an extended period of adjustment for domestic industry prior to any attempt to open the Indian economy to external competition. Second, the Bombay Club objected to government liberal policies toward private foreign investment. They especially expressed anxiety over the government's decision to raise foreign investment equity levels from 40 per cent to a controlling 51 per cent, the takeover of Indian local companies by foreign multinationals, and attempts by non-resident Indians (NRIs) to gain control of Indian companies by buying large blocks of shares and replacing the original promoters of the enterprise. The Indian business elite also charged that government was providing benefits to private foreign investors that were not being provided to domestic industry, especially in the case of infrastructure projects. Third, they opposed the planned reductions in protective tariffs on Indian industry and the opening up of the Indian economy to foreign goods. Since the tariff on finished goods would decline while local excise and sales taxes on industrial inputs remained high, the cost of Indian-made goods would become uncompetitive. This would result in unfair competition and would lead to plant closures and increased unemployment. Fourth, the Bombay Club charged that tight credit policies and high interest rates placed domestic industry at a competitive disadvantage compared to foreign capital. Finally, they charged that failure to reform India's complex labour laws, the failure to enact an exit policy which would enable unprofitable industries to close, and a failure to reform or privatize the public sector limited the impact and effectiveness of the reforms. Underlying the Bombay Club's critique of the reform package was a strong swadeshi tone which sought continued tariff protection, limits on foreign investment, and a desire to keep the Indian market closed to outsiders, at least for an additional decade or even longer.

While each of India's major apex associations applauded the Bombay Club's call for a level playing field, the strongest endorsement of the Club's policy critique came from the FICCI. In a series of speeches on behalf of the organization, Ajay K. Rungta, the President of the FICCI, has continued to emphasize the unhappiness of India's industrial elite with key elements of the reform package. Rungta has demanded a go-slow policy on globalization and has warned the government that a rapid policy of globalization would 'boomerang'. 'A drastic lowering of protective tariffs,' he warned, 'will bring in high quality, low priced foreign goods which will result in the closing of a large number of domestic industries.' India, he insisted, should adopt the Japanese and South Korean model of protectionism in which the economy was opened up only after 20 years of export-led growth. Rungta has also charged the government with tilting in favour of foreign capital and has insisted that the interests of domestic capital must be safeguarded against foreign direct investment.[52] Finally, the FICCI president has raised substantial doubts about the role of the private sector in the development of Indian infrastructure. Government, he insisted, cannot afford to abandon its responsibility for infrastructure development. 'The Indian private industry,' he warned, 'has neither the taste nor the experience of such high cost, long-gestation and low return projects.'[53]

While the FICCI has been the most open in its criticism of the government reform policies, the CII has taken a much more subtle approach. Publicly the CII has been a major proponent of the reform package both at home and, especially, abroad. Yet many of its most prominent members were leaders of the Bombay Club and the organization has been one of the most vocal supporters of the demand for a level playing field and continued tariff protection of the Indian engineering industry, its chief constituency. The CII has also fought for a reduction of tariffs on components, reductions in excise taxes and special price benefits for domestically produced goods.[54]

The policy reforms of 1991 were a response to a crisis brought on by external forces and severe domestic economic difficulties. They were initiated by a small technocratic elite within the bureaucracy supported by the prime minister and his finance minister. They enjoyed a shallow base of support in the government, the party, and the country. They were grudgingly accepted because of a widespread feeling that there was no alternative. The initial wave of reforms were, moreover, limited and had a minimal impact on key interest groups, including major business families, big farmers, union workers, public sector employees, and politicians dependent upon their ability to distribute benefits and patronage to constituents in the form of subsidies, cheap credit, public sector jobs and regulatory benefits. Once the immediate crisis had passed, therefore, opposition and resistance began to grow and the reform process began to slow down. While there was no real domestic pressure for reversing the measures already taken, the failure to build a large constituency in favour of reforms eventually resulted in a policy stalemate before the reforms could be completed. The shallow support base and the failure of government leaders to sell the reform package enables critics to block further action on such key elements of the reform package as exit policy, company law reform, subsidies, privatization, and transparency in the awarding of infrastructure contracts. In the words of the chief economic adviser to the Government of India,

Everyone thinks great reforms have been done, but that is not absolutely true...All that has been done is stabilisation. Proper reforms mean creating competition, creating an arms length relationship between government institutions and business, changing employment patterns, foreign trade. These things the government has hardly begun.[55]

The failure of the Rao government to build a strong constituency behind the reforms has had the effect of slowing the process of implementation and consolidation. Attracting support, therefore, requires substantial economic improvements. Since tangible results of the reform package take time, the entire process remains vulnerable. In addition, consolidation of the reforms requires the development of a more effective system of institutional consultation, especially between government and the private sector, in order to make the reforms more effective. Yet almost the entire system of government advisory and consultative bodies developed in the early years of planning has become all but moribund.

Throughout the post-independence period, major changes in Indian economic policy have seldom been a response to domestic political pressure. Rather, major changes in economic policy have occurred in waves or cycles triggered by external crises. Balance of payments crises in 1958, 1973, 1979, and 1991 each forced a major shift in domestic economic policies. Such reforms are usually initiated by a small technocratic elite in the bureaucracy supported by a small group of key political leaders. Since the reforms enjoy a shallow base of support, they become very difficult to sustain against charges that the policy represents a repudiation of the basic development consensus of the Nehru era. Consolidation of the reforms, therefore, becomes blocked and further change must await the next crisis, which again forces a new wave of change. As a result, the reform process in India has taken a long time. Reform of the Indian economy has been going on ever since the populist era of 1973, by which time India had created one of the most controlled and regulated economies in the non-communist world. India, unlike China, has never developed a Deng Xiaoping or a leadership committed to fundamental economic reform, and has, therefore, been forced to follow an incremental, cyclical model of crisis, adjustment, minor alteration, inaction, and crisis. The current stalemate in the reform process will continue until the 1996 national elections, and the character of the next wave of reform will depend on the results of those elections.

While the future of economic reforms in India remains uncertain, changes in government policy have fundamentally altered the business–government relationship and business lobbying. Collective action will become increasingly important and the ability of Indian business to work closely with government will become critical to Indian development. A closer partnership between business and government is, however, not absolutely assured. Indian reforms continue to meet resistance from politicians, bureaucrats and sectors of the business community that would like to see a restoration of the old iron triangle which provided benefits to each of the participants. If the process of reform does continue, however, the new set of informal relations between business and government must be translated into more formal mechanisms which would permit more frequent and continuing interaction. In short, while business–government relations have improved, the CII's vision of 'India Inc.' remains a distant dream. Although Indian business has become more effectively organized, is more vocal, and has become more pro-active, it remains divided and subordinate to government. It remains at best a junior partner, not an equal one, in a political system in which the state continues to enjoy considerable autonomy.

NOTES AND REFERENCES

1. This paper is part of a larger study of interest politics in South Asia and was supported by a Fulbright South Asia Regional Research Fellowship for field-work in India, Pakistan, and Bangladesh in 1993–94.

2. For a discussion of the relationship between public policy and interest group behaviour see Harry Eckstein, *Pressure Group Politics: The Case of the British Medical Association* (Palo Alto, Stanford University Press, 1960); and Theodore Lowi, 'American Business, Public Policy, Case Studies and Political Theory', *World Politics* 16 July (1964), pp. 677–715.

3. See FICC1 and Assocham, *Economic Refund in India: Highlights* (New Delhi, Joint Business Council, November 1993).

4. See Robert L. Hardgrave, Jr and Stanley A. Kochanek, *India: Government and Politics in a Developing Nation* (New York, Harcourt Brace Jovanovich, 1993), pp. 354–73.

5. Kyoko Inoue, *Industrial Development Policy of India* (Tokyo, Institute of Developing Economies, 1992).

6. Stanley A. Kochanek, *Business and Politics in India* (Berkeley, CA, University of California Press, 1974), pp. 9–193.

7. Ibid., pp. 289–302.

8. Rusi J. Daruwala, *The Bombay Chamber Story: 150 Years* (Bombay, The Bombay Chamber of Commerce & Industry, 1986), pp. 282–3.

9. *Financial Express* (New Delhi), 5 April 1986 and 30 January 1989.

MRTP refers to the Monopolies and Restrictive Trade Practices Act and FERA refers to the Foreign Exchange Regulation Act.

10. CII Press Release, 16 May 1995.

11. Gita Piramal, 'The Politics of Business', *Independent* (Bombay), 28 March 1991.

12. Kochanek, *Business and Politics*, pp. 98, 226, 266, 296.

13. Ibid., pp. 83–4.

14. C.S. Pandit, *End of an Era* (New Delhi, Allied Publishers Pvt., 1977), p. 113.

15. *Times of India* (Bombay), 30 August 1977.

16. *The Economist* (London), 8 January 1983, p. 65.

17. Sharad S. Marathe, *Regulation and Development: India's Policy Experience of Controls over Industry* (New Delhi, Sage Publications, 1986), p. 60.

18. Pandit, *End of an Era*, p. 70.

19. Krishan Bhatia, *Indira: A Biography of Prime Minister Gandhi* (London, Angus and Robertson, 1974), p. 267.

20. Prem Shankar Jha, *India: A Political Economy of Stagnation* (Bombay, Oxford University Press, 1980), p. 273.

21. Pandit, *End of an Era*, p. 189.

22. Margaret Herdeck and Gita Piramal, *India's Industrialists*, (Washington, DC, Three Continents Press, Inc., 1985), p. 385.

23. *Business India* (Bombay), 23 January–5 February 1989, pp. 50–6.

24. Ibid., p. 55.

25. Ibid., p. 56.

26. *India Today* (New Delhi), 15 May 1987, p. 18.

27. *New York Times,* 9 February 1986.

28. See *The Overseas Hindustan Times* (New Delhi), 4 April 1987, p. 4; *India Today* (New Delhi), 15 February 1987, pp. 15–18 and 15 May 1987, pp. 12–23; and *Ear Eastern Economic Review* (Hong Kong), 30 April 1987, p. 25.

29. R. Venkataraman, *My Presidential Years* (New Delhi: Harper Collins, 1994), p. 40.

30. Interview, New Delhi, August 1994.

31. *Economic Times* (New Delhi), 1 August 1994; and *Financial Express* {New Delhi), 26 June 1994.

32. *Economic Times*, 8 August 1994.

33. *Financial Express*, 1 August 1994.

34. *Business Standard* (Calcutta), 10 August 1994.

35. Ibid.

36. *The Times of India* (New Delhi), 5 July 1994.

37. *India Today* (New Delhi), 15 December 1994, p. 10.

38. *Financial Express* (New Delhi), 26 June 1994.

39. *Business India* (New Delhi), 22 July to 6 August 1994, 38–40.

40. *Business Standard* (Calcutta), 9 August 1994; and *Economic Times* (editorial) (New Delhi), 1 August 1994.

41. Ibid.

42. *Business Standard* (Calcutta), 10 September 1994.

43. *The New York Times,* 13 September 1995 and 20 September 1995.

44. See Stanley A Kochanek, 'The Transformation of Interest Politics in India', *Pacific Affairs,* 68, Winter (1995–6), pp. 525–50.

45. Based on interviews in New Delhi, August 1994.

46. *Business Standard* (Calcutta), 12 January 1992.

47. *Business and Political Observer* (New Delhi), 24 December 1994.

48. *Indian Express* (New Delhi), 1 June 1993.

49. *Patriot* (New Delhi), 25 July 1991.

50. *Times of India* (New Delhi), 15 August 1993.

51. *India Today* (New Delhi), 15 November 1993, pp. 60–5.

52. *Financial Express* (New Delhi), 12 February 1995.

53. *The Pioneer* (New Delhi), 30 September 1995.

54. Confederation of Indian Industry, *Economic Reforms and Industrial Growth – The Pending Agenda* (New Delhi, CII, 1994).

55. *Far Eastern Economic Review* (Hong Kong), 2 February 1995, pp. 42–6.

Select Bibliography

PLANNING

Bhagwati, Jagdish N. and Padma Desai. 1970. *India: Planning for Industrialization.* London and New York: Oxford University Press.

Chakravarty, Sukhamoy. 1987. *Development Planning.* Oxford: Clarendon Press.

Chatterjee, Partha. 1997. 'Development Planning and the Indian State', in Partha Chatterjee (ed.), *State and Politics in India.* New Delhi: Oxford University Press.

Hanson, A.H. 1966. *The Process of Planning: A Study of India's Five-Year Plans.* Oxford: Oxford University Press.

Lewis, John P. 1962. *Quiet Crisis in India.* Washington DC: Brookings Institution.

Nayar, Baldev Raj. 1972. *The Modernization Imperative and Indian Planning.* New Delhi: Vikas.

Patnaik, Prabhat. 1998. 'Some Indian Debates on Planning', in T.J. Byres (ed.), *The Indian Economy: Major Debates Since Independence* New Delhi: Oxford University Press.

GENERAL POLITICAL ECONOMY

Acharya, Shankar. 2006. *Essays on Macroeconomic Policy and Growth in India.* New Delhi: Oxford University Press.

——. 1988. 'India's Fiscal Policy', in Robert E.B. Lucas, Gustave Papanek (eds), *The Indian Economy: Recent Developments and Future Prospects.* New Delhi: Oxford University Press.

Bardhan, Pranab. 1984. *The Political Economy of Development in India.* Oxford: Basil Blackwell.

Bhagwati, Jagdish. 1993. *India in Transition.* Clarendon Press: Oxford.

Bhagwati, Jagdish and T.N. Srinivasan. 1975. *Foreign Trade Regimes and Economic*

Development: India, vol. 6. New York: National Bureau of Economic Research.

Bhambri, C.P. 1980. *India and the World Bank.* New Delhi: Vikas.

Corbridge, Stuart and John Harriss. 2000. *Reinventing India: Liberalization, Hindu Nationalism and Popular Democracy.* New Delhi: Oxford University Press.

Crouch, Harold. 1966. *The Indian Trade Union Movement.* Bombay: Asia Publishing House.

Dhar, P.N. 2003. *The Evolution of Economic Policy in India.* New Delhi: Oxford University Press.

——. 1988. 'The Indian Economy: Past Performance and Current Issues', in Robert E.B. Lucas and Gustave Papanek (eds), *The Indian Economy: Recent Developments and Future Prospects.* New Delhi: Oxford University Press.

Economic and Political Weekly. 2004. Special Issue on Globalization: New politics and old dilemmas, 3–9 January.

Erdman, Howard L. 1967. *The Swatantra Party and Indian Conservatism.* Cambridge: Cambridge University Press.

Fernandes, Leela. 2006. *India's New Middle Class: Democratic Politics in an Era of Reform.* Minneapolis: University of Minnesota Press.

Frankel, Francine R. 2005. *India's Political Economy 1947–2004* New Delhi: Oxford University Press.

Hankla, Charles. 2006. 'Party Linkages and Economic Policy: An Examination of Indira Gandhi's India', *Business and Politics,* 8, 3.

Harriss, John. 1987. 'The State in Retreat: Why Has India Experienced Such Half Hearted Liberalization in the 1980s', *IDS Bulletin* 18, 4.

India Review. 2004. Special issue on Second Generation Economic Reforms in India. 3, 4 (October).

Jenkins, Rob. 1999. *Democratic Politics and Economic Reform in India.* Cambridge: Cambridge University Press.

Jha, Prem Shankar. 1980. *India: A Political Economy of Stagnation.* New Delhi: Oxford University Press.

Kapur, Devesh, John P. Lewis and Richard Webb. 1997. *The World Bank: Its First Half Century,* vol. 1 (Washington DC: Brookings Institution Press, 1997).

Kohli, Atul. 1989 'Politics of Economic Liberalization in India,' *World Development* 17, 3.

Kudaisya, Medha M. 2002. 'Reforms by Stealth,' *South Asia* XXV, 2, August.

Manor, James. 1987. 'Tried and then Abandoned: Economic Liberalization in India', *IDS Bulletin* 18, 4.

Nayar, Baldev Raj. 1989. *India's Mixed Economy.* Bombay: Popular Prakashan.

Patel, I.G. 2003. *Glimpses of Indian Economic Policy.* New Delhi: Oxford University Press.

Pederson, Jorgen D. 2000. 'Explaining Economic Liberalization in India: State and Society Perspectives', *World Development* 28, 2.

Rubin, Barnett R. 1985. 'Economic Liberalization and the Indian State', *Third World Quarterly* 7, 4 (October).

Rudolph, Lloyd I., and Susanne H. Rudolph. 1987. *In Pursuit of Lakshmi.* Chicago: The University of Chicago Press.

Sen, Sukomal. 1997. *Working Class of India.* Calcutta: K.P. Bagchi and Company.

Sinha, Praveen. 1994. 'Indian Trade Unionism and Cross Road,' *Indian Journal of Labour Economics* 37, 3.

Shastri, Vanita. 1997. 'The Politics of Economic Liberalization in India,' *Contemporary South Asia* 6, 1.

Sridharan, E. 1993. 'Economic Liberalization and India's Political Economy: Towards a Paradigm Synthesis', *Journal of Commonwealth and Comparative Politics* 31, 3.

Thakurta, Paranjoy Guha. 2004. 'Ideological Contradictions in an Era of Coalitions: Economic Policy Confusion in the Vajpayee Government', in Bibek Debroy and Rahul Mukherji (eds), India: *The Political Economy of Reforms.* New Delhi: Rajiv Gandhi Institute for Contemporary Studies and Bookwell.

Vanaik, Achin. 1990. *The Painful Transition: The Bourgeois Democracy of India,* London: Verso Books.

Varshney, Ashutosh. 2007. 'India's Democratic Challenge', *Foreign Affairs,* 86, 2, March/April.

POLITICAL ECONOMY OF FINANCIAL CRISES

Ahluwalia, Montek S. 1986. 'Balance of Payments Adjustments in India', *World Development* 14, 8 (July).

Bhaduri, Amit and Deepak Nayyar. 1996. *The Intelligent Person's Guide to Liberalization.* New Delhi: Penguin Books.

Bjorkman, James W. 1980. 'Public Law 480 and the Policies of Self-Help and Short-Tether', in Lloyd I. Rudolph and Susanne H. Rudolph (eds), *The Regional Imperative.* New Jersey: Humanities Press.

Chaudhry, Praveen K., Vijay L. Kelkar and Vikash Yadav. 2004. 'The Evolution of 'Homegrown Conditionality' in India-IMF Relations', *Journal of Development Studies* 40, 6 (August).

Denoon, David B.H. 1986. *Devaluation under Pressure.* Cambridge, MA: MIT Press.

Joshi, Vijay and I.M.D. Little. 1994. *India: Macroeconomics and Political Economy, 1964 –1991.* New Delhi, Oxford University Press.

Muirhead, Bruce. 2005. 'Differing Perspectives: India, the World Bank and the 1963 Aid-India Negotiations', *India Review* 4, 1 (January).

Mukherji, Rahul. 2000. 'India's Aborted Liberalization – 1966', *Pacific Affairs* 73, 3 (Fall).

Singhvi, L.M. (ed.). 1968. *Devaluation of the Rupee: Its Implications and Consequences.* New Delhi: S. Chand and Company.

POLITICS AND ECONOMICS OF INDUSTRIAL POLICY

Agarwal, S.M. 1985. 'Electronics in India: Past Strategies and Future Possibilities', *World Development* 13, 3 (March).

Ahluwalia, Isher J. 1985. *Industrial Growth in India: Stagnation Since the Mid-Sixties.* New Delhi: Oxford University Press.

Athreya, M.B. 1996. 'India's Telecommunications Policy', *Telecommunications Policy,* 20, 1 (January–February).

Baru, Sanjaya. 1990. *The Political Economy of Indian Sugar.* New Delhi: Oxford University Press.

Chibber, Vivek. 2003. *Locked in Place: State Building and Late Industrialization in India.* Princeton, NJ, Princeton University Press.

Desai, Padma. 1972. *The Bokaro Steel Plant: A Study of Soviet Economic Assistance.* Amsterdam: North Holland.

Dubash, Navroz and Sudhir C. Rajan. 2001. 'Power Politics: The Process of Power Sector Reforms in India', *Economic and Political Weekly,* September 1.

Encarnation, Dennis. 1989. *Dislodging Multinationals: India's Strategy in Comparative Perspective.* Ithaca: Cornell University Press.

Evans, Peter. 1995. *Embedded Autonomy: States and Industrial Transformation.* New Jersey: Princeton University Press.

Grieco, Joseph. 1984. *Between Dependency and Autonomy: India's Experience with the International Computer Industry.* Berkeley and Los Angeles: University of California Press.

Ghosh, Jayati. 1998. 'Liberalization Debates', in T.J. Byres (ed.), *The Indian Economy: Major Debates Since Independence.* New Delhi: Oxford University Press.

Gupta, Rajni. 2002. 'Telecommunications Liberalization: Critical Role of Legal and Regulatory Regime', *Economic and Political Weekly,* 27 April.

Kochanek, Stanley. 1974. *Business and Politics in India.* Los Angeles: University of California Press.

Kudaisya, Medha M. 2003. *The Life and Times of G.D. Birla.* New Delhi: Oxford University Press.

Mahalingam, Sudha. 1989. 'Computer Industry in India: Strategies for Late Comer Entry', *Economic and Political Weekly,* 21 October.

———. 2005. 'Economic Reforms, the Power Sector and Corruption', in J. Mooij (ed.), *The Politics of Economic Reforms in India.* New Delhi: Sage Publications.

Marathe, Sharad S. 1986. *Regulation and Development: India's Policy Experience of Controls over Industry.* New Delhi: Sage Publications.

Mehta, Freddie A. 1988. 'Growth, Controls and the Private Sector', in Robert E.B. Lucas and Gustave Papanek (eds), *The Indian Economy: Recent Developments and Future Prospects.* New Delhi: Oxford University Press.

Mohan, Rakesh. 1992. 'Industrial Policy and Controls', in Bimal Jalan (ed.), *The Indian Economy.* New Delhi: Penguin Books.

Mukherjee, Aditya. 2002. *Imperialism, Nationalism and the Making of the Indian Capitalist Class: 1920–1947.* New Delhi: Sage Publications.

Nayar, Baldev Raj. 1971. 'Business Attitudes toward Economic Planning in India', *Asian Survey,* 11, 9 (September).

———. 1990. *The Political Economy of India's Public Sector.* Bombay: Popular Prakashan.

Nayyar, Deepak. 1981. 'Industrial Development in India: Growth or Stagnation', in Amiya K. Bagchi (ed.), *Change and Choice in Indian Industry.* Calcutta: K.P. Bagchi and Co.

Patnaik, Prabhat. 1981. 'An Explanatory Hypotheses on Industrial Stagnation,' in Amiya K. Bagchi and Nirmala Bannerjee (eds), *Change and Choice in Indian Industry* Calcutta: K.P. Bagchi & Co.

Pingle, Vibha. 1999. *Rethinking the Developmental State.* New York: St Martin's Press.

Ramamurti, Ravi. 1987. *State-Owned Enterprises in High Technology Industries: Studies in India and Brazil.* New York: Praeger.

Rao, S.L. 2002. 'Political Economy of Power', *Economic and Political Weekly,* 17 August.

Sridharan, E. 1996. *The Political Economy of Industrial Promotion.* Westport: Praeger.

Varshney, Ashutosh. 1984. 'Political Economy of Slow Industrial Growth in India', *Economic and Political Weekly,* 1 September.

Venkatsubbiah, H. 1977. *Enterprise and Economic Change: Fifty Years of FICCI.* New Delhi: Vikas.

Weiner, Myron. 1986. 'The Political Economy of Industrial Growth in India', *World Politics* 38, 4 (July).

Zagha, Roberto. 1999. 'Labour and India's Economic Reforms', in Jeffrey D. Sachs, Ashutosh Varshney and Nirupam Bajpai (eds), *India in the Era of Economic Reforms*. New Delhi: Oxford University Press.

AGRICULTURE: MOBILIZATION AND POLITICAL ECONOMY

Brass, Paul R. 1980. 'The Politicization of the Peasantry in a North Indian State: I', *Journal of Peasant Studies* 7 (July).

Chadha, G.K. and P.P. Sahu. 2002. 'Post-Reform Setbacks in Rural Employment', *Economic and Political Weekly*, 25 May.

Francine R. Frankel. 1967. 'Ideology and Politics in Economic Planning: The Problem of Indian Agricultural Development Strategy', *World Politics,* 19, 4 (July).

——. 1971. *India's Green Revolution: Economic Gains and Political Costs.* Princeton, NJ: Princeton University Press.

Gupta, Akhil. 1998. *Postcolonial Developments: Agriculture in the Making of Modern India.* Durham: Duke University Press.

Hasan, Zoya, and Utsa Patnaik. 1990. 'Aspects of the Farmers Movement in Uttar Pradesh in the Context of Uneven Capitalist Development in Indian Agriculture', in T.V. Satyamurthy (ed.), *Industry and Agriculture in India Since Independence.* New Delhi: Oxford University Press.

Parlberg, Robert L. 1985. *Food Trade and Foreign Policy.* Ithaca: Cornell University Press.

Varshney, Ashutosh. 1989. 'Ideas, Interest, and Institutions in Policy Change: Transformation of India's Agricultural Strategy in the Mid-1960s', *Policy Sciences* 22, 3.

——. 1998. *Democracy, Development, and the Countryside: Urban-Rural Struggles in India.* Cambridge and New York: Cambridge University Press.

GOVERNANCE

Appleby, Paul. 1956. *Public Administration in India.* New Delhi: Lok Sabha Secretariat.

Arora, Balveer and Beryl Radin, (eds). 2000. *The Changing Role of the All India Services.* New Delhi: Centre for Policy Research/University of Pennsylvania —Centre for the Advanced Study of India and University of Pennsylvania Institute for the Advanced Study of India.

Bhambri, C.P. 1986. 'Bureaucracy in India', in Kuldeep Mathur (ed.), *A Survey of Research in Public Administration 1970–1979.* New Delhi: ICSSR and Concept Publishers.

Chand, Vikram (ed.). 2006. *Reinventing Public Service Delivery in India.* Washington DC and New Delhi: World Bank and Sage Publications.

Das, S.K. 1998. *Civil Service Reform and Structural Adjustment.* New Delhi: Oxford University Press.

———. 2005. 'Reforms and the Indian Administrative Service', in Jos Mooij (ed.), *The Politics of Economic Reforms in India.* New Delhi: Sage Publications.

Herring, Ronald J. 1996. 'Embedded Particularism: India's Failed Developmental State', in Meredith Woo-Cummings (ed.), *The Developmental State.* Ithaca: Cornell University Press.

Kapur, Devesh and Pratap B. Mehta (eds). 2005. *Public Institutions in India.* New Delhi: Oxford University Press.

Kohli, Atul. 1987. *The State and Poverty in India.* New York: Cambridge University Press.

———. 1990. *Democracy and Discontent.* New York: Cambridge University Press.

Lewis, John P. 1995. *India's Political Economy: Governance and Reform.* New Delhi: Oxford University Press.

Mitra, Subrata K. 'Room to Maneuver in the Middle: Local Elites, Political Action and the State in India,' *World Politics,* 43, 3 (April 1991).

Mukherji, Rahul. 2004. 'Privatization, Federalism and Governance', *Economic and Political Weekly,* 3 January.

Roy, Rathin. 1996. 'State Failure in India: Political-Fiscal Implications of the Black Economy', *IDS Bulletin* 27, 2.

———. 1998. 'Debates on Indian Fiscal Policy' in Terence J. Byres (ed.), *The Indian Economy: Major Debates Since Independence.* New Delhi: Oxford University Press.

Varshney, Ashutosh. 2004. 'Why Haven't Poor Democracies Eliminated Poverty', in Ashutosh Varshney (ed.), *India and the Politics of Developing Countries.* New Delhi: Sage Publications.

Wade, Robert. 1985. 'The Market for Public Office: Why the Indian State is not better at Development', *World Development,* 13, 4.

FEDERALISM

Arora, Balveer. 1995. 'Adapting Federalism to India: Multilevel and Asymmetrical Innovations', in Balveer Arora and Douglas Verney (eds), *Multiple Identities in a Single State: Indian Federalism in Comparative Perspective,* New Delhi: Konark.

———. 2006. 'From Reluctant to Robust Federalism', in Mary E. John, Praveen Kumar Jha and Surinder S. Jodhka (eds), *Contested Transformations:*

Changing Economies and Identities in Contemporary India. New Delhi: Tulika Books.

Ahluwalia, Montek S. 2002. 'State-level Performance under Economic Reforms in India', in Anne Krueger (ed.), *Economic Policy Reforms and the Indian Economy.* New Delhi: Oxford University Press.

Baru, Sanjaya. 2000. 'Economic Policy and the Development of Capitalism in India: The Role of Regional Capitalists and Political Parties', in Francine Frankel, Zoya Hasan, Rajeev Bhargava and Balveer Arora (eds), *Transforming India: Social and Political Dynamics of Democracy.* New Delhi: Oxford University Press.

Chhibber, Pradeep. 1995. 'Political Parties, Electoral Expenditures and Economic Reform in India', *The Journal of Development Studies,* 32, 1 (October).

Guhan, S. 1993. 'Centre and States in the Reform Process', in Robert Cassen and Vijay Joshi (eds), *India: The Future of Economic Reform.* New Delhi: Oxford University Press.

Hanson, A.H. 1966. 'Power Shifts and Regional Balances', in Paul Streeten and Michael Lipton (eds), *The Crisis of Indian Planning.* London: Oxford University Press.

Jenkins, Rob. 2003. 'How Federalism Influences India's Domestic Politics of WTO Engagement', *Asian Survey,* 43, 4.

Kennedy, Lorraine. 2004. 'The Political Determinants of Reform Packaging: Contrasting Responses to Reform Packaging in Andhra Pradesh and Tamil Nadu', in Rob Jenkins (ed.), *Regional Reflections.* New Delhi: Oxford University Press.

Mooij, Jos. 2007. 'Hype, Skill and Class: The Politics of Reform in Andhra Pradesh, India', *Commonwealth and Comparative Politics,* 45, 1 (February).

Mukarji, Nirmal and Balveer Arora (eds). 1992. *Federalism in India: Origins and Development.* New Delhi: Centre for Policy Research and Vikas.

Nooruddin, Irfan and Pradeep Chhibber. 2004. 'Do Party Systems Matter? The Number of Parties and Government Performance in India States', *Comparative Political Studies* 37, 2.

Pai, Sudha. 2005. 'Populism and Economic Reforms: The BJP Experiment in Uttar Pradesh', in Jos Mooij (ed.), *The Politics of Economic Reforms in India.* New Delhi: Sage Publications.

Pani, Narender. 2006. 'Icons and Reform Politics in India: The Case of S.M. Krishna', *Asian Survey,* 46, 2.

Rao, M. Govinda and Nirvikar Singh. 2005. *Political Economy of Federalism in India.* New Delhi: Oxford University Press.

Saez, Lawrence. 2002. *Federalism without a Centre.* New Delhi: Sage Publications.

Sinha, Aseema. 2005. *The Regional Roots of Developmental Politics in India.* New Delhi: Oxford University Press.

GOVERNMENT REPORTS

Chakravarty, Sukhamoy (chair). 1985. *Report of the Committee to Review the Working of the Monetary System.* New Delhi: Reserve Bank of India.

Government of India. 1983. *Accountability.* New Delhi: Government of India, Economic Administrative Reforms Commission – Report No. 29 Phase 1.

——. 1985. *Long Term Fiscal Policy.* New Delhi: Government of India, Ministry of Finance.

——. 1997a. *Report of the Fifth Central Pay Commission.* New Delhi: Government of India, Ministry of Finance.

——. 1997b. *Action Plan for Effective and Responsive Government: The Conference of Chief Ministers.* New Delhi: Government of India, Department of Administrative Reforms and Personnel Grievances – Ministry of Personnel, Public Grievances and Pensions.

Hussain, Abid (chair). 1984. *Report of the Committee on Trade Policies.* New Delhi: Government of India, Ministry of Commerce.

Mohan, Rakesh (chair). 1994. *India Infrastructure Report.* New Delhi: Government of India and the National Council for Applied Economic Research published by Twenty First Century Prints.

Narasimhan, M. (chair). 1985. *Report of the Committee to Examine Principles of a Possible Shift from Physical to Financial Controls.* New Delhi: Government of India.

Contributors

MONTEK S. AHLUWALIA is Deputy Chairman, Planning Commission, New Delhi.

JAGDISH BHAGWATI is University Professor, Columbia University, New York.

C.P. CHANDRASEKHAR is Professor, Centre for Economic Studies and Planning, Jawaharlal Nehru University, New Delhi.

JOHN ECHEVERRI-GENT is Associate Professor, Department of Government and Foreign Studies, University of Virginia, Charlottesville.

ROB JENKINS is Professor of Political Science, Birkbeck College, University of London, London.

JASON A. KIRK is Assistant Professor, Political Science, Elon University, Elon, North Carolina.

LATE STANLEY A. KOCHANEK was Professor Emeritus, Department of Political Science, Pennsylvania State University, University Park, Pennsylvania.

RAHUL MUKHERJI is Associate Professor, South Asian Studies Programme, Faculty of Arts and Social Sciences, National University of Singapore.

BALDEV RAJ NAYAR is Professor Emeritus, Department of Political Science, McGill University, Montreal.

PRABHAT PATNAIK is Professor, Centre for Economic Studies and Planning, Jawaharlal Nehru University, New Delhi.

SUPRIYA ROYCHOWDHURY is Professor, Centre for Political Institutions, Institute for Social and Economic Change, Bangalore.

LLOYD I. RUDOLPH is Professor Emeritus, Department of Political Science, University of Chicago, Chicago.

SUSANNE HOEBER RUDOLPH is William Benton Distinguished Service Professor Emerita, Department of Political Science, University of Chicago, Chicago.

ANNALEE SAXENIAN is Professor and Dean, School of Information and Management, University of California, Berkeley.

ASHUTOSH VARSHNEY is Professor, Department of Political Science, Brown University, Providence, Rhode Island.

Index